The
Hemingway
Women

The Hemingway Women

BERNICE
KERT

W. W. Norton & Company

New York · London

The Acknowledgments on pages 537–38 are
an extension of the copyright page.

Printed in the United States of America.

First published as a Norton paperback 1986

The text of this book is composed in Janson Alternate,
with display type set in Torino Italic.
Book design by Bernard Klein

Library of Congress Cataloging in Publication Data
Kert, Bernice.
   The Hemingway women.
   Bibliography: p.
   Includes index.
   1. Hemingway, Ernest, 1899–1961—Relations
with women. 2. Hemingway, Ernest, 1899–1961—
Characters—Women. 3. Authors, American—20th century—
Biography. 4. Women in literature. 5. Women—
Biography.   I. Title.
PS3515.E37Z665   1983   813'.52[B]   82–18988

ISBN 0-393-30270-9

W.W. Norton & Company, Inc.
500 Fifth Avenue, New York, N.Y. 10110
W.W. Norton & Company, Ltd
10 Coptic Street, London WC1A 1PU

6 7 8 9 0

To my husband Morley
for his love and support

And to our children
Elizabeth, Kathryn, and Charles

Contents

Author's Note

Many critics, and some private observers as well, have accused Ernest Hemingway of being antagonistic toward women and of knowing nothing whatever about them. His fictional heroines, whether submissive or manipulative, seldom spring from the page as flesh-and-blood characters. And yet his personal world was alive with bold, resourceful, imaginative women whom he admired and very often married. They cared deeply for him and in most instances dedicated their considerable energies to creating the kind of environment he needed and demanded.

In the early 1970s, when I began to study the women, it became clear that no writer so far had focused exclusively on them. There was no dearth of books about Hemingway himself, but the women remained amorphous. Professor Carlos Baker, the preeminent Hemingway scholar, supported my conviction that these women merited a closer look. And so my examination continued.

My goal was neither a literary biography nor a psychobiography, but to seek out the women as individuals. What were the circumstances that brought Hemingway into their lives? How did they respond to him, and he to them? In the four marriages, what kept the partners together; what drove them apart? What of the other women who charmed him, did not marry him, but often appeared in his fiction: Agnes von Kurowsky, the Red Cross nurse; Lady Duff Twysden, prototype for Brett Ashley in *The Sun Also Rises*;

Jane Mason; and Adriana Ivancich, immortalized as the heroine of Hemingway's least respected book? Finally, was Grace Hemingway, the woman most often relegated to the category of "selfish and destructive mother," really the person her son claimed her to be, or has she been maligned?

From new depositories of unpublished letters, from the published literature, and from lengthy conversations with the principals themselves as well as relatives and friends, I came to know a remarkable population of women. Three of the Hemingway wives were reared in St. Louis; all but Hadley Richardson were working journalists before marriage. Even as their attitudes were in some ways a reflection of the culture in which they grew up, in other ways they had the courage and zest to pursue independent interests.

Gradually, I came to feel that the quality most common to the women was resilience. Their composite story seemed to be a study in relinquishment. For no matter what their degree of commitment, Hemingway could never sustain a long-lived, wholly satisfying relationship with any one of them. Married domesticity may have seemed to him the desirable culmination of romantic love, but sooner or later he became bored and restless, critical and bullying. The conflict between his yearning to be looked after and his craving for excitement and freedom was never resolved. Even so, he could not give up one woman until a new one was at hand; over a lifetime of wide-ranging correspondence he managed to communicate with —or about—his wives long after the intimacy had come to an end. And throughout, they displayed a generosity toward each other that was noteworthy.

In varying degrees, each of the women was fundamentally affected by Hemingway. Hadley Richardson, the wife of his early writing years, blossomed and was said to leave the marriage in better shape than she entered it. Pauline Pfeiffer suffered the most emotional deprivation, but when her marriage to Hemingway was functioning, some of his best and most enduring work appeared. Martha Gellhorn, who left him, became the scapegoat for much of Hemingway's vituperation and bitterness. And Mary Welsh, his last wife, remained loyal during the last debilitating years when, sick and old, he could not leave her and resented that this was so.

Of the women who were alive at the time of Ernest Hemingway's suicide, three have since died. Hadley Richardson Mowrer died on

January 24, 1979, in Lakeland, Florida, at the age of eighty-nine. She had been a widow since the death of Paul Mowrer in 1973. Jane Mason Gingrich suffered a crippling stroke in 1964 at the age of fifty-five but with intensive therapy regained partial speech and some mobility. By the time of her husband's death, however, in 1976, she was again confined to bed, although cheerful and in touch with the outside world by telephone. She died on December 28, 1981.

Adriana Ivancich married Count Rudolph von Rex, in 1963 and bore two sons. With her husband she managed a working farm in Orbetello, Italy, but each year she spent several months in Venice, the city of her youth, and her ties to her family continued to be a great comfort to her. In 1980 Mondadori published her memoir, *La Torre Bianca (The White Tower)*, a tender, often poetic reminiscence of her childhood as a Venetian aristocrat and, especially, of the time she spent with Ernest Hemingway. In the summer of 1982 Adriana wrote me that she was not feeling well— "even these few lines are a big effort." Some months later, on March 23, 1983, at the age of fifty-three, she took her own life.

Agnes von Kurowsky Stanfield moved to Gulfport, a seaside community near St. Petersburg, Florida in 1965. With forbearance and good humor, she battles the infirmities of one who has passed her ninetieth birthday and patiently answers the questions of scholars and others who return again and again to hear about her brief friendship with Ernest Hemingway. She perks up when she recalls her experiences as a Bellevue nurse and relates the activities of her husband's children, whom she raised as her own, and their children.

Mary Welsh lives in New York and Ketchum, Idaho. Martha Gellhorn has continued to live as she had before, and during, her marriage to Hemingway, following her career as reporter, writer of short stories and articles, and author of nine books. When she is not traveling, she resides in London and Wales.

Many people who played an important part in Hemingway's life have not been included in this book or appear only briefly. The Hemingway literature—novels, short fiction, journalism, and essays —is examined only as it reflects or contradicts the reality of the women's lives. The personal Hemingway world, spanning over half a century, is explored primarily for the light it sheds on the women. If anything new is discovered about the enigmatic man who married four times, had three sons, and always wanted a daughter, it will occur from seeing him through the women's eyes.

A work such as this could not have been accomplished without the help and encouragement of many people. My largest debt of gratitude is to Professor Baker, for the privilege of studying—over a period of five years—the interviews, correspondence, and other data that were the raw material for *Ernest Hemingway: A Life Story*.

A biographer who can meet her subjects face to face is fortunate. Hadley Mowrer, Agnes Stanfield, Jane Gingrich, Martha Gellhorn, Adriana Ivancich, and Mary Hemingway graciously extended me this privilege. Agnes, Jane, Martha, and Adriana permitted me to quote extensively from their unpublished letters to Ernest Hemingway. Regrettably, only a small number of his letters to the women exist. Most were destroyed or have been lost.

The enthusiasm expressed for the project by Jack and Patrick Hemingway made for a joyful experience. Perhaps it pleased them that I was inquiring about their mothers instead of their famous father. The value of the insights they provided during many hours of questioning cannot be measured. My thanks to Patrick Hemingway for permission to quote from the unpublished letters and African diary of his mother, Pauline, and from the unpublished letters of Mary Pfeiffer; and to Jack Hemingway for the right to quote from the unpublished letters of his mother, Hadley.

Carol Hemingway Gardner and Madelaine "Sunny" Miller, Ernest Hemingway's sisters, gave unstintingly of their time when I needed to learn more about their mother, Grace. To Ted Allan, Tillie Arnold, Connie Bessie, Betty and Otto Bruce, Peter Buckley, Arrigo Cipriani, Dr. Gregory Hemingway, Puck Hemingway, Al Horowitz, Jay McEvoy, Alice Sokoloff, and William Walton, my appreciation for enlightening personal conversations. On the telephone and via correspondence, Elicin Arguelles, Susan Edmiston, John Hart, Major General Charles T. Lanham, Jonathan Latimer, Lucille Lindsey, Mario Menocal, Jr., Karl Pfeiffer, Michael Reynolds, and Peter Wyden contributed valuable information.

For other kinds of help, each in its own way unique, I thank Leslie Andalman, Arno Bader, Anne Cazeneuve, Lawrence Frankley, Carol Hill, Kristine Kenner, Janet Miller, Melville Nimmer, Robert Parrish, Marilyn Sanders, Rhoda Schlamm, Richard Slater, the women of the Writers Group, and Barbara Zimmerman.

To Susan Fuchs and the late Robert Kirsch I owe a special debt, for they believed in me as a writer.

The complex nature of the research was aided by Audre Hanneman's exhaustive works: *Ernest Hemingway: A Comprehensive Bibliography*, and *Supplement*. Jo August, curator of the Hemingway Collection, John F. Kennedy Library, gave me continuous and indispensable help and guidance. Other assistance was provided by Jean Preston, curator of manuscripts, Princeton University Library, and her predecessor, Archibald Clark; the staff of the Lilly Library, University of Indiana; Ellen Dunlap, Humanities Research Center, the University of Texas at Austin; and the superior facilities of the Research Library, UCLA, and the Beverly Hills Public Library. Giovanni Trombetta, Department of Italian, UCLA, assisted me with the Italian text of *La Torre Bianca*.

For extending me the courtesies of the Hemingway Foundation and the necessary rights and permissions, I am greatly obliged to Charles Scribner, Jr., and Alfred Rice. Mr. Scribner also graciously permitted me to quote from the unpublished letters of the late Charles Scribner and other material from the *Scribner Papers*.

The quality of the text was enhanced by the tireless efforts of my editor, Carol Houck Smith, who brought her great skill and sensitivity to all phases of the editorial process. My friend and agent, Mary Yost, managed everything with tact and fortitude. And for her intelligent attention to detail in the preparation of the final manuscript, I offer thanks to Audrey Levy. To others, not specifically named, goes an additional heartfelt message of appreciation.

Bernice Kert
April 1983

The
Hemingway
Women

The better you treat a man and the more you show
him you love him, the quicker he gets tired of you.

Ernest Hemingway, To Have and Have Not

ONE

1872–1920

Chapter 1

"From my earliest days with EH," wrote Major General Charles T. Lanham (USA., Ret.) about his friend Ernest Hemingway, "he always referred to his mother as 'that bitch.' He must have told me a thousand times how much he hated her and in how many ways." At other moments in his mature years Ernest spat out the same invective. Grace Hemingway was a domineering shrew who drove her husband to suicide; she had to "rule everything." John Dos Passos said that Ernest was the only man he ever knew who really hated his mother.

It has also been said that Ernest's lifelong assertion of masculine power grew out of his emotional need to exorcise the painful memory of his mother asserting her superiority over his father, that his personal difficulties with women, even his submissive heroines, originated with his determination never to knuckle under, as his father had done. In the Nick Adams stories, Ernest portrays Nick's mother as a cloying, artistic woman who disdains her husband's interests and is insensitive to his needs. As a Christian Scientist, she cannot appreciate his medical training. Her advice in most situations tends to be sanctimonious, and her remarks often echo from the darkened bedroom to which she retires with headaches. As a reflection of Hemingway's dislike of his mother, both the personal remarks and the fiction must be respected. But as a fully realized portrait of Grace Hemingway herself, such evidence should be approached with caution.

"My mother was very much an English gentlewoman," Carol Hemingway Gardner, Ernest's youngest sister, said. "She liked to be waited on and expected her children to be well behaved. She thought of us as English as well, though of course we were all born in Oak Park." Grace herself was born in Chicago, Illinois, nine months after the great fire, on June 15, 1872. But her parents, Ernest Hall and Caroline Hancock, came from England, descendants of the enterprising English middle class. Her mother was the daughter of a widowed sea captain who took his three children around the world on his cargo ship before finally setting down roots in Dyersville, Iowa. She grew up to marry Ernest Hall, the dapper son of a farmer who had fought in the Iowa regiment of the Union Army. Disliking rural life, Ernest Hall took his bride to Chicago after the war and joined a wholesale cutlery business owned by a brother-in-law. After the fire he bought a clapboard house on Oakley Avenue, hired servants for his wife, and cultivated a life of travel and leisure. He taught Grace to play billiards and they played together every morning on the family billiard table. Impeccably turned out in formal clothes, he applauded the arias of grand opera in the company of his wife Caroline and his daughter Grace, who, as a girl not yet in her teens, possessed a fine contralto voice.

Music was the language of the Hall household. Ernest Hall was a baritone, Uncle Tyley Hancock a tenor. Caroline herself not only sang a good soprano but as a young woman in Dyersville had been the proud owner of the first organ in town, a melodeon that she took with her to parties, carried to Chicago after her marriage, and dragged to safety from the burning house at the time of the fire. It was this strong-willed mother who recognized her daughter's talent, arranging piano and violin lessons for her and, of course, voice coaching. Caroline ran an efficient kitchen but did not encourage Grace to learn to cook. "You tend to your practicing," she instructed the child. "There is no use any woman getting into the kitchen if she can help it."

Grace followed that dictum happily. The kitchen had no attraction for her. When she wasn't studying music she wanted to be outside with her brother Leicester, for she envied him his freedom, as well as his high-wheeled bicycle, considered a precarious device in those days. One afternoon, disgusted with female constraints, she put on a pair of his trousers, jumped on the cycle, and put on a jolly show for the neighborhood. "Come quick and look," gasped the shopkeepers. "It's a *girl* on a bicycle!"

When Grace was fourteen the Halls moved to Oak Park, Illinois, a sedate residential suburb known for its safe streets, retired clergy, and solid Republican majorities. Ernest Hall built a three-story turreted house at 439 North Oak Park Boulevard with a circular tower room, six bedrooms, and bath on the second floor and a library off the landing. The parlor boasted a fine bay window, tile fireplace, and Belgian carpet. The Halls owned one of the first telephones in town.

As a student in Oak Park High School Grace did not distinguish herself, barely passing Latin and the science courses, but she liked history and literature. She was tall and buxom with English coloring —clear blue eyes, rosy cheeks, and abundant brown hair. Her mother, devoted to velvet-trimmed hats, ostrich feathers, and lace-trimmed gowns, dressed Grace in fashionable clothes and directed her energies toward an operatic career. She obeyed her mother but was closer to her father. Well into her adult years, Grace's letters to Ernest Hall expressed with great intensity her love and concern for him.

Across the street from the Hall family, at 434 Oak Park, lived another high-school student, Clarence Edmonds "Ed" Hemingway. Ed Hemingway's father, Anson, was a deeply religious man who, like Ernest Hall, had served in the Union Army. While attending Wheaton College he had married Adelaide Edmonds, and he tried for some years to support his wife and growing family on the meager salary of a YMCA secretary. Ed never forgot the anxiety over meager rations and shabby clothes. Finally, however, Anson separated his ideals from his responsibility to six children and an overworked wife. He left the YMCA to found a successful real estate business and soon had enough money to move his family to the spacious house in Oak Park.

As he grew to young manhood, Ed Hemingway's fundamental drive became the need to serve. He looked after his brothers and sister, taking them on outings to the country when he was not needed at home. Interpreting literally the moral teachings of his parents, he disapproved of dancing, card-playing, and alcohol. The study of chemistry fascinated him, and a delight in mending the wings and legs of wounded birds and animals led him to medicine.

After receiving his high-school diploma he took his premedical training at Oberlin College in Ohio.

Grace Hall, urged on by her mother, went from her high-school graduation in 1891 to more voice lessons and a program of foreign language study in preparation for the operatic theater. She sang in the church choir, gave frequent concerts, and earned money as a voice teacher. Although only casually acquainted in high school, Grace and Ed struck up something more than a mere friendship when he was a medical student at Rush Medical College in Chicago. In her letter of November 6, 1893, addressed to him at Rush, Grace wrote in the tone of a young woman who was being courted and enjoying it. She asked coyly whether Ed was able to prescribe for the affections of the heart and apologized for implying that some doctors might be butchers. She urged him to write her father, adding that Mr. Hall would be delighted to hear about his work or anything else. And as an indication, perhaps, of a more serious aspect to their discussions, Grace asked him directly whether he believed attending the theater was wrong.

An Oak Park physician took the young Dr. Hemingway on as his assistant in 1894, the year Grace's mother became ill with cancer. Ed made many house calls at 439 Oak Park for the senior doctor. He was now a well-built young man, six feet tall, with penetrating dark eyes, a hawklike nose, and a trim beard that served to hide his youth. Grace was anxious about her mother's condition and depressed from the prolonged vigil at the sickbed. It was a great comfort when Ed Hemingway sat with her and they could talk of cheerful matters. He was a good listener, too, and always solicitous of her.

It is easy to understand the serious youth's romantic interest in the voluptuous young woman who was preparing for an exotic career. When he traveled to Edinburgh in the summer of 1895 to visit that city's great medical center, he wrote frequent letters to Miss Grace Hall. Returning to Oak Park at the end of August, he was eager to renew the relationship. But in September Caroline Hall died, and a few weeks later, to Ed's great disappointment, Grace left for New York, for this was the season that she had arranged to study voice with the renowned opera coach, Madame Louisa Cappianni. Neither Ed Hemingway's love for her nor her father's need for comfort in his bereavement deterred her from keeping that commitment.

In residence at the Art Students League, Grace took daily lessons and went about with other young singers as well as artists and dancers. Posing in a pink satin gown, she had her portrait painted by a fellow student. Madame Cappianni, who had prepared Amelita Galli-Curci for her spectacular career, believed that Grace possessed a remarkable voice. She arranged an audition for her pupil with the authorities at the Metropolitan Opera and there was the possibility of a contract for Grace.

During the winter of such excitement she also corresponded regularly with Ed Hemingway. That correspondence has not survived, but she later told her children that he was pleading with her to marry him. It was tempting. She saw him as strong and reliable, and no one in New York competed with him. Perhaps she was ambivalent about her career, hungering at times for love and protection and the satisfaction of bearing children. It was an unconventional course she had charted—to put her own work ahead of marriage to a suitable young man. The fight for musical recognition would be hard and risky. That she had even considered such a venture in 1896 was proof of her imagination and independence.

Even with her family's backing, Grace owed Madame Cappianni a thousand dollars for the lessons. To pay off this debt she scheduled a concert in Madison Square Garden. The press notices were good, but the experience of performing behind glaring footlights was hard on her weak eyes. (Her vision had been poor since a childhood siege with scarlet fever, but she refused to wear glasses.) Following the recital, her father invited her to travel with him in Europe for the summer. As a widower, perhaps he had reservations about his only daughter leaving Oak Park for an uncertain career. In any case, this sequence of events seemed to trigger Grace's decision to marry the boy across the street, who, in fact, was a boy no longer but a struggling doctor with strong opinions. His interests, apart from medicine, were in the outdoors. He was a skilled hunter and fisherman. He loved food and the preparation of it and was equally at home in the woods and in the kitchen. He dressed indifferently, was not above stoking the furnace or feeding the chickens, and probably assumed that marriage to Grace would be not unlike his own father's marriage to Adelaide Edmonds.

The ceremony was performed on October 1, 1896, in the First Congregational Church in Oak Park. The bride's gown was made of ninety yards of fine organdie. Her trousseau, carefully assembled during her summer in Europe, was lavish, with gowns, hats, and thirty-five pairs of gloves ranging from short red suede to long white. She persuaded Dr. Hemingway that they would live more comfortably in her father's six-bedroom house than in the kind of quarters Ed's small income could provide. Ernest Hall, retired from business, now subscribed to the gracious routine of a gentleman, looking after his investments, enjoying a late breakfast, and strolling on the boulevard, immaculately attired, with his Yorkshire terrier.

Grace had much more in common with him than with her husband, who rushed in and out at all hours, tending to sick patients, prescribing for them in his cluttered office off the second-floor landing of Ernest Hall's house, clattering off to the hospital in his horse and buggy. In rare moments of repose he dreamed of escaping to the wilds of Nevada or becoming a missionary in Guam. Grace had no sympathy for such notions. She wanted the cultural advantages of the city and the refined life enjoyed by her father. In arranging to live with him after her marriage she was able to postpone direct confrontation with a husband whose private yearnings were so different from hers. Ernest Hall was less volatile than Ed Hemingway, whose high-strung disposition was a surprise to Grace. The depth of his moral fervor was unexpected, too. Her own father had always led morning and evening prayers and the ritual was comforting. But he was less rigid than his son-in-law.

Ed seemed not to mind the arrangement. Ernest Hall held him in high esteem for being a physician; Ed in turn deferred to the older man in the hierarchy of the household. Grace had the companionship of her father and the loyal devotion of her husband, while earning money from her teaching of piano and voice.

In the first nine years of her marriage Grace bore four children, three within five years. The oldest, Marcelline, born January 15, 1898, was delivered by Ed himself in the second-floor bedroom when the attending doctor suffered a heart attack in the middle of the delivery. Ed, summoned home in a snowstorm, administered first aid to the unconscious doctor, kept his wife's anesthetic going, and performed a high-forceps delivery. Grace tolerated the crisis gamely and continued to view pregnancy and child-bearing as an elevating experience. Ernest was born eighteen months later, on July 21, 1899, Ursula in April 1901, and Madelaine in 1904, all in Ernest Hall's house.

Leicester Hemingway, who was not born until 1915, when Grace was forty-two, notes in his family memoirs that "From the start there was a succession of nurses and mother's helpers in the Hemingway household. For beyond singing lullabies and breast-feeding, our mother lacked domestic talents. She abhorred didies, deficient manners, stomach upsets, house-cleaning and cooking." Such an accusation leveled against a woman of Grace Hemingway's generation was meant to be pejorative. It was unseemly, especially to the men of the day, for a woman to "lack domestic talents," even when servants were present. Grace's daughters were not so perturbed. "She would certainly not do housework when she could avoid it," Carol Gardner has said. "She was not conventional for her day, but she gave a lot of herself to her children." Grace made no apology for her priorities—if she avoided the messiness of infant care, she eagerly embraced other joys of motherhood.

There was a meticulously annotated album for each of her six children. Ernest's five volumes, from birth to age eighteen, record his weight, height, and coloring, his eating habits, his verbal aptitude, and his emerging personality. At eight weeks he "behaved beautifully" when accompanying his scented, stylish mother to a local tea party. Of more consequence than the statistics of his walking and talking and the account of family gatherings, however, were Grace's own feelings as reflected in the albums. She relished the nightly presence of her infant son in her bed and the emotional satisfaction of having him feed at her breast, "for he is contented to sleep with Mama and lunches all night." She received his love joyously as he patted her face and squeezed up close. He laughed at her voice and wriggled delightedly across her bed. Before he was even a year old he slapped her when she didn't suit him, then quickly broke out into his big smile and in a rich, loving voice said "Fweetie, Fweetie," his favorite name for her. There was a strong element of romance in her narration of his early childhood—the pet names, the delicious dependency, even the small quarrels and happy reconciliations. She respected his displays of temper as manly. He had "good grit" and at two years displayed "wonderful courage and endurance" while fishing at Windemere, the Hemingway summer cottage near Petoskey in northern Michigan. Grace, favoring all things British, named the cottage after Lake Windermere, though the spelling became abbreviated through long family usage. The cottage was lit by oil lamps and heated with fireplaces. Simple cooking facilities included a wood-burning stove and a hand pump for water in the kitchen sink. In a clump of evergreens there was an outhouse and beyond the sandy beach was the clean expanse of Lake Walloon. It was a region of farmland, unspoiled forests, trout streams, and an occasional village.

Every summer saw the complicated Hemingway exodus from Oak Park, with fishing gear and whole hams, trunks of clothes, and noisy toddlers hauled aboard the steamer *Manitou* for the trip northward. Maids were brought from home or hired locally and Dr. Ed stayed for most of the summer, treating the local residents as well as the itinerant Ottawa Indians who camped nearby. Ernest Hall, christened "Abba" by the grandchildren, good-naturedly left the amenities of city life to be with the family. He was not a camping man, but he experienced grandfatherly pleasure in watching the naked babies frolic in the shallow water.

If the prevailing tone on Oak Park Boulevard was Victorian propriety, at Windemere it was an exultant freedom. Much of Ernest's character was formed there—"Ernest shoots well with his gun and loads it and cocks it himself," wrote Grace in *Album 2* a few weeks before his third birthday. His aspiration, she continued, was to be taken for a man, "a 'portsman,'" like his father. Ed did most of the cooking and preserving of local produce and communicated his love of fish and game to Ernest. He eventually taught all his children—the girls as well—to tie flies, cast bullets, and handle a gun and a rod.

Grace's activities at Windemere did not vary greatly from her routine in Oak Park. She read and sang to her offspring, recorded their activities, planned parties and picnics. Swimming was a favorite sport (if her husband stayed nearby to support her when she was afraid to touch bottom), as were nature walks and boating. At sunset, after the light evening meal, Ed would take her out on the lake, he rowing, she singing. The special milky blue of Walloon Lake was more beautiful, she insisted, than the Blue Grotto at Capri, and she composed a breezy melody, *Beautiful Walloona*, that was published by a Chicago firm to her own lyrics.

It was Ernest Hall's custom to visit his son, Leicester Hall, in Bishop, California at least once a year, and to spend some time in and around Los Angeles. In December 1903, Grace joined him for the trip west. There were visits to the missions, the orange groves, and the beach communities. Grace wrote letters to Ernest and Marcelline, as well as to her husband, reminding the children to behave and promising to fill her suitcases with trinkets and fruit.

This custom of gift-giving was an enduring tradition in the Hemingway clan. Christmas was celebrated with feasting and prayers and an outpouring of clothes, books, and toys. Ernest's first Christmas stocking looked like a "boa constrictor" that had just enjoyed a big meal. Birthdays were important, too. Not only was the birthday child feted but the one nearest in age as well. To Grace, who had been indulged by her parents, it seemed natural and proper that her life and the lives of her children be enriched by material things and full of celebration.

After her return from California, Grace became pregnant for the fourth time, confiding the news to Ernest, who had been asking for a baby brother. Ernest's later hostility toward his mother might have been due in part to the rapid displacement he suffered after the birth of the younger siblings—two in less than five years. With a mother whose attentions had been lavished so extravagantly, the abrupt sharing of that heady devotion could indeed be confusing and painful to a small child. Grace, however, so far as can be determined, did not recognize this as a problem. To her it only seemed that "her darling boy" welcomed each new baby. ". . . he came into my bed one morning [Ernest was then nearly five years old] and I told him the happy secret that God was going to give us another little baby. He wanted to understand all about it, so I explained and he felt the little one move and rejoiced over the good news. Our secret is *so* precious. Often he comes up and whispers to me, 'We know, don't we?' " Ernest waited anxiously for the new baby, imagining that this time it would surely be a boy. But another girl was delivered, Madelaine (later nicknamed Sunny), on November 24, 1904.

The swell of satisfaction that Grace experienced after childbirth came prematurely to an end in the spring of 1905. Abba Hall was stricken with a grippe that quickly worsened to nephritis. On May 10 he died of Bright's Disease. Grace was stunned and heartsick. He had been her bulwark in the complicated relationship with her husband. She held him up as a model for her children and lauded his virtues as long as she lived.

The inheritance that now came to Grace from her father's estate opened up an exciting prospect. She would build a *new* house, her dream house, and it would have a music studio where she could teach and organize recitals. With single-minded determination she moved to implement her decision, having read books on architecture and furniture design for years. In six weeks she sold the old Ernest Hall property, bought a large corner lot on Kenilworth Avenue and Iowa Street, and installed her household in temporary rented quarters.

Ground for the new house was broken before the first snow. By the spring of 1906 the framing was up. On a windy day in April everyone gathered before the hearth to lay the cornerstone. Ed produced a box of family relics to be cemented into the fireplace. The Hemingway grandparents watched proudly and Grace, who had a hymn for every occasion, burst out with "Blest be the Tie That Binds" and then served chocolate cake and milk in paper cups.

She stayed home from Windemere that summer to watch over the completion of her ambitious project. Delays and mistakes accumulated and the heat was enervating, but her zeal never wavered, for she had worked out every detail. In the basement were cement-lined closets for the home-canned fruits and vegetables, built-in tubs for laundry, plenty of shelves for Ed's many gadgets, and a handy gas hot plate for every family activity from melting lead for bullets to softening butterscotch for taffy pulls. All food and equipment was stored in cupboards built directly on the walls of the kitchen—a revolutionary idea for the time. Grace established the counter height —taller than average for her taller-than-average family.

The exterior of the oblong structure was gray stucco with white trim. A covered veranda extended the entire width of the Kenilworth side, while the main entrance and the service door, as well as a fine bay window, were on Iowa. There were eight bedrooms, none too many for an establishment that already included four children, Mother, Father, Uncle Tyley (who made his home with his niece when he was not selling on the road), plus the nursemaid and live-in cook. Patients calling on Dr. Hemingway could come in off the street without colliding with the family, for Grace had located his medical suite off a vestibule that was separated from the living room by a pair of leaded-glass doors. The waiting room (in the style of a library) displayed the doctor's collection of stuffed owls and chipmunks and his leather-bound volumes of nature books. As a general practitioner in an era of unsophisticated medicine, Ed Hemingway set fees, dispensed drugs, performed minor surgery, and listened to complaints in one examining room.

At the opposite end of the house, five steps down from the living room, was Grace's work area—a large, acoustically reliable music studio. In her reading she had discovered that the problem of echoes and faulty sound could be solved in a square room with the height equal to half the length of a side and with a balcony halfway up one wall. Her architect, applying this formula, built a room thirty feet square and fifteen feet high, with a balcony the length of the room. It was free of echoes in a day when many public concert halls were plagued with sound deficiencies. Huge galvanized containers of water, hung above the bronze radiators, acted as humidifiers to preserve the tone of Grace's Steinway. Caroline Hancock's melodeon appeared, and eventually Ernest's cello, Marcelline's violin, and Madelaine's full-size harp. Grace explained the purchase of a new dining table and twelve armchairs by saying ". . . no reason why the head of the house should be the only one to have a comfortable dining chair with arms."

Dr. Hemingway brought the children back from Windemere early in August so that they could complete the move into the new house before Marcelline and Ernest enrolled in Holmes Elementary School, one block away. There is no evidence that Ed had been dissatisfied with the old house. Raised in a Puritan background, he favored austere surroundings. When Grace wrenched him from the middle-class appurtenances of Oak Park Boulevard he was caught in a trap that would pinch and then tighten. Having a compelling need to please his artistic wife, he stepped into the trap willingly. But the seeds of dissension were sown. His personal satisfactions were realized in the rural atmosphere of northern Michigan, while she sought cultural and intellectual fulfillment in Oak Park and Chicago. The children could not appreciate the move upward and might have been better off in the comfort of familiar surroundings.

As his resentment of Grace hardened in his adult life, Ernest returned again and again to what he called the selfishness of her decision. Writing in 1927, he seemed to place the onus directly on her, reserving all his sympathy for the husband whose childhood mementos were carelessly burned by an insensitive wife.

In the north woods of Michigan. Grace Hemingway with Marcelline and Ernest, ca. 1900. From the John F. Kennedy Library

A family portrait, Oak Park, 1906. From left, Marcelline, Ed Hemingway with two-year-old Sunny, Ursula poised on Grace's knee. Ernest is at far right.
From the John F. Kennedy Library

The new house on Kenilworth Avenue, 1906.
From the John F. Kennedy Library

Grace displays her catch of the day at Walloon Lake, summer 1904. Looking on are Ernest, Ursula, and Marcelline.
From the John F. Kennedy Library

. . . after my grandfather died we moved away from that house and to a new house designed and built by my mother. Many things that were not to be moved were burned in the back-yard and I remember those jars from the attic [presumably the jars of snakes and other specimens collected by Ed Hemingway as a boy and preserved in alcohol] being thrown in the fire. . . . I remember the snakes burning in the fire in the back-yard.

For Grace, however, it had been an extraordinary experience to supervise a splendid house from drafting board to reality. Her inheritance was gone but her elation was unbounded. She would perform in surroundings that enhanced her talent. As many as three hundred guests eventually crowded into the music room and on the balcony for her recitals. She scheduled lessons and returned to musical composition. Her way of calling the family to supper was to sing out the summons. If any servant showed musical promise, she became a pupil and the regular fee of eight dollars an hour was waived. Leicester and Ernest were ambivalent about their mother's musical activities. They did not like to hear her even suggest that she had given up operatic stardom for marriage and motherhood. The daughters, on the other hand, perhaps not surprisingly, perceived her as a successful woman who enjoyed her success.

Rules of behavior within the household were established by Ed Hemingway. He enforced the Sabbath strictly—no play or games, no visiting with friends, and prayers and church attendance were mandatory. For infractions of behavior he used the razor strop liberally. His temper could flare up in a second. It was the unpredictability of his disapproval more than the punishment that was sometimes hard on the juvenile wrongdoers (and perhaps hard on Grace as well). Washing out mouths with bitter-tasting soap was routine for objectional remarks. Leicester Hemingway has described a kind of coventry as one of his father's most frequent punishments, with forgiveness reluctantly granted. He ascribes Ernest's ideological reverence for stoicism, his scorn for weakness, to the psychological banishment used upon him as a boy—the piercing moral disapproval that left the culprit squirming long after it would have been humane to lift the bans.

Grace brought other kinds of pressure to bear on the children. Before Ernest could read a word she had read to him from hundreds of books, had taught him to memorize Latin and German phrases and important lines of poetry. She poured the same energy that had been mobilized to build the house into creating a stimulating setting for her offspring. In turn she took each child to the opera, to the theater, and to museums, much as her father had. Before his ninth birthday Ernest had attended several performances of the Chicago Opera Company and was diligently sawing away on his cello. Grace saw her responsibility as primarily artistic—to exhort and inspire and open the souls of her children to the noble world of creativity.

Anthony Burgess has suggested that Ernest inherited from Grace the concern for tone and rhythm that was to make him into a major literary stylist, pointing out that James Joyce, too, had a musical background. Grace was lavish with praise when there was accomplishment, quick to criticize when she perceived a slacking off. Ernest learned that compliments came from excelling, sharp disapproval for floundering. His all-consuming desire to be first at everything was established early. Friends of the family noticed that the Hemingway children were achievers and believed that it was because their parents, especially their mother, wanted so much for them.

Marcelline once asked Grace how it was that she had time for professional interests, when none of her friends' mothers did. Grace replied airily that of course ability had something to do with it, but more important was the fact that she earned the money to pay for a cook and housemaid. But there was more to it than that. While her earnings contributed to concert tickets, extra trips, gifts, and parties, the basic household bills had to be paid out of the doctor's practice. He was never idle—he could not afford to be—and would not countenance idleness in others. He was critical when he saw the children daydreaming or reading a magazine. When free of his medical responsibilities, he taught Sunday School, led the Agassiz Club (a nature-study group), and hunted and fished whenever possible. The cellar was well stocked with canned and preserved fruits and vegetables. Ed's culinary skills were indispensable. Everyone ate well because of his interest in food. It might sound incongruous for a busy doctor on a house call to phone home about a pie in the oven, but for Ed meal preparation was one of the most satisfying aspects of his life, much more than the grind of medical practice. He worked long hours for meager fees with no tools to fight postoperative infections or such grim diseases as pneumonia and tuberculosis. Often he could do no more than prescribe simple elixirs. One Oak Park resident remembers Dr. Hemingway going into a spice cabinet and mixing herbs for a potion. Another time he paused during an examination to ask for the Bible and read a psalm.

He was negligent about fee collections, insisting that if people appreciated his services they would eventually pay up. His scolding of the children when they seemed lazy or uncooperative probably resulted from his anxiety about money. He worried more and more about financial security, and arguments with Grace over money matters became strident. With a careless confidence bred into her since childhood, she felt that there would always be enough money for important things. She was determined to protect herself against the wearing demands of headstrong children, expecting her husband and a series of housemaids to step into the breach. She loved to have people gather for large, informal parties. It was often difficult to support such largess even with Grace's earnings, and since it was hard for him to refuse her anything, Ed Hemingway felt increasingly pressured.

Most of the time, or so it seemed to Ernest, his father was the one to give in to Grace's wishes. And Grace, for her part, learned how to circumvent Ed's dicta if they seemed unfair, perhaps even lying a bit when the situation justified it. In a severe clash of wills, however, the stress was too much for her and she suffered periodically from migraine headaches. Ernest, recalling how she retired to her darkened bedroom after an argument in which she was the loser, evidently decided that the headaches were exaggerated to punish his father. From being a creative woman bent on enriching her children's lives, as well as fulfilling her own needs, she became, in the eyes of Hemingway the writer, a selfish wife who destroyed her husband.

Chapter 2

Ernest once claimed that his parents' marriage was preserved because they arranged to separate for some months each year. Carol Gardner, seven years removed from the older brood, did not perceive her parents as quarreling any more than other middle-aged couples she knew. "If there was an imbalance it was that my father was more devoted to my mother than vice versa," she said. "Not that she did not love him, but she was the one with the greater confidence in herself. She had a strong sense of freedom that went along with her self-assurance. Perhaps he did need her more, and was even a little bit in awe of her at times, but she depended upon him for his solidity, even as he was buoyed up by her effervescence." Sunny Hemingway Miller had this to say about Grace in an interview in 1978: "My mother was hard to get along with at times, since she held strong views. But my father adored her. When she entered a room everyone took note of her. She was the buoyant, creative one in the family, much like Ernie."

Ernest may have exaggerated the need of the elder Hemingways to separate periodically, but it is not unlikely that Grace, who sought to have things her own way, enjoyed herself when Ed was absent. Their longest separation occurred in 1908 when she gave her husband her accumulated earnings to pay for a four-month program of post-graduate medical education at the New York Lying-in Hospital. During his absence Grace led the annual trek to Windemere, enlarged now to keep pace with the growing family. For the most part she enjoyed the rough ease of life in the country. Housekeeping tended to be disorganized when Ed was not there, as boxes of ginger snaps and chocolate lay unopened all summer and preserving came to a halt.

Minor infractions were not always taken note of. It would not bother Grace, for instance, that young Ernest hid books under his mattress and then read surreptitiously after lights were ordered out. She encouraged daydreaming, believing it led to creativity. Since her religious faith was more sentimental than God-fearing, prayers were relaxed. She owned a .22 smokeless Winchester and knew how to use it, was photographed on the edge of Walloon Lake holding a seven-and-a-half-pound pike that she herself had caught, and in most family pictures was the dominating presence among her dimpled, blooming offspring.

This was the summer, also, that she decided to compete for cooking honors, since she was sometimes apologetic about her clumsiness in the kitchen. She practiced one recipe, for English teacake, a half-dozen times until she perfected it. Then she proudly served it to her family. For years thereafter the tasty, hot yeast-bread was baked for every social occasion. When Marce suggested that she might want to enlarge her horizons to include layer cake, Grace demurred. "I proved I could cook with my teacake, and I'm not going to take a chance of spoiling my reputation by trying anything else." With very few exceptions she did not.

In November Dr. Hemingway returned from his sabbatical, and seven months later, in the early summer of 1909, Grace took Marcelline to Nantucket Island. It was the first of five such junkets, for Grace believed that in a large family it was important for a parent to have time alone with each child. They left Chicago May 9 and explored historic Concord and Lexington before settling down in Nantucket. Grace was exultant to be back among artists and writers and struck up conversations with many of them. She attended meetings for women's rights and nodded approvingly while the tactics of the English suffragette Emmeline Pankhurst were explained. Prominently displayed in Grace's albums, along with valentines and group pictures of Grandfather Hemingway's Civil War cronies, were five suffragette posters.

A year later, on August 29, 1910, Ernest made the same trip with his mother. A comely child, with brown bangs over his forehead, he was properly attired in belted Norfolk jacket and porkpie hat. Grace, still small-waisted, wore an ankle-length serge suit and elegant shirtwaist. Ernest enjoyed his first swim in salt water and Grace, who always protected her fair skin, was decorously garbed in black stockings, bathing shoes, and elbow-length, full-skirted tunic. After a month at the seaside resort, they did the historic tour of Boston with Grace explaining to Ernest how a Hancock, from whom he was descended through his grandmother, was one of the first signers of the Declaration of Independence. Writing to Carlos Baker in 1951, Ernest attacked Grace as "a great snob" who had her facts all mixed up, at least about his English ancestors. "She just bowlderized and edited it into a wonderful respectability."

Ernest's first effort at fiction followed the Nantucket holiday. A short story entitled "My First Sea Vouge" appears in his mother's album, dated April 17, 1911. In the story the young hero's mother dies when he is four years old. Ernest apparently called upon the true-life story of his great-uncle Tyley Hancock, who went around the world with his widowed father, the sea captain, after his mother's death. In one important departure from the truth, Ernest's hero has a little brother, instead of Tyley Hancock's two sisters. When the story was written, Ernest's hope for a brother had not yet been realized, but Grace was pregnant again, so the possibility was awakened.

After the summer migration to Michigan she carefully explained to the four children her plans for the delivery and included all of them in her preparations. On the morning of July 19, when her labor pains began, the young people scattered to their assigned posts: Ernest went to the lake to fish, Marcelline was sent on a picnic, and Ursula and Sunny were entrusted to the care of a baby sitter. The day passed and at twilight the nurse imported by Dr. Hemingway to assist him with the delivery searched out the children to give them the news. Carol Hemingway had been born, tiny and dark-haired with perfectly formed features. If Ernest was crestfallen to have yet another sister, he took comfort from Grandfather Hemingway's birthday gift two days later—a single-barrel 20-gauge shotgun.

Four weeks after her confinement Grace was supervising the enlargement of the screened-in dining room and preparing for the reunion at Windemere of her husband's family. While twelve cousins frolicked in the lake and assorted aunts and uncles beamed with pleasure, she nursed baby Carol and directed games and conversation. Uncle Will told of his journey into Mongolia and Ernest recounted stories about the neighboring Indians.

At summer's end Grace braced herself for the return to Oak Park and a full schedule. The new baby did not cause her to scale down her activities. Housekeeping only became more slipshod as inept servants came and went. (Ed Hemingway complained, only half-humorously, that the fountain pen he lost in the living room was discovered three years later behind the sofa.) Grace worked long hours with the children's choir of the Third Congregational Church, continued to give recitals whenever possible, and retained a few pupils. She trained Marcelline and Ernest to lead discussions at weekly prayer meetings and coached Ernest in his first dramatic role, as Robin Hood in the seventh-grade school play.

No one was surprised to discover that Ernest was a good actor. From earliest boyhood he had entertained the family with imaginative tales in which he was the swashbuckling hero and had shown astonishing verbal aptitude, making puns and inventing nicknames. Like Grace he had an unusual power for projecting himself, and she watched his progress carefully. When he entered Oak Park High School in September 1913, and Latin was one of his subjects, she immediately hired a tutor for him.

At fourteen he was barely five feet four and still in knickers. All that winter he grumbled about his height and practiced marksmanship in spite of poor vision in his left eye. (He developed the habit at this time of blaming Grace for his defective eyesight, claiming that he had inherited it from her. Grace's problem was the result of her scarlet fever infection as a child, but the family saying persisted —Ernie's bad eyesight came from Mama.)

In a year Ernest grew six inches and graduated to long pants. Realizing that he was still shy around girls, Grace planned theater parties and concerts with young guests of both sexes. After Marcelline was humiliated at a local Unitarian Church party because she did not know how to dance, Grace decided that both Marce and Ernest should take lessons. Dr. Hemingway's attitude toward card-playing and alcohol extended to social dancing as well. Grace had many private quarrels with him before he finally consented to the dancing class. Marcelline was thrilled, Ernest less so, but he struggled into the required stiff collar and polished boots, still motivated to please his mother. He kept on with his cello and joined the school orchestra. At home there was the family orchestra, with Marcelline at the violin, Grace and Sunny at the piano, Uncle Tyley on the flute, and Ernest on cello.

By this time Grace was pregnant with her sixth child. Leicester has referred to himself as a completely unplanned-for baby, at first regarded as an embarrassment. Perhaps Grace was embarrassed by this evidence of sexual activity, presumably over by middle age. She was forty-two, with children ranging in age from newborn to sixteen. She had been married for eighteen years to a man of very different interests. To her family it seemed that Ed indulged her, treating her "like a baby." And to a degree she enjoyed being "babied." But she was too independent to think of herself as anyone's possession, even as beloved wife. Having satisfied her wifely duty to bear Ed healthy children and rear them according to his religious concepts, she expected to have her way in other matters —especially since she assumed her way to be the correct one.

After Leicester's birth on April 1, 1915, there were three sets of children on divergent schedules. The little girls, Ursula and Sunny, were in elementary school. Carol and Leicester were supervised in the nursery. Grace herself was interested primarily in the activities of the teen-agers, Ernest and Marcelline, as they raced from classroom to odd job to club meeting to church social. She began to dream of the day when they would go off to Oberlin College, their father's alma mater.

Ed Hemingway, too, was excited about the children's future plans, especially the possibility that Ernest would study medicine. "It will be only a few years," he wrote Ernest from the Mayo Clinic, where he was attending a meeting, "before you and Papa will be visiting clinics together." He was comforted as well by the birth of Leicester. It seemed that God Himself had intervened. At a time when Ed could expect to lose Ernest, his favorite, to the broader world, a new son was his to shape and love.

Ernest, who assured his father that he wanted to develop in accord with the highest Christian ideals, had not yet moved to that broader world. He shoveled snow and delivered newspapers, earned high marks at school, went to Sunday services and sang in the choir. At sixteen he was handsome and well built, with great strength and endurance, and was sweet with his younger sisters, who idolized him and vied for his attention. At various times, one or another was his favorite. Currently it was eleven-year-old Sunny, who accompanied him on various fishing excursions and even cleaned his fish.

Only Marcelline, as the oldest, could not be dominated. Her emerging womanliness—she was tall and handsome—and her fine singing voice as well as a tendency to take charge reminded Ernest too much of Grace. And she was at an age when she needed an occasional escort. If no one else was available, Ernest, to his frank dismay, was commandeered.

Grace and Ed celebrated their nineteenth wedding anniversary on October 1 and on November 15 Marcelline gave her first song recital, accompanied by her mother on the piano. Pinned to her collar was a fragrant corsage. Grace believed that the girl who received flowers and candy from her family was not so easily flattered by the first man who made a pretty speech to her. Good parties were important for a girl's popularity and Grace was a veteran at giving successful ones. On New Year's Eve 1916, she had a supper dance for Ernest and Marcelline and called it Marce's debut. Eighty-one invitations were printed on pale blue stationery, dance programs were distributed, and the food table was lavish. There were stunts and parlor games. Square dances alternated with the sedate fox trot and Grace herself saw to it that no young lady was a wallflower.

To the community at large, especially the young people, Grace was an unforgettable woman. Warm-hearted and hospitable, she took their problems seriously and opened her house to them. She was different from the other parents, pounding away on the piano while her husband and children served the food. She was amused rather than angry when Ernest smuggled his friends into her music room for boxing matches. "As the boxing began to degenerate into fighting," she wrote in *Album 5*, " 'The House' objected and 'the music studio' was restored to its pristine purity after mopping up the blood."

Ernest's devotion to the cello finally did pay dividends when the high-school musical clubs staged the opera *Martha* and from the pit he gazed abjectly at the Third Servant girl, "a dainty, adorable creature named Frances Coates," according to Grace. One of his classmates remembered him as joking and laughing but rarely turning up at school dances except in the company of Marcelline. The girls assumed that he was too busy fishing, hunting, and writing to bother with them. But it was not for lack of interest that he avoided dates and parties. His big feet got in the way of his dancing and he was not so confident that he could risk rejection. He became the butt of much family teasing as he brooded over his new feelings. But by May he had evidently found his tongue, at least with Frances Coates, for he invited her on an all-day canoe trip and picnic up the Des Plaines River with Marcelline and a high-school friend of Ernest's.

When the family gathered at Windemere for the summer of 1916 Ernest did not fall into the old routine. He still did heavy farm work and showed up for most meals, but he no longer hung around with the younger children. At Horton Bay, two miles from the Hemingway cottage, on Lake Charlevoix, he met a brother and sister named Bill and Katy Smith, summer residents from St. Louis, who lived with their aunt, Mrs. Joseph Charles (referred to always as "Auntie"), in a renovated farmhouse. Bill was twenty-one, four years older than Ernest, Katy almost twenty-five. Brother and sister were both slender and fair-haired, with sharp minds and droll wit. Katy read extensively and was a convenient source of books for Bill and Ernest. Though not pretty she had a definite style. Her hair was forever falling across her forehead, her nervous fingers continually brushing it back. She gazed out coolly from arresting green eyes and struck an attitude toward seventeen-year-old Ernest that was part flirtatious, part motherly.

Ernest was flattered by Katy's attentions, even when she told him to scrub his fingernails. Being in the company of an educated, high-spirited woman nearly eight years older was different from jockeying for the favors of a high-school girl. Nothing at all happened between Katy and Ernest that could be construed as sexual. In 1916, he was still a neophyte whose fantasies of " . . . plump brown legs, flat belly, hard little breasts . . . quick searching tongue" would come later in his development.

If Katy Smith was the out-of-reach older woman, however, Prudence Boulton, the nubile daughter of an Indian sawyer who worked in the area, was presumably more accessible. But there has never been corroboration of Ernest's 1932 fictional account in "Fathers and Sons" that it was Prudence (Trudy) who lay down in the hemlocks woods behind the Indian camp and initiated him sexually. His first complete sexual experience was consummated three years later. At seventeen he had received little sexual enlightenment from his doctor-father, who voiced the same garbled exaggerations as other parents of the days. Masturbation caused blindness, insanity, even death. Since prostitutes carried venereal disease, ". . . the thing to do was to keep your hands off of people."

Bill Smith noticed the hostility that was beginning to surface between Ernest and his parents. With her compelling way of seizing center stage, Grace was coming to be perceived as Ernest's rival. At times he seemed to resent his father as well. He was discovering the ambiguities in Dr. Hemingway's character; that the doctor's strict precepts could yield to his wife's demands or simply be forgotten out of moral fatigue. Some disillusionment on the son's part was not unexpected as part of the maturing process. But since Ernest's youthful relationship with his father was tantamount to hero worship, the disillusion was extreme. He brooded over his father's harsh discipline, occasionally expressing his rage in disturbing ways, as when he took up his shotgun and secretly drew a bead on his own father's head. He showed Bill Smith the tool shed in the garden from whence he had a clear view of an unsuspecting Dr. Hemingway working among his tomato vines.

But the young Hemingway who entered his senior year of high school in 1916 was generally not a sullen youth with a chip on his shoulder. He craved privacy, chafing under his father's watchful protection, but he did not yet openly disparage it. In freezing rain and snow the devoted Dr. Hemingway drove Ernest around on his paper route, and he watched him advance from lightweight football team to second-string, first team guard. Ernest still went to the opera (*Carmen, La Boheme,* and *Aida*) and in December traveled to Galesburg, Illinois for the YMCA Annual Older Boys Conference. He wrote for the high school newspaper, won a lead in the senior class play, Clyde Fitch's *Beau Brummel,* and published frequent short stories in *Tabula,* the school literary magazine.

Grace and Ed still hoped that Ernest and Marcelline would apply to Oberlin College, but only Marce went with her mother to visit the Ohio campus during the spring break. Ernest and a friend had gone on a canoe trip down the Illinois River. This was the week that Woodrow Wilson delivered his historic war message before a special session of Congress. By the time everyone was back in school after Easter, a state of war existed between the United States and the German Empire.

As commencement week approached there was much talk of enlistment. Dr. Hemingway was against such talk, believing that the boys were too young. Ernest himself seemed in no hurry. An uncle in the lumber business in Kansas City looked into the question of his nephew going to work for the *Kansas City Star* as a cub reporter. Word came back that there would be an opening in the fall. Ernest was elated, Grace less so. She still argued that he belonged in college, that his young mind needed the stimulus and the special knowledge of advanced training. Ernest, having decided to become a journalist and restless to be on his own, did not listen to her advice. How could college be better preparation for his career than the city room of one of America's best newspapers?

But first there was the sentiment and tradition of graduation week. In recognition of his literary achievements Ernest was Class Prophet. Marcelline spoke on "The New Girlhood." Grace applauded the program enthusiastically. On the Sunday following the formal exercises, Ernest delivered some sententious remarks before the Boys Club of the First Congregational Church, where a few weeks earlier he had been welcomed into membership. (It was the last time he would participate in church activities, but his name remained on the roster of the congregation until 1932.)

In June Dr. Hemingway decided to drive his Model T open Ford touring car the five hundred miles to Windemere. Grace, never one to pass up a new experience, packed up some personal items and two-year-old Leicester and joined Ernest and her husband for the journey. Six days after leaving Oak Park the dusty travelers reached their destination. Ed immediately went to work on his plans for Longfield Farm, a property he had bought across the lake. With Ernest and a hired hand, a team of mules, and a homemade stone-boat, he moved the old farmhouse off the property, built an ice-house, cut and cured twenty acres of hay, and planted the yearly vegetable garden.

Ernest crowded his fishing trips and social life into long, exuberant weekends. The Smiths from St. Louis were back, Bill and Katy, the latter nicknamed Butstein now by Ernest, known as Wemedge. Butstein was being courted by a thirty-two-year-old bachelor from

Kansas City, Carl Edgar, but in her droll, chiding way she fended him off, having no inclination at this time for marriage. Ernest, flattered to be an insider in this "older set," went to their nightly swimming parties off the dock at Horton Bay. He gave no sign that he dreamed of something more from Katy than sisterly joshing. But he watched intently as she evaded Edgar's overtures.

One of Ernest's early short stories, "Summer People," unpublished until 1972, tells of a midnight tryst under a grove of hemlock trees between Nick Adams and Katy. Since the tale remained unpublished in his lifetime, Ernest did not bother to hide the identities of his characters. Odgar (the nickname given to Carl Edgar) woos Butstein as Nick carries on an interior monologue about his erotic desires. ". . . Nick could get it if he wanted it. . . . He, Nicholas Adams, could have what he wanted because of something in him." What he wanted was Katy, and what she wanted was him. " 'Oh, Wemedge. I've wanted it so. I've needed it so.' "

Eighteen-year-old Ernest, still a virgin and in no position to seduce the twenty-five-year-old Katy, could not be blamed for imagining himself a sexual acrobat. In the fiction Katy spurns Odgar for Nick and there is the imprint of boyish fantasy as Nick brings food from his mother's kitchen and Katy drags blankets from her bedroom. It is a prompt and successful encounter. "He touched one of her small breasts with his lips gently. It came alive between his lips. . . . He felt the whole feeling coming back again and, sliding his hands down, moved Kate over." Kate in turn is as aroused as any young buck could dream of. " 'I love it. I love it. . . . Oh come, Wemedge. Please come. . . . Please, please. . . .' " At the dock, in the car, in all public places, the fictional Katy has the edge in the relationship. But in bed, where he is the master, Nick gives the orders.

This summer of 1917, Ernest and Marcelline, having graduated from high school, separated themselves from the household as much as possible. But Grace still had her hands full. Ursula and Sunny were adolescents now and less tractable. Leicester at three years required ceaseless vigilance or he would walk out into the lake or disappear into the woods. Only six-year-old Carol was at an easy stage. In August Marcelline brought her first serious beau to meet the family and Grace gave a series of potluck suppers to introduce him to friends around the lake. In September Marce left for Oberlin

College to study music and in October Ernest went to Kansas City.

For six months Ernest worked out of the *Kansas City Star's* city room. By the beginning of December he was sharing lodgings with Carl Edgar, Katy Smith's suitor. For $2.50 per week each they rented a comfortable room and sleeping porch, taking their meals at nearby restaurants. Grandmother Hemingway made Ernest a pair of thick socks and Grace sent cookies and cakes. He opened the box of sweets at the office. "The fellows said that Ma Hemingstein must be some cook and to give her their regards," he wrote to his parents. (In the high-school locker room Ernest had invented for himself the nickname of Hemingstein, one that he answered to all his life. It originated with a juvenile anti-Semitic joke about Ernest and his friends as Jewish pawnbrokers who dealt in "funds.")

Younger than the other staff men, Ernest was respectful of their experience, questioning them at length about how to write decent newspaper prose. Kansas City, only two decades from frontier days, was bawdy and wide open, a swift education for a church-going youth from the suburbs. He met prostitutes, lawmen, and hack politicians. He haunted the General Hospital for crimes of violence and the Union Station for underworld characters arriving from the East. But his good friends were clean-cut young men like himself and their topic of conversation, even more than women, was the war and how to get into it.

Ernest's poor eyesight seemed to make the decision whether or not to enlist an academic question. "We all have that bad eye like Mother's," he wrote Marcelline. But then he learned from a fellow reporter, Ted Brumback, that there was another route to the front, via the American Field Service. Brumback had spent four months in France with the Field Service, driving one of their ambulances, and now planned to reenlist. In January 1918 Ernest applied to the Red Cross as an ambulance driver. In April he gave notice to the *Star.* In May, while on a fishing trip in Horton Bay, he got the telegram from his father that he was to report for his physical examination on May 8 in New York. Dr. Hemingway had reluctantly dropped his objections when it was obvious that Ernest would not give up, but he could not hide his fears for his son's safety. He was sleepless with worry, praying hourly for his safe passage across the Atlantic.

Grace, on the other hand, exuded a calm confidence that no harm would come to Ernest. She had made her peace with his decision not to go to college and now complimented him, in her letter of April 17, on the superb way he had stated his position to enlist in the Ambulance Corps. However, when he made a casual reference to the possibility of becoming engaged, she was shocked and upset and did not know what to make of such a startling idea. Perhaps she had failed as a mother if he could not trust her with such important news as an engagement! On May 16 she warned him about the risk of marrying at such a young age, when he had no income and could return from the wars injured or disfigured. Would the young lady love him then? Coupled with her warning was a description of a real marriage—constant companionship, a cozy home, two loving souls experiencing a bit of heaven.

Ernest could not be blamed for snorting at such sentiments, coming as they did from a woman whose own marriage was hardly "a bit of heaven." But it was characteristic of Grace, to write and speak in hyperbole, making large and often inaccurate statements that she could just as easily contradict. Two days later her agitation subsided. She was addressing him once again as her darling boy and recalling the days when he was her yellow-headed lad and would hug her tight and call her "Silky Sockey."

One of the problems during this sequence of letters was that Ernest was writing infrequently. On May 20, when a telegram and a fine letter did arrive, both Grace and Ed were much relieved, Grace suggesting mildly in her letter of that afternoon that perhaps Ernest should let them know if he really was engaged. She wanted to learn to love the girl as though she were her own daughter and hoped that Ernest would tell her if he was joking. Apparently he was. It was hardly an innocent jest, troubling as it was to his parents. Years later Vincent Sheean remarked, after having spent time with him when the two were war correspondents, that Ernest created outlandish stories as unthinkingly as other people breathe. Most of the time his listeners could not separate his reality from his fantasy. In this case the "engagement" was entirely fantasy—a love affair with the actress Mae Marsh, who, when queried long afterward, replied that she had never met Ernest Hemingway but wished that she had.

Her worries over for the moment, Grace rejoiced that Ernest was now in uniform. She took a vicarious thrill in having two men in her family serving their country. The stars on the service flag that hung in the front library were for Ernest and for her brother, Leicester Hall, who was a supply officer in the 617th Aero Squadron. In her last letter to Ernest before he sailed, Grace was wistful about all the adventures ahead of Ernest, including the fine ocean voyage, but she would experience them through his letters. She invoked the Lord's blessing upon him, to watch "between me and thee, while we are absent, one from the other," and signed the letter "Your loving mother—Gracie."

Chapter 3

On June 15, 1918, three weeks after Ernest shipped out for Bordeaux on the old, small French liner *Chicago*, another Red Cross volunteer, twenty-six-year-old Agnes Hannah von Kurowsky, boarded *La Lorraine* for Le Havre. Agnes was born in the Germantown section of Philadelphia on January 5, 1892, the younger daughter of a German emigré and a pretty American debutante. Agnes Theodosia Holabird and Paul Moritz von Kurowsky had fallen in love as pupil and teacher in a German class at the Berlitz School in Washington, D.C. and married against the wishes of the bride's father, Brigadier-General Samuel Holabird, who, according to Agnes, was suspicious of anything German. "My mother was spoiled," she recalled, "but my father was a gentle soul. He could look fierce, but he wasn't."

Agnes's own taste for excitement and adventure was formed at an early age. Her father, as a civil service language instructor assigned to the U.S. Army, took his family to an army post in Alaska in 1898 and several years later to Vancouver, Washington. The Alaskan years especially were unforgettable ones for Agnes—to live in a white wilderness, make friends with Laplanders, ride in dog sleds pulled by reindeer. In Vancouver, however, illness struck the two von Kurowsky children. Agnes narrowly escaped death from diphtheria and her sister died from the complications of scarlet fever. A few years after this tragedy General Holabird retired and Paul von Kurowsky requested transfer back to Washington, D.C. so that his wife could live near her father. The general provided a private French tutor for Agnes and gave her the run of his immense library of seven thousand volumes.

The circumstances of the family changed dramatically following the deaths of Paul von Kurowsky, who succumbed to typhoid fever, and General Holabird. With the small trust fund left to her, Mrs. von Kurowsky moved with Agnes to an apartment. Agnes, who had graduated from Fairmont Seminary for Girls, became a librarian, influenced perhaps by the years of browsing in her grandfather's fine library.

For four years, until 1914, she worked in the cataloguing department of the Washington Public Library. She was a sociable young woman with curling chestnut hair and alert blue-gray eyes. Her expression seemed especially wholesome because of a slightly turned-up nose and friendly smile. She spoke in softly cultivated tones with a southern inflection. At about the time of the outbreak of the war in Europe, she began to get restless with library work and decided to take up nursing, applying to the only large city hospitals she knew of, Massachusetts General and Bellevue. The latter was her choice because her mother had grown up in New York. By the time Agnes earned her cap in July 1917, she had nursed alcoholics and psychopaths, worked in obstetrics and contagious diseases. She was not simply a nurse, she was a *Bellevue* nurse.

In her application to Clara Noyes, Director of Red Cross Nursing Service, on January 2, 1918, for consideration as an overseas Red Cross nurse, Agnes described herself as 5'8", 133 pounds, and fluent in French and German. Her recommendation from Bellevue gave her high marks for personality and executive ability. On March 14 Miss Noyes wired her to be ready to sail with Catherine DeLong, director of the Bellevue Nurses' Home. But the Bellevue contingent sailed without her because of a snarl having to do with her father's name. The German "von" threw the Italian consulate into a dither. Finally on May 22 the confusion was cleared up but then her departure was further delayed because, according to Agnes's recollection, "no ladies were travelling on any English steamer."

In her passport picture Agnes wore a broad-brimmed black hat and tailored coat and looked purposeful enough to deal with the war and its wounded. On board ship she was full of fun, making friends with many of the uniformed passengers. Behind her in New York

"My father could look fierce, but he wasn't." Paul Moritz von Kurowsky with Agnes, 1905. From the Michael Reynolds Collection, John F. Kennedy Library

was a doctor who considered himself engaged to her—apparently she led him to that conclusion after seeing him for some months. But she herself admitted that as soon as the ship sailed, she felt free to enjoy the company of other young men. She was the engaging prototype of the war nurse—pretty, reassuring, unattached. From Le Havre she went to Paris to take in the sights and then skirted the battle zones into Italy, reaching Milan safely on July 11, 1918.

In Milan the Ospedale Croce Rossa Americana (American Red Cross Hospital) was housed in a regal stone mansion at 10, Via Manzoni in the fashionable Piazza La Scala district, near the Duomo and the Galleria. On the fourth floor were fifteen private rooms, some with balconies, others opening to a wide terrace, all of them looking out to the heavy green summer foliage and mysteriously shuttered pensiones of this northern Italian city. "[It] had all the earmarks of [a] . . . country club," recalled Henry S. Villard, one of the original patients. "Under the striped awnings, which could be rolled up or down according to the temper of the sun, . . . patients were able to lounge at ease and have their meals brought to them. There were large wicker chairs, a chaise longue, green potted plants, and on the balustrade, decorative flower boxes." One floor below the patients' rooms were the comfortable nurses' quarters with their own dining rooms, kitchen, and teaching rooms. The ancient furniture had been polished to a soft luster and the walls were painted a cheerful pink. Catherine DeLong was the supervisor. Elsie Mac-Donald, another Bellevue veteran, ran the infirmary at the nurses' station and kept a watchful eye on the younger recruits.

Agnes took up her new routine eagerly. With Loretta Cavanaugh and Ruth Brooks, classmates from Bellevue '17, she carried her ill-fitting gray flannel street uniforms to a Milanese tailor for tightening and shortening and discarded altogether the gray chambray dresses and butcher aprons that were regulation issue but made the nurses look like scullery maids. She attended Italian language classes twice a day and was philosophical about the strict rules that regulated her personal life. American personnel were instructed to behave like Italian women—no unchaperoned dates were permitted, and when the nurses were unescorted they were to move about in pairs. Ruth Brooks, something of a flirt, exasperated Catherine DeLong by flaunting the rules, but Agnes gave that hard-working woman no cause for complaint, taking a friend with her even on a simple errand. Soon she became known as an angel of a nurse who was quick to offer a hot bath to a fretful patient or mix up a cocktail or eggnog for a sleepless one.

Less than a week after Agnes checked into the Croce Rossa Americana, the slow train from Mestre pulled into Milan, carrying a badly wounded Ernest Hemingway. It was 6:00 A.M. on the morning of July 17, four days before his nineteenth birthday. His ship had landed in Bordeaux at the end of May. Ted Brumback, from Kansas City, was with him, and he formed close friendships with two other youths—Howell Jenkins from Chicago and Bill Horne from Yonkers, New York. They had crossed the Italian frontier in a boxcar through the Mount Cenis tunnel, and in Milan their first assignment was to remove the dead and mutilated bodies from the explosion of a munitions factory. In his letters Ernest tried to describe the scene with a degree of detachment, but there was no way to remain detached in the face of such horror.

Two days later the entire contingent was assigned to ARC Section Four and shipped to Schio, twenty-four kilometers to the northwest in the foothills of the Dolomites. Their headquarters was an abandoned woolen mill. Seventeen lumbering Fiat ambulances and half a dozen smaller Fords were lodged in an open shed. For three weeks Ernest alternated with another driver at the wheel of a Fiat, maneuvering it up and down the hairpin curves of Mount Pasubio, evacuating the wounded to *smistamenti*, or distributing stations. Then the Austrians mounted an attack in the Piave River valley and the pace slackened. When some Red Cross personnel asked for volunteers to man a series of canteens on the west bank of the Piave, Ernest stepped forward. Under the command of Captain Jim Gamble, he was dropped off at Fossalta, a low-lying, heavily damaged village.

At first nothing happened—there were no supplies, no instructions, no action—only mosquitoes and the sound of gunfire. After about a week, however, canteen supplies began to trickle in. Ernest went back and forth on his bicycle, delivering cigarettes, chocolate bars, and tobacco to the men. On the hot and pitch-black night of July 8, when the only lights were the flowery bursts of star shells, he was in the trenches, practicing his imperfect Italian with some soldiers. Shortly after midnight an explosion tore the ground where he was standing. The Austrians across the river had fired a five-gallon, 420-caliber canister designed to explode on contact. Stunned, surrounded by dead bodies, bleeding in both legs from the trench mortar, Ernest heaved a grievously wounded man over his shoulder and staggered back toward the command post. A hundred yards away from the post a round of machine-gun fire tore into his right leg at the knee. Still he stumbled ahead, delivering the injured man to safety before losing consciousness himself. He had performed an authentic heroic action and would be recommended for one of Italy's highest honors, the silver medal of valor.

With the entire area under heavy artillery fire, stretcher bearers deposited him on the floor of a roofless shed. All night he lay there, surrounded by the dead and the dying. At dawn an ambulance transported him to a first-aid station near Fornaci, where the doctor in charge gave him morphine and antitetanus and removed some of the hundreds of steel fragments lodged in his legs. Another ambulance moved him to a field hospital near Treviso. For five days he lay in a bleak ward, swathed in bandages from heel to thigh. On the morning of July 15 he was carried aboard a slow hospital train that made its tortuous way through the summer heat and swarming flies of Venice and Verona. Finally on the 17th he was unloaded in the freight yard of Milan and delivered to 10, Via Manzoni.

Elsie MacDonald, short, middle-aged, and motherly, was the first nurse to greet the wounded Hemingway and the first to succumb to his charms, which were now considerable. His adolescent awkwardness was gone. His masculine good looks were enhanced by the bandages and his grinning aplomb. He had proved conclusively that he could be brave under fire and stoic in the face of pain and this had enlarged his confidence. Elsie, crooning softly in her faint Scottish burr, patted him as he was lowered onto the taut, clean sheets of a firm bed, bathed him, brought him breakfast, and kept a loving, if critical, eye on him. Soon he was joking with her and exerting his newly awakened sexuality to establish a teasing mother-son relationship. She accompanied him to the Misericordia Hospital for X-rays that confirmed that there was a machine-gun slug in his right foot and another behind his right kneecap. Both bullets would be removed in surgery when all danger of infection was past.

Ernest's first letters from overseas had begun to reach Oak Park early in July. On July 2 Grace wrote how everyone congregated when the postman shouted that there were letters from Ernie. She was delighted that he could see Paris, reminding him how everyone had two countries, their own and France. As for her, however, "Little Old England" was special. She had been writing Ernest at least once a week. He received most of her letters, carried them around with him, brought them back to America, kept them until he died. They were a chronicle of family life across the sea. Ursula was visiting Uncle George Hemingway at Walloon Lake, Marcelline was taking a summer course in typewriting, Dr. Ed had traveled to Camp Wheeler, Georgia, on a troop train—for the experience! It was a sweltering summer in town—ninety-eight degrees in the shade. Money was scarce. Grace hoped that there would be a good fall crop of potatoes and beans, enough to sell. Lately she was doing some of the cooking, preparing corned beef and cabbage and a special gingerbread for Sunday dinner.

Her imagination was fired up by the war effort. She arose at 6:30 A.M. to see the Oak Park draftees off on the train and viewed the war as a kind of spiritual uplift for the United States. At the same time her letters took on a stiff-upper-lip quality as she used such phrases as "life-sized scrap" and referred to Ernest as her "own Laddie boy."

When the dramatic news of Ernest's wounding was delivered by Red Cross cable and his heroic behavior was repeatedly described over the wire services, Grace's emotions rose to a fervid pitch. Was it really nineteen years ago that God had sent her a son? It seemed like yesterday that he had been dependent upon her for every want. How proud he must be that he had not been found wanting at the moment for heroic action. Everyone was telephoning, and she had even received a glorious bouquet of red roses. (Many years later Ernest remarked that the greatest disappointment of Grace's life was that he did not make her a gold star mother.) When a newsreel appeared at a local theater showing Ernest being wheeled out on the balcony of the hospital by a pretty nurse, she burst into tears.

From his letter of August 29, she learned of the attentions he was enjoying from the local Milanese. "They have been wonderful to me here," he wrote. "There isn't going to be any such thing as 'foreigners' for me after the war now." His friends from Section Four crowded around to hear his colorful tales and watch him pry the imbedded steel fragments from his legs with a pen knife. Everyone was impressed with his gay refusal to be cowed by the injuries. Italian porters bootlegged into his closet a steady supply of vermouth and cognac. ". . . he drank brandy all the time," recalled Agnes. "I think he slept very well." Catherine DeLong scolded him when she discovered empty bottles under his bed but he ignored her to do as he pleased.

The nurses spoiled him and he joked with all of them, but the one who attracted him seriously was Agnes. He began to write her from his fourth-floor room every day, sometimes twice a day, and the letters were delivered downstairs for her to read when she awoke from her afternoon sleep. "I think he was a sort of a one-at-a-time type," she explained later. "He was not the sort who flirted." At first she was merely diverted by him—his constant stream of visitors, his unruly ways. The flashing smile, the dimples, and the romantic Latin coloring—all made him a dashing figure. Then she found out that he was not just another eager young man contending for her favors. His magnetism went far beyond his physical presence. There was the tremendous vitality, the determination to be a free spirit, uninhibited by petty conventions. They were kindred souls, she discovered. During the long, quiet nights, when the hospital corridors were still and the sultry Italian air hung heavy over the balcony, she saw his gentle, serious side. The boasting gave way to modesty, the raucous humor to thoughtfulness. "I was on night duty most of the time," she said. "It was interesting, and it wasn't heavy, but the others just hated it. I didn't hate it at all." Noticing that Ernest was a night owl too, she sat with him in his room, talking and listening.

Villard related:

> I knew he had the inside track when I saw him holding her hand one day in a manner that did not suggest she was taking his pulse. I couldn't help noticing that he received an extra share of her attention, due partly to the special fondness that seemed to be developing between them, partly to his compelling . . . attitude which required her attendance at every conceivable turn.

In civilian life Agnes had enjoyed her men friends, flirting freely and refusing to be tied down. Even her doctor-fiancé realized he had no hold on her. In the Milan hospital setting, where most of the patients imagined themselves in love with her, she had been crisply unsentimental, striking a careful balance between professionalism and intimacy. But the romantic wartime atmosphere exerted its effect, and Ernest was different from the others. Three weeks after his arrival, her close friends began to sense what Henry Villard noticed, that Nurse von Kurowsky was interested in young Hemingway.

For Ernest, the relationship with Agnes was the crowning experience of an extraordinary year. It was the first time he was in love, and the fact that the object of his passion was pretty and accomplished and seven years older fed his ego. No one has suggested that it was a fully realized love affair. Even as Agnes was drawn to him, she continued to put limits on their physical closeness. And Ernest, although intensely aroused, was not so sexually advanced that he would seduce her. Ten years later, when he immortalized her as Catherine Barkley in *A Farewell to Arms*, she became his ideal heroine, submissive and fulfilled in love. Henry Villard, when he read the book, recognized the setting and most of the characters but was sure that Ernest dreamed a good part of the story. The part he dreamed, of course, was the fantasy of Agnes sleeping with him, becoming pregnant by him, and fleeing with him to Switzerland.

The real Agnes von Kurowsky appreciated the companionship that flavored their quiet nights, but most of the time she was mindful of the uncertain future. Sometimes Ernest tried to be nonchalant, as on the occasion when a blonde, English-speaking Italian officer, Captain Enrico Serena, pestered Agnes to go out with him. Ernest egged her on. "You be nice to the capitano, Ag," he said. Finally she agreed to ask Catherine DeLong's permission. "Ruth Brooks would not have been let out the door," said Agnes with a grin, "but with me she said, 'oh sure.'" She met Captain Serena in the park and he took her to a well-known Milanese restaurant, Lorenzo and Lucia, where he had reserved a private room with a piano and couch. No one played the piano and no one used the couch. Agnes made hurried conversation and then jumped up directly after dinner, insisting that she was due back for night duty. Ernest meanwhile was feeling hurt and neglected, for in the afternoon he had gone to surgery for removal of the bullets from his right knee and foot. When Agnes came around to his room at midnight he said accusingly, "You weren't here."

The heat wave continued into September and Agnes devoted herself to Ernest. When she finished her routine duties, they sat on the balcony outside his room, whispering, caressing each other, watching the swallows on the roof. It was an atmosphere rich in sensuality—Ernest lying about in his pajamas, Agnes tenderly solicitous. Lending an air of furtive excitement was the Red Cross hierarchy's disapproval of such special relationships between nurse and patient.

Agnes was discreet even in letters to America. Writing to one friend on September 28, she referred lightly to an outing at the San Siro racetrack with some of her convalescing patients from the Ambulance Corps. One of the patients in fact was Ernest, who had been fitted for crutches. The bright afternoon hinted of encroaching autumn when Agnes donned her high-crowned sailor hat and sweeping cape. Accompanied by Nurse MacDonald and two aviation lieutenants, the couple rode in an open carriage through the park and out along the tramway. After the races they stopped for dinner at the Gran Italia, where candles flickered on the outdoor tables and a dry, iced white Capri was served from a silver bucket.

Ernest wrote Grace that he was in love but assured her that she, Grace, was still his best girl. He took pains to explain that the nurse in the newsreel who had wheeled him out to the balcony was not Agnes. Ag was much prettier. Beyond the simple excitement of a first love, there may have been another dimension to his need for Agnes—and that involved his narrow escape from death at Fossalta, which exploded the youthful assumption that he was immortal. When Agnes was asked whether he was shellshocked or mentally disturbed when he was first admitted to the hospital, she replied only that he was frightened about the possibility of losing his leg from infection and amputation. To his parents Ernest wrote bravely that dying was a very simple thing, but the cold terror of the memory could not have been easy. Agnes's presence, her composure, her cool hand in the dark—such reassurance was probably more important than that the affair be sexually consummated.

Late in September Ernest was sufficiently recovered to go to Lago Maggiore for his convalescent leave, and on October 15 Agnes was called to Florence to nurse an American Red Cross officer with typhoid fever. The night before her departure they sat in the hospital library, talking of the separation and the letters that would have to console them. On the night of the 15th he rode with her in the carriage to the railway station and waited on the platform until the

Nurse Agnes von Kurow-sky. Ospedale Croce Rossa Americana, Milan, summer 1918. Courtesy Agnes Stanfield

An outing at San Siro race-track. Agnes (on Ernest's right), ca. September 1918.
From the John F. Kennedy Library

train from the south pulled in. They embraced, Ernest lingering as the train disappeared. Limping, he turned back to the carriage and returned in silence to the hospital.

Agnes set out for Florence cheerfully enough. Even when the train was three hours late and she had no dinner, her mood stayed high. She was met at the station by a Red Cross captain and put up for the night in what looked to be a converted palace. The next day she reported for work. Her assignment was night duty in a vast, nearly empty Italian Red Cross Hospital. She and her patient were the only ones on their floor. For one who thrived on sociability it was a depressing atmosphere. "And we weren't allowed to associate with the doctors at all," she recalled with some disappointment. "We had our own separate dining room."

Her relief nurse was Elsie Jessup, American-born but British in her ways. She wore her long blonde hair up in a "knob," carried a walking stick, spoke in a clipped English accent. To Agnes she seemed "wild" but intriguing. She smoked, had her own pensione for days off, and had served valiantly as the only nurse in a Serbian hospital during the typhus outbreak. Agnes wanted to see the sights of Florence with her, but since their patient was critical neither woman could leave him.

On October 17 Ernest's first letter came. Agnes wrote him twice, once in the evening, again in the middle of the night. "My poor patient is quite sick and so restless, he has not been able to sleep all night—so I've been able to stay awake and haven't had a chance to get cold, so I haven't really needed 'my furnace'—except for many other reasons than pure physical warmth." She admitted, however, that she was feeling desolate. Florence would be a different place if she only had him, and she would be a different woman when she saw his grin again.

If Ernest's letters were ardent and inconsolable (such opinion must remain conjecture since none of his survive), hers were not devoid of passion. "I think everyday of how nice it would be to feel your arms around me again," she wrote on October 21. "I am so proud of you and the fact that you love me, that I want to blurt it all out. . . . That is our war sacrifice, bambino mio, to keep our secrets to ourselves, but so long as you have no secrets from me and I have none from you . . . why should we worry about whether the old world knows." Throughout the letters, in her use of such phrases as *bambino mio, mon enfant,* dear boy, and so on, she made clear her self-consciousness about the difference in their ages. Sometimes she even called it directly to his attention, as when she addressed him as, "Ernie, My boy" and then wrote, "it sounds rather patronizing, but I meant it as proprietory."

She began to worry that he would leave for the front without her even seeing him. When she learned that Elsie Jessup was engaged to a British officer who had been missing in action since April, she was terrified. "Don't let me gain you only to lose you," she wrote on October 25. "I love you, Ernie. . . . Thank you for your Mother's message. I wish I knew her. . . . In spite of the sunshine, I am lost without you. I thought it was the dismal rain that made me miss you so." One night she dreamed about the doctor in New York. Feeling guilty over the careless way she had treated him, she confessed to Ernest that "the dreadful thought came to me today that maybe my punishment for this treatment of him would be to have you treat me in a like manner someday. I certainly need a dose of your presence, dear, to reassure and comfort me."

Such reassurance and comfort was out of the question, since Ernest, still limping, had left Milan to rejoin some of his friends from the Ambulance Corps. He located them in the vicinity of Bassano, where the huge Vittorio-Veneto offensive against the Austrians was about to be launched. Instead of chauffering the wounded, however, he came down almost immediately with a severe case of jaundice and dragged himself back to the Ospedale Croce Rossa. Events on the battlefields and in the seats of government were moving toward a climax. Trieste was taken by the Italians, the offensive was successful, and on November 3, 1918, an armistice was signed between Italy and Austria. In the north, peace terms were being negotiated between the Allies and Germany.

Agnes learned of Ernest's jaundice on November 1. "I just buried my face in my pillow," she wrote, "and laughed for joy to think I am going to see you in Milan when I get back. . . . Dear Kid, hurry up and get well so I shant worry about you. Just imagine yourself kissed goodbye—By your own Mrs. Kid, Aggie." During her patient's convalescence, as she shaved him and manicured his nails and gave him body massages, she reluctantly concluded that he was quite dull; "solemn as an oyster" was her description to Ernest. ". . . I can't imagine anything more awful than to have to live a life with anyone who hasn't got one [a sense of humor]. I think you are just about the most companionable man I ever knew, and if you do fly off the handle once in awhile, why even that is necessary to make life less monotonous."

With her American patient almost fully recovered, Agnes volunteered to nurse some of the Italian influenza victims who were coming into the hospital. Milan began to seem farther away again, "just when I want most to be there—when you are sick," she wrote on November 3. She was curious about a publicity job that he alluded to in his most recent letter. "Will you be in Rome all the time or travelling around Italy? I guess you don't trust me much, as you are unwilling to place the old Atlantic between us. I can't very well blame you, seeing what I did to the doctor—Well Ernie my darlin', some day you'll believe in me just as firmly as I now hold my faith in you."

There is little doubt that Ernest was holding the faith. As a sensible older woman reminiscing with the author, Agnes did not recall herself as being "crazy mad" for him, but during her three weeks in Florence she had written him every day, intimate letters that freely expressed her love for him and made no disavowal of his growing assumption that she would marry him. When asked how she viewed herself in those years she had replied frankly, "I was looking for adventure . . . and I was very fickle." Ernest, however, was not fickle. He believed what he read in her letters and did not catch such signals as she did send out—that she still had not officially broken with the doctor, that the age difference worried her, that she loved nursing and could not conceive of giving it up. Even when she brought Elsie Jessup to Milan and Ernest had no time alone with her, he made the best of it, probably rationalizing that in their situation they could not expect any privacy.

It was about this time that Jim Gamble, Ernest's captain from the lower Piave, made him an enticing offer. Ernest should remain in Europe with him for at least a year, traveling and pleasure-hunting at his, Gamble's, expense. Agnes argued vigorously against Ernest's embarking on such an odyssey. She explained years later:

My idea was to get him home to the United States because he was very fascinating to older men. They all found him very interesting. . . . I told him he'd never be anything but a bum if he sponged off someone else.

. . . I think I felt more or less an obligation to look after him a little bit because I was older. . . . he really would have gotten to be a bum; he had the earmarks.

But even as she was persuading him to return to America and emphasizing the importance of building his future, she included herself in that future. "I had the feeling that if I shoved him out, he would start off on that European tour." Her instinct was sound. The hurt of losing her might have pushed him into accepting Gamble's offer.

What also seems clear is that the mood of the lovers in that November of 1918 was not synchronous. Ernest, wholeheartedly in love, saw the situation from an uncomplicated perspective. In order to marry Agnes, he had to make at least a start toward a career. How else to do that but to return to Oak Park? Why not believe that Agnes would follow him? It had an attractive logic. Agnes, changeable in matters of love, was not so sure what she felt. She admitted later that she lost her nerve every time she thought of breaking off with Ernest. He was hot-tempered and jealous, and she dreaded his anger.

The problem of what to tell him or not to tell him was postponed when she and Nurse Cavanaugh were ordered to the American Army base at Treviso, near the city of Padua. They left Milan on November 20, nine days after Agnes had returned from Florence. Until she arrived, one medical corpsman had looked after the entire forty-bed ward, with no time to do anything but administer strychnine shots and take temperatures. Agnes gave the patients their first change of linen, their first bath, their first back rubs. "I am very happy indeed," she wrote to Ernest on November 25, "because I feel I am doing some really worthwhile work." On Thanksgiving Day she wrote that she missed him and wanted to see him badly. "Please don't think I am ashamed of you and don't dare to say it again. I thought I made you eat those words once, but you said them again in your letter and it hurts me."

This was a recurring theme in the correspondence. Perhaps it referred to the secrecy of their relationship—secrecy that Ernest was bound to resent. Or to the difference in their age, which made him wonder if she was really serious about him. Agnes, still caring for him, not ready to face her own ambivalence, wrote things that could only raise his hopes, as on December 1: "I sometimes wish we could marry over here, but since that is so foolish I must try and not think of it."

Ernest, who had recovered from the jaundice and was trying to arrange transportation to Treviso, surprised Agnes by limping into the ward one afternoon in early December. Leaning on his cane, covered with medals, he appeared a little ridiculous to the lounging doughboys, who had seen heavy action. Agnes, trying not to be embarrassed for him, introduced him to the other nurses. He spent the night in town, leaving the next day. "It doesn't seem like a reality at all that you were here yesterday," she wrote on the evening of the 10th, adding that her ward might be closed down in a few days and that if she wanted to she could think about going home. "We would have to sail from Italy . . . which is a bitter disappointment as I'd hoped to get back to Paris. . . . Do you think we'll be able to get over again some day—If so, I shant worry about seeing everything now." On the 13th she referred to their getting married. It was a light-hearted allusion. "I wrote to my mother that I was planning to marry a man younger than I—and it wasn't the Doctor so I expect she'll give me up in despair as a hopeless flirt."

Ernest, writing to Bill Smith from Milan on the same day, reported how he had driven up to Treviso to see his "missus," that she was "some girl," and that he was going to return to the United States to work for the "Firm." "Ag says we can have a wonderful time being poor together. . . . every minute that I'm away from that Kid is wasted." Three days later he wrote Agnes the same news— that he was definitely going back to America and would sail early in January on the S.S. *Guiseppi Verdi* out of Genoa. Though this had been her sober advice, vigorously recommended, the reality of it left her somewhat crestfallen, especially since her own chances for getting to Milan to see him before he sailed were remote. "I miss you more and more," she wrote on the 20th, "and it makes me shiver to think of your going home without me. What if our hearts should change? . . . and we should lose this beautiful world of us." That postscript to an emotional letter was the last intensely personal feeling she expressed. The next day she recovered her equanimity. "So you are really going," she wrote. " . . . can't hardly realize it, but I think you are doing right." She had some interesting news of her own. In a few weeks she would leave for a ruined section of the

Veneto to help supervise a small hospital and dispensary. "It is just temporary," she rationalized. ". . . as long as you are not in Italy what diff. does it make where I go. . . ."

When it became clear that Agnes was not going to return to Milan before he sailed, Ernest accepted an invitation to visit Jim Gamble at Taormina, on the east coast of Sicily. Later he said that he never reached Taormina but remained instead in a small Sicilian hotel where the female proprietor hid his trousers and kept him locked up for a week, serving him delicious food and her own fine body for their mutual pleasure. Nothing like that ever took place. Ernest's friends would recognize the yarn as typical of his tall tales. He did spend the Christmas season with Gamble and later wrote him a full letter of thanks from Oak Park.

By January 12, 1919, Agnes was at her new quarters in Torre de Moste, a Red Cross Hospital of eleven beds. The entire area had been devastated by shelling, and much of the population was homeless and starving. "I was the worst-looking mud-bespattered object you ever saw, when I arrived," she wrote Ernest that night. "But Cavie [Nurse Cavanaugh] gave me a royal reception. . . . she's had an awful time of it and has simply done wonders. She was so pleased with the book you sent her. As far as I can see, it's the only literature up here. So hurry up and write some, so you can send me copies, so I can improve my mind." The two American nurses and their two Italian colleagues did everything—home nursing, emergency care, even some of the cooking. While no longer writing Ernest every day, Agnes sent interesting accounts of small hospital crises and her reaction to the tragedy of the Italian displaced.

> Yesterday . . . I walked 3 kilometers through 1/2 foot of mud to the house of a little girl with typhoid. . . . our medico suggested that we try to clean up the place a bit. So I proceeded to remove the livestock from her hair, give her a complete bath, and a new bed, all clean. Well, I thought I had killed the child for awhile, . . . she screamed so. . . . please excuse the looks of this letter . . . my hands are cold and you're not here to warm them.

But she was not to be cold for long. Into this most unlikely setting of crowded hovels, pathetic orphans, and rain-swept mudholes stepped a new lover—Tenente Dominico Carracciolo, a handsome

Neapolitan who was the heir to a dukedom. Agnes was not aware of his noble lineage, only that he was " . . . very gentle, a gentle nice soul, much more interesting to me than a nineteen-year-old Hemingway at that time." The Italian officer found her gay and charming, a high-spirited American woman full of curiosity and humor, so different from the languid, sheltered daughters of the people in his mother's circle. He traveled with her to Padua, escorting her to the Valentine party of the American mission. When the sun broke through the stormy skies, they took long walks into the countryside.

From Oak Park came long letters from Ernest, full of anecdotes, overflowing with love for her. At first she said nothing about her new suitor, only that the future was a puzzle, that she did not know whether to go home or apply for additional foreign service. "Of course you understand this is all merely for the near future, as you will help me plan the next period, I guess." She was not yet prepared to break the news. But then she said something that carried a hint of the real situation. "Cavie has been very cruel to me lately, accusing me of being a flirt, which is putting me in [Ruth Brooks's] class. You know I don't do anything like that, don't you?" No longer did she refer to him as *meo tesoro* [my darling], her hero, her dearest. It was, "affectionately Aggie," or "your weary, but cheerful Aggie."

Into her letter of March 1 went the broadest innuendo yet that her life in Torre di Moste was not nearly as grim as the physical surroundings. Where did he get the idea that she was not having a good time? "I'm having the time of my young life," she wrote. She had learned to smoke, she played a fascinating gambling game called 7 1/2. "Oh I'm going to the dogs rapidly. . . . I'm not all the perfect being you think I am. But as I am, I always was, only it's just beginning to creep out. I'm feeling very *cattiva* [mischievous, evil] tonight. So good night, kid, and don't do anything rash, but have a good time."

It was Agnes, not Ernest, who was showing signs of rashness. Although she had known Domenico less than two months, she put aside her concerns about the difference in their background and agreed to become engaged. She burned all of Ernest's letters because the Tenente demanded it. At last in the middle of March she wrote Ernest the truth, that she had fallen in love with an Italian officer and expected to be married in the spring. She was very sorry and hoped he would forgive her. He would always be important to her for she believed in him absolutely and theirs had been a wonderful friendship. It was a huge relief, admitting the truth to Ernest. Now she could luxuriate in the fulfillment of the new love affair.

However, the romance soon foundered upon family disapproval. Although Carracciolo assured Agnes that his mother understood the depth of his love for her (I told her what a fine woman you are, she will be happy to receive you), that was not the whole story. The Duchess was outraged that her son should be involved with an obscure American, probably an adventuress shopping for an Italian title. When he returned to Naples on leave she was able to exert her influence. He was transferred out of Torre di Moste and Agnes did not hear from him again. A friend tried to find out what had happened and wrote the Tenente, but he never replied. Instead a stiff letter came from his mother, referring to the matter as a wartime experience best forgotten. By May the betrothal was off. Agnes returned all his letters. Dejected and bruised, she decided it was time to go home. Someday she would return to Europe, for it still held a great fascination for her, but for the present she needed to retreat. She booked passage on the S.S. *Re d'Italia* and reached the United States on July 9, 1919.

Chapter 4

Ernest, who had reached New York six months ahead of Agnes, was hailed as a celebrity. Reporters interviewed him, young women went dewy-eyed at the sight of him. It was heady stuff for an imaginative youth not yet twenty. But a week later, resting his aching legs on the green painted bed of his third-floor bedroom in Oak Park, fingering the brightly-knitted Red Cross lap robe that he had brought back from Italy, he too began to feel let down.

Grace tried to be solicitous, carrying his breakfast tray to his room, suggesting that he arrange his war souvenirs on the raised platform of her studio. She questioned him about the war, but Ernest believed, justly or not, that her interest wandered. He opened up to Marcelline when she came home from college on the weekends, offering her some kümmel from his secret cache, and he was kind to Sunny, who was still his favorite tomboy. But he was taciturn with Grace. How could he tell this woman of Victorian sensibilities about his Italian experience? As it was, he was irritated that she neglected the house and could cajole his father when he could not. Perhaps he wasn't even her favorite anymore. He was not prepared for the degree to which he had changed. He only knew that he felt estranged from everything that had been comfortable before.

In the morning he read in bed, listening for the mailman, hoping for letters from Agnes. More went out from Oak Park than arrived from Italy, but he tried to be satisfied, reading hers over and over. At noon he ate with the family. In the afternoon he wandered through the village, looking for friends who were no longer to be found, checking out books on military history, hanging around the high school because at least there he saw young people nearer to his age. He formed a new friendship with his next-door neighbor, eighteen-year-old Isabelle Simmons, and each confided to the other their displeasure with life in Oak Park.

He seemed resigned to being lonely and displaced, pinning all his hopes on the reunion with Agnes. Then in March came her devastating news. She loved someone else, a military man, a man of rank and privilege. She had pushed him out of her life without giving him a fighting chance, he raged. He was out of the running—too young, too poor, too far away. He was stunned, then sick, then furious. He grieved in his room for several days, not eating, running a fever, giving no explanation to his worried parents. Finally he confessed to Marcelline what had happened. As his anger escalated, he fired off a sizzling letter to Elsie MacDonald, telling the nurse how shabbily her friend had treated him—and bringing his own curse down on Agnes, that she should fall down on the dock when she got off the ship and knock out all her front teeth!

Ernest wrote bravely to his friends about cauterizing her memory with a course of booze and women, but the rejection continued to rankle, until it became an emotional injury of enduring consequence. He later returned to the event in three separate works (always altering it in some psychologically revealing way), the most noteworthy being *A Farewell to Arms.* As late as 1936, twenty years after the relationship ended, he was writing in "The Snows of Kilimanjaro" about " . . . the first one, the one who left him . . . how he had never been able to kill it."

A form of retribution came in June when Agnes wrote Ernest of the breakup of her romance. Magnanimously he referred to her as that poor, damned kid and wrote that he was sorry as hell for her. But there was nothing he could do for her now. For the present at least he slammed the door on a shuddering blow to his ego. "Vaguely he wanted a girl," he later wrote in the short story "Soldier's Home," "but he did not want to have to work to get her. . . . He liked the girls that were walking along the other side of the street. . . . But the world they were in was not the world he was in.

He would like to have one of them. But it was not worth it."

It is not clear how much Grace knew about Ernest's ordeal. She was angry when he gave his Italian cape to a young woman whom he dated briefly in April and May, so angry that she demanded he get it back. As for the nightmares and sleepless nights that were the legacy of the wounding at Fossalta, there was some awareness of that in the household. Leicester Hemingway, too young at five years to have much understanding of his brother's problems, observed enough to write in later years that Ernest was plagued with insomnia and could not sleep without a light on. He had chronic sore throats even after a tonsillectomy and was agitated more often than he was equable. Psychotherapy was unknown in Oak Park, but even if such treatment had been available it is unlikely that Ernest would have been receptive. At nineteen he was already committed to unflinching courage. The knowledge that his terror of the dark might be related to the bravest act of his life would have been intolerable. He set out instinctively to master the terror by repressing it, or failing that, to expose himself to repeated physical challenges, in effect refusing to admit that the danger existed. Ultimately he came to use his fiction as a way of dealing with trauma.

Grace, who had shown some intuitive psychological insights when her children were small, believed Ernest's idleness to be the cause of his emotional instability. She worried, as Agnes had, that he had no long-range goals, that he was not interested in going to college, that he spent his days aimlessly. Perhaps Dr. Hemingway could be excused for expounding the work ethic as a solution for neurotic behavior. But Grace was supposed to be the one who understood Ernie's sensitive, proud nature. When justifying to Marcelline her own need to be alone at times, away from her noisy family, she had even said, "Ernest is very like me. . . . When [he] gets through this period . . . of fighting himself and everybody else, and turns his energy toward something positive, he will be a fine man."

Although his experiences in Italy had removed him from the influence of his provincial parents, Ernest half-yearned to return to their protection. But Grace was in an emotional crisis herself. She was forty-seven, probably menopausal. Her musical vitality was ebbing and she was confused about her own needs. She had already raised four children and may have been ambivalent about the drain

"Gracie's house . . . on top of the world." Longfield Farm, 1919.
From the John F. Kennedy Library

the two younger ones imposed on her energies. In an era when it was unseemly for women to express anger, hers turned inward to depression. The return to her household of a sullen, self-willed youth who seemed to require special understanding at the same time that he shoved her to arm's length was a heavy burden.

For a number of years Grace had dreamed of building a tiny retreat of her own on top of Red Mountain, the knoll that was the highest point of Longfield Farm. Ed Hemingway was cool to the idea, but as the summers at Windemere became more hectic—with the comings and goings of the teen-agers—she felt more and more in need of such a retreat. She put aside money from her own earnings, drew up a simple, workable set of plans, and found a local carpenter who was willing to build the cottage for $1,000. Believing that she had her husband's tacit approval, she was full of pleasant anticipation. Then he tried once more to block a scheme that he looked upon as foolish.

In an undated letter of the period Grace framed a vehement reply that reflected her turbulent mood but was a logical and convincing rebuttal of Ed's objections. First she refuted his concerns about accessibility and wind conditions and other problems having to do with the site. Then she reminded him forcefully that she was using her own money and that she was desperate for a refuge. And lastly she made the point that her daughters, who believed excitement the only worthwhile form of happiness, might learn something from the simplicity and wholesomeness that the little cottage would represent.

Marcelline recalled how her mother defended her position. "I want the view from the top of the hill. It's worth going without water and food to have peace and quiet and a place to be alone. I love you all, but I have to have a rest from you all now and then if I am to go on living." Eventually the cottage was built and Ed resigned himself to her absences from Windemere for several days at a time. Grace believed that he was more patronizing than truly understanding of her needs. "He is . . . willing for me to have this cottage," she said, "but he feels he is giving in to a woman's whim." With an almost audible sigh she said to her daughter, "If I could wish for one great gift for each of my children, I think it would be that they each might find a mate who understands this need."

It did not worry her that the younger children were supervised by babysitters or that Windemere housekeeping was perfunctory. When she was ready to return to the cottage she either rowed herself back or, if she had no boat, sent up a Turkish towel to let someone know she was ready to be picked up. The older girls took turns staying overnight in the dormitory room of "Gracie's house." "With the big shutters propped open on three sides, the moonlight streamed in and the night wind blew over us. As we fell asleep we felt as though we were drifting on top of the world," recalled Marcelline.

During the summer of 1919 Ernest helped the crew of Hemingways and others to stain the clapboarding of the cottage a warm reddish-brown, but he scoffed at Grace having the need of such a place. The money should be used for Ursula's college education, he declared. Most of the time he absented himself from the family, as he was less and less able to tolerate parental restraint. Though he still was moody and uncertain at times, the natural setting of forest and lakes had a tranquilizing effect on him. In the evening he waited for Marjorie Bump, a chubby high-school student from Petoskey who was a summer waitress, to get off from work. She had red hair and dimples and was softly vulnerable and good-natured, the right degree of woman for Ernest. She packed their picnics for long evenings in front of a driftwood fire and trolled with him for rainbow trout.

When Marjorie returned to Petoskey, another, somewhat older waitress took an interest in him. One chilly night she walked with him down to the dock. In the shadows of the Potato House, where the harvest was stored, he had sex with her. She got a sliver in her buttock from the splintery planks. Two years later, Ernest fictionalized the incident in the story "Up in Michigan." Tame by the standards of the eighties, it was shocking to the New York editors of the twenties and was not published in America until 1938.

> The boards were hard. Jim had her dress up and was trying to do something to her. She was frightened but she wanted it. She had to have it but it frightened her. . . . "Oh, it's so big and it hurts so". . . . The hemlock planks of the dock were hard and splintery and cold and Jim was heavy on her. . . . [he] was asleep. He wouldn't move.

The story is told from the female point of view, but Ernest's presentation of that point of view seems prejudiced by the dichotomy of his own needs—the need to be assertive and to dominate versus the need to be soothed and cared for. When the seduction is over and Liz is shivering from the cold, her maternal instinct takes over. "Jim stirred and curled a little tighter. Liz took off her coat and leaned over and covered him with it. She tucked it around him neatly and carefully. Then she walked [alone] across the dock and up the steep sandy road to go to bed."

After the summer residents had dispersed and the wind from the north signaled the freeze to come, Ernest rode back to Oak Park with Bill Smith to retrieve his typewriter, a small cache of stories, and some warm clothing and return to Petoskey. He moved into a comfortable front bedroom in a boardinghouse and became a familiar figure in the beanery and the barber shop, with a visor cap pulled down over his forehead, big shoulders hunched inside his black leather jacket. He still walked with a noticeable limp. In the mornings he pounded the typewriter, determined to do some serious writing. In the afternoons he read in the library, waited outside the high-school auditorium for Marjorie, or lingered on the Bear River bridge to stare at the rushing water below.

In December Ernest gave a talk about his war experiences to the

Petoskey Ladies Aid Society and caught the attention of a visitor from Toronto, Harriet Gridley Connable, wife of Ralph Connable, head of Woolworth Ltd of Canada. Impressed by the demeanor and intelligence of the young veteran, she suggested to her husband that he would be a suitable companion for their nineteen-year-old son, Ralph Jr., who had been lame since birth and would be lonely in Toronto when the family went to Palm Beach later in the winter. Ernest liked the idea. He had not sold any stories and was short of money. After Christmas he returned to Oak Park to explain his plans to the family. The separation from his watchful parents had been healthy. He pleased his mother with a gift of white kid gloves and joined in the social life of Oak Park. By the time he left for Toronto, he had enjoyed a decent vacation and was ready to be the proper companion to a young gentleman.

From January 9, 1920, until late in May, Ernest lived with the Connable family at 153 Lyndhurst Avenue. There was a music room with a pipe organ, a billiard room, tennis court flooded in winter to serve as a skating rink, and a roofless loggia with fireplace and benches. Ernest escorted young Ralph Connable to hockey games and boxing matches and made friends with Ralph's older sister, Dorothy Connable, who thought him modest and a considerate guest. His schedule was flexible. He met Dorothy's crowd, played family hockey on the flooded rink, and paid visits almost daily to the editorial offices of the *Toronto Daily Star*. Before going south Ralph, Sr. introduced him to the chief of advertising, Arthur Donaldson, who turned him over to a pair of staff men. Ernest's way of ingratiating himself was to hang around, ask interminable questions, and be a good companion in sports. Finally one of the men took him in to meet the editor of the weekly edition, who hired him and gave him space rates and eventually a by-line.

Grace, writing frequently from Oak Park, congratulated Ernest on one of his feature stories and the ability to fashion something so lively out of the incidents of everyday life. In a well-meaning effort to share his interests, she mentioned stories in the *Atlantic* and other periodicals that she thought he would enjoy. On March 18 she reminded him rather emotionally how much she wanted to hear from him. He had written family letters but none to her personally since he went to Toronto. The winter had been hard on her—dark, dreary days, the temperature rarely above zero degrees. Even the social triumphs of her lovely daughters did not dispel her dark mood. In her depressed state she seemed to envy their youth and popularity as in the past she had envied Ernest his adventures abroad.

Often she seemed disconsolate. Ed Hemingway irritated her more than usual. Maybe some day Ernest would really come to know her, but in the meantime he was always in her heart. As for her, she knew that he would grow up to be a noble man, for he was, after all, the grandson of the finest, noblest man she had ever known, Ernest Hall. (The superlatives were always reserved for her father, not her husband.) On April 3, perhaps to make amends for his neglect, Ernest sent her a beautiful Easter lily. Such thoughtfulness brought tears to her eyes, she wrote, but they were tears of joy. She was rejoicing in his professional success and hoped he would send her some of his clippings. Would he try to remember that she was the same old mother, trying to do her best, not succeeding perhaps, but with it all never losing her faith in him?

Such feelings of inadequacy, never before expressed to Ernest, deepened her anguish. This was the season that she took up manual training in the sensible hope that some purposeful activity would help her fight despondency. She was on her fourth piece of furniture —a library table—she wrote him in the March 18th letter. She had made a settee, and was now planning a teacart. By April 12 she had finished the table. She seemed to gain genuine satisfaction from the newly acquired skill and announced that she was going to attempt a drawer, although she had been warned that it was a hard job.

Grace began to worry again about Ernest's lack of purpose when he announced, at the end of May, that he was going to Horton Bay for the summer and had no plans for the fall beyond a vague notion of taking a freighter to the Orient. She still wanted him to go to college and she was displeased, when she arrived at Windemere for the summer, to see that he refused to take over the heavy chores but came around mainly for meals. When she did gain his ear, she berated him for his careless habits, his rudeness, and his unwillingness to stay at a job, telling him she did not perceive his fiction writing as anything dependable.

Dr. Hemingway, too, was dissatisfied with Ernest's behavior and in letters from Oak Park kept up a drumfire of orders, which Ernest ignored. He countered Grace's demands by simply staying away. He was not going to take his father's place with her, however much she tried to maneuver him into such a corner. If anything, he expected to be placated himself. It was intolerable that he should be expected to play the father.

Both adversaries had a heightened sense of the dramatic. When a trifling incident finally brought on a confrontation, each one, mother and son, hotly defended her/his own position. There was hyperbole on both sides. Grace overreacted and blew up at least one situation beyond all reason, drawing a highly distorted picture of Ernest. Ernest, believing himself to be unjustly accused, had no tolerance for her exaggerations. Since he could barely tolerate criticism of any kind, least of all from her, he interpreted her disapproval as vengeful hatred.

It started with a midnight frolic. Ursula (age nineteen) and Sunny (age fourteen) decided to have a secret picnic with two youths from the neighboring Loomis cottage. They bought food, invited two more girls, and then inveigled Ernest and Ted Brumback to fill in. "Ernie went along with all these plans just to please Ura and me," Sunny recalled. After both families were asleep, the eight conspirators rowed over to Ryan's Point for several hours of uninhibited hilarity. But Mrs. Loomis woke up at 3:00 A.M. to discover that her teenagers were gone. She rowed over to wake Grace Hemingway, seeking an explanation. Grace, ignorant of the scheme, protested that everyone was asleep, but when her neighbor insisted, she checked Ernie's tent and her daughters' bedrooms. Embarrassed, she told Mrs. Loomis that they would talk in the morning. In the morning "the air was BLUE with condemnations. . . . Our innocent picnic," wrote Sunny, "was . . . judged to have been a disgraceful orgy. Ernie and his guest [Brummie] were blamed . . . because they were older and should have had more sense." The girls were grounded for the summer and Ernest and Ted were sent back to Horton Bay.

The next day, July 24, Grace mailed Ernest a scathing letter, the kind that could have been written in the middle of a sleepless night. She began by explaining why she was braving his anger in speaking out after trying to remain silent for so long. At the age of twenty-one it seemed that he was sadly in need of good guidance. Even his friends agreed with her. Then she digressed to draw a long, forced simile between a mother's love and a bank account—concluding that Ernest had overdrawn his account many times. For the first five years, she explained, the mother was a virtual slave to the child's every whim, as she lost sleep and bathed, dressed, fed, and amused the helpless infant (in her martyred state of mind Grace forgot about the succession of nannies in the nursery). Maybe someday the child will find a way to pay her back, thinks the mother. But for the next ten years, the bank continues to be heavily drawn upon for love and sympathy, nursing through illnesses, teaching, guiding, and developing. After that comes the trying time of adolescence, when the child sneers at her advice, thinking of her as a mere antique. Still, continued Grace in a burst of self-pity, the bank was paying out. Wasn't it about time that the child expressed something in the way of gratitude—a little respect for Mother's ideas, however peculiar, a bit of something pretty to wear, an occasional kiss and hug, a real appreciation for her singing and piano playing?

Having catalogued all her complaints, Grace then issued her warning and her threat. If Ernest did not give up his lazy, pleasure-seeking activities and his silliness with foolish little girls, there was nothing for him but bankruptcy. She invoked yet again the memory of her father, that model of chivalry and generosity. Ernest need not bother to return home until he had learned not to insult and bring shame to his mother. When he did learn such courtesy and sensitivity—and learn to be a mature man—he would find her ready to welcome him back.

It is possible that Grace was seeing some of her own undesirable traits in Ernest—his craving for excitement and romance, his tendency to exaggerate his experiences, his need to have things his own way. Beyond that dissatisfaction was the gnawing if barely articulated frustration with herself. It was her inner loss of control that left her vulnerable to Ernest's careless comings and goings. In her hypersensitive state, she developed a mild paranoia.

From a boardinghouse in nearby Boyne City, Ernest wrote Grace Quinlan, a fifteen-year-old friend in Petoskey, that he had been thrown out of his house. His mother hated him, he proclaimed, for getting in her way when she was building Grace Cottage. But he did not brood for long. Katy Smith was back in the area. He managed to get around with her and Odgar, who was still hoping for Katy's favors. By the time Grace was ready to return to Oak

Park a truce seemed to be in effect. She invited Ernest for lunch the day of her departure and did not make a scene when he disappointed her.

In October, Ernest moved back to Chicago. Bill Smith's brother, Y.K. (Yeremya Kenley), witty and sardonic like Bill himself, and Doodles, Y.K.'s wife, put him up in their near-North Side apartment until he found a job. However unfair her bruising letter of July 24 had been, Grace probably did Ernest a favor by booting him out of the house. "He had been loafing around all summer," Carol Gardner said, and "he needed a kick in the pants." It salvaged their relationship as well. With fifteen miles separating them, Ernest was able to go back and forth to Kenilworth Avenue without further quarrels. "I'm rating a terribly good drag with my family," he wrote Grace Quinlan in November, "and we go out there on Sundays."

After Thanksgiving Grace took six-year-old Leicester to California to spend the winter with her brother in Bishop. Whether the trip was undertaken for therapeutic reasons or whether she had already recovered her equanimity, she benefited from the change. She was always refreshed by the company of Leicester Hall, an amateur musician and Greek scholar, as well as a successful lawyer. Many of his clients were Japanese-Americans and native American Indians who needed his defense against discrimination of all forms and trusted him to take care of their interests. Grace wrote that she was disappointed in the unjust legislation being passed by the State of California against the Japanese. It seemed to her that some day all Americans would have to pay the penalty. These Japanese were good citizens. How unfair it was to see in nearly every town the ugly billboards that proclaimed: "Japs keep out, you are not wanted here!"

Not so many Americans in 1920 were sensitive to social injustice. Although he was of the younger generation, Ernest came out of Oak Park with prejudices that Grace herself never nursed. In another letter written from California she expressed an interest in Mary Bethune, the great black educator who was the daughter of slaves and had graduated from Moody Bible School in 1895. Grace considered her one of the rarest of women because she believed in doing things that other people simply pray to God to do for them.

Ernest was sending off good, gossipy letters in return. "I took Sun [Madelaine] to the foot ball dance," he wrote on December 22.

" . . . [she] looked great. Ura [Ursula] was there with Johnny and an apricot and white evening gown slashed like a court jester." He wondered whether his mother would swim in the bubbling mountain baths. " . . . they sound like when we used to swim at Nantucket [1910] and I'd go in with the kelp and the horseshoe crabs and you'd swim in the salt water baths." He wished her a Merry Christmas, but not a Happy New Year because the new year was "just one lurch nearer the grave. . . . " In spite of such a morose comment the tone of the letter was cheerful and friendly. Nothing in it evoked the tension of the summer. As 1920 came to an end Ernest was sounding less like the disgruntled son and more like an eager young man looking to the future.

TWO

1920–26

TWO

1950–56

Chapter 5

Before Katy Smith left Horton Bay in October 1920 she sent an invitation to her St. Louis friend, Hadley Richardson, to visit her in Chicago. Hearing of the death of Hadley's mother, Katy decided that a good long holiday was just the thing for her. Katy was moving into a hotel room at the Three Arts Club, but Hadley could stay with Y.K. and Doodles Smith in their spacious apartment. The women had met as classmates at Mary Institute, an exclusive preparatory school in St. Louis County. At twenty-nine, neither was married. But Elizabeth Hadley Richardson, delicately reared because of a childhood injury, dominated in her youth by a strongminded mother, was different in temperament and expectations from the bold, independent Katy.

She was born on November 9, 1891, the youngest of four children. Her father, James, was a genial man who had reluctantly assumed an executive position with the family drug company. Her mother, Florence, was a talented musician who often accompanied her husband on the piano as he sang out in his fine baritone voice. But in other important ways, they were incompatible. Florence had a driving intellectual curiosity, was never at ease in a frivolous setting, and was intensely interested in religion, especially psychic phenomena.

The injury that so inhibited Hadley's childhood was caused by a fall from a second-story window. Miraculously she was not crippled, but her injured back required months of bed rest. Her mother's overprotection undermined her natural good spirits, and it was years before she could learn to swim, so strong were the fears that she would catch cold. Hadley's father did treat her like a normal child and she worshiped him, although sometimes he seemed preoccupied and often he drank too much. However, when he was in a good mood he had endless patience for her childish games, and it was a terrible blow to her when, in 1903, James Richardson committed suicide by putting a revolver to his head following financial reverses. After his death, Hadley's memories of him grew dim. She only knew that the dullness of her life was intensified by his absence.

Florence Richardson moved with her two younger children—twelve-year-old Hadley and fourteen-year-old Fonnie—to a more modest house. The two older ones, James Jr. and Dorothea, had married and set up their own households. Florence's primary interest became the study of theosophy and science of the mind. She experimented with Ouija boards and automatic writing. A spiritualist who lived down the block convinced her of the power of the seance and in the evenings her friends gathered for discussions of the occult. No liquor was served. Nothing lighthearted was permitted.

Hadley, coming into adolescence in such a cheerless household, became painfully shy. Her only way of protecting herself from domination by her sister Fonnie and her mother was to retreat into music. She worked stubbornly, performing at music clubs and benefits, and even had a studio recital of her own. In 1910 she graduated from Mary Institute and entered Bryn Mawr College in the fall.

College should have been a liberating experience for Hadley, as freshmen crowded into her dormitory room to argue about Life, Love, and the Meaning of the Universe. At the same time she was under great pressure to keep up her grades, and by May was exhausted from sleeping so poorly and fighting a weak stomach. With the proper encouragement and a relaxing summer, perhaps she could have returned to Bryn Mawr for a second year. But it was Florence Richardson's firm judgment, expressed repeatedly, that Hadley had a delicate constitution. So she gave up and dropped out of college.

The next years were grim. Hadley's oldest sister, Dorothea, who had been badly burned in a fire the summer before Hadley went to Bryn Mawr, died after giving birth to a stillborn child. Florence and

Fonnie, the latter now married but living in an apartment down-stairs, seemed to be in league against Hadley, directing her life, telling her what to think and what to do. Once again she turned to music, and reached a high level of competence with a new teacher, Harrison Williams. Before long Williams came to personify all the qualities of an ideal man, but he never returned her ardor. His rejection was a blow, but Hadley did begin to reevaluate her commitment to the piano, admitting that perhaps she did not have the drive for a serious career.

So now she was in limbo again, sharing an apartment with a mother whose interests had nothing in common with hers, estranged from the old friends who had fallen away when she was immersed in her musical studies. Constantly reminded of her delicate health and half-believing the precarious state of her body, she sank into a kind of torpor.

Four years later in 1920, Florence Richardson contracted Bright's Disease. Over the next nine months Hadley nursed her dying mother. By the time of her death at the end of the summer of 1921, Hadley was emotionally spent. Katy Smith's invitation to come up to Chicago seemed premature, but the more Hadley thought about it, the more she wanted to go. She was free of her mother, but free to do what—be a spinster aunt to Fonnie's four children, a fill-in at her friends' dinner parties? She yearned for some deeper fulfillment, even though she could still not articulate her yearnings.

The apartment in which Hadley found herself a house guest was a furnished sublet at 100 East Chicago Avenue, negligently cared for, occupied not only by Y.K. and Doodles but a series of floating boarders—glib, high-spirited young men who called each other by everything but their given names and parried in a kind of private pig Latin. When she arrived, she barely had time to unpack and put on something fresh before it was time for the evening party. All kinds of people surged into the living room. She could hardly sort them out but shyly joined in the word games and after some urging played the piano.

One young man emerged from the babble. He was the best-looking one in the room and his disarming smile stretched from ear to ear. He had a string of nicknames—Hemingstein, Nesto, Wemedge—but the proper name was Ernest Hemingway. His flattering habit of focusing his entire attention on a person, gazing out from watchful brown eyes, was not a pose, for he was an alert listener. And on this particular night he concentrated on Hadley. She noticed that all the women in the room, including her friend Katy, were intrigued by him, but he gave no sign that he was interested in anyone but her. She enjoyed the evening enormously, the laughter and the jokes, the reassurance that she was accepted by the group and not least by the "hulky, bulky something masculine" who rarely left her side. What, she wondered, did he see in her, that excitable fellow who seemed to be the leader of the crowd? That she had red hair and good legs? Wait until he knew her better. He'd find out she was not his type. She went to sleep that night assuming that he was not her type either, too restless, too dashing, and certainly too young.

But her assumptions were wrong. She underestimated his many-sided nature and her own susceptibility. At twenty-nine she was still a bottled-up creature of vague dreams. Ernest, at twenty-one, had already made his way through the tough wards of Kansas City, survived the wounding at Fossalta, and put the restrictions of Oak Park behind him. He had mastered the wilderness and the city room. In breadth of experience he was the mature one, Hadley the neophyte. But more important to her than his adventures, or even his brilliance, was his vitality, his unflappable conviction that he could get what he wanted. Her reserve and her tentativeness began to dissolve under the heat of his boundless energy.

For three weeks, as boarder and house guest, they roamed about together, deep in conversation, exchanging confidences. Hadley heard about his quarrel with his parents, he about the trials with her mother and the tragedy of her father's suicide. Back at Y.K.'s apartment he sometimes showed her his latest literary effort. "How I did love to have you roll in from Yen's room and just have to read it to me," she wrote in one of her subsequent letters. "Your stuff has both rhythm and the right word. . . . I am quite keen about it."

One morning he came into her room "panting and seething" to tell her about the girl he had loved so much and who had given him so much and then went away. She listened as he ranted, pacified his bitterness, finally advised him not to get married for a long time, saying he wasn't ready. As open as he was with her, she was equally direct and comfortable with him. "Maybe the nicest feeling I have about you," she explained, "is that you now and probly always will have a true response to anything I say or feel."

A twenty-one-year-old unproven writer was hardly a promising suitor for a sheltered woman nearing thirty. But Hadley sensed that her friendship with Ernest was no mere romantic interlude and she returned to St. Louis at the end of October refreshed and even a little bit excited.

His first letter was so "nice over and above the . . . personal angle" that she read whole sections of it to her friends. He wrote her a "peach" of a letter on her birthday and she responded with eleven pages. When he confided that he had been aroused by some flashily dressed and seductive young women at a party, she replied that she could sympathize with his physical reaction to such people.

> . . . I understand . . . how many different grains of personality must go to make up the experience of an intelligent and normally curious man and perhaps you really *are* young, Ernest. . . . Can't imagine, personally, shining up to a man who didn't attract me other ways than physically . . . so glad you did tell me—anything goes, doesn't it, between honest men?

When a friend, Letticia Parker, invited Hadley to go to Chicago as her guest for a weekend in early December, Hadley seized the opportunity. To her relief there was no letdown in this second visit with Ernest, and she returned to St. Louis to begin a daily correspondence. Occasionally she wrote about the various men who were taking her out, including a persistent one, referred to only as "Dick." "I decided," she announced on December 13, "that you were a thousand times to be loved above Dick, by me that is, because, as you say, we complement each other." She did not try to hide it when she was lonely or depressed. "The only thing I could think of that would possibly console me was you to be very close and loving, the way you are." She began urging him to visit her for the New Year's holiday. When he did not respond affirmatively, she made further references to Dick. "We had a jolly good time," she wrote on the 20th. "He's an awfully good sport . . . that must make you very jealous." She indicated that Dick would be her New Year's Eve date. On the 23rd she mentioned another attentive escort—"a male name o' Rowland . . . awfully nice slouchy sort—knows enough to gas about books and music. Bro't me home and we have now two engagements—you'd better come down here. I'm a very fly [by-night] girl sometimes."

On December 27, in her last letter of the old year, she thanked Ernest profusely for the exquisite evening bag he sent her—soft to the touch, beautifully ornamented with stones. Then she described her walk along the icy, quiet neighborhood streets and the glow that came over her when she imagined being swept up in his arms.

Yes, I think you are the nicest lover a person ever had. . . . I feel snatched up and appreciated and taken care of the way I did the night I rolled so fast and scaredly down the sand dunes in the dark and you whirled me up and kissed me—I want to be picked up *now* . . . if you were here you would be around me and [I would be] domestic and needing to be necessary to you. D'you ever feel that way about me? Big and lonely, only, and needing. Huh? Good night, Ernest dear, dear. Your Hash.

"The moment she entered the room . . . an intense feeling came over me. I knew she was the girl I was going to marry." This from a ruminating Ernest Hemingway, looking backward through the prism of other marriages and love affairs to his initial meeting with Hadley Richardson. Whether he actually experienced such a revelation is problematic. But by the time he had known her three weeks he was indeed talking about marriage, and it was obvious to his friends and his family that he was very much attracted to the woman from St. Louis. She was right about his liking her red hair. He thought it was terrific. Like his mother he always admired beautiful hair, especially if it was blonde or titian. He enjoyed her unaffected sense of fun, her sportsmanship, her frank appreciation of his spirited ways.

Edmund Wilson cited as the wifely qualities most suited to Ernest innocence and an awed appreciation for his exploits; his wife should be "the female bird, shy and retiring, entirely devoted to the splendid and brave and adventurous cock-pheasant." There was an element of this in the initial interaction between Hadley and Ernest. But the Hadley Richardson of 1920 was not "the little school-teacher type" suggested by Wilson as the ideal wife for the posturing Hemingway. Shy, yes, reserved, yes; but the strength beneath the reserve was impressive, and Wilson himself, who liked Hadley, described her as not beautiful but then not exactly plain either—rather, she was "wholesome and level-headed."

It was not altogether a coincidence that the first woman who engaged Ernest's serious attention after Agnes von Kurowsky was also eight years older. There was in Hadley a gracefulness that was evocative of Agnes and a nurturing instinct that met Ernest's needs. But chronological numbers in Hadley's case were deceiving. Unlike Agnes, Hadley was the sleeping beauty ready to be awakened by an intrepid prince scaling the wall. She often thought of Ernest as Chaucer's "very parfit gentle knight." (Long after her divorce, married happily for thirty years to her second husband, she could describe Ernest as a prince, a beautiful man, and an impish smile would spread across her face.)

Hadley was back in St. Louis only a few days when her "parfit knight" began to bombard her with letters. He also wrote his mother in California about "Hash," his wonderful new friend. "She wants me very badly to come to a big New Years eve dinner and party at the University Club in Sin Louis—but I can't negotiate the grade. Being about as well seeded as the navel orange [seeds meaning money]." He bragged to his sister Marcelline that Hadley was a great sport, hobbling to a football game with him on a badly sprained ankle in a red felt bedroom slipper on her bandaged foot. "Anybody else would have been embarrassed," he boasted. "She went along as though nothing had happened."

In December Ernest moved out of Y.K.'s apartment into another with his old friend, Bill Horne, from Schio. A few days later he nailed down his first steady job—forty dollars a week writing for a slick monthly magazine known as *The Cooperative Commonwealth*. He wrote Hadley everything he was thinking and doing. Sometimes he asked himself whether she could go on loving him for a little while at least, or whether it would all end too soon. Hadley chided him. "Don't you expect to hold out very long yourself . . . do you mean . . . that you don't feel the capacity to stand the long strain of . . . our companionship?" After an initial drawing back, she was beginning to let her own feelings run free. "You are mine," she wrote, "my own. . . . I do love you very much. And I want to love you more."

Life in St. Louis was changing. Two St. Louis friends moved in with Hadley. She began to practice at the piano again, walked for miles in the snow, ice-skated in the park, saw the great Pavlova dance. Each new day was hers to fill as she wished. Interesting men took her out. But even as old admirers and new ones gathered around her, she was longing for her Nesto. "At the party last night [New Year's Eve] . . . I danced with everyone . . . [but] I was feeling so blue thru all this and thinking so hard of you—wondering where you were. . . . Dick was very sympathetic and . . . considerate . . . [he] did kiss me good night in the quietest way—and I let him —cause I do like Dick and . . . feel sorry for him."

When Ernest wrote her that his old friend Jim Gamble, the Red Cross captain, had invited him to Rome, Hadley wrote dreamily about the delicious temptation of going with him. "Rome sounds so wonderful. I would be so envious of you! The mossy old fountain of the Tritons, Mont de Pincio . . . Castello Angelo and the river. . . . I would miss you pretty frightfully. . . . I hope it's not too unfair to say so." Then he wrote her that they should get married and go to Italy together. Such an idea was "pure madness," she admitted, but suggested that money would be no problem, in "the bold penniless dash" for Europe. She could take tickets at the movie house in Milan or try her hand at sweeping chimneys. But in every letter she reiterated that most important to her was his writing. His ambition must be their guide. "I'm not at all the woman [who] wants her practical future guaranteed."

By the end of January, she was thinking of him every waking moment, seeing him in every situation, saying his name to herself when others were talking. "Just think," she wrote on the 18th, "of loving somebody so heavenly that it's absolutely right and good to love—and he even needs it." She appreciated the interest he showed in her music. "It makes a separate and personal thrill for me. Harrison [Williams, her piano teacher] tho't I could do something good, but last year when he came back from Boston he 'llowed I had reverted to type. Quite a nail to drive in, n'est-ce pas? But your loving it makes a new pleasure."

The difference in their ages, however, was becoming a nagging concern. At the ice-skating rink an attractive sixteen-year-old reminded her of Ernest—something about his face and build. The boy sensed the woman staring at him, so he showed off for her until she broke into a grin. "Guess he wonders who's the old girl with the second-hand come hither in her eye," she joked. In other letters she dealt with the subject soberly, wondering if Ernest wouldn't be better off finding someone younger. He protested that it made no difference at all. She admitted that it was a kind of testing of him, that she had to be absolutely sure he didn't mind. It would be awful to think she could lead him about. "Ernest," she wrote, "*I* have never taken an attitude of olderness to your youngerness in anything that mattered, have I? . . . I don't feel that way. . . . I can learn from you every minute of the time. . . . "

In January, Ernest had moved back with Kenley, this time to a seven-room apartment on Division Street. Ernest's friends were beginning to question his romance with Hadley. Why should Hemingstein succumb to the marital state when his life was so pleasantly unencumbered? Y.K. gave him a long afternoon's worth of advice on the way into the city from Oak Park one Sunday. When Ernest referred to the conversation in his letter as "unusual for us men," Hadley felt a tug of anxiety. It was the beginning of February, two months since she had seen him. "Terribly low lately," she confessed, " . . . am dull, am dull. Would pay a thousand for—not just one kiss —that would bring me just to normal—but two—that would make me very very happy. Don't you know the way you put your arm around me in a taxi? I want it. Brute!"

In Chicago Ernest was struggling with the finances and logistics of arranging to visit her. Finally, on February 19, his special delivery letter seemed to indicate that a trip was really going to materialize. Trying to encourage him, Hadley wrote:

> . . . it will all be smooth as a mill pond. . . . you're to have my room, and I'll have to keep coming to get things. And you'll stay awhile Ernest, won't you. I want you to eat lunch with me at our little table in the den and get breakfast with me—or sleep late, as you will—and sit by the fire with me and read lots of your things to me. . . . And we can hustle off to the Park some sunny, springy day with oranges and bread and butter . . . and wander around or sit around. . . . Come along, Ernest, it'll be sweet anywhere you and I are together. . . . you gotta come now, dearest heart, cause I gotta have you.

Everything was at last worked out. Ernest and Katy Smith came down for a three-day weekend beginning March 11. Prudish relatives had been told that Ernest was Fonnie's guest, put up for convenience in the apartment above. Hadley had little patience with such subterfuge. All that mattered now was that they were together at last. When she saw him in his brand-new Brooks Brothers suit, she was overcome with shyness. Then he paraded about in his Italian cape and she forgot her reserve. "How I love that cape," she wrote later. He brought news of a possible job in Toronto and left her his scrapbook of *Star* articles. They talked long and seriously about whether to take off for Italy or stay on this side of the Atlantic. Hadley felt brave enough not to worry about which it would be. " . . . [Why] wait around and make hoards and piles, instead of working and living along in the . . . way we want and people should —with the person they love. . . . " At the end of the visit, they decided that Hadley would go to Chicago in two weeks.

The only one to raise an objection to the romance was Fonnie Usher. "For Ernest and my sister," Hadley recalled, "it was not love at first sight or second." In spite of his courteous manners and good looks, twenty-one-year-old Ernest Hemingway did not fit in with Fonnie's idea of a proper match for her twenty-nine-year-old sister. She could hardly be blamed for thinking them an ill-suited couple. But she kept her reservations in check.

Several of Hadley's friends, George and Helen Breaker and Ruth Bradfield, accompanied her on the Chicago trip, but even with this reinforcement she suffered an acute attack of stage fright upon reentering Y.K.'s apartment. Ernest's exuberance rescued her. He gave her the confidence to crack jokes, be familiar with the guys and affectionate, even bold, with him. (Passers-by on Division Street were startled when Ernest and Hadley passionately kissed in full view on the sidewalk.) Ruth Bradfield was struck by the excitement young Hemingway generated everywhere he went. Everything that happened took on a heightened quality because of his enthusiasm— the food they ate, the books they argued over, the small supper clubs they visited.

Ernest took Hadley to Oak Park to meet his family, and modest though she was, she could see that she was making a big hit. "I must have looked tame to them," she said. Their biggest worry seemed to be that headstrong Ernest might not know how to care for a "sedate little bride." Dr. Hemingway, who had been suffering from angina pectoris, rushed around talking fast and exuding enthusiasm. Hadley was made somewhat uneasy by Grace, who reminded her of her own mother in her self-importance and strength of bearing.

"We were not made to be friends," she admitted, "but she worked at it."

On their last evening together, before she boarded the night sleeper for St. Louis, Hadley explained to Ernest about her trust funds. There was a modest one from her mother, and her grandfather had left her a capital account that yielded an income of about twenty-five hundred dollars a year. It seemed logical to her to use that patrimony to back Ernest in his career. His work was a powerful catalyst in her love for him. "I never expected to find anyone into whose life I could fling my spirit—and now I can—every side of me backs you up," she vowed. She could not imagine loving someone wholeheartedly who was not himself devoted to art. She rationalized that a few years earlier they could not have expected a successful marriage because she was still consumed with ambition. "Ambition as well as passion for music would have kept me unhappy, because married . . . I could never satisfy either." Her own struggles for a career made her a thousand times more understanding of his agonizing doubts. " . . . you're honestly the first one that's ever satisfied me . . . intellectually and spiritually."

Two months went by before she saw him again. The separation seemed less intolerable, however, now that they were at least tacitly betrothed. Her favorite new word was *together*. "I want to be with you together." She promised him a Corona typewriter for his birthday. "I will give you a Corona and you will consequently marry me . . . man marries girl who gives him Corona, is rumor." Ernest, distorting even further the truth about how Grace financed her Longfield retreat, now complained that he had been cheated out of a Princeton education because his mother squandered the family savings on the cottage. Hadley assured him that he needed no university—he was smart without it. She praised him for saving so much out of his weekly salary—"Don't see how a . . . mortal man can save $42 out of $52 a week."—and began to send him some of her own checks to be invested in Italian lire. Italy was still their most likely destination, although a friend of Y.K.'s, the novelist Sherwood Anderson, suggested that Paris was a better city for serious writing. Hadley repeated that she would follow Ernest anywhere—Italy, Paris, Toronto, or the near-North Side of Chicago.

The living situation at Y.K.'s had deteriorated for the bachelor boarders. Ernest began to sleep on the roof to avoid the stuffy little room he shared with Bill Horne. He had worked up an intense dislike for Doodles Smith, whom he suspected of carrying on a clandestine affair with one of the young men in their crowd. According to Ernest, she was a slothful housekeeper and a bad pianist and was the first of a long list of his friends' wives who became the target for his disapproval. Hadley, on the other hand, epitomized what was most beguiling and reassuring—her devotion, her belief in him, her unaffected trust. But a wife was different from a pal. As he drew about him the warming mantle of her love, he looked nervously behind him to the freedom of trout streams and wilderness. "Guy loves a couple or three streams all his life," he wrote to Bill Smith. " . . . falls in love with a girl and the goddamn streams can dry up for all he cares."

Something of this underlying tension persisted in all Ernest's marriages, as he reserved for himself the freedom to wander off in search of "the goddamn stream." Hadley, from the beginning of their relationship, seemed to understand these needs. She believed that she could fill them, and in the act of so doing, satisfy her own as well. "I love your ambitions," she wrote on April 30. "Don't think I am ambitious except to be a balanced, happy, intelligent lady, making the man happy and using everything lovely he has to give me, very hard."

On May 20, Hadley wrote that she could put her mind to nothing except his Memorial Day visit. A few pages into the same letter she described a book on sex relations that her sister lent her:

> . . . some good stuff in it . . . mature-minded people have to gauge things for themselves but think we're crazy enough about each other to look out for one another if things aren't good for us. . . . I feel the way you do—want you to be happier than anybody ever has been—in *all* the beautiful ways there are.

On Saturday morning, May 28, Ernest and Bill Horne arrived in St. Louis. Now the wedding plans were discussed openly. Ernest suggested a church in Horton Bay for the ceremony, and Hadley liked the idea. She did not want Fonnie to take charge of the arrangements and she did not like the memories evoked by St. Louis. "I was dull in St. Louis," she remarked. "Everything was dull in St. Louis." She hoped that the occasion would be simple and quiet.

" . . . can't we 'give' it ourselves," she suggested wistfully, "and do our 'reception' sort of round about the church door . . . [then jump into] that doity motor[boat] of Bill's [Smith]. . . . go—git out, run!" (In the end, it did not turn out that way. Four hundred and fifty guests attended the marriage ceremony and the dinner afterward. But at least Hadley had the satisfaction of taking the control out of her sister's hands.) She was furious when she learned that Fonnie had suggested to Ernest that she might not be strong enough for marriage and child-bearing. In strong terms she told Fonnie to mind her own business. Fonnie protested that she was really crazy about him, and Hadley relaxed, proud that she had not wilted under family pressure.

Ernest's friends were still concerned about his getting married. They had nothing against Hadley. Bill Smith, for one, liked her very much, though he tried to talk Ernest out of marrying her because he thought she was too old. The other men emphasized that marriage per se was a bad idea for a talented young man on his way up, which was plausible except that it did not apply to Ernest. The best thing for his talent was Hadley's faith in it. And the emotional stability of marriage was important to his youthful psyche. In his early relationships with women he was as old-fashioned as any Oak Park churchgoer. As soon as the first stirrings of passion seized him he thought of marriage.

Hadley understood Ernest much better than did his friends. She knew that she was right for him. She would follow him anywhere. She would never jam him into any rigid mold, having known too many stultifying traps herself to spring one on him. She never doubted that he would make a good husband and bring honor to her. When Ernest passed along some of the naysayers' doubts, she reacted sharply. "We're PARTNERS," she reminded him. Maybe she wasn't the perfect woman for him, maybe the whole thing was a vast mistake. God hadn't told her any secrets, and she doubted He had told anyone else either. ". . . if I hadn't been aware of my ability to back my single self financially . . . I wouldn't have let you, ever, take me on." Perhaps she was also implying that if she had not had her own money, she would not have taken *him* on.

It was a rainy June 14 when Hadley formally announced her engagement. " . . . only the best friends arrived at all," she wrote

Ernest the next day. "Had a lovely time. . . . Telegram in the midst of the party from Dr. and Mrs. C.E.H. Awful nice? Here are the two notices [from the local papers]. . . . Dearest love—you're awfully easy to talk about to people."

During the humid weeks that followed, she assembled her trousseau, packed up the accumulated belongings of a lifetime, and made the myriad decisions required when one leaves a place "apparently forever." She selected a creamy bolt of imported lace for the wedding dress, which she and her friends cut from a pattern then handed over to an expert dressmaker for the sewing and finishing. There was a small contretemps with Ernest over her veil. He was afraid she would be overdressed for his ushers. She exploded:

> You practically tell me . . . that I can't wear a veil because Bill Smith hasn't any dressy clothes. . . . seems to me I've heard of brides wearing veils even at morning weddings—oh well—I'll inquire around and tell you what I think in a few days—you know St. Paul says it about women's heads—what variety of church is this anyway? . . . Wot kinda bathing soot do'you like me in? . . . I immediately note anything you don't like me in. So tell me.

Nothing was too private to share with him. In her letter of June 7 she ruminated over a girlhood friendship with a lesbian, a Mrs. Rapallo.

> I appealed to her . . . [and her companion] as a helpless little somebody. . . . she managed to show me how much pleasanter life was [with them] . . . then this rotten suggestion of evil [from Hadley's mother]. . . . being very suggestible I began to imagine I had all this low sex feelin' and she for me—quite sure now it was nothing. . . . but if home had been different I wouldn't have wanted them. . . . By George, I'm fond of her still. She was a lady to the end—never insulted my family . . . and she knew what they tho't of her. . . . you needn't fear on that side, my dear. There was a time when someone liking me that much made me think I liked them that much but I know now that I don't. I like other kinds better—very few women and a great many kinds of men.

She did like men. While she turned up hems and sorted out books, male friends would drop in for a chat. What they mostly heard from her was her unaffected praise of her fiancé. With such easy camaraderie in her own life, she did not seem disturbed that Ernest dropped hints about Katy Smith and about what may or may not have gone on between them in the past. She suggested mildly that such things were perhaps better left unsaid and slyly suggested that he might like to postpone the wedding. That ended the subject.

When Ernest sent Hadley his first poems and then a satirical short story, "A Divine Gesture," her breathless praise was exactly what his ego needed. He was too severe with himself to be spoiled by it. Now and again she tempered the compliments with some detached good sense. "It takes a lot of humbleness to hold yourself down to truthfulness in an art," she wrote on June 27, "and up to the day of your death you'll probably find yourself slipping . . . into poor psychology . . . it's just as hard for you as for anyone else to be honest . . . but no one has a better chance than you because you've the will to be."

She accepted with alacrity Grace's offer of Windemere for the honeymoon. "Already," Hadley wrote her future mother-in-law, "Ernest and I have long romantic conversations about getting the groceries." Grace deserved their gratitude. It would take a gigantic effort to move her large brood out and clean up the place for the newlyweds. Letters now began to increase between Oak Park and St. Louis as Grace pressed Hadley for some decisions. There were numerous problems in moving an entire wedding party from St. Louis to northern Michigan, but finally, to Grace's relief, the date and hour were set—September 3, 1921, at 4:00 P.M.

Ernest was not handling the distance from Hadley as well as she. Perhaps the rejection by Agnes von Kurowsky was still too fresh for him to feel entirely safe in Hadley's absence. He was beginning to demonstrate his need for continuous reassurance and the pattern of wide mood swings between ebullience and depression was evolving. Hadley already knew about his nightmares. "Wish I were there," she wrote, "to rub you [and] sit by you till you just sailed softly off to sleep—then would kiss you very tenderly and go away —not very far and listen for when you weren't maybe happy in the dark night, if the dreams came again." Now in his loneliness he was writing morbidly of "mortage" [suicide]. She decided that her repeated declarations of love were not enough for his sagging morale and arranged to go to Chicago for a weekend in the middle of July.

All tensions evaporated when they touched one another. They went dancing and drank white wine, gossiped with friends, imagined what life would be like when they finally got to Italy. Y.K. and Doodles invited Hadley to move in with Ernest (who was still their boarder) after the honeymoon. If Hadley had reservations about such an arrangement she did not share them with anyone. After returning to St. Louis she sent Ernest the much talked about Corona in time for his twenty-second birthday, under the mistaken impression that he was twenty-three.

Preparations continued, and by the end of July Hadley was back in Chicago again. This time she would not return to St. Louis before the wedding. It was joyous and sad all at the same time, for she was saying goodbye to dear friends and familiar sights and a way of life that offered a comfortable continuity even when it was etched with frustration. But she was heeding her own instincts, approaching this large step with a sure-footedness that was impressive.

For one delirious week in Chicago she gave herself up to the pleasures of being in love, following Ernest about from office to luncheon to boulevard, "wonderful times of hand-in-arm breathing together, stepping together." In the evenings they slipped away from the crowd in Y.K.'s living room to seek privacy on the rooftop. "I wish I could have you now to pet," she wrote later from the fishing camp in Wisconsin where she would stay until it was time to go to Horton Bay. "Remember how we both tried to be the little, small, petted one the last night on the roof? There wasn't ever a petter like you, Oin." In her bemused state she had left souvenirs of her presence everywhere—her umbrella in Y.K.'s apartment, her jewelry in the hotel safe, Ruth Bradfield's bridesmaid's hat in the compartment of the train, and she caught cold as soon as she hit the chilly air of Wisconsin.

Meanwhile, Ernest was beginning to suspect that something shady was going on in the operation of *The Cooperative Commonwealth*, but his financial situation was so precarious that he hung on, hoping to earn a few more dollars before the organization collapsed. Compounding his anxieties during the weeks before the wedding was a quarrel with Y.K. over the activities of Doodles and Don Wright. Y.K. angrily withdrew his invitation to Hadley and Ernest to move in after their marriage, and Ernest rented an apartment for them in an old house on North Dearborn. Hadley, typically optimistic, wrote that it sounded jolly and perfect, and went to work on a new budget—$75.00 a month for rent, $30.00 for meat and vegetables, $8.00 for milk and eggs, and always something set aside for the lire.

The barrage of letters that had begun with Ernest's and Hadley's accidental meeting in October 1920 was drawing to an end. Had they not been prolific letter writers, the meeting in Y.K.'s apartment would likely have come to nothing. But both parties had an unusual capacity not only for relating the minutiae of their daily lives, but for confiding their deepest yearnings. And so the love affair had prospered. Their weeks together probably numbered no more than six in the entire eleven months of the courtship. Planes did not fly between St. Louis and Chicago. Telephone connections were primitive. Visits had to be chaperoned and carefully financed. Only a stream of special delivery letters made up for the miles that separated them. One of Hadley's last was hastily scrawled on the afternoon of August 21 in a burst of passion. "I need you in *every* part of my life. I wanta be kissed. I wanta pull your head down on my heart and hold it very close and cradle you there for hours, you blessed thing—love you, love you—your ownest in the world."

Ernest reached Horton Bay on Sunday, August 28, irritable and hollow-eyed from lack of sleep. He greeted the family at Windemere then took off at dawn for a three-day fishing trip, his last as a bachelor. Grace, meanwhile, was directing the refurbishing of the house, including a new roof for the porch and fresh varnish on the wood floors. It was not likely that Hadley would take special note of a new roof, but Grace was not satisfied until everything passed inspection. Not only did the house have to be groomed but her husband and children as well. There were light summer dresses for Ursula and Carol, a flowered frock for herself, a slightly baggy white linen suit for Leicester, and a wing collar for the doctor. A complicated schedule of packing had been worked out so that all the Hemingways could vacate the house on the morning of the wedding. Sunny, at summer camp in Minnesota, would proceed directly to Oak Park to stay with the grandparents. Marcelline, who was still in Maine, would learn about the festivities from her mother's letters.

Ernest returned on Thursday from fishing the Sturgeon River. He looked sunburned and fit but it seemed to Grace that he was

Ernest Hemingway at the time of his courtship of Hadley Richardson. Spring 1921.
From the John F. Kennedy Library

Hadley Richardson, moments before the 4:00 P.M. wedding. September 3, 1921.
From the John F. Kennedy Library

apprehensive and had to be encouraged every step of the way. On Friday Hadley, the Breakers, and Ruth Bradfield arrived to warm greetings from Auntie Charles, who was putting them up in her home and held a dinner party in their honor Friday night. She omitted from her guest list all the Hemingways except the groom. Grace was hurt by this curious snub but not surprised. She knew that Auntie thought of herself as socially superior to the other summer people.

From the hilltop setting of the Charleses' house Hadley drank in the vistas of blue water and green hillside and sniffed the clear September air. She had overruled Fonnie's objection to the word "obey" in the marriage vows—its implications did not bother her —and challenged Auntie's warning that Ernest would be a difficult young man to live with. She went for an afternoon swim, forgetting how long it took for her thick hair to dry, and was a little late for the ceremony, arriving with damp hair. But the ivory lace dress hung beautifully on her stately frame. The soft veil, held in place by a wreath of flowers, cascaded down her back, and she carried a bouquet of babies' breath.

The church was decorated with swamp lilies and balsam boughs. The children squirmed in the heat. Leicester swears that his brother's legs were shaking as he walked down the aisle. The family's perception of Ernest as an uneasy bridegroom seems confirmed in a sketch, "Wedding Day," not published until 1972, in which Nick Adams is the bridegroom. After a swim, Nick's friends stand about nervously as he puts on his blue wedding suit and knots his striped tie. Everyone takes a long gulp from a bottle of whiskey. "He enjoyed their nervousness," the story goes. "He wondered if it would be this way if he were going to be hanged. Probably. He could never realize anything until it happened." Ernest's ushers wore blue jackets and white flannels and there was the usual horseplay as Ernest was teased about Kid Hemingway now going to the mat and a radiant Hadley posed for pictures for an hour in front of the church.

The honeymoon began after dark with a quick getaway in a borrowed Ford and a long row in the damp night air across Walloon Lake. Ernest beached the boat and helped Hadley scramble ashore, and then the lovers embraced. "Nick kissed her," Ernest would write later in the same sketch. "She kissed him back hard the way he had taught her with her mouth a little open so their tongues could play with each other. They held tight to each other and then walked up to the cottage. . . . Nick unlocked the door and then went back to the boat to get the bags. He lit the lamps and they looked through the cottage together."

At Windemere the temperature dropped and the poorly insulated house was difficult to heat. Hadley could not find the proper cooking utensils. A careful letter of instruction, drawn up by Grace to prevent such frustrations, was not discovered for two weeks. Ernest was suffering from a recurrent throat virus and Hadley still had a hacking cough. The magnificent Indian summer of northern Michigan mocked them in their sickly state. They were too ill to enjoy water sports or hikes into the woods. Dragging themselves across the lake in a borrowed motorboat to bring in provisions was a big nuisance. But after a few depressing days, their spirits lifted. They took long naps in Grace's oversized bed, kept a fire blazing on the hearth, and nursed their fevers with a home brew of mulled wine.

In a week they had recovered sufficiently to have lunch with Grace and ten-year-old Carol at Grace Cottage and wander about Petoskey greeting Ernest's former girlfriends. With her mother-in-law Hadley brought forth her best manners. She was charming and deferential, later sending off a proper letter of thanks. She was "busting with gratitude" and charmed with Windemere—was terribly sad to be leaving it.

About the girlfriends she was not so enthusiastic. It seemed to her in bad taste to go from house to house meeting the young women who had not won the competition. Hadley did not hide her disapproval of Ernest's vanity and was not appeased by his explanation that the reason for the introductions was to elevate him in her estimation. It may have seemed a lame excuse to Hadley but it was probably close to the truth. In spite of Ernest's good looks and unusual talent, he was seized frequently with sharp feelings of inferiority. At the same time that he was trying to impress her with his conquests he was telling her that she was the first woman he had ever slept with. She believed this to be true. And in the sense of its being his first sustained sexual relationship no doubt it was. His affair with Agnes was not consummated and the encounter with the waitress in the shadows behind the Potato House was very brief. Both Hadley and Ernest brought a kind of innocence to their love-making and there is every indication that each satisfied the other as they set up housekeeping in the fifth-floor walk-up on North Dearborn.

The apartment was cramped and shabbily furnished. Hadley tried to brighten it with wedding gifts, but family silver and bone china did not make up for leaky pipes and a lumpy Murphy bed. Her buoyancy was further tested by the run-down neighborhood and many hours of being alone. Although Ernest had finally left *The Cooperative Commonwealth* to avoid being embroiled in its financial shenanigans, his habit was not to stay home and brood but to wander about the city in search of new faces and new scenes. Hadley's best friend, for a brief period, was the grocery man around the corner. "He could smell a lonely woman," she recollected.

Grace Hemingway came to call but the visit was not a success. Knowing the depth of Ernest's hostility toward his mother, Hadley was cool to Grace's pious lectures about love and marriage. Probably she overreacted, since Grace was at heart a generous-spirited woman. Hadley played out her irritation by showing up at the Hemingways' twenty-fifth anniversary party in an unflattering outfit, thus depriving Grace of the satisfaction of introducing a stylish new daughter-in-law to Oak Park society. A week later she stepped out, more suitably attired, at a public Fireman's Ball in Chicago.

Later in the fall, Sherwood Anderson and his wife invited the young Hemingways to dinner. Anderson, a friendly, warm-hearted man, spent the evening extolling the advantages of Paris over Italy for Ernest's career. He had just returned from six months in the French capital, living and working on the Left Bank, meeting the famous expatriates Gertrude Stein and Ezra Pound. In Paris Ernest's imagination could run free, said Anderson. And the exchange rate was favorable. It was absolutely the place to go.

Hadley listened closely. She had recently inherited eight thousand dollars after the death of an uncle. Such a windfall would provide the necessary cushion. She trusted Anderson. With her strong encouragement Ernest was convinced that they should go. John Bone, the managing editor of the *Toronto Daily Star*, then agreed to publish Ernest's dispatches about European events. He could cover sports and politics. Passage was booked on a French Line ship that sailed out of New York on December 8, 1921.

Sherwood Anderson wrote in behalf of the young couple to all his influential friends, letters that were full of superlatives about this extraordinary writer of promise named Hemingway and his delightful wife. He recommended the Hôtel Jacob et d'Angleterre on the Left Bank as a cheap, comfortable roost until they located something permanent. Grace presented them with a check, Ed Hemingway packed them a box of food. Katy Smith, Bill Horne, and the rest came to the train platform on a freezing December day. Marcelline tossed Hadley her woolen gloves and one of the men followed with a muffler for Ernest. His friends were sniffling with sentiment, but Ernest was elated. Reinforced by Hadley's unwavering faith, he could not contain his excitement that finally he was on his way.

Chapter 6

The old ship *Leopoldina* pitched and rolled on the heavy winter sea. Hadley wrote home that she and Ernest "took turns being laid low," though she was bothered more by the vibration of the engines than the swell of the ocean. Ernest made friends with everyone and there were times when Hadley resented so much sociability. She wanted to believe that she and her husband were "all in all to each other." But rather than mope, she played the ship's piano and practiced her schoolgirl French with some of the crew. She even gathered up some admirers of her own—an elderly French gentleman and three dapper Argentinians. By the time the brown mountains of the Spanish coast came into sight the weather had turned calm and it was warm enough to sunbathe on the deck. The weather turned cold once again as they sailed across the Bay of Biscay and northward past the French coast. Hadley got a sore throat in spite of layers of sweaters, but she would not stay below. She did not want to miss a moment of the ship's approach to Le Havre.

Paris was nearly as cold as the north Atlantic. At the Jacob et d'Angleterre was a letter of welcome from Anderson. His description of the hotel was accurate—clean, inexpensive, crowded with Americans. Hadley did not mind their noisy presence. It was a comforting sound in the vast, strange city. In a few days it would be Christmas and this was her first not only in a foreign country but any place at all without close family. Ernest's way of combating

homesickness, his own or Hadley's, was to get out and walk, learn
the streets, observe the people, line up a bistro. They found a good,
cheap place to take their evening meal, Le Pré Aux Clercs, on rue
Bonaparte around the corner from the hotel.

This was the Sixth Arrondissement, the Paris of writers and
painters, stretching from the left bank of the Seine to the Boulevard
Montparnasse. At the intersection of Boulevards Raspail and Montparnasse were the three cafés that Malcolm Cowley has called the
"heart and nervous system of the . . . literary colony"—the Dôme,
the Select, and the Rotonde. On an afternoon before Christmas,
weary of sightseeing, Hadley and Ernest rested on the terrace of the
Dôme, drawing warmth from the burning coals of a charcoal brazier
and sipping delicious hot rum. " . . . we've been walking the streets,
day and night, arm through arm, peering into courts and stopping
in front of little shop windows," wrote Ernest to Sherwood Anderson, his pen moving quickly in the cold air. "The pastry'll kill Bones
[Hadley] eventually I'm afraid. She's a hound for it. Must have
always been a suppressed desire with her I guess. . . . we're terrible
glad we're here and we hope you have a good Christmas and New
Year. . . . " Hadley added her own note. "Every word he says is true,
especially the wishes for the jolliest kind of Christmas season. It feels
anything but strange here . . . what with your note of welcome and
the feeling that you too have lived here so lately . . . we're going out
now to shop for each other's Christmas stockings. I will try to keep
from buying pastries for him. Here we go."

On Christmas morning, cheered by letters and gifts from home,
they decided to explore the Right Bank, the Paris of the rich and
fashionable. Still respectful of their slender budget and unsure about
public transportation, they set out on foot, crossing the Seine at
Pont Neuf and walking the entire length of the Avenue de l'Opera.
The Louvre was closed for the holiday. The Jardin des Tuileries in
all its stately expanse was deserted save for a few lovers like themselves. The shops around the Place Vendôme were nothing like the
ones in the Latin Quarter. Here were the matched jewels—rubies,
emeralds, sapphires—gaudily set in tiaras and chokers to attract
international money. On the rue de la Paix they decided it was time
for Christmas dinner. The menu of the Café de la Paix looked
manageable. They ordered judiciously but when the *addition* was
presented their spirits drooped. Somehow they had misinterpreted

the prices. Ernest did not have enough money in his pocket to pay the bill. So he sprinted back to the hotel, leaving Hadley to sit alone in the restaurant. She feigned poise as best as she could. But she morbidly imagined his being hit by a car or struck down in some way that would keep him from rescuing her. Of course he returned, having run as fast as he could both ways. But they went to sleep that night somewhat subdued.

The first one of Anderson's friends to call them was Lewis Galantière, a slightly built, witty young man of twenty-six with a finely developed taste for antiques and engravings. Hadley was comfortable with him immediately. His flair for mimicry amused her and she appreciated the care with which he had furnished his flat in the rue Jean Goujon. He took them to a fine restaurant, Café Michaud, for their first gourmet meal since the Christmas fiasco. Galantière liked the Hemingways—Ernest for being a gay companion and Hadley for her all-around niceness. He promised to help them find an apartment when the holidays were over.

Ernest had already started to work up a piece for the *Star* about tuna fishing in Spain, based on his observations when the ship had docked briefly in Vigo harbor. He could expect about thirty-five dollars per article. But since nothing was coming in yet, Hadley's checks from St. Louis were crucial. With Lewis to guide them they looked at rentals in the Latin Quarter off Boulevards Montparnasse and Saint-Michel, the neighborhood they already knew something of from living on the rue Jacob. This was the popular place to be. But Hadley soon realized that desirable places in the Quarter were more than they could afford. Ernest wanted to spend their little store of money for travel and recreation, not fancy digs. Hadley was as enthusiastic as he was about exploring other parts of Europe. Finally Lewis directed them to a fourth-floor walk-up at 74, rue du Cardinal Lemoine, in an archaic, working-class district of the Fifth Arrondissement, far from the good cafés and restaurants. Hadley agreed with Ernest that they should take it.

Paris was still wet when they moved in on January 9, 1922, and Ernest proposed that they have a holiday in Switzerland instead of settling down immediately to work and housekeeping. The article on Vigo was finished and mailed. They could eat as cheaply in the mountains as they could in Paris. He heard that train fare was nominal. He could write anywhere and the dry air would be good for Hadley's cough. What did she think? Hadley thought it was a good idea. She could be ready anytime. Perhaps the weather in Paris would even clear up by the time they got back. They outfitted themselves with skiis and boots (an example of how they found money to do the things they considered important) and bought third-class railway tickets for Montreux, the winter resort on Lake Geneva. In Montreux were shops, fashionable hotels, and many members of the old and new French aristocracy. They stayed long enough for Ernest to form impressions for future *Star* articles and then rode the small electric train straight up the side of the mountain to their pension at Chamby.

It was a brown wood chalet, owned by a pleasant German-Swiss couple named Gangwisch. A large, comfortable room, as clean as Hadley could have hoped for, and three good meals for two came to less than five dollars. Every morning while they still dozed under the blankets, Mme. Gangwisch came in with armloads of wood for their tall porcelain stove. She closed the windows, tended the fire until it was roaring, and then returned with the breakfast trays. From her perch against the pillows, Hadley could see the lake in the distance. The mountain dropped steeply to the little plain along the water. It was a white world. Fields and slopes and rooftops were blurred into soft shapes by the drifting snow. Hadley was enthusiastic about the skiing and learned easily, making better progress at first than Ernest, who was still bothered by stiffness in his knee from the war wound. For the long hikes through the dark pine forests she wore hobnailed boots and carried a steel-tipped walking stick. The snow was packed down and the air was clear and sharp. Once or twice they saw deer tracks. Another time they surprised a fox. There was an inn at the Bains de l'Alliaz that served *glühwein*, a hot red wine with spices and lemons in it. Some days they lounged at the chalet, reading, writing letters, playing two-handed card games, and, if the sun was hot, eating their lunch on the porch.

Back in Paris the rains had stopped and a winter sun warmed their tiny flat. "It certainly is crowded," wrote Hadley to Grace on February 20, 1922, "but it is undoubtedly comfortable." It may have been more crowded than comfortable, but she tried to be optimistic whenever she wrote Ernest's mother. She knew that the apartment was a sorry affair in many ways. "The steep winding staircase had a niche on each flight for a step-on-two-pedals toilet," she recalled.

Hadley and Ernest at Chamby. Winter 1922.
From the Patrick Hemingway Collection, Princeton University Library

"We had a living-bedroom of odd shapes and queer angles, a nice black mantel and fireplace, a huge fake mahogany bed with lots of gilt decoration. The mattress was good." She rearranged the furniture and left space in the dining alcove for the small, upright Gavian piano. From the concierge she learned of Marie-Cocotte (Marie Rohrbach), who, for two francs an hour, emptied the slop jars and hauled the garbage, took care of the laundry, and taught Hadley the rudiments of French cooking.

The flat, made comfortable by Hadley's efforts, was still too small for Ernest to work in solitude. He rented a bedroom for sixty francs a month on the top floor of a hotel in rue Mouffetard and there struggled every day to write simple sentences that would meet his stringent standards. He was striving for truth and economy of style. His own acute ear and his detached way of observing others were slowly finding their way into his writing. None of it came easily. His blue notebooks were filled with scratched-out phrases, false starts, and endless corrections. He was impatient to be published but not at the expense of being derivative or pandering to public taste. He was going to forge his own style and it would come from serious, hard work.

With Ernest strict about his working hours, Hadley was alone most of the day. She ate breakfast with him, if she was awake, but it was a silent meal, for Ernest was already preoccupied with the accusing blank pages that awaited him in his hotel room. In spite of many solitary hours, however, she never suffered from an isolation of the spirit that had so oppressed her when she was living with her mother. When she was lonely, it was the practical result of being thrust into a rough neighborhood where she was the foreigner. She thought that her red hair made her conspicuous and she was self-conscious in American clothes. Though plain enough, they were very different from the shapeless coats worn by the laborers' wives. Her schoolgirl French was inadequate to the swift argot of the tradespeople and she was cautious about venturing far from home. Ernest had written his friends that he was living in the best part of the Latin Quarter and enjoying a fine view of the Seine from the living room. What Hadley actually saw from her living room were glimpses of the tiny shops and walls of other buildings.

As the good weather continued, she moved outward in ever widening circles. From the top of rue du Cardinal Lemoine she could walk straight down to the river as the street descended sharply to the busy beginning of the Boulevard Saint-Germain. Here the quai was bleak and the wind seemed always to blow cold. Nothing attractive beckoned on the right, only Halle Aux Vins, the vast forbidding warehouse for storing wine from the provinces. Straight ahead, however, was the graceful small Isle St. Louis with its elegant, narrow houses carefully preserved, its healthy chestnut trees, and its quiet park at the very tip of the island that merged with the granite span of Pont Sully. There was a stairway down to the park where the fishermen of Paris put out their lines for the excellent catch called *goujon*, delicious when fried.

Far from this bucolic river scene, at the other end of Cardinal Lemoine, a radically different world seethed, the world that had so intimidated Hadley. At the top of the street in the old cobblestone square known as Place de la Contrescarpe were the bistros, some of them smelly and awful. Bundles of rags blocked the doorways. Then the rags moved, revealing themselves as wine-soaked men and women. The green autobus careened around a corner. Flower vendors dyed their flowers, the purple dye running into the gutters. On the market street, rue Mouffetard, where Ernest worked in the room once occupied by Paul Verlaine, housewives shouted and shoved and fought for cheap goods. Tired beggars bleated for alms in front of Église Saint-Médard. This was the Paris of Racine, the dramatist; Rabelais, the wit. Descartes had lived close by, not on the street named for him, but another one, rue Rollin. The buildings had aged. But the occupants still lived meagerly, fought a harsh existence, drank to forget their disappointment.

Hadley never developed a love affair with Place de la Contrescarpe to the degree that Ernest later did. But she learned to move about it with ease, no longer frightened by the squalor. Her stilted French was loosening up. Ernest's vitality was contagious. She thought again how handsome he looked in his worn jacket and cap, how well built, and felt fortunate that in this enormous, strange city he made friends so easily.

On a winter afternoon he rushed home to tell her of an important discovery. He had found a good rental library in a bookstore called Shakespeare and Company. The owner was Sylvia Beach, an American woman from New Jersey, who gave him a library card on credit and an armful of books. Hadley smiled. She knew Ernest for a voracious reader. Sometimes when he nuzzled and hugged her and she assumed his attention was lost in such pleasures, she would peek around to see him reading a folded-up newspaper behind her back. She asked him if Miss Beach had books by James, a favorite of hers. Ernest replied that she did, and they prepared to go out for their late afternoon walk, their drink at a café, and dinner at a neighborhood bistro.

At first Ernest had resisted calling on Anderson's important friends. His friendliness with the plain people of Paris did not extend easily to literary figures with established reputations. Until he was sure of acceptance he could be defensive, but eventually he and Hadley did have tea at Ezra Pound's studio and Hadley noticed that in the actual presence of the poet he became respectful and modest, with an attractive shyness. "He listened at Pound's feet as to an oracle," she said later. "I believe some of the ideas lasted all his life." The room was large and cold, the only heat radiating from a stove in the middle of the floor. Ugly shelves were haphazardly stacked, strange Japanese prints lined the walls. A great deal of tea was drunk. Hadley counted seventeen cups served the poet by his pretty wife, Dorothy. Hadley preferred Dorothy Pound's charming British reserve to Ezra's magisterial ways and his studied Bohemianism, though she appreciated his reputation for helping young writers he believed in. "He was quite cantankerous in temperament," she recalled. "Not at all lovable."

In March they met Gertrude Stein, who lived with her devoted companion, Alice B. Toklas, at 27, rue de Fleurus, a sharply angled street adjacent to the Jardin de Luxembourg. A correct French maid ushered them into a long, well-proportioned room that contained the jumble of good antiques typical of an affluent family and paintings worthy of a great modern museum. Hanging on every wall of the two-story apartment were the works of the innovators, now recognized masters—Cézanne's watercolors, Matisse's Fauve pictures, Picasso's sober green-and-tan Spanish landscapes.

Alice Toklas (whom Ernest persisted in calling Miss Tocraz) took them down the length of the room to meet Gertrude Stein, who was seated by a large fireplace where coals glowed and hissed. Hadley thought the shape of her head "absolutely beautiful" and her soft brown eyes not unlike Ernest's in the way that they saw everything. Ernest was struck by her solidly built body and heavy breasts, and he compared her "lovely, thick, alive immigrant hair" and mobile features to those of a northern Italian peasant woman.

Gertrude, forty-eight years old, twice Ernest's age, responded to his dark good looks in the same way that she enjoyed the masculine appeal of men such as Picasso and Juan Gris. She beckoned to him to sit beside her. Hadley prepared to sit there as well but was firmly steered by Alice to the other end of the room. This was the ritual at number 27. It applied only to wives. Nonwives, unmarried women, were admitted to Gertrude's intellectual discourse, but wives were expected to talk of domestic matters to Alice, whose piercing black eyes took in everything even as she served delicious liqueurs and tiny cakes or from her station across the room worked on a lapful of needlepoint. Hadley would have much preferred to hear what Gertrude was saying to Ernest, but since that conversation was out of earshot she resigned herself to Alice's monologue.

As they walked back to their quarter both the Hemingways admitted that they felt somewhat like two well-behaved children who had been forgiven for being in love and married. Hadley found Alice's steel control rather frightening, but the open attachment between the women did not trouble her. She enjoyed their colorful life, their taste and intelligence. She respected their effort to confront their emotional needs openly. Ernest was scornful of aberrations and at twenty-three had already expressed a strong dislike for homosexuals, but he was eager for Gertrude's friendship.

A few nights later Gertrude and Alice climbed the steep staircase to the Hemingway apartment. Gertrude, who was keeping her promise to look at some of Ernest's work, arranged her large bulk on the mahogany bed and read everything that Ernest handed her —poems, a novel fragment, some short stories. She was mildly pleased with the poems but did not care for the novel. " . . . a great deal of description," she stated, "and not particularly good description. Begin over again and concentrate. . . . " She liked the stories, all except "Up In Michigan." That one was *inaccrochable*, which literally means unable to be hung, as with a painting. The story was good, but the explicit seduction scene made it unpublishable. Ernest did not bridle at this adverse reaction. What interested him was her support of his efforts to write strong declarative sentences stripped of overweight description.

From literary criticism Gertrude turned to lecturing her young friends about the importance of buying pictures. "You can either buy clothes or buy pictures. . . . It's that simple. . . . Pay no attention to your clothes . . . buy [them] for comfort and durability and you will have the clothes money to buy pictures." Hadley averted her eyes from the strange "steerage" garments worn by Gertrude. Ernest's wardrobe consisted mainly of cheap fishermen's T-shirts and patched sneakers. Hadley had not spent any money on herself since she assembled her St. Louis trousseau. She could not see how pennies saved from their clothes shopping could pay for valuable art. In spite of such unsolicited advice, however, she considered the evening a success. She began to look forward to other visits with the women. One evening when Picasso was at Stein's he read some of his poetry to the hushed group, none of whom dared to say anything when he was finished. There was a long silence. Hadley noticed how he was fidgeting. Still no comments from the other guests. Finally Gertrude said, "Pablo, go home and paint."

Ernest continued to enjoy Gertrude's interest in him and was drawn to her powerful personality. "It was easy to get into the habit of stopping in at 27 rue de Fleurus late in the afternoon for the warmth and the great pictures and the conversation," he recalled. "Often Miss Stein would have no guests and she was always very friendly and for a long time she was affectionate." Twenty years later he paid her the ultimate male compliment. " . . . I always wanted to fuck her," he wrote W. G. Rogers, "and she knew it and it was a good healthy feeling. . . . " He added that Alice was always jealous of Gertrude's men friends.

When their talk turned to literary personalities, he was fascinated, but when she attempted to instruct him on the subject of sex, he became uncomfortable. She was implacable about the differences between male and female homosexuals. Men were to be pitied. "The act [they] commit is ugly and repugnant and afterwards they are disgusted with themselves. They drink and take drugs, to palliate this," explained Gertrude, "but they are disgusted with the act and they are always changing partners and cannot be really happy. . . . In women it is the opposite. They do nothing that they are disgusted by and nothing that is repulsive and . . . they can lead happy lives together." Ernest thought Gertrude's analysis too simple, and he did not like being patronized. Later, when he went home to rue du Cardinal Lemoine, he shared his newly acquired knowledge with Hadley. "In the night," he wrote, "we were happy with our own knowledge we already had and other new knowledge we had acquired in the mountains."

Everyone who came to know Hadley during her early years in Paris was struck by how happy she seemed and how much in love she was with her young husband. The passions that he had awakened in her were being fulfilled and her appreciation in turn elicited great tenderness from him. Worry over money matters, long hours of being alone, even the recognition that he could be ruthless in his ambition, mercurial with friends, and given to bouts of self-pity and depression did not affect her devotion. She believed that he was right for her and repaid him over and over, in loyalty and good spirits and a remarkable selflessness, qualities that he came to demand of his friends and especially of his wives.

When Hadley wrote to Grace that they were having a wonderful whirl with new friends, she did not add that Ernest was quarreling with Bill Smith, his crony of six years and best man at his wedding. It had started the year before when Y.K. ordered Ernest out of his apartment for his blunt remarks about Doodles and Don Wright. Bill tried to stay neutral, but Ernest, who knew how to hold a grudge, continued to insult Y.K. in his letters to Bill, who finally had written Ernest that blood was thicker than water and that he did not care for the attitude of his old friend. In spite of that he was sending regards to Hash.

Hadley was dismayed. She loved the Smith family. Katy had brought her and Ernest together and Y.K. had provided the setting. Couldn't Ernest overlook Bill's outburst, or at least be satisfied with a gently reproving letter that left room for a reconciliation? Apparently he could not. Hadley learned that forgiveness came hard to him. Once he believed himself to be ill-treated, or the behavior of the other party displeased him, the quality of the relationship changed. Even as he was feuding with Bill, however, he was wondering how to keep up his friendship with Katy Smith. It was important not to break with her. She was holding about eight hundred dollars in drafts of Italian lire in her safety deposit box. Ernest needed some of it to finance an assignment in Genoa, but since he could not bring himself to write her at this touchy time, he asked a mutual friend to intercede for him.

Ernest's April 1922 trip to Genoa to cover an international economic conference was the first separation for him and Hadley in their seven months of marriage. The *Star* paid him seventy-five dollars a week plus expenses, but there was no allowance for wives. Hadley made the best of it but was lonely and edgy during much of his three-week absence. Spring was coming, her first spring in a most romantic city. How could she not yearn for him when the rains turned soft and the horse chestnut trees faintly bloomed and the air was fragrant? It was an impatient marking of time until he returned.

But eventually he did return and Hadley was delighted to learn of the new friends he made among the correspondents. An American editor, Max Eastman, liked some of his prose sketches well enough to send them to his magazine, *The Masses.* Lincoln Steffens, the grizzled muckraker, invited him to join a group that gathered frequently at a neighborhood trattoria. Paul Scott Mowrer, European correspondent for the *Chicago Daily News,* suggested that he charge his dispatches to the *News* account until he could establish cable credit.

After filing fifteen dispatches on the conference, Ernest was able to return to his own work without feeling guilty. He was making some progress at last. Half a dozen poems went out to Harriet Monroe in Chicago, editor of *Poetry: A Magazine of Verse.* Margaret Anderson, editor of the American literary quarterly *The Little Review,* had come to know of him through Pound, who had sent her one of Ernest's stories. "A Divine Gesture," the fable he had written during his courtship of Hadley, was accepted for publication in May by *The Double Dealer* of New Orleans. Most significant in terms of his goal was the gradual evolution of a style—not journalism, not rhyme, but a carefully pruned narrative prose.

As the days grew longer Ernest started his work earlier, often stealing out while Hadley was still asleep, when the tall old buildings were still shuttered and only the goatherd was on the street blowing his pipes. Sometimes on his way home he would pick up a racing form. The horses were running at Enghien-Les-Bains, where steeplechasing was Hadley's favorite because the jumpers were so graceful. They went by train from the Gare du Nord through the slums of Paris to the small pretty track outside the city. Hadley would spread a picnic on Ernest's raincoat in a grassy bank near the grandstand. First they ate, then they studied the odds, then they placed their bets. When they were lucky Ernest divided the winnings—one quarter for each of them to spend, half for the racing capital.

A sporadic correspondence continued between the young couple in Paris and Ernest's parents in America. Ernest concentrated on sporting events, politics, and fishing; Hadley on current fashions, the people they were meeting, and Ernest's success with the *Star*. At home in Oak Park, Grace Hemingway was trying to become an artist. First she registered in an adult education course. Then she joined a children's class because she thought the instruction was better. Now she had progressed to being an extension student at the Chicago Art Institute, struggling to sharpen her powers of observation and develop a technique. Her family was relieved that her energies were channeled into something useful that kept her from interfering in their lives, but they did not take her seriously. Sometimes they smiled at her efforts, sometimes they ignored them, but she worked doggedly, converting the big music room into a studio and painting four and five hours a day. She wasn't lulled into believing she had extraordinary talent. Landscapes were easier for her than catching likenesses. But she signed her pictures Hall Hemingway and used the art, as she formerly had with music, to give her life some direction.

With summer approaching, Ernest decided that he was ready for a big trip. Hadley concurred. This was the time of their lives to be extravagant, when they weren't hemmed in by responsibilities. Later they could be prudent. For a change there was extra money in the bank. Ernest's payment from the *Star* for the Genoa articles was over five hundred dollars, and some trust fund checks had come in. So they decided to spend a month at the Gangwisch pensione in Chamby for mountain climbing and trout fishing. Then they would hike down to Milan, where Ernest could show Hadley the scene of his wartime adventures. Chink Dorman-Smith, Ernest's Irish military friend from Milan, would join them, for he was in Paris on leave.

Hadley liked Chink from the start. He was tall and spare, with a small auburn moustache, twinkling blue eyes, and "excellent manners and British courtliness." More significant to her, however, was the genuine affection he felt for Ernest, like that of a benevolent older brother. She was aware of Ernest's need for different kinds of friends. In Chink she saw someone of integrity who did not goad Ernest's competitive drive, and for whom he had genuine respect, the kind of respect he reserved for the good professional soldier. Dorman-Smith agreed that Hem was indeed like a younger brother. "He seemed to make up for all the friends I had lost during the World War." He liked Hadley, too, and promptly christened her Mrs. Popplethwaite. "They were very much in love," he recalled in 1961, "and Ernest used to disturb my bachelorhood at breakfast coffee by reciting blow by blow the events of their nights."

For Hadley the days around Montreux and the Rhone Valley were supremely happy ones. Preferring the company of good men to most women, she appreciated the presence of two attractive males. Together they climbed high peaks and drank dark beer in weather-beaten mountain inns. They slid down the broad snow fields by simply sitting down and letting go. It was narcissus time. The hardy blooms sprang up between the jagged crevices and on small bare patches of warm earth. When Ernest fished his favorite stream, the Stöckalper, near the juncture of the Rhone River and Lake Geneva, Chink and Hadley waited for him in the garden of an inn at Aigle. Hadley appreciated Chink's small attentions. "When you [Ernest] and Chink talked I was included. It wasn't like being a wife at Miss Stein's."

Chink had the idea to cross the St. Bernard Pass and go down to Aosta on foot, not realizing the difficulties for hikers when the pass was still under deep snow. They agreed to carry the minimum of gear—most of their baggage went ahead on the train—but Hadley could not believe that the minimum did not include her toiletries. Ernest insisted that the bottles be left behind. Hadley balked. Poor Chink. To keep the peace he offered to pack them in his already heavy knapsack. "We tramped thirty kilometers in snow knee-deep, up, up, up," recalled Hadley. "Vanity and ignorance induced me to wear a light pair of American oxfords, suitable for neither terrain nor weather. I believe I wanted Chink to admire my trim legs."

The journey became something of a nightmare, as they climbed and stumbled. Ernest was bothered by the altitude and Hadley's feet were soaked. Finally, however, the gaunt Hospice of St. Bernard, boldly outlined in the moonlight, came into view. The monks put them up for the night. The next morning Hadley could barely squeeze her swollen feet into the shrunken leather oxfords. Ernest, who had had the good sense to wear stout boots himself, expected Hadley to endure physical discomfort without complaining, especially since she had shown such poor judgment in her choice of shoes. She tried to oblige, but it wasn't long before one of her shoes split open and Chink had to slit the other one. They walked twenty minutes and rested ten, all the way to Aosta. "I was a human blister," she said. "The boys practically carried me the last few miles. I did not leave my bed for two days." But she had shown remarkable endurance for one who had been written off as having a delicate constitution and that was important for her self-esteem. Had she had the proper boots, as her companions did, she probably could have sailed through the expedition without mishap.

After Chink left them in Milan, Ernest interviewed Benito Mussolini, the new Fascist leader, and together Hadley and Ernest visited an Italian nobleman who had been kind to Ernest in 1918. "We were welcomed hospitably," reported Hadley, "and shown through the family mausoleum which was handsome and impressive. There was a charming young daughter who thought Ernest at least as good as a prince. She behaved beautifully. If her heart was broken, at least it was a very young heart." Hadley's favorite late afternoon refreshment was the fruit cup at Biffi's in the Galleria, fragrant with wild strawberries, laced with Capri, chilled in frosted glasses. If the homecoming touched off a yearning for Agnes, his first love, Ernest as yet gave no sign. Hadley was giving him the full measure of her admiration. When a black mood was upon him, Agnes's rejection would rankle. But he seemed cheerful in Milan, with romantic impulses all going in Hadley's direction.

When they returned to Schio, where the Ambulance Corps had been stationed in the summer of 1918, Ernest's spirits sank. Nothing was as he remembered. The mill had been reconverted to producing wool and the stream was polluted. The good hotel that he remembered was now a shabby hostelry with fly-specked walls and poor food. Perhaps the food had never been good. Ernest was beginning to distrust his memories. He was anxious to move on to Fossalta and the river bank where he had been wounded. In a hired car they crossed the desolate wastelands of the Adriatic marshes, only to find that Fossalta, which had been a heap of rubble when he left it, was now a rebuilt village, an ugly collection of garishly painted cottages. Ernest did not begrudge the peasants their meager comforts, but it was disquieting to see everything so completely back to normal. Then they drove to the bank of the Piave River, where the screaming, whining shell had almost killed him. He looked about, bewildered. Here, again, nothing was the same. The trenches and dugouts were gone. Not a piece of rusty equipment remained. Sloping to the water was a smooth, grassy bank. Out on the peaceful river bargemen guided their cement flatboats.

Hadley sensed his frustration, although for her the trip had been a success. Since their very first meeting, she had listened, spellbound, to his tales of the Italian front. She was deeply touched by his desire to share it all with her. That Schio was tawdry or the countryside healed over may have surprised her but it did not alter the central fact—that she felt closer to Ernest for having seen everything. But this was not enough for him. On this very spot he had nearly died. For years he had awakened in the night in a cold sweat, and the compulsion to return to the scene had been overwhelming. It was a shock to find that nothing was the same. Had the place been strewn with debris, had the ground been torn up, perhaps his demons would have been exorcised. But this did not happen, and he could not relive the event, even from time's safe distance.

Paris had turned warm and humid by the time the Hemingways returned from Italy in mid-June. People who could afford to left the city, those who could not took to the streets. In front of the decaying buildings on rue Cardinal Lemoine children played sidewalk games while their mothers shouted warnings and fanned themselves in the heat. The café terraces along Montparnasse were crowded from early afternoon until dawn, the French women quietly drinking lemonade as their escorts cooled off with inferior French beer. The bateaux mouches plied the Seine as far out as Saint-Cloud. Five nights a week the neighborhood dance halls were packed with merrymakers.

Next door to the Hemingway apartment was such a dance hall —a *bal musette*—and Ernest gleefully exaggerated its character, populating it with roughnecks and whores. But Hadley knew that it was respectable in a picturesque French way and, except for the incessant noise of the accordion, enjoyed its proximity as a convenient place to entertain visitors and friends. If the visitor happened to be a snobbish relative from the States, she mischievously flaunted her newly acquired Latin Quarter manners and made a point of dancing with the roughest sailors who asked her. The *javam de Fox* had recently been imported and was beginning to catch on. There was some fine waltzing. Ernest reveled in the smoky, smelly, noisy atmosphere, though he was still not much of a dancer. Guy Hickok, head of the Paris office of the *Brooklyn Eagle*, later wrote that Ernest's idea of dancing was to shuffle around the floor with anyone he could get his hands on. During the Bastille Day celebration in the week of July 14, 1922, the accordionist moved to the street under Hadley's window. Together with two drummers, a bagpiper, and a cornetist he formed a quintet that played for four nights, with the neighborhood revelers taking full advantage.

In August the Hemingways went on a fishing trip to Germany with Lewis Galantière, his fiancée, and Bill and Sally Bird. Bill Bird ran the Paris office of *Consolidated Press* and had first met Ernest on the train to Genoa. "A wonderful friend and intimate from the start," said Hadley. "He and Sally embraced us both into their friendship." News items were scarce and Ernest had been scrounging without much success for human interest stories. He was itching to get out of the city and calculated that inflation-ridden Germany could provide him with some fresh material. Instead of taking the train with the others, Hadley and Ernest flew in a small silver biplane from Paris to Strasbourg, where they all stayed at a Gasthaus on the cobblestone square. Across the Rhine at Kehl in occupied Germany they saw firsthand the devastating inflation that gripped the defeated nation. Kehl's best hotel served a five-course meal for 120 marks, amounting to fifteen cents in foreign currency. Ernest, alert to the effect of the tragedy upon ordinary people, saw a bearded old man shake his head sadly when he could not buy some apples from a street vendor. Five apples cost less than two cents, but the old man, his life's savings eroded, could not afford the twelve marks.

As the six Americans began their hike into the Black Forest, their sympathy for the local citizens dropped off. A five-hour train ride to Triberg was made unpleasant by rude, pushing Germans with shaved heads and *Lederhosen* and in one country dining room the Americans were denounced as *schieber* (profiteer). The vaunted

German cleanliness was misleading. Outside, the inns were indeed freshly painted and attractive. Inside, the rooms were often dirty and the proprietors surly. After one arduous hike on a steep, rocky trail, when Hadley and the others were especially hungry and tired, the owner of the only Gasthaus in the valley refused to serve them a simple lunch.

But they had some wonderful picnics and Ernest took copious notes for future articles. In addition there was the fishing. The other two women were not interested, but Hadley listened carefully to everything Ernest told her. She was a good pupil and he was an excellent teacher. The first time she worked seriously at it she caught three fine trout. It was nearing the time of their first anniversary—September 3. If she felt at all contemplative, she must have been astonished by what had transpired in twelve months. She had married a complicated young man, followed him across the ocean, and was living in what amounted to a garret. It was a bewildering contrast to her staid, well-ordered past. She had not merely survived the challenge, she seemed to thrive on it.

Upon her return to Paris, however, Hadley's mood darkened dramatically. She had scarcely unpacked when Ernest announced that he was going to Constantinople, ordered there by his editors to cover the war between Greece and Turkey. With an intensity that surprised her, Hadley begged him not to go. When he had had to leave her in April for Genoa, she had grumbled but accepted it. Perhaps it was the great distance between Paris and the Dardanelles. Perhaps it was the fear for his safety that set her off. A brutal war was raging in the countryside, and there were reports of fearsome epidemics. They quarreled bitterly, the situation made worse because Ernest could not conceive of turning down the assignment and Hadley was nearly incoherent with disappointment. She was not able to account for her reaction except to remember how lonely she was and how much she dreaded his going. Although she had made a conscious decision to adapt to everything in her new life, to be faced with one more test seemed grossly unfair. For the moment she had run out of patience.

When Ernest went ahead with his preparations for the trip Hadley stopped talking to him. "It was just awful," she admitted years later. He suffered terribly, but she never budged. He left on the night of September 25 without a word from her. As soon as he was gone she was overwhelmed with grief and guilt. She had treated him cruelly and broken her vow never to interfere with his work. It was a dismal month. She tried to occupy herself sensibly, but much of the time she brooded and wept, imagining that he would never want to see her again.

By October 5 she mobilized enough energy to write Grace but left out any details that would give away her anguished state. Even allowing for this self-censorship, her underlying good spirits were slowly returning. "I did think of you on the first with great affection," she wrote, referring to Grace Hemingway's twenty-sixth wedding anniversary. "And it was so dear of you to write us on our own day [September 3]." Lightly she described herself as "gadding about with gay young people . . . and moving furniture about to make things even nicer." She boasted about Ernest's fine work, not only for the *Star* but for other papers as well. This was a touchy subject. She skipped the important detail that work for other papers was negotiated in secret. Although Ernest was under exclusive contract to the *Star,* he agreed to file spot news for International News Service under a pseudonym. Hadley rationalized at that time that they needed the extra money but admitted years later to Carlos Baker that such actions seared her "puritan soul." The arrangement caused Ernest some problems. He had to lie his way out of a sticky situation when items for the INS hit the wire service ahead of his "exclusives" for the *Star.*

At 6:35 A.M. on October 25, Ernest stepped off the train at Gare de Lyon, exhausted, feverish from a bout with Malaria, and covered with bug bites. Hadley was so relieved to have him safely home that she forgot all about the quarrel, but Ernest eventually put it to use in "The Snows of Kilimanjaro." As Harry Walden, the failed writer, lies dying of gangrene at the African camp base, a kaleidoscope of remembrances rattle about in his head, reveries that are strongly autobiographical. One passage has Harry reviewing a quarrel that he had with his wife before leaving for Constantinople. He remembers that he "whored the whole time" after leaving Paris but that the whoring "had failed to kill his loneliness." There is much erotic fantasy in the prose, as Harry dances with " . . . a hot Armenian slut, that swung her belly against him so it almost scalded. . . . They got into a taxi and drove . . . along the Bosphorus . . . and went to bed and she felt as over-ripe as she looked but . . . smooth-

bellied, big-breasted and needed no pillow under her buttocks."
And in another passage ". . . back at the apartment with his wife that
now he loved again, the quarrel [was] all over, the madness all over."

Ernest later confessed to Bill Smith that he was unfaithful to
Hadley only once, during the fall of 1922 in Constantinople. In any
event, he had remembered to bring her some presents—a bottle of
attar of roses, an ivory necklace and another of amber—and gratefully accepted her smiling attentions. Later he would write Bill
Horne that Hadley was more beautiful than ever, that they loved
each other very much and went everywhere together.

Chapter 7

On November 22 Ernest left for Lausanne to cover the Peace Conference convened to settle the territorial dispute between Greece and Turkey. Hadley, recovering from the grippe, stayed behind. He commiserated with her misery, wiring her on two successive days that the weather was gorgeous and to hustle down to Lausanne as soon as she was well enough to travel. If she was really sick, she should advise him instantly and he would come home.

Following the wires he wrote a long letter full of pet names and loving baby talk. The tone contrasted sharply with his offhand public manners. Hadley was Wicky Poo, he her little wax puppy. He, too, was sick, with green sputum and a stuffed head, but he could not take care of himself as she could. Instead he had to race down the hills, running a twenty-four-hour coverage for two Hearst agencies. He complained bitterly of the sweatshop wages and the difficulty of covering news breaks in areas distant from one another. The letters were also sprinkled with references to Mums and Mummy, characteristic of Ernest when he was in poor health and feeling sorry for himself.

> I love you dearest Wicky—you write the very best letters. Anyhow both being laid out with colds we haven't lost so much time on the time of the month because you've probably been too sick. I do so hate for you to miss what is the most comfortable and jolly time for mums. Won't

we sleep together though? . . . Deer sweet little feather kitty with the castorated oil and the throwing up, I think it is so pitiful I could just cry.

As soon as Hadley felt strong enough, she gathered up her ski clothes—they were going to Chamby when the conference was over —and in a separate small valise packed all of Ernest's manuscripts that she could find, assuming that he would want to get on with his writing during the winter holiday. At the railroad station she gave her luggage, including the valise, to a porter. When she reached her state room her personal bags were there but the valise was missing. She could not believe it. First she thought wildly that she was in the wrong compartment. With a sick feeling she raced up and down the cars, but the awful truth held.

Notifying the conductor and asking other passengers was an empty formality. Hadley's well-meaning intentions had boomeranged; everything was in the case—originals, typescripts, carbons. She was so upset when she saw Ernest on the station platform in Lausanne that she burst into tears. "She had cried and cried," he recalled later, "and could not tell me. I told her that no matter what the dreadful thing was that had happened nothing could be that bad, and whatever it was, it was all right and not to worry." Finally she did tell him, breaking down again as soon as the words were out of her mouth. Lincoln Steffens, who had accompanied him to the train station, thought that Ernest was tender and patient and seemed less upset than Hadley. But Hadley was not fooled. She, more than anyone, knew what those stolen manuscripts represented. She knew the degree of anger and frustration that must be boiling up inside. Part of the horror of the experience was watching him gamely pretend that it didn't matter. She watched numbly as he boarded the day train for Paris. He needed to see for himself that everything was really lost.

During the 1960s and early 1970s, when she was being interviewed repeatedly about the Paris years, Hadley still shuddered over the memory of the stolen manuscripts. "That painful subject again!" she wrote Carlos Baker when he inquired in 1965 what Ernest might have told her about his search through the apartment. "I think he went through a collection of old papers—duplicates or originals of his writings—in a box or valise, but I had been through them all and to be perfect, took all with me on that ill-fated trip."

Two stories escaped. Ernest found "Up in Michigan" in a dusty corner of a bureau drawer, and the racetrack story, "My Old Man," was in New York being read by the editors of *Cosmopolitan*. The poems were gone except for the six he had sent to Harriet Monroe. The Paris sketches, a novel fragment, and everything else had been packed in the valise. His friends tried to comfort him. Gertrude and Alice fed him a nice lunch before he returned to Switzerland. Ezra Pound tried to analyze the loss for him objectively. If the form of the story was right he should be able to reassemble it from memory. Ezra was not so far wrong. Much of the novel fragment was about Nick Adams in northern Michigan and Ernest was able to use all of it in later short stories. But he never forgot the blow. He would become visibly tense whenever the subject was mentioned, still referring to it in 1959 when he was celebrating his sixtieth birthday. It was the only context in which he ever criticized Hadley.

There was nothing more to be done. When Ernest returned to Lausanne to finish up his coverage of the conference, instead of brooding openly, he adopted an air of raffish gaiety, laughing louder, exclaiming over the great skiing that lay ahead of them, making up free verse caricatures of the statesmen attending the meeting. Hadley wrote to Ernest's mother on December 11 and was effervescent as usual, making no mention of the heartache over the lost work. Her Christmas shopping excursions had been fruitless. She had found nothing that remotely resembled an American Christmas card and any important gift she tried to send back would carry a stiff duty. "The outcome of . . . my wanderings is this little Swiss linen hankie for you mother and for father, a copy of the Xmas number of l'Illustration. . . . The small cheque enclosed is for the kids. . . . We shall think of you all on the great day."

And a great day it was! Chink Dorman-Smith, on his first Christmas leave since 1914, took a room directly above the Hemingways at Chalet Chamby. On Christmas morning they fell upon their presents, piled at the foot of the porcelain stove. "We ate breakfast in the old, untasting, gulping early morning Christmas way," wrote Ernest later, "unpacked the stockings, down to the candy mouse in the toe, each made a pile of our things for future gloating."

Then they threw on their ski clothes, ran for the train that chugged up the mountain, and shouted and cheered as it stopped at each jammed platform, finally reaching the top. During the morning hours they climbed, single-file, sliding smoothly across the snow on strips of sealskin harnessed on their skis, occasionally hitting a short downhill run. Lunch was a rucksack picnic with a bottle of white wine and a short nap for Hadley, whose face was already sunburned, "even through the last crop of freckles and tan." Chink suggested, straight-faced, that she use lampblack, as the mountaineers did. She just laughed and went to sleep, while the men removed the sealskins and waxed the skis. As the afternoon sun waned, they took off, "in one long dropping, swooping, heart-plucking rush. . . . " At the point where the cogwheel railway stopped, hundreds of skiers converged, shooting down the road. Hadley disappeared ahead of Ernest. Sometimes as he went hurtling down he caught a glimpse of her blue beret. They took a few falls, none serious. In the onrushing darkness the windows of the chalets that dotted the hillsides glowed with candlelight.

All over Switzerland, holiday turkey was served at night to accommodate the skiers. For Hadley there was none of the strangeness of the first Christmas in Paris. This time it was like coming home, to be at Chamby, greeted warmly by the proprietor, snug and comfortable and cared for. The hated subject of the stolen manuscripts had been put aside, at least for the present. Ernest was too eager for a good outdoor vacation to worry about his work. Chink was going to stay for another week. Hadley liked that, for he had become her friend as well as her husband's.

In the mail forwarded from Paris there was an interesting item for Ernest—a long letter from Agnes von Kurowsky. In October Ernest had written to her, but that letter has never turned up. Perhaps the impulse to write was touched off by his trip to Milan the previous spring, or by a sense that things were so good for him now that he could afford to reach out. Agnes herself, thirty years later, described Ernest's words as friendly but restrained. He said that though he was happily married, he still thought of her, especially when he had returned to Italy.

"After I recovered from the surprise," Agnes had written on December 22, "I was never more pleased over anything in my life. You know there has always been a little bitterness over the way our comradeship ended, especially since I got back and Mac [Elsie Mac-Donald] read me the very biting letter you wrote about me. . . . Anyhow I always knew that it would turn out right in the end and that you would realize it was the best way, as I'm positive you must believe, now that you have Hadley. Think of what an antique I am at the present writing." (Evidently Ernest did not tell her that Hadley was also seven years older than he.)

The letter continued with a long account, larded with personal reflections, of Agnes's travels since 1919. "In the first place—to dig up the ruins—I came back from Italy a sadder but wiser girl— feeling that I'd like to break something and preferably somebody, and life really wasn't worth living" (a reference to being jilted by her Italian lover). After working at Bellevue for six months, she returned to active duty and sailed for Paris with the expectation of being sent to Russia. " . . . didn't dare tell my . . . relatives it was to be Russia, as they all had an idea it was certain death as a suspected spy to venture over the borders of that poor land." When the announcement came that the Russian borders were suddenly closed to women workers, Agnes and two other Red Cross nurses were sent to Bucharest instead. "I will never forget that trip on the Simplon Express," she wrote. . . . we landed after four days on the train at 1:30 A.M. . . . nobody to meet us . . . no street lights, no cabs." Conditions in the city were terrible. Food was scarce and medical care unreliable, and there was constant turmoil in the government.

Agnes and her companion did infant nursing and Aggie learned to speak Rumanian. She stayed on the job, difficult as it was, until September 1920, when she took a long leave that satisfied in some measure her thirst for travel. At Constantia she boarded a freighter that took her across the Black Sea to Constantinople, Athens, Corinth, and, finally, Naples. "And there," she wrote, "I was surprised and relieved to find I landed without any of the feelings that tormented me on my previous visits—Naples being the home of a certain dashing young Artillery Officer." She did not tell Ernest that she had caught a glimpse of that officer as she was walking in Naples with an Englishman. A fine carriage rolled by. In it were two people, an older woman and a young man. Agnes recognized the man as Domenico Carracciolo, but when he moved to greet her she pretended not to know him, moving haughtily ahead with her escort. She smiled to herself, pleased that she had had one last opportunity to satisfy her wounded pride.

From Italy Agnes went to Paris. "Oh my," she admitted to Ernest, "I'm homesick for the smell of chestnuts on a grey, damp Fall day—for Pruniers . . . and my pet little resturant behind the Madeleine—Bernard's where I ate creme chocolat every night."

She finished her letter on a sensible note, in exactly the tone one would expect, though it gave no comfort to Ernest, who may have hoped for a sign of regret.

It is so nice to feel I have an old friend back because we were good friends once, weren't we? And how sorry I am I didn't meet and know your wife—Were you in Paris when I was there a year ago this Nov.? Is there any chance of knowing when your book will be out? [In November Ezra Pound had asked Ernest to write some prose sketches for a series of books he would edit under the imprint of Three Mountains Press, a project of Bill Bird's. Evidently Ernest mentioned this in his letter.] How proud I will be some day in the not-very-distant future to say, "Oh yes, Ernest Hemingway—Used to know him quite well during the war."

She brought up the possibility of hearing from him occasionally, and wrote that it was "priceless" to have such a long talk. "With my best wishes to you and Hadley. . . . And a strong grasp of the hand, as they say in Rumania. Your old buddy. Von (Oh, excuse me, It's Ag.)"

Six months after receiving Agnes's letter, Ernest tried for the first time to write a short story about the love affair. On one level "A Very Short Story" is a straightforward account of a wounded American soldier's relationship with his nurse. He loves her; they part; she writes him a Dear John letter. But one stroke at the end of the story discredits the relationship. "A short time after he [the American] contracted gonorrhea from a sales girl in a loop department store while riding in a taxicab through Lincoln Park." And so Ernest turned his emotional crisis into a sordid joke. Luz, in the story, comes through as one of his earliest "bitch" heroines. She lies when she tells Nick she loves him; she goes to bed with another man as soon as he is sent home; and then she writes the abominable letter. Even those who knew Agnes's flirtatious ways and the ambivalence of her feelings in the winter of 1918–19 would understand that she is not the Luz of the story. Ernest, the writer of fiction, was reshaping reality. But the impact of the ending suggests that in 1923 he still harbored some of the feelings of a rejected lover.

It was well into January when the annual Christmas package

arrived from Oak Park. Grace had handstitched an elegant purse for Hadley. There was a book for Ernest and a homemade Christmas card from Leicester. Carefully wrapped in many layers of waxed paper and cotton was Grace's English teacake, the first of many that she shipped to Ernest's households over subsequent years.

Marcelline, the second of the younger generation to leave Kenilworth Avenue, had married Sterling Sanford of Detroit. Hadley, in her January letter to Grace, promised to write to Marce herself, to "thank her for the little rosebud pins and to show how interested I am in all their first days of the new life lived far from her family and old companions and spent entirely for a new person that can't quite absorb you all at first." Such a quiet remark, written about another could have been Hadley's expression of her own deep involvement with Ernest, and wistfulness that Ernest could not, as she put it, "absorb" all of her eagerness.

Shortly thereafter, Hadley discovered that she was pregnant. She had conceived sometime in January and was thrilled with the news. But Ernest, who thought that they had been taking the necessary precautions, was upset, fearing that the baby would inhibit his freedom of movement and ability to work. "Cross Country Snow," written a year later but placed in this period, dramatizes his ambivalence toward the sudden change in his life. The surface texture of the story is that skiing is wonderful fun, but the underlying tension is how to reconcile an exhilarating phase of masculine life with domestic responsibility. " 'It's hell, isn't it?' " asks George, referring to the fact that Helen is pregnant and that she and Nick are leaving Paris for the dull life in America. " 'No. Not exactly,' " replies Nick. The tone of the story is one of resignation rather than bitter regret, as the young husband prepares to meet new demands. What is not reflected in the story, but which lurked, unstated, in the lives of Ernest and Hadley, was the difference in their age and frame of reference. Ernest at twenty-three—enjoying his freedom, depending on Hadley to satisfy all his personal needs—could not but chafe at the prospect of fatherhood. Hadley, nearly eight years older, found the prospect marvelous. It was the first serious challenge to the unity of the marriage.

By February the snows of Chamby gave way to slush, and the clear days to a gloomy chill. Ezra and Dorothy Pound in Rapallo had been urging the Hemingways to join them under the warm

Mediterranean sun. At first Ernest procrastinated, unenthusiastic about Ezra's scheme for the four of them to do a walking tour of the area. Then Hadley suggested that the sea air might be good for her. Ernest booked them on a train to Milan, where they celebrated with a fine meal at Compari's, and then went to the Hotel Splendide on the waterfront of Rapallo. The rates were cheap, since it was not the tourist season. Their room was on the second floor facing the sea.

The Pounds went off for a few weeks, but Mike Strater and his family, friends of the Pounds, were living in the area. Hadley, playing vigorous tennis with Ernest and the Straters, noticed that Ernest was as competitive about tennis as anything else. ". . . whenever he missed a shot he would 'sizzle.' His racquet 'would slash to the ground and everyone would simply stand still and cower,' . . . until he recovered himself with a laugh." She tried to humor him, believing that his churlish behavior was a screen for intense frustration over his meager output of writing. He had written nothing original since November. He blamed his dispirited attitude on the humidity, the paltry waves of a boring sea, even Strater's sprained ankle, which put a stop to tennis and some good boxing. Hadley blamed it on the loss of the manuscripts. The damage to his momentum had been shattering. No wonder he contrived one feeble excuse after another to avoid the blank notebooks.

She was immensely relieved when Edward O'Brien, the editor of an important yearly anthology of the best short fiction, who was living in the hills above Rapallo, asked Ernest if he had any material on hand to show him. Ernest gave him "My Old Man." O'Brien read it, judged it an excellent piece of work, and told Ernest it would appear in his next edition, thus breaking the precedent that all selections be reprints from magazines.

Whether it was this sudden recognition from an unexpected source or a spontaneous quickening of his interest, Ernest began to write again. He made some notes that later were the basis for a short story called "Cat in the Rain." The story perhaps tells something of Hadley's mood during the early months of her pregnancy. It is a rainy, boring afternoon at the Hotel Splendide. A young American, George, is propped up in bed, reading. His wife stands at the window, wishing she could rescue a kitty crouched under one of the dripping green garden tables. Finally she goes downstairs, hesitating to step out into the rain but assisted finally by a kindly maid who holds an umbrella for her. " . . . she walked along the gravel path until she was under their window. The table was there, washed bright green in the rain, but the cat was gone. She was suddenly disappointed." Back in her room the disappointment mounts. " 'I wanted it so much,' she said. 'I don't know why I wanted it so much. I wanted that poor kitty. It isn't any fun to be a poor kitty out in the rain.' " With her husband still absorbed in his book, the young woman sits in front of the mirror, studying her profile, wondering if she should let her hair grow. Then she bursts out with a spate of irrational desires. " 'I want to pull my hair back tight and smooth and make a big knot at the back that I can feel. . . . I want to eat at a table with my own silver and I want candles. . . . I want it to be spring and I want to brush my hair out in front of a mirror and I want a kitty and I want some new clothes.' " The husband continues to read, not listening. " 'Anyway, I want a cat,' she said, '. . . I want a cat now. If I can't have long hair or any fun, I can have a cat.' " A moment later the maid comes to the door with a tortoise-shell cat in her arms. The padrone has sent it to the young woman as a present.

Ernest asserted to Scott Fitzgerald that the story had nothing to do with Hadley but was based on a Harvard youth and his girlfriend whom he had met in Genoa. Carlos Baker has suggested that such an assertion be viewed with suspicion. Except for the gift of the cat from the manager, which was the clever final stroke of the author, the young wife's yearnings seem to belong to Hadley. Pregnant, far from home, irritable on that gloomy afternoon with the lack of domestic comforts, her longing disparaged by a preoccupied husband, she cries out for a cat. The warm kitty would be the substitute for all that she has given up over many months. In none of Ernest's later sentimental tributes to her does Hadley spring to life as in this fragment. The young wife is neither idealized fantasy nor a stereotype of the author's prejudices, as were some of his later heroines, but a flesh-and-blood woman drawn with insight and objectivity.

When Ezra and Dorothy returned to Rapallo, Ernest and Hadley joined them for the walking tour. With rucksacks on their backs, they hiked southward in fine weather to Pisa and Siena, lunching al fresco on fresh figs, cheese, and olives and drinking the local wines. Ernest was enchanted with Dorothy, one of the rare wives he did not disparage, and Hadley thought Ezra in good form, less patronizing than usual, full of sage remarks. He lectured learnedly on the terrain, on Renaissance history, and especially on the fifteenth-century Italian prince, Sigismondo Malatesta, the subject of a new set of Cantos. From Orbetello they took the train to Sirmione on Lago di Garda. There the two couples parted, the Pounds to return to Rapallo, the Hemingways continuing north-ward to Cortina d'Ampezzo, a ski resort in the Dolomites.

With the big season over, there were plenty of inexpensive rooms all over the village. Hadley continued to ski, selecting her runs carefully. Ernest, when he wasn't on the slopes, worked on a project for *The Little Review*, whose foreign editor, Jane Heap, had asked him to contribute to the April "Exiles" number. He went back to the idea of the simple sentence, the "I have seen" sentences that he had tried to compose in his tiny room on rue Mouffetard. This time he wrote paragraphs, each one constructed to communicate a single powerful impression. One was an account of a bullfight, another described a bloody skirmish on the western front in 1918. The only one based on his personal experience was a stunning, understated word picture of the retreat on the Karagatch Road that he had witnessed in Turkey. He worked and worked over the paragraphs, calling them miniatures in motion. When he was called away unex-pectedly to the Ruhr to cover Franco-German problems, he stopped off in Paris and delivered a set of six to Jane Heap.

He returned to Cortina in the middle of April to find the snow melted and the weather more suited to trout fishing than skiing. One day he hired an unsavory local character to show him where the good fishing was. Unhappily the guide was a liar and a cheat and scorned by all the villagers. By the time Ernest realized that he had been tricked into breaking the local fishing laws, they were already on their way to the stream. Hadley and Ernest had quarreled at lunch. No one seems to remember the cause of the argument, but Hadley, upset that Ernest was willing to break the law, walked behind, holding the rods. Ernest tried to cajole her into walking with him, then suggested that she go back to the hotel if she so strongly disapproved. At first she refused, taunting him with the accusation that he didn't have the nerve to turn back. " 'I'm going to stay with you,' " said the American wife in the story he would write. " 'If you go to jail we might as well both go.' " But finally Ernest did prevail. Hadley turned around and disappeared over the hill. A few minutes later Ernest was saved from an embarrassing illegality because the guide had forgotten the lead for the bait. With a sigh of relief he put away his rod, joined the old man in a long drink of marsala, and warmed himself in the sun.

When he got back to the hotel room he sat down to work. " . . . [It] was an almost literal transcription of what happened," he would explain in 1925 to Scott Fitzgerald when they were analyzing each other's work. He called the story "Out of Season" and passed it off as a simple story. It was not. "It was a kind of gateway," wrote Carlos Baker, "to the best writing of his career . . . a new narrative technique [in which] two intrinsically related truths [were developed] simultaneously." The "out of season" theme applies with equal force to the husband's relations with his wife and to the insistence of Peduzzi (Ernest's fictional name for the guide) that the young man fish for trout in defiance of the local fishing laws. It is a metaphor that works, an esthetic discovery that forms the basis for some of his best short fiction.

The Hemingways returned to Paris at the end of April, and Hadley began to cut and stitch many of the items for her layette. She was assisted by Janet Phelan, who had helped to cut the pattern for her wedding gown. It was decided that the baby would be born in Toronto. Ernest knew that he could get temporary work on the *Star* and believed that it might be easier to ensure the child's citizenship as American. "I also liked the idea," said Hadley, "because I believed, correctly as it turned out, that doctors, nurses, hospitals, would be better there than in Paris." The occasional quarrels recorded during the winter and spring were a reflection of her increasing confidence in speaking her mind. Most of the time she still thought Ernest right, and even if not right, so lovable and so smart that she supported his opinions. But when she believed he was wrong, she said so. The vitality and sparkle of their life in France, the travel, the interesting people they met, plus the continuing challenge of athletic pursuits had caused her to flower. Ernest had been good for her. Being pregnant was good for her, too.

On July 5, Hadley went with Ernest to Pamplona in the Basque country of Navarre for the Fiesta of San Firmin—six wild days of bullfights, street dancing, fireworks, and round-the-clock celebrations. Late in May he had left her behind to make a brief trip to Spain as the guest of Robert McAlmon, a twenty-six-year-old poet whom Ernest had met at Rapallo. Joined by Bill Bird, the three men had visited Madrid, Seville, and the spectacular village of Ronda, with its ancient bull ring high in the mountains above Malaga. Ernest returned from that holiday converted to the Spanish bullfight as the most beautiful thing he had ever seen. Not just a sport, he insisted, but a tragedy, requiring more courage and skill than anything possibly could. "It's just like having a ringside seat at the war with nothing going to happen to you," he wrote Bill Horne. Since then he had dreamed of returning to the bullfights, especially after Gertrude Stein had told him about the fiesta. His exuberance was contagious. Hadley thought it sounded like something she would not want to miss, that the experience would be good for her, might even be a favorable prenatal influence on the baby, whom they were now convinced would be a boy.

They arrived in Pamplona at night and after some difficulty found a room in a private house. Their window opened to a balcony of wrought iron and the walls were as thick as a fortress. "Music was pounding and throbbing," Ernest wrote. "Fireworks were being set off from the big public square. . . . Bands of blue-shirted peasants whirl and lift and swing . . . in the ancient Basque Riau-Riau dances." The wild music never stopped until daylight, when there was a roll of drums, and a military band took over. At 5:00 A.M. Hadley went out on the balcony. On the street below a great crowd milled about. At six, all the bulls that were to fight in the afternoon were set free to race through the town for the mile-and-a-half run to the pens at the bull ring. Ahead of them sprinted and ran and stumbled the men and boys of Pamplona, "[to give] the bulls a final shot at everyone in town . . . before they enter the pens. They will not leave until they come out into the glare of the arena to die in the afternoon."

Hadley mingled with the crowds, her heart leaping to the shrill sound of the fifes. In the afternoon the consummate struggle between man and beast took place—the man a professional torero, brave and dignified, the beast a carefully bred fighting bull, strong, speedy, vicious. Even if the actual event did not confirm Ernest's perception of it as tragedy, it seemed to Hadley an exciting and colorful spectacle. As Ernest explained it all to her, suggesting that she turn away from the worst parts, she quietly featherstitched garments for her baby—"embroidering in the presence of all that brutality," as she later described herself.

Unfortunately, she contracted a heavy cold when she got thoroughly soaked in a sudden heavy downpour at the bull ring. Ernest worried about her when they returned to Paris. She was in her seventh month now. In four weeks they would set out on a ten-day sea voyage to Montreal. She looked pale and was bothered with insomnia. Indigestion, the plague of pregnant women, drove her to nighttime eating. Ernest vacillated between concern for her and worry about the constant interruptions to his work. In an unpublished sketch of the period he described himself as dribbling away the day in domestic trivialities such as running out for the breakfast rolls and emptying the slop jars. He was lucky if he could find an hour a day for his writing.

In spite of disruptions Ernest did manage to do some good work. He wrote ten more prose sketches, similar in character to the ones he had written for Jane Heap. This set of sixteen would make up a small book, *in our time,* to be printed by Bill Bird. As it turned out, this was not to be Ernest's first book. Robert McAlmon offered to publish him ahead of Bird. Ernest gave him three stories—the two that had not disappeared on the train ("Up in Michigan" and "My Old Man") and the new one from Cortina, "Out of Season," as well as some poems. The friendship between McAlmon and Hemingway had deteriorated after their trip to Spain in May. McAlmon was a homosexual who had married for convenience and Ernest disliked his effete ways and cold, hard eyes. McAlmon regarded Ernest as a hypocritical amalgam of bully and small boy. (Apparently his personal opinion did not affect his professional judgment.)

James Joyce once remarked that the two men were confused about each other. "Hemingway posing as tough and McAlmon as sensitive, should swap poses and be true to life." Joyce was noticing what Hadley and others had observed—that much of Ernest's swagger was a protective cover for a deeply anxious nature.

To his old friend, Bill Horne, Ernest confided some of his current feelings about the prospect of becoming a father. Before sailing in mid-August he wrote,

We are going to have a baby sometime in October. We hope he'll be a boy and that you'll be his god father. He's spent the first six months of his life on skis and he's seen . . . 5 bull fights so if prenatal influence can do anything it's been done. We're both crazy about having the young feller. Hadley hasn't been sick a minute or even nauseated all the time. She's never felt better and looks wonderfully. . . . Gee, we've had fun, Bill. It doesn't seem possible we're going to leave it all. But when there were just the two of us it didn't make any difference how near broke we were. . . . But I figure I've got to have a steady job during The First Year of the Baby and expenses etc—anyway. Soon as he gets old enough he can take his or her chances with the rest of the family.

In commenting on Bill's latest love affair, Ernest revealed something of his own attitude toward love. "So you're in love again. Well, it's the only thing worth a damn to be. No matter how being in love comes out it's sure worth it all while it's going on."

Chapter 8

The baby was not expected for a month, time enough to get moved and settled. Dr. Hemingway was shipping the wedding presents, long stored on Kenilworth Avenue, and Grace would include Ernest's own christening robe and baby blanket. In Toronto, a suitable apartment was found and moving day was set for Saturday, September 29. Then Hadley began to worry that Ernest might not be on hand to help her. Instead of writing by-lined articles for John Bone's *Star Weekly*, he was working for the hard-driving editor of the *Daily Star*, Harry Hindmarsh, who had decided that Ernest was too cocky and deserved his comeuppance. "He is greatly overworked," Hadley wrote Grace. "So many trips, no sleep and countless unimportant assignments." She apologized for Ernest's infrequent letters, explaining that he never got home until two and three in the morning and had not even had time to open a checking account.

Nor did he have time to see her moved and settled. David Lloyd George, the British Prime Minister, was arriving in New York the week of October 1 and Ernest was dispatched there. Hadley's only helpers during the move were an ancient janitor and an inexperienced cleaning woman. This was the beginning of her hatred of Harry Hindmarsh. She was close to full term now and saw Hindmarsh as conducting a personal vendetta to keep her husband away from her. On October 9 she went to dinner at the Connables. When Harriet began to play sentimental tunes on the piano, Hadley was overcome with loneliness for Ernest, and almost simultaneously her contractions began. Ernest had worried constantly about the possibility of being away when she went into labor. Now it was happening as they both had dreaded.

At two o'clock on the morning of October 10, 1923, John Hadley Nicanor Hemingway was born at Wellesley Hospital. The next morning at nine o'clock Ernest rushed in, wild with anxiety. He had been with the Lloyd George party on the Montreal-Toronto train, knew nothing about Hadley's condition or the baby's until someone told him that a boy had been born. Handing his notes to a *Star* man he headed for the hospital. When he saw her, he broke down, "but then pulled together," wrote Hadley to Isabelle Simmons, "and was as sweet as you and I know he can be."

John Hadley was a perfect baby, named for the Spanish matador Nicanor Villalta (whom Hadley had seen in Spain) and for both parents (John Hadley being the pen name Ernest sometimes used). To Grace, Hadley described the first grandchild as well built and strong with perfect ears and lots of dark brown hair falling in sideburns "à la Rudolph Valentino." He looked like his grandmother, like Ernest, and "a tiny bit like me." The tone of the letter to Isabelle turned somber when she described Ernest's troubles with Hindmarsh. Still groggy from the anesthetic, nursing her two-day-old infant, she reflected that they might have to leave Toronto much sooner than expected. Hindmarsh was a brute. He had been furious with Ernest for going straight to the hospital instead of delivering the Lloyd George material to the city room in person. Dramatizing the grim alternatives, she added that "it is too horrible to describe or linger over. . . . our hearts are heavy just when we should be so happy. . . . I haven't the faintest idea but what I'd come out an old, care ridden *thing* from another big move—and staying is hell."

Ernest continued to obey Hindmarsh's orders, covering stories as far north as Sudbury and Cobalt, halfway to Hudson Bay, but he now believed that the editor's exploitation was destroying his literary life. In fact, Ernest had little good to say about Canada. It was a dull, dreadful country, " . . . against the law to sell Candy in the drug stores on sunday," he joked grimly to Sylvia Beach. "You have to smuggle it out." John Hadley had taken to "squawling," he wrote his family, "and is a fine nuisance. . . . It seems his only form of entertainment." Early in November he wrote Gertrude Stein that they were definitely returning to Paris and already had a sailing date, in January. He was going to "chuck journalism" and go all the way with serious writing.

During the first two years in Paris, Hadley's income had provided them with modest luxuries, but Ernest had earned good money. Now, when there was John Hadley to care for, her income would be their sole support. Hadley, however, was determined to put Ernest's needs first, especially as they related to his work. When her darling cried out that he could not stand it (in Toronto), she agreed that there was only one thing to do, and that was to get out. She and John Hadley must never get in the way of his writing.

The baby was now called Bumby, so named by Hadley for his warm, solid, Teddy-Bear-like feel in her arms. His eyes were still blue, but she was sure they would turn brown, after his father—a father who seemed now to have forgotten his misgivings about parenthood. Hadley wrote frequently to Ernest's parents, who had sent a generous check that took care of all hospital expenses. To Grace she described how she was putting fresh ribbon and lace on Ernest's christening robe for the baptism, now expected to take place in Paris. With Dr. Ed she discussed feeding schedules. Should she cut out the middle of the night feeding, since Bumby would probably sleep through until 5:30 or 6:00 if she let him? Early in December the big question was whether she and Bumby should go to Oak Park with Ernest for Christmas. Hadley thought not, even though Ed Hemingway offered to pay her fare. "Most of all," she explained, "on account of the baby's feeding—the least little fatigue or worry on my part so often pretty nearly ends the supply [of milk] and we feel that I *must* be able to nurse him on the ocean trip."

Grace swallowed her disappointment at not seeing her new grandchild by gathering up gifts and trinkets for him and his mother. The most lavish was a tiny, exquisite dress, not unlike the one Ernie wore in his infancy, with silk stockings and small pink shoes lined in quilted silk. The family gathered from near and far to welcome Ernest. Grace, always emotional, was so overcome that she retired to a quiet corner of the music room to shed tears of happiness. Writing Ernest a few hours after his departure, she tried to express how much his visit meant to her. Once again she likened him to her own father, especially in the maturity of his judgment.

Earlier in the fall, the package containing copies of *Three Stories and Ten Poems* from Robert McAlmon's printer had reached Toronto, and soon after that, there were the proof sheets from Bill Bird for *in our time*. The first American critic to take notice was Burton Rascoe in a small item in the *Sunday New York Tribune*. Edmund Wilson, who reviewed books for the influential quarterly, *Dial*, had brought to Rascoe's attention Hemingway's six prose miniatures in the "Exiles" issue of *The Little Review*. Rascoe called them amusing stuff and admitted that he had not gotten around to reading a new book by the same author. Ernest was livid at Rascoe's negligence. He sent Wilson a copy of *Three Stories and Ten Poems* with a letter asking for the names of other reviewers who might read it.

Before Ernest left Oak Park he had given Marcelline a copy of *Three Stories and Ten Poems*, with the strict warning not to show it to their parents. He knew that "Up in Michigan" was much too sexually explicit for them. She respected his wishes and they never saw the book, but he did not realize that they would be just as upset by the contents of *in our time*, especially his father, who had ordered several copies directly from Paris. When Ed Hemingway read the prose miniatures he erupted into grim-faced rage and insisted that all the copies be returned. He would not tolerate such filth in his home, he declared. Grace tearfully suggested that she would like to keep one copy since it was Ernest's first book. But her husband was adamant. He said to one of his friends that he would rather see Ernest dead than writing about such seamy subjects—the subjects being, among others, the unpredictable tragedy of war, as demonstrated by fleeing refugees; the cold-blooded nature of public executions; the savagery as well as the bravery of the Spanish bullfight.

The entire shipment was returned to Bill Bird in Paris sometime after New Year's with a note penned by Marcelline that the contents were not suitable for Christmas presents. She had predicted to her parents that Ernest would learn of the incident and resent it bitterly. She was right. He remembered the insult for the rest of his life. And he seemed to reserve his deepest hostility for his mother.

It is not clear whether Grace ever realized the depth of that hostility. She seemed to feel that a mother's obligatory role included honest criticism of her offspring. Ernest, however, was not interested in her literary opinions. What he wanted and expected from her was unqualified loyalty and approval. When anything less was forthcoming he lashed out like a wounded adolescent. This in spite of the fact that he understood her Victorian sensibilities and occasionally even protected them.

In January the Hemingways, loaded down with luggage and boxes and baby paraphernalia, sailed from New York for Paris. After passing up several desirable apartments because of the high rents, they located one that they could afford, at 113, rue Notre-Dame-des-Champs, up the street from the Pounds, four blocks from Gertrude and Alice, and an easy stroll from the Luxembourg Gardens. It was a neighborhood of attractive buildings, well-kept trees, and stylish cafés. The Dôme and the Select were almost directly behind, on Boulevard Montparnasse. If the tone was more refined than rue Mouffetard, the accouterments of the flat were still far from elegant. There was no electricity, though the plumbing was a modest improvement over 74, Cardinal Lemoine. The owner of the building, who lived on the ground floor, operated a lumberyard and sawmill adjacent to his property. No loud accordion from a *bal musette* disturbed the night, but the whine of the circular saw and the racket of the donkey engine were unremitting from 7:00 A.M. until 5:00 P.M. Hadley rented the use of an out-of-tune upright piano located in the cellar of a musical instrument shop on the Boulevard Montparnasse.

Chink Dorman-Smith, visiting from Germany, joined Hadley in urging Ernest to set the date for John Hadley's christening, and conversation turned to what church should be the scene of the baptism. Gertrude Stein and Dorman-Smith were to be godmother and godfather. Ernest thought that Gertrude's Judaism and Chink's Catholicism canceled out each other. One of the Protestant denominations should be selected. Gertrude came up with Episcopalian as the least dogmatic. Ernest balked at interviewing the minister and stood outside reading a scrap of newspaper he had picked up from the gutter while Chink made the arrangements.

On March 10, 1924, Hadley dressed her placid boy in the lace-trimmed robe worn by his own father nearly twenty-five years before and the party walked to St. Luke's Episcopal Church in the rue de la Grande Chaumerie. After the ceremony everyone returned to no. 113 for champagne and sugared almonds, traditional fare at French christenings.

Hadley was still nursing Bumby and not supplementing his diet with solid food because Ernest (the son of a doctor and privy, he thought, to special medical insights) convinced her that nothing more was necessary. It was William Carlos Williams, the physician-poet, invited to dinner one night, who noticed that the child was listless and pale. Hearing Hadley admit that her supply of milk had dwindled, he told her to wean the baby from the breast and pre-scribed a diet that "would have done for Jack the Giant Killer." Almost at once Bumby's cheeks fattened and his muscles grew strong.

Sometimes Ernest looked after Bumby in the early mornings. He prepared the formula, boiled the nipples, and filled the bottles, then spread his work across the dining room table, with only the satisfied gurgles of the baby to intrude upon his concentration. He taught the child to put up his fists and assume a ferocious expression and to thrust out his tiny hand to catch passing flies. Sometimes he gave Bumby a bath, and sometimes he carried him off on an outing. (Sylvia Beach remembers the two of them in her bookstore, Ernest holding the baby ever so carefully while engrossed in reading some-thing on one of the shelves.) But such fatherly tasks were not per-formed with any regularity. Ernest was pouring most of his energies into his work. Slowly he fashioned the short stories that were sent off regularly to American magazines—and just as regularly came back with rejection slips. If home was too distracting or he craved a change of scene, he took his notebooks and sharpened pencils to a quiet café, Closerie des Lilas, where it was warm inside and no one knew him. He read copy for Ford Madox Ford, the distinguished novelist and editor who had come to Paris to start a new literary magazine, the *transatlantic review*.

Ford, known for his kindness to young writers, had heard of Ernest from his friend Ezra Pound, who lauded Hemingway as the finest prose stylist in the world and a disciplined journalist. Ernest vindicated Pound's confidence. He did a first-rate job for Ford, who soon recognized Ernest's talent. "I did not read more than six words of his," he wrote in his memoirs, "before I decided to publish everything that he sent me." In the April issue of *transatlantic* was the first review of *Three Stories and Ten Poems* and an early Nick Adams story, "Indian Camp." Other reviews soon followed. This recognition by *transatlantic* gave a significant thrust to Hemingway's career. It made his name known in Paris literary circles, lifting him above the dilettantes who were pouring into the Quarter, and opened up a respectable outlet for his work. There was another reason for the importance of the April issue. Ernest had persuaded Ford to bring out Gertrude Stein's *The Making of Americans* in serial form and this was the first installment. Gertrude was enormously pleased. The manuscript had lain on her shelf, unpublished since 1911, never revised because she hated such drudgery. She turned that job over to Ernest, who put it into readable form and gave Gertrude fresh reason to dote upon him.

Ford, whose English wife, Violet, refused to divorce him, lived down the street from Hadley and Ernest with his new love, an Australian painter named Stella Bowen. Hadley and Stella quickly became friends, Hadley often walking over to Stella's studio for the elaborate lunch that Ford fancied, and to watch Stella at work. Hadley enjoyed Ford and was amused by him. Not so Ernest. In spite of the editor's generosity to him, Ernest worked up an ardent dislike for his appearance and his mannerisms. Poor Ford was unathletic and flaccid, with lusterless eyes and the shape, to quote Hemingway, of an "up-ended hogshead." He had an unfortunate penchant for exaggerations and small pomposities. Hadley's fondness for the couple did not temper Ernest's scorn. He wrote a biting miniature about Ford and Stella arguing over wines. Only his own shrewdness had led him to play for a time the game of deferential novitiate. Ford ignored his barbs and seemed genuinely proud when Ernest condescended to show up at his Thursday literary teas in patched jacket and sneakers.

It was on one such afternoon in the *transatlantic* editorial office, in the back shop of Three Mountains Press on Quai d'Anjou, that Ernest met Harold Loeb, a Princeton graduate and editor of another magazine of the arts, *Broom*. Loeb was fascinated with everything he observed about Hemingway—the shy disarming smile, the shabby clothes, the fervent dedication to his craft, the air of casual disinterest. " . . . never before had I encountered an American so unaffected by living in Paris," he wrote. Ernest was more ambivalent, for Harold Loeb was Jewish, an automatic disadvantage in forming a close friendship with Ernest.

Anti-Semitism was common among Ernest's friends. In his private circle, it was the rare gentile who did not disparage Jews. One of the most candid statements in this regard was made by Donald Ogden Stewart, who did not claim any superiority in tolerance. " . . . I have no doubt," he said later, "that I was really basically anti-Semitic in those days, as probably also was Hemingway. People had Jewish friends who, *mirabile dictu*, were nice people. . . . I am only saying what most everybody else would say if they spoke the truth. . . . I renounced all this claptrap a long time ago." Stewart acknowledged that he had been " . . . cruel to Harold, perhaps not to his face, but even worse behind his back, since he remembers me with kindness." Harold did treat most people with kindness; he was a gentle man with a streak of romantic idealism. His anxious desire to please exasperated Ernest, but his athletic prowess was a compensation. He had wrestled in college and played a good game of tennis.

Hadley appreciated Loeb's gracious manners and noticed that he treated women in a way that her husband often did not—Harold's way was soft and respectful. When she met him, he was in the company of Kitty Cannell, an expatriate from Ithaca, New York who had been educated at the Sorbonne. Slender and fashionable, with the erect carriage of a ballerina, she was "all pink and white and gold," Hadley observed. Her fragile beauty, however, concealed a sturdily independent turn of mind. Through her husband, Skipwith Cannell, a poet, she had moved in London literary circles, and she had published fiction in quarterlies. Though she and Harold Loeb were lovers, they did not live together. He had been unhappily married and wanted no permanent relationship. Kitty, not yet divorced from Cannell, was satisfied with the loose arrangement.

She was immediately drawn to Hadley. No two women could have been more different, yet Kitty was full of admiration for the relaxed, plainly-dressed woman with the fresh complexion. "A very attractive example of the American girl," thought Kitty. In later communications with Carlos Baker she emphasized Hadley's sense of humor and lack of pretense. "Not a bit prissy," she said. "Maybe the Doris Day of the intellectual world, as Doris is in films, not in Hedda Hopper." Everyone respected Hadley, recognizing that her quiet management of his domestic life contributed to Ernest's stability. Donald Stewart for one believed that Hadley was the perfect wife and the Hemingway marriage so ideal that there was a holiness about it.

Kitty Cannell, who was beginning to distrust Ernest, dissented from such a lofty judgment. To her there was something suspect in Ernest's determination to keep Hadley in such mean surroundings. It riled her that a woman should be so supportive of her husband while asking nothing for herself. When Kitty made occasional small gifts of jewelry to Hadley, Ernest was furious. "He felt I was a bad example to a submissive wife," she believed. Kitty Cannell was one of the first observers to hypothesize that Ernest disliked women. She admitted that Ernest had a small-boy quality that could be endearing, but she warned Harold Loeb that his new friend could suddenly turn on him, and not to be unprepared.

In the spring of 1924, the financial hardships of the Hemingways were compounded by the mishandling of Hadley's trust fund. On the advice of Hadley's friend George Breaker, who was managing her investments, the Hemingways had sold off $19,000. worth of United Railway four percent bonds for $10,000. and put the money into some Arkansas Road Bonds. For eight months there had been no income at all from the bonds. Now it looked as though the new investment was shaky. It was ironic that this occurred not when Ernest was a well-paid journalist but when he earned scarcely anything from his writing. There was no money coming through from the *Star,* and Ford paid nothing for Ernest's editing.

These were the days when Ernest picked up a few francs sparring with professional heavyweights and Hadley walked miles out of the way to locate the least expensive groceries. But there was no question of complaint. She could see the growing number of short stories. And she was not one to be overly concerned about money matters. They were young and indulged themselves as they could. Sometimes they went by bus to follow the bicycle races and joined the villagers in beer-drinking contests. On long trips, now and later, Hadley would rely on Marie-Cocotte (Rohrbach) to care for Bumby. For short outings Ernest suggested that Feather Puss, their handsome black cat who often curled up at the foot of the crib, watchful and alert, could act as temporary baby sitter. Hadley did not argue the point but arranged for her landlady to look in on the child. Ernest's urge to take charge affected all the decisions in their daily life. On one occasion when he was being especially lordly, Hadley teased him into admitting that he would like to be a king. But though she might chide him gently, she still followed his lead.

Early in the summer, Ernest decided that they should withdraw three hundred dollars from their dwindling savings account for a month's vacation in Spain. In Madrid he took Hadley to the bullfighters' pensione in the Calle San Jeronimo, where he had stayed with Robert McAlmon the year before. Now he was an insider, exchanging heated opinions with the matadors. At Aranjuez, twenty miles south of the capital, they watched a spectacular corrida that featured Bumby's namesake, Nicanor Villalta, and six bulls from the Martinez ranch. From there they went north again to the mountains of Navarre, for the fiesta of San Firmin, checking into the Hotel Perla in the city of Pamplona.

Despite the presence of two wives (Sally Bird had come down from Paris with her husband, Bill), the week at Pamplona had a distinctly male tone, almost that of a fraternity revel, with dancing in the streets and long lines in front of the whore house. Donald Stewart, won over by Ernest's enthusiasm, was there, as were John Dos Passos, Robert McAlmon, and Chink Smith. Unlike Sally Bird, who was so upset by the brutality in the bull ring that she stayed away from most of the events, Hadley took her seat in the stand every afternoon.

The rest of their crowd drifted off before the festival was over, but Hadley and Ernest stayed until the last reveler had slept off his orgy and the town returned to its former lazy state. At noon on July 14, a baking hot day, they boarded a double-decker bus jammed with Basque farmers drinking wine from leather wineskins. A few miles out of Pamplona the bus began to climb, stirring up a good breeze as it crossed the rocky hills and sloping grain fields. Their destination was Burguete, high in the mountains near the French border. Ernest wrote later:

> We went through the forest . . . and out ahead of us was a rolling green plain, with dark mountains beyond it. . . . The green plain stretched off. . . . As we came to the edge of the rise we saw the red roofs and white houses of Burguete ahead strung out on the plain, and away off on the shoulder of the first dark mountain was the gray metal-sheathed roof of the monastery of Roncesvalles.

Hadley was eager to make this leg of the trip because Ernest had told her of the great trout fishing in the Irati River a few kilometers from the village. Sally and Bill Bird and Bob McAlmon were waiting for them at the inn in the center of the town. Hadley, seeing her breath in the cold mountain air, wondered how it could ever be warm enough for fishing. All night the wind blew against the shutters of her second-floor bedroom, but in the morning the clouds had vanished and the warm sun encouraged her to believe that a hike to the river was possible after all. The innkeeper packed them a good lunch and some wine. They crossed meadows and rushing streams and followed a narrow road through beech forests. It was a strenuous hike for a day's fishing, but Ernest urged them on. The road dropped steeply out of wooded hills into the valley of the Rio de la Fabrica, and then the Irati River, framed by steep bluffs, came into view. Hadley made the best catch in the icy water—six fine trout, firm and hard. She shucked the insides, gills and all, as Ernest had taught her, washed them in the quiet water of a damned-up pool, and packed them carefully in her bag between layers of ferns.

A few days later Chink Smith and Dos Passos arrived to take McAlmon on a walking trip to Andorra on the Spanish side of the Pyrenees. Ernest went along with them for a few hours, then retraced his steps back to Hadley. He promised her that they would return to the Irati next year with sleeping bags and cooking gear, and camp by the side of the river. That would be fine, she thought, but right now she was ready to go back to Paris. She missed Bumby. A month was a long time in a small child's life.

Ernest's writing output since moving back to Paris had been remarkable, nine stories in all, each one glinting "with the hard factual lights of the naturalist," none of them straying very far from personal opinion and experience. For the first time, in "The Doctor and the Doctor's Wife," Ernest wrote about the interaction between his parents. The incident in the story is based on a log-cutting episode that took place at Windemere in 1911. Dr. Adams (Ed Hemingway) backs away from a confrontation with a tough Indian sawyer who accuses him of keeping the logs that have washed up on his beach instead of returning them to their rightful owner. Dr. Adams then is evasive to his wife about what happened. She, lying in her bedroom with the blinds drawn and a copy of *Science and Health* beside her, quotes Bible verses to her irritable husband as she tries to wheedle the truth from him. It is an unsentimental portrait of both Hemingways but Nick's sympathies are clearly with his father.

In a coda to the story "Big Two-Hearted River" Nick speculates upon some of the moods that bring out his best work. "He always worked best when Helen [his wife] was unwell. Just that much discontent and friction." It would not startle Hadley that some irritability between them motivated Ernest to creativity. She had considerable patience for his gyrating moods and was philosophical about her place in his scheme of things. It only worried her that his work was not being appreciated where it really counted—in America.

Then, in the October *Dial*, Edmund Wilson singled out Ernest's prose as "of the first distinction. . . . [it] conveys profound emotions and complex states of mind . . . and is strikingly original." Ernest wrote to Wilson, thanking him for his praise and informing him that he had just finished and was sending off a full-length book of stories to New York. He was referring to a manuscript that he had mailed to Don Stewart, who was trying to place Ernest's work with publishers. The miniatures from *in our time* were placed as interludes among twelve longer pieces—the original ones from *Three Stories* and nine recently completed ones.

"We will probably be in Paris all winter," Ernest continued to Wilson. "Not enough money to get out." He seemed to enjoy dramatizing their pinched circumstances. To the families in St. Louis and Oak Park, Hadley wrote of a different and possibly more realistic scenario. Life was an exciting mélange of famous friends and exotic travel. The grandparents were supposed to be relieved by the fact that Gertrude Stein, who had gone to Johns Hopkins Medical School, checked up on Bumby.

By this time the shock of Ernest's explicit prose had apparently worn off, as both Grace and Ed doted on his progress. When Ford Madox Ford visited Oak Park and looked up Grace, she invited him for tea and, according to Leicester's memoir, pressed Ernest's baby books and high-school stories on the curious Ford. Ed Hemingway conscientiously mailed Ernest all the sports magazines and literary reviews that might interest him, though there is no evidence that any checks were slipped in with the letters. The doctor was close-fisted with money, but if he had been aware of their poverty he would very likely have helped the young Hemingways.

Grace, no longer earning her own money, was dependent on her husband for the private art lessons that she now took from a well-known Chicago artist, Pauline Palmer. When her skills had developed sufficiently, she asked Ernest to investigate the Paris art scene for her and send her some good art catalogues. She would be so grateful to him for looking out for her interests. What Paris thought of her was not as important as making it in the eyes of her own countrymen, but some recognition from Paris would be a tremendous boost.

In the fall of 1924, Grace persuaded Ed to take her to Florida because she was getting better at landscapes and wanted to be able to paint out-of-doors all the time. She wrote Ernest from St. Petersburg that the boom in population was most impressive and that the beauties of the area certainly justified it. At the urging of real-estate promoters, the Hemingways began to invest much more than they could afford in undeveloped Florida land. Ed took out a mortgage on his Oak Park house and pyramided his holdings with small down payments. Grace encouraged him in this dream of easy money and rationalized that it would be good for his health. He was looking gray and tired and had even taken to smoking a pipe for relaxation. When he successfully passed the examination for a medical license in Florida, she began to plan for an eventual move to the south.

Ernest attacked Grace throughout his life for manipulating and dominating his father. But his own dominance of Hadley's life and his instinctive habit of putting his own needs ahead of hers, with Hadley as willing accomplice, were not so different from Grace Hemingway building the Kenilworth House as a monument to herself or arranging Florida vacations for the sake of her art. Years earlier she had predicted that Ernest would be more like her than any of her other children. Both were restless and imaginative, with strong competitive instincts and the drive to dominate their environment. Ernest could never acknowledge this. The qualities that he thought admirable in a man—ambition, an independent point of view, defiance of his supremacy—became threatening in a woman. Ernest was interested in women for their sexuality, their companionship, and their tenderness, their capacity to serve his best interests. But he was made uncomfortable, was even angered, when they did not play out the traditional role assigned to them by society. He was convinced that his mother was guilty of such role reversal and was suspicious of any woman who reminded him of her.

None of these negative feelings applied to Hadley. She managed their lives in a way that gave Ernest all the freedom he craved. "She is the best guy on a trip you ever saw," he wrote his friend Jenkins, who had originally opposed the marriage.

> She is keeping her piano up and runs the house and the baby damned smooth and is always ready to go out and eat oysters at the cafe and drink a bottle of Pouilly before supper. We have good whiskey in the home and a swell lot of books, open fire places and it's comfortable, and a guy can read or lie around and go out when he feels like it.

Hadley, of course, did not have the actual mobility Ernest enjoyed. Very often she stayed behind in the flat, reading by gaslight, or climbed alone into the big double bed when heat from the fireplaces was inadequate against the winter cold. She was not present on the night that Harold Loeb and Kitty Cannell took Ernest to meet Leon Fleischman (literary scout for the publishers Boni and Liveright), a connection that Harold wanted to open up for Ernest. Fleischman greeted his guests warmly, served them good liquor, offered Ernest some business advice, and behaved in an altogether charming way. But something in the New Yorker's manner sent Ernest into a seething rage. Perhaps he sensed a faintly patronizing tone in Fleishman's offer to read his stories and send them on to his publishing house if he liked them. Ernest was still the envious outsider, craving approval from the literary establishment but too proud to curry favor.

After they left the apartment, he called Fleischman a low-down kike and other epithets. Kitty was disgusted but not surprised. Harold chose to ignore what he heard, preferring to think that the slurs had nothing to do with him. His admiration for his new friend had taken on a kind of hero worship, and he fretted over the number of rejection slips Ernest had been receiving. Having sold his own novel, *Doodab*, to Horace Liveright's company, he thought he possessed some insights that would benefit Ernest. At L'Avenue on Montparnasse, Loeb suggested that perhaps Ernest's stories were not selling because he, Hemingway, had not suffered enough. Ernest was indignant. To cite the misery he had experienced, he described the crushing disappointment over losing Agnes. He told

Loeb how they had fallen in love, but that she had left him, gone away. He could not rid himself of her memory. "In short words . . . he described her hair, her breasts, her body. . . . I was quite convinced," wrote Harold.

With Ernest's penchant for self-pity and exaggeration it is difficult to assess the seriousness of such remarks. He told much the same story to Lincoln Steffens, adding that if the nurse from Italy were to come back into his life he would give up everything for her. The most that can be said about such remarks is that the rejection still rankled and he had a rich imagination. Both Don Stewart and Loeb regarded him as a puritan who never chased women, who was remorseful if he stared too hard at the girls of Montmartre. Although few of their friends lived in tranquil domesticity and liaisons were easily broken, Ernest did not as yet seem susceptible to the hedonism that surrounded him. Archibald MacLeish, the poet from Illinois who met him at this time, found him to be sensible as well as perceptive, not one to fall for the shoddy. Ernest never became the typical sidewalk-café writer; the amateurs and pleasure-seekers resented him and were made uncomfortable by his diligence.

Gloomy though Ernest's expectations had been for the winter, he always managed to find money for the activities he liked best. This was the year that he discovered Schruns, a little-known village in the Austrian Voralberg where lodging was cheap and the skiing superb. The Hemingways went there a week before Christmas, to stay at the Pensione Taube in the picturesque Montafon Valley. In February, while they were still enjoying the good life of vacationers, Ernest received momentous news. After a thrilling ski jaunt to the Vermunt-Stausee ("frozen glacier"), he and Hadley were resting at the inn at the foot of the glacier. At nightfall a messenger arrived from their pensione, bringing two cables from New York—one from Don Stewart, the other from Harold Loeb. Horace Liveright wanted to publish *In Our Time*. When Ernest returned to the pensione, there was a cable from Liveright himself, with some of the details. The publisher thought the stories were splendid, except for "Up in Michigan," which he felt was too sexually explicit for American taste. The stories would be published in October.

This major breakthrough for Ernest was followed by an incident that ultimately was to be of even greater significance for his career. On the recommendation of F. Scott Fitzgerald, already a well-respected author, Maxwell Perkins, his editor at Scribners, wrote Ernest to inquire about his work. Ernest replied that he had signed a contract with Liveright, but he left open the possibility that some day he might have something to show Perkins.

Although Ernest and F. Scott Fitzgerald knew of each other's work, they had not met at this time. That first meeting was to take place in late spring, in a bar. Soon Hadley and Zelda Fitzgerald also met. Hadley admired Zelda's beauty and style but knew at once that they had nothing in common except literary husbands who had struck up a friendship. She sensed that Zelda was jealous of Scott's work, and that he was jealous of her, and noted the continuous tension between them. Hadley also understood why there might be an underlying hostility between Ernest and Zelda. "He was too assured a male for her. Maybe she caught this and resented it. . . . He was then the kind of man to whom men, women, children, and dogs were attracted. It was something."

What Zelda came to resent was her husband's noticeable hero worship of Hemingway. At one point, she told Scott that Ernest was a phony and that he should not go out of his way to help him. Ernest, with his talent for picking up the weaknesses of others, believed that Zelda was emotionally unstable and blamed her for Scott's excruciating self-doubt. (Some years later, when Scribners published a slender volume of Zelda's fiction, Ernest pronounced it "unreadable" and warned Maxwell Perkins that if he ever published a book by any of his, Ernest's, wives, "I'll bloody well shoot you."

In spite of the coolness between Zelda and Ernest, the Fitzgeralds became part of a widening circle of Hemingway friends. Bill Smith, now reconciled with Ernest, arrived to spend the spring and summer and met most of them. After dinner, they strolled down to the Select, or the Closerie, where they ordered double-strength drinks and chatted. In the afternoon there were tennis games with Harold Loeb or long bike rides into the Bois de Boulogne with Archibald MacLeish. Two newcomers had recently joined the group, sisters from the Midwest whom Bill Smith remembered. Their names were Pauline and Virginia Pfeiffer; Pauline, the older of the two, worked in the Paris office of *Vogue*. They had been to some of Harold Loeb's parties and had asked to meet the Hemingways. On that first meeting, Ernest had paid more attention to Jinny than to Pauline, giving her a spirited account of his recent winter holiday at Schruns. Later, when the sisters visited the Hemingway apartment, Pauline was shocked by the sight of Ernest, unshaven and sloppy, reading as he lay on the rumpled bed. She was not impressed. But subsequently she came to see him in a different light—tall and handsome as he strolled on the boulevards, working quietly at the Closerie des Lilas, making wonderful jokes. She cast about for ways of catching his interest. Her gambits were often clumsy, however, as when Bill Smith heard her say, "I was talking to someone about you just the other day," to which Hemingway, rising to the bait, answered, "Oh? And what did he say?"

It did not appear to Bill that Ernest was more than mildly interested in Pauline's admiration. Indeed, his attention seemed to be concentrated elsewhere. Over the winter and spring he had formed the habit of buying drinks for a titled Englishwoman, Lady Duff Twysden, and the young Scotsman with whom she was living while waiting for her divorce decree to come through. Duff, born Dorothy Smurthwaite on May 22, 1892, was the daughter of a plain man who kept a wine shop in Yorkshire, but her mother, an elegant woman, aspired to social position. Duff took her mother's maiden name of Stirling after her parents were divorced.

In preparation for a good marriage, Duff had been educated in Paris, where she became fluent in French. She was fairly accomplished at drawing in pen and ink. Summers were spent at her grandmother Stirling's home in Scotland, a solid stone house with uniformed servants. Duff, whose accounts of her childhood tended to be fanciful, described a setting of mist and heather, horses and stately neighborhood teas. She hinted at ties to minor Scottish nobility. And it was true that her mother was able to arrange for Duff to be presented at Buckingham Palace. Photos of this period show her as tall and angular, with a high forehead, narrow Roman nose, and small exquisite head on a slender neck. She was beginning to demonstrate the self-possession, the indefinable air of breeding, and the natural style that became characteristic of her.

During her first marriage, to Luttrell Byrom during World War I, Duff carried out volunteer assignments for the British Secret Service and flirted with naval officers who were considerably younger than her husband. One such officer was Sir Roger Thomas Twysden, tenth baronet, commander, Royal Navy, whom she met at a ball in Exeter. Sir Roger was drawn to Duff at once, and the fact that she was already married gave a provocative edge to the chase. The Twysden family watched with growing alarm as Sir Roger dropped other women in favor of Duff. To them she was a mere adventuress, scheming to get her hands on Roger's title and his money, and Roger's mother did everything she could to sever the attachment. Only Roger's sister grudgingly admitted that Duff could stir a man's imagination.

When Duff was divorced by her husband (on the only possible grounds—adultery), she slipped quietly out of London with Sir Roger and they were married in Edinburgh on January 25, 1917. Thirteen months later Duff gave birth to a son. The Twysdens still scorned her, perceiving her as a grasping woman who drifted from lover to lover, cared nothing for her child, and corrupted her young husband with her drinking. The story Duff told later was quite different. According to her, Roger was an ugly drunk who continually harrassed her. Whether he actually kept a sword in his bed, or ordered her to sleep on the floor, as she was to tell Ernest, was never established. But the marriage was stormy. She frequently took the child to Paris or to her grandmother's home in Scotland to get away from Roger. During this time her young cousin, Pat Guthrie, consoled her, and she became increasingly attached to him.

Pat was an alcoholic who had already been institutionalized. He had no money and left a string of bad debts wherever he traveled, but Duff fell in love with him anyway. He was good-looking and amiable, full of fun when he was sober. The fact that he was a renegade may also have attracted her. In due time, she left Roger to go to Paris with Pat, leaving her only child to be cared for by his two grandmothers and her titled husband to sue her for divorce, naming Guthrie as correspondent.

It was in Montparnasse that the legend of Lady Duff Twysden began. She wore her dark brown hair closely cropped and favored loose sweaters, pulling them over simple blouses with tiny Eton collars, and plain Scotch tweed skirts. Her love affair with Guthrie engaged everyone's attention. When checks arrived from one or the other family, they moved to the Ritz and ordered champagne and caviar. When the money ran out they repaired to a third-rate hotel. In either instance they haunted the cafés. When Pat was too drunk to accompany her, Duff made the rounds with his tight circle of English homosexual friends.

Duff drank as much as anyone—it was the thing to do—but no one ever saw her make a fool of herself. Her attraction for men seemed less a matter of her own sensuality than her ability to fulfill their fantasies about themselves. She may even have been frigid, but her talent for satisfying her partners was considerable. Although half the men of Montparnasse fancied themselves in love with her, she remained uninvolved, flirting lightly with everyone, letting no one know where her real feelings lay. She seemed ready to marry Pat when her divorce became final and suggested various schemes for getting her child back, including kidnapping, but as a practical matter she did nothing. This habit of drifting with the tide, putting up with abusive treatment as though she deserved it, caring nothing for money except as a convenience for satisfying her temporary needs, were the traits Duff shared with the floaters who formed her clique.

Ernest, who disdained the emptiness of the café life, did not fit the mold of Duff's admirers. But the same qualities that attracted others attracted him—her insouciance, her style, her unerring charm. Occasionally he brought her around to the apartment. Hadley liked Duff for her broad, unaffected sense of humor and her delightful manners, and especially because she was sweet to Bumby. "When she laughed," Hadley said, "the whole of her went into that laughter. Lots of broad language, certainly, but it went over with all kinds of people." Hadley found something else attractive about Duff, the implicit assurance that husbands were not fair game, that in spite of being a man's woman, she would respect the code. Ernest may not have appreciated such a distinction. Though he could write Sherwood Anderson on May 23, 1925, that he and Hadley were as fond of each other as ever and got along well, he was beginning to feel the first stirrings of a new passion. He was not free to take up with Duff but he encouraged her friendship and her confidences, suspecting that the confidences might not be cherished secrets at all but harmless lies.

Harold Loeb, who had been Duff's silent admirer for months, was free to take up with her. Over the past months he had told Kitty Cannell that a restlessness had taken hold of him and that their old relationship was over. Kitty, surprised and hurt, did not know what had gone wrong but made it clear that she wanted nothing from him. He could have the freedom he craved. It was at the Select, on a quiet afternoon as he worked on his novel, that Harold had first noticed Duff.

> I heard a laugh so gay and musical that it seemed to brighten the dingy room. . . . She was not strikingly beautiful, but her features had a special appeal for me . . . the expressive eyes and the fresh complexion . . . [the] grace about the way she held herself. . . . she moved around in a muck of lost souls without losing a certain aloof splendor.

Belonging as they both did to the same small world, he caught glimpses of her at cocktail parties and bars. But the opportunity to talk to her did not present itself until months later, again at the Select.

This time they made an appointment for the next afternoon at a café where no one would recognize them. After that rendezvous, Duff took Loeb to a friend's apartment, where they made love. He invited her to go away with him and the next day they boarded a compartment on a wagon-lit for Spain. Harold, full of romantic illusions about her troubled past, treated Duff with a delicacy that bordered on awe. For her, his sincerity, rugged good looks, and solid education were a welcome escape from weary British aristocrats. She responded generously, drinking much less to suit his moderate ways, always preserving the mystery that so enchanted him.

"There was a sadness in her smile," Loeb later wrote in his memoir of the love affair. " 'I think . . . that you see me as someone that I'm not,' she said. ' . . . I could disappoint you terribly.' " After a few days of walking on the beach and swimming in the ocean, dancing and gambling at the casino, they went to a secluded mountain inn near Ascain. Loeb moved in a kind of trance, bewitched by her. Duff seemed relaxed and happy. She showed Harold a portfolio of her drawings. He was impressed with her talent and encouraged her to work harder, but she only laughed. Work was not suited to her. "I have nothing against work . . . for those who like it," she conceded. They talked about Ernest Hemingway, and Harold wondered if there was more to that friendship than she admitted. Duff was evasive, calling Ernest a good chap, not denying that she had once said she liked him but would never go off with him because of Hadley. Gently she reminded Harold that Pat Guthrie expected her back in Paris, and she must prepare to board the night train.

" . . . the thought of losing her pierced like a knife thrust," he wrote later.

Harold went on alone to St. Jean de Luz and a few days later Duff wrote that she missed him terribly and was miserable without him, and that their interlude had been a glorious little dream. "Now for a doubtful glad tidings," she added. "I am coming on the Pamplona trip with Hem and your lot. Can you bear it? With Pat of course. If this appears impossible for you, let me know and I'll try and get out of it. But I'm dying to come and feel that even seeing and being able to talk to you will be better than nothing."

Harold agreed with that and took comfort from the fact that she could still express such tenderness for him. He seemed philosophical about the fact that Guthrie would accompany her. It was Ernest, not Pat, who worried Harold, for it was Ernest's friendship that he valued, and it was Ernest's anger that could be so searing. But a letter from Hemingway, on June 21, gave no hint that trouble might be brewing. "Pat and Duff are coming too," Ernest wrote. "Pat has sent off to Scotland for rods and Duff to England for funds. As far as I know Duff is not bringing any fairies with her. You might arrange to have a band of local fairies meet her at the train carrying a daisy chain so that the transition from the Quarter will not be too sudden."

By this time not even Hadley believed that Ernest's interest in Duff was entirely innocent, although she calmly went ahead with preparations for the summer holiday and ignored his jealous scowls when anyone spoke of Harold's new infatuation. During the winter she had left the cafés early, feeling like an intruder when Ernest was preoccupied with Pat and Duff. But lately she tried to drink along with him, reminding herself that there was nothing to be gained by sulking. Ernest wrote Harold that he and Hadley were getting very tight and having a swell time. On the way to the feria they would stop at Burguete for a week of trout fishing with Don Stewart and Bill Smith and were expecting Harold to meet them. Ernest took charge of all the arrangements, buying the railroad tickets, reserving the rooms at Pamplona, instructing Bill especially, who had not seen a bullfight before, in the subtleties of the spectacle.

In St. Jean de Luz Harold had received a second letter from Duff, written three days after her first. This time her remarks were much less veiled. "It will be a great joy to see you again," she wrote, "though I expect I shall have a bit of time managing the situation. Hem has promised to be good and we ought to have really a marvellous time." What did she mean—Ernest had promised to be good? Now Harold was worried. He had to know more about it. Impulsively he wired Hemingway that he would not meet him in Burguete for the fishing but would wait instead at St. Jean for Pat and Duff, who were already on their way. It was a curious situation he had invited and he could not account even to himself why he had done it.

When Harold met their train, he put up as best he could with Pat's surliness, recognizing that the Scotsman had good cause to resent him. Over a martini at the hotel bar, when Pat was absent from the room, Duff explained that things were not the same so far as Harold was concerned. "Pat broke the spell," she said. "He worked hard at it." This was her way of letting Harold down gently. By the time Harold rented the car for the trip to Pamplona he felt more and more like the outsider. Duff's attitude toward two of her lovers seemed clear enough. She was in love with Pat, and bound to him, however bleak the prospects for their marriage. She was no longer intrigued with Harold, although the two-week idyll had been a welcome balm to her wounded spirit.

But what about Ernest? Most of his friends thought he was infatuated with her. When she turned to him for help and drew him into her orbit, he was buoyed up. When she solemnly told him that his sexual magnetism tested her self-control, he was all the more excited by her. Whether she was in fact aroused by him in any appreciable degree is uncertain, however. Kitty Cannell believed that Duff did not want to sleep with him and was using her loyalty to Hadley as the excuse for staying out of his bed. Duff may have confirmed this when she later told her third husband, Clinton King, that Ernest did not interest her sexually, though this remark too could be taken as the remark of a wife who wanted to protect her husband's pride.

"The question of Hem and Duff is a tricky one," observed Donald Stewart, who was questioned many times by various writers trying to form a conclusion.

> I was such a naïve romantic at the time [of Pamplona] that the possibility of Ernie and Hadley not being happily married was not allowed to enter

my mind. I sensed that there was something between Hem and Duff; he was angry that she had spent a week at St. Jean with Harold Loeb. But whether she had fallen for Hem . . . I was not sure and did not want to be sure. . . . everything was somehow changed and for me, spoiled. I wanted Hem and Hadley to be as they had been.

In Pamplona Duff's presence changed a fraternity revel into a nervous festering of sexual jealousies. Pat Guthrie, the only one whose position could be interpreted as unambiguous, was sullen in the presence of his rivals, Loeb and Hemingway. Harold was in low spirits, but hung around. Ernest gave everyone the uncomfortable impression that he lusted after Duff but could not, or would not, satisfy his longings. Hadley maintained her air of cheerful composure in the face of the crosscurrents. When Ernest was conspicuously absorbed by Duff she went to her room on the pretext that she was tired or had a headache.

Duff seemed to understand her priorities, even if no one else did. She shared her fourth-floor bedroom at the Hotel Quintana with Pat. She and Ernest wore matching berets and held long, whispered conversations, with Duff doing more listening than talking. In case Harold still harbored any illusions, she went down to his room to tell him that her passion for him was over. By this time Harold had learned from Bill Smith that Ernest knew all about Duff's holiday with him in St. Jean, that Ernest's reaction had been a string of curses. "You mean he's in love with Duff?" asked Harold. "I didn't say that," said Bill. Harold felt sick. Of course Ernest was in love with her. Everyone was. If Ernest thought Harold had gone away with her, knowing that he wanted her too, the friendship was finished.

When Harold had given up all hope of rekindling her interest in him, Duff suggested that he join her for a quiet after-dinner drink. Central to her personality was Duff's need to generate competition for her favors. They spent a pleasant hour together, but then Duff wandered off by herself, to become the center of attraction at an all-night revel at a private club. The next day at lunch she appeared with a bruised forehead and black eye. One can assume that the party got rough or that Pat beat her up because he thought she was with Harold.

"When I asked her about it," recalled Harold, "Hem interrupted,

Ernest, Lady Duff Twysden, and Hadley with friends at Pamplona. July 1925.
From the John F. Kennedy Library

saying that she had fallen against the railing. I boiled, but could think of no retort. Pat was sour, ugly. Hadley had lost her smile. Don tried a quip that went lame. Bill looked grim." At the afternoon bullfight Duff and Pat sat with Ernest and Hadley. A new matador from Ronda, nineteen-year-old Cayetano Ordoñez, had the crowd mesmerized. Ernest analyzed everything for Duff step by step, as he had done in previous years for Hadley.

It had drizzled all day but by nightfall the moon shone bright on the square. At an outside table, where the group sipped brandy and watched the lines form for the morning sale of tickets, Ernest began to bait Harold for his disgust with the brutality of the afternoon's spectacle. Pat joined in. Harold made a retort unflattering to Guthrie. Ernest sprang to Pat's defense. "You lay off Pat," he said grimly. "You've done enough to spoil this party." Harold gripped the edge of the table. It did not matter that Guthrie hated him. He disliked him, too. But he was shocked by Ernest's hostility.

"Why don't you get out?" shouted Pat. "I don't want you here. Hem doesn't want you here. Nobody wants you . . ."

Harold looked straight at Duff. "I will . . . the instant Duff wants it."

Duff, engaged in quiet conversation with Hadley, looked up and slowly shook her head. "You know . . . that I do *not* want you to go."

"You lousy bastard," said Ernest. "Running to a woman."

Hadley shuddered. Bill Smith, who had grown fond of Harold, was dismayed. But Harold knew only one way to settle the matter. He asked Ernest to step away from the table. Ernest obliged silently, and the two men walked to the end of the street, past the last lighted shop. Harold was frightened. Ernest was forty pounds heavier than he was, and Harold was sad over a good friendship coming to this. Suddenly, with a broad smile stretching across his face, Ernest offered to hold Loeb's glasses for him. That broke the tension and Harold knew the worst was over. They walked back in silence to join the others. The next morning Harold found a note of apology from Ernest in his hotel mailbox. He was relieved to get the note but he knew that things would never be the same.

Before settling her hotel bill, Duff took Donald Stewart aside to borrow some money. She and Pat had come down from Paris without enough to finance the holiday. Ernest could not help her—he

was on a tight budget himself and had already borrowed from
Stewart. Without saying why, she had apparently decided against
asking Loeb to take care of her debts. Stewart, who liked Duff and
thought her great fun, "really quite a dish," bailed her out. In
retrospect he decided that he had been used—not by Ernest, who
paid back every cent, but by Pat Guthrie, whose irresponsibility was
well known.

Goodbyes were overly hearty and everyone separated. Hadley
and Ernest left for Madrid, Stewart for the Riviera. Harold drove
Bill Smith, Duff, and Pat to St. Jean in a rented car. At the casino
that night Duff once again began to flirt with Harold, sitting close
to him at the bar, her smile curling with promise. But both knew
it did not mean anything.

Ernest began to write about the events at Pamplona as soon as he
and Hadley reached Madrid on July 14, 1925. He had decided to
make the young matador, Cayetano Ordoñez, the hero of a novel.
His fictional name would be Pedro Romero and the action would
take place during the Fiesta of San Firmin at Pamplona. But by the
time the Hemingways moved on to Valencia for the great annual
feria on July 24, Ernest was dissatisfied with his opening pages. He
moved the locale to Paris and sketched in the background of a new
protagonist, Jake Barnes, an American newspaperman who fought
in the war and in 1920 came to Paris as the European Director of
the Continental Press Association. The heroine was Brett Ashley,
a titled Englishwoman who had "hair . . . brushed back like a boy's
. . . wore a slipover jersey sweater and a tweed skirt . . . [and had
a way] of looking that made you wonder whether she really saw out
of her own eyes. They would look on and on after every one else's
eyes in the world would have stopped looking. . . . 'chap she got the
title from. . . . Ninth baronet. . . . Always slept with a loaded service
revolver.' " Brett's companion in the novel is a dissolute Scotsman,
Mike Campbell, and her abject admirer is Robert Cohn, middle-
weight boxing champion of Princeton, member of one of the richest
Jewish families in New York, editor of a review of the arts, author
of a published novel. Barnes, impotent from a war wound, burns
with futile desire for the fascinating, pleasure-seeking Lady Ashley.

In the early mornings Ernest filled his notebooks with recollections of the last year in Paris, including Loeb's love affair with Kitty

and Bill Smith's arrival from America. At midday he and Hadley packed up their bathing suits and rode the trolley to the beach. Hadley fell into the routine gratefully, relieved to be away from the strained atmosphere of Pamplona. She loved the Spanish food and drink—fat prawns sprinkled with lime juice, pastries filled with fish, paella, cold beer in pitchers—served off long buffets in the pavilions on the sand. Refreshed by the swimming, they went every afternoon to the Plaza de Toros to see Ordoñez perform his heroic feats. In the evening before the late Spanish dinner they made love to the sound of fireworks and the scent of the flower markets in the street below.

Early in August they went to Madrid for a few days, then on to San Sebastian for more ocean swimming, and finally to Hendaye, across the border in France. All the while Ernest was working well and Hadley was cooperating with his mood, which was increasingly one of bursts of creativity—writing late into the night, dropping off to sleep for a few hours, then waking to get on with it. By August 12, when she went ahead of him to Paris, he had filled two notebooks with his large, boyish script. Reading it as he handed sections over to her, she had praised him lavishly. The novel was rich in detail, exciting, different from anything he had done, perhaps his best work so far. That it was based on actual events and real people did not surprise her. But she later admitted that subconsciously she kept a distance from the book, especially as it delineated the intensity of Jake's feelings for Brett Ashley. Perhaps as she waited for him to join her, it gave her pause that Ernest put nothing of her in the book but used Duff Twysden as the model for his first fully developed heroine.

Chapter 9

On September 21 Ernest declared the first draft of his novel finished and a week later chose the title *The Sun Also Rises*. He had taken his characters from Paris to Burguete, from Burguete to Pamplona, to San Sebastian, and, finally, to Brett's seedy hotel room in Madrid. His rendition of Brett Ashley remained faithful to her prototype, Duff Tywsden—in appearance, the details of her disorderly life, and much of her personality. But he fantasized an unconsummated love affair between Jake Barnes and Brett, and drew from his own past the circumstances of the original meeting. Barnes falls in love with Brett when she nurses him at a hospital in England after he has been wounded on the Italian front. The love affair collapses because she cannot remain sexually faithful to a maimed lover. Frustrated and helpless, he is the miserable witness to her demeaning relationship with Mike Campbell, her inexplicable tryst with Robert Cohn, her headlong rapture for the matador, Pedro Romero. In his loyalty to the marriage vows—at least as regards fidelity—Ernest had still not strayed from the morality of his parents. Not wishing to admit this, he may have substituted the condition of Barnes's impotence for his own reluctance to betray Hadley. Other fallout from the same dilemma was his gnawing resentment of Harold Loeb. He wanted Duff, Harold got her. So Ernest took out after Harold, defining him as a complaining bore. Kitty Cannell as Frances Clyne becomes a fading beauty with coarse, nagging ways, and Duff's attachment for

Pat Guthrie is reduced to a neurotic compromise for money.

Duff herself had run into further financial problems when she and Pat returned from Spain. In desperation she wrote to Ernest late in September, a scribbled note on the back of a bar check.

> Ernest my dear. Forgive me for this effort but can you possibly lend me some money? I am in a stinking fix but for once only temporary and can pay you back for *sure*. I want 3000 francs—but for Gods sake lend me as much as you can. I hate asking you—but all my friends seem to be in the same boat—broke to the wide.

No one seems to know whether Ernest was able to help Duff, but she made no other effort to see him, relying on chance encounters to catch up on his activities. He had set aside the *Sun* manuscript for later revision but continually thought about ways to improve it. After receiving her letter he set down some fragments of monologue that could be attributed to her or were another example of his wish-fulfillment. "You must make fantastic statements to cover things. . . . It is like living with fourteen men so no one will know there is someone you love. . . . We can't do it. You can't hurt people. It's what we believe in in place of God." Only the last sentence appeared in the book verbatim, but the implication of a woman made desperate by a thwarted love affair was present throughout Ernest's portrayal of Brett Ashley.

Whether Duff slipped out of his life as a natural consequence of her dwindling interest or Ernest grew weary of an untenable situation, by the fall of 1925 their friendship was at an end. Ernest was concerned with other matters, among them a decision about what to get Hadley for her thirty-fourth birthday. They had been admiring a large painting by the Spanish artist, Joan Miró, "The Farm." Ernest's friend Evan Shipman, a sometime poet and gambler, had been promised it by Miró's dealer if he ever came up with the money. Learning that Hemingway wanted it for his wife, Shipman offered to throw the dice for it. Ernest won, then borrowed enough (mostly from Hadley herself) to pay the 5,000 francs. Dos Passos and Shipman and Ernest carried the canvas back to number 113 in a slow-moving Paris taxicab and hung it over the living room couch.

Hadley appreciated the uniqueness of such a gift, but a different —and perhaps deeper—satisfaction came with the publication of

Ernest's first American book and its dedication to her. *In Our Time* had a first printing of 1,300 and a laudatory comment by Sherwood Anderson on the jacket. Although the book did not attract much popular response, all the influential New York dailies reviewed it. The consensus seemed to be that here was an original voice, expressing itself with "merciless bareness." This man Hemingway "looks out upon the world without prejudice and records with almost terrifying immediacy exactly what he sees." Ernest liked the praise but took umbrage at the one dissenting voice. Herschel Brickell, writing in the *New York Evening Post*, complained that the stories were too thin to be considered anything but sketches, although the best one was "My Old Man," which Sherwood Anderson himself could not have improved upon. Ernest began to fume. He was sick of being compared to Anderson. He knew he owed something to Anderson's influence and wanted to live down the connection as soon as possible.

During the gloom of November he sat down to write a parody of Anderson's latest book, *Dark Laughter*. Hadley watched this project with misgivings. She remembered, even if Ernest preferred to forget, that Sherwood Anderson had befriended them when they were nobodies in Chicago, that he had gone far out of his way to help Ernest's career, and that he was a kindly man who did not deserve such treatment. Ernest ignored her protests. He borrowed the title *The Torrents of Spring* from Turgenev and composed a fable in which he took aim at Anderson's weaknesses—the tricks of style, the naïve sexual promiscuity of his characters, their chaotic wanderings and pseudophilosophy. In a week he had finished the book and was reading it aloud in preparation for submitting it to Liveright.

Dos Passos was amused, agreeing that Anderson could be silly sometimes, but wondered why Ernest was taking the trouble to "double-cross an aging champion." Hadley agreed with Dos, only more emphatically. She thought the whole idea "detestable." She suspected that the writing of it was a deliberate ploy to break his contract with Liveright and go over to Scribners. Gertrude Stein was furious that Ernest should betray someone so much a part of her inner circle.

Only Pauline Pfeiffer gave *The Torrents of Spring* unqualified approval. She doubled over with laughter, insisting all the while that it was a brilliant parody. In the face of such enthusiasm, Hadley felt like a "thoroughgoing wet blanket" for trying to restrain Ernest. Pauline's support had an effect. Ernest decided that she was a good literary critic and began to notice her with increased interest. Her lips were full, in a winsome if not conventionally pretty face, and her dark brown eyes were alternately thoughtful and impish beneath heavy, ungroomed brows. She was an avid reader who knew what she liked and why, the difference between trash and quality in prose. She was slender and well built, unlike Hadley, who had not lost the weight gained during her pregnancy and who gave the settled appearance of approaching middle age, even though she was only thirty-four.

Ernest began to feel like the young man married to the older woman. Although Pauline was in fact older than he by four years, having just turned thirty, she seemed younger because she was unencumbered by responsibilities and her enthusiasms were young. Her frank admiration for him was especially flattering in the context of her own original turn of mind and highly developed intelligence. And he liked her friends, that select circle whom both Hadley and Ernest now referred to as "the rich"—Dos Passos, Scott and Zelda, Archie and Ada MacLeish, and now the Murphys, Gerald and Sara, who had left the States in 1921 to create a special life in France for themselves, their children, and their friends. Pauline was at home with these people. Hadley was not. Pauline knew all the private jokes and flavorful gossip that so fascinated Ernest. And Pauline had the money to move about freely. Her father had made a fortune on the St. Louis grain exchange and by the time she moved to Paris was one of the richest landowners in northeastern Arkansas.

One day in December Kitty Cannell ran into Pauline, who was carrying a new pair of skis. Pauline explained that she was going to spend Christmas at Schruns with the Hemingways. The couple would be there for three months, and Ernest had promised to teach Pauline to ski. Kitty was surprised. She did not know that Pauline had become such a friend of the Hemingways, and she most certainly did not know that Pauline was now in love with Ernest. Only her sister, Jinny, was aware of Pauline's intense new feelings—that she wanted Ernest more than anyone she had ever met and believed that her life would be empty and wasted if she couldn't have him. She had even begun to rationalize that she would be better for him than Hadley. She was much more stimulating, had a special feeling for his work, and might make his life easier so far as finances were concerned. As she departed for Schruns, she knew that she would go to any lengths to become his wife. Ernest, who had narrowly averted an illicit relationship with Duff Twysden, seemed ripe for his first serious act of adultery.

Paul Pfeiffer, Pauline's father, had never cared for city life. A fairly accurate family story has it that he and his wife were on their way from St. Louis to California in 1913 when their train broke down at Greenway, Arkansas. Paul, who had achieved his first success with a chain of drugstores in small towns, stepped out into the fresh air and took a walk down the roadbed to nearby Piggott. Looking about, he quickly calculated how much money could be made by converting the slashed, timbered-out flatlands to cotton. With land selling for a dollar an acre the possibilities were exhilarating. Over the next few years he would acquire as much as 60,000 acres. His crew of two hundred would prepare the land for cotton, corn, wheat, and, eventually, soybeans. Pfeiffer representatives would fan out to Iowa and Illinois to recruit the tenant farmers. Eventually Paul owned the cotton gin and the local bank and exerted an influence on the area that was virtually feudal.

The Pfeiffer house in Piggott was a sprawling white frame structure, set in a grove of oak trees, surrounded by wide, shady porches, furnished with massive, German-style furniture, and filled with objets d'art from St. Louis galleries. There were five family bedrooms, maids' quarters, good well water, and a red barn for the rubber-tired family buggies. Paul Pfeiffer converted one room of the house into a chapel for his wife, Mary Downey, who was a devout Catholic. Himself an agnostic, he left the religious education of his four children to her.

Pauline spent the war years as a journalism major at the University of Missouri in Columbia, returning to her family in the summer and for winter holidays. She adapted to Piggott's sluggish pace, but the townspeople assumed that when she graduated she would migrate to a more cosmopolitan environment.

By the time of the armistice in November 1918, Pauline was working at her first job—on the night desk of the *Cleveland Star*. From there she went to New York and the *Daily Telegraph*, and finally to *Vanity Fair*, the magazine of the arts, where she became a fashion reporter and publicist. Paul Pfeiffer generously supplemented her scribbler's wages. Her St. Louis uncles had acquired the controlling interest in the Richard Hudnut Company, eventually forming the Warner-Hudnut Company, a leader in the pharmaceutical industry. She was a particular favorite of Uncle Gus Pfeiffer and his wife, Louise, who maintained a New York apartment. Pauline had come a long way from Piggott, but her basic attitudes had not changed. She was serious about her religion and about her work, and she retained a traditional view of love and marriage.

The tattlers in Paris who claimed that Pauline Pfeiffer had come abroad to find a husband did not know the whole story. The offer from *Vogue* to be assistant to their Paris editor, Mainbocher, was a reward for her experienced eye for fashion as well as her good journalism. While in New York she had become engaged to her cousin, Matthew Herold, a successful lawyer who was the rising star in the family enterprises. It would have made a fine marriage of convenience for the Pfeiffer interests. But Pauline was not sure that she loved Matthew, and their intellectual interests were different. So the offer from *Vogue* gave her a chance to put off making the decision.

Virginia Pfeiffer accompanied Pauline to Paris. Jinny was the one with the rapier wit, less restrained than Pauline about speaking out. With a proud set to her head she made a distinguished appearance and played the role of the aristocrat who is above working and, furthermore, does not need to work. Ernest's remark after meeting the sisters—that he wouldn't mind taking Jinny out if she wore Pauline's chipmunk coat—amused Jinny. But actually she had little interest in male suitors. She had already expressed a strong preference for women friends, though she could be "one of the boys" when it came to drinking beer and dancing at the *bal musettes*. Otherwise, she shied away from commitment to another person, unwilling to take the risk that might lead to dependency. The way she attached herself to Pauline was somewhat parasitic, but the sisters were close and Pauline's life and friends—including the men —became a source of great interest and entertainment.

At Schruns Pauline did everything to keep up the fiction that she was there to visit both Hemingways. She admired Bumby's childish charms and Hadley's piano playing. She stayed behind with Hadley when Ernest took off on strenuous excursions into the high country. But the isolation of the hotel, the weather, and the holiday ambience all contributed to a much closer relationship than Ernest and she could manage in Paris. In spite of his later disclaimers, he was not the passive innocent, preyed upon by a scheming Pauline. He was sexually aroused by her and they were intellectually compatible, and that was a powerful combination. Hadley was his good and devoted wife, but Pauline was the strange, wonderful new girl (as he later described her), and he did nothing to cool his infatuation. His long afternoon walks were reserved for Pauline. Hadley rarely joined them. Pauline recognized the ambiguity of her position, and sometimes she brooded over it, but like Ernest she did not withdraw.

She was still at Schruns on December 30 when a cable arrived from Horace Liveright. He was rejecting *The Torrents of Spring* (which Ernest had mailed to him before leaving Paris). Pauline expressed disappointment, but Ernest was neither surprised nor upset. He understood that Boni and Liveright could not publish a book that so blatantly satirized their most important author. His agreement with them clearly stated that their option on his first three books would lapse if they rejected book number two. Hadley has suggested that the ruse to break the agreement was Pauline's idea, but Ernest was perfectly capable of devising such a scheme himself. He may not have written *The Torrents of Spring* for that express purpose, but he quickly saw its possibilities for setting him free. He wired Liveright to hand the manuscript over to Don Stewart at the Yale Club. Don could then submit it to Perkins. Other publishers were beginning to court him, but he wrote Fitzgerald that his inclination was to sign with Scribners. He decided to make a quick trip to New York to settle everything in person.

Pauline, who had returned to Paris to cover the upcoming designer collections, was writing to Schruns almost daily, sometime to Hadley alone, sometimes to both of them. She made no secret of how much she missed them. "Oh my soul, I wish I woz in Schruns. I miss you two men. How I miss you two men!" It was an odd choice of words but perhaps her way of disguising the relationship, suggesting that theirs was a friendship among comrades. Upon learning that Ernest's anticipated trip to New York would take him through Paris, she urged him to bring a copy of the revised *The Sun Also Rises* for her to read. What she put into words, in her friend-to-

Pauline Pfeiffer in her Vogue *reporting days. 1918.*
From the Patrick Hemingway Collection, Princeton University Library

Hadley at Schruns.
Winter season, 1925–26.
From the John F. Kennedy Library

A relationship develops. Pauline and Ernest at Schruns, Christmas week, 1925.
From the Patrick Hemingway Collection, Princeton University Library

the-whole-family letter, carried a mixed message. "I feel he should be warned that I'm going to cling to him like a millstone and old moss, and winter ivy." She then urged Hadley to leave the adorable Bumby and come too. Addressing Hadley as "Cherishable," Pauline wrote, "I've missed you *simply indecently*. . . . and I couldn't restrain the impulse [to lure you here]. . . . Better brood well over the you-coming-to-Paris idea. I am not a woman to be trifled with and I shall behave badly if trifled with."

If Hadley was startled by such hyperbole, she kept her opinions to herself. She had come to think of Pauline as a friend. "She was always a good companion in those days," she has acknowledged, "and always nice to me." Bracing herself for some lonely days without Ernest, Hadley helped him to pack up for the mid-winter ocean voyage.

In Paris Pauline worked "like a mad thing," writing up her notes after midnight for delivery the next morning before the 10:30 A.M. fashion showings. Ernest stayed at the Hotel Venetia on Boulevard Montparnasse but went around to Pauline's flat in the rue Picot whenever she had time away from work. They hoarded the hours until his ship sailed, catching a few art exhibits, eating quietly in obscure bistros, their appreciation in being together whetted by Ernest's imminent departure. After he left, Pauline wrote to Hadley on February 4 that "your husband, Ernest, was a delight to me. I tried to see him as much as he would see me and was possible."

For Hadley, waiting uneasily in Schruns, February 1926 was a time of foreboding. She practiced the Bach-Busoni chaconne until her fingers ached. It was to be a surprise for Ernest. But as the days stretched into weeks she began to despair of his ever hearing it. Her mood had not been so dark since the month in 1923 when he went to Constantinople. In an effort to fend off her anxieties, she went mountain-climbing and skiing until her legs gave out.

Meantime, Ernest's news from New York was all good. Maxwell Perkins thought *The Torrents* a "grand" book and offered him a $1,500. advance on both the satire and the unfinished *Sun*, and a flat 15 percent of royalties. There were so many interesting people to pal around with that Ernest stayed for three weeks instead of one. Hadley tried not to begrudge him the excitement, but she yearned to be a part of it, especially when she learned that he had seen their good friend, Isabelle Simmons, married now to a classical scholar named Francis Godolphin. On March 1 Hadley wrote Izz that she was fighting a horrible depression caused by the news that Ernest's ship on the return voyage, *The President Roosevelt*, was still delayed on the high seas. "I'd thought to have my liebling here this very day," she fumed. "I hope storms aren't brewing. . . . I don't see how I can live thru another few days! Because he'll surely have to stop in Paris for money and to do something about the apartment— please excuse me if I wail—it's such a dark day, inside and out." She had not been cheered by the news from Pauline that she, too, was getting letters from Ernest and expected to see him when he passed through Paris.

Pauline did indeed see Ernest when he stopped over in Paris. Whether they were having sexual relations by this time is unclear. Years later he wrote that " . . . where we went and what we did and the unbelievable wrenching, killing happiness, selfishness and treachery of everything we did gave me such a terrible remorse." However overwrought or self-serving such recollections seem, it is likely that Ernest did suffer some pangs of guilt. He had not philandered during his marriage. The episode with Duff Twysden had been a passing thing. Now for the first time he was tangled in a web of unfaithfulness.

For Pauline an affair would present problems of a different nature. She was a practicing Catholic, and extramarital sex was clearly a sin. In more practical terms there was the threat of pregnancy, since Pauline had grave reservations about contraception. But with Hadley safely in Schruns and Ernest free to come and go, the opportunity to consummate the relationship was irresistible. She welcomed him back with fierce ecstasy. When she finally saw him off at the Gare de l'Est, she knew that he returned her love and she must keep up the pretense of a friendship with Hadley to protect their secret.

Hadley, in turn, was so relieved to have him safely back that she asked no embarrassing questions. Sara and Gerald Murphy and Dos Passos came up for a week of skiing, their gaiety a welcome antidote to her simmering anxiety. "Everybody kidded everybody during that week at Schruns," recalled Dos Passos. "We ate vast quantities of trout, and drank the wines and beers and slept like dormice under the great featherbeds." Ernest was persuaded to read a few chapters from *The Sun Also Rises*, which he had been sporadically revising all winter. The Murphys were highly complimentary. Ernest and

Gerald vied for supremacy on the skis, with Ernest persuading everyone to make the long, bracing trek to the Madlenerhaus. With the warm sun there was the threat of avalanches, but there were no incidents. The sun was hot and the nights cold, and the purple shadows lengthening across the snowy peaks were a pleasure to Gerald's painterly eye.

Pauline, miles away, made sure that no one forgot her. Letters from Paris reached Schruns regularly and were replete with news of small events. She had arranged for a bright new carpet in her apartment, and in a fond domestic note added that it was "about the colour of Bumbi's beret," a good color for a beret but perhaps a bit much for the entire floor of a room.

By the time the Hemingways returned to Paris, a sudden mild spell had caused early buds to burst into green bloom. Ernest dedicated *The Sun Also Rises* to Hadley and to John Hadley Nicanor and gave the manuscript to a professional typist. On April 24 he mailed it to Scribners. After the period of sustained work he was ready for diversion—bicycle races, horse racing, a polo match between St. Cyr and Sandhurst. At about this time Pauline and Jinny invited Hadley to drive with them through the Loire Valley. Hadley accepted gladly, for she had never seen the chateau country. "We had lots of fun at first," she recalled, "stopping at good places, eating deliciously and of course the old castles were a delight. Then Pauline began to get very moody, quite often snapping at me when I tried to make conversation." It was strange and uncomfortable. Jinny tried to cover up by explaining that her sister had always been subject to moods, ever since she was a child. Hadley could not be satisfied with such a lame excuse. She knew she had to force the issue. "Is Ernest any way involved?" she asked Jinny. "Has Pauline fallen in love with him?" When Jinny replied that she thought they were very fond of each other, Hadley could not bring herself to ask anything else. She knew more than enough already.

Ernest by now was making plans for another summer in Spain, but Hadley could not concentrate on the preparations. It was impossible to forget what Virginia Pfeiffer had told her. Close to tears, she blurted out that she had reason to think Ernest was in love with Pauline. He denied nothing but instead of sounding contrite or comforting, rebuked her sternly for bringing "the thing" into the open. "What he seemed to be saying to me," recalled Hadley, "was that it was my fault for forcing the issue. Now that I had broken the spell our love was no longer safe." For a woman as straightforward as Hadley this was a mean blow and carried with it an implicit threat. She backed off immediately, hurt and confused, but determined to do what he asked, which was to go on as before.

As it turned out, Ernest went to Spain ahead of Hadley. The excuse was that she had to stay behind to nurse Bumby, who was suffering from a bad cough, but some kind of separation was inevitable after their quarrel over Pauline. During a few hot days in Madrid he completed three stories, "Today is Friday," "Ten Indians," and "The Killers." "I was in love," he explained years later, "and the girl was in Bologna [Pauline was in Italy] and I couldn't sleep anyway, so why not write." A letter to his father on May 23 was a garbled comment on the bizarre state of his personal life. Saying nothing about Pauline, he wrote instead that he was going to bring Hadley and Bumby to the United States for a visit in the early fall, and referred to spending the winter in Piggott, Arkansas! They would go to Oak Park for several days, then stopover in St. Louis for Hadley to see her family. " . . . one day of facing the relatives [in St. Louis] before we shove to Piggott. . . . Pauline Pfeiffer, who was down in Austria with us . . . lives in Piggott . . . and is getting us a house there." He closed the letter with the remark that he had attended Mass and was going to a bullfight in the afternoon.

With Ernest in Spain, Hadley accepted Sara Murphy's invitation to visit Cap d'Antibes with Bumby. She convinced herself that the warm Mediterranean sun would cure the little boy of his cough, and she was excited at the prospect of seeing the magical Villa America, which Gerald and Sara had bought primarily for its garden, a dazzling profusion of plants and trees carried there by its former owner, a widely-traveled French army officer. Crooked paths intersected the many levels and the night air throbbed with nightingales. The gardener's cottage had been converted into a small studio for Gerald, and the farmhouse, or *bastide*, into a guesthouse. Zelda and Scott were living nearby at Juan-les-Pins. Ada and Archie MacLeish were down for the season. Every morning the friends gathered at the Garoupe, a tiny beach at the foot of the steep gardens, laboriously cleared of seaweed by Gerald, who directed the daily ritual of mid-morning sherry and sweet biscuits. Bumby frolicked on the sand with the Murphy children. Hadley gave herself over to sun and swimming and mouth-watering meals under the giant silver linden tree. It almost seemed possible in such a setting to forget that her marriage was coming apart.

The slow-paced luxury bolstered Hadley's morale, but unfortunately Bumby's cough did not improve. Sara and Gerald, concerned about their own children, summoned their British doctor, who made the diagnosis of whooping cough and quarantined Bumby. Scott and Zelda, who had decided to move to a larger villa, St. Louis, helped Hadley out of a difficult situation by offering her the original villa for the six weeks that remained on the lease. Marie-Cocotte was summoned from Paris to help with Bumby, and Ernest came from Madrid. Every afternoon at cocktail time the Murphys, the Mac-Leishes, and the Fitzgeralds would drive over with food and drink and sit in their cars, separated from the Hemingways on the piazza by an iron grille.

Ernest quickly realized that the Riviera was no place to work. Too many friendly distractions. Only occasionally did some fit of truculence hint at his personal conflict. One day the whole crowd went on a day-long sail aboard the Murphy sloop, *Honoria*. (Evidently the quarantine was not always enforced.) When everyone went ashore at Monte Carlo for teadancing, and gambling at the casino, Ernest asked Ada MacLeish to dance. She accepted. Archie turned to Hadley. She demurred. Later Ernest returned to the table to demand reassurance that MacLeish had not snubbed Hadley. No, explained Hadley patiently, all was well. She simply did not feel like dancing. Mary Hickok, Guy Hickok's wife, who also came down to visit, remembered that Ernest and Hadley seemed to be kissing a lot, and except for Sara Murphy, who was Pauline's very good friend, no one suspected the truth.

Ernest was writing daily letters to Pauline, who was happy to hear that *The Torrents of Spring* was popular with the reviewers but felt as though she were in exile, far from the center of things. What if she came to Juan-les-Pins and shared the quarantine with them? She was not afraid of the whooping cough, having had it as a child. Ernest encouraged her to do that. What better way to cheer up his days? She arrived while the Hemingways were still in the villa. When the lease was up, Pauline and the Hemingways took rooms at the nearby Hotel de la Pineda. "Here it was," recounted Hadley, "that the three breakfast trays, three wet bathing suits on the line, three bicycles were to be found. Pauline tried to teach me to dive, but I was not a success. Ernest wanted us to play bridge but I found it hard to concentrate. We spent all morning on the beach sunning or swimming, lunched in our little garden. After siesta time there were long bicycle rides along the Golfe de Juan."

It was a shabby episode and no one came out of it untarnished—neither Pauline, with her disregard for Hadley's position, nor Ernest, nor even Hadley, who should not have allowed herself to be demeaned so. But Pauline had thrown down the gauntlet months ago. And Hadley believed, perhaps correctly, that if she told Pauline to leave, Ernest would follow her. The one on the spot was Ernest himself. He wanted both women and was ready to give up neither.

Chapter 10

Hadley saw nothing in Ernest's actions to point toward a reconciliation. "We went to Madrid, Valencia, and San Sebastian, all the time bitterly unhappy," she said. Aside from her own pain, Hadley has referred again and again to the suffering Ernest endured during that period. She seemed genuinely moved by his misery. Since she was the person closest to him she has to be taken seriously. At Pamplona, Pauline, too, looked forlorn and depressed, and Hadley felt a stab of pity for her as well. Perhaps the uncertainty of the affair was wearing her down. But when the week of festivities was over and the adversaries returned to their respective corners, Pauline mobilized her energies. "I'm going to get a bicycle and ride in the bois," she wrote on July 15 with a show of bravado that was somewhat forced. "I am going to get a saddle too. I am going to get everything I want. Please write to me. That means YOU, Hadley." Hadley was silent but Ernest wired Pauline that "Today's still Pfeiffer day in Valencia."

On their way back from Madrid Hadley and Ernest stopped off to visit Sara and Gerald Murphy. Dos Passos was there and Don Stewart and his bride, spending their honeymoon at the Villa America. All were shocked to learn that their favorite couple was splitting up. Only weeks before, Gerald had written admiringly of them as "close to what's elemental," with "values . . . hitched up to the universe." Now he tried to be supportive, offering Ernest the use of a studio he kept in Paris at 69, rue Froidevaux. Ernest accepted, but the sense of what it all meant still had not penetrated. As they resumed the journey home, Hadley conversed with an American woman who was carrying a canary as a gift to her daughter, whose love affair she had broken up. Ernest brooded upon all the images of destruction that passed outside the window of the lit salon compartment—a burning farmhouse with the rescued furniture stacked haphazardly by the roadside, Avignon with its collapsed bridge, the wreckage of several baggage cars outside Paris. The entire experience was later transferred almost intact into a short story Ernest called "A Canary for One," of which the poignant last sentence was: "We were returning to Paris to set up separate residences."

In Paris Ernest spent most of his time at Pauline's apartment, using Gerald's studio as a convenient working address. Hadley took a room at the Hôtel Beauvoir across from the Closerie des Lilas. She had no appetite for their empty apartment. The last six months had exhausted her, and she could not avoid well-meaning friends who were full of pity and concern. She alternated between tears and anger and a small degree of detachment. Don Stewart, who escorted her home from a party one evening, recalled that she cried all the way to her hotel. Even as she wept over losing her husband, however, there was an undeniable relief in being alone for a while, as her thoughts began to take shape.

Hadley believed that Ernest was especially susceptible to Pauline's adoration. He was almost weak, she explained, in the sense that when someone reached out to him with love he responded, even if he was not in love with that person. Her way of testing his vulnerability was to ask him to stay away from Pauline for a specific period of time. Much later in her life, Hadley wondered if that had been a mistake. Perhaps she should have encouraged them to go off together to let the infatuation burn itself out.

But she did the reverse—she wrote out an agreement on a small slip of paper, signed it formally, and presented it to Ernest, feeling, as she admitted in retrospect, like "the Emperor Tiberius." If Pauline and Ernest would stay apart for a hundred days and were still in love by the end of that time, she would give him a divorce.

Pauline saw no choice but to acquiesce. Ernest wondered if the misery of being separated was worth Hadley's approval. Perhaps they should simply defy her and go away together and wait for her to capitulate. He was fearful that Pauline would buckle under her mother's expected disapproval and be forced to give him up. But Pauline swore that she would never give him up. She would get a good rest at home, get healthy and strong, and it would be okay. If her mother made too much trouble she would simply leave. She believed she was winning the fight for him. Three months was not an eternity; it was only one-fourth of a year. So she booked passage on the Red Star liner *Pennland,* due to sail for New York on September 24. Ernest went with her to Boulogne to board the ship. They spent their last night together at the Hôtel Meurice, dining on sole and partridge and deciding on a set of code words for use in their transatlantic cables including the name "Pilar" for Pauline. They could protect their privacy at the same time that they cut the cost of the cables.

Pauline did not like sea voyages even in the best of circumstances. Being without companionship among 1,200 passengers was worse than she imagined. She sent Ernest a cable before the ship was out of port and again when she left Southampton, but in her first letter at sea mustered some optimism, as much for her morale as for his. She wrote,

> I am feeling very comfortable and warm and solid, and I love you more than ever . . . writing you everything, I can keep you very close to me and very much in my life until I see you again. . . . I'm cockeyed happy that I have you. . . . I look at all the people on this boat and wonder how they can get on without Ernest. . . . From the looks of them I think perhaps they don't get along without Ernest very well.

Studying French helped to pass the time and there were shipboard conversations about everything from Mussolini's politics to the harbors of Brazil. Her dreams about Ernest were good but waking up was torture, though she hastened to assure him that she straight-talked herself into a sound mental state. She even tried to pretend that she was just a young matron who had left her husband in Paris to visit her parents in the mother country. But ten days out she caught a cold, which did not help, and she began to wonder why she was going to New York.

The ship docked on Monday morning, October 4. On hand to welcome her were her Uncle Gus and a favorite cousin, but when

they left her at the Waldorf she was told that her room was not ready
—too many people had stayed over to see the World Series. She
wandered about in a daze, picking up medicines to dose her cold,
eating alone in the vast hotel dining room, feeling "very frightened
and homeless and dead." The panic dissolved only when she was
handed her room key and a letter from Ernest. " . . . and now I'm
swell again, with lots of endurance. . . . tomorrow it will 89 [days]."
She stayed in New York a week and ran into Robert Benchley, who
questioned her eagerly about Ernest. "I think maybe the Murphys
told him something," she wrote Ernest. Gerald had become Ernest's
most enthusiastic advocate in the separation, depositing $400. in his
depleted bank account and advising him not to suffer remorse—he
was a genius and nothing must be allowed to interfere with his
work.

Whenever possible Pauline thought up errands that would make
her feel closer to Ernest. She bought some fine white shirts for him,
and stopped in at the Scribners office to learn that *The Sun Also Rises*
was coming out on October 22. To further distract her from useless
worry, she bought a "printing" of boats and their sailing dates and
studied those departures that would most expeditiously carry her
letters to Ernest. Before boarding the train for St. Louis, she received her third fat letter from him. Maybe it was worse for him,
she mused, being the one who stayed behind, than for her, the one
who was in a new place.

Pauline was right when she imagined that it might be worse for
Ernest than for her. He was 3,000 miles away, living in an unheated
garret and fighting a guilty conscience. " . . . the deliberate keeping
apart when all you have is each other does something bad to you,"
he wrote Pauline, "and lately it has shot me all to hell inside." Some
of the suffering was a pose that he fell into easily, but Archie Mac-
Leish confirmed that Ernest dreaded being alone, especially at night.
"Nothing faked about that," said MacLeish. "It was real and touching. He was mad about Pauline, but saw himself as a son of a bitch
for leaving Hadley."

Ernest still managed to work, however. He wrote "A Canary for
One" and "In Another Country," the latter recalling an incident at
the Ospedale Maggiore in 1918. Edward O'Brien wanted to print
"The Undefeated," which had been translated into both German
and French, in *The Best Short Stories of 1926* and *Scribner's Magazine*

paid $200. for "The Killers." Ernest saw Bumby as often as he wished and continued to complain how painful it was to be separated from Pauline. Hadley listened patiently, but so far she was not disposed to release him from the agreement.

"I'm home [in Piggott] since yesterday at 4:30 a.m.," wrote Pauline to Ernest on October 14.

> Mother met me. Papa was in Memphis trying to send up the price of cotton. I told Mother about me and she felt terrible. She's awfully . . . unworldly and awfully good. . . . The first thing she said was "And how does she feel?" . . . we talked it over and then she said perhaps the best thing to do was not to mention it anymore. So we aren't going to. She asked me not to tell Papa until later. So that's that.

She was not surprised by her mother's reaction but wondered why it was necessary to keep the news from her father, the more worldly of the two. Surely he would suspect something, with his daughter writing a letter a day to Paris and sending and receiving cables.

Her letters were perfectly revealing of her character—that attractive mix of qualities that so stimulated and satisfied Ernest. A letter was a failure if it did not entertain, and compliments were sprinkled throughout. Ernest was smart, Ernest was perfect, Ernest made everyone else seem stale and profitless. But transcending the wit and the praise was her deeply felt emotion about the quality of her love. It was a love that submerged her being into his. ("We are one, we are the same guy, I am you.") She would be strong for him, healthy for him, solid for him. Wherever Ernest was, there would be Pfeiffer. Never again would she leave him. If he wanted to go away from her, he could, for she was part of him and would be there when he returned.

Early October in Arkansas was for the most part "very much on the bright side with a swell kick in the air," wrote Pauline. She loved the countryside for its overgrown, not quite cared for look, so different from "smug New England." The biggest local excitement was the drilling of an oil well. It was started in September but the money gave out after twelve hundred feet. Now fresh money had been raised and Pauline was thinking of buying some units for her and Ernest and Jinny, at ten dollars a unit. " . . . if there is oil," she explained, "it will make anywhere from one thousand to five thousand dollars. . . . We could have a house in all the countries in the world, with servants keeping them open for when we came along —with our five or seven sturdy offspring, all of them speaking language germaine [sic] to the country." Her father, however, did not own any units and sternly advised the townsfolk not to give any leases to the oil men who were sniffing around. "If leases are mentioned, Papa foams at the mouth. He says that everyone is a fool and that oil men are crooks." Her father's opinion notwithstanding, Pauline continued to send Ernest weekly reports from the rig and eventually did invest thirty dollars.

An interesting proposal had come from the editorial office of *Vogue*—would Pauline work in their New York office from Christmas until March? "They don't know that I am marrying out of all that," she wrote Ernest. "I said I didn't think I could do this. But they said they would write me to Piggott." Ernest, dispirited and lonely in Paris, was not so sure that Pauline would say no to *Vogue*. Perhaps she really wanted the job, he wrote. Perhaps the separation wasn't as hard on her as it was on him. In a fit of despair he seemed ready to assume the worst—that she would accept the *Vogue* offer, that their separation would stretch on interminably and what he called his horrors would never come to an end. Yet Pauline had never indicated that she thought seriously of taking the job. As early as October 11, before leaving New York, she had written that "without benefit of clergy or anyone else" she had decided to arrive in Paris before Christmas. The *Volendam* was sailing out of New York for Boulogne on December 11, and she wanted to be on that ship.

On a melancholy Monday, after a weekend of rain had soaked the freshly-tipped autumn leaves, Pauline experienced her own version of the horrors. "A madhouse depression" enveloped her like a poisonous cloud. Her conscience, goaded by her mother's innocent, heartbroken face, demanded payment. She rode a neighbor boy's bicycle on the muddy roads to recover her poise but returned to the house to break down with uncontrollable fits of weeping. In the afternoon she wrote her daily letter to Ernest. The tone and content were totally different from anything she had previously expressed.

You got your terrible hell being day after day with Hadley and I think I'm getting mine with Mother. . . . in addition to feeling that her daughter has broken up a home and feeling so terrible about Hadley, she worries about me. . . . I can't comfort her because I don't seem to be able to find any comfort for her. . . . if there is anything Hadley wants you to do for her or Bumby, ever, no matter what, you gotta do it don't you. And any amount of money settlement. And I am not going to mention to you again about Hadley not liking me, because if she hates me it will be alright. . . . you . . . know . . . that I love you more than ever and two months from today I shall be in Boulogne. But if Hadley should want us to stay apart, or do anything else, no matter what, that is what you, or I, or we, will do.

Pauline's mother tried clumsily to comfort her, with such words as, "What's a mother for, if not for a daughter to come home and cry on?" But she said nothing to ease her daughter's guilt. Before mailing her Monday letter Pauline added some reassuring words, knowing how demoralized Ernest would be by her state of nerves. But the sentences had a hollow ring. The misery and remorse did not abate. She could think of nothing but Hadley and her open-hearted goodness and kindness in the face of her own wicked scheming. She collapsed on the bed, frightening her mother into writing Jinny that her sister had "gone to pieces."

On Friday, October 29, Pauline dragged herself to her typewriter and tried, for herself as well as for Ernest, to put the painful catharsis into perspective.

Maybe what I am going to say to you now is going to be pretty bad . . . because I went through hell to get it and I am writing it because I must write it and because we are the same guy. . . . Ernest and Pfeiffer, who tried to be so swell (and who were swell) didn't give Hadley a chance. We were so . . . scared we might loose [sic] each other—at least I was—that Hadley got locked out. Hadley was just locked out. I don't think you did this the way I did. . . . I think the times Hadley doesn't hate me she must know that I was just blind dumb.

Dearest, you and I have something that only about two persons in one or several centuries get. . . . And having it, when we say we can't face life without each other and then deliberately make some one else face life alone, it makes me very afraid about us. Because having all there is, it seems to me, really ought to make us stronger instead of weaker.

She closed the letter with the pledge that she loved him and trusted him and in seven weeks would see him again, but reiterated that

Hadley was wise to require them to wait the three months, however tough it had been, and that just sticking it out wasn't enough; they had to think about all three, Hadley too.

It took two weeks for Pauline's anguished letters to reach Ernest. Predictably he was upset by their contents and spilled out his anger, self-pity, and frustration in his reply. It was her mother's fault for giving her the silent treatment. Pauline, whom he loved more than anything and had betrayed everything for, and killed off everything for, was being destroyed. Hadn't she promised to leave Piggott if things got too horrible? Where would it all end? What if Hadley never gave them the divorce but only stalled again? In the fall when he had first fallen in love with her—he now admitted—he had contemplated suicide, soberly and upon reflection, for it seemed the only way to remove the sin from Pauline and spare Hadley the necessity of a divorce. Now he felt all out of control again. He was neither a saint nor built like one. He was perfectly willing to go to hell after he was dead rather than now, but not both. " . . . I pray for you hours every night and every morning when I wake up. I pray so for you to sleep and to hold tight and not to worry." When he visited Hadley at her new flat at 35, rue de Fleurus he spared her none of the details of Pauline's misery. (If he was true to form he probably dramatized her despair even beyond its actual state.)

Hadley, who had been doing some thinking of her own, now asked Ernest to move in with Bumby for a few days so that she could go away for a period of quiet reflection. At first no inspiration came. Everything she recalled about him and Pauline only filled her with heartbreak and disillusion. But finally, in the peaceful surroundings of the Hôtel de France, in Chartres, she came to terms with her torment. On November 16, 1926, she wrote Ernest that she had reached a decision. "The entire problem belongs to you two—I am not responsible for your future welfare—[that has been proven] from the length to which you have carried things in asking for a divorce. . . . I took you originally for better, for worse (and meant it!) but in the case of your marrying some one else, I can stand by my vow only as an outside friend." There was, in these thoughtful ruminations, a significant clue for the future relationship between Hadley and Ernest. In addition to loving Ernest she cared for him —that is, was concerned for his future welfare, no matter what she said. It had been an essential part of her marriage. And it accounts for the sensitivity and concern that she continued to express long after they were divorced. "Please, Ernest," she concluded, "get hold of some valid information about legalities. I want to find out several things from the States before I start on all this so things may go slowly for awhile. However, the three months separation is officially off."

Ernest rushed over to Jinny Pfeiffer's apartment with the news but held off sending the cable to Pauline. First he wrote Hadley that her letter, like everything she had ever done, was brave and generous. He would write both Scribners and Jonathan Cape, his British publisher, to assign her all the royalties from *The Sun Also Rises.* "I would include In Our Time and Torrents but I believe the one is on the deficit side still and the other not likely to make money." (He did instruct Max Perkins about the royalties but never got around to informing Cape.) To be absolutely sure that he was not misinterpreting her letter, did it mean that she was actually starting the divorce, and was it agreeable to her if he communicated her decision to Pauline?

Hadley replied on November 19:

> Haven't I yet made it quite plain that I *want* to start proceedings for a divorce from you—right away.... Whether you communicate with her [Pauline] about any or all of your and my arrangements makes no difference to me. If you ... feel any hesitation, I will start things myself tho I think you are much more likely to find a *good* lawyer quickly. ... The gift from you to me of your royalties on *The Sun Also Rises* is very acceptable and I can't see a reason just now why I should refuse it. Thank you a lot.

She encouraged him to see Bumby as much as he wished, never letting the child feel that anything out of the ordinary had happened. "She made it easy for me," recalled Jack Hemingway, "by explaining that they [Pauline and Ernest] were simply very much in love." She ended the second letter with a list of personal articles and furniture that she wished Ernest to send over to her new flat, and in a softer tone closed with "Mummy's love" and the hope that he would eat well, sleep well, keep well, and work well.

Archie MacLeish recommended a lawyer who would move quickly, and Ernest rented a handbarrow to move Hadley's possessions from Notre-Dame-des-Champs to rue du Fleurus. He made several trips hauling the furniture, family silver, and china, and finally the Miró painting that had been his birthday present to her the year before. She pretended to be unmoved each time he burst into tears over some sentimental item. It would not hurt him to suffer remorse. As for herself, she was beginning to feel a little excitement about the possibilities in her own future. "I didn't know what was going to happen to me," she recalled, "but I had plenty of good friends. Some of them thought I let go too easily. Perhaps I did. But I would not try to hold on."

THREE

1926—36

Chapter 11

On a quiet Sunday evening, the telegraph office delivered a momentous cable from Jinny to the Pfeiffer house. "THREE MONTHS TERMINATED AT HADLEY'S REQUEST SHE STARTING IMMEDIATELY OWN REASONS STOP COMMUNICATION RESUMED STOP SUGGEST YOU SAIL AFTER CHRISTMAS WHAT ABOUT ME." Pauline was jubilant. She did not understand why Hadley had relented unless she was in love with someone else, but whatever the reason this was enough to revive her faith in prayer. She was only sorry that she had upset Ernest with her wailing. "And as I didn't lose my mind," she rationalized to him, "I don't think I ever shall, and that ought to be some comfort to a man when he is going to marry me."

Her sense of humor had returned. "I went down this morning to see about air mail, if it was routed from St. Louis to New York, and I asked the mail clerk if he knew anything about air mail and he said he thought it went by airplane!" Now that everything was wonderful what did he think about her staying through Christmas? And negotiating with *Vogue* for a hundred dollars a week for the six weeks? She could make six hundred dollars, which would pay for her passage. "I really think it is perhaps better for you to make the plans as you know what is happening." Then she wrote to Jinny to say how much she appreciated all her cables and letters.

Pauline subscribed to a clipping service so that she could keep up with the reception accorded *The Sun Also Rises*. By November 27 over fifty mailings had arrived, some of them adulatory, some critical. "I should think . . ." she wrote to Ernest, "that *The Sun* ought to sweep. A lot of the critics think it is as epic-making as *This Side of Paradise,* which if it doesn't mean sweeping, doesn't mean much to me." A sweep was indeed in the making. The novel was already into its second printing and Perkins looked for a strong performance through the spring. Edmund Wilson believed it to be the best novel by anyone of Ernest's generation and Malcolm Cowley noticed that young men in Greenwich Village were talking, walking, and shadowboxing like Hemingway, and young women from the eastern colleges were modeling themselves after Brett Ashley.

The prototype for Lady Ashley, Duff Twysden, was living quietly in Montparnasse. Her divorce from Sir Roger became final in the summer, and the baronet was awarded custody of their son, Anthony. This was a bitter disappointment to Duff, who loved the child even though her only contacts with him were the occasional visits to Scotland. Marriage to Pat Guthrie seemed farther away than ever. He had moved in with a rich American woman twenty years his senior, who threatened to report him to the police over a bad check episode if he left her. It was a contemptible performance, but Duff continued to see him from time to time and hid her hurt beneath a pose of unconcern. She lived with friends and invited her sister to visit her. Harold Loeb, back from New York, took them out several times. Duff's charms were still considerable. Newcomers to the Quarter were drawn to her, and with Hemingway's book immortalizing her she had acquired the additional luster of a legend. When she read *The Sun* her own fortunes were at a nadir, but she managed to be wryly amused. One night at the Café Dingo she told Ernest that her only criticism of the story was that she had not in fact slept with the bloody bullfighter.

Kitty Cannell was furious with the book—not so much for the portrayal of herself ("I'm really tougher than the big he man [Ernest] and I can stick up for myself," she recalled), but for Ernest's treatment of Harold Loeb. She was not surprised, however, for Ernest once told her that he was writing a novel and that "that kike Loeb is the villain." Harold was hurt and confused. He believed himself to be a loyal friend to Ernest (which no doubt he was) and could never understand why Ernest singled him out for such a malicious portrait. It was the betrayal of a friendship that Harold had cherished.

In Oak Park *The Sun Also Rises* was causing the elder Hemingways a different form of anguish. They " . . . were as bewildered and shocked as convent girls visiting a bawdy house," Leicester Hemingway wrote. A work that eventually took its place in American literature as a genuine classic was referred to on Kenilworth Avenue in horrified tones as "that book." Dr. Hemingway, uncomfortable in the presence of capricious sex and wanton drinking, confined his remarks to the hope that Ernest's future books would be more elevating. Even so, he could not help but be proud of a son whose works were displayed in Chicago bookstores and reviewed by the most prestigious magazines.

Grace, however, reverted to her old self-righteousness when she criticized the book in terms that Ernest never forgave. She was pleased that his work was financially rewarding but deplored the use of his great talent to write about such degenerate people. Was it some kind of honor to have produced one of the "filthiest books of the year?" Every page filled her with sick loathing. It was impossible, she felt, to keep silent when a word from her might help him to find himself. The fact that she prefaced such a harsh judgment with the coy reminder that he used to call her "Fweetie" did not mollify Ernest. He did not expect her to admire his disreputable set of characters, but he had tried in an earlier letter to justify the ugliness of his subject matter. " . . . I'm trying in all my stories to get the feeling of the actual life across," he had written in the spring of 1925. " . . . You can't do this without putting in the bad and the ugly as well as what is beautiful." Now he reminded her that as an artist she should not force him to defend his choice of subject. He regretted her lack of loyalty, but he understood "absolutely" that she believed she owed it to herself to correct him in a path that seemed to her disastrous.

Highly sensitive to criticism, determined to achieve literary recognition only by adhering to his own stern sense of what was authentic, Ernest was irrevocably offended by his mother's disapproval. There seems little doubt that he perceived her as more powerful than his father and as having higher expectations for him. Yet while Grace realized that he was becoming a writer of great promise, to her at times he was simply her artistic if slightly wayward boy who needed a good scolding. That was the tone of her letter and Ernest could not be blamed for reacting. When she castigated him he lashed back.

Contributing to the discomfiture in Oak Park was the suspicion that something was wrong with Ernest's marriage. Grace had written him that she was worried about his happiness and the rumors of some cooling off of affection between him and Hadley. She promised to say nothing to anyone, however, unless he wrote something specific. Isabelle Simmons Godolphin, visiting her parents' home next door to the Hemingways, recalls the doctor quoting Ernest as writing that it was pure hell to be in love with two women at once. (Dr. Hemingway dismissed such a dilemma as nonsense.) Ernest referred obliquely to his plans having been shot to pieces and wrote that Bumby had recovered from the whooping cough and was living in a comfortable, well-heated apartment, but he said nothing about any separation.

While his own parents were expressing concern about Ernest's marital state, Pauline's mother, Mary Pfeiffer, was beginning to take a more benign view. She admitted that her future son-in-law was a good-looking man. The most recent picture he had mailed to Pauline showed him as having shed some weight, the chiseled face more striking for being thinner, the rich black hair combed neatly. When Pauline gave her mother a copy of "In Another Country" to read, she was impressed. Like her daughter, she was an avid reader and could recognize talent.

Pauline's letters to Ernest reverted to whimsy and loving anticipation and the enormous pleasure of knowing the worst was over. "It won't be very long now until this glorious life starts. I am going to look out for you and after you and I won't have anything else to do but try to please you. And when a person only has one thing to do she ought to be able to finally get to do it with reasonable consistency."

The *Vogue* job fell through, which was more of a relief than a disappointment, and she booked passage on the *New Amsterdam* sailing out of New York for Cherbourg on December 30. The money situation was eased when her father deposited $900. to her account. Hadley was still on her conscience. "Since I know now that Hadley isn't in love with anyone else . . . what would you think of my going away again?" she wrote on December 3. "Not far, some place like Dijon or Toulouse, until the divorce is over. It seems pretty thick to me for two people who are putting her through this alone to go away together and get strong and happy."

Hadley, in fact, was no longer an object of pity. Her days may have lacked some of the excitement of a Hemingway marriage, but she was free of its demands. As an adult, Jack Hemingway recalls his mother saying that her divorce was not the terrible letdown she thought it was going to be, but a kind of relief. "He was a handful," said Jack, "for all his wives and for everyone."

Eligible men and married friends brightened up Hadley's evenings. Then one day at a local tennis court she met Paul Mowrer, Paris correspondent for the *Chicago Daily News* and head of their foreign desk, whom Ernest knew from Genoa. Cultivated and unobtrusive, Mowrer was a seasoned journalist as well as a poet of unexpected subtlety. He was a public man with a deep craving for privacy, preferring classical music on records to the commotion and excitement of the symphony hall. The depth of his knowledge was attractively cloaked in modesty and reserve. He remembered Hadley from an earlier meeting when she had the air of a woman in serious trouble. But at the time of the second meeting she was animated and relaxed. "I liked the clean way she hit the ball," recalled Mowrer, "her barbless wit and generous good humor. After tennis, she and I went sometimes to the Cafe de l'Observatoire for a beer." When Paul met Hadley he was forty years old, married to Winifred Adams, and the father of two teen-age sons. His marriage was in trouble, too, not from any dramatic confrontation but from a slow drying up of common interests. It was a period of transition for him and he began to look forward to time with Hadley.

Ernest was at Cherbourg to meet Pauline's ship, as were Ada and Archie MacLeish, who came down with him from a week of skiing in the Swiss Alps. The four friends stopped in Paris to pick up Jinny and then proceeded as a group to Gstaad for a long winter holiday. Ernest's friendship with Virginia Pfeiffer had flourished during his three months' separation from Pauline. She comforted him when he despaired and amused him when he was in the mood to welcome distraction. If it bothered him that she was a lesbian, he put aside his prejudices because she was Pauline's sister and because she herself was so attractive and sharp. Jinny would be free to travel with them, to help Pauline with all sorts of mundane matters, to be a companion to her when Ernest wandered off. He was not averse to having more than one attentive female in his ménage, if they were careful not to cross him. The reluctance with which he gave up Hadley, even as he was falling in love with Pauline, gives credence to the notion that he, like many men, would have enjoyed "having it both ways." He wrote Isabelle Godolphin that his marriage to Hadley broke up because he got into a jam with her over loving someone else. "Naturally I didn't want to do anything about it," he explained lamely, " . . . but Hadley said I should."

Still, he seemed to hang back from setting the date for his second marriage. There was a suspicion that this process of falling in love was risky. Even as Pauline was protesting with such fervor that she would oppose him in nothing, that he could have his own way all the time, he knew that compromises would be expected of him. In his life as well as in his fiction he had nothing but scorn for men who permitted dominance to pass into a woman's hands. Equality in a relationship had no appeal for him.

Hadley's divorce, on grounds of desertion, became final in Paris on January 27, 1927. There was no alimony settlement other than Ernest's letter to Perkins that *The Sun* royalties should be paid to her. Occasionally, from then on, he sent her gifts of money and paid for most of Bumby's schooling. Her private income was now about two thousand dollars a year. Before her investments had been mismanaged, it had varied between four and five thousand a year. In March, when Ernest brought Bumby to Gstaad, Pauline and Jinny supervised the child's meals and naps while Ernest made day long ski runs. "I'm swell now," he wrote Isabelle on March 5. "I'm cockeyed about Pauline and going to get married in May. . . . I felt like hell before, but now everything is very very good and everybody feeling swell."

Perhaps Pauline felt less than swell. When they returned to Paris, Ernest decided to make a trip to Italy with Guy Hickok, a last-minute bachelor fling much like the three-day fishing sortie he made before marrying Hadley. Pauline was fed up with separations, even a little tired of Jinny. She wanted some time alone with Ernest. Her description of the plan was "that Italian tour for the promotion of masculine society." But she swallowed her disappointment in a flurry of unpacking and laundering (both hers and Ernest's) and set out to find an apartment. Ada MacLeish steered her to one at 6, rue Férou, a picturesque lane behind the Church of St. Sulpice. There they would have a large bedroom, salon, and dining room, a superb kitchen, two bathrooms, a small study for Ernest, and an extra room for a maid or an infant. The apartment was freshly painted and in good repair. Pauline wrote Uncle Gus Pfeiffer about it, assuming (correctly) that he would advance the money to pay for it.

The next order of business in Ernest's absence was an investigation of the necessary documents for their Catholic ceremony. Both of them would need a certificate of baptism. Pauline had hers. Perhaps since Ernest was now in Italy he could locate the priest who had baptized him. The only other document required would be his certificate of marriage to Hadley, which would be judged invalid since that event had taken place outside the church. Ernest did encounter the priest, Don Guiseppe Bianchi, who had anointed him while he lay wounded in the Piave valley in 1918. There is no evidence that Ernest produced any baptismal papers, but he evidently was able to persuade the church of his affiliation. Hadley's only comment, for publication, was that it seemed strange to find that one's marriage, if it took place in a little Methodist church in Horton Bay, wasn't a marriage at all.

Meanwhile Hadley was ready to take Bumby to America for a long trip. She would visit friends in New York and California as well as both families—her own in St. Louis and the Hemingways in Oak Park. While she was away at Chartres for a weekend with Winifred Mowrer, Paul Mowrer invited Ernest to his apartment for lunch. At one point in the conversation he asked Ernest if his marriage was really over, or whether something could still be done to patch things up. Ernest's recollection, reported later, was that Paul told him he was in love with Hadley. Paul denied saying that. He did not believe that he would have spoken so frankly then, when he had known Hadley only a short time and had not made a formal break with Winifred. Since he did initiate the meeting, perhaps he was sounding out Ernest about Hadley's true situation.

In New York Hadley went out with various men and was graciously received by Max Perkins, who arranged for a portion of *Sun* royalties to be deposited to her account. From St. Louis on May 21 she wrote Ernest that she still missed him. " . . . I get sore once in awhile, and have bad dreams. . . . do write an ex-playmate. . . . not a beau in this god-forsaken town for me." She added that his name was known everywhere and she was accorded a royal welcome because of it. Before going out to California for the summer she would take Bumby to Oak Park to see the grandparents.

The Hemingways had finally learned the truth from Ernest after Hadley's divorce decree became final. In language quite removed from her previously expressed views of romantic love, Grace wrote him her reaction. She was sorry to hear that his marriage was over, but as far as she was concerned very few marriages deserved to survive. She admitted that she held rather heretical views on marriage but usually kept such opinions to herself. This is a strong statement from Grace—denouncing her own marriage, even indirectly, and taking a caustic look at the ones around her. And she was blurting out such "heretical views" to a son who had little sympathy or affection for her. Such a passionate expression underscores the degree to which she may have felt trapped in a society that sanctioned only the most narrowly defined female role.

In the same letter she tried to defend herself against Ernest's accusation that she had been disloyal for criticizing *The Sun Also Rises*. He was confusing her concern about sin with her concern for his welfare. (Two weeks later, in her letter of March 6, she made a point of praising "The Killers" and bought the O'Brien collection with its reprint of "The Undefeated.")

All Grace's letters of the period describe her euphoria over the local attention her own work was receiving. Some paintings had sold for as much as $250. She decided to ask $600. for her latest, a large mountain landscape, and had recently been voted into the Chicago Society of Artists—a high honor, one that would open many doors in the art world to her. Even with allowances for her exaggerated perception of herself, such accomplishments were not inconsiderable, especially as they were achieved at a time when she was worried about her husband's health.

Recently Ed Hemingway had made the self-diagnosis of diabetes. He was also suffering from severe attacks of angina. The prognosis was disturbing, since diabetes is a common cause of arteriosclerosis of the brain, heart, kidneys, and lower extremities. Grace tried vigorously to persuade him of the importance of diet, even preparing special dishes for him. But the dieting came hard—he liked rich food too much—and he stubbornly refused to change his work habits, saying that he was under increasing financial stress. When Hadley brought Bumby to visit, Grace was pleased to see him take the child everywhere in his Model T. But after the visitors left his mood reverted to one of depression and fatigue. Frustrated by her inability to change the situation Grace poured her energies into her own work.

Pauline and Ernest were married at L'Église de St-Honoré d'Ey-lau, at 9, Place Victor-Hugo May 10, 1927. The groom wore a three-piece tweed suit and button-down shirt and the bride, a soft silk dress and single strand of pearls. Her black hair was combed across her forehead and bobbed above her ears. Jinny Pfeiffer witnessed the Catholic ceremony and a few close friends gathered afterward for the wedding luncheon. No other relatives could be present, but cables, letters, and checks arrived from across the ocean. Paul Pfeiffer sent the bride a thousand dollars and a sprig of bridal wreath, the first to open in his garden. Mary Pfeiffer wrote that it was a strange sensation for one's daughter to be married across the sea where they could neither look upon her face nor clasp her hand, "but my dear Ernest, if you are all that those who know you best believe you to be, we are glad to give our heart's treasure into your keeping." Aunt Harriett in Cedar Falls, Iowa, writing on May 24, three days after Lindbergh made his solo flight to Paris, wondered facetiously whether Pauline might not fly over with her husband "and spend the day with us now that it's such an easy matter getting over the sea."

The generosity of Pauline's relatives and the comfortable way she lived herself always brings up the question of Pauline's money. She did not as yet have a large, independent income, though the backing was there and it gave her an edge, permitted her to take some risks, supplied the mobility that was critical to the love affair. But to assume that Ernest married her for her money, or that it was even a major factor, is to undervalue greatly Pauline's originality and depth. As much as anything, it was her conviction that they were kindred spirits, uniquely right for one another, that aroused him. She was the other half that would make him complete. She was one with him and would be *for* him in a way that no other woman could.

For their honeymoon they went to the small fishing village of Grau-du-Roi near Aigues-Mortes at the mouth of the Rhone estuary. The weather was mild and the beaches unspoiled. One day they stained their faces with berry juice, disguised themselves as gypsies, and rode their bicycles to a local festival. Pauline encouraged Ernest to work at his own pace and fish and swim whenever he wanted. They both flourished until Ernest cut his foot and developed an anthrax infection (a deep-seated abscess difficult to treat) that necessitated a ten-day stay in bed after their return to Paris.

Under Pauline's influence Ernest began to dress more like a young guardsman and less like a Left Bank fisherman. He ordered handsome suits from a rue St. Honoré tailor and took care that they fit properly. Pauline and Jinny completed the furnishing of the apartment and then helped type the collection of stories that Ernest was sending off to Perkins for October publication. Ernest wrote the first of his frequent reports to his new mother-in-law—that Pauline weighed 114 pounds, ate all they could pay for at any time, rode sixty-eight kilometers on the bicycle without getting tired, and was now in the other room copying a story.

On June 17 Sara Murphy wrote Pauline from Cap d'Antibes that she and Gerald were terribly pleased about her and Ernest. It was an immense relief to them and everyone else who was so fond of Ernest that he had put a very bad time behind him. Sara was clearly on Pauline's side throughout the breakup and believed that Hadley's insistence on the hundred-day separation was too harsh. She went on to invite them down to the Riviera, but Pauline could not accept the invitation. Ernest was already planning a summer in Spain— Pamplona, then San Sebastian and Valencia, finishing up at one of the peaceful small towns for some concentrated writing.

Hadley, who had been in Spain with Ernest every year since 1923, was now in California, "having one day a bum time, the next day a grand one—how can a person tell when they are pulling out of the woods?" She had rented a house in Carmel ten minutes from the beach and hired a schoolgirl to help with Bumby. " . . . my *time* at least is full," she wrote, "even if my life isn't. There are possibilities —but all a little bit wrong—you know." The person she took care not to mention was Paul Mowrer. The Mowrer family was in America, too, on leave from Paris, and Paul kept Hadley apprised of his whereabouts. While their growing friendship was not openly acknowledged, both knew that they were strongly attracted to one another. When she referred to possibilities that were a little bit wrong, Hadley was thinking of Paul. Since he was still married, she kept a tight rein on her feelings as the prospect of returning to Paris drew near.

Hadley reached New York on October 8, a few days before she was to sail back to France. Paul Mowrer was in town. They met privately and talked frankly about their future. Paul explained that he and his wife were going their separate ways. Winifred wanted to share a small studio with a close friend in Paris. Paul meanwhile was looking for some property in the country, preferably around Crécy, an easy commute to the city. There was still no talk of divorce. Winifred would help him get settled and visit him on weekends. But it was understood that he wanted to see more of Hadley if she could accept, at least for the present, certain ambiguities. Hadley assured him that she could. Having just emerged from a bruising divorce, she needed his warmth and admiration more than an immediate proposal of marriage.

After six months of traveling, Hadley was physically weary, but her morale was good when she reached Paris in mid-October. The flat she finally leased was on the sixth floor of a modern building at 98, Auguste de Blanqui, above the noise of the elevated, with large windows and a small wrought-iron balcony. Jack's adult memories of it were tender. "I came to love the sound of the rain on the slate mansard roof, and the reassurance of sleeping so near to her, going from my little alcove to her big warm bed in the early morning."

In November Ernest helped to gather up and move Hadley's belongings, which had been stored with various friends. He also presented her with a copy of his new collection of short stories, *Men Without Women*, which had recently been published. There were fourteen in all—the three that he had composed during the hot days in Madrid in 1926, when Pauline was in Bologna, two written when she was in Arkansas and he was fighting off the loneliness in Paris, and various others of the past year. One of the recent ones, "Now I Lay Me," contains the scene in which Nick Adams's mother callously burns her husband's collection of Indian artifacts in the back yard of their old house before the move to the new house. Another, "Hills like White Elephants," is unusual for its effective identification with the female point of view. Neither the incident nor the woman involved came out of Ernest's experience. Rather, they grew out of a remark made by Robert McAlmon about a college friend who had had an abortion. In dialogue, the story tells of a fatuous American's effort to persuade his frightened young mistress to have an abortion. As they sit drinking beer outside a

Spanish railroad station, the characters spring to life with dramatic clarity and Hemingway communicates with great sensitivity the fear and submerged anger of the pregnant woman.

Ernest dedicated *Men Without Women* to Evan Shipman, but his first choice had been Jinny Pfeiffer for her support during the bad months of the separation from Pauline. As he later explained to Mary Pfeiffer, it had seemed to him that with the book being called *Men Without Women* and containing fight stories and so forth, it would be in better taste to dedicate it to a man. He wanted to give Jinny something she would like, but thought a dedication might possibly be an embarrassment. For Pauline, who was now in the early months of her first pregnancy and would come to depend on Jinny more and more, it was a great relief that Ernest liked her sister. Jinny never catered to him the way Pauline did. But she was not the wife and Ernest seemed to understand that. It was enough, at least for the present, that she was loyal to Pauline and amusing with him.

During Pauline's pregnancy, Ernest evinced none of the ambivalence that had come to the surface during Hadley's pregnancy. He did not have the same kinds of financial worries, and from everything Pauline had demonstrated, he sensed that he was in no danger of being displaced. They went to Berlin for the six-day bicycle races and to Gstaad for their second season of winter skiing. As often happened, Ernest stayed on to ski by himself for a few days. By this time Hadley's resentment of Pauline had dissolved and with Jinny's stamp of approval the three women constructed an amicable friendship based on shared concerns for Bumby and Ernest.

"I am feeling simply swell everywhere but in the heart, which cries out for you," wrote Pauline to Ernest in Gstaad. "The energy is simply tremendous. I rise at dawn and hop about like fleas." She had plenty to do in the apartment. It was flooded because of a broken pipe, which had burst in their absence and knocked out the heating system. It was still not repaired when Ernest arrived. He went to bed with an attack of grippe, grumbling that it had been a miserable year for his health.

Early in March Ernest was struck by a curious mishap, one that seemed to bear out the opinion that his poor eyesight and physical awkwardness combined to make him accident-prone. At two in the morning in the bathroom of the apartment he accidentally pulled a cord that controlled a decrepit, cracked skylight. The whole window fell on his head, leaving a two-inch gash above his right eye. Pauline rushed to staunch the blood and then in a panic called Archie MacLeish, who took him to the American hospital to be stitched up.

Whether it was the result of so many discomforts or a simple case of homesickness, Ernest then decided that he wanted to go back to America for a while. Pauline was willing. She preferred to have her baby in the United States, close to her family. Ernest's attention was drawn to Key West, Florida by Dos Passos, who described it as tropical, maritime, and unspoiled. Pauline decided that they should keep the rue Férou apartment. She had furnished it handsomely with antiques and did not want to dismantle it.

And so they set off, to discover that Dos Passos's description was accurate. Flowering shrubs and trees grew luxuriantly. There was water everywhere—the Atlantic Ocean on the south, Gulf of Mexico to the north, the entire island only one and a half miles wide and four and a half miles long. It was accessible by ferry boat, steamer, or railroad. Most of the 7,000 people scratched out a bare living from fishing, or serviced the saloons and bordellos that catered to wealthy Cubans who came over from Havana to gamble or carouse. The U.S. Naval Installation, once a major employer for the Conches (native-born Key Westers of Caucasian stock) had sharply curtailed its operation. The streets were half-paved. Most of the dwellings were unpainted cottages with tin roofs, privies, and collapsing front porches. But there were some hard-working families who had prospered in business and law and in their neighborhoods there were quiet tree-shaded lanes and comfortable two-story homes in Conch architecture (faintly Georgian, strongly Spanish, with elaborate latticework, balconies, and overgrown gardens).

By the end of the first week Ernest had met some of the locals. He formed a close friendship with a young man named Charles Thompson, who was the same age and shared his interests—especially hunting and fishing. Educated up north, Charles had returned to help run the family enterprises—the hardware store, fish market, tackle shop, ship's chandlery, and a small cigar factory.

Charles's wife, Lorine, a high-school teacher from Richmond, Georgia, was a lifeline for Pauline, whose sagging spirits in the sixth month of her pregnancy perked up somewhat in the cool shade of the Thompson side porch. Lorine often invited the Hemingways to her house for dinner. Evenings for the most part were quiet. There was plenty of action on Duval Street, where the bars and gambling joints were clustered, but Ernest avoided the drinking and the brawling. He was more content than he had been in months, for in the quiet mornings he was working on a new novel. Fitfully begun in Paris, then set aside during the transition to Key West, it was now proceeding well. It was to be the full fictional treatment of his wartime experience in Italy.

Ernest was working so well that Pauline decided to go to Arkansas ahead of him. A few days before her departure, Ernest's parents arrived for the day, though not unannounced. Grace's letter forwarded to Ernest from Paris had explained that they were going to Florida and Cuba and would sail back to the mainland via Key West. While in Florida they had investigated their real estate investments and were shocked to learn how much the value of their lots had declined. Ed, depressed from his physical disabilities, was in no condition to act decisively. Instead of selling out, which would have left them with their original capital and a small profit, they decided to hang on, encouraged perhaps by their glib-talking agent.

The reunion took place on the C & O docks and Pauline joined them for lunch and a tour of the island. Grace said little to Ernest about her personal worries. Instead she talked with great animation of a painting tour of the Pacific Southwest that she had taken with her brother, Leicester, who had driven her out into the desert for four day excursions.

Ed Hemingway had none of her spirit. Next to her ruddy robustness, he looked wan and wasted. His beard was white and thin, his eyes seemed filmed over with a faraway sadness. He wiped tears from his eyes as Pauline kissed them goodbye, promising to write frequently and to let them know when the baby came. It seemed to Ernest that his father's strength was waning as his mother's was being regenerated.

Chapter 12

From Jacksonville, Florida, enroute to Arkansas, Pauline wrote that "Little Pilar loves travelling and kicks constantly and I've taken to kicking back." In late May Ernest drove across the country to join her, accompanied by her father, who had gone to Key West to fish with him. He was able to form a cautious friendship with Paul Pfeiffer. With Mary Pfeiffer he was much more spontaneous and affectionate. Her transparent sincerity was so appealing that he immediately relaxed. She was a genuine Southern storyteller in her droll observations of village life, and Ernest was vastly entertained. She reported to him in a letter after the visit:

> The town was shocked by the suicide of that poor old man, Mr. Keith, father of Lawanda, Laverne, Lenore, Ruth, Myra and Doris. They were too much for him, as a new grandchild was arriving almost monthly for him to look after. . . . Laverne had recently eloped under peculiarly trying conditions and Mrs. Keith was away looking after Ruth who had had her third operation. Myra, the deaf and dumb screamer, was managing the household. Brother Maris at the funeral in making a resume of his life said, "I think God's mercy will cover this case." There was an audible Amen.

Ernest did not find the rest of Piggott as entertaining. The weather was oppressive. It was the wrong season for quail hunting and he could not control the domestic arrangements of the household to fit in with his writing routine. Pauline, four weeks from term, was more concerned with where she would deliver the baby. In trying to figure out the solution to that problem Ernest wrote to his father. How about if Pauline had her baby in Petoskey? How was the medical care? Could they have the Loomis cottage at Walloon Lake? What about servants? Behind such practical questions was Ernest's yearning for the green forests and sparkling lakes of northern Michigan. Dr. Hemingway's reply was prompt but stiffly worded. The queries seemed to offend him deeply. "You would best consider having your new baby in Kansas City or St. Louis as the Petoskey Hospitals are really only best for local emergencies. Nurses and maids are very scarce up there. . . . If you want to have me attend your wife at the Oak Park Hospital, I am glad to offer you my services." He signed his letter "Lovingly, your father" and below it wrote "C.E. Hemingway, M.D."

Ernest seemed disappointed that his father did not welcome him to Walloon Lake and Dr. Hemingway was hurt that Ernest did not agree to put Pauline in his care. But it was Pauline's decision that prevailed. She chose Kansas City because it was a medical center. Her friends Ruth and Malcolm Lowry invited them to stay at their spacious estate across from the Country Club, and Ernest liked the sound of that arrangement. He drove Pauline from Piggott to Kansas City in searing heat. Pauline put herself under the care of a local specialist, Carlos Guffey, who calculated that the baby would be born before the end of the month. Ernest worked on his novel and followed the events of the Republican National Convention, which had convened in Kansas City to nominate Herbert Hoover for its presidential candidate.

Pauline's labor pains began on June 27, 1928. She was admitted to Research Hospital in downtown Kansas City but did not deliver nine-and-a-half-pound Patrick Hemingway until eighteen hours later by Caesarean section. It was a long and difficult labor and the postsurgical days were full of misery. The doctor warned them that Pauline must not become pregnant for at least three years. (If she did not want to become a cripple or a corpse, wrote Ernest graphically to his mother-in-law.)

Ernest was relieved that the ordeal was over, but he was fed up with disruptions to his work. Fatherhood was no longer a novelty and he dreaded the stopover back in Piggott. What he yearned for now was cool weather, tranquility, good streams, and a momentum that would propel the book into a mighty finish. Three weeks after the baby's birth, he escorted a bellowing Patrick and the convalescing mother back to the Pfeiffer home. Jinny Pfeiffer returned from Paris and supervised Patrick's routine. Mary Pfeiffer kept a dragon's watch on Pauline, who was still not permitted to climb the stairs. Ernest wrote Waldo Peirce, a painter whom he had met in Paris, that he could not understand why the latter ever wanted to be a father. He made plans to escape to Wyoming until Pauline was well enough to join him. On July 25 he took the train back to Kansas City, where he picked up his old friend Bill Horne to accompany him across the plains.

Pauline seemed philosophical about the separation. She understood that Ernest needed the right environment for the book and she knew why he found Piggott so stultifying. She did not resent it that he was bored with bottles, feeding times, and intermittent screaming (she was not all that taken with it herself). She did not fancy having him moping about when she was too restricted to join him. Her first priority was to get strong and fit so that she could go to Wyoming, too.

Jinny had already volunteered to stay behind with Patrick. The pattern was now forming that would be a model for the ensuing years. Jinny liked mothering—that is, if the final responsibility lay elsewhere. Pauline prepared to turn Patrick over to her as soon as she could travel. "With you away," she wrote Ernest on July 31, 1928, "it seems as tho I was just a mother, which is certainly not very gripping. But in three weeks I'll begin to get ready to go to Wyoming, where I shall be just a wife." Pauline's maternal instinct did not run as deep as Hadley's. "We raised the formula [Patrick was weaned from the breast when Pauline left the hospital]," she added. "We have a little slogan to keep Patrick a good boy. It is Raise the Formula." By August 4, she was climbing the stairs and admiring her new flat abdomen. "Hurry up and send for your wife," she wrote. "I'll even pay my own passage."

Patrick was baptized by Mary Pfeiffer's local priest on August 14. "He didn't make a noise," reported Pauline, "until the priest said, 'Patrick, do you renounce the Devil with all his works and pomps?' and he gave a little groan and a little whine of protest." Most of the time she described him as though he were someone else's child. "Jinny was cutting out the two o'clock feeding because the doctor said he gained too fast and he has started on orange juice. I think we may like him very much." He was her first-born, but her passions were and always would be reserved for his father.

After the baptism Pauline left for Wyoming, stopping over in St. Louis long enough to see the dentist and to hear some amusing if grossly distorted gossip. The local wags were saying that the character of Lady Brett Ashley was clearly based on Ernest Hemingway's second wife. With her own friends Pauline set the story straight, explaining that there was a Brett Ashley but that her real name was Duff Twysden, not Pauline Pfeiffer. Pauline, of course, did not know that Duff was then living her own sequel to Ernest's fictional re-creation of her troubled life. In the summer of 1927, after finally breaking off with the dissolute Pat Guthrie, Duff fell in love with a young American painter, Clinton King, who made his home in Paris. King, drawn to her at their first meeting, arranged to go in her company to Tréboul and then invited her to move in with him at his studio in the rue Boissonade. Duff confided to him that she was hurt by Ernest's portrayal of her, in spite of her flip remark about the bullfighter. She wondered sorrowfully whether that portrayal finished off whatever faint hope she had of wresting custody of her child away from the Twysdens.

King was thirteen years younger than Duff and financially dependent upon his wealthy father, who ran the King Candy Company in Fort Worth, Texas. She worried about the age difference and the difficulty of making the transition from Montparnasse to Texas. But finally she did throw in her lot with him. This time her judgment was sound. King was absolutely loyal to her. He defied his family to stay with her and on August 21, 1928, three days after Pauline was reunited with Ernest in Wyoming, Duff Twysden and Clinton King were married in a London Registry Office.

In Sheridan, Pauline was so grateful to be with Ernest again that she fell easily into his routine. When he was too restless to work in the early morning, they went out to shoot sharp-tailed grouse and then picnic on the car fender by the side of the road. The near fields glowed with newly ripening grain. A long way off the mountains rose up stark and gray-brown. By the end of August the first draft of the war novel was finished, and Ernest wanted a real vacation. The wilderness to the west—the South Fork of the Yellowstone, the Snake River Valley, the Grand Tetons around Jackson Hole—drew him. The weather was glorious now, a perfect early fall when the sun still warmed the back and the air had the bracing sniff of winter. Pauline was, in Ernest's words, "strong as a goat." She fished the Snake for trout and shot at prairie dogs from the moving car with Ernest's Colt pistol. They did not stay in any one place for more than a few days, but toured the whole magnificent area, finally turning east at Casper, Wyoming for the thousand-mile trip across the plains to Arkansas.

There the heat was insufferable, with temperatures registering 108 degrees in the shade. Pauline began to yearn for their Paris apartment, having had enough of small towns and forests. Ernest missed Paris, too, but he missed Key West more. As he jogged over the back roads, he formulated his plans to be back there when the good winter weather set in. But first he must pay a visit to the elder Hemingways in Oak Park.

When he saw his parents he was jolted by the deterioration of his father's health. The doctor's diabetes was worse and his angina attacks more frequent. Either he was silent and depressed, or irritable with everyone, taking offense at even the mildest remark. Grace pleaded with him to rest, but his insomnia made the nights as exhausting as the days. He had never taken Grace into his full confidence about money matters, and only he knew how dependent she and the children were on the earnings from his practice. All his savings had been poured into the Florida land, which paid no income and required heavy interest payments. Grace confided to Marcelline that he now locked his drawers and closet and spent many hours alone behind the closed doors of his office. The only person to enjoy his trust and affection was thirteen-year-old Leicester, whom he kept at his side as much as possible, even resenting the hours the boy was at school. Ernest tended to blame Grace for not understanding his father's needs, but his sisters perceived otherwise. They believed that their mother did her best in a terrible situation and was puzzled and hurt by Ed's rejection; some of her frenetic activity at this stage was a mask for the constant anxiety about his condition, but it was characteristic of her to read hopeful interpretations into even the most ominous signs.

On the morning of December 6, several weeks after Ernest's visit, Ed Hemingway awakened with a bothersome pain in his foot. As a doctor he projected vividly what such a pain could mean—an arterial obstruction, possibly gangrene, and beyond that the specter of amputation. In his depressed state he was especially frightened, and confessed as much to Grace over breakfast. She pleaded with him to consult one of his colleagues immediately. He replied that he would but the fact is that he did not. Perhaps he was too fearful to seek the truth about his condition, or was so despondent that such an obvious step was too much for him. Only a few days earlier he and Grace had decided, upon the advice of his banker brother, George Hemingway, to sell off some of the Florida lots, but Grace knew that nothing had been done. Ed came home at lunchtime, drawn and pale, asking after Leicester, who was home with a cold. When Grace assured him that the boy was much better and was sleeping, Ed Hemingway went down to the basement to burn some personal papers and then told her he would rest in his room until lunch was ready. The next sound in the house was a single sharp gunshot. He had shot himself behind the right ear with Anson Hemingway's old Smith and Wesson revolver.

Because of the nature of the death the police had to be called. Carol was summoned home from high school and made all the necessary phone calls—to Marcelline, Ursula, and Sunny. Grace, already sedated and on the verge of collapse, was able to tell Carol that a letter addressed to her father, still unopened, had arrived that morning from Ernest. From the contents of the letter Carol learned that Ernest had gone to New York to pick up Bumby and was at that moment traveling south on the Havana Special.

Carol's telegram with the news of his father's death intercepted Ernest at Trenton. He had only $40. in his pocket and wired several friends in New York for money. Scott Fitzgerald's hundred dollars reached him at the railroad station in Philadelphia and paid for his ticket to Chicago. Ernest left Bumby in the watchful care of a Pullman porter with instructions to wire him of the child's welfare at every stop.

By the time Ernest reached Oak Park, Marcelline had arrived from Detroit to help Grace with the funeral arrangements. Ernest led the family in the Lord's Prayer in the music room where the body lay. Funeral services were held in the First Congregational

Church and half the town was present. In spite of some mutterings about the nature of the death, most of the mourners seemed genuinely moved by the loss of the doctor who had tended them for so many years. Ernest's siblings turned to him for comfort and some explanation. He told them that there was nothing to be ashamed of in their father's death. He had been too sick to know what he was doing. Nothing would have made any difference to a man who had been temporarily knocked out of his head, said Ernest.

Grace was still grieving and in a shocked state when Ernest left for Key West, but he repeated—until she understood—that he would give her all the help possible to educate the two younger children and provide for her security. Right now, he explained, he had a big job to finish. If his novel became a financial success everyone would benefit.

On December 21, Hadley wrote to Ernest.

> I sent a telegram to Pauline at Key West on hearing of Dr. Hemingway's death. I hope it got there. That seems a very fragile address. I wanted you to know I was thinking of you. . . . Taty, I felt so sorry for you, the mixture of emotions! I remember how affectionately you talked of him to me in New York. What a hard thing that he had such bitter blows just when he, such a hard-working man, had surely earned a respite.

There were echoes of sadness for Hadley in the tragedy. Twenty-five years earlier her own father, James Richardson, who had filled such a special place in her life, killed himself in the same way as Ed Hemingway, and perhaps out of some of the same experience—financial reverses, an incompatible marriage, deepening depression.

For Ernest, identifying with his father, bitterly critical of his mother, the suicide set off a continuing search for a villain. Eventually he cast Grace Hemingway in that role.

Sunny was the only one of the Hemingway children who could not attend Dr. Hemingway's funeral. Ernest later told her the details, explaining about Ed's heart disease, his diabetes, and the financial stress, but they talked little. "Dad had always told us," she wrote, "that only a coward commits suicide. We found, though, that when someone you love commits the acts, it's easy to find comforting excuses. And you regard him none the less for it." Whatever gentleness and intimacy Ernest expressed with Sunny during the time after Ed's suicide did not translate into the feelings he shared with others. He suffered deep shame and disappointment over the tragedy and found it necessary to distance himself behind a harsh stance. "I would esteem it a favor from you," he wrote to Mike Strater, "not to shoot yourself nor have any Caesarian [sic] operations nor anything of that sort until old Hem the writer has finished this book." When he learned that the *Brooklyn Eagle* had been sold and Guy Hickok's job was in jeopardy, he wrote Hickok on January 9, 1929, that he could count on Ernest for next year but that this year his father had killed himself and left him with the whole family to support. He would give his relatives some of his advance from Scribners, he added, if they promised never to write him. Such heavy sarcasm, if applied to Grace, seems particularly unfair, since she was making a credible effort to understand the reality of her new economic situation. In working over her husband's accounts with Marcelline she discovered that Ed had lost control of his affairs months before his death. Unpaid bills were ignored and the check-book was not balanced. Although Grace had never earned the repu-tation of being a good manager of finances, she was intelligent and resourceful and adapted quickly to the changed environment. Her brother-in-law, George Hemingway, and her son-in-law, Sterling Sanford, paid the funeral expenses. In a letter of February 2, she wrote Ernest that she had taken on three private painting pupils and two voice pupils, and hoped to rent out rooms. Three weeks later he responded with the promise of permanent financial help. He would send her $100. a month.

Ernest would never know, she replied emotionally on the 24th, what an enormous relief it was to receive the news of such substan-tial material help. (She admitted that she had been almost sleepless with worry.) It was nothing short of a reprieve. The difference between $100. a month and $200. was the difference between being poor and being comfortable. Until she received his good news, she had been scrimping on everything—magazine subscriptions, church socials, even the children's allowances.

She then explained how she had invested the $21,000. from Ed's life insurance to earn an average interest of 6 percent and used money from the sale of her paintings to pay the taxes on the Kenil-worth house. Sterling would take care of the mortgage payments.

The next problem was to settle the tax bills on the Florida property. Dr. Hemingway had forgotten to pay the first installments during the previous years, incurring large penalties for 1928. (Ernest subsequently sent her $578.93 to cover the entire amount due.)

The last item in that letter was to follow through on a request that Ernest had made. He had asked her to send him the revolver that had been Ed's suicide weapon. She finally succeeded in getting it back from the coroner; it was the old Civil War "Long John" that she had learned to shoot when Ernest was just a baby. Leicester asked for it too, she wrote, but Ernest had first choice. (This exchange of letters should serve to end the rumors, long-circulated, that Grace shipped the revolver to Ernest for malign reasons of her own.)

The revolver went into a carton that contained a chocolate cake, some cookies, a book for Bumby, and a roll of Grace's two best canvases of desert scenes, whose safety was her greatest concern. She could not bear to think of losing the paintings and reminded Ernest of her dream that at least one find its way to a Paris salon. She repeated in each letter how grateful she was for everything.

For the remainder of the year she hoped for some sign of recognition from Paris. The art scene in Chicago was disillusioning. It seemed that influence meant more than talent in the awarding of prizes and honors. Would Ernest do his best for her? No one else seemed to care. Her need for sympathy called for this bit of grandstanding, but in fact she was continuing to "do" for herself with perseverance and some modest results. She rented four rooms in the house. A painstaking search through Dr. Hemingway's medical and index cards turned up some accounts that were collectible, and she managed to earn a small honorarium from a series of art lectures.

At Ernest's suggestion Sunny Hemingway had come to Key West in November of 1928 to type the final manuscript of *A Farewell to Arms*. In two months she finished, and Ernest wired Max Perkins to collect it in person. Between fishing excursions Perkins read the manuscript, pronounced it magnificent, and suggested that *Scribner's Magazine* might serialize it before publication. The magazine's editors agreed and offered Ernest the largest sum in their history, $16,000., for the first serial rights.

Ernest, following the advice he once gave Fitzgerald to use in his writing the things that hurt him badly, had made use of two personal, traumatic experiences—his wounding at Fossalta and Agnes von Kurowsky's rejection, both experiences significantly altered from their real-life context. Lieutenant Frederic Henry is an American ambulance driver attached to the Italian Army. After his wounding in the trenches, he is transferred to an American Red Cross hospital in Milan, where he falls in love with a beautiful English nurse, Catherine Barkley. When he returns to the front, it is to experience the misery and violence and treachery of the retreat from Caporetto. (Hemingway, the journalist, covered the retreat in Thrace in 1922.) Sickened by the sight of Italian carabinieri shooting their own officers, Lieutenant Henry flees with Catherine, now pregnant, to Switzerland, for a brief idyll at Chamby before she delivers a stillborn child and then dies.

Frederic Henry is a fully developed, realistic character, young, careless, and selfish, reluctantly learning the meaning of sacrifice. The gradual development of his consciousness as he makes the commitment to Catherine parallels the inevitability of death in the human condition. All life ends in death, Henry learns, and all commitment in loss, but the commitment must be made nevertheless. "That was what you did. You died. You did not know what it was about. You never had time to learn. They threw you in and told you the rules. . . . But they killed you in the end."

Catherine Barkley is an idealized Hemingway woman, selfless, brave, and erotic—part mother, part sexual partner. She asks nothing of her lover except that he love her in return. Those critics who defend Ernest's heroines claim that these ideal creatures are superior to his heroes—more faithful, more loving and more responsible. This does not seem to satisfy the objection, however, that Ernest had little interest in exploring the needs, aspirations, and conflicts of flesh-and-blood women.

Agnes von Kurowsky has come to be identified as the prototype for Catherine Barkley. But in fact Ernest drew on many sources for his doomed heroine. Her Scottish origins and mannerisms were derived from Duff Twysden, her troubled past from Agnes's co-worker, Elsie Jessup. Her name, Catherine, and its abbreviation, Cat, came from Ernest's nickname for Hadley—Feather Cat, shortened to Kat or Cat. And the idyll at Chamby was also based on winter scenes from his time with Hadley.

This Catherine, or Cat, resembles Agnes in physical description, but she can barely understand Italian, whereas Agnes became fluent in Italian. The nurse is war-weary and susceptible and is quickly aroused by her handsome patient. " 'I'll say just what you wish and I'll do what you wish,' " she assures him. " 'There isn't any me any more.' " Such abnegation of self was entirely alien to Agnes von Kurowsky. Intrigued by the opportunities for nursing in distant lands, Agnes was unwilling to become the worshipful partner in an unstable liaison.

If Catherine's rootlessness belongs to Duff Twysden, the Swiss Alps setting to Hadley, and the warm August nights on the balcony of the British Hospital to Agnes, this heroine's tragic death is clearly related to Pauline's Caesarean section in Kansas City. Critics have noted that Ernest wrote the death scene of *A Farewell to Arms* a month after his wife suffered a long and dangerous labor, but they have generally attributed Catherine's saintliness to Ernest's perception of Hadley. However, Ernest's idealization of Hadley came much later, thirty years later, in *A Moveable Feast*. When he wrote *A Farewell to Arms*, he was more likely basing his portrait on Pauline.

Catherine's way of expressing her love for her lieutenant has the identical ring of Pauline's letters to Ernest in 1926. "Remember especially that we are the same guy. . . . I am only half without you. . . . these three months [of their separation] I'm hardly even alive. . . . how lovely you are, dear dear dear dear dear Ernest. . . . time without you is useless." Catherine in *A Farewell to Arms* says, " 'Oh, darling, I want you so much I want to be you too. . . . I want us to be all mixed up. I don't want you to go away. . . . I don't live at all when I'm not with you.' " Guy Hickok, who had read the novel in manuscript, picked up the similarity at once, without being privy to Pauline's letters, when he noted such a passage as " ' . . . why don't you let your hair grow? . . . I could cut mine and we'd be just alike only one of us blonde and one of us dark. . . . Then we'd both be alike.' " Hearing that Pauline had dyed her hair blonde, he wrote to Ernest on July 26, 1929. "How is Pauline as a blonde? She talks a lot like Catherine as a brunette. Hennaed-up she would be Catherine if you could stretch her up height-wise a few inches."

With the manuscript delivered to Perkins and a solid advance on its way to his bank account, Ernest urged his friends to come on

Pauline, Ernest, and his big fish. Key West, 1929.
From the Patrick Hemingway Collection, Princeton University Library

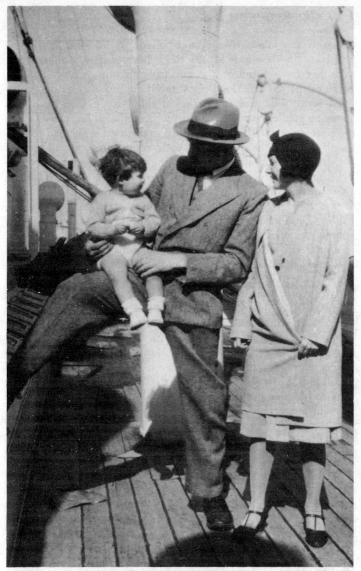

On board the liner Yorck. *Ernest, Pauline, and nine-month-old Patrick, April 1929.*
From the Patrick Hemingway Collection, Princeton University Library

down to Key West. Mike Strater obliged, as did John Dos Passos and Katy Smith, whose loyalty to Hadley apparently did not prevent her from forming a comfortable friendship with Pauline. Strater departed and Dos Passos stayed on, beguiled by the green-eyed Kate, who was unmarried at thirty-seven. She liked Dos Passos, a gentle, near-sighted man who reminded her of her reclusive, professorial father. Katy still treated Ernest as she had at Walloon Lake when he was sixteen, with teasing affection and none of the deference that others were beginning to show him. In his memory she was one of his first girls. Now that he was a seasoned, twice-married man, he followed Katy's romantic life with interest. It was time she took a husband. Ernest agreed that the kindly, balding Dos Passos would make a good one. (The two were married six months later.)

As the visitors came and went, Pauline managed the household with the help of local domestics and in late March began preparations for the trek back to Europe. They crossed the straits to Havana early in April, boarding the ship for Europe on April 5. Ernest took Jinny and Guy Hickok to Pamplona in a new Ford furnished by Uncle Gus, while Pauline waited in Paris until Patrick could go to Compiègne with his nursemaid. With Gus Pfeiffer's largess, and Ernest's advance from *Scribner's Magazine*, stringency was no longer necessary, although Ernest wrote his friends that he was still dead broke. He was openly grateful to Gus Pfeiffer, not only for the gifts and money but for his high regard, and was alert to ways of showing his appreciation. He had already given him the original manuscript of some short stories and now dedicated *A Farewell to Arms* to G.A. (Gustavus Adolphus) Pfeiffer and made him a gift of that manuscript as well.

On August 30 in Madrid the travelers, joined by Pauline, saw the performance in the bull ring of a new phenomenon. This was Sidney Franklin, the Jewish matador from Brooklyn, and Ernest was impressed enough by Franklin to follow his major corridas for the next two weeks. Franklin was a nerveless, exuberant youth with an unquenchable talent for showmanship. He became one of Ernest's most devoted admirers and extended his loyalties to include Pauline, who was amused by Franklin in spite of his bumptiousness and accepted him as one of Ernest's buddies.

The Hemingways returned to Paris on September 20, 1929, with

Pauline and Ernest follow the corridas *in Spain. September 1929.*
From the John F. Kennedy Library

the publication date for *A Farewell to Arms* less than a week away. Perkins wired them that the first reviews were "splendid." Percy Hutchinson, writing for the *New York Times*, labeled the love story of the English nurse and the American ambulance driver a high achievement of the new romanticism. Clifton Fadiman called it "the very apotheosis of a kind of modernism." Grace Hemingway seemed genuinely moved by the book, writing to Ernest on October 5 that it was his best work so far and deserving of the critics' praise. A month before publication 33,000 copies had already been advanced and Ernest predicted that the sales would top 100,000. If the profits were big he was going to set up a trust fund for Grace. Uncle Gus had already promised to contribute to it.

Agnes von Kurowsky, living in Port-au-Prince, Haiti, learned some months later that Ernest had transposed their wartime romance into a best seller. For Agnes, reading the book was a vivid reminder of an exotic episode from her past. It felt strange to see herself metamorphosed into a beautiful, ill-fated heroine. But she was much too clear-headed to be taken in by Ernest's artistic imagination. In Catherine, Agnes saw more resemblance to the flirtatious Elsie Jessup than to herself. A fellow nurse who had been with Agnes at the Ospedale in 1918 was a much more trusting reader. After reading the novel, the nurse was positive that such a scandal had taken place under her nose. Agnes was never able to convince her otherwise.

In the spring of 1926, restless for new horizons, Agnes had reenlisted in the Red Cross. On July 4, after four years of private-duty nursing, she sailed for Haiti. The American military government on that island needed French-speaking nurses to train Haitian probationers. On May 15, 1927, Agnes was made director of the nurses training facility at the Haitian General Hospital and was commended by the hospital administrator for the high standards she imposed. "The heat was terrific," recalled Agnes, "but we managed to be comfortable in pleasant cottages. We slept under netting—there were no screens on the island—and I wore a summer cotton instead of the hot grey flannel worn by the French nurses. I had my own horse, which was nice, and I learned to drive a Model T Ford."

The next year, returning by steamer from a vacation on the mainland, Agnes met Howard Preston Garner, a civilian auditor from Georgia who worked in the American Army's financial department. A muscular, round-faced man with a black moustache (his photographs show him as resembling the Ernest Hemingway of the thirties), "Pete" Garner had served as U.S. representative on various European Claim commissions, and seemed lively and attractive. "Short men always liked me," Agnes commented. On November 23, 1928, when she was thirty-seven, they were married by the bishop of Haiti in the Episcopal Church of Port-au-Prince. "We are avoiders of publicity," Agnes wrote to Clara Noyes in the Washington, D.C. Red Cross office, "so it was all very quiet." Clara Noyes sent her blessings. "Times have changed," she wrote. "Once it was regarded as not quite proper for a nurse to marry while she was working. Now of course our attitude has undergone a complete adjustment."

When Bumby rejoined Hadley in 1929, he carried, as a gift from Ernest, a copy of *A Farewell to Arms*. " . . . it *is* attractive," Hadley wrote on October 7. "Congratulations and thanks." She had been writing Ernest frequently during the past two years, and the tone of her letters was that of an affectionate friend. When Ernest had cabled her of Patrick's birth and followed with a letter replete with the traumatic details, Hadley had answered, "What a horrible time you must have had. . . . I have felt sick for you, baby, and poor little old Paulinos . . . now give [her] my love and Bumbi's, and heartfelt congratulations on the size and sex." She cautioned him to "try and ease up on the tired mind and heart . . . and forget all the women and children and the various woes they have bro't you. I have tho't about you a great deal and I am sure you need a great rest and as usual have had the good sense to look in the right place for it." As for her, it had been an ideal summer. With Paul Mowrer and his sons, she had climbed mountains, fished, picked blackberries, and taken over the household in Winifred's absence. Bumby was brown and strong and everyone's friend. "I like you very much, Papa," wrote his mother for him, simulating his childish patter. "I like you better than all the world so I'll send you a flower pot so you can buy flowers to put in it."

There were no complaints in the letters, no sarcasm, no lingering bitterness. Hadley was still proud of Ernest's accomplishments but more interested in the growing recognition being accorded Paul Mowrer. In May 1929 he had been awarded the Pulitzer Prize for his work as a foreign correspondent. He was beginning to talk to Hadley of retirement from the service and was at the point of liquidating his considerable investments when the stock market crash on October 3 put an end to such dreams. (When he sold out in 1930, his securities were worth $8,000, instead of $100,000.)

She was also grateful to Paul Mowrer for his attentions to her boy. "Bumbi and Paul and Dos and I spent an afternoon at Versailles, mostly on the lagoon and had a priceless time." Paul had located a country house in Crécy-en-Brie, forty-five minutes from Paris. Forty yards upstream was a mill. It was a bourgeois country place perhaps twenty years old, with four bedrooms upstairs, a large kitchen, and French doors that opened out to a walled garden. Most of the year the river was calm enough for canoeing, and the fishing was good for pike and perch and goujon—paddling and the fishing were favorite sports of Hadley and Paul. On washday the river was sudsy where the local women scrubbed laundry on the stones beside the bank.

While the house was being renovated Paul and Winifred, who still had not formally separated, leased a chalet on Lake Annecy in the French Alps. Hadley and Bumby were to share it for part of the summer. Unselfconsciously Hadley accepted her place in Paul Mowrer's life, giving no sign that she was restless for the divorce that would free him to marry her.

Years later, she responded to questions about her first marriage with the simple reply, "He gave me Bumby." Recollections of her past life with Ernest brought no more pain. Sometimes she was even able to joke about it. When the Godolphins visited her, in the late summer of 1929, Isabelle had reminisced about growing up in Oak Park. "If Ernest had not been brought up in that damned stuffy Oak Park environment," Hadley had said with a smile, "he would not have thought that when you fall in love extramaritally you have to get a divorce and marry the girl."

Chapter 13

Ernest complained to Waldo Peirce that he had to support a wife, a mother, two sisters, a brother, an ex-wife, two sons, and three servants, and that if he didn't get to work soon, thousands would starve. In truth, Pauline frequently received extra money from her family, Sunny supported herself, and Hadley used her own income to supplement the irregular payments from Scribners. Ernest was touchy about financial dependence. Money as proof of worth was too fundamental to give up easily.

Alliance with the Pfeiffer family seemed to put him more on the defensive than had his marriage to Hadley. He and Hadley had been young and resourceful and had lived, most of the time, like poor people. But Ernest was a conspicuous figure now. He and his entourage traveled back and forth across the ocean and throughout the United States like rich gypsies. Pauline preferred to subsidize their life style rather than sacrifice their accustomed comforts. As the Depression deepened and fewer and fewer people could live as they did, Ernest became more prickly and tended to exaggerate the extent of his expenses and the number of people dependent on him.

On January 10, 1930, the Hemingways and Henriette, Patrick's French nurse, sailed out of Bordeaux, reaching Key West early in February and moving into another rented house, this one on Pearl Street. In March, Ernest's gang arrived for spring fishing. He fumed about the disruptions but was the last person to discourage anyone from coming down. Actually he was still in no mood for serious work. The fishing was too good and there were too many lively companions to drink with. Sloppy Joe's, owned by Josie Russell, became his favorite bar, and the tropical lushness of the island continued to please him. "It's the best place I've ever seen anywhere," he reported to Hickok, "flowers, tamarind trees, guava trees, coconut palms . . . got tight last night on absinthe and did knife tricks."

In an exchange of letters with Hadley, Ernest brought up the question of Bumby's religious training, remarking that he and Pauline would like to make him a little Catholic if Hadley did not mind. She replied:

> My long pondered answer is this, old dear. I *do* mind—he belongs to the Episcopalian Church by baptism and I hope will grow up free of judgment and full of faith in these matters. He can make up his own mind when he is eighteen and be as many Catholics as he wants *then*. In the meantime I am teaching him Bible stories . . . and all the kindness, consideration and uprightness I can summon from my own beliefs. . . . I don't want him to join any church until he's old enough to think or *feel* rationally for himself.

For his annual voyage to New York, Bumby was entrusted to Jinny Pfeiffer's care. Early in June Ernest and Pauline left Key West separately—Ernest for New York to meet Bumby's ship, Pauline and Patrick and Henriette, by train, for Arkansas. A robust, chattering Bumby was excited at the prospect of traveling across the country with his beloved papa. They drove west to Piggott, picked up Pauline, and crossed the plains in the hot midsummer. On July 13 they checked into the L-Bar-T dude ranch just inside the Wyoming state line, where the owner, Lawrence Nordquist, put them in his prime double cabin, with a fine view of the great peaks to the west. Ernest spent most mornings on an idea that had been incubating for several years. He wanted to do a full-length big book on the Spanish bullfight, complete with photographs. It must be interesting and wholly accurate. He started slowly but in the next two months wrote two hundred pages. When he was not working, Pauline and Bumby rode and fished with him. Small and slim in her jeans, her hair cut in a boyish style, Pauline sat well on her high black mount. Slowly they would file out, following a worn trail that angled up the slopes, the horses stepping carefully around the fallen timber. As the sun dipped behind Pilot Peak they would begin the long descent by another trail, finally trotting across the meadows to the ranch buildings.

During the few clear days, when the fishing was good, they took a large catch of rainbows and cutthroats. On September 13 Ernest and Pauline executed new wills leaving everything to each other. Ernest specifically entrusted Pauline with the responsibility for the maintenance, education, and support of his two sons, "John H.N. Hemingway and Patrick Hemingway." The next day Pauline and Bumby left for New York to meet Henriette, who would return with the boy to France.

On the morning of November 2 Pauline received bad news from Wyoming. Ernest was in St. Vincent's Hospital in Billings with a fractured right arm. The night before, while driving the Ford on a narrow, two-lane gravel highway, he was blinded by the lights of an oncoming car that had pulled out to pass another car. Ernest's Ford careened into a deep ditch and flipped over, and Ernest was pinned upside down behind the wheel. Dos Passos (who had come out in October) and one of the hands from L-Bar-T were thrown free with only minor bruises. They eased Ernest out of the wreckage and flagged down a passing motorist.

Ernest's injury was diagnosed as an oblique spiral fracture, nearly compound, three inches above the elbow. After surgery, the break was bound with kangaroo tendons and the long incision sewn up. For a month he was immobilized in the hospital bed. Pauline, who had come to Billings immediately, sat with him all day, every day, reading to him and sending notes to friends all over the world. "The poor fellow has had a very tough time of it, with pain practically all the time, and sleepless nights. It's been more than four weeks now since he changed his position," she wrote to Grace and Sunny. "The numbness in the elbow and the paralysis of the wrist still persist, but the doctor seems to think these will clear up later. But it will be a long time before the arm will be ready for active service again."

When Ernest's pain began to subside and he was sleeping better, Pauline offered to take dictation for the bullfighting book. That did not sound practical to Ernest, but he did enjoy dictating long, single-spaced letters, which she took down on the typewriter. In mid-December he was discharged from the hospital and they returned by train to Arkansas in time for Christmas. Pauline was in a fine mood, grateful to be out of the depressing hospital atmosphere, but Ernest was still grouchy from the long inactivity. Finally in mid-January they departed for Key West. Pauline settled Ernest, Jinny, Patrick, Henriette (back from Paris), and herself into a rented house on the corner of Whitehead and United Avenues and hired new household help. His arm almost completely healed, Ernest returned to the bullfight manuscript and began to formulate plans for a trip to Spain later in the spring.

In February, Grace Hemingway came to Florida to visit her youngest daughter, Carol, who was a freshman at Rollins College, and to enjoy her first look at her grandson, Patrick. In their travels back and forth to Arkansas, neither Pauline nor Ernest had brought Patrick to Oak Park, although Grace had suggested such a visit in many of her letters. Patrick remembers his Pfeiffer grandparents as a significant presence in his childhood. But he perceived his Hemingway grandmother as a large, strange woman whom his father disliked. At the time of this visit to Key West, the trust fund conceived by Ernest, Pauline, and Gus Pfeiffer was in place. Pauline and Uncle Gus together contributed $20,000. and Ernest put in most of his earnings from *A Farewell to Arms*—$30,000. It was a generous decision and he was proud of it. As he once wrote Fitzgerald, "The only thing in life I've ever had any luck being decent about is money so am very splendid and punctilious about that."

Grace was full of gratitude. She had written Ernest again and again that she was overwhelmed by Pauline's munificence as well as his. But the nature of the relationship between mother and son was such that frequent misunderstandings cropped up in their correspondence. Grace would pontificate and Ernest would take umbrage. Then Grace would try to apologize. She realized that she had a penchant for saying the wrong thing—things that irritated him— and she conceded that it was an unfortunate weakness on her part. Would he try to be understanding? After all, life was so short; why remember only the criticisms and disagreements?

Unfortunately, Ernest was too hardened to change his harsh view of her. And there was another addition to his list of grievances—the conviction that his mother had driven his father to suicide. He would suggest such a possibility a few years later in the short story "Fathers and Sons," in which a mature Nick Adams is driving across the country from Key West to Arkansas accompanied by his nine-year-old son. Nick ruminates about his father, describing the same flaws in Dr. Adams's character that had so disturbed the young Hemingway—his nervousness and sentimentality, the unexpected cruelties, the foolishness of the so-called sex instruction. Obeisance, however, is paid to the big frame, the quick movements, the magnificent eyes. There is everlasting gratitude for the fishing and the shooting, " . . . a passion that had never slackened. . . . [It seemed to Nick that] his father was as sound on those two things as he was unsound on sex."

But casting a shadow over all the reminiscences and brought up to the surface for the first time in "Fathers and Sons" was the painful subject of his father's suicide. "If he wrote it he could get rid of it. He had gotten rid of many things by writing them," says Nick to himself. Now Ernest was seeking to reconcile the hated flaw of cowardice in the once-adored man who had sired him. He was not yet prepared to put the blame on his mother. But there was a hint of such blame in his groping for absolution of the victim. "He had died in a trap that he had helped only a little to set, and they had all betrayed him in their various ways before he died." "They" later became "she" as Ernest continued to brood over the shameful deed. (Carol Gardner, who lived at home for two years after her father's death, believes that her mother's grief was genuine, that Ernest was wrong-headed to insist that Grace did not love and appreciate her husband when he was alive.)

If Grace became aware of this aspect of Ernest's hostility, she never acknowledged it. At this point of her widowhood she was absorbed by her many interests. The economic jolt of Dr. Hemingway's death was now alleviated by the trust fund. She bought a second-hand Pontiac and learned to drive it. As she traveled around the country with sketch pad and brushes and paints, she painted seascapes in Nantucket and desert mesas in New Mexico. Sometimes she worked from inside the car to escape the flies and mosquitoes. When her paintings failed to sell, she tried to get satisfaction from her pupils' accomplishments.

No one heard her complain of loneliness. She drove from place to place, visiting the children and the grandchildren, but only for a few days at a time, always appearing in long dresses and high, white, laced boots. The new freedom she enjoyed probably compensated in some ways for the loneliness that she kept to herself. Even as she grieved for Ed, there was a sense of relief, a release of creative energy. As she adjusted to the changes after his death, the force of her own ego sustained her. The qualities that had alienated Ernest and irritated even the most devoted of her children—the stubborn belief in her own opinions, the self-importance, the pride and vanity —these traits were the same qualities that rescued her from a timid, bereft old age.

In March Pauline missed her period and a local doctor confirmed that she could expect a baby sometime in November. At once she began to house hunt, this time with feverish urgency. Their needs were becoming clear. There must be a place for Ernest to write in seclusion, rooms for Patrick, the new baby, and visiting older brother, and a semblance of luxury in the master bedroom. Next to reading, gardening was Pauline's favorite hobby. So there must be plenty of yard space. And whatever its basic design, the house must be European in flavor to provide the right background for her fifteenth-century Spanish antiques.

The least prepossessing property turned out to have the most possibilities—a neglected mansion that Pauline had seen the year before and had referred to since as that "damned haunted house." It was at 907 Whitehead, on a fine corner lot, built in 1851 by a shipping tycoon. Behind the decay was a structure of dignity and sound materials—white stone, heart of pine shipped from Georgia, delicate wrought-iron railings. The windows were long and graceful, with old shutters that could be restored to their original beauty. The steep staircase rose to a second-floor center hall separating the master suite from a children's wing that included a sitting room and high, old-fashioned bathroom, intricately tiled. Tall French doors opened to a loggia that surrounded the entire second floor. There was a carriage house, a twenty-thousand-gallon cistern, and open fireplaces in several rooms. Gus Pfeiffer came down to provide the cash and negotiate the sale. It was consummated on April 29, 1931, for $8,000., with the title made over to Ernest and Pauline. Ernest was somewhat self-conscious that his first house was paid for by his wife's uncle. And Pauline knew enough to be apprehensive about the problems that could come from trying to renovate an eighty-year-old house. The windows were broken, the plaster crumbling, the plumbing antique. Every door in the house was warped and the floor sagged.

But there was no time to be anxious about the future. Too much was happening in the present. Ernest left a few days later for Havana to board the S.S. *Volendam* for Vigo, Spain. Pauline would leave for New York with Patrick and Henriette to make a late May sailing of the S.S. *President Harding* for Cherbourg. The plans called for Ernest to work in Madrid while Pauline packed up the Key West house, tended to business matters in Paris, and eventually met him in Hendaye Plage. "I am going to be a good girl and be sweet and patient and try to love Motherhood, but what will make me really content will be you," she wrote on May 6 from Key West. There was no troublesome nausea with this pregnancy and she operated in the oppressive heat with great energy, along with Jinny, who had come to help wind things up. On May 13 she wrote Ernest, "I miss you all the time and I don't care about daily events and all I want is you. You are the punctuation and grammar as well as the exciting story."

When she arrived in New York Uncle Gus showed her his new Hudnut headquarters and laboratory in the old B. Altman Building on Eighteenth Street and Aunt Louise went with her to the top of the Empire State Building, recently opened. "I hate to take this fine stationery to tell you," she reported to Ernest on the ship's letterhead, "that we are now at sea with 150 Gold Star mothers. . . . the boat is very dull without you, even though those gold star mothers are little cutups."

In Paris she found thirteen letters from Ernest, "each more lovely than the rest, full of love, and neat, which is the ideal combination." She prepared at once to send Henriette and Patrick to Bordeaux, made arrangements to ship the furniture, stored in Paris, to Key West, and then succumbed to the temptations of Paris shopping. "Spending still pretty bad," she confessed, "but I don't want nor expect any birthday present and will turn in any birthday checks received." She described her new permanent wave, hoping Ernest would not be disappointed. She thought it was lovely and soft and not at all like artificial curling. "I think you will like it. Hurry up and grow yours and I will make braids or buckles in the back on rainy afternoons."

At this time Pauline began to refer hopefully to the coming child as Little Pilar, "a nice small girl who will be easily gotten into the world." Since she had already borne a son, it was now her open and fervent wish to present Ernest with a daughter. He made no secret of the fact that this was his wish as well. He wrote Waldo Peirce that he wanted a girl "very much, but so far have never had a legitimate nor illegit daughter so don't know how to go about it." Having grown up in a household with four sisters, he was accustomed to the company of females, especially if he could assume the bossy role of big brother, and he had seen the devotion of his sisters to Ed Hemingway. There was a protective instinct at work in Ernest, a paternalism that lately came to be expressed in his using the term "daughter" with his wife and woman friends. An old superstition about a man who could not beget daughters being less than a man may also have had some relevance, since Ernest could be as superstitious as a medieval peasant. As Pauline's belly grew, she fantasized with greater intensity the satisfaction to be enjoyed if she were the lucky wife who gave him the daughter. Her strict Catholic upbringing left her no choice in the matter of pregnancy and contraception, but there is scant evidence that she hungered for motherhood. What she hungered for was Ernest. Whatever pleased him was sure to please her.

Early in June Ernest had journeyed to Paris to escort Bumby back to Spain for a holiday. It was the first time the boy had seen his father and mother together since the divorce. "I want your advice," Hadley had written Ernest in April, "and [your] opinion as a friend, on Paul's and my situation, particularly a propos of Bumbi. We have been up hill and down dale since last I saw you. Will you let me talk and you listen and then if you'll talk, I'll listen. Maybe you can help clarify things for me." Evidently he did, for on June 15 she wrote him a letter that overflowed with gratitude. "There was never anything did anybody so much good as that visit of yours did me. Bumbi was *mad* about it, but I just want especially to speak about myself. It literally did my heart good and my heart wasn't in a good state at all."

Ernest had left to meet Pauline in Madrid, and it was there that they met Jay Allen, a reporter for the *Chicago Tribune*. Ernest, alone at a local bar, had struck up a conversation with Allen. When Allen compared Hemingway's fiction to that of Chekhov, Ernest decided he should meet Pauline. The two men walked over to the dining room of the Biarritz, a hostelry selected by Ernest because it was frequented by matadors. Pauline, who had expected Ernest some two hours earlier, was in no mood to be placated. "Here's a guy named Allen who likes "Hills Like White Elephants," said Ernest proudly. Allen's recollection was that Pauline could not have been less interested. "Haven't you noticed that the place is closed? We won't get any lunch here," she said frostily and marched out ahead of them.

Allen did not realize that such a display of pique was out of character for Pauline. The heat, the pregnancy, and their fleabag accommodations had done nothing for her disposition. In reality what troubled her most was the decision about where the baby should be born. Should they go to Paris or to Piggott and then on to Kansas City, where Dr. Guffey, who knew her medical history and whose judgment she trusted, could perform the Caesarean? Mary Hickok supplied detailed information about French hospitals and medical care, but on September 7 Ernest reported from Spain that a compromise had been worked out. "Pauline left last night for Paris. We are going to play the overture in Kansas City [bypassing Piggott], leaving around the last of September."

They sailed on the *Ile de France*, and with them went an exciting material acquisition, *The Guitar Player*, a painting by the Spanish cubist Juan Gris, who had died in 1927. Ernest, who had a shrewd eye for art, stated that he had used up most of their passage money to pay for the painting. This was a typical Hemingway exaggeration, since it was not really that expensive, but it was a valuable work, even in 1931. Pauline was now in her seventh month, still handling the pregnancy well but in no condition to appreciate the ship's cuisine or wine list or merrymaking. Donald Ogden Stewart was on board with his pregnant wife, and the two expectant fathers cavorted with a passenger from Havana, Jane Mason, wife of G. Grant Mason, head of Pan American Airways in Cuba.

At twenty-two Jane was already a recognized beauty. She was of medium height, with a slender, well-proportioned body, exquisitely formed features, and blue eyes. Her strawberry-blonde hair was parted in the middle and drawn demurely away from her face to create an illusion of serene purity. There was nothing demure about her personality, for she danced and drank with great verve. Born Jane Welch in Tuxedo Park, New York, on June 24, 1909, she took

*Jane Kendall Mason. From a
portrait by Simon Elwes, 1936.*
Courtesy Jane Gingrich

the name Kendall when her mother remarried. As an art student at
the Briarcliff School in New York, she had begun to show a talent
for sculpting and painting, but her studies were secondary to her
social life. She was presented to Washington, D.C. society at not one
but two debuts, and after the season, at eighteen, she married Grant
Mason, whose career was as promising as his family connections
were impeccable.

By the time the *France* dropped anchor in New York harbor, not
only Ernest but Pauline and Jane Mason had become friends, and
they exchanged addresses. Ernest and Pauline checked into the
Brevoort and entertained callers in their suite as they balanced
breakfast or dinner trays on their knees. Late in October it was time
to go to Kansas City "to play the overture" as Ernest had put it.
Pauline went into labor on Armistice Day, November 11, 1931, at 6:00
P.M., and subsequently was admitted to Research Hospital. She was
in severe labor for nearly twelve hours while the doctor stood by,
hoping for a normal delivery, but finally it was necessary to perform
a Caesarean section.

Ernest provided all the details in the form of a log to his mother-in-law, explaining angrily that Pauline had suffered terribly for seven fruitless hours. When the ordeal was finally over, however, Pauline had none of the postsurgical misery that she had experienced after Patrick, and a blissful amnesia about most of the agony Ernest had witnessed. Gregory Hancock (the "Hancock" from Grace's mother) weighed nine pounds, had a full head of blue-black hair, and a strong little body. He was named Gregory after any number of bad popes, joked his father. There was no mention that either parent was disappointed because of the child's sex. That seemed sensibly put aside as they rejoiced over his excellent health.

Chapter 14

"Depression and all," Hadley wrote Ernest on December 16, 1931, "Bumby and I are going to the Hotel Edelweiss at Combloux for three weeks." This was the region called Haute Savoie, so evocative of past holidays with Ernest. North into Switzerland was the Gangwisch pensione at Chamby, where she had first learned to ski. A few kilometers to the east was the St. Bernard Pass, scene of the famous springtime hike with Chink Dorman-Smith in 1923. But this was not the season for nostalgia. On her immediate horizon momentous changes were in the air. Paul Mowrer was at last able to go ahead with his divorce proceedings. Winifred had moved to a small Normandy dairy farm, leaving the house at Crecy for Hadley and Paul. Legal matters moved slowly in France, but Hadley expressed no complaints to Ernest as 1932 approached, only wished him the merriest of holidays and the luckiest of New Years. ". . . better eyes, more books, and no more infants" was the way she signed off.

Amen, muttered the new father in Key West as the French nurse, Gabrielle, took to her bed with homesickness, and an angry Patrick sprayed his baby brother with mosquito powder. Pauline, directing her crew of workmen from a makeshift bed in the living room, quickly read Ernest's mood and ordered the workers to set up a study in the old carriage house. On January 21, 1932, Ernest wired Perkins that the rewrite of *Death in the Afternoon* was finished and would be typed by Lorine Thompson, Jinny Pfeiffer, and some of Lorine's high school students.

With Jinny's help Pauline continued to direct the renovation, which proceeded slowly. When the ceiling plaster began to fall into the babies' cribs, Jinny draped bolts of cheesecloth to protect their eyes. Everytime it rained the roof leaked. Meals were casual, since kitchen plumbing and wiring were obsolete. When he was not fishing or working on the bullfight book Ernest, who assumed the medical wisdom of his late father, lectured Pauline on how to preserve her insides, or confided in Mary Pfeiffer. "There is no way a woman can be more completely and utterly ruined," he wrote, "than by not being careful for eight weeks after a baby is born. Until the placental site is healed."

He also began to fret to Mary Pfeiffer about the book and the quality of the revision.

> If this book is punk, it won't do any good to take the readers if there should be any, aside and say, "But you ought to see what a big boy Gregory is and just look at the big scar on my arm and you ought to see our wonderful water-work system and I go to church every sunday and am a good father to my family" . . . . I happen to be in a very tough business, where there are no alibis. . . . Taking refuge in domestic successes, being good to your broke friends etc. is merely a form of quitting.

By February some order had been restored to the house and the completed manuscript, *Death in the Afternoon*, was mailed off to Perkins. A cabinetmaker, Otto Bruce, was commissioned to build an oversized bed for Pauline and Ernest and some special handcrafted pieces to complement the imported ones. Jinny was preparing to sail for Paris, and Pauline, ruefully admitting that Gabrielle would never adjust to Key West, paid her passage back to France and went to New York to locate a new nurse. The city was full of misery, she reported to Ernest, with bread lines forming and a pinched look to many of the people. But their own situation was snug and comfortable. A thousand dollars had just been deposited to her trust account and she was trying to get tickets to see *The Barretts of Wimpole Street* with Katherine Cornell before leaving. She reported her good fortune in locating an authoritative Yankee woman named Ada Stern who came highly recommended. In addition to being nanny to the boys Ada could manage the domestic help.

As soon as she returned to Key West, Pauline assembled an

adequate staff from the many unemployed islanders, most of whom were short on training but eager to earn a livelihood. She paid top wages and Ernest gave tips. Pauline was polite to the townspeople but remained aloof, for she had an aristocratic sense of her place in life. Her natural wit did not always assert itself, even in the presence of Ernest's friends, but it was there, as evidenced by her letters and the testimony of her intimates. Perhaps it was self-protection that moved her to maintain a certain watchfulness.

Guests were mercifully scarce during the spring and Ernest took off in April to fish Cuban waters on Josie Russell's small fishing boat, the *Anita.* In his absence Pauline gave her undivided attention to household matters. Workmen were still swarming about. The kitchen, formerly separated from the main house by a breezeway, was being moved forward to become adjacent to the butler's pantry, which could then become the children's dining room. The floors were stripped and then left unfinished until special ceramic tiles could be imported from Cuba. The place was habitable but far from finished. Pauline was in no hurry. She had a clear picture of the effect she eventually wanted to create—a Mediterranean atmosphere in an aging but carefully restored American residence. When Ada, the new nanny, was sufficiently trained in the ways of the children and staff, Pauline joined Ernest in Havana. He had made a marvelous discovery—the sport of marlin fishing, "utterly satisfying as a sport, a living, a spectacle, and a form of exercise." Between fishing trips he read proofs of *Death in the Afternoon* and made progress on some short stories. After Pauline's arrival the pace of social life quickened. From her sunny second-floor room at the Ambos Mundos Hotel she called up Jane Mason, their fellow passenger from the *Ile de France.* The Masons introduced the Hemingways to Cuban café society, with dancing under the royal palms of the Sans Souci and midnight gambling at the roulette tables. Grant Mason owned Jaimanitas, a fine estate west of the city, and maintained a forty-six-foot Matthews cruiser, the *Pelican II.*

Jane was passionately devoted to sports fishing and was one of the few women in Cuban society who participated in pigeon-shooting at the Club de Cazadores. She was at home in the company of men and insisted upon being treated as "one of the boys." This was not always possible. Her beauty stood in the way of such a hope, as the men jumped to bring her a drink or hold her special lightly loaded

The "aging but carefully restored" residence of Pauline and Ernest, 907 Whitehead Street, Key West.

Ernest at Nordquist Ranch, 1932.

shells. Ernest, however, treated her as an able sportswoman who was eager to learn and wanted no special consideration. Slipping easily into the brotherly role, he patiently taught her everything about marlin fishing as he learned it.

Jane quickly became friends with both Hemingways. She admired Pauline for the way she took care of Ernest and sensed a stability in the marriage that was lacking in her own. Perhaps she had married too young. Certainly her husband's stolid personality clashed with her own restlessness. Though she enjoyed deep-sea fishing and all sports and performed them well, these activities were not enough to satisfy her. She had adopted two little boys and loved them dearly, but she entrusted them to the care of an English nanny. In an attempt to develop other interests, she began to sculpt again and tried opening a craft shop, since she had an eye for native art. But the restlessness persisted.

Periodically, Jane struggled with deep feelings of inadequacy, and her moods could swing sharply from elation to despondency. Her husband sensed that she was bored with him—and with her life— and wondered whether her frequent consultations with doctors were a form of weakness. Privately he believed that she sought attention from doctors and that they coddled her. The physicians, however, realized that she was deeply disturbed and suggested hospitalization on a number of occasions, not apparently for any specific psychiatric treatment but to remove Jane from her troubled atmosphere.

Pauline, who did not care for ocean fishing, saw that Ernest was stimulated by Jane Mason, but she did not yet feel threatened. For the time being, Jane really did seem more interested in friendship. Pauline believed, probably correctly, that Ernest did not have much patience with high-strung women, and this may have made her feel that the friendship would be short-lived.

This was the situation for the week of Pauline's stay in Havana. After she left, Ernest stayed on, writing fairly steadily in the early mornings and fishing in the afternoons and on weekends with Jane and Josie off the *Anita*. Someone, not Ernest, wrote in the ship's log, "Ernest loves Jane." What did pass between them probably was not love—it very likely was too soon for that—but the agreeable sexual excitement they had enjoyed on the *France*. The fact that they were both married did not inhibit them because strictly speaking they had not yet broken any rules. Jane was a perfect fishing partner. She was beautiful to look at, she was amusing, she handled the rod expertly. She never got seasick and she could help with the cooking. It was an ideal setup and Ernest relished it.

On May 10, his fifth wedding anniversary, Ernest was still in Havana. Pauline was in Key West, and Jane was en route to New York to be hospitalized, not for an emotional problem this time but for surgery. Her mood suggested an edge of hysteria as she fired off oddly-worded cables to both Hemingways. From Jacksonville, Florida she cabled Ernest. "FELICEDADES. BOTTLE THROWING VERBOTEN IN PLANE. WAVED TEARY HANDKERCHIEF INSTEAD . . . LOVE TO ELEPHANTS AND GOCARTS. JANE." A second was addressed to Pauline. "YOU'LL FIND ANNIVERSARY PRESENT PAIR OF FLAMINGOES AWAITING YOU IN HAVANA STOP I MAY ACCEPT YOUR INVITATION AND STOP A NIGHT EN ROUTE IF CONVENIENT FOR YOU. LOVE JANE." The next day from New York she cabled Ernest again. "HU VOY PARA EUROPA SHOW STARTS FRIDAY MORNING DOCTORS HOSPITAL." Pauline's reaction to all this was to go to Havana for the weekend and obediently escort the birds back to Key West and make a home for them in her garden. After sending Ada and the little boys to Piggott, she was free to spend the rest of the month with Ernest in Havana.

By June 6, Jane was convalescing at her mother's estate in Tuxedo Park. "ARRIVING SATURDAY MORNING," she wired Ernest in Havana. "MAY I FISH SUNDAY. LOVE JANE." Pauline was on hand to greet her and then left for Arkansas. Again, Ernest stayed on for a few more weeks. From the tone of Pauline's letters at this time she was now reacting to her husband's rising interest in Jane Mason. When she heard from Ernest that on his last day at sea with Josie and Jane he played a big marlin for two hours and then lost it, she wrote, "Next year we'll go over and get enormous ones, you and me, and when you come here I'm not going to leave you again for a long long time. . . . I miss you very much and all the time and will follow you around like a little dog and so will Patrick. Gregory looks too swell with his four teeth and his silky, curly hair. . . . Hurry, hurry, hurry, can't wait any longer than is possible. I think you'll like me." This last reference was to a new hair style, with the flattering bangs she had worn when she first met Ernest in 1925. In Madrid in 1929 she had dyed her hair blonde, her first of many experiments with tints and new hair styles. This periodic attention to her hair generally occurred in response to Ernest's eyeing other women.

But the current other woman—Jane Mason—was temporarily out of his life, since he had set off for Arkansas in a new Ford V-8 roadster. After greeting his in-laws, he took Pauline to Wyoming for a long, golden summer at the Nordquist Ranch. "Well Pauline is cockeyed beautiful," Ernest reported to Guy Hickok. "Figure lovely after Greg born—never looked nor felt better." For a week he finished reading the galley proofs on *Death in the Afternoon.* Pauline wandered down to the corral to watch the horses being saddled up, hiked over sun-warmed pine needles, and sampled books and magazines from the big, closely-packed boxes that followed the Hemingways everywhere. A few days after their respective birthdays (Ernest thirty-three on July 21; Pauline thirty-seven on July 22), the galleys were mailed to Perkins. From then on the days disappeared easily, one into the other. Pauline was up with Ernest in the early morning, Stetson in place, to ride over the familiar trails. On September 22, she left reluctantly for Key West to attend to household decisions. Ernest and Charlie Thompson followed in the Ford roadster on October 16, driving the first three days in a blizzard so severe that Ernest rigged a candle in a tin can to defrost the windshield.

In Key West Pauline had arranged everything for Ernest's arrival. A welcome-home banquet was laid out—green turtle steak, black beans and rice, conch salad, good French wine. The workmen were called off the job and a grinning, affectionate nine-year-old Bumby, visiting from Paris, was reunited with his papa. But Pauline's own joy at seeing Ernest again was cut short by a frantic call from Piggott. Both Patrick and Gregory were down with whooping cough and neither Ada Stern nor Mary Pfeiffer could cope without her. So Pauline departed immediately for Arkansas. Ernest was left to wait anxiously for the reviews of *Death in the Afternoon* due in from the clipping service.

The book had come out in October and was enjoying good sales in spite of the poor state of the economy. Its dedication was simple —"To Pauline"—and it was no longer a straightforward account of the history and current condition of the Spanish bullfight but a discursive and highly personal text. Ernest uses the device of a dialogue between an old woman and the author to express his opinions on everything from male sexuality ("Three things keep boys from promiscuous intercourse, religious belief, timidity and fear of venereal diseases") to his enemy, the literary critic. When the old woman asks what he means by love, he replies, indirectly evoking the pain associated with leaving Hadley, "I would sooner have the pox than to fall in love with another woman loving the one I have." And with feeling and clarity he communicates his impressions of the Spanish landscape and personality.

The reviews of the book were lukewarm, nothing like what Ernest had hoped for. Some critics chided him for his crude vocabulary, others objected to what they called his morbid preoccupation with death. Robert Coates in *The New Yorker* accused him of petulance in his gibes at fellow authors such as William Faulkner and T.S. Eliot. And Max Eastman, who had praised his prose sketches in 1922, wrote a long critique in which he attacked Ernest's "juvenile romanticism." In a recent discussion of the book, Anthony Burgess accepts the remarks of Eastman and Coates as valid but believes that it "sheds many of its faults as it becomes weathered by time" and contains "insight and truth . . . not a book easy to shrug away."

From the left came rumblings of a different sort. Paul Romaine, a bookseller from Wisconsin, urged Ernest to stop writing about the lost generation (the generation that came of age during and immediately after World War I) and bulls, implying that there were more fundamental political concerns now, of which he should take note. Ernest replied that in writing there was neither right nor left, only good and bad. He had written the bullfight book, he explained, to organize and remember all that he had learned, and he was not going to follow fashions in politics.

After the first of the year, Ernest went to New York for business conferences. During that visit there occurred a family incident that for its unpleasantness and lasting consequences was one of the most disagreeable Ernest ever precipitated. It involved his sister Carol, and it was an example of the proprietary attitude he adopted toward people—especially women—for whom he felt responsible. During her tenure at Rollins College, Carol had become Ernest's favorite. She was the prettiest of Grace's daughters and the most literate— as a high-school student she had been editor of the literary quarterly and was honored at commencement for her writing ability. When Carol came to Key West she loved to fish with Ernest and would hold the rod patiently for hours in the broiling sun.

As an undergraduate, she had fallen in love with another student, John Gardner, and although she was now in Vienna studying French and German, she and the young man kept in close touch. Aware that she looked to Ernest as the head of the family, Gardner came around to the New York hotel where Ernest was staying to explain that he and twenty-one-year-old Carol had decided to get married. Ernest flew into a rage. He took an instant dislike to Gardner, who apparently gave the impression of being more idealistic than practical, and threatened to knock his teeth out if he made any more overtures to Carol.

Undeterred by Ernest's opposition, Gardner hurried off to Vienna and married Carol at the end of March. A relationship that Ernest had come to enjoy now came to an abrupt end. He never forgave Carol for marrying against his wishes. "Ernest was supporting me financially," said Carol Gardner, recalling the episode with a degree of forebearance. "And he believed himself to be exercising his duty. Besides," she added with a smile, "John and I decided to go into education and Ernest would hate that, you know. He heartily disapproved of teachers."

Carol's elopement was a shock to Grace as well, but she tried to make the best of it, recognizing that Carol was a strong-willed young woman, like all of her children. It was clear that Carol put her own happiness ahead of Ernest's objections. As for Grace, she thought this was rather "sporting of them."

Out of gratitude for the trust fund, she had offered to deed the Windemere cottage over to Ernest and begged him to make use of it. She made new curtains and rugs and painted special pictures for the walls. It had meant so much to his boyhood; wouldn't it be fine if his sons could enjoy it, too? If money was a little low for Ernest, Windemere could save his renting a place in Montana.

She was now following his career proudly, reading every story and news item as it came out. She made a special note about the story that appeared in the May issue of *Cosmopolitan*—how really good it was. (Her taste had developed. "After the Storm" is the terse account of a hard-bitten diver-sailor who is the first to find a sunken ship but, for want of adequate equipment, loses out on the chance to recover the booty.) When *Time* ran a photo of Ernest and a black marlin he landed, Grace was ecstatic. As far as she was concerned he was as great a success at fishing as at everything else. After months of frustration she was finally able to boast, just a little, about herself. She had been invited to exhibit ten or twelve of her pictures at the Chicago World's Fair. What a wonderful adventure, she exclaimed. Things were looking better.

In spite of carpenters and painters, noisy children, and a tropical menagerie (four raccoons, eighteen goldfish, a possum, three peacocks, and now two flamingoes), Pauline labored with good humor to create an environment in which Ernest could flourish. Her reward was his departure on April 12, 1933, for another two months of fishing along the Cuban coast. Although she knew that Havana meant more of Jane Mason she passed it off with a rueful joke. "Am having large nose, imperfect lips, protruding ears and warts and moles all taken off before coming to Cuba," she wrote Ernest on April 28. "Thought I better, Mrs. Mason and those Cuban women are so lovely. Bumby is wondering whether he is going to see Mrs. Mason in Cuba. Says Bumby, 'I certainly hope I do.'"

Bumby soon got his wish. On May 3 Pauline escorted him to Havana. It was lonesome and wet, she wrote, with "no papa to admire with red-orange brown skin and handsome moustache over tightly closed mouth." He must not worry about money, she wrote, for she had received an interest check from her father and would keep the house accounts separate.

"The place is again in the hands of my enemies, the workmen," she lamented toward the end of May. She was sublimating her loneliness by improving the garden, which now bloomed with fig and lime trees and lush palms gathered from distant keys. Gregory was thriving physically but lonesome for Ada (who had now taken Patrick to visit his father). According to Pauline, Gregory had turned into "the lousiest type of mama's boy" in Ada's absence, clinging to Pauline and howling when she was out of sight. She bragged about his adorable ways, but it was beginning to rankle that he was not the daughter she had prayed for.

In Havana, Ernest was fishing in the Gulf Stream and writing about it for Arnold Gingrich, whom he had met in New York in January and who had persuaded Ernest to do a series of articles for his new men's magazine, *Esquire*. The first one, "A Cuban Letter," recounted the magic of pulling away from San Francisco wharf in the early morning, and described the pleasure of hot lunches cooked over an open fire on a deserted beach and the thrill of battling a 750-pound marlin. What Ernest did not share with his *Esquire* readers, but which lent a special zest to the days on the water and the nights in town, was the presence of Jane Mason.

"Finest life you ever saw," he wrote happily to Janet Flanner, the Paris correspondent for *The New Yorker*. And it was, for him at least, the best of all worlds. The words were flowing, the fish were biting, and back in Key West was the house, the lovable children, the devoted wife, to form that warm and welcoming refuge for which he periodically hungered. Havana, where he docked his boat and worked and sometimes prowled, was a wide-open city, but it was not Ernest's habit to look for casual sex. Whatever he might proclaim in rough talk to his men friends, he was sensitive and proud and entered into sexual liaisons warily.

Although twice married, his experience with women had been limited. From a brief, intense worship of Agnes, he had rebounded to a traditional marriage with Hadley. Duff had come into his life when he was not prepared to be unfaithful, and deceiving Hadley with Pauline had left him bruised and guilty. But now he was older, more sophisticated, and he could rationalize that his sexual relationship with Pauline was not entirely satisfying. Accepting the strict admonition of her Kansas City obstetrician that she not become pregnant for a third time, Ernest claimed that it was necessary to practice coitus interruptus, since other forms of birth control were prohibited by her Catholicism. In his memoir, Gregory Hemingway questioned this reasoning, finding it strange that a doctor's son would not know that there were certain times when couples can have satisfactory intercourse without undue anxiety about pregnancy. But some sexual coolness had set in, as their long separations might suggest. Ernest, not Pauline, initiated the separations. It is possible that absence for him was a form of birth control.

Jane Mason found it easy to be drawn to Ernest. Their life on the sea was stimulating, and Ernest at this time was at his most engaging. He was a literary celebrity and sportsman combined. There was the flashing wit and the unexpectedly quiet sensitivity, the dazzling smile breaking over the dark, piratical face. Patrick Hemingway has postulated that Ernest, who had read Turgenev's *Torrents of Spring*, may have likened Jane to the Russian heroine, Maria Nikolaevna, herself twenty-two and rich, locked in a marriage of convenience to the heavy-lidded Polosov. In the society of twentieth-century America, no less than nineteenth-century Russia, a wealthy woman preserved her freedom of movement best by being safely married. Discreet affairs were tolerated. So Jane saw Ernest freely, with and without Grant, mostly on the *Anita*, but occasionally around the city and at her home.

Exactly how they conducted their love affair is unclear. "Not on the boat," said Jack Hemingway. "Too much was going on, and Papa would not carry on in front of the crew. They were his buddies." Ernest later bragged to Jack that Jane liked to climb through the transom into his hotel room at the Ambos Mundos, where he kept a room when he went to Cuba to fish. Almost fifty years later, after the death of her fourth husband, when she was incapacitated from a crippling stroke, Jane replied haltingly to questions by the author that she had almost married Ernest. There were no arguments between them, she said, only good-natured teasing, and if neither one had been married at the time, perhaps they would have married each other.

On May 27 the first of two incidents occurred that put Jane in jeopardy for the rest of the year. As she was driving Bumby and Patrick back to Jaimanitas in her large Packard, she was forced off the narrow country road by a Ford bus out of control. Her car rolled down a ravine, landing upside down. Miraculously the automobile was not seriously damaged, and the boys were not hurt. With great presence Jane turned off the ignition and helped them out of the car. But she herself was badly shaken, wondering over and over if somehow the accident was her fault. She did not believe she was speeding, though she often drove her car very fast.

A few days later she fell or jumped from the second-story balcony of Jaimanitas and broke her back in what may have been a suicide attempt. It was not the first time she had tried suicide, but her husband had not been particularly alarmed by any of the previous incidents. None had caused serious injury and he tended to regard them as a further bid for attention. This time, however, Mason recognized the severity of the situation and sent Jane, accompanied by a nurse, to New York on a Ward Line vessel. Their stateroom was equipped with special bars on the portholes. In New York, Jane was hospitalized for five months and agreed to psychoanalysis with

Dr. Lawrence Kubie, a prominent Freudian of good reputation who enjoyed Grant Mason's trust. Jane's back eventually healed, though she was in a brace for a year, and she cut back on her drinking.

The evidence for Ernest's reaction to Jane's acts of desperation is contradictory. When questioned about the enigmatic title of his short story, "A Way You'll Never Be," he had said it was an effort to cheer up a hell of a nice girl going crazy from day to day. The implication was that Nick Adams, suffering from nightmares, was "much nuttier" than this girl was ever going to be. Everyone assumed that the "nice girl" he referred to was Jane. Ernest's explanation in a letter to his mother-in-law was more concrete. He said that Mrs. Mason had broken her back in an accident with the children, and that continued to be the impression shared by Ernest's sons. But in a crass joke to Dos Passos, he later referred to her as the girl who fell for him literally. Perhaps the tasteless joke helped to deflect the anxiety that any suggestion of suicide triggered in him. Ernest resisted falling in love with women who had emotional problems. He liked to describe his various wives as "happy, healthy, hard as a rock." So while he may have been greatly attracted to Jane, even in love with her, he carefully avoided taking any responsibility for her disturbed state.

Ernest did not see Jane again for the rest of the year. Coming up in a short time was a trip of major significance that he had been planning for months—a safari to East Africa preceded by a long European holiday. Gus Pfeiffer had offered to finance the trip in the amount of $25,000, a vast sum in 1933 when banks were failing, millions were out of work, and factories were shut down. Charlie Thompson would accompany Ernest and Pauline for the African leg of the trip. In July Ernest returned to Key West to make last-minute preparations, and Pauline moved ahead decisively with all the details of servants and child care. The Hemingway party that sailed out of Havana on August 4 was composed of Pauline, Ernest, Jinny, Patrick, and Bumby. Gregory was left behind with Ada, a situation that loomed large in the bitter memory of the adult Gregory Hemingway in forming his belief that his brother, not he, was his mother's favorite.

In Bordeaux, Patrick's former nurse, Henriette, looked after the two boys while Pauline and Jinny stayed in Madrid with Ernest. In October the women left for Paris. "Who do you think called up?"

wrote Pauline to Ernest on October 19. "Mrs. Mowrer! . . . Hadley is very happy, grand, big fur coat. Didn't see Paul as he had not returned from Geneva." Hadley and Paul had been married in London on July 3, 1933. Hadley now had no doubts about her future. She and Paul had been lovers and friends for five years. Not the least of her respect for him grew out of his tender concern for Bumby, who would now come under his influence.

After Hadley's marriage a relationship began that, for Pauline at least, vindicated her early determined efforts to win Hadley's friendship. No longer were her motives suspect. Everybody could see that Hadley was more compatible with Paul than she had been with Ernest. And Ernest had, in the long run, been more of a help to Hadley than a hindrance. Dos Passos put it simply. Hadley had been at loose ends when she met Ernest. He had given her a sense of belonging and had been more of a "builder-upper" than a "tearer-downer" for his first wife.

Upon his arrival in Paris Ernest read the batch of reviews that greeted the publication of his latest collection of short stories, *Winner Take Nothing*. There is great diversity among the stories. In "Fathers and Sons" he explores the relationships between the generations, especially as it related to him and his father. "A Clean Well-Lighted Place"' is a symbolic rendition of the universal struggle against loneliness and despair. "Homage to Switzerland" takes an ironic look at the shamefaced feelings of embarrassment that accompany divorce. But most of the critics passed over these stories to attack him for themes in some others—castration ("God Rest You Merry, Gentleman"), prostitution ("The Light of the World"), lesbianism ("The Sea Change"). T.S. Matthews accused him of writing about the kind of "abnormalities that fascinate adolescents but really have nothing to do with the price of bread." Ernest had predicted such a reaction, to Mary Pfeiffer. "I don't expect anybody to like the present book of stories. . . . [they] are mostly about things and people that people won't care about—or will actively dislike." But his pride was stung nevertheless.

When Charlie Thompson arrived in November for the imminent departure for Africa, Ernest became the good Paris guide. Much had changed since the twenties. Montparnasse had been taken over by the bourgeoisie and the Dôme was crowded with refugees from the

Nazi terror. Duff Twysden had long since left Paris. For a time she and her husband, Clinton King, lived on the shores of Lake Chapala in old Mexico. "We lived a different life from the rather senseless Montparnasse days," recalled King. "I worked all day at painting while Duff drew her amusing sketches in watercolor, or posed for me, or read a great deal." The economist, Stuart Chase, and his wife met the Kings while vacationing in the area. " . . . we met together every night for conversation and . . . drinks," they recalled. Duff would arrive wearing a big Spanish hat and looking terribly attractive. One night she sang "sea shanties" for them. Another time she cried because it was her son's birthday and her former husband's family would not let her see the boy.

In the summer of 1933, Duff and Clinton moved to New York. Clinton's allowance from his family had been cut off when he married Duff and his resources were nearly exhausted. They were reduced to living on small checks that occasionally arrived from Duff's relatives in England and the rare sale of one of King's paintings. Clinton signed on as a WPA artist and they lived in a remodeled brownstone on East Ninth Street. One night at a party Duff came to the door to stand face to face with Harold Loeb. Harold later professed to be shocked by her appearance, implying that she had lost her looks. Duff's friends vehemently denied such a judgment, insisting that Duff was still elegant and lovely. Certainly she had never lost her spirit. She dyed her pepper-and-salt hair blonde and wore it cropped. She put together individual ensembles from remnants and odd, ornamental jewelry. Her appearance and style were not so different from the Lady Twysden of Montparnasse. But there was a contentment about her, a sense of her own worth that had been sadly missing in her Paris days.

Nine years later, on June 27, 1938, Duff Twysden King died of tuberculosis in Santa Fe, New Mexico, at the age of forty-five. According to her wishes she was cremated; there was no ceremony and no funeral. She had refused treatment for old tubercular lesions, presumably healed over, but at the very end permitted herself to be placed under the care of the sisters at St. Vincent's Hospital. Her life with King had been gracious and quiet, and if Ernest in *The Sun Also Rises* portrayed her wild years, what happened after Pamplona was quite the reverse. The legend of Duff Twysden was enshrined in the literature of the lost generation. The facts of her life were quite different.

Ernest's own love affair with the French capital had worn off. "It was a fine place to be quite young in," he wrote for *Esquire*, "and it is a necessary part of a man's education. . . . But she is like a mistress who does not grow old and she has other lovers now." He had proclaimed his preference for the great mountain peaks of Wyoming, the blue waters of the Dry Tortugas. Now he was poised to explore the part of East Africa that was the playground of the rich, an exotic enclave organized for the pleasure of white Europeans. He was in the process of constructing a new persona, that of rugged international sportsman.

Chapter 15

On December 10, 1933, a photograph of Ernest and Pauline appeared in the New York *Herald Tribune* over the announcement that the well-known couple had departed for Africa. Accompanied by Charles Thompson, they had sailed out of Marseilles harbor on November 22. Their vessel was the S.S. *General Metzinger*, slovenly and slow-moving. Pauline and Charles came down with food poisoning three days out of Marseilles but Ernest, who drank steadily during the cold, rainy passage, escaped with a mild form of diarrhea. At Mombasa, the port city of Kenya, Ernest put on a wide-brimmed Stetson and rolled up his shirt sleeves for the disembarking. Pauline, not to be outdone, wore an ankle-length white dress and gloves and carried a ruffled white parasol. "Pauline and I looked like missionaries," recalled Charles, "while Ernest had the distinct look of a whiskey drummer." After spending the weekend with a young British couple in the modern section of the city they rode the train to Nairobi, three hundred miles to the west. There Tanganyika Guides Ltd. assigned to them the experienced British white hunter, Philip Percival, who had been a resident of Kenya since 1919. He and his wife operated a large farm at Potha Hill in Machakos, twenty miles south of Nairobi. While preparations for the safari were under way, Pauline and Ernest and Charles stayed at the farm, hunting gazelle, impala, and guinea fowl on the Kapiti Plain. A friend of Jane Mason's, young Alfred Vanderbilt, was also staying at Potha Hill, and when he told Ernest he wanted to be a writer, Hemingway lectured to him paternally.

On the morning of December 20, four weeks since the Hemingway party had left Marseilles, they departed on safari. The crew included Ben Fourie, the white mechanic; a Kikuyu driver; and two gunbearers, or trackers, plus the porters and kitchen staff. Two lorries held the gear. The hunters rode in a high-clearance, open-sided vehicle. The destination was the vast game preserve of the Serengeti Plain to the southwest, where the lion was the prized trophy.

Two nonfiction accounts have come down to us from the safari —Ernest's published work, *Green Hills of Africa*, and Pauline's diary. "The writer has attempted to write an absolutely true book," explains Ernest in his introduction, "to see whether the shape of a country and the pattern of a month's action can, if truly presented, compete with a work of the imagination." Whether it does in fact compete with a work of the imagination was later a subject of controversy among the critics. But Hemingway certainly gives the reader the shape of the East African country and the pattern of the action. He also includes his own philosophy of the hunt, a long discourse on the grim challenges facing the honest writer, and a shamefaced analysis of his hunting competition with his friend Thompson. And although he invites his reader "to insert whatever love interest he or she may have at the time [of reading]," he himself would supply it only in the form of the comaraderie between him and Pauline, "P.O.M." (Poor Old Mama). By this time Ernest was Papa, or Poppa, originally Bumby's form of address but gradually adopted, with Ernest's encouragement, by his entire circle.

The other report of the safari is Pauline's log, written as she moved from camp to camp. Crammed with details of geography and wildlife, it hints rather than dwells on her changing moods and always communicates her highly personal reactions. At the border crossing into Tanganyika, while the guns were being dismantled, inspected, and stamped, she watched a flirtation heat up between a handsome black man and two women. When the older, less attractive woman left the scene, the young couple laughed and wrestled and finally retired to a nearby hut. For the first time she saw Masai warriors, shiny black and "snooty." At a rest camp she enjoyed a good night's sleep in a plastered hut under a wide mosquito net and awoke the next morning to begin the long, dusty ride to Arusha. "Kilimanjaro kept appearing and disappearing high in the air like a Cheshire cat."

In Arusha there was a good hotel with a swimming pool, comfortable rooms, and a continental menu. From there they drove west, climbing to the high region of Ngorongoro Crater, and on Christmas day descended to the Serengeti plain. Temporary camps were set up along the three-day route. The first view of the Serengeti was spectacular with great herds of wildebeest moving in all directions, zebras, gazelles, and an enormous bird population. Pauline shot five sandgrouse herself, "two on the wing." Christmas dinner was served at the campsite, a clearing in a clump of shade trees at the foot of a rocky hill. Evenings were the best—first, the warm bath prepared by the porters in a canvas tub; then, good whiskey in front of the fire. In blue dressing gown and mosquito boots Pauline listened to Ernest and Philip exchange anecdotes. She liked Percival for his modesty, skill, and equable temperament.

There was no shortage of lions in the area. The only question was which ones to go after. Mr. P. examined them all with his powerful field glasses, eliminating the females, the ones that were too young, the ones with unimpressive manes. Everyone agreed that Pauline should have the first shot when the right one came along.

Eventually Percival selected the lion for her, "a light lion, old, with not too big a mane," she wrote. With her small Mannlicher she shot from a kneeling position but missed. Then Ernest shot with his big Springfield and the animal went down. M'Cola, the squat, black, bald gunbearer who had christened Pauline "Mama" and was devoted to her exclusively, drew up close and determined that the lion was dead. Ernest's account in *Green Hills* has M'Cola shaking Pauline's hand most solemnly, then announcing to all, "Mama hit . . . Mama piga. Piga Simba." When they reached base camp the porters, the cook, the skinner, and the boys, hearing M'Cola shout "Mama piga Simba," commenced dancing. Keeping time, and chanting from down in their chests, they produced a sound that began as a cough and then came out as "Hey la Mama! Hey la Mama!" Pauline was lifted high in the air, very carefully, carried round and round the fire, and finally at her tent set down gently.

The entry in her diary was straight to the point. "Very splendid; wished I had shot the lion. Gave everybody a shilling." Ernest supplied some dialogue in *Green Hills:*

Until P.O.M.'s license ran out, she was [M'Cola's] favorite and we were simply a lot of people who interfered and kept Mama from shooting things.

"Good old Mama," I said. "You killed him."

"No, I didn't. Don't lie to me. Just let me enjoy my triumph."

Ernest's own triumphs were more elusive. He still expected to be first in everything. But as they moved from camp to camp and the targets changed from waterbuck to eland to buffalo to leopard it was Charlie Thompson who turned up with the phenomenal trophies. Even Ernest's lion, which he finally shot on January 11, 1934, though handsome and light in color, was not as large as the one Thompson had bagged the week before. Pauline, who understood his competitive urges, noted that Ernest's lion at least did not smell so bad as Charlie's, "which smelled like a vampire." To add to his discouragement Ernest began to suffer from diarrhea. At first he ignored it. Then he tried dosing himself with various remedies, none of them effective. He became weak and dehydrated. Pauline lost her enthusiasm for the sun-baked plains and the continuous killing. She began to worry that he would collapse in some remote place where there would be no help.

On January 14, 1934, after hours of vigorous bird-shooting, Ernest returned to camp in such great pain (from a prolapse of the lower intestine) that Philip decided he must be flown to Arusha for immediate treatment. "Ben [Fourie] went off to the nearest station (on Lake Victoria—115 miles away) to send the wire [summoning the plane]. Ben will get there tonight," wrote Pauline, "and the plane will be here in the morning." Ernest stayed in bed all day, moving to the campfire at sundown. The next morning he woke up claiming that he was better. But when he tried to walk, he was overcome with weakness.

When the plane did not come, Pauline went out bird-shooting with Charles and Ernest stayed in bed reading English magazines. Now there was intermittent discussion about whether he should be treated in Arusha or Nairobi. Where was the better hospital, the better doctors, or did he have to go to a hospital at all? Perhaps the doctor could take care of him in a hotel. As debilitated as he was, everyone assumed that a few days' treatment would restore him. When the plane finally arrived Tuesday morning and picked him up, Pauline's understanding was that he would be set down in

Arusha. She managed a cheerful face and wished him luck. "Ernest went off very gay and handsome," she recalled, "(partly due to extreme thinness) in a small silver plane with a tiny pilot belonging to the weasel family."

With the plane out of sight, the safari broke camp, for the schedule called for a return to hill country. Leaving Serengeti, they had one last encounter with lions. The shooting was sloppy, but Pauline, at least, was happy with the results. "I think mine [downed after at least ten shots] is the best of all the 85 [lions] we've seen. . . . wish my performance could have been a little more brilliant." By evening her mood had darkened. She missed Ernest, Percival had indigestion, and her sleep was ruined when at 2:00 A.M. a beetle bug the size of a small bird got into her mosquito net. "Hit him many times with the search light but like native he was unstunable." The rest of the journey was "a sorry affair." Percival was now feverish and the hunting not up to his standards—twenty-eight shots to down one topi. They reached the Ngorongoro Crater on January 18. The next day while picking some flowers, Pauline fell into a thorn bush. "Very painful taking out thorns from fatty part of anatomy," she wrote.

On January 20 Charles and the rest moved ahead to set up a base camp from which to hunt kudu, sable, and rhino, while Pauline and Percival headed for Arusha. "Mr. P. and I . . . went on the hot, dusty road to Arusha to surprise Ernest. . . . we got to Arusha about 3:30. . . . very dirty. Dashed . . . into the hotel and asked for Mr. Hemingway from the Hindu clerk. Mr. Hemingway not here he said and had never heard of Mr. H." The mystery was solved by the proprietor's wife, who remembered that Ernest had rushed in five days earlier to collect the mail and had then continued on to Nairobi for treatment. "Don't know who was more crushed," wrote Pauline. "Mr. P. took to drink and I took to my bed." She tried to keep herself busy all day Sunday, except that there was nothing to do in Arusha. The pealing church bells gave her "a guilty start, but had no stockings," she wrote. "Only alternative was wearing trousers. Had doubts about trousers."

After an exchange of telegrams, it was determined that Ernest would return to Arusha Monday morning. Pauline and Philip drove out to the airstrip that had been put into shape for the arrival of the American secretary of state. An ebullient if slightly peaked Ernest appeared on schedule. In Nairobi, he had taken a series of emetine injections, the drug of choice for amoebic dysentery, and he began to improve almost immediately. From his bedroom at the New Stanley he had sent out a piece for *Esquire* and enjoyed all the mail, especially the news from Perkins that *Winner Take Nothing* had sold 12,500 copies by Christmas.

Pauline, Ernest, and Philip Percival now joined Charlie Thompson and the rest at the new base camp. It was a terrain of forest and rushing water, and every day Ernest was up at dawn, following the rhino trails deep into the grassy wilderness. Out of this exhilaration came an affecting tenderness for Pauline, later expressed in *Green Hills of Africa.* When she napped on the trail after the midday meal, "She was always lovely to look at asleep, sleeping quietly, close curled like an animal, with nothing of the being dead look that Karl [Charlie Thompson] had asleep." When there was a fuss between husband and wife, Ernest's recounting of it was self-effacing. On the subject of a limp Pauline developed, first there was a

> highly-righteous-on-both-sides clash . . . on unwearable . . . boots . . . [with] the situation . . . un-helped by the statement that men's new boots always hurt for weeks before they became comfortable. Now, heavy socks removed, [she was] stepping tentatively, . . . the argument past, she wanting not to suffer . . . me ashamed at having been a four-letter man about boots, at being righteous against pain, at being righteous at all.

Pauline was with Ernest on January 29 when he shot his first rhino. She wrote:

> Called in what seemed to be the middle of the night but which turned out to be a little after 5. . . . Ernest got up in bed and said "I think maybe I won't go," but he finally got up, and it's a darn good thing he did because we went up the hill back of the camp after breakfast about 6, and stayed there . . . on Mr. P.'s advice. . . . suddenly . . . along came a rhino down the hill very fast like locomotive toward the water and the forest. . . . the range was too far [but Ernest shot him anyway]. . . . when he came out again from under cover E. shot him again, 2 times, but the range was too far. . . . we went running along without much hope of finding him. We finally . . . heard the old rhino breathing heavily (what turned out to be his death rattle) and finally came upon him, feet in the air, dead. . . . then there was the celebration and even the cook came out

and innumerable pictures were taken. . . . Mr. P. much impressed. Said longest away he'd ever seen a rhino shot (first shot about 250 yards away) and said it was best shooting he had seen E. do.

But Ernest's pride was once again cut down by Charles Thompson, who brought in a much bigger kill a few days later. "He had made my rhino look so small that I could never keep him in the same small town where we lived," wrote Ernest, ashamed of his jealousy but unable to contain it. Percival, sensitive to the bad feelings, reduced the tension by sending Charles out the next day for oryx, while Ernest and Pauline went for more rhino and buffalo.

The drama of the last two weeks was Ernest's stubborn search for a kudu bull. Percival guided them out of the rugged hill country back to the Cape-to-Cairo Road and two hundred miles south to the region around Kibaya in the Masai steppe. On the way they hunted oryx and zebra, briefly escaping the dust and tsetse fly to be the house guests of an Englishman, Colonel Richard Cooper, who was a friend of Jane Mason's and a great admirer of Ernest's work. Pauline wrote:

It is a charming place, high and cool and swimming in flowers and vines. With a lovely view of Lake Manyara. Also has slow-running water and rather uncertain electric lights. We played the graphaphone [sic] and drank on the veranda . . . Mr. P. in his stork dressing gown and Dick Cooper's manager (a nice boy with nice manners) and so to bed in a big double bed. *Think Jane would like this place.*

At first Charles's luck was no better than Ernest's. Then on February 11 two local trackers reported that there were fresh kudu tracks at a salt lick five miles down the road. From her tent Pauline heard an argument between Ernest and Charles—who would go to the salt lick, who would go to the hills? "Distinctly heard 4-letter word," wrote Pauline, "and Charles went to the lick." That night Charles came home with a respectable kudu and Ernest with nothing. "No kudu" was Pauline's closing entry of the day.

Now the hunt became a dogged contest for Ernest, who would consider the entire journey a failure if he couldn't match Charles. Only a few days were left before the rains made the roads impassable. Pauline loyally identified with Ernest's frustration and stayed behind at the camp with Philip waiting for shots. "It is now 9:30," she wrote on February 13, "and Mr. P. and I are waiting for a possible gun report. This kudu business is a waiting game—and now another of the five hunting days left is gone."

Ernest returned late at night with nothing. The next day he went out with bags, flask, citronella, mattress, and trackers to a far salt lick. In his absence Pauline and Philip went out to "shoot some meat for the pot. . . . turned out to be no game for us to shoot so here we are at 9:20 [A.M.] waiting for—what do you think—kudu news! A lot of cows are mooing at the side of the camp, sounding exactly like I feel." In the afternoon she took a walk with Philip. Again Ernest came back empty-handed. Mealtime was a dismal affair. The rains were imminent. Three days later, on February 16, scouts reported that two fine kudu bulls had been spotted in a herd. "There was immediately rejoicing where there had been gloom and consternation, and Ernest started out once more with the mattress, citronella, whiskey et al. And Mr. P. and I are left to our own now too familiar occupation of waiting. Both very restless. Weather gloomy."

The next day they broke camp and started off to join Charles and Ben, who had gone east after sable and were now due back. With a sinking feeling Pauline heard Ben describe a magnificent kudu that Charles had shot on their sable hunt. Seeing it only confirmed Ben's description. The horns had a spread of at least fifty-seven inches, "like a cathedral," observed Pauline. How would Ernest rationalize such a defeat? But then, at ten o'clock, after she was in bed for the night she heard a tremendous racket. A moment later she recognized Ernest's shouts over the noise of the klaxon, and a gun went off. She dashed outside to be grabbed by Ernest, who held her tight. ("she feeling very small inside the quilted bigness of the dressing gown, and we were saying things to each other."—*Green Hills*) Spilling out of the car were fine-looking kudu horns and those of a sable cow. "Food and drink were had by all," concluded Pauline, "and the story of the chase. Very fine ending to the safari."

After relaxing on the East Coast of Africa, with plenty of deep-sea fishing, the Hemingways and Charles Thompson boarded the *Gripsholm* for the return voyage to the Mediterranean. Vanderbilt and his white hunter, Baron Von Blixen, an urbane European formerly married to the writer Isak Dinesen, were also on board. This Swedish ship was the antithesis of the untidy, cramped *General Metzinger*. A luxury liner with private suites and a salt-water pool, it carried a roster of millionaires and titled Europeans. Ernest, the middle-class boy from Oak Park, was enjoying his new friends in this monied set. He spent most of his time lounging by the pool with Vanderbilt and the baron, or drinking at the Ritz bar in the stern of the ship.

They docked at Haifa on March 16 and Lorine Thompson, who had come over on a cruise ship from New York, joined them for the trip across the sea to Villefranche. When she showed Pauline some recent snapshots of Gregory and Patrick, Pauline's eyes filled with tears at their solemn expressions. "Poor little lambs, she said. I can see they miss Mummy." How much she missed them is debatable. Certainly she wrote nothing in her diary to indicate that she yearned to be back in Key West with her children. But after a seven-month absence it was time to go home. They stayed in Paris for nine days and then sailed on the *Ile de France* for New York. One of the passengers was Marlene Dietrich, who recalled her first meeting with Ernest in an article written many years later. "I entered the dining salon to attend a dinner party. The men rose to offer me a chair, but I saw at once that I would make the thirteenth at the table. I excused myself on grounds of the superstition, when my way was blocked by a large man who said he gladly would be the fourteenth. The man was Hemingway."

One important task remained after landing in New York. Eight months earlier, Ernest had read in the Wheeler Shipyard brochure of a thirty-eight-foot, gasoline-powered boat with twin screws, double rudders, and ample bunk space. All winter he had planned and dreamed about how he could buy such a seaworthy craft. He wanted to pay for it himself, but it cost $7,500. When Arnold Gingrich advanced him $3,300. against his future contributions to *Esquire*, Ernest and Pauline rode in a taxicab to the Brooklyn shipyard to place the order. The Gingrich check was the downpayment. Delivery was promised in thirty days.

Pauline was flattered that Ernest named his proud new possession the *Pilar*, after their secret name for her during their courtship, but she recognized that there would be even longer separations now between Ernest and her and the boys. The *Pilar* was built for serious fishing, not pleasure boating, and Pauline had not been able to work up any sustained enthusiasm for the sport. She put aside her reservations, however, to cheer when Ernest maneuvered the ship into Key West Harbor from Miami early in May of 1934.

For the next two months Ernest alternated between fishing excursions on the *Pilar* and morning stints with the African manuscript. Pauline excused him from the obligatory visit to Piggott when she took Patrick to visit her parents on May 31. Three-year-old Gigi (Gregory) went with Ada to her home in Syracuse, New York. Even if Pauline believed that Ada was a reasonable mother substitute, it was a mistake to separate Gigi from Patrick. Such separations only intensified Gregory's sense of isolation and rejection. As an adult, he comforted himself with Pauline's remark that probably she did not have " . . . much of what's called a maternal instinct. . . . I can't *stand* horrid little children. . . . That is why Ada always took care of you. But I loved you, darling, I really did, though I guess I didn't always show it."

En route from Jacksonville to Piggott, Pauline wrote Ernest. "Patrick is a fine boy, but not, I am learning, you. . . . My but it is dismal here in the rain. . . . I am so sleepy and we are getting another berth tonight as we bumped like elephants all last night." In Arkansas Patrick liked the Pfeiffer routine. His Aunt Jinny took him swimming in the river and his grandfather, Paul Pfeiffer, filled his pockets with coins after morning visits to the family bank. Pauline, too, came upon unexpected windfalls whenever she was around her father. This time she received $2,308. from a long-forgotten childhood savings account. "It was Papa's idea to take the savings," she wrote. "Nobody to pay back and can bring along some more if you wish. Have no end of this filthy money. Just leave me know [if you wish me to bring more money] and don't get another woman, your loving Pauline. Poor Papa, rich papa." Pauline tried not to be the heavy-handed rich wife, and made jokes about her money, but Ernest continued to be self-conscious about it.

In April, Hadley had written from Chicago to inquire whether Bumby could spend the summer in Key West. She and Paul had left Paris in January after Paul became managing editor of the *Chicago Daily News*, and they were gradually getting settled in a large, sunny duplex. "A Philco radio is supposed to arrive today," she wrote, "so you can see how American we are getting. We will then be supplied with everything except a car and electric sewing machine to make ideal citizens." Bumby was a "popular student" at Chicago Latin School. " . . . his holidays begin Friday, June 8. . . . I don't think school-less days with Paul busy and me able to do so few sporting things will be wise for him. Give me an idea as soon as you can."

By the time Pauline reached Piggott the plans were laid. Pauline would meet and escort Bumby to Florida on June 21. "I will be so glad to get back [to Key West]," she confided to Ernest. "I'll love you all the way home and we won't be separated anymore."

But that was wishful thinking. From mid-July, when he set out for Cuban waters, until October 26, when he returned to Key West for the winter, Pauline would see little of him. The woman he saw much more of was Jane, who seemed to have recovered in health and was back in Havana when Ernest arrived there with the *Pilar* on July 18.

Pauline had flown over to meet him and spend a few days. Carlos Gutiérrez was signed on as first mate and a pickup cook was hired who could double as steersman. The next day Jane and Grant came aboard to toast the sleek black cruiser's arrival. Pauline caught the first marlin, a forty-four-pounder, with Ernest coaching. They celebrated his thirty-fifth birthday party at El Pacifico, the exotic four-story restaurant where hash was smoked in the basement and the food and patrons improved in quality as they progressed to the rooftop dining room.

For the rest of the summer Pauline was in Key West. With Ada and Gregory away, she spent a good deal of time supervising Patrick's meals and baths and reading time. The hardest part of the day was after five o'clock, when even a nice little boy becomes tiresome. Pauline had begun to fuss with her hair again, trying to get it just the right shade of deep gold. She even postponed a scheduled weekend flight to Havana so that her hair colorist could correct the pink tint of the dye. "I would like it a little gold before showing it off to friends in public demonstrations. . . . wish you were here for the process," she wrote Ernest. Despite Pauline's attempts to catch Ernest's wandering attention, coloring her hair was probably a mistake, since her friends agreed that her own dark hair looked best.

When Pauline did fly back to Havana in September, Jane Mason had left for Tuxedo Park. She wrote to both Hemingways:

Darlings, . . . there is something about this place which forces even the most robust and gutsy to dash about in whispers. . . . I have taken the gun of my sister-in-law, as a French grammar might put it, and have tried to shoot skeet. . . . As for the writing I have done one piece which may, or may not, turn into something which could double for a portion of tepid hash with an underdone egg. . . . I have placed an order for your firsts. I have a few, but I wanted to get *The Sun Also Rises* and *The Torrents of Spring*. So when I come back will you take the plume in hand and sign them?

As usual, Pauline's stay with Ernest was brief, and she returned to Key West alone. When Ernest arrived she had him to herself for about a week before Katy and Dos arrived for the winter. They occupied a pleasant bungalow nearby but took most evening meals with the Hemingways. During these evenings, Ernest was full of complaints. He had never caught the big marlin he coveted and he was nervous about the African book, which he pronounced finished on November 16. Many nights he retired to his bed before supper, as Pauline and the guests gathered around him to eat from trays. Katy, the oldest friend, poked fun at his princely airs and Dos wrote later, "We called it the *lit royale*. I never knew an athletic vigorous man who spent as much time in bed as Ernest did."

Around Thanksgiving the safari trophies began to arrive from the taxidermist in New York—leopard and lion rugs, mounted heads of sable and roan antelope, impala and oryx, with kudu and rhinoceros to follow. From Chicago came a much different wall decoration, Miró's *The Farm* that Ernest had bought for Hadley in 1925. When the Century of Progress Exposition opened its second year in Chicago, Paul and Hadley had allowed the painting to be shown publicly. After a press release reminded Ernest of its existence, he asked Hadley if he could borrow the painting for five years. She agreed and it was hung in the place of honor on the dining room wall. Pauline liked it much better than the animal heads. (Ernest may have, too. He never returned it to Hadley.)

During the 1934 Christmas visit to Piggott, Ernest hired Otto "Toby" Bruce, the young cabinetmaker who had built Pauline's furniture, to work for him on a permanent basis, taking over the jobs that Ernest disliked—driver, maintenance man, secretary. Ernest was now the most famous person in Key West and came back from Arkansas to find his house listed in the local guide book as a principal tourist attraction. (With 80 percent of the townspeople on relief, tourism was the last desperate measure to bring in some form of prosperity.)

In the seven years since Ernest had moved to Key West his muscles had hardened and bulged, and the girth of his belly had thickened considerably. On the *Pilar* he was the captain giving orders, legs braced widely, green eyeshade pulled down, white pants stained with grease and fish blood. In Sloppy Joe's his bearing changed as he became the observant writer once more, watching Josie's hard-drinking, belligerent customers for future material. Ernest was a hard drinker too, and not without his own moments of belligerence. But his great tolerance for alcohol kept him from being a drunk and his belligerence was sporadic. If he picked a fight in a nightclub and embarrassed Pauline, he was so contrite in the morning that she could not remain angry.

He continued to worry about *Green Hills* and handed Perkins a fresh typescript to read when the latter arrived for a brief holiday. Max praised it but seemed reluctant to commit *Scribner's Magazine* to a high price for serialization. "I am broke," wrote Ernest to Gingrich on February 4, 1935, "and need money for my taxes and 300 bucks I had promised to send for Bumby's schooling." Of course he was not broke. But as Ernest became increasingly antagonistic toward "the rich" he was more anxious to pay his way. In the end *Scribner's Magazine* paid only $5,000., which Ernest thought was niggardly in view of all he had done for the company since 1926. To compound his disgust he had a recurrence of amoebic dysentery and was forced to take another series of emetine injections. Katy stopped teasing him and Dos meekly took his orders. Finally the infection subsided and he got over his disappointment about the low price for serial rights. He was off on a new enthusiasm—tuna fishing.

Forty-seven miles due east of Miami (two hundred thirty nautical miles northeast of Key West) lay the tiny cluster of islands in the west Bahamas known as Bimini. There was talk of a magnificent wide beach, a run-down wharf, coconut palms, and native shacks. A Pan American seaplane made occasional stops. Trim yachts from Havana and Miami floated into the small harbor. But the big attraction for Ernest was the rumor of giant tuna. On April 7 he set out with his crew of two, and three passengers—Mike Strater, Katy, and Dos. The trip was suddenly aborted when Ernest accidentally shot himself in both legs while pumping bullets into a shark. Katy was furious, believing that Ernest was too free with his pistol and that only a miracle had prevented some horrible fatality. Ernest was humiliated. The pain was intense but the embarrassment was worse. He stayed at home for a week to recuperate and then on April 14 set out again. This time the trip was made without incident.

Two weeks later Pauline flew over to see Bimini for herself. She agreed with Ernest. It was just about perfect. She would make all the arrangements for moving her brood over at the end of June.

Chapter 16

When Jack Hemingway was a boy growing up, he felt sorry for children who had only one mother. In effect he had two, for Pauline always treated him as one of her own. She accorded him the same good-humored attention she gave Patrick and Gregory and exacted the same high level of decorum. When Uncle Gus Pfeiffer was setting up trust funds for the younger members of his family, she persuaded him to make one for Bumby. "He is a lovely child," wrote Pauline when Bumby came down from Chicago in 1935, "not spoiled nor self-centered nor silly, but a handsome, well-mannered intelligent fellow with a fine sense of humor. . . . he is trying to keep girls out of his life this summer because they get in your hair and cause jealousy. You figure out what he means."

Earlier in the spring Grace had written Hadley to invite Bumby to a Hemingway family reunion. "It seems to me quite natural and right and he is quite curious also about his grandmother," explained Hadley to Ernest. "I promise I shall never press him toward dutifulness in that direction, however." Jack Hemingway is not sure that he made it to the reunion, but he does remember occasional visits with Grandmother Gracie, as everyone then called her. His most lasting impression, and the only one formed independently of his father's bitterness, emanated from a day he spent alone with her. "Do you know how to drive a car yet?" she asked her twelve-year-old grandson. When the answer was no, she marched him out to her car (then a Model A Ford), put him behind the wheel, and showed him how to shift gears and move the clutch. With his grandmother at his side, Jack drove around the block. "Any lady that would do that with a boy can't be all that bad," he later remarked to the author.

It was during his first summer at Bimini that Jack learned more about Ada Stern's complex personality. Her origins were obscure. She was unmarried, with a fairly conclusive story that her husband had deserted her on her wedding night. Patrick, nearly four when he had come under her care, was old enough to know that "my mother was my mother and Ada was simply a woman whom I hated." But Gregory was only three months old when Ada had taken charge of him. He became dependent upon her for all his needs—especially for love and approval. He knew that she withdrew both when he misbehaved, threatening to leave him if he did not obey her. The face she turned to Pauline was one of efficiency and loyalty. But on the other side was an unpredictable temper and secret drinking. (The further question of homosexuality was not recognized by Bumby at the age of eleven but as adults all the Hemingway sons concluded that she was homosexual.) Each of the children had his own tactic for coping with Ada. Jack, the oldest, was the most resourceful. He bribed her with thimblefuls of liqueurs siphoned from the pantry. Patrick, a finicky eater who never forgave Ada for the unpleasant messes she cooked, prayed that she would burn in hell. Gigi, who clung to her skirts when she threatened to abandon him, was too emotionally dependent to challenge her authority. None of the brothers seems ready to blame Pauline for failing to rescue them from Ada, although they acknowledge that out of her own peculiar needs, Ada turned Gregory against Pauline by playing on his fear of being unloved.

That same summer of 1935, before Pauline put in an appearance, Ernest was living on the *Pilar* in Bimini harbor. He wrote Jane Mason to come over and fish with him. He had not seen her or heard from her for many months—her explanation for not writing was that she had made a long trip to Africa during the winter. Some of Ernest's irritability of that winter may have been caused by their separation and the fact that she was interested in another man— Colonel Cooper, the Englishman who owned the house at Lake Manyara. Jane wrote on May 17:

It was fine [the trip to Africa] and I did love the whole trip. "My Mr. Cooper" sent salutations and such, and I imagine Blix has given you all the tiresome details so I shant go into that. . . . I have done no more on the writing. "The New Yorker" rejected "A High Windless Night" saying that the characters were a little too far from home and that I seemed to have been reading a great deal of Maugham and Hemingway. . . . Perhaps Blix has told you that I have given up the bottle for a long time. . . . I don't even tipple cider.

Jane did go over to Bimini in June, bringing wine and tinned delicacies, and fished for tuna off the *Pilar*, but Dick Cooper was still on her mind. "My sunburn hurts and Mr. Cooper is lovely," she wrote Ernest from Miami on June 20. "He's off to Wyoming so pl–ease keep your fingers crossed so that things will go well for him. *Erregardless* [sic] *of me* and what the 'future holds' he deserves a break."

She ended the letter in a burst of emotion over a disagreeable argument she was having with her psychiatrist, Dr. Kubie, that concerned Ernest. At the suggestion of his friend, Henry Seidel Canby, editor of the *Saturday Review of Literature*, Dr. Kubie had written a series of articles in which he attempted to apply the principles of psychoanalysis to "the modern literature of neuroticism." The first article, dealing with William Faulkner's *Sanctuary*, and the second, with Erskine Caldwell's *God's Little Acre*, had already been published. The third one was to deal with the works of Hemingway —*The Sun Also Rises, A Farewell to Arms, Death in the Afternoon, Men Without Women*, and *Winner Take Nothing*.

In a summary of his lengthy analysis, Kubie formulated a series of propositions. For the Hemingway hero, women are unworthy of any emotion save hostility and dislike. In his attempt to prove that he really has no fear of her, the hero is constantly driven to assert his superiority. The warmest attachments in the stories are formed between young men and gentle, tender, older men, with the older figure repeatedly made to represent the threat of overt homosexuality. As a result of all this—the fearful conception of women and the exaggerated love of older men—the hero behaves as though life were "beset with danger." It is not enough to accept risk, he must seek danger, even violent death, to prove his manhood. "The underlying struggle remains the same: i.e., the struggle of all men to overcome the terror which is engendered in their complex relationship to the image of the father." When the confused battle is over, Kubie wrote, the symbols of victory are empty and the underlying angers and anxieties remain.

Kubie sent the article to Ernest for his opinion. Ernest, as one might expect, was furious. He threatened to sue both the psychiatrist and the editors of the *Saturday Review* if the article was printed. Jane, who felt she was caught in the middle, was frantic. Had she revealed intimacies about Ernest that could become grist for the psychiatrist's analysis? "Papa," she wrote on June 29, "you were lovely about it all [the Kubie affair] and I'm feeling ever so much better for having told you about it. . . . your friendship, and this goes for you too Madame, *means* a great deal more than either of you can know and I'd never, never, *never* do anything intentionally that would make it . . . messy. And I'm sorry, as anything, that I was too scared to tell you right off. I'll send the letters so you'll get them right away."

Early in July the letters reached Ernest. In the one from Dr. Kubie to Jane, he had written her about Ernest's threat to take libel action and his own opinion that such a course of action would be childish. He then remarked that Ernest's handwriting was amazingly like Jane's and suggested that in the last few years perhaps she had unconsciously begun to imitate his handwriting to an extraordinary extent. The other letter, written May 12, was Jane's reply to Kubie. Her handwriting had never been any different from what it was now, she insisted. She was disappointed and hurt by such a suggestion, and she reminded the doctor how opposed she had been from the beginning to the idea of his doing the article. Because she knew it would make Ernest angry, particularly when he found out that Kubie was her analyst, and since she cared greatly about her friendship with Hemingway, the whole affair was most distasteful to her. In her last letter to Ernest on the subject Jane quoted Kubie as saying he would not publish the article and that he was sorry he had been persuaded to write it in the first place. But in defense of his own integrity he reiterated that nothing about Hemingway that came to him from Jane played any part in the final article.

The Kubie affair, coming close on the heels of Jane's infatuation with Richard Cooper, very likely cooled Ernest's ardor. Pauline was now in Bimini and Ernest moved off the boat into a cottage with her. Occasionally Pauline went out on the *Pilar*. Once she even caught a respectably large sailfish. But she preferred to stay on the beach with Jinny, who was also visiting, and with Katy and Dos, who had arrived for the season and whose languid routine differed sharply from Ernest's. They acquired a shell collection, swam in the clear water, and fished for bonefish in the shallows between the coral heads. For the cocktail hour everyone went down to the dock to welcome the *Pilar*. Pauline brought all the ingredients for the bar and the boys hung about to finish the dregs. All three children adored their papa, who radiated a kind of magic for them. Jack believed Ernest to be an authentic hero, and until he was a man automatically assumed that all of Ernest's opinions were correct.

In August, when Bimini turned sultry and unpleasant, the Hemingways headed back to Key West. With *Green Hills of Africa* scheduled for October publication, Pauline persuaded Ernest to go north with her. She wanted to shop with Jinny and she also wanted to visit her Pfeiffer relatives, who gathered periodically at the Homestead, in rural Connecticut, where Uncle Gus had bought up and restored twenty-one colonial farmhouses for the use of family and friends. Ernest stayed in the country for a week after Pauline went back to Manhattan.

On the evening that he returned to their suite at the Hotel Westbury, Pauline was entertaining three callers—bullfighter Sidney Franklin; Ward Merner, her cousin from San Francisco; and Merner's friend, Jay McEvoy. Sidney had appeared bearing boxes of ill-fitting, ready-made dresses for both children and adults from his brother-in-law's factory in Brooklyn. Pauline, assuring him that a machine-knitted, bright blue dress was exactly what her wardrobe lacked, put it on and stood patiently as he pulled and tugged, pointing out how she could take it in here and let it out there. McEvoy, who had never met the Hemingways but had heard a great deal about them, noticed that Pauline's manner changed as soon as Ernest arrived. From being lively and full of wisecracks, she turned meek and apprehensive, as though she was uncertain how her husband would react to a stranger. McEvoy's recollection is that Ernest was pleasant to all of them and made no references to the reviews that were now coming out about *Green Hills of Africa*.

Ernest had predicted that the critics on the political left would not be pleased with his continued lack of interest in social problems, and he had already taken pains to state his position in *Esquire*. "The hardest thing in the world to do," he wrote, "is to write straight honest prose on human beings. First you have to know the subject; then you have to know how to write. Both take a lifetime to learn and anybody is cheating who takes politics as a way out. . . . Books should be about people you know, that you love and hate, not about the people you study up about." But few critics were convinced. One, from the American left, urged Ernest to find more important themes than "the pursuit and dismemberment of animals and fish, no matter how big." Ivan Kashkin, a Soviet critic and a serious student of Hemingway's work, thought his writer's face was a mask for some tragic disharmony within. The reviewers for some of the major newspapers and magazines were more favorably disposed. Edward Weeks found the book "absorbing" and Carl Van Doren liked the "magical prose." But Edmund Wilson thought the book weak, and T.S. Matthews indignantly asked if Hemingway thought he could write about "anything and get away with it."

On November 4, 1935, *Time* complimented Hemingway for writing candidly and with delicacy of his love for his wife. Many years later, the critic Robert W. Lewis Jr., in *Hemingway on Love*, suggested that Ernest's love for Pauline as conveyed in *Green Hills* was a "good" love, mature and harmonious. Pauline, experiencing that love from the duration of a nine-year-old relationship, undoubtedly tried to believe that everything was as solid between them as when he had left Hadley in 1926, and that their frequent separations were not significant. At Christmas she decided to celebrate the holiday in Key West instead of Arkansas. Ernest wrote to Mary Pfeiffer in January, 1936:

> Pauline has the same energy as always and manages to put in a good eight hour day every day and then in the evening . . . goes sound asleep at nine o'clock and sleeps like a child all night. . . . She was talking of going up to make a retreat with you but lately she has been reading James Joyce's *Ulysses* and has taken such an admiration for Mr. Joyce that she may be going to make a retreat with Ulysses instead.

Ernest was not doing as well. The pattern that had taken shape early in his life, of great swings in mood between euphoria and depression, once more asserted itself. For three weeks he was sleepless and anxious. To fight off insomnia, he would leave his bed in the middle of the night and work in his study until daylight. To his mother-in-law he confided that he had never had " . . . the real old melancholia before and am glad to have had it so I know what people go through. It makes me more tolerant of what happened to my father."

By the time he wrote to Mary Pfeiffer he was over the worst of it. " . . . have been going out and driving myself in the boat . . . in any kind of weather and am o.k. now . . . " To prove it he invited her to come for a visit. " . . . this place really runs very smoothly and we eat very well and we would love to see you." He bragged about four-year-old Gigi now adding three-digit numbers and remarked how toughened up Patrick had become against seasickness. "I was never a great child lover," he confessed, "but these kids are really good company and are very funny and I think (though may be prejudiced) very smart."

Even as he was inviting Mary Pfeiffer to visit him (on the assumption, perhaps, that she would never come) he complained to his friends that the number of visitors to Whitehead Street was driving him nuts. This was characteristic of Ernest, to protest loudly before the guests arrived; he enjoyed them once they were there. Early in March, Jane Mason arrived for a short visit. When she heard that Ernest and Josie were going to sail the *Pilar* to Cuba late in April, she volunteered to be in Havana in May and make the return trip with them. "Mrs. Mason," wrote Hemingway to Dos Passos, "is almost as apt at going places without her husband as Mr. Josie is without his wife."

When Jane arrived, the atmosphere aboard the fishing vessel was tense. Ernest was morose and unpredictable. The marlin were running scarce and he took his disappointment out on poor old Carlos Gutiérrez. Carlos, not as sharp in eyes or ears as in former days, but utterly loyal to Ernest, was hurt by his captain's barbs. Knowing that the crew was embarrassed, Jane eased the situation by lightly scolding Ernest and comforting Carlos in private. Her tact and good humor paid off. By the time they docked in Key West at the end of May, Ernest's black mood had dissipated and he even decided to sign Carlos on again.

As his ambiguous relationship with Jane was coming to an end, Ernest created a female character whose prototype—or so he confided to some of his Cuban friends—was the woman they all knew as Jane Mason. In appearance, Margot Macomber with her perfect oval face and hair drawn back in a knot at the nape of her neck is without doubt modeled after Jane. So, too, is her eagerness to participate in the hunt for the lion, and the bleak state of the Macomber marriage. The story, published in *Cosmopolitan* as "The Short Happy Life of Francis Macomber" is the tale of a young American sportsman on safari in Africa. Francis Macomber—tall, clean-cut, and vapid—panics in the presence of a dangerously wounded lion and flees the scene. Margot, his wife of eleven years, shows her contempt for his cowardice by leaving their bed in the middle of the night to visit the tent of the laconic white hunter, Wilson, who had bravely killed the lion at close range after his client ran away. The next day, as Macomber conquers his fear and faces down a charging buffalo, Margot aims her Mannlicher at the buffalo but kills her husband instead.

Critical opinion is divided over Margot's motivation, although the majority opinion seems to be that she is driven, if only unconsciously, to destroy her husband, because she sees her power over him coming to an end. If, through the act of bravery, he achieves a sense of self-worth, her freedom to cuckold him would presumably be curtailed. Edmund Wilson believed her to be an example of Ernest's growing antagonism toward all women. Certainly her marriage is the kind that Ernest had come to detest, where the husband is rich and weak, the wife beautiful and predatory. According to this point of view, the story is a severe indictment of wives such as Margot, who exert their power through beauty and sexuality (in their situation, married to wealthy men, they have no other power), and become deadly when threatened with loss of power. Jackson Benson, writing in 1969, believes Margot to be "clearly bent . . . on maintaining her dominance over Macomber" but acknowledges that she is "a monster created by circumstances at least partly beyond her own control. Considered from Mrs. Macomber's point of view, this is a very sad story, but Hemingway does not allow us to take that perspective."

Warren Beck, a critic who titled a 1955 essay "The Shorter Happy Life of Mrs. Macomber," dissents from such negative views of Margot. "Perhaps what Mrs. Macomber fears," writes Beck, "is a further challenge to herself as a human being and a wife [after Francis reasserts his moral authority]. . . . " This would seem to be a natural reaction for one who has met repeated disappointments in a relationship. To Beck it appears that she does want to save her husband from the buffalo, who would have mangled and perhaps killed him—after all, he was only two yards away. "If this be the meaning, "he continues, "it is a more profound story, more humane in substance, and . . . more subtly executed. . . . " Such an interpretation should be taken seriously in light of what probably transpired between Ernest and Jane. Ernest understood the severe estrangement between Jane and Grant, and at various times he felt genuine compassion for her.

The Hemingways were currently in Bimini occupying the most luxurious house on the island, lent to them by the millionaire sportsman Mike Lerner. When Arnold Gingrich came down to fish with Ernest and to read his latest fiction, Ernest showed him some new material about Harry Morgan, a solitary charter boat captain, operating out of Key West, who had been the hero of two previous stories. The first, "One Trip Across," published in *Cosmopolitan* in 1934, tells of Morgan's difficulties with unscrupulous smugglers who involve him in murder. The second story, completed in December 1935 and sold to *Esquire*, is "The Tradesman's Return." Here Ernest chronicles a rum-running episode that leaves Morgan severely wounded. In both narratives Morgan, the man who from economic desperation functions outside the law, is seen as having more courage and integrity than the so-called law-abiding citizens of the story.

Gingrich was enthusiastic about the new material and persuaded Ernest to put it all into a novel. He was not so enthusiastic about the fishing. He grew weary of Ernest's competitiveness aboard the *Pilar* and was preparing to leave when Pauline introduced him, over a drink at the Compleat Angler Bar, to Jane Mason. His interest suddenly revived. He was immediately drawn to Jane and began to plan how he might see her again when they were both in New York.

On July 5 Pauline flew back to Key West with Ada and the boys, leaving Jinny to stay on at Bimini with Ernest as he made a last effort to salvage a miserable marlin season. Jinny made few concessions to Ernest's temperament. She thought him a "great big selfish chap," and it is possible that he respected her all the more for not being intimidated by him. The fact that she was lesbian removed the problem of sexual tension between them, although Ernest still wondered if there wasn't a man someplace who might interest her. It bothered him that she would not write seriously. " . . . Jinny has as much talent or more for writing than I have," he wrote Mary Pfeiffer, "only she has no confidence and won't work at it. She really has talent and has been around enough so she has something to write." On his thirty-seventh birthday, he wrote Arnold Gingrich that he cared truly for only two people in the world (other than his kids)—Pauline and Jinny.

"The Snows of Kilimanjaro" had just appeared in the August 1936 issue of *Esquire,* and letters of admiration began pouring in from friends all over the world. Katy Dos Passos, who was not the most tongue-tied of Ernest's friends when it came to deflating him, wrote that it had made more people cry than anything since the Armistice.

The action of the story is minimal. All the emotional intensity comes from the internal landscape of the writer, Harry, who has contracted gangrene while on safari and lies dying in an African base camp as his wife, Helen, looks on helplessly. His recollections of the past involve places that had captivated him—the snow at Schruns on Christmas Day so bright it hurt his eyes, the trout streams in the Black Forest, the sprawling trees and white plastered houses of Place Contrescarpe. Another memory vividly evoked is the heartbreak of a lost first love.

> . . . he had written her, the first one, the one who left him, a letter telling her how he had never been able to kill it. . . . How when he thought he saw her outside the Regence one time it made him go all faint and sick inside, and that he would follow a woman who looked like her in some way, along the Boulevard, afraid to see it was not she, afraid to lose the feeling it gave him. How every one he had slept with had only made him miss her more. How what she had done could never matter since he knew he could not cure himself of loving her.

Much more traumatic for the dying writer, however, is the awareness that he will die before his best work is done. The scapegoat for his failures is his current wife, Helen—rich, middle-aged, conscientious Helen, whose wealth he blames for corrupting his creative impulse. Patrick Hemingway believes that his father borrowed certain details about Margot Macomber from Lorraine Shevlin, a regal beauty married to a man who had extensive lumber interests in the Pacific Northwest and who fished and hunted with Ernest. But there are disquieting messages for Pauline in much of Harry's bitter reverie.

" . . . you [Harry talking to himself] said that you would write about . . . the very rich. . . . But he [Harry] would never do it, because each day of not writing, of comfort, of being that which he despised, dulled his ability and softened his will to work so that, finally, he did no work at all." That was Ernest's abiding fear, that he would go soft and lose his talent. Pauline, who was his "kindly caretaker" in much the same way the fictional Helen was, left him no excuse for failure. " 'I'd have gone anywhere [said Helen]. I said I'd go anywhere you wanted.' " " 'Your bloody money,' he said." A distortion as applied to Pauline, but as Ernest's anxiety over his work deepened and he believed himself to be stagnating, he lashed out angrily. Years later he wrote that the idea for the story began with a rich woman who had invited him to tea in New York in 1934 and offered to finance another safari. Harry Walden was the image of himself as he might have been had he accepted the woman's offer. But the finished effort goes beyond Ernest's resourceful imagination to reveal truths about himself that would significantly affect his relationship with Pauline.

This story, of course, is also noteworthy for the references to the first love. For the third time in his fiction, seventeen years after the episode, Ernest was still examining the pain of Agnes's rejection. Agnes herself was now married to William Stanfield, a widower with three children. Her previous marriage to the auditor, Howard Garner, had begun to unravel when she found that Garner had a violent and unpredictable temper and, almost as disillusioning, no sense of humor. In retrospect, she wondered why she had become involved with him and concluded that at thirty-seven she had grown tired of living alone and had married in haste. In 1930 she moved out of their house in Haiti, vowing not to ask Garner for a penny, and went to Reno to seek a divorce.

By the end of the next year, the divorce had been granted and she returned to New York to become assistant supervisor of nurses at a tuberculosis sanitarium in Otisville, New York. There she met Bill Stanfield, a hotel manager. This time she moved carefully, and it was four years before they married. When "The Snows of Kilimanjaro" was published, Agnes was living in Virginia Beach, helping her husband run a small resort hotel. She has no recollection of having read the story at that time.

In the fall, Ernest began to talk of going to Spain, where a bitter civil war had just broken out. Five years earlier, after a long period of economic misery, dictatorship, and revolution, the Spanish monarchy had abdicated and elections were called. But with no tradition in constitutional democracy, factionalism was rampant and extremists from the right and the left seemed bent on disrupting a government that, however ineffectually, was trying to steer a middle course. In 1936 a Popular Front composed of Republicans, trade unionists, socialists, and some leftists was elected by a popular majority, but the police, the officer class of the army, the church hierarchy, and the aristocracy never accepted the election. It was this rebel coalition, calling itself Nationalists, that provoked a war with the Loyalist government.

At first Ernest was of two minds. He had good friends on both sides of the conflict and did not seem anxious to go to war. But he told a young writer friend that his sympathies were with the democratic government and the common people. In September he admitted to Max Perkins that he would hate to miss the Spanish thing.

Pauline was apprehensive, afraid for Ernest's safety. Her natural leanings were conservative and she had no interest in the intellectuals of the left who had been chiding Ernest for his lack of commitment to political issues. But she understood, better than anyone else, what he demanded of himself as a writer and as a man of action. She repeated her objections as forcefully as she dared, but with a gloomy premonition that events would overtake them.

As if to confirm her fears, a letter arrived in Key West on November 25, 1936, from Harry Wheeler, general manager of the North American Newspaper Alliance. The news service wanted Ernest to cover the war for them. Pauline was silent as Ernest wrote back that he was interested. He then took the *Pilar* over to Cuba for a week to visit Sidney Franklin and returned with grand news. Sidney had agreed to accompany him to Spain, which should please Pauline, he thought. Pauline acknowledged that it would be comforting to have Franklin along, but she was not ready to become a cheerleader for the project. She reminded Ernest that he should be thinking how to reassure the other women in his family, especially Grace, who had seen newspaper reports that Ernest was going to Spain. Ernest passed that task off on Pauline. He had a more important problem. Max Perkins, less than enthusiastic about the fact that his most celebrated author was going to war, was asking for the completed Morgan novel. Ernest had been struggling with Gingrich's idea to meld the Harry Morgan stories into a loosely-constructed novel form. His new material reflected his hardening attitude toward most of the people he and Pauline had associated with on Bimini, including Jane Mason. He had already written the novelist Marjorie Kinnan Rawlings that women who fished seriously were both the worthiest and dullest bitches alive, while 90 percent of their husbands were the same. To that category he added the parasitic rich and their sycophants who inhabited the yacht basin at Key West. Now Ernest was holding the manuscript back, suddenly worried that he had not sufficiently disguised the rich sportsmen and their wives. He wired Gingrich to come down from Chicago and also invited his lawyer, Maurice "Moe" Speiser, from New York. Together they would examine the manuscript for possible libel.

Gingrich, having already read most of the material, was of the opinion that Ernest had good cause for worry. "The week was funny," he wrote years later in *Esquire*.

> It was like those Paris riots, where the rioters and the cops would lay down their brickbats and nightsticks respectively, and adjourn for two hours for lunch, then come back and pick up again. It was just like that with us. Ernest and Pauline and Moe and I would "riot" all morning, then Ernest and I would go out fishing for the afternoon, then in the evening we would "riot" again.

Arnold thought he had been summoned for his sage advice. But when he suggested that Jane and Grant Mason were "libeled right up to their eyebrows" as one of the married couples in the book— Helene and Tommy Bradley—Ernest shrewdly sensed that Arnold's interest was not entirely impersonal. "Goddamn editor comes down to Bimini and sees a blonde and he hasn't been the same since," taunted Ernest. Gingrich squirmed. Since June, he had been seeing Jane in New York—secretly, he thought. But then he remembered that later in the summer Jane had traveled with Jinny Pfeiffer. "Maybe what one knew, they all knew," he reminded himself miserably.

By the end of the week Ernest hinted that he might fix up the offending passages, but what eventually remained was hardly flattering either to Jane or Grant. Helene Bradley is a rich and lustful woman who " . . . collected writers as well as their books." Openly unfaithful to her inept husband, Tommy, she lashes her current lover, Richard Gordon, for going limp when they are surprised in the sex act by Bradley.

Generous relatives were not exempt in this latest manuscript. The "pleasant, dull and upright" family asleep on one of the yachts seemed openly fashioned after Pauline's relatives, especially for their patent medicine fortune. " . . . and where did the money come from that they're all so happy with and use so well and gracefully? The money came from selling something everybody uses by the millions of bottles, which costs three cents a quart to make, for a dollar a bottle." And through the voice of a woman married to a Hollywood director, Ernest issues a warning to all women who expect their men to be monogamous:

> But they aren't built that way. They want some one new, or some one younger, or some one that they shouldn't have, or some one that looks like some one else. Or if you're dark they want a blonde. Or if you're blonde they go for a redhead. Or if you're a redhead then it's something else. A Jewish girl I guess, and if they've had really enough they want Chinese or Lesbians or goodness knows what. . . . Or they just get tired, I suppose. You can't blame them if that's the way they are. . . . The better you treat a man and the more you show him you love him the quicker he gets tired of you. I suppose the good ones are made to have a lot of wives but it's awfully wearing trying to be a lot of wives yourself.

One can only theorize how much of this fictional musing reflected Ernest's own state of mind, but coming on the heels of "Kilimanjaro," it seemed to be another warning to Pauline. One afternoon in late December as he prepared to leave the cool sawdust interior of Sloppy Joe's, a trio of tourists walked in. One was a young woman with beautiful hair—tawny-gold, loosely brushing her shoulders. She wore a plain black cotton sundress whose simplicity called attention in a well-bred way to her long, shapely legs. Ernest listened with interest to her eastern seaboard diction and the low, husky tone of her voice. He formed the hasty conclusion that she was married to the young man with her and that the older woman was her mother. The thought flashed across his mind that he could get her away from the young man.

The next afternoon he returned to the bar, hoping to see her again. When he noticed her in the company of the same companions he introduced himself. She said that she was Martha Gellhorn, and Ernest recognized the name. She was a writer from St. Louis, whose recent publication, *The Trouble I've Seen*, was a literary work of distinction. He was wrong about her being married; the young man was her brother, Alfred. The handsome woman, however, was her mother.

Skinner, the black bartender, later described the meeting of Martha and Ernest as between beauty and the beast. He was right about Martha. She was indeed a beauty. To describe Ernest as the beast, however, was well off the mark, though big and slovenly he was, with a hemp rope tied carelessly about the waist of his Basque fishing shorts. According to prim Key Westers, he looked as if he'd just pulled his pants on and planned to take them off again any second. But with his skin burnt mahogany and his thick black hair falling across his forehead he cut an impressive figure. The dimples flashed and the warm brown eyes were intent and responsive.

The conversation was friendly, and there was the coincidence of Martha's being from St. Louis, where both Hadley and Pauline had gone to school. Ernest lingered into the evening, offering to show the visitors around the island and point out the good swimming spots. At home Pauline was holding a fine crayfish dinner for Ernest's arrival. She had an extra drink with her guests, the Thompsons, then asked Charles to fetch Ernest. Charles did as he was told but could not retrieve Ernest, who introduced Martha Gellhorn as a literary fan and sent the message to Pauline that he would meet her at Pena's Garden of Roses later in the evening. Charles reported back that the reason for his host's delay was a beautiful blonde in a black dress.

FOUR

1936–44

Chapter 17

Martha Gellhorn was born on November 8, 1908, the only daughter of remarkable parents. Her father, Dr. George Gellhorn, one of the most important gynecologists in St. Louis, held professorships of obstetrics and gynecology at both Washington and St. Louis Universities. Her mother, Edna Gellhorn, a graduate of Bryn Mawr College, had a strong sense of responsibility to the community and worked tirelessly for social causes that she considered important. Dr. Gellhorn was full of pride in everything she did. "They had marvelous men," said Martha, referring to the husbands of her mother and grandmother. She remembered how her father would sit in the high-school auditoriums and lecture halls where his wife was speaking out for suffrage. And nod approvingly. Martha considered it her greatest good fortune to have been brought up with her three brothers in a "loving, merry, stimulating" home.

After completing her secondary education at the John Burroughs School in St. Louis, Martha attended Bryn Mawr but left at the end of her junior year, against the wishes of her father, who expected her to graduate as her mother had done before her. She accepted gladly the principle that if you wish to live your own life you must pay for it and from then on earned her own shoestring living. After two brief jobs in the summer and fall of 1929, on the *New Republic* and the *Hearst Times Union* in Albany, she wrote an article for the Holland America trade paper, which paid her passage to France.

Three summer holidays in Europe during school and college years had given her a passion for France. Her aim was to become a foreign correspondent, as her livelihood. She wrote somewhere that "my plan for life was to go everywhere, see everything, and write about it."

Martha's first job in Paris was with an advertising agency, her second with *Vogue,* her third with *United Press.* As a free-lance correspondent for the *St. Louis Post-Dispatch,* she went to Geneva to see the League of Nations in session, interviewed important women in League politics and eventually worked up a series that was prominently featured.

Unlike Hemingway, immersed in the expatriate Parisian world of writers and artists, Martha lived and worked entirely with the young French. Money was minimal. Unemployment, underpaid and badly treated workers, the cynicism of the old politicians—such were the concerns of Martha and her friends, though the rich, fashionable life of Paris was not unknown to them. Martha continued to support herself with her writing, traveling extensively though very cheaply in Germany, Italy, Spain, and England.

She was the only woman in a delegation of young French, mostly from the Sorbonne, who went to Germany at the invitation of young National Socialists. The politics of the French ranged from communism to right-wing Catholicism, but all had a fierce desire to prevent another Franco-German war. The journey was hardly a success; the young French found the young Nazis intellectually absurd and therefore unimportant. As a special mark of favor some of the delegation were invited to lunch by Baldur von Shirach, then head of the Hitler Youth, who lived with a Rumanian male companion. Having thought the young Nazis infantile, Martha felt this setup to be strangely repellent and von Shirach himself odious. When he hit his soldier servant for spilling a cup of coffee, Martha left the house.

During the summer of 1933, she went to Capri to work on her first novel. Fiction was her real aim and ambition; journalism was a means to see and learn about the world. The book became the story of three American students who leave their prestigious women's college to look for meaning in their lives. She borrowed the title *What Mad Pursuit* from John Keats and the watchword "nothing ever happens to the brave" from Ernest Hemingway.

In the autumn of 1934, belatedly realizing that her own rich country was in grave trouble—unemployment not being limited to Europe—Martha returned to America to help. "The great beauty of being young," she wrote later, "is that you always believe you can help. You have only to plunge in and work and thus move mountains: make the world a fairer, finer place."

Armed with an introduction from her friend Marquis Childs, Washington reporter for the *Post-Dispatch*, she offered her services to Harry Hopkins. Her idea was to find out how Relief actually worked, how the unemployed were treated as people, how they managed to live. Hopkins hired her as a relief-investigator for the Federal Emergency Relief Administration [FERA], of which he was head, and sent her to the depressed mill towns of New England and the South. When she brought her first reports of terrible suffering back to Hopkins, he introduced her to Eleanor Roosevelt, who was always concerned about the real human condition and therefore interested in Martha's work. The First Lady in turn introduced Martha to the president, who thereafter for the rest of his life always made time to see her, as did Mrs. Roosevelt whenever she had the kind of grass-roots information she believed they ought to know. Martha and Eleanor Roosevelt became lifelong friends.

For the rest of the winter of 1935 and well into the summer, at a salary of $35. a week and per diem for travel expenses, Martha crisscrossed the country, interviewing hundreds of people who had lost their jobs, their savings, their homes. She learned more about hunger and despair and frustration than most bureaucrats. But eventually she left the job, feeling that her reports were not helping the tormented people she was seeing. She decided instead to write a book about them, believing that if she could make them come alive as people, rather than statistics, she could serve them better.

The result was *The Trouble I've Seen*, carefully planned to represent the four age groups who were victims of unemployment—the old, the middle-aged, the young, and children. The book is divided into the four parts of the country—South, East, West, and Midwest. Martha's sensitivity and instinct for understatement let the people speak for themselves. And the result is as fresh and as moving today as it was forty years ago. Ruby, whose sordid story achieved tragic proportions, was based on a waif Martha had encountered in a Hooverville, Illinois shanty. H.G. Wells, who had met Martha at the

White House, was so impressed with her work that he offered to write a preface. Martha did not want this, feeling no need for anyone's sponsorship, and did not like what he wrote but was too young and inexperienced to know how to refuse the great man. "Enlarge this book a million times," Wells said, "and you have the complete American tragedy." He recommended it to the English publisher, Putnam, who bought the book for their spring list.

The Trouble I've Seen was well received by the British critics. The highest praise, reflecting a prevalent masculine viewpoint, came from Graham Greene in *The Spectator*. "Her stories are quite amazingly unfeminine," he wrote. "In 'Joe and Pete' . . . the tale of a union organizer . . . it is quite impossible to detect that a woman is writing. She has none of the female vices of unbalanced pity or factitious violence; her masculine characters are presented as convincingly as her female, and her writing is hard and clear."

On June 3, 1936, Martha sailed for England and Germany. In July she was working in Stuttgart, checking background facts for a novel based on her years of involvement with all her French friends in the political life of France. The central characters of her novel were an extraordinary young French couple whose experiences ranged from police brutality shared with striking coal miners to elegant Parisian receptions. They were pacifists and idealists who believed that only a Franco-German rapprochement could prevent another feared war.

The new Nazi regime already mocked such hope. When she wasn't working in the *Weltkriegsbibliothek*, Martha was reading German newspapers and watching life in the streets—the swaggering Nazis, or brown shirts, the cowed people—not fully understanding it but knowing it to be much more "alarming and vile" than it had been during her last visit to Germany in 1933. Whatever the Nazis were for, she absolutely opposed. When she read of the outbreak of the civil war in Spain and the Nazi newspapers described the democratically elected government of the Republic of Spain as "Red Swine Dogs," she knew immediately which side she was on.

Eleanor Roosevelt, who had received an advance copy of *The Trouble I've Seen*, was proud of her young friend. Three times during the week of August 5 she wrote about Martha in "My Day," her syndicated column. In her direct, artless way she explained how she had read the book one afternoon for two hours while cruising on the U.S.S. *Potomac* and on the evening of August 3 read it aloud to some guests at Hyde Park. During the week of September 17, she read again from the first section of the book, this time before a group of publishers and editors at the Colony Club. She explained in her column:

> It was little enough for me to do, not only for a friend, but for a book which I feel on its own merits should be read by many people in the next few months. . . . The American edition of *The Trouble I've Seen* will come out on the 23rd of this month. I cannot tell you how Martha Gellhorn, young, pretty, college graduate, good home, more or less Junior League background, with a touch of exquisite Paris clothes and "esprit" thrown in, can write as she does. She has an understanding of many people and many situations and she can make them live for us. Let us be thankful she can, for we badly need her interpretation to help us understand each other.

The acclaim for the book was universal. The *Boston Evening Transcript* called it compelling in its simplicity and fearlessness. The *San Francisco Chronicle* compared it to *Little Man, What Now*, the Hans Fallada classic about the ordinary German who is crushed by destructive economic forces. Full-page reviews appeared in the major New York papers, including an exhaustive one in the *New York Herald Tribune* by Dorothy Thompson. Martha's photograph, in which she looked proud, serious, and full-lipped, adorned the cover of the *Saturday Review of Literature* on September 26.

Lewis Gannett, whose column "Books 'n Things" was syndicated across the country, highlighted the Gellhorn book and Martha herself the day after publication. Gannett likened her promotional picture on the dust jacket to that of a Hollywood actress posing for a film to be called *The Virgin's Prayer*. (Others used the words young and wistful to imply the same thing.) His critique of the book was wholly favorable. "Who is this Martha Gellhorn? . . . Her writing burns. . . . Hemingway does not write more authentic American speech. Nor can Ernest Hemingway teach Martha Gellhorn anything about economy of language." The book's publisher, Morrow, continued to advertise it extensively, for they saw a best seller in the making.

On November 1 Martha was back in the United States lunching with the Roosevelts at Hyde Park. On November 17 she appeared on a panel sponsored by the *New York Times* National Book Fair at Rockefeller Center. Charles Poore was the moderator, the subject for discussion was "Listening to America," and her fellow panelists were Edgar Lee Masters, Morris Ernst, and Burgess Meredith. Disliking the promotional hoopla that went along with publication, Martha fled to St. Louis as soon as she could. But the acclaim did not die down. Gannett, who had praised her in his September column, was still impressed. On November 26 and again on December 6 he selected her book as the one to cut deepest into his memory in 1936 and said that a stinging poetry lurked behind the despair. An attempt was being made to dramatize the book for Broadway, and the new magazine *Book Digest* would condense it for one of their winter issues.

At Christmas—the first one without her father, who had died early in the year—Martha suggested that the family take a trip south. Her brother Alfred, on vacation from medical school, Edna Gellhorn, and Martha herself took a train to Miami, which they hated on sight. Alfred, out scouting, saw a bus marked Key West. The name appealed to them; they had never heard of the Florida Keys and knew nothing of Key West. The bus driver said it was farther south and they took the bus as a simple way of escaping from Miami. When they arrived in Key West, Edna Gellhorn spotted a bar with the curious name of Sloppy Joe's. She took the young people over to investigate.

Alfred and Edna Gellhorn left Key West after New Year's, when Alfred's academic holiday ended, but Martha stayed on at the Colonial Hotel on Duval Street for an extra week of sunshine and swimming. While her mother and her brother had been there, she saw Ernest only in the company of Alfred and only in the daytime. Her introduction to Pauline took place as Ernest was driving Martha and Alfred around the island. Pauline happened to be walking on the street and Ernest, stopping the car, asked her to get in. "She was very grumpy," Martha recalled, and "he was very sharp. . . . It never occurred to me that she could be jealous, and who knows if she was; may have had other reason for being cross."

After the departure of her family Martha saw more of Ernest, though still during the day and mainly for swimming. Having already decided independently to go to Spain, she talked to him at length about the dangers to the Spanish Republic. She never saw him in the evening and remembers only one visit to the Key West house. Neither by word nor gesture did Ernest show anything beyond friendly interest. Such is Martha's recollection. Pauline's friends believed otherwise, at least insofar as Ernest was concerned. To them he seemed more than casually taken with Martha. Dressed in shorts, and with her hair hanging loose, she looked much younger than her age, twenty-eight. Yet she was already a person in her own right. The publicity generated by her recent book had not subsided. Harry Hansen, another syndicated columnist, tabbed her as the discovery of the year among young writers. She was selling her short stories to *The New Yorker* and *Harper's Bazaar*. Her first meetings with Ernest Hemingway must have impressed her. Since her college days she had thought of him as a great writer; and, he looked so much older than the nine years that separated them. He talked older. He acted older.

By comparison with Pauline, the odds were in Martha's favor. For five years Ernest's extramarital energy had been absorbed in Jane Mason, herself beautiful and daring. But Jane was married and Martha was not. Jane had intimate ties of friendship with Pauline that, according to her own recollections, inhibited her intimacy with Ernest. Martha was a stranger to the scene. "The world was her oyster," recalled Patrick Hemingway. She would always find a way to do what she wanted and follow her instinct where it took her.

On January 5 Martha wrote Eleanor Roosevelt that she was seeing Hemingway, who was

an odd bird, very lovable and full of fire and a marvelous story teller. (In a writer this is imagination, in anyone else it's lying. That's where genius comes in.) So I sit about and have just read the mss of his new book and been very smart about it; it's easy to know about other books but such misery to know about one's own. So Hemingway tells me fine stories about the Cuban revolution and the hurricane and then I come home and . . . try to make a solid plan for a book. . . . If there is a war then all the things most of us do won't matter any more. I have a feeling that one has to work all day and all night and live too, and swim and get the sun in one's hair and laugh and love as many people as one can find around and do all this terribly fast, because the time is getting shorter and shorter every day.

In the same letter, Martha told Mrs. Roosevelt that she had thrown out everything she had written for her new book. The book must be just right, or she would not do it.

Martha left Key West around January 10, 1937, and Ernest took off for New York abruptly the next day, overtaking her in Miami, where they had a steak dinner and then rode the train together as far as Jacksonville. She now recognized this pursuit as more than ordinary interest, but their behaviour was decorous as they faced each other in the railway car and talked about Spain.

From St. Louis, Martha wrote Pauline that it was worse than she remembered. "It rains and freezes on the way down. You cut your way through the smoke with an acetylene torch. . . . But it is going to be brief. My new system of the daily dozen (pages by God) is going to finish this book in no time. . . . perhaps then I shall take a cutter (now would it be a cutter) and sail about the Horn, or maybe the Himalayas are the place for an ambitious girl." She concluded with words of appreciation for Pauline's hospitality. " . . . if I kept a diary it would be full of fine words about you."

Pauline, accepting Martha's letter for what it was—a fulsome thank you message—shipped Ernest's cold-weather clothes special delivery to New York and overexercised at tennis and swimming so that she could fall asleep at night. Telegrams arrived almost daily from the chairmen of hastily formed committees to aid the Spanish Loyalists. She wrote to Ernest:

> I'm trying to have a busy chatty life, but I'm really just marking time until you get back and life starts again. . . . Would love to be with you instead of being here with nobody and the sea. And all those telegrams about Spain and ambulances bring my situation of impending doom pretty near the front door where I am only used to the wolf and the stork. . . . So goodbye big-shot-in-the-pants, good luck and why not start keeping me informed? Your loving wife, Pauline.

One night to "fill the horrible dinner gap," she went to Josie's with friends.

It was milling with swing and undulating citizens. And as we had only had two drinks, I imagine we sort of stood out, straight and tall like young saplings only not swaying, and immediately became the center of a lot of very admiring gents and were soon dated until the last dance. But after dancing once we left. Partly to relieve Josie and partly because I was afraid that you might run into one of those citizens when you got back and they might say "I danced with your wife the other night" and you would have to sock them.

Most of her evening hours, however, were filled with nothing more exotic than letter writing, quiet games of parcheesi with Ada and the children, and straightening her accounts.

A new friend of Pauline's in Key West was a young writer named Jack Latimer. She went bike riding with him and offered to proof-read his manuscript, a mystery thriller, for Doubleday. He accepted gratefully because he had heard that she was a good editor and had helped her husband with similar tasks. "She reminded me more than anything," Latimer recalled, "of Helen Hayes. She was not pretty, but very winning, very bright. Her face was not beautiful, but so intelligent and alert that she became attractive."

In New York, at an afternoon conference with Perkins, Ernest promised to deliver the Morgan novel by summer and then suggested that Max read a good story called "Exile" by Martha Gellhorn. Perkins, who admired *The Trouble I've Seen*, took Ernest's suggestion, and a few days later *Scribner's Magazine* bought the story. Ernest signed a contract with the North American Newspaper Alliance [NANA] for his Spanish coverage and wrote a fresh commentary for a propaganda film, *Spain in Flames*, for Prudencio de Pereda, a young writer whose fiction he respected. At the same time he was writing Martha and telephoning her, urging her to come to New York, saying that he could fix it up for her to get into Spain, too. Martha, because he had been her hero as a writer, was flattered and amazed by such attentions.

When Ernest returned to Key West, Pauline was not prepared for the feverish urgency that overtook him. Although separations in the past had been an acceptable part of their marriage, she had the uneasy feeling that this one would be dangerous. She began to say that perhaps she should go with him to Spain. Ernest stated emphatically that she could not go. The most she could do was to meet him in Paris when he came out of the country. In a belated Christmas letter thanking Pauline's parents for some stock and a check, he tried to explain his feelings—first with a half-hearted joke ("This is from the leader of the Ingrates battalion on the wrong side of the Spanish war"), then with a statement of conscience (" . . . you can't preserve your happiness . . . by putting it away in moth balls and for a long time me and my conscience both have known I had to go to Spain"), and, finally, with an emotional declaration of his love for Pauline, ("I'm very grateful to you both for providing Pauline who's made me happier than I've ever been.")

Martha, meanwhile, was corresponding from St. Louis. "I hope we get on the same ark when the real deluge begins," she wrote. "It would be just my luck to survive with the members of the St. Louis Wednesday Club." Her publisher, Morrow, was treating her wickedly. Was there a chance that Ernest could show her manuscript to Perkins? Her last letter to reach him before he left Key West was written on February 15, 1937. She began on a lugubrious note. "This is very private. We are conspirators [a reference to their effort to get into Spain, the Franco-British Non-Intervention Pact having made it very difficult to get any kind of visa] and I have personally already gotten myself a beard and a pair of dark glasses. We will both say nothing and look strong." Then she turned jumpy. "Angel, I have so much to tell you, but suddenly I find that there is no time even to think straight. . . . please, please leave word in Paris [in case she missed him in New York]. Give my love to Pauline." She concluded in a last burst of anxiety. ". . . write if you can. Please don't disappear. Are we or are we not members of the same union? Hemingstein, I am very very fond of you. Marty."

Sinking ever lower into her St. Louis "horrors," Martha decided that her novel was a failure. She finished it but shoved it into a desk drawer. "You do get yourself into a state of jitters," wrote Eleanor Roosevelt. " . . . Mr. Hemingway is right. I think you lose the flow of thought by too much rewriting. It will not be a lifeless story if you feel it, although it may need polishing." Worst of all was the frustration of not being able to find an editor who would give her an official reason for entering Spain. When the female employees of the National Underwear Co. went out on strike, Martha joined the picket line and was a member of the committee of faculty wives at Washington University who negotiated with the factory owner on behalf of the workers.

She arrived in New York at the end of February, several days after Ernest had sailed for France, accompanied by Evan Shipman and Sidney Franklin. Disappointed that Ernest had not left clear information for her about entry into Spain, she looked up various people who might help her. Finally, on March 3, Kyle Crichton of *Collier's* gave Martha a letter that identified her as a special correspondent for that magazine. Actually she had no position with *Collier's*, but the letter might satisfy the authorities. An item in the *St. Louis Post-Dispatch* on March 17 noted that Miss Martha Gellhorn was en route to Europe to try to get into Spain. "She has made arrangements to join Ernest Hemingway and other Americans seeking entrance into that country." It was the first time that Martha's name was publicly linked with Ernest's.

In Paris she sought out the French authorities to apply for the papers required before leaving France. "The French fonctionnaire [sic], as all know who have dealt with him," she wrote later, "is a certified brute. He sits, unlistening, behind a grille, scratching away with a sharp governmental pen and pallid ink. I cannot have come out well with this type, as I only remember studying a map, taking a train, [and] getting off at a station nearest to the Andorran-Spanish border. . . . " She walked the short distance from France to Spain, then found a second train to Barcelona. This one, with antiquated wooden carriages, was moving soldiers of the Spanish Republic, who looked hardly as old as her brother Alfred and were equally friendly and decent. They offered her garlic sausage and hard bread and taught her Spanish songs. Barcelona was bright with sunlight and brilliant with red banners. So early in the war the people still believed in victory. A taxi driver refused to take her money. "Since few people have lived in such an atmosphere, even for a minute, I can report that it is the loveliest atmosphere going. I was handed around like a package, with jollity and kindness; . . . "

Sidney Franklin, whose own exit from France was an obscure operation involving mysterious meetings with strangers at street corners, later claimed that Ernest instructed him to look after Martha in Paris, that she met him in a cab loaded with suitcases and he put her on a train for Toulouse. Martha pointed out the absurdity of such a tale. Ernest had no idea when she would get to France; she did not know herself. If he gave such instructions to Sidney, it was to pose as the insider who could pull strings. As for suitcases, that was another myth that grew up about her. She had a knapsack and the clothes on her back—grey flannel trousers, sweater, warm windbreaker. One of her personal reasons for being happy at war was the freedom from possessions, no responsibility beyond "seeing and writing."

Martha and Sidney did, however, arrive in Valencia at approximately the same time, by widely-divergent routes. Constancia de la Mora, who was in charge of the government press bureau, assigned both of them to the same car and chauffeur for their transportation to Madrid. On the morning of March 30 the driver, with Franklin at his side, swung by the Hotel Victoria to pick up two more passengers, Martha and Ted Allan. Constancia had asked Allan, a young correspondent for the Federated Press, to ride to the capital with the *Collier's* correspondent (Martha) and brief her on policy matters. Allan made a face. It sounded very dull. Constancia smiled. "You will not be sorry," she said, "when you see her." She was right about that, recalled Allan. "I absolutely flipped for her—the wonderful smile, the hair, the great figure." They settled themselves in the back seat and before long were giggling and cuddling for warmth under the baleful eye of Franklin, who turned around frequently with disapproving looks.

In Madrid, Martha followed Sidney to the dining room in the subbasement of the Hotel Gran Via, the only designated eating place for correspondents, where Ernest was having a late dinner. The menu was an abomination—malodorous fish in yellow, mealy rice, and millet-and-water soup. The only appetizing item was an occasional orange. But because of the food shortage in Madrid everyone was hungry all the time, and ravenously ate what was served.

"I knew you'd get here, daughter," said Ernest, getting up from the table to put his arm around her, "because I fixed it up so you could."

Martha looked at him in astonishment. What did he mean? He had fixed nothing. This was the first of his many little attempts at self-aggrandizement that she began to notice. That night, however, he was the epitome of strength and authority, burly and radiating good health. Seeing Marty, young and dusty and cold, he expansively took the credit for her safe arrival. But Martha was not one to cater to his illusions. She proceeded to tell him exactly how she had managed to get there.

Madrid had been under siege for nearly five months. The Hotel Florida was in the direct line of fire from Franco's heavy artillery and most of the rooms facing the square were too badly damaged to be used. The hotel lift seldom ran; chairs were abandoned in dusty corners; hot water was unreliable and some weeks it scarcely flowed at all. Soldiers on leave from the International Brigades came around to Ernest's room for a meal and a bath. The talk was good, and plenty of women (Ernest's "whores de combat") hung around the hotel. Sidney Franklin, who had brought ham, coffee, and butter from Paris, cooked over a hot plate and kept Ernest's tall armoire stocked with food. Martha and the bullfighter did not become friends. His loyalty remained with Pauline, and Martha disliked his ignorance of politics and his posturing. But others enjoyed him. He could crack jokes when everyone was down. He found bargains in furs and perfumes. When he visited a village, the word spread like wildfire. Children tagged after him, grownups stood about entranced, even the mayor came out to shake his hand.

After her arrival in Madrid, Ernest tried to take charge of Martha in ways that were sometimes heavy-handed. On her second night, during a heavy bombardment, she woke up and, seeking company, found her door locked from the outside. She banged and shouted but to no avail. Finally, when the shelling stopped a stranger unlocked the door. Who had locked it, she wondered. She located Ernest in one of the back rooms playing poker. He had locked it, he admitted sheepishly, so that no man could bother her. In retrospect, Martha wondered why she put up with such possessiveness, when she was wary of any man who tried to take over. Somehow, Ernest's attentions felt like a command as he put his hand on her and claimed her. But she never catered to him the way other women did. Sefton Delmer, of the *London Daily Express*, who spent a lot of time with them, said that she behaved with just the right note of humorous indulgence. It was soon obvious that they were sleeping together; one night a shell burst the hot-water tank at the hotel, and a number of couples fled from the bedrooms, Ernest and Marty among them.

At first Martha did not file any stories, "I tagged along behind the war correspondents, experienced men who had serious work to do," she wrote in 1959 in *The Face of War*. " . . . I went with them to the fronts in and around Madrid. Still I did nothing except learn a little Spanish and a little about war, and visit the wounded. . . . " Then one day Ernest asked her why she wasn't writing. She was a writer, wasn't she? So she wrote a piece about Madrid, pecking it out on an old, borrowed typewriter, and sent it to *Collier's,* not expecting it to be published. Indeed it was. *Collier's* titled it "Only the Shells Whine," her name appeared on the masthead, and once that was accomplished she was a bona-fide war correspondent.

With the donkey carts rumbling across the streets and the peroxide blondes loitering in front of Chicote's Bar, the atmosphere seemed as unreal at times as a stage setting. A few movie houses were still open. People moved gaily about, as cool to the havoc as trained soldiers. One afternoon, as Martha lingered in a shop that had no merchandise to sell, she suddenly heard the "huge, stony, deep booming of a falling shell." The bombardment lasted about thirty minutes. And in the food lines that stretched along the sidewalk no one moved, for no one dared to leave his place in line, even when the shelling started. As Martha watched, mesmerized, an old woman, holding the hand of a terrified child, ran into the square. A moment later the child was killed. Two hours after that, the debris had been piled into neat stacks, the shopkeepers had rearranged their wares, little boys collected pieces of shrapnel as souvenirs, and once again people sauntered arm in arm in the sunshine.

After such a day Martha would welcome a drink with Ernest at Chicote's or Molinero's. Then it was possible to forget, if only for an hour or two, that the front was 1,200 yards away. They laughed over the famous people who were turning up in the beseiged city —movie stars, Bloomsbury intellectuals, even the Dean of Canterbury. Martha listened avidly to the military talk, admitting that she knew next to nothing, not even how to read a map. But she paid attention and learned quickly.

As Martha went about with Ernest she noticed immediately that he enjoyed special privileges because of his stature as a writer. Even with the extreme shortage of cars and drivers he had the use of a beat-up taxi and easy access to gasoline. When he volunteered to work in the field on a documentary film, *The Spanish Earth,* to be distributed in America, Martha met the film crew and Ernest's special friends in the Twelfth International Brigade—the Hungarian general, Lucasz; Werner Heilbrun, a German-Jewish doctor; and Gustav Regler, the political commissar of the Brigade. Regler, especially, became very fond of her.

During the last week of April Martha went with Ernest and a driver on a tour of the four central fronts. It was a strenuous effort. When they could not return to Madrid to sleep, they pulled up at the side of the road or accepted the meager hospitality of a field headquarters. Once they made a foray in an armored car that was hit four times by bursts of machine-gun fire. All her life Martha remained grateful to Ernest for teaching her about the different sounds of gunfire and when to fall flat. He began to say that she was the bravest woman he had ever met, braver than most men, including himself. Her courage was not tempered with caution, as his was, for she had never been traumatized as he had been at Fossalta. He understood and respected the booby traps of the battlefield in a way she could not, but her lack of knowledge in no way diminished his respect for her.

Since courage had come to be the yardstick by which Ernest judged people, Martha's possession of this quality dramatically enhanced his admiration of her. She in turn saw him at his best. "I think it was the only time in his life," she remarked, "when he was not the most important thing there was. He really cared about the Republic and he cared about that war. I believe I never would've gotten hooked otherwise."

Chapter 18

During the two months that Ernest was in the civil war zone, Pauline received a number of cables from him but only one letter. That letter finally reached her on April 15 and contained the suggestion that he might be leaving Madrid in two weeks. "If that is really true," she wrote, "cable me when you get this and I'll start to let down. If it isn't true I'll not let down." She had heard from Jane Mason, in the hospital for the repair of some torn ligaments in her back. Jane, sounding subdued, had asked Pauline to send her Ernest's novel in manuscript.

Pauline wrote to Ernest on the 20th:

> I am pretty sure Gingrich has said something to her, although maybe not. . . . I said I had promised you to give it only to two people while you were gone and not to let anyone else have it and of course that didn't apply to her, I knew, but just the same I didn't feel that I could let it out of my hands. If you put "Jane" in the next cable after you get this, that would mean she could read it. She didn't seem to think much of this plan but I said that was the best I could do. So there you are.

Grace Hemingway had written to ask if Ernest liked the tapestry she wove for him, and the Shevlins had wired that they would be in Cat Cay the first of May. Pauline apologized to Ernest for a dull recapitulation of such uneventful happenings. "You must remember that I am really a very funny woman in real life. . . . I am going to say right now that I am sick and tired of all this. . . . I wish you were here sleeping in my bed and using my bathroom and drinking my whiskey. . . . dear Papa, please come home as soon as you can."

Pauline now embarked on a big project for improving the property. It was to be a surprise for Ernest—a high wall to protect his privacy, a salt-water swimming pool (the only one—salt or fresh—between Miami and Key West) and a small pool house for changing rooms. The days dragged on, the weather turned hot, there were no more letters. Pauline began to wonder why she had not insisted upon going to Spain. "There is evidently something wrong with me somewhere," she confided to Max Perkins, who had written to ask if she needed any help, financial or otherwise. "I am told that when I was a very young baby I could be left alone on a chair and would never fall off. I seem to be still at it." She reassured Max, however, that she was really fine. "At the moment, all goes well on the widow's peak and there is little reason to think such a state won't continue."

On April 24 Ernest cabled to say that he would reach Paris May 9 and arrive in New York May 18. Pauline was so excited that she threw a dinner party for twenty people on the patio, under a full moon, with café tables and plenty to drink. The last guest left at 4:00 A.M. "Now I am cold sober," she wrote Ernest on the 26th, care of the *Normandie*, "and missing you as much as ever."

The film footage for *The Spanish Earth* was complete and ready for cutting when Ernest and Martha left Madrid. They traveled separately but expected to meet in New York in June. In Paris Ernest told a NANA correspondent that he was returning to the United States to finish the revision of a novel but would go back to Spain later in the summer. This time, he was quoted as saying his wife would accompany him. He was not self-conscious about the reference to Pauline. Although it was an open secret in Madrid that he and Martha were intimate, the rest of the world had not caught up to the gossip. For a brief period he had enjoyed a heady combination—illicit lovemaking and the dangers of war—but now he was returning to security and the warm hearth.

It is not clear how much Pauline knew. Ernest later told Martha that she knew nothing until she discovered a snapshot of Martha in his luggage after his second trip to Spain. Most of Pauline's Key

West friends, however, thought she suspected something and admired her for putting up a good front. Patrick Hemingway, in reminiscing with the author, described his mother as the responsible older woman, married to a younger man, who believed that it was up to her to make the marriage work. If her husband was attracted to another woman, then she must wait for his interest to wane. This rationale had worked well in his relationship with Jane Mason. Now it would be tested again.

Pauline looked forward to Ernest's taking up his fishing-and-writing routine. Perhaps Spain would recede safely into memory now. But there was too much Spanish business at hand for such a hope to be realized. She became increasingly tense as telegrams began to arrive in rapid succession from Joris Ivens, the documentary filmmaker who had directed *The Spanish Earth*. Ivens was reminding Ernest that he had promised to write the narration for the film and also to address the coming Writers' Congress in New York.

Martha, who had reached New York in mid-May, urged Ernest to do everything Joris asked. "I suppose I will bleed and die for the damn man," she wrote, "on account I admire him so." She was not so admiring of other communists she encountered and watched with some skepticism their maneuvering to infiltrate all situations and committees. "These communists are sinister folk and very very canny. . . . " On May 28 over lunch at the White House with Eleanor Roosevelt, Martha asked the First Lady to invite her and Ernest and Ivens to show the film to the President. "Martha Gellhorn seems to have come back with one deep conviction," wrote Mrs. Roosevelt in her daily column, "that the Spanish people are a glorious people and something is happening in Spain which may mean much to the rest of the world."

On a sweltering June 4 Ernest flew from Bimini to New York to appear before the Writers' Congress and to be reunited with Martha at the Hotel Gladstone. The League of American Writers, ranging in political philosophy from center to far left, convened the congress with an open meeting at Carnegie Hall. Thirty-five hundred people jammed the auditorium and another thousand were turned away. Ernest, sweating in his heavy clothes, pulling nervously at his tie, sat through the early speeches in the company of Archie MacLeish, who was chairman, and Martha. After ten o'clock

Pauline, acting as barber. Bimini, 1937.
From the John F. Kennedy Library

he strode to the podium to deliver a seven-minute speech that electrified the audience. "There is only one form of government that cannot produce good writers," he said, "and that system is fascism. For fascism is a lie told by bullies. A writer who will not lie cannot live and work under fascism." The sheer power of his presence took the place by storm. Waves of applause swept the hall as Ernest rushed to the wings. "He was astoundingly good and so simple and honest," Martha wrote later to Eleanor Roosevelt. He had vindicated her faith that he would put his reputation on the line for a cause "that was bigger than his own cause."

The next afternoon Martha delivered her own address before the afternoon closed session of the Writers' Congress at the New School for Social Research, in which she said:

> The writers who are now in Spain . . . were just brave, intelligent people doing an essential job in war . . . completely unaware of *themselves.* . . . A man who has given a year of his life, without heroics or boastfulness, to the war in Spain, or who, in the same way, has given a year of his life to steel strikes, or to the unemployed, or to the problems of racial prejudice, has not lost or wasted time. He is a man who has known where he belonged.

As soon as the congress was over Ernest and Martha separated once again, Ernest returning to Bimini to complete his revisions of the Morgan novel, now titled *To Have and Have Not,* and Martha remaining in New York. She badgered her friends in the government and the labor unions to take notice of the Spanish situation. Crackpot committees sprang up everywhere. It was a never-ending exasperation to fend them off. Then on June 17 she learned to her horror that Lucasz and Heilbrun of the Twelfth Brigade had been killed and Gustav Regler severely wounded. "I thought I knew everything about war," she wrote sadly to Ernest, "but what I didn't know was that your friends got killed."

A few days later, Ernest arrived in New York to record the spoken narrative for *The Spanish Earth.* "It seemed to me," recalled Prudencio de Pereda, the novelist who was working with Hemingway on the sound track, "—and I think to Joris [Ivens] . . .—that Martha was doing most of the courting. That was a natural enough thing to do. . . . I think she is a woman of spunk and would be willing to consider the point." De Pereda and the others may have noticed how spontaneous and open Martha was at this time. She seemed able to trust Ernest with her feelings. Her friends had always enjoyed her because she was full of life, full of fun. She was generous, went out of her way for people, and all this came together as she fell in love.

On July 1 Ernest was back in Bimini, having given Perkins the go-ahead to publish *To Have and Have Not* in the fall. On July 5 he received a letter from Martha. The letterhead read, "Emergency Ambulance Committee; Ernest Hemingway, President; Martha Gellhorn, Secretary; Thomas Shevlin, Treasurer." "Dear President," she began, " . . . of all the things attached to this war that I have found funny, this paper is . . . the funniest. . . . it looks so phony that you would suspect the treasurer of absconding with the funds, the president . . . of being an imposter . . . and the secretary a cretin with homicidal leanings." She was feeling more and more depressed about her own writing. "I write lousier and lousier and longer and longer each day. Before I die they are going to think I am Dreiser. . . . the book is so bad I wouldn't be surprised if I sold serial rights. . . . Salud, Marty."

Five days later Ernest left Cat Cay again, for the third time in less than two months, to meet Joris and Martha for the flight to Washington to show the film at the White House. At Newark Airport Martha bought sandwiches for the group, explaining to the surprised men that the food at the White House was awful and it was a good idea to eat something before going there for a meal. She knew because she had "stayed there a lot," Ernest explained later to his mother-in-law, identifying Martha as "the girl who fixed it up" for the film to be shown.

From Washington, Ernest and Joris flew to Hollywood to raise money from the film community. Martha, still in Manhattan, wrote to Eleanor Roosevelt. "I am the scribe for that group [Hemingway and Ivens] and so am delegated also to thank you for them, warmly. . . . If I hadn't felt so like a mother with her two infant prodigies and been so nervous lest anything go wrong with the film, I'd have felt brighter. . . . you were heavenly to us and I hope you like my two trench buddies, both of whom I adore."

Ernest returned to Bimini in time to celebrate his thirty-eighth birthday on July 21 and went through the motions of domesticity with an air of martyrdom. Open fighting with Pauline over Martha had not yet erupted. What did take place were tearful pleas from Pauline not to risk his life in Spain and dogged insistence from Ernest that Spain was where his duty lay. If she really loved him she would cooperate. Reports from the battle front were all bad. On the 26th a gloomy letter arrived from Martha in New York. In spite of endless nagging and arguing she had made little headway with the movie distributors on releasing the film. She hated being treated like a "cuckoo idealist up and down the Great White Way." A box of books was on the way for his birthday. In the meantime, she was off to St. Louis to visit her mother.

Pauline watched helplessly as Ernest prepared to return to Spain. Ernest could say little to his children, but he did try to defend his actions to Mary Pfeiffer. Writing on August 2, he admitted that after two weeks in Spain he had felt like a man who had no wife, no children, no house, no boat, nothing. Over there that was the only way to function. Now he was home and valuing all things again. But he had lost his fear of death and knew that to think of his personal future when the world was in such a bad way was simply egotistical. Having thus rationalized his separation from Pauline, he departed for New York to meet Martha. " . . . in that pre-historic past," she wrote forty-four years later, "we tried steadily though in vain to be discreet."

Ernest sailed from New York on the *Champlain* on August 17, 1937. Martha left two days later on the *Normandie*. She booked tourist class because that was what she could afford. There was no question of taking money from Ernest for hotel rooms or passage on ships or anything else. Nor did Ernest press any money on her. He was not inclined to spend money on women. (Martha could not recall that he ever gave her anything except a shotgun and long cashmere underpants from Abercrombie and Fitch suitable for duck-shooting on cold days.)

In Paris, Ernest and Herbert Matthews of the *New York Times* were waiting for her. She made last-minute preparations for Spain, then went alone to swim at le Lavandou on the Riviera, where the sea was warm and calm and the beach clean. There were a few days back in Paris before the three of them left on September 6 for Madrid. Immediately after checking in at the Hotel Florida they drove to the Aragon Front. Two-thirds of Spain was in Franco's hands, but Belchite below Zaragoza had just been recaptured by the

Loyalists. Martha walked about the smoking ruins, watching the soldiers bury their dead, then joined some Americans who were lounging on a stream bank under the olive trees. She could taste the yellow dust of Aragon on her tongue and feel it settle over her clothes and eyebrows and hair. "It was a strange thing," she wrote in *Collier's*, "walking through that olive grove, . . . seeing the faces from Mississippi and Ohio and New York and California and hearing the voices that you'd heard at a baseball game, in the subway, on any campus. . . . "

From Belchite the three companions moved on to the heights above Teruel. Crawling on her hands and knees over clean-smelling straw in a pitch-black dugout, Marty looked down through a slit in the wall onto a pretty, peaceful scene. "Even in war, . . . " she noted, "nothing can spoil this handsome land." For three days they climbed steep mountain trails over newly cut military roads, visiting the highest mountain positions. They were the first correspondents permitted to survey this front. Traveling in an open truck that was equipped with mattresses, blankets, and cooking utensils, they parked at night in the courtyards of farmhouses with the cattle and the donkeys. Hospitable peasants shared with them their small stocks of food and wine.

With the fascist firepower concentrated in Aragon, the artillery bombardment of Madrid had decreased in intensity. The weather was fine and the bars were crowded. Life was agreeable for the lovers. In 1981, in the *Paris Review*, Martha wrote of Ernest that in Spain and in China " . . . he made good jokes and was valuable cheerful company . . . and no more boring than we all are the rest of the time." On rainy days they gambled at dominoes, on Sunday mornings they went to the flea market to buy canaries in paper bags and silver watches that never ran. In an affecting short story Martha described a zoo located behind the carved iron gate that opened into the Parque de Madrid. "It is a very sweet zoo, intimate and absurd, with little cage-houses hopefully imitating the architecture of the original country of the animals. The elephant lives in an odd-looking sort of Hindu temple; the monkeys are in a thatched affair . . . the peacocks are housed in tile." With finely-controlled emotion she evokes for the reader the contrasts created by war. " . . . how incredible it was to have everything mixed up together, the zoo and the gun positions behind the statue [of Alfonso XIII], and the café that grew up in one half of a shelled building. . . . "

On October 15, *To Have and Have Not* was published. It quickly became a national best seller, but the reviews were mixed. Ernest was never able to successfully reconcile the Harry Morgan sequences with the ones about the yachtsmen and their love affairs. Despite a handful of superb scenes, Louis Kronenberger wrote that the book displayed "shocking lapses from professional skill." Praise came mostly from reviewers on the left, who were pleased with Ernest's emerging social consciousness. But Edmund Wilson disparaged even that praise, chiding the critics for lauding one of Hemingway's least credible works as a brilliant social commentary.

As for Pauline, there can be little doubt that she was jarred by Ernest's brutal delineation of a collapsing marriage. The role reversal (of Helen Gordon, the wife, walking out on Richard, her writer-husband) seemed at times to be a transparent disguise of Pauline's true situation. Helen says:

> "I've tried to be a good wife, but you're as selfish and conceited as a barnyard rooster. . . . you were a genius and I was your whole life. . . . Slop. Love is just another dirty lie. . . . Love always hangs up behind the bathroom door. It smells like lysol. To hell with love. Love is you making me happy and then going off to sleep . . . while I lie awake all night afraid to say my prayers even because I know I have no right to anymore. . . . All right. . . . I'm through with love. Your kind of pick-nose love. You writer."

It was all there, the sexual tensions and Pauline's Catholic conscience, her loyalty and care of him, his conceits and demands. She sent him the reviews and the sales figures, but privately she was confused and depressed.

With nothing to report from the front, Ernest stayed in Madrid and began to work again—this time on his first full-length melodrama. The hero, Philip Rawlings, is loaded with Ernest's own habits and opinions. A secret agent working for the Loyalists, his cover is that of a rowdy journalist who eats raw onions, walks like a gorilla, and is plagued with insomnia and nightmares. He is in love with a beautiful American correspondent, Dorothy Bridges, who is ignorant of military matters and wishes he would exchange his tattered uniform for a handsome suit and bowler hat. The stage directions are a precise description of Ernest's room at the Florida, and the actress who plays the correspondent should have blonde hair, look very young without make-up, and wear a silver fox wrap.

Ernest was not secretive about the manuscript. Everyone who read it recognized the caricature of Martha. But Marty, who was having a fine time and not worrying about the future, took it good-naturedly. If he needed to portray her in such a light, perhaps it had something to do with his own conflicts. Philip Rawlings's curious reply, when asked why he continued to fool around with the flirtatious Junior Leaguer, is that he wants to make an absolutely colossal mistake. Ernest may have been suggesting, to himself if not to the reader, that he was *going* to make a colossal mistake.

In bed together in the dark, Philip Rawlings confesses to Dorothy that he loves her. " 'Listen, I want to say something else. Would you like to marry me or stay with me all the time or go wherever I go, and be my girl?' " Of course she would like to marry him, replies Dorothy. " 'I'd like us to be married and work hard and have a fine life.' " But the fictional lovers do not marry. Philip leaves for dangerous espionage work and Dorothy stays behind. In the climactic scene, there are caustic references to the time it took to get tired of one another and the "thousand breakfasts come up on trays." All the memories evoked here, with a certain mournful finality, belong to his ten years with Pauline—the Crillon and the Ritz, Nairobi, the long white beach at Lamu, Sans Souci on a Saturday night in Havana. " '. . . I've been to all those places,' " says Philip contemptuously, " 'and I've left them all behind. And where I go now I go alone, or with others who go there for the same reason I go.' " If he was not quite ready to leave Pauline, Ernest seemed to be using the forum he liked best—his own fiction—to prepare her for trouble ahead.

Chapter 19

In November the weather in Madrid turned dismal. It rained steadily and the streets were mustard-colored with mud. There was much talk of a coming offensive. Everyone seemed gripped by a brooding paralysis that only lifted during the noon hour, when the bars could sell beer. Chicote's was still the place to go. "The smoke from black tobacco was choking," Martha wrote, "the noise deafening; . . . the indomitable girls with dyed hair and amazing high heels waved and smiled; people walked in through the sandbagged door and stared and saw no one they knew or nothing they liked and walked out again." One day, during a particularly heavy shelling, Ernest was at lunch with the chief of the secret police and some other functionaries. Suddenly he got up and left, fearful for Martha's safety. Where was she? At the hotel? On some dangerous street corner? He rushed through the mud and rubble to find her. Martha did not object to this show of concern—she appreciated it—but it seemed to her that he was amazingly unconcerned most of the time.

Generally, Martha and others walked to the nearest front, ten to fifteen blocks from the hotel. "No matter how often you do it," she wrote for *Collier's*, "it is surprising just to walk to war, easily, from your own bedroom where you have been reading a detective story or a life of Byron, or listening to the phonograph or chatting with your friends." They would move forward through the shallow, muddy trenches with some difficulty. Mortars exploded, machine guns clattered their reply, but to Martha the young soldiers on duty seemed as casual as people at an outdoor summer concert.

There was no good news, only rain and rumors and the interminable wishful thinking that somehow an offensive would break the stalemate. During October and November Martha was one of the correspondents asked by foreign networks to send out shortwave broadcasts from the soundproof building in the diplomatic quarter. One of them was rebroadcast in the United States by NBC and heard by her mother in St. Louis. In December Martha began preparations to leave Spain. With some reluctance, she had agreed to make a lecture tour in the United States, with her fees going to Spanish medical aid. Ernest hated the idea of the tour and insulted her steadily, although he never explained why.

A week before Christmas, when Martha and Ernest were in Barcelona, the news came through that the long-delayed offensive was at last under way. The government troops had launched a surprise attack against Franco's forces defending Teruel. Ernest raced to the front with Herbert Matthews and Sefton Delmer. The assault raged for several days in a blinding snowstorm, as the three correspondents watched the troop movements from a command post on a mountaintop, where a fifty-mile-an-hour wind blew. At night they rushed back to Valencia to file their dispatches. By day they scrambled from ridge to ridge to get a better view, finally entering the town with Loyalist officers behind two truckloads of young soldiers with dynamite. Ernest commuted daily from Valencia to observe the Loyalists' mopping-up operations, then returned to Barcelona to celebrate the victory over Christmas dinner with Martha at the Hotel Majestic.

The next day Marty left for Paris, expecting to enjoy the change. Instead she became ill from the rich food and resented the indifference of her friends to events in Spain. She settled her debts to Ernest with the royalty check that was waiting for her at her Paris bank, listing their accounts and how she was handling them, always meticulous about paying her share. " . . . you may know," she wrote him, "that this book [*The Trouble I've Seen*], which is the best thing I ever wrote, paid for Spain which is the best thing I ever did." A few days later she wrote again from the *Normandie*. Her luggage had been temporarily lost and she had a foul cabin but would try to work. The tone of the letter was subdued. "I hope all is well with you and that the yuletide season is the yuletide season. See you sometime, greetings, Marty."

In the meantime, Pauline had left Key West early in December, having convinced herself that she could patch up everything if only she could see Ernest. She had taken the train to New York, hoping to be in Paris, perhaps even Spain, by Christmas. But nothing went right for her. The ocean crossing was stormy and then there were the frustrating delays in Paris as she waited for a visa that never came through. She saw Jay Allen and told him tearfully that it was terribly important to get to Ernest, for she now understood how critical it was for her to learn something about the war and what it meant to her husband. When Jay returned to Barcelona he told Ernest how Pauline had been trying in vain to get the visa. Ernest put Allen through a kind of third degree, for hours and hours. "He seemed amazed and flattered too, that his wife would risk the dangers of war in order to see him," recalled Allen, "and mightily displeased with me for not making it possible."

By the time Ernest reached Paris, Pauline was exhausted and edgy with disappointment. The reunion quickly degenerated into a bitter quarrel. She stormed and raged, promised to get even, to make him pay dearly, threatening to jump off the balcony of their suite at the Hôtel Elysée. Ernest, who tolerated people who stood up to him if they were good-humored and easy about it, did not budge. He wondered why she bothered to come looking for him if she was going to be so disagreeable.

The trip from France to New York was no better. The winter seas were stormy and their ship, the *Gripsholm*, was an ironic reminder of happier days, when they had sailed out of Africa in 1934. But in the familiar surroundings of Key West Pauline relaxed. Even when Ernest took the *Pilar* to Havana she did not object but simply said that the swimming pool would be filled when he returned.

At the Ambos Mundos Ernest tried to work, but the words would not come. Hadley heard from him on January 31, a frank letter full of laments and ending with the tribute that of all the people in the world, he admired her and Paul the most. His marriage to her was beginning to seem like an island of tranquility, as Hadley herself assumed more and more the guise of someone who never caused him a moment's trouble. In none of his letters to friends did he refer to Martha directly, although to Perkins he admitted that he was in a gigantic jam, mostly of his own making.

On March 15 Ernest heard in a phone call from Europe that there was a new fascist drive across Aragon to the Mediterranean. Immediately he wired Max Perkins to book him on the *Ile de France* and enlisted Pauline to help him with his packing. As she assembled his heavy clothes for the cold mountain fighting, she announced that she would go on the plane with him to Newark. Ernest, relieved that she did not berate him, reverted to his former term of endearment, Poor Old Mama, and they left together.

The day after Ernest's ship sailed from New York, Pauline had tea with Max Perkins and his wife Louise. She said nothing about her personal agony to the Perkinses but with her friends and with Jinny she was decidedly upset. Ruth and Jay Allen tried to reassure her, but Jinny's consolation took the form of sharp criticism of Ernest's behavior. As far as Jinny was concerned he was a rat for treating Pauline so shabbily, and she warned her to be prepared for a drastic change for the worse. She should be tough with him. It was the only language he understood. Pauline poured out her grief but doubted the wisdom of Jinny's advice. Instead, her letters to Ernest adhered to a light and loving tone. He should not hurry home if staying would help beat the fascists. "Don't be sucked in by the fixed date racket," she joshed. "Remember how it was when we had to get to Piggott by Christmas." Occasionally a wisecracking sense of foreboding crept in. "Remember that tragedy comes from within, not from without, and remember me without you within limits (figure that out)."

Martha, who kept her commitment to the Post Agency to go on the lecture circuit across America in behalf of the Spanish Republic, was finding it more and more painful to be a so-called celebrity. On January 7, 1938, she spoke before 3,000 people on the campus of the University of Minnesota. On January 19 she addressed the Des Moines Women's Club. Under the auspices of the League for Industrial Democracy she greeted an overflowing crowd at the Sheldon War Memorial in St. Louis on January 29 and reminded them that famous writers from all over the world, including Ernest Hemingway himself, had gone to Spain to do what they could for a desperate and brave people. "She spoke as an honest partisan," reported the *Post-Dispatch*, "and called Franco a butcher." (Martha did not tailor her opinions to the politics of her audience. St. Louis, conservative Catholic and heavily German, heard the same views as liberal New York.) At an interview in her mother's home, Martha predicted that the defeat of the Loyalist government would lead to a world war. Her last stop, early in February, was Chicago, where her forum was the Nineteenth Century Women's Club. An enthusiastic member of her audience was Grace Hemingway. On the margin of the newspaper clipping reporting the speech Grace wrote Ernest how much she enjoyed meeting Martha.

After two months of speechmaking in America, Martha had forfeited the fees and fled to Harbor Island in the Bahamas. The futility of trying to persuade her well-fed audiences that the Spanish people really needed their support was finally too much for her youthful idealism. She was back in Paris when Ernest arrived. With only the briefest of reunions they boarded the train for Perpignan, the French coastal town near the Spanish border. From March 31, when they departed, until the middle of May, when they were back in Paris, they were inseparable, though often not alone. Vincent Sheean and Jim Lardner rode with them to Barcelona. After two days at the battered Hotel Majestic they joined up with Herbert Matthews for the dangerous journey south to Tarragona and the Ebro Delta, now the target of Franco's drive to cut off Valencia.

The gray hills visible from the coastal road were splashed with the pink of almond blossoms. But the peaceful horizon was a mirage. Half a mile from Reus, Martha and her companions dove from their small, open car into a ditch to avoid being strafed by a Rebel monoplane. When the road became clogged with refugees and carts, plodding animals and weary soldiers, they were forced to turn back, to make the same effort the next morning. This time they managed to keep very close to the unstabilized battle lines. In the afternoon they headed for Tortosa, maneuvering their little car through boxes of dynamite set to mine the small stone bridges on the narrow road. Ernest could not find enough words to describe Martha's courage, repeating that she was the bravest woman he had ever met.

At 4:00 A.M. on Good Friday, April 15, joined now by Tom Delmer, the correspondents left Barcelona under the illumination of a full moon that silhouetted the jutting cypresses on the rocky Catalan hills. Again they hit the ditches as the silver and white Italian Savoia-Marchettis came over to bomb the area. Nine days later Martha would describe the scene in a letter to Eleanor Roosevelt. " . . . we watched thirty-three silver Italian bombers fly in wedges over the mountains across the hot clear sky to bomb Tortosa: and anywhere and everywhere is proof of the huge amount of new material sent in for this drive, and everywhere is proof of the unbending resistance of Loyalist Spain." Crossing the last steel bridge that was still standing, they reached Ulldecona, only to learn that the Moorish and Navarrese troops that supported Franco were approaching from the next village. Ernest liked to boast about Martha's poise and would tell his friends that in spite of the frightful practice of some Moors with prisoners of either sex, she did not leave his side.

Back in Barcelona at midnight, Martha washed and slept and was ready again at dawn to drive with Ernest to a point on the Ebro River that faced across to Amposta, now also in enemy hands. She followed him through an irrigation ditch. A line of young boys lay on their bellies below the railroad tracks, their bayonets aimed across the river. These children were the fresh Republican troops. Suddenly the clatter of machine guns was much closer, and there were sudden spouts of stone dust. The sharp slant of the bayonets angled above the rails. The "dress-rehearsal quality" of the scene was gone. Making a run for it, Martha and Ernest jumped into the car and sped off, feeling drops of rain on their cheeks and hair. Heavy rains would be good for the Loyalist army, for it would slow down the fascist advance.

In trying to analyze Ernest's attraction for her, Martha has spoken of his unselfishness and generosity in the cause of Spain. But she met other men who were serious and selfless about Spain. Only Ernest became her lover. Her own answer explains it. Ernest generally got what he wanted. He was always at her side and a tower of strength. He understood war from experience, he spoke easy Spanish, he was her guide and teacher. And he was wonderful, funny company in those days. If making love gave him intense pleasure, good; it was, to her, the least important part of their relationship. She had the most fun with men who became her buddies, "the chaps" as she later called them, who wanted no special lien on her.

In the spring of 1938 Ernest still had no special lien on her. But the companionship they shared, the jokes, the political allegiance to Spain, her respect for his literary genius—all that was enough to win her. If she was chary of marrying him—for at this stage he did suggest marriage—it was because she knew that the demands he would make as her husband were different from the ones he could make as her lover.

They lingered in Barcelona, then in Paris, reluctant to separate. Martha was uncertain when she would see him again. She was facing important assignments for *Collier's* in Czechoslovakia, England, and France. " . . . my daily bread may drive me out for awhile," she wrote to Eleanor Roosevelt, "but then I'll come back. What goes on here [Spain] seems to me very much the affair of all of us, who do not want a world whose Bible is Mein Kampf."

As the time neared for them to part, Ernest grew gloomy about their chances for a reunion. He was sinking into the same state of helplessness that had overwhelmed him in 1926, when he was tied to one woman, in love with another, and wishing for something wholly unpredictable to rescue him. It was at this time that he cast about for someone to blame—other than himself—for the mess in his personal life. Once he had held Sara and Gerald Murphy responsible for his leaving Hadley. This time the spoiler was his sister-in-law. He was right to suspect that Jinny would side with Pauline against him, but to cast her in the role of deliberate troublemaker was patently unfair.

When he passed through New York on his way to Key West he went around to the Allen apartment in Washington Square. First he questioned Jay and Ruth about Pauline—what they knew and what they had heard. Then he accused Jinny of turning Pauline against him. Jay was sympathetic, but he had no particular advice except to suggest that Jinny had nothing to do with it. Everyone felt sorry about what was happening to the Hemingways. Even Hadley, when she saw Jay in Chicago, had asked him if there wasn't something she could do, "write to Ernest or something." But really there was nothing anyone could do.

Pauline was polite when Ernest finally got home, but there was no lightheartedness left, only a bruised and battered pride. In public she was worn out from the effort to ignore what was now obvious. In private, it was impossible for her to keep her dignity. She stormed at him, he lashed back. Though friends sided with Pauline, they could see that Ernest was as miserable as she was. He seemed unable to leave her and unable to mount a fresh courtship. All his energies poured into his work. From the creative impasse of the winter he moved to a steady output of material—short stories based on his recollections of Madrid and some political articles for *Ken*, a new magazine.

Pauline described Ernest to her mother as leading a quiet life of working and fishing, "perhaps too quiet." She stayed out of his way as much as possible but reacted angrily when he made trouble. In the midst of her last-minute preparations for a costume party at the Havana Madrid nightclub, Ernest burst in from a fishing trip to announce that his study door was locked and the key missing. He fired his pistol at the ceiling, then went outside to shoot the lock off the door and barricade himself inside. Pauline sent the children to stay with the Thompsons, went to the nightclub as planned, and then asked Charles to check on Ernest.

Now recovered from his tantrum, Ernest decided to join the guests at the club. For a while he was attentive to Pauline, who was seductively attired in a hula costume. Later, however, when one of the male guests began to paw Ernest's dancing partner, Ernest clobbered the man with his fists. In the ensuing fracas furniture was broken. In the old days Pauline might have shrugged off such an incident, but this time she went into a frenzy that lasted even after a shaky truce.

In August the heat and dampness became oppressive, and they set off for the Nordquist ranch. Husband and wife bickered constantly, neither giving an inch as the arguments droned on. Pauline would try to give Ernest road directions and Ernest, ignoring them, would blame her when he took a wrong turn. "I recorded it just like a tape recorder," recalled Patrick, who was ten at the time. "Only later did I assimilate what it all meant." Martha's name was still not evoked but she was the unspoken presence. At the ranch torrential rains confined them to their cabin. For two weeks Pauline and Ernest read proof and discussed what to do about publication of *The Fifth Column*. Ernest finally decided to publish the play in the same volume as a collection of forty-nine stories—a few new, most old— that Scribners was bringing out. Perhaps someone else would re-write it for the stage.

On August 20, he mailed the galleys to Perkins along with a dedication that read, "To Marty and Herbert with love." Although this tribute was later dropped, the statement was most likely Ernest's way of certifying his new feelings. He hinted of trouble when he wrote Mary Pfeiffer that if he had hired someone to run his life badly he could not have done a more complete job of it. Pauline, reading in front of the fireplace, called across the room to him to add a postscript that she was really fine. "Fine" was hardly the word, but she kept her composure until he broke the news that he was leaving for Spain. Again she begged him to reconsider. Again he reiterated that he must do what he was doing.

A week later Ernest was in New York preparing to rendezvouz with Martha in Paris. On August 30, the night before sailing on the *Normandie*, he had dinner with Jinny and Jay McEvoy, who observed how lonely he seemed. Suddenly Ernest turned to Jinny and asked her to sail with him. "We could cable for your passport," he suggested. It was a strange invitation and probably reflected the skittishness that took hold of Ernest when he was going from one woman to another. Jinny, who treated the idea as a joke, later remarked to Jay that perhaps she should have gone. Maybe things would have been different; she implied that she might even have saved the marriage.

Martha's summer had been both strenuous and sobering. On August 6 *Collier's* had published her report from Czechoslovakia. It was heavily documented and disquieting. She had traveled to all the frontiers and understood well the geography of the small nation. "Czechoslovakia is shaped like a badly-made kite and its head [the Sudetenland, where two million German Czechs lived] rests in Germany. Since Austria was absorbed into Germany [March 12, 1938], Czechoslovakia is surrounded on three sides by the Reich." The well-equipped Czech army was determined to defend its democratically-elected government but the Nazis were exerting tremendous propaganda pressure.

> All these people [the citizens whom she interviewed] are united in their will to go on as they are. They want to work and make their country bloom; they want to be quiet. . . . [But] Czechoslovakia's tragedy is that it is in the way. If the somber procession is to continue—China, Ethiopia, Spain—then Czechoslovakia is next.

Martha covered England in the same thorough manner, visiting the country towns and the cities, listening to working people in pubs as well as industrialists in their factories. The British generally frowned on talk of the possibility of war as war-mongering, yet preparation on a national scale was going on. "The English have always had the privilege of fighting their wars someplace else, but now England is preparing to fight in her own air, over her own fields and cities, and the prospect is pleasing to no one," Martha wrote in "The Lord Will Provide for England."

Two years later Martha published a novel, *A Stricken Field,* whose heroine is Mary Douglas, an American journalist working in Europe. When Mary visits her lover in Paris, she describes her mood as

" . . . free as air, and bright as a whistle . . . drinking coffee with John on the terrace of Weber's, and watching him read *L'Auto,* and he'll stop reading and see you watching him and smile, and you'll hold hands probably for a moment in the sun, and then he'll go on reading about the boxing at the Salle Wagram, and you'll look at the women passing to see if you can pick up any ideas for your fall clothes, and after breakfast you'll take his arm and walk down the rue Royale, stopping at all the expensive shop windows. . . .

One can speculate that this mood reflects in some measure Martha's own mood of September 1938, even though Martha is not Mary Douglas and has stated emphatically that real life in Paris with Ernest was in no way as lovely as the fiction.

Leaving Ernest occupied with his own work—he was making a tentative start toward a novel about the Spanish Civil War—Martha set out by car to gather material for the third of her *Collier's* assignments. She drove south to the Spanish and Italian frontiers. In the isolated mountain village of Massat she talked to the mailman; in Marseilles she had coffee with metal workers; in the fortified town of Briancon, thirteen kilometers from the Italian border, she visited with the mayor. Nowhere was there any appetite for war. "There were over eight and a half million men killed in the last war," she wrote for *Collier's.* "The French do not want it ever to happen again: there are enough graves to last them for all time. And they know that there is neither victory nor defeat; there is only catastrophe."

On November 3 Martha and Ernest returned to Spain one last time. Together with Herbert Matthews and Vincent Sheean they went every day to the crumbling Loyalist front. On the occasion of the birthday of the Soviet Union a noisy party was held at the Hotel Majestic in the suite of the assistant Pravda correspondent, Boleslavskya. At midnight everyone became silent. It was a moment to remember the ones who had died. Martha and Ernest stood quietly, heads bowed. They had lost dear friends and been the sorrowful witnesses to terrible tragedy. Their cause was lost, the cause that had brought them close. A fascist victory was imminent, even if it could be staved off for another few months.

It was time to move on. Ernest was going to New York to face Pauline and everything he dreaded. Perhaps the second time around would not be so tough. Perhaps Pauline would be graceful after all, like Hadley, and the boys would be like Bumby, full of love and obedience. He was not so much contrite as apprehensive, writing Perkins that he was " . . . sick of conflicting obligations which seems to be the product that I have the greatest supply of."

Martha stayed on in Barcelona for a few weeks, visiting hospitals and the homes of ordinary citizens. Food lines stretched for blocks; rations were pitiful—a handful of dried peas, a sliver of codfish. In the childrens' wards of the huge hospitals there was near-famine. The young patients played listlessly with makeshift toys. At the sight of their faces, shrunken and old before their time, Martha went numb with rage but wrote of them lovingly, with a discerning eye for their mischief and a special insight into the dramas between parent and child. In one vignette she told of a miserable, wounded little boy whimpering with loneliness in the hospital. Only when his haggard witch of a mother appeared at his bedside was he pacified. She filled his eager ears with all the horrors of her life—bombed-out house, stolen belongings, nothing to cook with. Martha wrote for *Collier's*:

> . . . he listened with . . . sympathy and wasn't homesick any more. Then she took a pot from some pocket, it materialized like a rabbit from a hat, and gave it to the child. . . . He began to scoop up cold rice from the pot. . . . He ate it . . . spilling a little on the bedclothes and stopping only to collect the grayish rice grains with his fingers. He seemed happy then and at home.

In September at Munich, England and France had appeased Hitler by withdrawing their commitment to Czechoslovakia and in effect forcing the Czech government to cede all of the Sudetenland to Germany. Again Martha wanted to see for herself what was happening. When she reached Prague she found the Czech people bitterly ashamed of their rulers for capitulating to Hitler's hideous terms. A fine army had been forbidden to defend itself, a rich industrial area lost. For *Collier's* Martha examined the tragedy in economic and political terms. Grimly and with barely concealed anger she mourned the loss of democracy. In *A Stricken Field* Mary Douglas ponders the random tragedy of a war that dooms one pair of lovers even as it spares another.

> They're just like us, Mary thought. They love each other the same way. Only they are smaller and with no luck. We have the jobs and the passports: we can always get on trains and meet each other, we can talk about how it will be when we're old and we can make plans for next year. She could imagine John sitting where Peter was, this could be their home, she could be Rita: in another country, perhaps, and in danger for other reasons. The reasons didn't matter. If you were always and naturally on the side of the oppressed, you would always and naturally have reasons for danger.

Martha left Czechoslovakia on the last civilian plane, carrying secret documents that testified to the Nazi terror. Months later, in trying to formulate her own statement of faith, she wrote to Eleanor Roosevelt, "Myself, alone, I have a wonderful and privileged life and am deeply aware every minute of my benefits and good luck. But that doesn't let me out. Or maybe that is what lets me in. . . . the only way I can pay back for what fate and society have handed me is to try, in minor totally useless ways, to make an angry sound against injustice."

Chapter 20

Two months with Jinny had stiffened Pauline's resolve not to let Ernest get away easily if he insisted upon a divorce. (Make the bastard pay, would be a fair summary of Virginia's sisterly advice.) At the same time, the stimulus of New York City was restorative. Jinny's friends included her in their round of luncheons and openings. When time dragged, she went to the Pfeiffer compound in Connecticut to be pampered by her doting aunts. The pain of losing Ernest was like a sentence that could never be lifted, but she had found a way to get through the days. Ernest was not always so good an actor. When Jinny invited both of them to her apartment for dinner, Ernest fixed his eyes blankly on a painting that hung between the windows and moped like a jealous small boy who is being ignored.

After the Christmas holidays in Key West, Ernest was once again in New York. He read Benjamin Glaser's adaptation of *The Fifth Column*, prepared for the Theater Guild, and spent a few days with Martha, who had returned from Europe and would be going south with her mother. Jack came down from prep school for the weekend. His father, meeting him at the train, mentioned that they would see *The Spanish Earth* and drop in at the Stork Club. "Who should go to the movie with us but this absolutely glamorous creature?" recalled Jack. How, he wondered, could his "old" father have anything to do with someone so young and beautiful? She wore a long, lustrous fur coat and used four-letter words with a flair that impressed the fifteen-year-old preppie. He did not realize until many months later that Martha was someone special in his father's life.

Grace had written Ernest in December that she would drive down to Lake Wales, Florida to visit Carol and her family. It would be nice to see him, too, for it had been seven years since they had been together and Gigi was the only one of her ten grandchildren whom she had not met. Ernest was back in Key West when her visit took place in early February of 1939. He put her up in handsome quarters at the Casa Marina on the other side of the island and refused to let on that anything was wrong. Grace was not fooled but realized that she had better not offer any unsolicited advice. So she painted and walked and tried to get better acquainted with both grandchildren. Patrick was embarrassed when she took him aside one afternoon to hand him a small penknife that she described as the valued possession of his grandfather, the doctor. Patrick was old enough to recognize the knife as one that Grace had bought that very morning in the Key West dime store. The incident planted in the boy's mind the unhappy suspicion that his grandmother was a liar, an idea that was often reinforced by Ernest's caustic remarks. What Patrick did not consider, at least until he was much older, was that there might be considerable pathos in his grandmother's deception, a desire on her part to bring something of his grandfather into his life.

Grace at sixty-six was still queenly, and in public appeared to be indomitable. She still wore the flowered chiffon gowns that had long since gone out of fashion but were inseparable from her image. "It was like royalty arriving, when she entered a room," recalled a woman who met her then for the first time. "She spoke eloquently, often in metaphysical terms. . . . radiated such zest and enthusiasm that for me it was as if some exotic bird of paradise had flown into our midst and we were all brown sparrows by comparison." Four years earlier, in 1935, Grace had come to a hard decision, which was to allow foreclosure on the big house that she had created with such excitement and ingenuity twenty-nine years before. It was not possible to pay off the $10,000. mortgage that was then due, and the taxes and upkeep were prohibitive. She explained all the figures to Ernest by letter and he accepted her logic. She then officially deeded over the Windemere property to him and Pauline. At that time she admitted to being depressed but decided to stop feeling sorry for herself and go to a doctor instead.

Six months later Grace moved to a small house in River Forest, Illinois. The change was good for her. She improvised a studio, painting the walls white to display her pictures, and left the old, dark furniture behind. Only her mother's melodeon, some special antiques, and personal books and possessions followed her to the new home. She made friends quickly and attracted a new following of art students, mostly adults. Her elation at these developments was fed by an occasional prize for a landscape or an invitation from a local college to present one of her illustrated lectures. The honoraria were important. Even with her trust fund, money was scarce, and it was her ingrained habit to give checks to any of her children in a financial bind. She liked to remind Ernest that she was holding up her end by taking in a roomer or two or selling a picture.

Before Ernest had gone to Spain he was writing Grace about twice a year—a Christmas letter and check in December and a birthday thank-you in July. But during 1937 and 1938 she heard nothing, except indirectly. When she sent a 1937 holiday gift package to Piggott, Paul Pfeiffer sent word that Pauline was on her way to spend the New Year with Ernest. Hadn't he done enough for Spain? she wrote on December 17. If the worry was hard on her, how much worse for Pauline? Even one war was too much in a man's life. No longer did the battlefield seem elevating to her, as it had been in 1918, when her pride in Ernest's heroism assumed exaggerated proportions. Her point of view was now more mature. She grieved for the defeat of his cause. He had not spared himself, she wrote on July 14, 1938, yet Evil seemed to be triumphing on every side.

On December 24, 1938, she received a letter from Ernest. Replying the next day, Christmas, she thanked him for his large check but repeated emotionally that much more important to her than the money was his love, as expressed in his letter. She gave him the news of his brother and sisters, and the nieces and nephews that he had never seen. She reminded him that he still had not visited Windemere and told him again how sorry she was for the Loyalist defeat and that she had been giving whatever she could spare for Spanish children.

As soon as his mother's 1939 visit was over, Ernest took the *Pilar*

to Havana to await Martha, who had promised to join him in the
spring. He was now writing five and six hours a day on the war
novel he had started in the fall. The more pages he finished the more
excited he became about the quality of the work. It seemed to him
that he was going better than at any time since *A Farewell to Arms*.
In April Martha arrived, and the hours when he wasn't working
were no longer lonely. In the late afternoons they swam and played
tennis. Evenings were quiet. They avoided Havana's night life,
confining their outings to a good meal at the excellent French and
Spanish restaurants. Martha, like Ernest, had material for a novel,
hers based on the experience in Czechoslovakia during the tense
days following the Nazi invasion of the Sudetenland. She watched
the diligent care with which Ernest wrote, never undervaluing what
that apprenticeship meant to her. "I owe him the painstakingness of
writing," she said.

The only problem was the hotel. Ernest had holed up with his
beat-up typewriter and fishing gear in a small second-floor room,
although he had promised to find them a suitable house to share
when she came to Cuba. Marty was willing to endure discomfort
cheerfully if there was a reason. But it seemed ridiculous to her to
live in squalor in Havana. "I am really not abnormally clean," she
mused. "I'm simply as clean as any normal person. I've lived in
places and been in places where to keep even faintly clean was a
sinister thing. But Ernest was extremely dirty, one of the most
unfastidious men I've ever known." It was only in comparison to
him that she seemed like Dutch Cleanser.

Refusing to accept the disorder, she went around with real estate
agents to look at rental properties. Finally one of them appealed to
her, a dilapidated house fifteen miles east of downtown Havana near
the impoverished village of San Francisco de Paula. It was a sprawling, one-story Spanish structure with some good features—a sixty-
foot living room, fifteen acres of lush farmland, a swimming pool
filled with unfiltered greenish water, and a fenced-in area, overrun
with weeds, that had once been the tennis court. It's name, La Finca
Vigia, derived from the ancient watch tower that used to stand on
the property. The view of Havana to the west was magnificent and
the rent, $100. a month, was reasonable enough. Although the inte-
rior colors and furnishings were ugly and tasteless, Martha saw that
it had possibilities.

The place looked hopeless to Ernest, however. He went off on a fishing trip, leaving Marty to do the work. The house was not too different from the Key West house when Pauline first saw it. And like Pauline, Martha used her own money for the restoration. She did not mind finding the place and fixing it up, because that had an element of creation. A local painter whitewashed the walls and a carpenter built some simple furniture. Two gardeners took care of the grounds and she installed a cook in the kitchen.

In a later short story, "Luigi's House," Martha's American heroine describes her satisfaction with the newly-restored domestic order of an old Corsican house.

> . . . there would be cool things to drink under the mimosa trees and at night they would read in comfortable chairs with good lamps beside them. . . . She would walk about her house in the morning, opening the linen closet for the joy of seeing the sheets piled so stiff and white together, the knubbly heaps of bath towels, the flat squares of the table napkins. She would stand in the living room, with new flowers in her hands, admiring her work and wondering how she had lived before with no house to tend and watch over. . . . soon this would be a home for two people, a real place.

In such a way, perhaps, did the Finca become a home for two people. Ernest, quite pleased with the results of Martha's efforts, lived with her for the rest of the season, though out of consideration for Pauline he received his mail at the Ambos Mundos. They split the household expenses fifty-fifty, apart from the costs of his liquor, which was his business. "Nor did Ernest suggest any other way," said Martha. She always insisted that the question of money be clearly defined, and this gave her the absolute right to go off and earn her own living. She asked nothing of him financially and continued to support herself as she had always done. Cuba may not have been her first choice but since it was Ernest's she tried to make it work for her too. " . . . you followed your man wherever he had to go; you stayed near him or waited close by: there was nothing strange in that." So concluded the American woman in "Luigi's House" and so, perhaps, concluded Marty at this point in her relationship with Hemingway. Ernest's Cuban friends—Mario G. Menocal and his cousin, Elicin Arguelles, both of them wealthy sportsmen—were pleased to see Martha treat Ernest with tenderness and respect, although they wondered privately why it was necessary to break up his good marriage to Pauline. Couldn't a man keep a wife and a mistress simultaneously?

Pauline's letters during this period were careful and correct. If they were ironic, it was in a low key as she remarked that he had left three sets of underwear behind or described in detail what was served for Sunday lunch. At the end of May 1939 she took Patrick and Gigi to New York and outfitted them for summer camp. When Ernest complained that she had not consulted him about her plans, Pauline replied, "I thought I was so good not to bother you about plans, but it seems from recent letter of yours that I should have told you plans. Also, sweetie, I didn't just shove children in camp to be rid of them as you seem to think." Her careful defenses were beginning to crumble. Using Patrick's birthday as the excuse, she asked Ernest to fly up for the Joe Louis-Tony Galenti heavyweight boxing match. She urged:

> Hope that you will wire that you are coming up. You've been working pretty steadily and you could fly up over night in blond hair and beard. . . . It would please me very much if you can do this. P.S. just realized you couldn't possibly receive this in time, so sent cable—1st message was "Would you come up to fight," amended to "wish you would come up to Louis-Galenti fight" as did not want to frighten you.

But Ernest did not come and Pauline drove to Nantucket to look for a summer rental. While there she began to experience some rectal bleeding. A Boston doctor suggested a battery of tests to rule out the possibility of a malignancy, and she went to New York for the examination. All the tests proved to be negative, and she was so relieved that, along with two friends, she impulsively booked passage for Europe instead of idling in Nantucket for the summer. She wrote to Ernest on July 12 before sailing:

> Just a note in great haste. . . . am very excited, rather frightened and certainly wish you were going. Maybe next time you will be and we will look like the enclosed [a newspaper clipping of an ancient, stout Scottish couple—the woman wearing a dowdy suit, the man in kilts—sailing on the *Mauretania*]. Don't worry, sweetie, and write well and aside from

a few crazy ideas you've got there's nobody like you and nobody smarter, so you're bound to come out right in the end.

During Pauline's ordeal of the tests, Ernest had not heard from her. Concerned about her silence, he finally reached her by phone on the day that the first examination (of the stomach) was negative. While she waited for the results of the next day's X-rays, he made preparations to fly to New York in case she had to undergo surgery. When the good news came that she was fine he went back to work. "I think . . . the jolly trip on the Normandie with the Willerts . . . was a fine thing," he wrote Pauline's mother on July 21, the occasion of his fortieth birthday. "There is plenty of money for a European trip," he boasted, "as I had just deposited the proceeds of sale of To Have and Have Not to the pictures. . . . They ought to have a fine time and this may be the last chance at Europe before it blows up."

Ernest was also corresponding with Hadley at this time about their arrangements for meeting in Wyoming later in the summer. There was no mention yet of Martha, but he made many references to his financial straits and criticized Pauline for having spent all the money in their joint account. He must not take the easy way out, he wrote, " . . . like your and my noted ancestors [referring to the sad coincidence of both Hadley's and Ernest's fathers having committed suicide]." He praised her as the member of her sex whom he most admired and compared their holidays in the Black Forest and on the Irati River to heaven on earth.

That Ernest was worrying over one wife's health while idealizing the other's character did not disturb Martha. Jealousy of other women was not one of her problems. So far there was little friction between them. She was sweet when she chided him and in most matters abided by his decisions. The greatest boon to their harmony was his ability to work spectacularly well. By the time they left Cuba in mid-August his novel had reached 76,000 words.

After stopping briefly in Key West to pick up his car, Ernest drove Martha to St. Louis to visit her mother. He then continued on alone to Cody and there detoured to visit Hadley and Paul, who were fishing at Crossed Sabres Ranch. It was a cordial reunion. Paul gave Ernest a mess of grayling and all three of them remarked how nicely Jack was maturing. Hadley radiated contentment. She harbored no bitterness against Ernest and would be the first to agree with Dos Passos that he had left her in better shape than he found her. Now that he was trying to shed Pauline he discovered that not all women were so good-natured. Bumby was always the reason for writing her, but there was a deeper motivation—the desire to keep her generous spirit in his troubled life.

On September 1, 1939—only a few days after Ernest and his sons gathered at the Nordquist Ranch in Wyoming—war broke out in Europe. Hitler's troops marched into Poland, and England declared war on Germany. Ernest was not surprised; he had predicted it for several years. But he postponed any question of getting involved.

Pauline called from New York. She had just come off the ship and wanted to fly out to be with him and the boys. From Europe she had written him frequently. Only rarely did her real feelings creep into her letters, as on August 5 when she had confessed to finding at the bottom of her suitcase a little fly-fish hook. "Don't know how it got there," she had written, "but when I saw it had just read your letter. I burst out crying."

On the flight west Pauline caught a cold and within a few hours of landing at Billings her throat was raw and she was aching and feverish. The weather at the ranch was bad, and Ernest treated her as though she were a vaguely familiar acquaintance in need of temporary succor. He tried to prepare some simple food, all the while looking black and distant, while she huddled under blankets and dosed herself with rock and rye. There seemed no way for her to get past her misery and Ernest's impenetrable rejection. He made it clear, without actually saying so, that she should give up and go home.

Patrick, long his mother's favorite, though so sensible and cooperative that he had a good relationship with both parents, witnessed an incident during that unhappy week that seemed to him to be the "knock-out punch." When Pauline finally struggled out of bed to unpack some of her clothes, she discovered that the wax buttons on a favorite Paris suit had melted all through the fabric. In front of the disconcerted boy, who tried awkwardly to comfort her, she sobbed uncontrollably. After that Ernest took over. He instructed Toby Bruce to escort Pauline and his sons back to Piggott and Key West. Then he called Martha to meet him in Billings.

Ernest's black Buick convertible was packed with gear—sleeping bags, fishing rods, gun cases, and boxes of books—when Martha joined him in Billings, Montana. It was after midnight on September 20 when they finally reached their destination, the Sun Valley Lodge in central Idaho. Since leaving Craters of the Moon National Monument, they had driven in total darkness, uneasy about the drive ahead, unwilling to turn back. From Hailey on, the road was dusty and unpaved. The tiny old mining town of Ketchum, a mile from Sun Valley, had been shut up tight. At the Lodge a room clerk, dozing over his register, sprang up to show them to number 206, a small corner suite with a fireplace in each of two rooms and a fine view of the mountains. Steve Hannagan, the publicist, had conceived the idea of offering Ernest the hospitality of the new resort, which Averell Harriman, the president of Union Pacific Railroad, was developing as a ski and summer resort. Although he was wary of being exploited, Ernest was well aware of his publicity value. If the weather was mild and the wing-shooting good enough, it might be worthwhile.

Early the next morning the photographer for the hotel, Lloyd Arnold, noticed a young woman with loose blonde hair and loping stride walking across the lawn with Hemingway. He noted that she didn't look like Mrs. Hemingway, of whom he had seen photos, and was told that Pauline and Ernest's marriage was on the rocks. Later the two men approached Martha and Ernest in the dining room. Ernest, standing up politely, introduced Martha and then lapsed into an awkward silence. Martha smiled and asked the men to sit down, and the atmosphere thawed.

Two days later Martha was out in hip-waders, slithering through a swamp with Lloyd Arnold and Ernest as they explored the marshland of Silver Creek. Though the day was windless and hot and there was not a duck in the air, Ernest was ecstatic. He could tell that this valley floor supported a gigantic population of game birds —mourning doves, partridge, mallards. Sliding their way back to the road, the two men half-dragged and half-carried Marty, who struggled for a toehold in the mud.

For the next six weeks Martha adapted her routine to Ernest's—work in the morning, then riding, tennis, and some shooting in the afternoon. She never became enthusiastic about shooting but knew that Ernest was proud of her quick progress. Her favorite recreation with him was their afternoon ride into the mountains with some sandwiches and a bottle of wine in the saddlebag. The Sun Valley people were all impressed with her good sportsmanship and her sense of humor. Tillie Arnold, Lloyd's wife, liked her immediately and called her a "barrel of fun and sharp as a tack." Clara Spiegel, a frequent visitor, became a loyal friend to both Martha and Ernest. Her husband, Fred Spiegel of Chicago, had driven ambulances with Ernest in Italy in 1918.

In the middle of October Martha received a telephone call from Charles Colebaugh of *Collier's*. He wanted to send her to Finland, where the Soviet Union was making threatening moves along the Finnish-Russian border. Martha was uncertain whether to go. "I talked to E.," she wrote her mother on October 18, "who is always so grand about these things, never thinking about himself at all, but only of me and what will give me satisfaction." Ernest said she could do the Scandanavia thing quite well, and they decided that she write to Colebaugh and agree to leave Sun Valley in two weeks. If Ernest could get away, he would meet her over there; if not, she would meet him back in Cuba after the first of the year.

Martha made the point clearly in her letter to Edna Gellhorn that money was the overriding reason for taking the assignment. " 'This may be the last time you [Martha] will have to do it,' " she wrote, quoting Ernest. " 'Because what with that nest egg you can write and sell short stories. And that would be enough money and you wouldn't have to do journalism.' " "Also," Martha continued, "we'd be married by spring, he thinks, and once married I'd have a swell excuse not to be separated from him. I can just say [to *Collier's*] my husband and I work together." She told her mother that she hated the idea of leaving Ernest, for she was so happy in "this paradise," but that she was afraid to throw away a certain means of making money.

When the travel orders came through, Ernest went around complaining that he was being abandoned. "What old Indian likes to lose his squaw with a hard winter coming on?" he asked everyone within earshot, saying nothing about money as the reason for the separation. Believing that it was Martha's ambition and restlessness that caused her to accept the offer, Tillie Arnold tried to dissuade her. Why leave Ernest now, she asked, when things were going well? Was it really necessary? Martha replied simply that there was no way she could pass up such an opportunity. She did not add that she needed to earn money as much as any self-supporting man. Ernest seemed to enjoy the martyred air he affected over her so-called desertion, but finally he dropped that act and told everyone how courageous she was. On the eve of her departure he gave a farewell party for her, and before she was driven to the train at Shoshone, everyone gathered for lunch. "Keep your eye on this big clown," Martha said to Tillie and Clara. " . . . see that he's shaved and cleaned up when you go out on the town. . . . I'm depending on *you.*" She had said the same thing to them privately, that it would be hard on him without her and they should be solicitous of his welfare.

On November 10, 1939, Martha sailed out of Hoboken, New Jersey on a small Dutch vessel carrying American wheat to Belgium. The food was "as interesting as boiled cardboard," Marty wrote in "Slow Boat to War," " . . . so people began to keep queer hours, floating around at five in the morning and sleeping until three the next afternoon. . . . " Most of the passengers were anxious Europeans returning to countries in the path of the Nazi juggernaut, and everyone was apprehensive about the inauguration of a new German weapon—the magnetic mine. On the eighth day the ship, posting huge signs that proclaimed its neutral registry, entered the English coastal waters that had been heavily mined. It all seemed idiotic to Martha. How did one proclaim one's neutrality to a floating mine? Two days later they dropped anchor in the Downs, a free stretch of water (free of mines, that is) approaching Ramsgate on the channel, where the English blockade was enforced and cargo inspected. From the ship's radio came continuous reports of sunken vessels, even in the so-called safe zone.

When the captain finally received clearance and the ship got under way only two English-speaking passengers were left, Martha and a young man from America. In the sea around them dead bodies still wearing life belts floated face-down. Basketball-shaped mines bobbed on the choppy water. Then the fog came in and there was nothing more to see until evening, when the lights of Ostend, Belgium came into view. The boat, bathed in moonlight, moved slowly into the Scheldt River. "Suddenly the whole trip seemed long ago and only a thing to remember," Martha reported. Cabling Ernest and her mother that she was safe, she flew to Helsinki November 29, arriving only hours before the Russians dropped their first bombs. "It is cold as hell and rainy, like Gary, Indiana," she wrote Ernest the next day. "At 9:15 a.m. I was dressed and ready to go downstairs to breakfast when I heard the siren. . . . it is going to be terrible. They [the Finns] are about as well off as Spain from the point of view of material." It was appalling and all too familiar —the stunned civilians, the fires, the lost children. On the second day the Russians came again, this time with leaflets as well as bombs. Helsinki would be flattened if Soviet demands were not met. The people were marvelous, Martha added in the same letter, fearful but with a kind of frozen fortitude. Unlike the Czech government, the Finnish leaders decided to fight a defensive war, " . . . rather than lose their country and their hard-working unaggressive decent way of life," she reported for *Collier's*. With her acute eye and ear for the innocent good sense of children, Martha concluded that dispatch with an anecdote about a blond, plump boy of nine, standing outside his home in Helsinki, watching the Russian bombers. When the bombers had left, he said, "Little by little I am getting really angry."

Grateful for two cables from Ernest that reached her on December 4, Martha responded with a long emotional letter. " . . . I am so happy you are proud of me, although I don't know what for. I am just surviving." He must keep on with his work, for it was what would last. " . . . Without the book our work is wasted altogether and as I love you I love your work and as you are me your work is mine." She added that she was getting wonderful material, the best war stuff of the year, but would be glad to be home with him where she belonged. " . . . I'll never leave you and you can go anywhere you want and do anything you like, only please, I'll come too."

The next morning at dawn a young military chauffeur drove Martha to the southern frontier in freezing darkness over unmarked icy roads and heavily mined bridges. Hidden in the unending forests were the armies. Gun flashes illuminated the sky. She was in the middle of the first big night operation of the war and the Russians were less than three-quarters of a kilometer ahead. Suddenly an officer came out of the darkness to order them back. "This is the height of stupidity," he said in German. Martha's guide laughed but obeyed. In the bombed city of Viipuri she visited captured Russians and later was taken to the airfield where the small, crack squadron of Finnish pursuit planes was based. "As always," she wrote for *Collier's*, "one is astounded by the age of the pilots [so young]." In their dugout, camouflaged by pine boughs, one aviator serenaded her with a sad Finnish love song, to the accompaniment of another's guitar. The colonel of the regiment briefed her about the Russian bombers and the flight lieutenant said tersely, "They will not get us as a present."

By Christmas Eve, Martha had completed the Finnish assignment and written her *Collier's* pieces in Sweden. Now she was on her way to Lisbon to board the Pan American *Clipper* for Cuba, but first there was an urgent task in Paris. Gustav Regler was interned as an enemy alien in a French prison with no citizenship but the useless one of the doomed Spanish Republic. Martha went to her friends in high government places to see who among them would work for his release but was unsuccessful. She gave money to Regler's wife and later asked Eleanor Roosevelt to intercede with the French, which the latter did. That led to Regler's eventual release. She then prepared to leave Paris for Portugal, but after cabling Ernest to expect her on the first day of the new year—1940—she ran into a tangle of red tape about her exit visa and her transit visa to Portugal. There was the added uncertainty of not knowing whether French planes would fly at all. The only comfort in the endless waiting was the beauty of Paris.

A few days before the end of the year Martha finally reached Lisbon, only to meet another delay. Bad weather was holding up the *Clipper's* take-off. On January 2 she cabled Ernest. "CLIPPERS STOPPED, NO CHOICE EXCEPT REX ARRIVING 11TH STOP DID EVERYTHING POSSIBLE TO KEEP PROMISE BE HOME FIRST STOP ASHAMED DISAPPOINT YOU STOP MISERABLY UNHAPPY."

Ernest had stayed on in Sun Valley for another month after Martha had left. He had rolled ahead with the novel—474 pages of typescript were finished by November 15. The locale is a Loyalist guerrilla camp in the Sierra de Guadarrama range and the hero is Robert Jordan, an American professor who had gone to Spain to fight the fascists. The heroine, Maria, was based on a lovely, dignified young Spanish nurse whom Ernest had met at a coastal hospital near Barcelona in the spring of 1938.

Ernest wrote Perkins that Martha had crossed the mined North Sea and was getting shot at in Finland so that he could afford to write his book. "I imagine it did not take her long to realize," he added facetiously, "that those bi-motored Katuskas were no longer our planes." He fretted over the dangers she faced. "I've been so worried, can't eat or sleep thinking about the Marty," he wrote Clara Spiegel on December 9. "The boats ahead and behind hers in the channel were sunk by mines."

The one who heard from him the most frequently was Hadley, and with her he aired his miseries. Pauline had crossed him up by objecting to his wanting to spend Christmas with her and the boys in Key West. He complained that the behavior coming out of Key West was wicked, but it was only what he had come to expect of people who thought only of themselves. Hadley, always soft-hearted about his predicaments, invited him to spend Christmas with them. He demurred, explaining that he had to go south. "Here is a joke to show you that I can joke still," he added. "I think if one is perpetually doomed to marry people from St. Louis it's best to marry them from the best families."

Meantime Tillie Arnold kept her promise to Martha to look after Ernest in Sun Valley. One evening when she and Lloyd and Ernest went to dinner, the conversation turned to parents. Ernest remarked that his father had had no patience with him when he was small and that he always missed the companionship and competition of brothers when he was growing up. Tillie teased him for feeling sorry for himself and this put him on the defensive. He described the details of his father's suicide and from that launched into a diatribe against Grace. "She had to rule everything," he said vehemently. "She was a bitch." Tillie was shocked and said so. But he never backed down, simply repeated that it was true, no matter what Tillie thought, and then went on to blame Grace for his father's suicide.

Carol Gardner, whose marriage Ernest had opposed, recalled to the author that after she defied his wishes he began to tell lies about her also. If someone asked Ernest how Carol was, he would say that she was divorced or that she had died. Ernest knew how to hold a grudge, said Carol, especially against someone who had defied him. As for blaming Grace for Dr. Hemingway's death, she pointed out that Ernest had blamed their Uncle George Hemingway, too (for being insensitive to his brother's financial plight), and that some-times he blamed himself. All the children at one time or another asked themselves whether they had contributed to the tragedy. A reconciliation was probably not possible between Ernest and his mother, since his feelings had hardened past the point of reexamination. Carol, who saw Grace frequently in the years when Ernest was not seeing her, heard her repeat many times how proud she was of him. Grace no longer seemed bothered by the so-called immorality of his early novels.

On a drizzling day in December Ernest left for Key West. En route he mailed a letter to Pauline's mother, dated December 12, 1939. He apologized for not visiting her in the fall and admitted that this kind of letter was no fun to write and less fun to read. He tried to justify the estrangement between himself and Pauline by implicating Jinny. It was a lame defense. "Virginia's version of my life and conduct," he wrote, "is a very fantastic one. But she spread it sufficiently and at the right time to break up my home. . . . I do not mean that I have ever been in the right in *anything* but the true version would be very different from anything you have heard." He had been lonely working on the book, but so far there was not a bad word in it. Assuring her that he would look after Pauline's interests as though they were his own, he said he would take good care of the children and added that they got along very well with him.

This was not mere vanity on his part. Ernest was as much a hero to Gigi and Patrick as to Bumby. "When you were with my father, it was the Crusades," recalled Pat. "He was Richard the Lion-Hearted, and my mother was the woman you left behind in the castle with the chastity belt." It was confusing that their mother and father should separate, but one good thing seemed bound to come out of it for the younger boys—they could spend all those glorious holidays and summers with Ernest, as their brother Jack had been doing for so many years.

When Ernest arrived in Key West he found that Pauline had discharged the servants and left for New York. Only the boys were there with Ada waiting to go to Cuba with their father for Christmas. For a week Ernest stayed in the house, slowly packing up his personal possessions. He stored manuscripts and private papers in a damp basement below Sloppy Joe's saloon. On the 24th the Buick was loaded onto the Key West-Havana ferry, along with boxes and fishing gear and clothes, and the two boys and Ernest sailed to Havana and the Ambos Mundos. One of the last pieces of mail he opened before setting out was a sad letter from Mary Pfeiffer. "Your father and I are deeply grieved," she wrote. "As a member of the family for so many years I have come to regard you as one of my own. This is the saddest Christmas I have ever known. A broken family is a tragic thing, particularly so when there are children."

Chapter 21

Martha's Czechoslovakian novel would be published by Duell, Sloan & Pearce, and Ernest handled the negotiations. "It is a hell of a good book called *The Stricken Field*," he wrote Perkins on January 10, 1940. "I did not want to show it to you because I think it is a bad idea for people in the same family . . . to be published by the same firm." He was suspicious of the contract sent to him by Duell. It was full of what seemed to be "jokers." Would Max send him their toughest contract so that he would have a basis for comparison? On the 18th, having studied the Scribners sample, he sent a heavily red-penciled Duell contract to Perkins with his own shrewd analysis of clauses that seemed objectionable.

By this time Martha had arrived in Cuba and they moved together to the Finca. Ernest had hated being alone; it had made him feel abandoned. She must not do that again, he told Martha, and one afternoon he wrote up a mock contract for her to sign. What seemed like tomfoolery on the surface had a serious undertone.

I, the undersigned Mrs. Martha, or Mrs. fathouse Pig . . . hereby guarantee and promise never to brutalize my present and future husband in any way whatsoever. . . . I recognize that a very fine and sensitive writer cannot be left alone two months and sixteen days during which time many trying and unlikely things are put upon him voluntarily and involuntarily, and that I . . . was a great cause for his uneasiness of mind during this long period of solitude. . . . I also state for witnesses that far from putting him out of business, he and his business are what matter to me in this life. . . . I am deeply sorry therefore and shall attempt . . . to make up to him for the wretchedness he has gone through and shall also attempt to protect him against same wretchedness in the future. This statement is given of my own free will and in my rightest mind and with love. Martha Gellhorn. Witnesses: Judge R.R. Rabbitt, Judge P.O. Pig.

With Martha safely at his side Ernest immersed himself once again in his novel, cutting back on the drinking, going to sleep at sensible hours. The phonograph was well stocked with records. On Sundays a group of expatriate Basques—Loyalist soldiers who had fled Spain after Franco's victory—came to the Finca for tennis and swimming. Gambling, pelota, marathon drinking at the Floridita—all such favorite diversions were put off until weekends. It was a cold and stormy January but by early February the weather turned mild. Martha, worn out from her travels, could not yet concentrate on her own work. So she did "hausfrau" tasks and sometimes went off by herself to hunt doves in the fields. "It is wondrously beautiful," she wrote to Clara, "and I look about the house and the land and cannot figure out how I happened to be so lucky in my life with such a place to live and such a one to live with."

In March *A Stricken Field* was published, with its dedication to Ernest. Martha believed that she had seen the phrase from which the title was taken in the *History of the Peninsular Wars.* "I . . . knew exactly how I wanted to use it; the meaning is altogether clear. So I searched and searched and it was not there." Ernest stepped in and wrote a medieval epigraph to fit the phrase, as he had previously with his own title *Winner Take Nothing.* The events of the story approximate Martha's experiences of the previous winter. The fictional Mary Douglas is a young journalist devoted to the cause of freedom and democracy, full of admiration for the Czech people, disgusted and horrified by their betrayal in the Munich Pact, when Chamberlain and Daladier in effect gave Czechoslovakia to the Nazis. There are references to an absent lover, John, who was with her in Spain. On March 7, 1940, Eleanor Roosevelt recommended the novel in her column as an important book. It was respectfully and widely reviewed but not acclaimed unanimously as had been the case with *The Trouble I've Seen*. The dissatisfaction rested mainly with the book's wavering blend of fact and fiction. "Yet its material is so poignant and so well-handled," wrote the *New York Times*, "that it cannot be dismissed lightly."

Time did dismiss it lightly, in one paragraph, as a romanticized autobiography. Martha was "a novelist with a legend." The news magazine was the first to break the public silence about "her great and good friend, Ernest Hemingway." Ernest, writing to Jay Allen, said disgustedly that the great and good friend stuff was what *Time* used instead of serials. The many facets of Martha's personality came into dramatic focus in the photographs that showed up about the time her book was being promoted. In *Time* she was all slick glamour—with a scarlet slash of lipstick, plucked brows, and fashionable haircut. In the *Saturday Review of Literature* she was the contemplative artist—serious profile, hands folded, austere attire. Finally there was the third Marty, photographed so many times in tennis shorts or riding pants around Sun Valley and the Finca, who wore no make-up, whose hair was flying, and whose round, rosy face was shown breaking into the relaxed grin. This was the Marty that Ernest loved the most and naturally found the least threatening. He tended to forget that she was also independent and touched with wanderlust, and he reacted sharply when he came up against these qualities full-force.

On March 20 Patrick and Gigi arrived at the Finca. For the first time since the winter of 1936 they would have a chance to see the lively woman who was now their father's dear friend. They responded to Marty's warmth with a rush of affection, especially Gigi. Ernest's permanent move to Cuba provided him with the perfect escape from Ada and Pauline. The Finca came to seem like a paradise where his father became his playmate and the enchanting Martha, a new mother.

Early in April, Bumby joined the group. To the sixteen-year-old youth it seemed extraordinary good luck that the woman who had so impressed him in New York the year before was to be his daily companion. The vacation was good fun, the best ever, recalled Jack. There were tennis games and fencing lessons and one of Ernest's Basque friends taught him how to play pelota. Everyone agreed that Jack was a natural with a racket, and all the taxi drivers and bartenders and common folk who adored Ernest wanted to shake the hand of this handsome boy who was the oldest son of Ernestino. Best of all were the long conversations with Martha: She told him of her adventures in Finland and nicknamed him "Bumble."

Martha wrote to Hadley after he left:

> We talked and talked, about any number of things. As I remember with horrid clearness all the business of college boards and high school, I felt very chummy with him on those problems and I listened respectfully to the trout fishing talk and was ashamed to admit I have never caught anything and did not know the names of the flies in his little tin box. He said, though, to cheer me up, that you didn't care how you caught them, whether with a fly or a grasshopper and so I realized that I could learn and I certainly am going to try. . . . I count myself unbelievably lucky to have him as my friend, through inheritance. I don't see how a woman could produce a better or more beautiful boy than you did.

Patrick, quiet and observant, believed that the special relationship between Jack and Martha was formed because both had been such handsome young people, blonde and radiant and pleasing everyone with their charm and high spirits. Martha was a loving stepmother to all three boys. "I think they accept me as part of the gang," she continued in her long letter to Hadley. "Ernest's gang, another one of the large family who dashes about obeying Poppa and having a fine time." Laughingly she did obey. Ernest adored her, bragging in every letter that she was beautiful as hell and he was the luckiest guy in the world. Her mood was always the most pliant after she was home from a killing assignment, as though she had earned the right to be frivolous.

Since returning from Europe Martha had written only one story. She bemoaned her undisciplined ways as the fatal mark of an amateur, but finally she was halfway through her second, about the recent Christmas visit to Paris. Ernest warned her about sinking into the "permanent gloom class" as a writer. It was no good to be branded a herald of disaster. She agreed with him. *Collier's* was after her to go back to the war zone, "which I won't do," she reiterated, "because will not leave my home and himself."

In spite of enthusiastic praise from everyone who had read chapters from the big Spanish novel, Ernest was beginning to wish that Pauline would read it. He valued her literary judgment above anyone's. Patrick believes that in such matters his father did work best in conjunction with his mother. There is no evidence, however, that Pauline read any of the chapters. On April 21 he found the title for the novel in *The Oxford Book of English Prose:* " . . . any man's death diminishes me, because I am involved in Mankinde; and therefore never send to know for whom the bell tolls; it tolls for thee" (John Donne). He cabled Perkins the provisional title *For Whom the Bell Tolls* and pushed ahead, confident that the end was in sight.

If *The Fifth Column* reflected his ambivalence about a love affair with Martha, the new novel carried no such negative message. There is a moving passage about the value of love as expressed by the hero, Robert Jordan. "You never had it before and now you have it. What you have with Maria . . . is the most important thing that can happen to a human being. There will always be people who say it does not exist because they cannot have it." And the physical description of Maria could very well be a tribute to Martha.

> She had high cheekbones, merry eyes and a straight mouth with full lips. Her hair was the golden brown of a grain field. . . . Her legs slanted long and clean from the open cuffs of the trousers. . . . Every time Robert Jordan looked at her he could feel a thickness in his throat. . . . She moved awkwardly as a colt moves, but with that same grace as of a young animal.

No one would suggest that the docile Maria bears even a distant relationship to Martha psychologically. No personalities could be more different. But in its reflection of Ernest's emotional state when he was writing it, this book may be said to belong to Martha. "I am so damned happy with Marty," he had written Perkins, "that everything has gone better."

Martha's work was not going as well. She was finding it "ghastly hard to write," spending fruitless hours trying to improve her plotting and dialogue, exhausted from the "grim, grinding business" of trying to make sentences say what she wanted them to say. For a while it had been better. Ernest had boasted to Max that she was writing well. Now that she was in a funk he muttered that all writers were crazy and concentrated on his own deadlines. Worst of all for Martha was the grim news from Europe. In April, Hitler's war machine invaded Denmark and Norway, knocking out the Danes immediately and Norway in a few weeks. In May came the crushing defeat of the low countries. Martha traced the disasters on wall maps and bought a radio so that she could hear the horrors first-hand.

"It is extremely pretentious to take the world's troubles as your own," she wrote Clara on May 30, "but I must say they concern me more gravely than anything else. I feel itchy in my skin, sitting here and knowing nothing." It had been raining for three days, and then the water-logged living room ceiling collapsed in a sea of plaster dust. Bumby and Patrick, arriving for a summer visit, found the house in a disheveled state and the weather still unpromising. They hung around waiting for the rain to stop. Ernest, ignoring both family and surroundings, plunged deeper into his work. Martha, fed up with the isolation, flew to New York. She was there on June 22 when France surrendered. Everyone expected Marty, as a working journalist, to have an opinion. She was still bitter about the British sellout at Munich, but now that England had to fight Hitler alone she felt that President Roosevelt was right to support them with materials. She was not sure about sending American troops.

Edna Gellhorn, who came to New York from St. Louis, accompanied Martha back to the Finca for a visit; soon she and Ernest became good friends. "He loved my mother," Martha recalled. "Both of my husbands loved my mother, always. . . . they loved her more than me . . . and they were absolutely right." She was surprised —and somewhat irritated—to hear her mother say that she felt sorry for Ernest. How could anyone feel sorry for such a bear of a man, who had known such success? Edna Gellhorn dropped the subject but Martha wondered later if perhaps her mother sensed an emotional instability in Ernest that had not yet surfaced. Her mother was also more tolerant of Ernest's casual habits than she was. One afternoon when the three of them had made plans to meet and Ernest failed to show up, Martha stormed into the Floridita, where he was having drinks, and berated him for his thoughtlessness. "You can stand me up," she cried, "but you can't do that to my mother." Mrs. Gellhorn was amused but Martha demanded an apology. She would not defer to him. His sons had already noticed that, and so did his Cuban friends. There was something attractive about her facing him down and he seemed to accept it good-naturedly. Grinning sheepishly he followed her out of the bar.

Late in July Ernest went to New York for a few days to deliver the finished manuscript to Scribners. On September 1, he and Martha departed for Sun Valley, Ernest from Key West, in a new car, and Martha by train via St. Louis. With Ernest's divorce still pending it seemed better to travel separately whenever possible. On the day of the departure Martha wrote Clara that sometime in the fall she and Ernest would be married. They had expected to go through that formality while still in Cuba, but things got held up. Martha conceded that being married was perhaps simpler all around but she herself thought living "in sin" wonderful. "We are now on our 4th contented year," she wrote in the same letter. As the date for the wedding drew near she began to feel trapped.

Ernest had grumbled all year that his divorce was being held up by Pauline's tricks. He alluded again and again to her wanting to "put him out of the book business." He meant financially, for she was grim about his sending her monthly checks. That she did not need them was beside the point. Money symbolized his admission that she had been wronged. Feeling deeply aggrieved, and urged on by Jinny, she was not going to make the situation easy for him as Hadley had done. Now, after months of stalling (according to Ernest) she agreed to a separation settlement proposed by her Uncle Gus, only to turn around and demand more money. Ernest's caustic advice to Max Perkins was to marry as little as possible, but never to a rich bitch; he said they had a way of sensing your soft spots and upping the price. He later spread nonsensical reports of what the divorce had cost him, maintaining that Pauline took valuable property in Ketchum (which in fact did not exist), the Key West house, and a large share of his past earnings. Actually the only monies exacted so far were the $500. monthly payments, which he continually protested.

That Pauline had shared her money with him, generously and discreetly, did not mitigate Ernest's resentment. That he was on his way to considerable financial success (*For Whom the Bell Tolls* had already been chosen as an October selection of the Book-of-the-Month Club), did not soften his determination to give her as little as possible. She was standing in the way of his marriage to another woman. The more she delayed the more he insisted that her devout Catholicism had ruined his sex life. ("Papa would suffer for a long time with a woman who was giving him problems sexually, but in the end he would make her suffer more," wrote Gregory Hemingway in 1976.) And since Pauline had stolen him from Hadley, so went Ernest's logic, she had simply got what she deserved.

In Key West Pauline finally hammered out an agreement that was acceptable to both parties. The house would be divided sixty-forty, even though Uncle Gus had originally put up the money to buy it. The Florida National Bank in Miami was appointed trustee with Pauline having the right to lease or rent the house, provided she paid the taxes and the insurance. In the event she chose to sell it, Ernest had first option to buy it, with the provision that he pay 60 percent of the asking price as downpayment. If he declined to buy it, he would receive 40 percent of the sale price, with Pauline receiving the balance. In the event of Pauline's death, Patrick and Gregory would divide her 60 percent equally, with Ernest receiving the other 40 percent. The $500. monthly payments would continue.

Pauline tried to hide her misery, insisting that it would be wonderful to be a free woman at last. She had filed for the divorce in Miami, where she was not as well known as in Key West, and then went to San Francisco. With Jinny's help she found a comfortable apartment on Telegraph Hill, looking out to the Bay and Alcatraz Island. Having promised never to keep the children from their father, she made plans for them to go by train to Sun Valley at the end of the summer, to remain with him and Martha at least through the duck-hunting season.

On September 10 Ernest sent the last batch of corrected galleys of *For Whom the Bell Tolls* to Perkins with a careful checklist of Spanish spellings and phrases and the dedication "This book is for Martha Gellhorn." Three weeks of rain quashed his hunting plans but not his drinking as he celebrated the end of eighteen grueling months of work. When the weather cleared, he organized a packtrip with Martha into the wild Middle Fork region of the Salmon River. "Good but rough trip," was his comment. "23 miles of trail to get in." Martha, hopelessly outclassed in wilderness experience, gamely carried on without complaint.

Ernest came back from the trip refreshed and cheerful, but Martha had the flu. For two weeks she languished under the covers, aching and gloomy. On October 23 she wrote Clara that deep within her was the cesspool of gloom that accompanies the grippe. "If I ever get over my miseries I am looking forward to walking about outdoors and breathing the sun." She made no direct references to her marriage plans, only that she was planning to leave around

November 15 and was doing her damnedest to get a Far East assignment from *Collier's*. Ernest took a glum view of such an idea. For him it was a question of keeping her away from "war, pestilence, carnage and adventure." Suspecting that this was an empty hope, he contacted Ralph Ingersoll, editor of the newspaper *PM*, about his own willingness to cover the war in China if Martha did get the nod from *Collier's*. He could not let her go on such a rough trip by herself. It was not his idea of a honeymoon, he wrote Charlie Scribner. They had been arguing about it for a month, and everyone had urged Martha to change her mind, but she would not budge. "I want that assignment more than anything in the world," she said.

From her sickbed Martha kept track of the excited talk about the movie potential of *For Whom the Bell Tolls*. Gary Cooper, who had already played Lt. Frederic Henry of *A Farewell to Arms*, wanted to play Robert Jordan. Ernest was all for that. As the book publication date approached, he became more and more nervous. Unable to wait for reviews, he called Jay Allen in East Hampton and asked him to read the first reviews over the phone. When he was assured that they were favorable, he put Martha on the extension and had Jay read them to her all over again. At Sun Valley Lodge, a private switchboard was assigned to take the Hemingway calls and a special bellman to deliver the Hemingway mail.

Ernest's confidence in the book was not misplaced. The structure is successful, the theme of a people betrayed is powerfully realized, and the characters, except for Maria, are complex and believable. Many of Ernest's friends from Spain appear as themselves or are thinly disguised. One of the least disguised is the hero, Robert Jordan, whose political judgments and personal qualities are very like those of Ernest. Jordan is an anti-fascist libertarian who respects the communists for their discipline but has no use for their ideology. His father, like Ernest's, has killed himself with a Smith and Wesson pistol. The death of the father is now judged openly as an act of cowardice. "I understand it, but I do not approve of it. . . . I'll never forget how sick it made me the first time I knew he was a *cobarde*. Go on, say it in English. Coward . . . and that was the worst luck any man could have." Not only was the father's death a cowardly act; his life was as well, for he never stood up to "that woman." Whatever the truth of Grace and Ed Hemingway's lives, Ernest seemed dedicated to fixing the blame according to his own vision.

Most of the critics praised the book lavishly as an important addition to American literature. Edmund Wilson wrote in *The New Republic* that "Hemingway the artist is with us again; and it is like having an old friend back." But in a subsequent essay he acidly disposed of the "amoeba-like" Maria as resembling too closely the docile native wives in Kipling, who lived only to serve their lords. The love affair in the sleeping bag between Robert and Maria completely lacks the "give and take" that goes on between real lovers, wrote Wilson, who went on to suggest that Hemingway heroines seemed doomed to embody one of two extremes, either the deadly (Brett Ashley, Margot Macomber) or the saintly (Catherine Barkley, Maria.) The former were his fear-projections, the latter his wish-fulfillments. (Carlos Baker, without trying to exonerate Hemingway, makes the point that in polarizing his heroines in this way, Ernest did no worse than most of the writers of English and American fiction who preceded him.)

On November 4, 1940, the announcement came over the A.P. wire that

> Ernest Hemingway, the novelist, was divorced in Miami by his second wife, the former Pauline Pfeiffer, on the grounds of desertion. The uncontested divorce awarded custody of their two children, Patrick and Gregory, to Mrs. Hemingway with the provision that the father could see them at any time. . . . Mrs. Hemingway was in New York when the decree was signed by Circuit Judge Arthur Gomez and Hemingway was on a hunting trip near Sun Valley, Idaho.

The next day a reporter from the *St. Louis Post-Dispatch* reached Martha by phone. She denied rumors that she and Ernest expected to be married in the near future. "I am just finishing a book on which I have been working for some time," she told the reporter. "When it is finished I will go to New York and that is as far as my plans go at this time. My mother, who is visiting me here [at Sun Valley], will return to St. Louis in a few days."

In River Forest, Illinois, Grace Hemingway received a warm, carefully phrased letter from Pauline. She would always look upon Grace as her second mother. She knew how upsetting the news had been to her, as indeed it had been a shock to her own parents. She was glad it was all finally behind her. Comparing the heart of another to a dark forest, she wrote how amazing it was that people did anything right in this world, considering what they had to contend with. Martha, in what seems a startling coincidence, was to choose *The Heart of Another* as the title for her new book of short stories. On the title page the following words appear: "The heart of another is a dark forest."

Formal denials notwithstanding, the wedding plans moved ahead. Early in November, Robert Capa, who knew Martha and Ernest from Spanish Civil War days, arrived to do a photographic essay about them for *Life*. Ernest was host at a prenuptial party at Trail Creek Cabin and the couple were married on November 21, 1940, in Cheyenne, Wyoming, before a justice of the peace.

In New York they took a suite at the Lombardy. Martha sent a wire on December 9 to Tillie and Lloyd Arnold "PICTURE US TWO ERNEST POINTING DARK FUTURE WITH RIGHT HAND TAKEN BY HARPER'S FULL PAGE SPREAD EXCLUSIVE WITH BYLINE YOURS. . . . EVERYTHING FINE HERE CLOSELY RESEMBLING LIFE IN RUNAWAY ELEVATOR STOP AM OFF TO BURMA ROAD SOONS POSSIBLE STOP ALL THIS AND HEAVEN TOO LOVE TO THE GANG. MARTY." Most of the time Martha was tolerant of Ernest's claque. But she also cherished her privacy and sometimes resented the publicity that was a by-product of his fame. "I do not believe that the private person has to be public property," she declared years later. "The work, yes; the person, no." Ernest then agreed with her, but his was an irresistible force. Wherever he appeared reporters, old pals, children, and literary and sports personalities flocked around him. If he was in a receptive mood he welcomed them. On this trip he welcomed everyone. He had a new wife at his side and a novel that was a huge success. The door to the Lombardy suite stood ajar as the liquor flowed and the telephone rang incessantly. Ernest sent for Bumby to celebrate with them and to take a series of boxing lessons at George Brown's gymnasium, where Ernest liked to work out.

H.G. Wells, who was in New York on a lecture tour, came around for an afternoon visit when he learned that Hemingway, whom he had never met, was in town. Wells enjoyed all the hullabaloo and the assorted characters wandering about, but Martha was disappointed with the conversation, waiting in vain for something scintillating to come out of a Hemingway-Wells verbal joust. Ernest liked to pretend that he knew nothing and had read nothing, hiding his omnivorous knowledge behind the pose of the unlettered sportsman. It seemed to Martha that he disliked conversing with people who could read and write. She may have been too hard on him. Many of his generation thought it was bad form to indulge in literary shoptalk. Movies were another form of entertainment that Ernest avoided but Martha enjoyed. If she nagged, or if he wanted to make up to her, he took her to a film or a play. But most of the time it was jai alai, boxing, bullfights, horse races—anything he could bet on that tested a man's skill. Billy Conn, the light heavyweight, was the favorite of the moment.

By Christmas they were back at the Finca. The run-down estate that Martha had discovered and refurbished in the spring of 1939 was now their own. Ernest had purchased the property for $12,500. Martha concluded her agreement with *Collier's* to go to China and then hurried to put the finishing touches on her volume of short stories, which Scribners was going to publish. (Ernest's earlier opinion that two authors in the same family should not be with the same publishing house—was now set aside.) Reluctantly Ernest prepared to go with her. Money was not currently a problem for him, with 180,000 copies of *For Whom the Bell Tolls* already sold and David Selznick offering $100,000. for the film rights. Five trips to Spain, four years of wrangling with Pauline, a backbreaking effort with the novel—all that had put him in the mood for the kind of life the Finca now offered. He wanted to fish and shoot and drink with his friends, have fun with his sons, perhaps even sire a daughter, since he had never given up on that particular dream.

But none of this had any appeal without Marty. And she was determined to go to the Orient. "I felt a driving sense of haste: hurry, hurry, before it's too late; . . . I was determined to see the Orient before I died or the world ended or whatever came next," she wrote in 1978 in *Travels with Myself and Another.* Ernest knew all about her curiosity when he married her. It was what made her a first-class journalist. And since he offered her no money, it was necessary for her to work. Though Ernest had no prior experience with a wife who led a life independent of his, he would try to adjust, at least for the present.

It was mid-January 1941 when Martha and Ernest left for New York on the first stage of the journey to the Far East. Everything was the same as in December, with Jack down from school for weekend boxing lessons, open house in the suite at the Lombardy, and drinking parties with old friends. Ernest had written Hadley

Martha Gellhorn. Sun Valley, Idaho, 1939.
From the John F. Kennedy Library

Martha on a pack trip in the Middle Fork region of the Salmon River. October 1940.
From the John F. Kennedy Library

that it was wonderful to be legal again, but his guerrilla sleeping habits had not changed; he was still up at dawn. He encouraged her to let Jack have a year off before going on to college. It could be a maturing experience and teach the boy that education was a serious business. In a postscript he wrote that he would like to take Jack as a dependent in 1940, since he was now in the 62 percent tax bracket due to the success of *For Whom the Bell Tolls*. Clara and Freddie Spiegel came to town, as did Edna Gellhorn. One evening there was a champagne dinner, followed by the Tony Zale fight at Madison Square Garden and then another celebration at Toots Shor's. Martha and her mother finally gave up and went to bed, but Ernest and Jack stayed out all night.

Martha delivered her volume of short stories to Max Perkins for Scribners' fall list and received last-minute instructions from *Collier's*. Earl Wilson, the columnist, asked her to arrange an interview for him with Ernest. She set up the meeting and promised to be present, but when Wilson arrived Ernest was alone, propped up in bed, aching from typhoid shots. The interview went well, Wilson having been coached by Marty on which subjects to press, which

Martha and Ernest in the season of their marriage, November 1940.
Robert Capa/Magnum Photos, Inc.

The Hemingway sons with Ernest and Martha at Sun Valley. Autumn 1941.
From the Patrick Hemingway Collection, Princeton University Library

Martha Gellborn, Sun Valley, 1941.
From the John F. Kennedy Library

The Finca Vigia, San Francisco de Paula, Cuba.
From the John F. Kennedy Library

to avoid. Martha eventually appeared, loaded with magazines that she dropped at the foot of the bed. She was smiling and cordial until Ernest asked her whether he should tell the columnist how he was busted and she went to Finland to make some more money so he could go on writing his book. Her expression darkened and she said curtly not to believe him, that that was just one of his jokes. Wilson was puzzled and Martha did not elaborate. What irritated her was that Ernest interpreted everything in terms of himself. The simple fact that she supported herself, that journalism was her job, was not satisfactory to his ego. He preferred to believe that she was doing it for him.

The January 6 issue of *Life* featuring Robert Capa's photographic essay entitled "The Novelist Takes a Wife" was now on the newsstands. Capa had caught an especially tender moment with Ernest gazing down with open adoration at Marty, whose own face bears a modestly mischievous smile. The article notes that the leather hunting bag slung over his shoulder was the gift she had brought to him from Finland. In San Francisco en route to the Orient they had lunch with Ingrid Bergman, with whom Ernest discussed the possibility of playing Maria in the Selznick film. The *Life* men turned up again and there were shots of Ernest and Bergman at their table at Jack's on Sacramento Street, as well as one of Marty, standing in front of the landmark restaurant.

The sailing across to Honolulu was miserable, with giant gray waves, falling trays, and crashing bottles. Honolulu was hardly an improvement. Neither Martha nor Ernest appreciated the island custom of lei-draping and continuous entertaining. "This is a place," wrote Martha to her mother, "where hospitality is a curse and no one can be alone." What she had hoped for in vain was a haven of sunshine and seclusion. Ernest adopted his illiteracy pose as the guest of honor at a literary luncheon and almost got into a fistfight at a luau. He was drinking so much that Martha tried to intercede when one of the hostesses refilled his glass. He waved her aside imperiously. Lunch with his aunt and a gathering of missionaries was a failure since no liquor was served at all, but Martha thanked the aunt politely for a snapshot of Ernest fishing at Horton's Creek in 1904. On the back of the photo was the inscription "To our lovely new niece, Martha Gellhorn Hemingway, Honolulu, February 15, 1941."

Chapter 22

In 1978, Dodd, Mead published Martha Gellhorn's book, *Travels With Myself and Another,* an exceedingly funny and perceptive account of journeys she had made to various parts of the world. The first chapter, "Mr. Ma's Tigers," is her recollection of the trip to China with Ernest, who is identified throughout only as U.C. (Unwilling Companion), since Martha did not want to trade on the celebrated name. This book may contain the most discerning and engaging portrait of Hemingway ever drawn, at least as he was in 1941—crackling with humor and wisdom, sturdy and forbearing. For those who wonder what Martha loved about him, it is all there, told in the first person, with affection and appreciation. She wrote:

> U.C. took to Hongkong at once. . . . in the twinkling of an eye, [he] collected a mixed jovial entourage, ranging from local cops . . . to fat wealthy crook-type Chinese businessmen. . . . U.C. . . . never tired of true life stories. . . . It was a valid system for him. Aside from being his form of amusement, he learned about a place and people through the eyes and experiences of those who lived there.

Martha, who was a moderate drinker, had no desire to do what Ernest did—drink and listen through most of a day and a night. When she slipped away from the talkathons to gather material for her assigned articles, "U.C. used to say, kindly, 'M. is going off to take the pulse of the nation.' "

Her assignment from *Collier's* was to report on the defenses of Hong Kong, Singapore, and the Dutch East Indies, take a look at the Burma Road, and find out something about the progress of the China-Japan War. The British military authorities in Hong Kong were determined to defend the Crown colony, but there were terrible problems in protecting the area, what with a potentially severe shortage of food and water, frequent outbreaks of cholera and crowded streets that could become death traps in an aerial or sea bombardment. The government had devised a number of schemes to evacuate the populace but none seemed practical. "If you considered these facts," wrote Martha in "Time Bomb in Hong Kong," "life on top of the time bomb would be extremely unpleasant."

Four days after their arrival, Martha left for the Burma Road. Leaving Ernest behind she boarded a DC-2 that was owned jointly by the Chinese government and Pan American and operated by U.S. personnel. The plane took off for Lashio on the Burma border in the predawn darkness of a freezing February night. The first stop was Chungking, the capital of China, 770 miles away. With seven Chinese passengers, Martha found a seat in the unlighted cabin. Thirty minutes out they encountered a storm. Tilting and plunging, with hail beating against the wings, the plane bucked the wind. As ice formed on the propellers (there was no de-icing equipment) the pilot climbed out of the storm through clouds that were like dense steam. Of their steep descent into the Chungking area, Martha wrote the following for *Collier's:* "Suddenly, from being lost in cloud, we were so low that we could see washing hanging in the courtyards." The airfield, only 1,900 feet long and 100 feet wide, was on an island in the middle of the Yangtze River.

While the plane was being refueled for the next leg of the trip, the weather improved. Now, instead of heavy cloud cover against Japanese bombers, a bright sun shone in a blue sky. They took off anyway, so that the pilot could keep to his schedule and reach Lashio by midnight. Martha tried at least to appreciate the scenery —rice paddies brilliant in the sunshine, delicate purple hues of terraced fields, narrow gorges of riverbeds—as the pilot kept his craft below the rims of the mountains out of sight of enemy planes.

At dusk they reached Kunming, where they stayed only long

enough to take on gasoline and further passengers. Now they would fly over the highest mountains at an altitude of 14,000 feet.

> The DC-2 behaved as if it were a runaway roller coaster. . . . When you could see at all, you saw great, round rings of fire on the mountains, where the peasants were burning brush. . . . It was very weird and handsome: a vast blackness . . . breaking into lines and circles of red light. . . . I did not even see the Lashio field until we had landed on it.

It was 10:00 P.M. Fourteen hundred miles of narrow dirt road, spiraling over the highest and most rugged mountains, linked Chungking and Lashio. That was the Burma Road. Vehicles navigating its treacherous curves took two weeks to make the journey. Pilots of China National Aviation flew it regularly in less than four hours. It was the lifeline of China.

At the hotel there was hot water for bathing and a mattress that rested on a board. Martha slept soundly. In the morning she saw what there was to see in Lashio—a lively country fair, native women washing themselves modestly at the public water taps, an Indian jewelry store managed by a Hindu merchant who seemed proud of the city's crime rate—just like Chicago, he explained. A few hours later she flew back to Kunming, where the pilot timed his landing at dusk, after the last Japanese daylight bombing. Gas mains in Kunming had been hit, and the sewers and the miserable houses, split open, gave off their accumulated stench of dirt and refuse. A grunting coolie pulled Martha and the pilot to the Hotel de l'Europe in a ricksha. In the darkness thousands of dislocated people who had fled to the hills now plodded back after the raid.

At six-thirty the next morning she boarded the plane for the final time, flying through clouds that were like "volcanic white soup." At Chungking some notables came on board for the final lap back to Hong Kong. In three days Martha had flown twice the distance from Chicago to San Francisco, under conditions that made this the most dangerous commercial flying in the world. "Glowing with adrenalin and high spirits, I would gladly have started again on the next flight," she wrote in *Travels*.

During the next three weeks she gathered more information and wrote up her articles for *Collier's*, while Ernest loafed and waited for their clearance to visit the Canton Front. U.C. acquired "an ever-growing band of buddies," enjoyed huge Chinese feasts, and was charmed by local customs, "for instance ear-cleaning," Martha wrote in *Travels*. "The Chinese passion for firecrackers also delighted him. U.C. bought them every day and was very disappointed when I insisted that he stop lighting them in our rooms. . . . From the first he was much better at the glamorous East than I was, flexible and undismayed." The noise, except in the exclusive environs of the very rich, was deafening, a combination of Times Square on New Year's Eve, a three-alarm fire, and the subway at rush hour. Coolies shouted and grunted, housewives shrieked at the food vendors, brass bands struck up loud tunes for the passing Chinese funerals. And above this permanent bedlam, firecrackers exploded regularly in celebration of some wedding or birthday.

In her *Collier's* article of June 7, 1941, Martha described the hideous overcrowding of poor people who slept ten to a room in dark, airless, filthy cubicles. Even those destitute souls were better off than the thirty thousand squatters who lived in the streets, cooking, begging, sleeping, or simply leaning against crumbling walls. In sad little corridors, coolies paid four American pennies for three pipes of opium. A fourteen-year-old girl who prepared the pipes and tended the bunks kept a small turtle for a pet and earned twenty cents a day.

Martha shouted at U.C., " 'We're all living on slave labour! The people are half starved! I want to get out, I can't stand this place!' "

U.C. looked at her "thoughtfully. 'The trouble with you, M., is that you think everybody is exactly like you. What you can't stand, they can't stand. . . . How do you know what they feel about their lives? If it was as bad as you think they'd kill themselves instead of having more kids and setting off firecrackers.' " Martha describes herself in *Travels* as follows. "From agonizing over the lot of my Chinese fellow men, I fell into a state of hysterical disgust with hardly a pause. 'WHY do they all have to spit so much?' I cried." Martha knew the answer—the spitting could be due to endemic tuberculosis—and she knew she was being "contemptible," but to avoid further scenes Ernest moved her out of the old downtown hotel to an English hotel at Repulse Bay, where there were no spitting and no smells. He teased her about her contentment in the British enclave but he enjoyed it too, satisfied to read quietly and take long walks through the hills.

On March 24, everything seemed in order for the Hemingways to visit the Canton Front (the nearest sector that Chiang Kai-shek's Army of the Kuomintang was holding.) They flew to Namyung, 200 miles north of Hong Kong, where they were greeted by two Chinese escorts. There was Mr. Ma, the political interpreter, and Mr. Ho, the transportation officer, who accompanied them in an ancient Chevrolet over rutted mud roads to Shaokwan. Accommodations at the local hotel consisted of two planks for sleeping, a spittoon and a washbowl, and a hole-in-the-floor toilet down the corridor.

Martha wrote in *Travels:*

I wondered aloud about the washing arrangements: how exactly were two people to manage with one bowl of water? . . . U.C. told me earnestly not to wash at all and if I dreamed of brushing my teeth I was a nut case. I had better control my mania for keeping clean. "Cheer up," U.C. said. . . . "Who wanted to come to China?"

The burden of politeness and speechmaking fell directly on Ernest, who managed to survive the ordeal by drinking the yellow rice wine that to Martha tasted like kerosene. As a woman, she was expected only to smile. "Thinking it over, after these many years," she wrote in her travel memoir, "I put a proper value on U.C.'s patience and courtesy, neither his most familiar qualities. . . . "

To reach the mountainous battle front, a hundred miles from Shaokwan, required the complex navigation of rutted roads, the swift current of the mud-colored North River, slippery mudbanks, and interminable hours astride mean-spirited Mongolian ponies. Always the wind blew, the fine cold rain fell, and the dampness penetrated the layers of heavy garments. River transportation was a dilapidated Chriscraft that was pumped every two hours to keep it from sinking. Towed in its wake was a sampan that carried an armed escort of two officers and five soldiers and the sampan family. At four-thirty in the afternoon the first meal was bowls of rice, and at six darkness fell. The Chinese passengers curled up on the floor of the sampan, but Martha and Ernest moved to the small, sloping roof of the motorboat to sleep on the coiled ropes and boathooks. He slept and she stayed awake, watching the boat run aground on sandbars.

Twenty-four hours after they left Shaokwan, the downriver trip was over. Now came the transfer to the ponies. "A platoon of soldiers in soaked cotton uniforms and eight stable coolies with eight diminutive horses stood at attention to receive us," Martha wrote. "Men and beasts shook with cold." There was no easy way to ride the ponies. Mr. Ma was knocked down in the mud. Martha's horse kicked viciously. The coolies would strike the ponies and scream at them, and the horses would attempt to bite the coolies. The footpath was like a mixture of grease and glue. Rain came down in sheets, and the entire procession "jolted forward in sodden silence."

For a week they traveled on narrow footpaths from village to village, from outpost to regimental headquarters. This was the Seventh War Zone and it was left to Ernest to make the daily speeches to the troops. Together Martha and Ernest viewed parades, studied maps, and watched political entertainments. The sleeping accommodations never varied—bedboards and bugs. One night, with the mosquitoes and flies swarming, and no whiskey due to the general's enthusiasm for it, Martha "said in the darkness, 'I wish to die.' "

" 'Too late,' answered U.C. from across the room. 'Who wanted to come to China?' "

On the trip back to Shaokwan, Martha felt numb and oblivious to the landscape. "After you have seen three rice paddies you do not need to look anymore." At night she slept inside the sampan with the Chinese families. During the day, as U.C. read, she perked up and began to imagine that things would get better. "I shouted above the clanging of the Chriscraft motor, 'The worst is over!' U.C. glanced at me and returned to his book. 'Mr. Ma says we'll be at Shaokwan by noon tomorrow. . . . He says we can get anything we want to eat on the train. . . .' U.C., reading, had begun to wag his head like a pendulum."

Forty-three hours later they climbed out of the sampan. A few hours after that they were settled in a hot, airless, first-class train compartment littered with fruit skins and cigarette butts. Twenty-five hours and four hundred miles later they were in Kweilin, where they were to be picked up for a flight into Chungking. But, of course, it did not work out as planned. The plane did not show up and the two travelers were marooned in Kweilin's Palace Hotel with bedbugs, filthy water, and overflowing toilets. "I cannot imagine how we passed those days," Martha wrote, "clinging to the remnants of sanity."

Eventually the plane did come, an unscheduled flight on a freight trip, and Martha and Ernest remained in Chungking for several weeks. This was the period when Martha began to suffer from an intractable fungus on her hands—China Rot was its distasteful name —and she had to wear large white gloves over a smelly salve. The Hemingways were invited to lunch alone with Generalissimo and Madame Chiang Kai-shek, the rulers of China, and through a furtive meeting in a marketplace they were led to the secret quarters of Chou En-lai, the communist leader. "We thought Chou a winner, the one really good man we'd met in China. . . . " Martha wrote. She and Ernest parted in Rangoon, Hemingway to return by the *Clipper* to the United States, Martha to fulfill her commitment to *Collier's* to visit the military and naval installations of the Netherlands East Indies, and Singapore. She praised Ernest for his generosity in coming to China with her. It was even possible, she wrote, that given more time, and with her not around, he might have developed into a happy Old China Hand. He was not reduced to despair by the disease and the filth. "He saw the Chinese as people, while I saw them as a mass of downtrodden valiant doomed humanity."

At Surabaya naval base in Java, Martha watched submarines being repaired at the naval yard. "The Dutch are not only preparing to defend their islands," she wrote later for *Collier's*, "but they are ready to destroy everything the Japanese want, in case they cannot keep them out. Mainly right now, the Japanese want oil . . . and the Dutch of the Indies have plenty of oil." A government functionary flew her to one of the oil fields on Tarakan, an island off the northwest coast of Borneo, "not one of the world's beauty spots," she added, " . . . hotter than the inside of a steam boiler." There was much disagreement over the aims of the Japanese. Some doubted that they would start a war; it was not logical, when they could buy all the oil and sell their own goods in return. Others said it was not a matter for reason. The Japanese military clique was demanding a "New Order" in Asia. But everyone agreed on one thing. The United States fleet was the most important influence in the Pacific.

Martha's last stop before flying back to the United States was Singapore, a startling contrast to Dutch efficiency in Java. The red tape was horrendous, the censorship oppressive, but "if you relax and decide you are part of a movie—an extra, perhaps," she reported, "you can have a wonderful time." On the plus side every luxury was available, from fresh caviar to champagne. She went with gallant young British officers to cocktail parties in the officers' mess, dances at the country club, moonlit drives around the Gap overlooking the harbor. There were relatively few white women in Singapore, she soon noticed, and she did not lack admirers.

Ernest, staying over in Hong Kong for a few weeks, was on a cocktail party circuit of his own, but his letters of the period do not read as though he was enjoying it. To provoke his absent wife, however, he did recount with apparent glee an incident of questionable veracity involving three young Chinese beauties, presented to him as a gift from a Cantonese war lord. Returning to his room one night he found them waiting for him, giggling and bowing. Uncertain of the protocol, he suggested that they take a communal shower. After that, still uncertain, he turned out the lights and learned, as well as he could, what to do with three young women.

Before flying out on May 6 he visited an old friend from the Spanish Civil War, Ramon Lavalle, an Argentinian pilot who had flown for the Loyalists. At his house in Kowloon Ernest met Lavalle's four-year-old daughter, whom he cradled in his arms and watched with great tenderness. Lavalle was moved by the sight of the leathery, robust man holding the delicate child. He recalled earlier conversations, in which Ernest had expressed his longing for a daughter.

Ernest would not see Martha again until they met in New York in June 1941. His letters followed her from Manila and Guam and in flight over the Pacific. Repeatedly he wrote how much he missed her. To Max Perkins he reported, perhaps wishfully, that she was weary of globetrotting and ready to stay home with him. Whether or not Martha was serious about chucking her work to stay home with her husband, she told Tillie Arnold that she wept with relief and gratitude when she finally saw the Golden Gate Bridge, and that if it had not been for Ernest she could never have made it. After joining Ernest in New York, she went with him to Washington, D.C. for a briefing session with Colonel John W. Thomason at the Office of Naval Intelligence. Colonel Thomason later wrote Max Perkins that he liked Ernest and that Martha was quite a person in her own right. He listened respectfully to her critique of the inadequate British defense system at Singapore.

In Key West, Ernest spent some time with Gigi and Patrick before the two boys left to meet their mother in San Francisco. Pauline wired him at the Finca that the boys had arrived safely, and he replied, thanking her for the wire but chiding her for signing "regards." With all their fights he still missed her and would sign his letters with love, "if you know what I mean." He had sent her some jade pieces and a wooden carving from China and wished her a happy birthday.

Such gestures made no dent in Pauline's hostility. For comfort and companionship she had turned to Jinny, who divided her time between San Francisco and Los Angeles. Jinny could not help exerting a subtle influence on Pauline and Pauline now wondered if any man was ever to be trusted. At one point during the summer, she accused Ernest of not spending enough time with his sons and refused to budge in her insistence upon the monthly checks. Irritated, Ernest replied that if he was to salvage any income at all from the government he must maintain six-month continuous non-resident status. Three months in the Far East and the summer in Cuba would meet that requirement. The boys were in camp in California and would meet him in Sun Valley in September. "I have to have a little money of some kind to run things you see," he wrote sarcastically. "I pay over $15,000 tax on the $6,000 you get tax free. . . . If anyone asks the children what their father did in Mr. Rooseveldts war they can say 'He paid for it.'"

By July Ernest was writing to Max Perkins that Martha was now well-rested, and since neither of them was working, there was plenty of time for their social life. Their best friends were Robert and Jane Joyce, he a first secretary at the American Embassy and she, a handsome young woman who formed a close friendship with Martha. They often came to the Finca for impromptu late dinners and Sunday swimming parties, as did the ranking officer at the embassy, Ellis Briggs, and his wife. "It was fun to be a guest there," recalled Briggs, "and Ernest could be the kindest of hosts, but it must have been undiluted hell to try to have any organized life with him."

Martha's temperament was suited to the Spanish way of midnight suppers and late rising—that timeless existence that does not recognize deadlines. And she enjoyed Ernest's numerous cats. "What I did not like to do was run the house," Martha said to the author. "The servants were hopeless and I did not know how to boil an egg. I couldn't teach people how to cook because I didn't know anything except when it wasn't edible. . . . what drove me crazy was when I had to cope with chauffeurs and servants and loonies, the whole lot, and I never stopped complaining about that."

In September Martha and Ernest were back at Sun Valley Lodge as guests of Union Pacific. Jack, after crisscrossing the country with friends from his high-school graduating class, arrived for trout fishing, and Gigi and Patrick came by train from San Francisco. Ernest, still riding the triumph of *For Whom the Bell Tolls*, was determined to make this 1941 vacation a banner one. He organized several canoe runs and took Marty and the younger boys on pheasant hunts and duck shoots. There were gambling in Ketchum and continuous parties with vacationing Hollywood personalities—the Coopers, Howard and Slim Hawks, Barbara Stanwyck and Robert Taylor. However, the gaiety was shadowed by an awareness of ominous events in Europe. The Germans were advancing into the Russian heartland and Ernest was betting everyone that the United States would be at war by the new year.

In October Martha's volume of short stories, *The Heart of Another*, was published. Ernest pressed her to write under her married name of Martha Hemingway and was irritated when she declined. He had worked hard with Perkins to design the dust jacket properly and to prepare the jacket copy. About the cover photo he was facetious, explaining to Max that as he snapped her picture he wondered if the Hays office ban on sweaters extended to writers. About promotion of the book he had some thoughtful advice. It seemed to him that the critics had not fairly distinguished between Martha's journalism and her fiction. Her best stories, such as the "Ruby" one, wrote Ernest to the editor, were so convincing that people assumed they were true, in much the same way as readers believed everything in *A Farewell to Arms* had happened to him. It was necessary for sales purposes to identify her by her journalistic reputation, he acknowledged, but at the same time a distinction had to be made between her imaginative work and her factual effort.

Ernest's efforts paid off. The critics did treat the book as serious fiction, but Martha's refusal to be classified as a Hemingway did not spare her from being identified as one. *The New Yorker* called the stories intelligent and affecting but added that she had read too carefully the works of Mr. Hemingway, "an amiable trait in a wife but dangerous for a writer of fiction." Robert Littell in the *Yale Review* said that she had heart and substance and wished that she would lose "her pronounced but not incurable Hemingway accent." Rose Field, writing in the *New York Herald Tribune* on November 2, 1941, also believed that Gellhorn had been influenced by Hemingway but said she did not consider this a derogatory statement. "It would be strange indeed if two writers, emotionally and intellectually drawn to each other, did not consciously and sub-consciously influence each other's work. . . . These stories are pure Hemingway—romantic under a surface of hardness."

Such comparisons seem exaggerated. Martha's latest stories were not so different stylistically from the ones written in 1935, when she did not know Ernest. There is an autobiographical feel to the stories in *The Heart of Another*; the various settings correspond roughly to places Martha visited. "Slow Train to Garmisch" takes a sharp look at a young woman traveling through Germany in the early thirties after a broken love affair. "Luigi's House" tells of an adversary relationship between a woman who had recently come from the Spanish Civil War and an illiterate Corsican peasant. The long piece, "Portrait of a Lady," is crammed with detail about the Finnish war front. And in "Good Will Toward Men," she makes a cool appraisal of Paris and Frenchmen on the eve of the war. Like Ernest, Martha was a good observer, using the sights and sounds of real experience and then putting her imagination to work on relationships.

She was good-natured about the comparisons to Hemingway and wrote Clara Spiegel that she knew exactly what there was still to do (in her work) even if she did not always know how to do it. She was not interested in the book's promotion, believing that the business of a writer was to write and the business of the publisher to sell the book. She wanted good sales, the money being important, but she would not know at least until after Christmas how it was faring.

On December 7, 1941, the Hemingways were sipping daiquiris in a local bar outside Tucson, Arizona when the news of the Japanese attack at Pearl Harbor broke. "A tattered Indian child came in, with some clutched newspapers, and said, 'Con la guerra, la guerra,' mildly," Martha wrote in 1959 in *The Face of War*. Veterans though they both were of international crises, they were horrified to learn the extent of the American defeat. Ernest fumed that Frank Knox should resign as secretary of the navy and that those responsible at Oahu should be shot. Martha, until she finally reached London late in 1943, would continue to be " . . . paralyzed by conflicting emotions: private duty, public disgust and a longing to forget both and join those who were suffering the war. It is too hard," she wrote, "to sit on the outside and watch what you can neither help nor change; it is far easier to close your eyes and your mind and jump into the general misery, where you have almost no choices left, but a lot of splendid company."

"This winter we both have to get back to work," Martha had written Clara from Sun Valley. "We have done an awful lot of rushing around, but the real hard work is when you sit still alone." She did begin a new novel when they returned to Havana, but Ernest, who had not done any serious work in over a year, gave no sign that he intended to start writing. However, he told Max Perkins that he wanted to do something for the war effort close to home. He had agreed to edit and write an introduction to a volume of war stories for Crown Publications. While balking at writing propaganda, he thought that a book illustrative of war might generate support from the public. Then he conceived an idea that was much more suited to his personality. He would form a private intelligence network to gather information about Fifth Column activity in and around Havana. Spruille Braden, the American ambassador, gave the plan his support. Ernest recruited as agents several pelota players, some anti-fascist Spanish noblemen, waiters and fishermen, and a few wharf rats. The small guest house at the Finca, recently remodeled by Martha from the old garage, became the secret headquarters. Information was funneled to Ernest, who then translated and processed it and delivered it himself to Robert Joyce at the embassy. The code name was Crime Shop but Ernest humorously referred to the network as the Crook Factory.

In May, Martha went to Florida to meet her mother for a holiday. The most enduring love of Martha's life was for Edna Gellhorn, and she was closer to her than anyone else. She admired her and, most important, trusted and could rely upon her. They met at a resort on the Gulf coast not far from Pensacola. Sweet and uncomplaining as usual, Edna Gellhorn was also weary. She would not admit how much Martha's company meant to her, for fear of seeming dependent, but Martha understood the significance of the visit. With serious talk that the government would soon put an end to private pleasure travel, this might be their last trip for the duration of the war.

Martha had carried her work with her and was eking out a few pages at a time. She believed that the writing was good but feared that the novel was turning into "a well-written, meaningless" story about people she did not really understand. This was perceptive of her, for she was creating a heroine, Liana, who was quite unlike herself. Uneducated and instinctual, Liana is an exquisite mulatto child-woman married to a middle-aged white entrepreneur but helplessly in love with a French teacher. The setting, lush and indolent, is a small Caribbean island. The period was contemporary.

Martha wrote Ernest every day. When a week went by without any word from him she became anxious, and then frantic. Was he sick? Was he in an awful mood? Worst of all, was he out in the *Pilar* with the motors dead and no one to check up on him or notice that he had not returned? "If you are cross with me," she wrote on May 27, "I will understand. Just tell me and I won't sit here thinking desperate things. I feel so cut off." Finally she sent him cablegrams, pleading for some word. On May 30 she received a cable and a good letter. Writing immediately, she asked if he needed her. If so, he should wire her and she would return at once. "I'm counting every day until I come," she wrote. "I guess I love you very much or something."

When she read some mail that Ernest had enclosed from Spanish friends, Martha realized once again that for her Spain had been the best of all. She had been young and bold, the cause had been just, and Ernest had been her hero. "There will never be anything like it again," she wrote. On June 1, as she was preparing to leave for the Miami airport, she received another cable explaining that he had written her eleven letters. She had received three. So she left her forwarding address and hoped that eventually the letters would be returned to the Finca and she could read them over breakfast.

While Martha was away, Ernest had asked Ambassador Braden to support another of his ideas for fighting the Nazis. The *Pilar* should be armed as a Q-boat and Ernest would be the commander. Braden, an imaginative man, was interested. Martha, through her friendship with the Roosevelts, was able to get permission from the President for a Marine radar operator and the weaponry. "The President loved . . . derring-do and jokes," she recalled. "He would have done it himself if he could." The equipment was assembled and Ernest formed a crew that included Winston Guest, who had lately been visiting the Hemingways, Gregorio Fuentes, the *Pilar*'s veteran mate, and some exiled Spaniards. Martha thought the whole operation had the ring of fantasy and teased Ernest about some of the crazy things that could happen, but Ernest told her she was a feeble strategist and went off to cruise the northern coastal waters.

With the annual arrival of Patrick and Gigi in June, Ernest analyzed all his sons in a letter to Hadley. Jack was healthy and cheerful but knew nothing about money and absolutely had to have a college education in order to get any kind of a job after the war. Patrick was intelligent and sound. Only Gigi puzzled him. "He [Gigi] has the biggest dark side in the family except you and me," he had written to Pauline, "and I'm not in the family. He keeps it so concealed that you never know about it. . . . " Ernest's insight may well have been correct but there was a coldness about it. His judgment became a burden for Gregory, who suffered more than Patrick from Ada Stern's presence and from his mother's divorce. Ernest picked up on the "dark side" of Gregory without giving consideration to the possible source of the boy's difficulty. He valued toughness, not pity. He wanted his sons to be good athletes, well educated, morally sound. It was an embarrassment to him that any one of them might have an emotional problem, or that he, himself, might in some measure be responsible.

All three boys continued to find Martha a devoted companion. Patrick, perhaps the most reserved so far as affection was concerned, readily admitted that they had an easy, adult relationship. Gigi worshiped her and was the most upset when Ernest lost his temper with her. In the heat of one argument over writing, he roared, "I'll show you, you conceited bitch. They'll be reading my stuff long after the worms have finished with you." Martha knew that it was foolish to cross him, except in the most good-natured way, but as his mood had become increasingly bellicose she was less willing to rein in her own temper. He had greeted her ecstatically when she returned from Miami. But after the loving reunion he resumed his own pursuits and pleasures. During this summer his clandestine activities with the Crook Factory were disrupting even her minimum requirements for orderliness, as his various informers appeared and disappeared at all hours.

Six weeks after she came home, Martha prepared to leave once again, this time for a two-month sweep of the Caribbean to investigate for *Collier's* the effect of submarine warfare on the life of the islands. "During that terrible year, 1942, I lived in the sun, safe and comfortable and hating it," she wrote in *Travels*. Like so many others, she could not realize, because of censorship, the extent of Allied shipping losses everywhere, including the Caribbean, where 251 ships were sunk in one year and 71 lost during the two months of Martha's assignment. Though she intended to do her best "with the mild material at hand" she assumed, mistakenly, that the watery area in which she would roam was a "sideshow."

Ernest did not want her to leave him but admitted that they could use the money. At least his sons were with him. They were good company and, unlike Marty, trained not to talk back. He signed them on as apprentice crew to sail on an "Operation Friendless (code name)." If he was sometimes irascible at home (finding it more and more painful to write), he was good-humored and relaxed at sea. With the boys aboard, the voyage became an innocuous idyll of fishing, stargazing, and island explorations, aptly described by Gregory as "Don Quixote vs. the Wolf Pack."

Chapter 23

On July 20, 1942, one day before Ernest's forty-third birthday, Martha sent him greetings from Port-au-Prince, Haiti. She felt refreshed and content. The island was a most agreeable place even in the stifling heat. She enjoyed the luxury of traveling light, with no plans and with every day a surprise. "It does not make for depth of wisdom probably," she wrote on the 23rd, "but it keeps the mind light and limber and full of jokes. And I think I would rather feel young than be Jane Austen." In Ciudad Trujillo the customs officials were perturbed about her typewriter, but after studying her passport closely they asked her if she was related to the "grande escritor." When she replied that she was, they made no more trouble about the typewriter. "I am embarrassed to profit by your fame, very embarrassed," she said to Ernest. In Haiti she had started off by saying that she was Miss Gellhorn, but that was too complicated, for if that was her name, how did it happen that her passport said Hemingway? No matter how much she explained, or what she did, it was in vain, for his name followed her everywhere. Ernest thought that her attitude was mere foolishness, but she was serious about it. Finally an Austrian refugee waiter in a Haitian restaurant asked her to autograph his copy of *A Stricken Field* and she enjoyed experiencing her own identity again.

By the time she reached San Juan, she was worrying about not hearing from Ernest and began sending off cables. On August 1 she even cabled a Cuban friend to find out if he was ill and unable to write. She was greatly relieved when four letters and two cables were delivered. She had been imagining that he was about to cut her off without a word. Such fluctuating moods were typical of Martha's feelings for Ernest. When she was away she longed for him. When she was home she found it difficult to put up with his exasperating habits. At the same time that she scolded him for not bathing, or for drinking too much, or for telling some silly lie about his exploits, she would make an impressive effort with his sons, his cats, his parties, his guests. When nothing changed she boiled up with frustration and knew only one way out, to get away for a while. "All is well here, now that I know you haven't renounced me," she wrote on August 2 in reply to all the good mail.

Her pace in San Juan turned hectic, as she worked twelve hours a day visiting water-front dives, slum housing, and naval installations. "I seem to be driven to this unceasing looking . . . not for Collier's," she wrote, "but because of some terrible curiosity, a desire to know what it is all like and all the time knowing that I will not know. . . . I am so tired and so full of new and useless knowledge." That Sunday she had a chance to rest and sort out her papers and clothes. She had run short of books to read. For years, she wrote Ernest, she had been carrying Proust around. Finally she could admit that he bored her and she would give him up.

A week later she reached St. Thomas in the Virgin Islands. It was a joy after the squalor of Puerto Rico—the wonderful houses of soft colors, the winding stone streets, the magnificent views of the sea. She wrote a long article, mailed it August 12, and engaged a run-down native potato boat to take her through the Windward Islands. Her account, as published in Travels, is further testimony to her tolerance for harrowing travel conditions and her unquenchable appreciation for raffish characters. In the context of her marriage to Hemingway and the responsibility for him and their household, some of her personal remarks seem to take on an added dimension. "I hadn't felt so carefree," she wrote after a solitary swim off a beach at St. Martin's, "since my girlhood travels with a knapsack, discovering Europe." Yet too much idle contentment was not for her either. "Since I was living in perfect comfort," she wrote of another island, Saba, "and eating good food, I began to fret. . . . For I wasn't all that enamoured of peace thirty-four years ago; I was enamoured of surprises and excitement and jokes and risks and odd people. . . . "

Ernest's reaction to all this was open sarcasm. "Marty, my Marty," he wrote Evan Shipman, "is down in the Caribbean on a thirty foot sloop with a crew of three negro comrades doing some pieces for Colliers. Last heard from by cable from St. Kitts yesterday. If she gets sunk with all hands I think Colliers pay double for the article. Or maybe instead they get me to write a Tribute To Her."

Ernest may have been lonely, but he was rarely alone. Everyone flocked to the Finca for the swimming, tennis, food, drink, and good talk. The boys were included in all their father's grown-up activities —shooting at the Club Cazadores, lunch at the Floridita, wine and beer with their meals, gambling at the jai alai games. Hadley sent birthday greetings from Minnesota, where she and Paul were fishing, and Ernest replied in his usual vein. His principal problem was financial, having paid out $103,000. in income tax in 1941, 80 percent of his earnings. Since he was not writing or selling fiction, Pauline's $500. monthly payments came out of capital. It was his bad luck to have made a fortune when whatever one made was confiscated by the government. But the good luck was to have had all the wonderful times with Hadley at Enghien and Pamplona and Cortina D'Ampezzo. "Good bye Miss Katherine Kat," he wrote. "I love you very much. It is all right to do so because it hasn't anything to do with you and that great Paul; it is just untransferable feeling for early and best Gods."

In Antigua, Martha found her idea for the final *Collier's* article. She would go south to Surinam, a remote Dutch colony on the northern coast of South America that was of vital importance to the American war effort because of its rich deposits of bauxite. The Dutch territorial forces guarded the mines and the U.S. Army and Air Force personnel manned the military airfield. An hour's ride from the airport was the capital city, Paramaribo, carved out of the jungle, bustling with shops and restaurants and bars. There was one hotel, small and shabby and mosquito-infested but hospitable to travelers and to American servicemen who gathered around Marty, eager to buy her a beer and show her their dog-eared snapshots from home. Her presence in the desolate outpost was conspicuous and her cool acceptance of the harsh living conditions greatly admired.

From South America Martha flew to New York for two weeks. "Got no sleep on the plane so look haggard and awful," she reported to Ernest on the 10th of October from her room at the Lombardy. "Feel like a dying cow, but am *very happy*. The town is beautiful and exciting and the weather marvelous." She was worried about Patrick, who was spending his first year away from home at the Canterbury School in New Milford, Connecticut. "Just talked to Mousie," she wrote. "Like talking to some one in jail, boys never allowed out except for dentist." She had a medical checkup, and a good haircut at Elizabeth Arden, and did some shopping for Ernest. Eleanor Roosevelt invited her to dinner at her Manhattan townhouse, and she had lunches with Charlie Scribner and with her editor at *Collier's*, Charles Colebaugh. "He [Colebaugh] is sweet, sends you love," she wrote Ernest on the 21st, "and is crazy about me." (Ernest always greeted sourly the news of Marty's luncheon dates with her editors. To read that someone was crazy about her, even her own editor, was not the kind of news he relished, especially when he had not seen her for three months.)

On the 22nd Martha accompanied the First Lady to the White House for the weekend. Suddenly she was overcome with homesickness. More than anything, she wanted to be at the Finca with Ernest, but alone! Not pressed upon by people. "We'll have to divorce in order to see each other as lovers," she wrote plaintively, acknowledging that the blame did not rest altogether with Ernest. Already she had invited two friends from Spanish Civil War days to come in January.

By the time Martha returned to the Finca late in October, Gigi had left for Key West. The date of his departure had seemed to Ernest to be tailored to Ada's convenience, not his. His letters of the period were liberally sprinkled with irritated references to Pauline's lack of consideration. To Patrick he alluded darkly to "the way things are managed." To Hadley he had written that he was trying to get a European bicycle of his shipped to Jack at Dartmouth. " . . . with a little co-operation from Key West will do so," he wrote. "But that is not the headquarters of co-operation." Pauline believed that she was most cooperative. She consulted him about the children and saw to it that they visited him often. It was time he realized that there was more to her life now than maneuvering everything for his benefit. (Ernest would never accept that. Apparently, even after the divorce, he became jealous when Pauline showed affection and attention to others.)

After the outbreak of the war Pauline went into business with two friends and opened up a fabric shop, Bahama House, where they sold drapery and upholstery materials. She worked as a Gray Lady at the local hospital and made friends among the officers attached to the Seventh Naval District. One, a commander Campbell, came often to take her out, and she seemed quite fond of him. Patrick in later conversations expressed regret that his mother did not remarry and create the kind of life she had enjoyed with his father. She liked to manage a household for a man, he said, and did it very well. But it seemed to him that she became more like her mother, an older woman who was no longer interested in a sexual relationship. She would continue to have men friends but with no heart left for marriage. The hurt of Ernest's desertion was too deep. Jay Allen and his wife noticed this too, when Pauline visited them in the fall. The conversation turned to Spain and Pauline suddenly burst out, with great bitterness, "Spain! Don't mention Spain to me. That war lost me the man I loved." And, as Patrick phrased it, "there was always the sister. . . . Aunt Jinny was lesbian and she was quite keen on getting my mother to be homosexual as well. . . . There was always this undercurrent with Jinny."

Gigi's reaction to his mother's suitor was immediate and negative. "When she made the mistake of asking me what I thought of Campbell," Gregory said years later, "I quickly made a big face and objected strenuously." He suggested, in retrospect, that his antagonism probably had something to do with his hero-worship of his father. How could anyone fill Ernest's shoes? And the possibility of sharing Pauline's affections with a stranger was less than appealing, since he was still trying to win her himself.

Martha was pleased when Ernest turned the "Crook Factory" operation over to Gustavo Durán, a former Loyalist colonel whom she and Ernest had known in Spain. She liked Durán, but since she was fighting for privacy in which to work she was annoyed that he brought his wife, Bonte, to stay with him at the Finca. Tensions mounted between the two couples. Bonte Durán thought Martha arrogant, Martha thought her dull. Ernest had fits of guilt about the disruptions to Martha's work. When the Duráns' driver carelessly blew his horn under her window in the middle of the night, Ernest threatened to put a gun to the man's head. The Duráns moved to a hotel and Martha and Ernest returned to quarreling.

Jack, who was now staying at the guest house, noticed how much more his father was drinking and that his outbursts against Marty were unpredictable and often took place in public. In Havana one night he upbraided her severely for what he considered to be paltry Christmas gifts to the servants and then stalked out of a party, leaving her to find her way home alone. Another time, when he was roaring drunk after an evening on the town, she insisted upon driving them back to the Finca. All the way out he cursed her and then slapped her, not hard, but enough to send her into a cold rage. Never one to be cowed, she deliberately slowed the car—his beloved green Lincoln Continental—to ten miles an hour, then drove it into a ditch and a tree, leaving him to walk the rest of the way.

Martha accused Ernest of using his Q-boat patrols as a pretext for getting scarce gasoline for fishing trips. She suggested that this submarine chasing was all "rot and rubbish." At times the atmosphere aboard the *Pilar* did seem to be a mockery of wartime, as when Winston Guest recited bad poetry and grenades were hurled aimlessly at buoys in the Gulf Stream. Martha, who had originally joined Ernest's fishing trips to please him, now seemed unmoved by his childlike satisfaction in planning such trips. She would agree to go out then would leave at the first port. The behavior that began to disturb her was his need for self-glorification. If reality did not provide him with continuous triumphs, he drew on his fantasies. His Cuban friends did not see such tale-telling as harmful. They simply turned aside until he recovered his good sense. But to Martha it was lying and it sickened her, she admitted later, "making the ground shaky under the feet."

As soon as Patrick and Gigi arrived to spend their Christmas holidays with Ernest, Martha went to St. Louis to be with her mother. She had not been away twenty-four hours when she was writing of missing Ernest terribly. She carried her unfinished novel with her, but the American censors took it from her in Miami, promising to send it to St. Louis. For the first time in writing to him, Martha referred to Ernest as her darling, housebroken cobra. No one knows when a cobra will strike next. If such a metaphor was Martha's growing perception of her husband's behavior, then the marriage was in serious trouble.

On the last day of the year 1942, she wrote Ernest a three-page typewritten letter. December 31 made her almost as sad as her birthday, not from thinking about the future but remembering the past. Her manuscript finally arrived from the censor and she was going to try to work on it. She had been reading Dostoevski's letters to his wife. She hoped Ernest's next trip out would be successful and promised to be home "as quick as a winklet."

On January 8, 1943, Martha left for Chicago on the first leg of her return trip to Cuba, only to wait all day in Chicago for the plane to Miami, which never took off because of a new storm. She checked into the Palmer House and at one o'clock in the morning wrote Ernest about the awful day and then explained that since there had already been this delay she would stay with her mother for three extra days. Ernest was leaving January 12 to go submarine hunting, and she could not possibly get back in time to see him. She was only going for the book and that seemed wrong and shameful in the wake of her mother's sad, hurt face. "I guess I am not a real writer," she wrote, "because Mother's feelings are more important to me in the end. . . . I know you will think I am right. . . . the story is safe inside me, all that is necessary now is the discipline to finish it and I know I will do it." She ended in a burst of emotion. Ernest and her mother were all she had to love in the world, so she had an enormous amount of love to divide between them. If anything happened to him while she was away, an accident or an illness, she would kill herself. Theirs was a marvelous life, they should be so grateful for it, for their beautiful house, for the sunshine. She admitted that it had not been a good year. Though not a Catholic, she had gone into the cathedral to light a candle for him and for the boys. Perhaps the candles would protect them.

In the new novel, Martha had placed three characters in an untenable situation and now led them to a crashing resolution. Liana, trapped in a loveless marriage with Marc Royer, experiences her first romantic rapture with the introspective French schoolteacher, Pierre. When Royer discovers that Pierre is having an affair with his wife, he takes his revenge in a more subtle way than merely beating the wife and shooting the lover. He manipulates Pierre into abandoning Liana, who is so devastated by the betrayal that she slashes her wrists.

Ernest wrote Max Perkins that he was enjoying reading the chapters as Martha finished them, "like in the good old days when there were good magazines and good installments." He was dreading the time when she would want to go off to war again, but it was a good thing she liked going to war. With Pauline's demands about money, Martha had to do it whether she liked it or not. In the same letter he added that all the money Martha made the year before from the Caribbean trip was used up. Martha has pointed out that this was patently untrue. Ernest greatly exaggerated his financial problems during this period. He always had enough money for the things he wanted to do—for the boat, liquor, trips, and so forth. Martha worked to support herself and her share of the Finca's expenses.

In April Martha began to think about Patrick's and Gigi's travel arrangements for the summer. "We are probably being too far ahead of time, doing all this," she wrote Patrick from the Finca, on the 26th,

> but it never hurts to get things done and anyhow Papa will probably be going away for a month at the end of the week. I will get Gigi's round trip plane ticket at the same time [as yours] and send it to him. . . . I assume you will be ready to take the plane from Miami early a.m. June 7. Do not worry or think of this anymore. It will all be attended to, in plenty of time, and you will come right here like a knife cutting through butter, if I may invent a phrase.

On May 21, after a series of exasperating delays, Ernest and his crew took the *Pilar* out to sea for two months of sub-hunting. They would drop anchor at various islands to pick up supplies and mail. In his absence Martha began a series of repairs to the house. She haggled daily over the prices, worrying that Ernest might think her extravagant, and kept careful records for him. She did not see how he could complain when for less than two hundred dollars the floor would be retiled, roof and tennis court repaired, outside and inside walls painted, new electrical wiring installed, and furniture and trees bought. While cleaning Ernest's room she discovered hundreds of past due lottery tickets. Sorting them out, she was able to collect sixty dollars. "After this trip you may even enjoy tidiness and space and cleanliness," she wrote him hopefully.

Her biggest struggle was to finish the novel. To escape the workmen she locked herself in the Little House with the manuscript. One day, feeling optimistic, she gave a fiesta for the pelota players. "It was a great success," she reported, "seventeen men, three children and me. We were all as drunk as goats." She assured Ernest that he was sorely missed and that her drunkenness was the kind she always wanted, no dizzying wheels within wheels, and a marvelous, laughing feeling. His gang of friends was more fun than their Havana society friends. But the next day, nursing a hangover, she finished the letter in a chastened mood, depressed that she would never be a real writer.

> Writing like that evidently comes from strengths I do not have. . . . I seem to myself merely clever and facile, with a kind of spurious slickness, but the knowledge, the ear, the juices are lacking. If I can't be a good writer I would rather not publish. It is an unhappy way to be thinking about oneself. I do so love you. Love me please. I am an efficient woman with no confidence.

Gigi and Patrick arrived as arranged and were considerate of Martha's need for work, as they swam and read and amused themselves with the cats in the oppressive heat. Unending feline pregnancies and a stream of incestuous kittens were no longer a blessing. Martha felt that probably some family decision should be made about spaying the females and having the males neutered.

On June 13 Winston Guest brought the *Pilar* into the harbor to pick up a cache of supplies assembled by Martha and to take the boys aboard to spend the next month with their father. Martha sent word with Winston that Paramount Pictures wanted Ernest on hand in New York for the opening of *For Whom the Bell Tolls* in July. Knowing his sentiments about such appearances, she had replied in his behalf that her husband could not sponsor the film because he had not seen it. She firmly refused to go there herself, "having no natural talent for being a celebrity even by marriage." Her mother was coming to the Finca on July 9 and that was much more important than any public relations stunt. She wrote to Ernest on June 14:

> I love you. I *am* tired. Don't know why. But the end of the book is wonderfully clear in my head. . . . Liana is a poor woman really, a poor stupid lost woman without a place to live. So in a way it is the story of two men who finally go home, in their various ways, and a woman who has no home. If that is a moral?

Heavy June rains delayed the outside painting, but the floor was installed, the roof fixed, and the pool freshly filled, while Martha pushed ahead with the final chapter of the novel. On June 27, sitting in the Little House, she looked at the last page. It was finished, finished. Over and over she repeated the simple words, trying to believe them. Jane and Bob Joyce came over to swim with her that evening in the dark, while she talked and talked, getting higher and higher with exultation. At five in the morning she woke up full of doubts. Was the novel really good, or was she imagining it? Writing it during the last two weeks was the finest feeling she had ever had, maybe the finest feeling there is in life, in spite of the fatigue and the forty cigarettes a day. Could it really only be a pile of shit? She did not think so. If it had to be worked over yet again she would do it.

All day on the 28th Martha experienced the fatigue of having finished the book. How odd it was, she wrote Ernest, that she, who had started with the dream of writing, a dream that never changed, who lived so meagerly in Paris, romantically buying violets to wear instead of buying breakfast when out looking for a job, would end up "in this perfect, safe beauty," finishing her fifth book. But there were no real rewards for time passing. She did not want to grow old. She would trade this perhaps excellent fifth book for her wretched first one, if in the exchange she could be twenty again, with that time's fears and surprises and hopes.

> I wish we could stop it all now, the prestige, the possessions, the position, the knowledge, the victory. And by a miracle, return together under the arch at Milan, you so brash in your motorcycle sidecar and I badly dressed, fierce, loving. . . . That loud . . . reckless . . . disheveled girl was a better person. . . . By God, how I wish it, . . . the days hard, but with that shine on them from not being sure, but of hoping, of believing in fact in just the things we now so richly have.

As she sat in the living room after supper, with the cats chasing over the furniture and the one called Friendless purring in her lap, she went back to the very long letter begun earlier in the day and tried to put into words her uneasiness about their marriage. "You have been married so much," she wrote, "and so long, that I do not believe it [marriage] can touch you where you live and that is your strength. It would be terrible if it did because you are so much more important than the women you happen to be married to." As for her, she had come to believe that marriage was a rare and good thing and more of an instinct than otherwise, since it happened everywhere in nature, but it was a "brutalization, too. . . . One is safe. Two people live together . . . and slowly for each other become the common denominator. They agree without words to lay off the fantasy and passion, the difficult personal private stuff. They find some common ground which is green and smooth and there they stay." But what if they (or she) is "a quite odd and burning sort of person?" At what moment can they (or she) be wild and free as she really is?

And then she repeated the essence of what she had written in the afternoon, this time in words that were more significant for what they said about her conflict.

> I would like to be young and poor and in Milan and with you and not married to you. I think that I always wanted to feel in some way like a woman and if I ever did, it was the first winter in Madrid. There is a sort of blindness and fervor and recklessness about that sort of feeling which one must always want. I hate being so wise and so careful, so reliable, so denatured, so able to get on.

More disturbing than her own uncertainties about their relationship was the fear that he would not understand what she was driving at and that real communication was becoming impossible. She wrote:

> I will almost bet twenty dollars that this letter makes you angry, doesn't it? "What does she mean," you will say, "complaining and crying for some other time and place and life? What the hell is the matter with that bitch? Haven't I enough problems without her?" I am no problem, Bug, never think that. . . . I only write to you tonight as I feel or think, because why not? We cannot be so married that we cannot speak. Love, Marty.

In the morning the reliable, efficient Marty took over. The manuscript went to the typist. The exterior walls of the house were painted a frosty pink. She organized a schedule for the garden crew, nagged the chauffeur about the care of the cars, and urged the housemaids to do a thorough cleaning for Mr. Hemingway's return.

"I have begun to diet according to Harper's Bazaar," she wrote Ernest on July 4. "Will you like me, short and curly-haired, brown and thin, sitting in front of our nice shiny, pink house? . . . It will be lovely to babble to you in person instead of into the typewriter." Everything was in perfect readiness for his homecoming in two weeks. The cats were looking beautiful as they lay about the back terraces like wonderful animals at some elegant water hole. Edna Gellhorn had arrived and was comfortable in a refurbished guest room. Marty went into town for the newest books and the latest newspapers and magazines. She promised to spoil him with too much attention, scattering rose petals wherever he walked!

For a week after Ernest's return, everything was gay and affectionate between them. Edna Gellhorn's sunny presence had a soothing effect and Ernest complimented Marty on the fine improvements to the house. But then she received the official word that she was going to London in the fall. *Collier's* was sending her to the European Theater of Operations. Wouldn't it be splendid if he took on a similar assignment and they could go to war together, as they had done in Spain? The more he hung back from the idea the more she pressed him, openly scorning his Q-boat operation, insisting that he must go to Europe where he could do some good in the war against Hitler. Nothing was more important than destroying Hitler, and she reacted sharply to Ernest's notion that she should stay home and look after him. That sounded all wrong to her. Listening to him make up stories about the *Pilar* and its sub-chasing made her feel sick. She knew that she was losing respect for him. And she argued that not only his ideals but his genius would be better served by going to war.

Secretly Ernest may have believed some of what she was saying. He knew how in the thirties he had been accused of going stale and then returned to action and wrote a masterpiece. But he did not want to leave the comfortable life that was organized around his needs. And increasingly he was assuming the pompous "Papa" role, fed by the obsequiousness of his many admirers. Martha seemed to be the only one who defied him. So the quarrels became shrill and Ernest drank and grew more truculent. Gigi, especially, was mortified when his father began to bait Martha, especially since it seemed to him that so often she was right and Ernest wrong.

The degree to which they were not sexually compatible probably contributed to the growing tension and bitterness. One of the great bonds in marriage—"with my body I thee worship"—was always lacking for Martha, who, through ignorance and self-doubt, never discussed it with Ernest. Though his physical ardor was constant, he was totally insensitive to Martha's feelings. In such a one-sided situation, love-making could not provide the balm that softens so many marital quarrels. Their Cuban friends speculated that Martha might be having an affair with a handsome Basque pelota player, but Martha said no, she never dreamed of not being faithful all the time, and "expected no praise for it." Jack Hemingway remarked to the author that his father should have been flattered that Martha's loyalty lasted as long as it did. Jack believed her to be a spirited woman who would never be bound by the conventional double standard.

Ernest always expected a woman's morality to be different from a man's. In his introduction to *Men at War* he wrote that a writer " . . . should be of as great probity and honesty as a priest of God. He is either honest or not, as a woman is either chaste or not, and after one piece of dishonest writing he is never the same again."

That meandering essay was the last writing Ernest had done, in August of 1942. The long layoff bothered him deeply. He was quick to explain to everyone that his war work was responsible for the lapse. He told Max on August 18, 1943, that he wanted to write so much that sometimes it was worse than being in jail. He had given up all semblance of his strict morning routine. If he did anything in the morning, it was letter-writing. The one reason for his belligerence that might have seemed legitimate to Martha was the painful loss of his literary powers. But even that disappointment and frustration did not condone his rancor toward her, not in her eyes. She had too much self-respect to tolerate his abuse.

Early in August Ernest was preparing for a three-month sub-hunting expedition that was supposed to coincide with Martha's European assignment. But various foul-ups delayed his departure. He was still at the Finca when she left for New York on September 20 and he was miserable as soon as he was left alone. He did not seem to mind the quarreling as much as Martha did, perhaps because he initiated so much of it. Mario (Mayito) Menocal, Jr., the twenty-year-old son of Ernest's close friend, was an unwilling witness to the dissension because he spent so much of that summer reading in Ernest's extensive library. He believes that Ernest never stopped loving Marty, whatever form his bullying took.

In New York Martha settled some editorial problems with Scribners and waited for her visa. She went to Central Park to pose for the photo that would appear on the jacket of her recently completed novel. Her favorite picture was a pensive one, posed against the curve of park benches, but Perkins selected a wind-blown one that made her look like an aging Colette. Charlie Scribner promised to make *Liana* (the official title) his first big book of 1944. Paramount and the Book-of-the-Month Club were showing some interest. Martha wrote Ernest that she would be thrilled with a hunk of money if it would relieve his financial strain. Nothing she was now doing was as important as her love for him. " . . . I am yours first of all and you are my main concern. . . . You tell me what you want and that is what I will do." What he wanted was for her to be at the Finca. Loving him in New York was no help for his depression.

On October 8 Martha learned to her dismay that it might be as late as the 25th before she could embark. She went to see the old movie version of *A Farewell to Arms*. Though it was phony and wrong she wept buckets, for their lost youth and everyone's. Her most precious visits in New York were with her younger brother, Alfred, who was now a doctor teaching medicine at Columbia Medical School for the usual meager academic salary. With time still to use up, she went to Lakeville, Connecticut for a few days in the country. The foliage was a brilliant purple-red and gold. Everything reminded her of places where she and Ernest had been together. The water was as clear and cold as Silver Creek, and the tiny village as unspoiled as the French one near the Loing Canal. As she walked around the lake she imagined what she would do with a fifteen-thousand-dollar bonanza from the Book-of-the-Month Club. A huge slice of it to Ernest, of course, then some to the Reglers in Mexico, and lastly to Alfred and his wife and their children. She was ashamed of her own bad management. Already she had used up her entire Scribners advance.

The next day, an embarrassed Charlie Scribner told her that the Book-of-the-Month Club had passed over *Liana*. "In my heart," she wrote Ernest, "I always knew I was not destined to be a best seller." (When *Liana* was published a few months later it sold briskly across the country and did make the best-seller lists. The critics were generally pleased. Diana Trilling, writing for *The Nation*, found sensitive reverberations beneath the simple story, and *The New Yorker*'s reviewer noted that the characters were credible and touching.)

Martha sent Ernest a box of new detective fiction instead of a fat check and waited restlessly for mail from him and some word of her papers. On the 15th two long letters came, which she read over breakfast and again on the night train to Washington, D.C. On White House stationery, as a guest of the Roosevelts, she begged Ernest to protect his eyes from the sun's glare. "I don't mind being your daughter, but don't want you to be Milton." She was having a fine time in the capital, admired by attractive men who made her feel stylish and charming, not at all like an old Bryn Mawr girl. The film of *For Whom the Bell Tolls* was shown at the White House for President and Mrs. Roosevelt, Elmer Davis, Harry Hopkins, and an array of generals. Everyone loved it and was fascinated to learn that Martha was married to the author of the novel. Hopkins pulled strings to circumvent the red tape she was experiencing in getting her papers, and the way seemed clear at last for her departure. On the 21st she wrote Ernest another long letter. "Please know how much I love you. . . . you are a much better man than me, but I hope I am not too bad a wife even if I have gone away when I thought you would be away too. . . . I feel ashamed of being happy unless you are. And tonight, just going, just feeling ahead the strange places, I am happy like a firehorse. . . . But like woman, and your woman, am sad; only there isn't anything final, is there? This is just a short trip and we are both coming back from our short trips to our lovely home . . . and then we'll write books and see the autumns together and walk around the corn fields waiting for the pheasants."

Chapter 24

"It is great fun to see the world at 250 miles per hour," Martha wrote from Estoril on October 29, 1943. The flight via Bermuda and the Azores had been uneventful and now there was a four-day layover. She stayed at a deluxe hotel and went out dancing two nights, escorted by the *Clipper* captain, the co-pilot, the young radio engineer, and a scientist from Montana. "They were all solid drinkers and good dancers and very attentive to your wife, so I am having a fine, brainless time." The last stop on her flight plan was Ireland. After ten days of travel—two nights on planes, eight on the ground —she reached London by train at 11:00 P.M. on November 3 and got a room at the Dorchester.

" . . . and now," she wrote Ernest on the morning of November 4, "I am waiting for Ginny [Cowles] to come to breakfast. . . . The room somehow reminds me of Madrid, same color walls, same cretonne curtains, same cold. It is kind of nice therefore. Outside it is gray and chilly and many chimney pots." The weather was nothing like Cuba, but she did not mind. In two days she received her official war correspondent I.D. card with its simulated rank of captain and attendant privileges. Everyone was taking her out and treating her beautifully. When Raymond Guest (Winston's brother) offered her the use of his apartment she accepted. Hoping that by flattering Ernest she could persuade him to leave his "shaming and silly" life in Cuba, she wrote him on November 6 that he was the big local hero and everyone wanted to see the movie [*For Whom the Bell Tolls*]. "I think people like me because you chose me and so puts on me the mark of superior approval."

Martha's first assignment took her to an airfield at Woodhall Spa, where the British Lancasters were based for their missions over Germany. From the Control Station (a painted trailer) out on the field, she watched thirteen of them take off, like enormous "deadly" black birds. "First you wait for them to go and then you wait for them to get back," she wrote in her first piece for *Collier's*. Watching the off-duty pilots read detective stories in the ugly country hotel, she was reminded of tidy school children doing their homework. The pilots wondered, silently and fearfully, which of their friends would return. Only their weary eyes distinguished them from boarding school boys.

She returned to London with a nasty cold but tramped through the most battered, heavily bombed neighborhoods to report on the working children who now performed myriad jobs left vacant by men who were at the war. In shabby clubs, the boys played table tennis and the girls knitted on their off hours. They were cheerful and tough and reminded Martha of young leopards strolling in their home jungle.

Repeatedly, wherever Martha was—on the trains, in clubs, at airfields—ordinary people poured out their warmth and admiration for Ernest's writing. "It's like being married to some one mythical to be affiliated with you," she wrote. An RAF officer had read everything. A young Dutch refugee confided that he knew all the stories from his classroom in Holland. And this was not the literary shoptalk that Ernest found so annoying. "I wish you could hear all of this for yourself," she added. It was beginning to worry her that she had received no mail.

> Try to send me at least a cable every two weeks just to say that all is well. I have your pictures on my desk and try to remember all about you from them but I cannot. I have talked too much about you, I mean about your work and what you like to do and how you look. . . . In a way I've talked you away from me, just like talking away a story. . . . with this distance between us you become monumental, not quite human. And I am sort of an oddity, the very ordinary wife of an extraordinary man.

When her cold turned into a chronic infection, Martha vacated Raymond's poorly heated flat for a room at the Dorchester. In an interview with three Polish refugees she learned of the terrible exploitation of Polish workers by the occupying Germans, of mass shootings by the Nazis, of whole villages wiped out. One of the men was a Jew, formerly an official with the League of Nations, now a private in the British Army. For the first time Martha heard of Jews being herded into cattle cars, and of conditions in the Warsaw Ghetto, where 550,000 souls were packed behind walls to die of disease and starvation. "He spoke now," Martha wrote in her *Collier's* article of March 18, 1944, "for the dead—for the two and a half million Jews who were killed in Poland alone. He had watched the greatest organized destruction the world had known and he refused to believe in it." Poland seemed very far away, she continued, " . . . and the Germans had tried to make it into a cemetery."

From her sickbed she tried again to persuade Ernest to come over to England. He could be accredited by one of the wire services and later make better contracts. "Everyone knows you and wants you to come, and it would be especially wonderful for me. . . . remember how we wanted to drink the coffee and read Le Sport in Paris." In his next letter to reach her he disagreed sharply, citing his own war work as the main reason not to leave. So she dropped the subject and, still feverish and aching, returned to the hard work of journalism.

Through Ginny Cowles Martha met charming and elegant people, all involved in the war, as well as writers who were excluded from military service and doing their share in London. But victory over the flu proved to be elusive. An acute gastritis on top of the respiratory ailment sent her to bed for another week. Now the panic set in. Only one article was written. How would she ever finish the others? There were no more letters from Ernest. "I keep hoping unreasonably that I'll get some whopping news from you," she wrote on the 5th of December, "and it will also say you'll be over. . . . don't think for a moment that I am not understanding of your long job there, but I'm so ashamed not to be there keeping you company, or keeping the place comfy, that I keep hoping you'll have a vacation."

By the 9th, while still weak and frail, she was feeling better. Her spirit returned. It was even possible that she could finish seven articles, which would provide a nice family nest egg. It would be great if she could get to the Italian Front. Herbert Matthews was there. It would be like being back in "the old racket." Her determination to pry Ernest loose from the Finca swelled. In a long letter of December 12 she appealed to him on all levels—his career as a writer, his role as a novelist-historian, the importance to their future relationship of his participation in these momentous events.

She wrote:

> You will feel deprived as a writer if this is all over and you have not had a share in it. . . . the place is crying out for you, not for immediate stuff but for the record. . . . I beg you to think this over very seriously. . . . I say this not only because I miss you and want you here, but I hate not sharing it with you. . . . It would be a terrible mistake to miss this, for both of us. . . . I would never be able to tell you about it because I could never do the things that you can. You would be the one who would see for us.

She suggested that he contact Harry Hopkins. He admired Ernest and would give the forms a helping push. She repeated that she worried every minute that he was alone. "Wouldn't the easiest, wisest, happiest and best thing be for you to come to me for a bit, especially at the season when the climate makes it so difficult for you to write?" (Censorship forbade her referring directly to the sea operation.)

The next day, December 13, four letters arrived from Ernest, "so it is a national holiday." In all of them he declared emphatically that he was not going to leave Cuba. She read and reread them, swallowing her disappointment, and tried to respond frankly and thoughtfully. Journalism might not be a good trade for him, but it was very good for her, providing many things for her eyes and mind to feed on. "I am neither Jane Austen nor the Bronte sisters," she declared. "I have to see before I can imagine." As for his coming or not coming to London, she made her peace with that. "I won't urge you to come anymore. . . . I think you will regret it and it will be a great general loss for all the people who need and love to read . . . but I will not speak of it again. . . . I see now that you will not have time free that I thought you might have."

Then she wrote from her heart how she felt about what she was doing.

You have a life there because you have a useful work. It is what you believe in and feel right about doing. But I believe in what I am doing too and regret fiercely having missed seeing and understanding so much of it these years. I would give anything to be part of the invasion and see Paris right at the beginning and watch the peace. . . . I have to live my way as well as yours or there wouldn't be any me to love you with. You really wouldn't want me if I built a fine big stone wall around the Finca and sat inside it.

But perhaps he did want to build a wall and keep her inside it. Ever since he had been his mother's "precious boy" and then saw her divide her love among her other children, he wanted the woman in his life to stay in one place where he could always find her, and to put him first, all the time, ahead of anything else.

Ernest wrote everyone—Perkins, MacLeish, Scribner—that he was sick lonely without Martha, like someone with his heart cut out. If anything happened to her he would be in a bad way. Staggering into the gloomy, neglected Finca straight off the *Pilar*, he would gulp some whiskey and then fall asleep on the Samoan mat in the living room as the wind blew outside and the cats spread themselves across his chest. At daybreak he brewed some tea while waiting for the cook to prepare him a decent breakfast. Later in the morning his chauffeur drove him to the Floridita bar, where he put away double frozen daiquiris and repeated old yarns to anyone willing to listen. He gambled more than he could afford to and drank until his speech thickened.

In spite of the loneliness Ernest did not, so far as any of his Cuban friends could recall, seek the companionship of other women. He was not interested in a substitute for Martha. He simply wanted her back. "I never had so damned much time to think in my life," he wrote Hadley on November 25, "especially nights on the water and here when I can't sleep. . . . thought about you with great pleasure and admiration and how wonderful you were and are. . . . Paul can't mind me still loveing you because knowing you he would know I would be crazy if I didn't. . . . "

Hadley wrote to Ernest in December, and again in January. She had injured her back but was recovering and sent Christmas greetings. "Your condition sounds much worse than mine," she wrote on January 14, 1944. "My back may be slow in healing and I may poke around in a brace, but at least I'm not lonely. Twas rotten luck to have Marty dash away for these months assured that you couldn't be home anyway." She was touched that he had invited Paul and her to visit him but explained that Paul was working seven days a week as well as trying to finish a book at night.

Martha had sent holiday greetings from a village beside the Thames, where she had gone to do a story on an English Sunday during the war. She attended church with the very old and the very young. Everyone shared the grief of families who had lost their sons. There was a wintry sun, and wild ducks on the water, and a gentle, smoky haze in the atmosphere. Cuba seemed like the other end of the earth. She could hardly even imagine it. "You are real and my own," she wrote on December 22, 1943, "but everything else, the good boring loving people, and the life, is remote, somehow awful, and I dread it. Please forgive me. When I think of it, it is like being strangled by those beautiful tropical flowers that can swallow cows!" What a contrast to the ecstatic words she had written to Clara Spiegel four years ago. ("It is wondrously beautiful and I look about the house and the land and cannot figure out how I happened to be so lucky in my life with such a place to live and such a one to live with.") The langurous paradise had now become a tar pit and the heroic lover a drunken scold.

For Ernest, still in love with her, the letter represented a crushing rejection. Was there no way to win her back but to take out after her? That seemed to him grossly unfair. Had he not already proven himself in Italy and in Spain? "My father was always much more frightened of getting killed than Marty," Patrick has said. "He felt that he was entitled to stay behind, living in a place that he liked, and enjoying himself." To Pat, who came to the Finca for part of his Christmas holiday, Ernest poured out his resentment. Drinking ever more heavily, he accused Martha of being selfish and ambitious. At no time did he mention the practical reason for her absence— that she needed to earn money. With the respectful boy as a poignant reminder, Ernest even experienced a twinge of regret for what he had given up when he divorced Pauline. But most of all he was frustrated and angry over what he insisted was Martha's callous treatment of him. Her New Year's cable repeating that she loved him did not make him feel any better.

As she was preparing to leave for the Italian Front and North Africa in the middle of January, Martha heard from Raymond Guest that Winston was coming over shortly. "What does this mean?" she demanded of Ernest agitatedly. "Where will you be early in February? [The significance of Winston's coming over was that the sub-hunting crew was being dismantled]. . . . it would be a disaster of all time if you were on your way over here when I was on my way home." She promised to be back at the Finca by March if the connections worked out.

Ernest continued to be churlish about her activities, announcing loudly that he had married her for a wife, not a distant ideal, or "even the Unknown soldier." But in public he still praised her, especially in the March 4, 1944, issue of *Collier's*.

> Her pieces are always about people. The things that happen to her people really happen, and you feel it as though it were you and you were there. . . . All right, I'm prejudiced. So I will tell you some more. She hates to get up in the morning. She needs 12 hours sleep, and has to have ten. But when she is at the front or getting there, she will get up earlier, travel longer and faster and go where no other woman can get and where few could stick it out if they did. . . . She gets to the place, gets the story, writes it and comes home. That last is the best part.

From a press camp near a shelled village outside Cassino, Martha and other war correspondents traveled by jeep over the mountainous Italian Front. Villages had been leveled as though by a cyclone, but the children still played in the dust and their mothers scrubbed their shredded clothes in the streams. A French soldier drove her around to the battallion aid stations, where she saw the horribly wounded—men with severed legs, others newly blinded. Ernest's cables were following her down through the divisions, read each step of the way by the censors with much amusement. "ARE YOU A WAR CORRESPONDENT OR WIFE IN MY BED?"

In March, as she had promised, Martha returned to the Finca, but not to settle back into the old routine.

> I was not received with loving tender care though I was absolutely exhausted; the flight from Tangiers in the freezing aluminum belly of a bomber with a few sick G.I.'s being sent home was bad enough. But Ernest began at once to rave at me, the word is not too strong. He woke me when I was trying to sleep to bully, snarl, mock—my crime really was to have been at war when he had not, but that was not how he put it. I was supposedly insane, I only wanted excitement and danger, I had no responsibility to anyone, I was selfish beyond belief. . . . it never

stopped and believe me, it was fierce and ugly. I put it to him that I was going back, whether he came or not, and through Roald Dahl, he could get a plane seat.

(On her way back from Italy Martha had stopped off at the White House, where she met Roald Dahl, who was the assistant air attaché at the British Embassy. If Ernest would mention the R.A.F. in his reporting Dahl would get him a priority seat on a plane.)

After two years of defending himself, Ernest now gave in. Perhaps his personal sense that it was time for a change, as well as Martha's powers of persuasion, pried him loose. He was fed up with the long sea voyages that accomplished nothing. The deterioration around the house was unnerving. And it is possible that his competitive instinct was finally aroused. Martha might as well know that if he entered the contest of foreign correspondents he would be a formidable adversary. She soon found out what that meant. With his choice of any newspaper or magazine in the world to represent, Ernest deliberately offered his services to *Collier's*, the magazine that had been hers since 1937. By the rules for the U.S. Press Corps in the European Theater of Operations, a magazine was allowed only one front-line correspondent. "Therefore," said Martha, "I was totally blocked. . . . having taken *Collier's* he automatically destroyed my chances of covering the fighting war [in an official capacity]."

In April they left for New York, where Ernest's "hideous and insane reviling" of Martha continued. "He was going to get killed, doubtless, and hoped I'd be satisfied at what I'd done. . . . I told him in New York that he was making it impossible for me to go on loving him." She was learning that Ernest had various ways of getting even when he believed himself to have been mistreated. She was too proud to ask for a seat on the plane for herself, but she thought that he would speak up for her. "Oh no," he said blandly, "I couldn't do that. They only fly men." (Later she learned that Beatrice Lillie and Gertrude Lawrence were passengers with him.) So she sailed on May 13, the only passenger aboard a freighter with a cargo of dynamite. "It was a very good and interesting experience," explained Martha wryly, "but it was long, believe me."

As she had predicted, Ernest received a hero's welcome in London. Old friends turned up—Freddie Spiegel, Lewis Galantière, as did Ernest's brother Leicester (attached to a documentary film unit in London) and *Life* photographer Robert Capa. Ernest's celibacy in Havana did not carry over to London. A few days after his arrival he was at the White Tower restaurant for lunch. On his way through the dining room he stopped at a small table to greet Irwin Shaw.

"Introduce me to your friend, Shaw," he said, eyeing Shaw's female companion.

Shaw complied. Her name was Mary Welsh Monks. She was an American based in London and wrote feature stories for *Time*. She was small and shapely. Her hair was a curly honey-brown and she had chiseled features and a cleft chin. Her voice was soft and musical. Her husband, Noel Monks, was covering the South Pacific Theater of Operations for the *Daily Mail*. Later, Mary recalled that Irwin Shaw had pointed Ernest out to her before he came over to their table and that he looked hot and uncomfortable in his heavy woolen R.A.F. uniform. She knew that he was married to Martha Gellhorn. Diffidently Ernest suggested that perhaps Mary would have lunch with him. She agreed, responding perhaps to a shy warmth in his manner. But their first date was nothing special, merely a return engagement at the same restaurant.

Mary's third encounter with Ernest was in the Wertenbaker suite on the third floor of the Dorchester. Charles Wertenbaker had come over from New York to direct *Time*'s coverage of the coming invasion. Lael Wertenbaker remembered vividly that Mary, again accompanied by Irwin Shaw, came around to their suite for a drink. Ernest dominated the conversation with rambling conceits and tasteless jokes. His mood during his early days in London was characterized by strident gaiety, a telltale sign that inwardly he was in turmoil. When he called out to Mary that he would visit her in her room later, she secretly hoped he would not show up. But he did, made himself comfortable on one of the twin beds, and then talked for a long time to Mary and her roommate, Connie Ernst, about his Oak Park boyhood. When he finally stood up to leave, he stared at Mary. "I don't know you, Mary," said Ernest. "But I want to marry you."

Mary assumed that he was merely drunk. He repeated the proposal, and she made a remark to the effect that they didn't know each other and were both married.

"This war may keep us apart," he continued. "Just please remember I want to marry you."

FIVE

1944–61

Chapter 25

Martha's ship docked in Liverpool on May 27, 1944. She gave a rather cheerful account of the voyage in *Travels with Myself and Another*, but in truth the conditions were exceedingly hazardous. The hold was filled with high explosives and there were no lifeboats.

It was freezing, there was almost perpetual fog, and the captain worried . . . about collisions due to the inexperienced captains of the U.S. Liberty Ships. [Martha's freighter was part of the last great convoy to England before D-Day.] The crew and the captain were Norwegians; every man had been torpedoed off a ship in the north Atlantic at least once. None had heard any word from their families since the Nazi invasion of Norway in April, 1940. The captain's only brother, in the Resistance in Norway, had been caught by the Gestapo and vanished into a Nazi concentration camp, sure death. Yet no one complained, no one made heroics out of their job, plodding through those dangerous waters for four years.

At the wharf some English reporters crowded around Martha to talk about her husband's accident. What accident was that, she inquired, grateful to be on solid ground at last. An auto accident involving a collision with a street water tank was the reply. He was a patient at St. George's Hospital. (Three days earlier, on May 24, after a party at Robert Capa's apartment, a Dr. Gorer had offered to drive Ernest back to his hotel in the blackout. Ernest's scalp was gashed after he was thrown against the windshield and he had suffered a concussion as well.)

Martha checked into the Dorchester, taking the room adjacent to Ernest's, one that he had reserved in a "safe angle" on the second floor, and then went to the hospital. She found him with a huge turban around his head; champagne and whiskey bottles were under the bed, and he was holding court as usual. The entire scene infuriated her. "If he really had a concussion he could hardly have been drinking with his pals or even receiving them. He did not look the least ill anyway." It was not the way to behave at a war, she felt. The fact that she had just spent seventeen days on a dynamite-filled ship did not concern him at all. Right then, in outraged indignation, she told him she was through, absolutely finished. She considered herself free from then on. She had had seventeen days to think about all of it—his egotism and "Q-boat play-acting" in contrast to the real bravery and suffering she had witnessed in London and Italy, his "ceaseless, crazy bullying" in Cuba and New York, the accusations about her ambition and her selfishness, which hurt her deeply because they were so unfair and untrue. Ernest, who imagined that he had narrowly escaped death, wanted sympathy and reassurance. Martha, who was tired and disgusted and coldly critical, stalked out of the room. (After she had seen him, she moved up to the top floor of the Dorchester, in a "wonderfully exposed" room, far from his on the second floor.)

After such heated disapproval, Mary Welsh's armful of tulips was a comfort to Ernest's wounded pride. His compliments to Mary on the May evening in her hotel room had left her nonplussed. She remembers telling Connie Ernst that he was probably too big for her, meaning both in "stature and status." But she was feeling let down after an unsatisfactory reunion with her husband, and when he left for a secret assignment on June 1 she decided to pay Hemingway a visit. He greeted her with gusto and invited her to see him at the Dorchester when he was discharged in a day or two. She agreed.

Mary Welsh was born in the same year as Martha Gellhorn, 1908, but her origins were very different, not only from Marty's but from Hadley's and Pauline's as well. Adeline and Tom Welsh were plain people of limited means, both of them largely self-educated. Tom

Welsh, a logger, supplemented his earnings by operating a Mississippi riverboat, the *Northland*, taking local groups on day-long trips. Mary was an only child, born in the village of Walker, Minnesota but raised in Bemidji, a town only slightly larger. Winters were long and quiet and snowy, but summers were time for adventure, as she moved to the riverboat for three months and lived with her father in a rugged, exclusively masculine atmosphere. If at times she thought it would be better to be a boy, it was only because she wanted to be like her father. "Maybe it was not so much that he treated me like a boy," she later remarked to the author, "but rather like a human being, who could do anything and try anything."

Her mother, Adeline Welsh, a Christian Scientist of genteel ways, stayed behind to follow a more sedate routine. Mary sensed a basic incompatibility between her parents and respected their loyalty in staying married.

The logging business had declined alarmingly by the time Mary graduated from high school in 1926. Everyone admired her pluck when she announced that she was going to major in journalism at Northwestern University. With no financial help from her parents, but a great deal of encouragement, she went off to Evanston, Illinois, supporting herself with part-time jobs.

In her junior year Mary fell in love with a drama student from Ohio. He was poetic and played a good game of tennis, and they were married by a justice of the peace after a brief romance. Mary dropped out of school to take a job on a small trade magazine known as *The American Florist*. In one week she learned more about copy editing and the mechanics of publishing than in her three years of college. Her marriage, however, floundered. She believed in hard work and achievement; her husband could not keep a job. He was satisfied to live off her salary and some money from his family. After two years she finally had to admit that marrying him had been a youthful mistake. They were divorced quietly.

During the Depression years of the early thirties Mary worked a ten-hour, six-day week. From the magazine she went to work for a firm that published throw-away weeklies. The wages were paltry but the experience enabled her to move on to the *Chicago Daily News* as a society reporter. Colonel Frank Knox had bought the paper and Paul Mowrer was brought back from Paris to be managing editor. Mary wanted to cover City Hall and the crime beat, but she could not be picky. The *News* had a distinguished staff, and for Mary it was a large step up from the publishing sweatshops of the North Side. Occasionally there were staff parties at the Mowrer duplex at 1300 North State, but it did not come out in conversations there that Hadley Mowrer was the former Mrs. Ernest Hemingway.

In 1936 Mary visited England and Ireland and then crossed over to Paris, where the bureau chief of the *London Daily Express* invited her to dinner. As she was bemoaning her return to Chicago he persuaded her to call his London boss, Lord Beaverbrook, and ask him for a job on one of his papers. Beaverbrook seemed less than intrigued by the young stranger's call, but he agreed to arrange an interview for her with his Fleet Street editor.

After her return to Chicago Mary tried for a year to persuade the *Daily News* people to send her to one of their foreign desks. Finally she got the break she wanted. Lord Beaverbrook came to Chicago and invited her to lunch. A week later he called from New York, offering to pay her fare if she would visit him. She did not accept his offer, but obtained a round-trip ticket through her press connections. From his huge bed in the chilly Waldorf Astoria suite, a spindly, asthmatic Beaverbrook began to lecture his visitor. First he invited her to accompany him on a trip up the Nile. Then he chided her for her doltish Midwestern refusal and reminded her irritably that romantic love was a waste of time, that a woman's goal should be to please a man. Mary phrased a polite reply to the effect that her father had warned her never to mix business with affection. With that Beaverbrook gave up in disgust and promised that if she did come to London he would try to find her a job.

Three months later, on July 2, 1937, Mary reported for work at the *London Daily Express* editorial office. Lord Beaverbrook had kept his word and found her a place in his organization. Her first assignment was to write a one thousand-word story about the disappearance of Amelia Earhart over the South Pacific. Other features quickly followed—some serious, some frivolous—and before long she had a by-line. Her basement apartment was in Chelsea, and her men friends were her co-workers. Noel Monks, a red-cheeked Australian who had been a champion swimmer and now worked for the *Daily Mail*, began to take her out. In her autobiography, *How It Was*, Mary described him as "abstemious" and "conservative," qualities not noticeably present in Mary herself, who drank freely and was liberal in politics as well as uninhibited in her personal life. But the attraction held up and in the summer of 1938 Mary Welsh became Mary Welsh Monks.

Her assignments became more interesting and she crossed the Channel frequently. She covered the birth of Princess Juliana's first child in the Netherlands and flew to Munich in September 1938 to report on the meeting between Neville Chamberlain and Adolf Hitler. In March 1939 Chamberlain announced the mutual defense pact with Poland, and in April compulsory military service went into effect in Great Britain. Mary and Noel had only just returned from their August holidays when the German Army marched into Poland, and at 11:00 A.M. on September 3, England declared war on Germany.

When Noel went to northeastern France to cover the R.A.F., Mary arranged to be sent to Paris. She rented a studio flat behind Les Invalides and studied conversational French in her spare time, feeling as though she were going " . . . through the steps of a minuet in a house that was about to burn down." The burning began in May. The Germans swept over the Lowlands, the French retreated, and the British Expeditionary Force was cut off. On a humid Sunday in June, Noel learned that Paris was about to surrender. Packing a few essentials, they grabbed a taxi for Austerlitz railway station. Via train and bus, requisitioned vehicle and free-floating taxi, they worked their way to Bordeaux and the safety of a small ship that was carrying refugees to England.

In London Mary inquired of *Time* London bureau chief Walter Graebner, an old friend from Chicago, whether he might have a job for her. Two days later, as the German Luftwaffe was launching its devastating attack on England, Mary was hired as a *Time* correspondent. On September 7, 1940, Air Marshal Göring ordered the nighttime blitz of London. On September 22 Mary's building in Berkeley Square, Lansdowne House, was firebombed. Although Winston Churchill later wrote that the Germans had lost the battle for Britain by November 1, Mary remembers the winter of 1940–41 as one of terror and destruction. Every night the bombers came and the fires raced from rooftop to rooftop. In the morning as she walked to work she passed the plain gray vans being loaded with dead bodies.

Mary's crisp no-nonsense attitude has been likened to that of the

*Mary Welsh as a war corre-
spondent in London, 1943–44.*
From the John F. Kennedy Library

British Wren—resilient, always able to cope, "not given to complaining." When the windows in her penthouse were smashed, she
calmly packed a small load of possessions and the Monks moved to
55 Park Lane, behind the Dorchester. However unpredictable the
future, she had reason to be cheerful about the present. *Time* ran her
cover story on her old friend Beaverbrook, who was now minister
for Aircraft Production, and people in official circles noticed her
good-natured way of getting things done.

On December 7, 1941, as Mary and Noel were sitting in the
restaurant of their Park Lane building, a *Daily Express* reporter
rushed in to tell them that the Japanese had bombed Pearl Harbor.
Within a short time Noel was sent to the South Pacific to report on
Australian troop movements and Mary returned to America, temporarily transferred by *Time* to their New York foreign desk. Her

office mate on the seventeenth floor of the Time-Life building was a young writer named William Walton. Mary discovered, to her chagrin, that in matters of rank men were the "writers," women the "researchers." When her stories began to appear in the magazine, the women on the staff resented her and the men avoided her. A cheering note was the arrival of Noel, on his way back to the European Theater via New York. They celebrated Christmas together before leaving America separately.

Somewhat to her surprise Mary now found that it was a relief, even fun, to live by herself. She had to admit that she and Noel were not as close as they had been. They had talked about having a child, but with the war and separations, the time never seemed right. Perhaps it had less to do with the war than with her changing feelings. She believed, without making an issue of it, that she was a much better reporter than Noel and moved much faster to solve a problem. His sweetness did not make up for the dullness in him that she now frankly recognized.

When word came to her through meddlesome friends that Noel was seeing another woman in Cairo, Mary only shrugged. With the Americans arriving, no woman in London had to be alone if she chose not to be. And Mary chose not to be. "She was full of laughs and full of lovers," recounted Bill Walton, who had arrived in London from New York to cover the U.S. Air Force. "She was very little, very attractive, and always seemed to be the one to dash out into the blackout for the taxi." Walton was impressed with her reporting. It was first-class, creative journalism, and he recognized what a long road she had traveled, on her own, from Bemidji to *Time.* "I think it was a marvelous period for her," he continued, "perhaps the best time in her life." She was confident with men. If one of them flirted she was ready, but she never ran after anyone. "If the chase was on," as Walton put it, "it was the guy's chase."

As Americans crowded into London's West End in the fall and winter of 1943, Mary's inner circle began to form—Robert Capa photographing the war for *Life,* literary and film people including Henry Hathaway, William Saroyan, and Irwin Shaw. By the next year her circle of friends and acquaintances was considerable. On April 5, 1944, they gathered in her tiny living room to celebrate her birthday, ordinary G.I.s elbow to elbow with generals and bureau chiefs. The conversation turned to the question of the invasion—

when, where, and how soon. One after another of the English ports was being closed off. Later, Mary studied the Almanac and decided that the tides were favorable for June 4–6. When she confided her calculations to a friend at the admiralty, he was astonished and threatened to have her jailed.

As the German bombers returned in force during the warm spring nights, Mary experienced an uncomfortable chill of loneliness and wondered if it was simply the fear of being alone at a time of extreme danger. Irwin Shaw introduced her to a young woman from New York, Connie Ernst, who was also on her own, and the two moved in together, taking a huge room at the Dorchester. Mary welcomed Connie into her Time-Life gang. "Mary had been in London so long," recalled Connie, "that she knew everybody, and had wonderful connections. There was this great sense of liveliness about her and she always spoke her mind. I was no threat to her in any professional sense and became the woman friend she seemed to trust."

Before Mary's move to the Dorchester, Noel had come to London and stayed in her flat for two weeks. For Mary there was no denying that it felt good to have his familiar solid presence in her narrow bed. She shared her news with him and listened politely to his, but underneath the gossip and the love-making was a distance that could not be breached. On June 1 Noel left for a secret assignment having to do with the coming invasion, and Mary, hearing that Ernest Hemingway had been in a car accident and was at St. George's Hospital, decided to pay him a visit.

Chapter 26

With hundreds of others from the working press, Martha Gellhorn learned of the Allied invasion—launched a few hours before—at a morning briefing in London. Ernest was not present. He and all the correspondents accredited for the first D-Day crossing had been taken a few days earlier and in secret to a staging area. Late on the night of June 5, he boarded the attack transport *Dorothea L. Dix.* By 5:00 A.M. on June 6 he was transferred to a landing craft, and from his station beside the commander of the vessel watched the battle-ready troops wade ashore. Allied battleships hurled salvos from fourteen-inch guns and the Germans laid down murderous cross fire. Moments later the commander, Lt. Anderson, roared away, putting Ernest back aboard the *Dix.* On July 22, 1944, *Collier's* would publish the D-Day dispatches of its famous husband-and-wife team. Ernest's eyewitness account of the Normandy landing was the cover story. Martha's description of the first hospital ship to reach Normandy was modestly featured.

Martha, who had wheeled transportation to the embarkation port, hung around until after midnight and then locked herself in the toilet of an unarmed hospital ship that would cross the Channel at dawn. The ship, painted white, decorated with huge red crosses, and with 422 beds empty and waiting, sailed slowly through the mined channel. For thirty-two hours wounded American and German soldiers were hauled from Omaha beach to water ambulances, to LSTs, and, finally, to the decks of the ship. "I acted as an un-trained nurse's aid. . . . they had not thought of food, so I organized the boy stewards to make corned beef sandwiches, the only available food for those wounded who could eat, carried ducks [urinals], called nurses when the situation was drastic." Under cover of dark-ness on the night of June 7, Martha went ashore with the stretcher bearers to collect wounded men.

So it was that she actually walked on the Normandy beachhead, picking her way through mine fields and barbed wire, while Ernest had been confined to the bridge of a landing craft. This so infuriated Ernest that he convinced himself it never happened, explaining that Martha could not have made the landing because she did not have the proper credentials. Martha, back in London and hoping to get to Italy where she could report on the war with non-U.S. forces without the need for official papers, sent a note to Ernest. "I'm leaving for Italy on a hopeless Cook's tour," the note read. "I came to see the war, not live at the Dorchester." Ernest marked up the margins of the note with sarcasms.

In the steady company of Mary Welsh, Ernest became somewhat less testy. Over long lunches and dinners in West End pubs and restaurants they exchanged opinions and the details of their past. The love affair proceeded in such a satisfactory way that Ernest composed a poem, "To Mary in London," free-verse reflections on past triumphs, present miseries, and future hopes. When he told her that her legs were strong, like Prudy Boulton's, she seemed to enjoy the compliment and wrote quaintly, "[Prudence] was the first fe-male he had ever pleasured." Mary liked being a good sex partner. Love-making was easy for her and apparently she did not place any demands on Ernest that he was unable to fulfill. Such easy accept-ance was exactly what he needed after Martha's outspoken rejection.

Two months after he met Mary in the White Tower restaurant, Ernest went to France to cover American troop movements. By August 24, as General Jacques Leclerc's armored troops converged on Paris and the Germans retreated, Mary had persuaded Graebner to send her to France, too. She was airlifted to the French coast and then rode in an American jeep to Paris. Lugging bedroll and type-writer, she made her way through the shouting mob celebrating the liberation of the city. At the Ritz she inquired for Mr. Hemingway and was sent to Room 30, where Ernest was celebrating with his friends of the Resistance. As the champagne flowed, he settled back to recount his own adventures.

After checking in late in July with the American General, Raymond Barton, 4th Infantry Division, Ernest had set out to meet some of the officers in Barton's command. On the 28th of July, in a small Normandy farmhouse near the village of Mesnil-Herman, he met Colonel Charles T. "Buck" Lanham, commander of the 22nd Infantry Regiment. Colonel Lanham, whose wide-ranging interests included an appreciation of literature and art, was intrigued with the unkempt Hemingway, whose physical presence and watchful eyes reminded him of an eighteenth-century pirate.

Nine days later the two men met again, this time in Villedieu-les-Poëles. Shells were bursting and buildings burning as Lanham's men battled the retreating Germans. The colonel, roaring through the main street of the town in his jeep, spotted Ernest on a street corner, casually poised on the balls of his feet. With him was a red-haired private, Archie Pelkey, who had attached himself to Ernest as personal aide-de-camp. Ernest's London mood of self-pity and sarcastic pessimism had evaporated in the crisis atmosphere of an advancing infantry. Dodging bullets, sleeping in farm carts, scrounging for food—these were activities he understood and performed handily. At Villebaudon he had expropriated an abandoned German motorcycle, a battered Mercedes, and Pelkey. He was in his element, taking for himself privileges reserved for men who faced extreme danger. On August 18 he and Pelkey met up with two truckloads of Resistance fighters. By the 20th Ernest had his own command post at the Hôtel du Grand Veneur in Rambouillet and was directing the partisans in intelligence gathering. Pinned inside his shirt was an official authorization from an OSS colonel, David Bruce, to carry arms and direct the clandestine activities of his small band. He and his *maquis* (Free French) followers made their way to Paris along the route of the liberating armies and reached the capital on the same day as Mary.

Heady from champagne and Ernest's warm welcome, Mary took to the streets to cover the first day of the Liberation. She was at the Arc de Triomphe when Leclerc men made their historic march down the Champs Elysées. On the reviewing stand was Charles De Gaulle himself. At the Hotel Scribe, headquarters for the Allied Press, she filed a long cable. The rest of the evening was a blur. Too exhausted to unpack or find her way to her own room, number 26, Mary fell asleep on Ernest's bed amid the rifles, the hand grenades, and Pelkey's cooking utensils. The next morning she returned to room 26 with its dove-gray walls, rose brocade chaise lounge and marble mantelpiece. Charles Ritz appeared not to notice when his good friend Hemingway left his overcrowded quarters for Mary's orderly boudoir.

Though she had to meet her own deadlines as a reporter, Mary joined Ernest's continuous champagne celebration as often as she dared. Naturally he expected to show her his Paris. So there was an introduction to Picasso at his studio, and a visit to 27, rue de Fleurus, where they were told that Miss Stein and Miss Toklas were away. After a stiffly formal visit to the working-class family of a French *maquisard* who was devoted to Ernest, when Mary thought she had behaved properly under difficult circumstances, Ernest cursed her and accused her of being clumsy and patronizing. She flinched under the sting of his words. For the first time since meeting him she found herself in the role of "whipping boy." Martha had resisted the role forcefully, finally refusing to live with Ernest. Mary, however, reacted to his insults with a self-abasement that was puzzling. "I never learned to play it as gracefully and dispassionately as I should have liked," she wrote. Such humility seemed unnecessary. But perhaps she had decided that the most important trait in a relationship with Ernest was the ability to take it. "Papa can be more severe," said Capa, remarking on Ernest's bullying tendency, "than God on a rough day when the whole human race is misbehaving."

On September 4 Ernest left Paris to rejoin Lanham and his 22nd Regiment, which was advancing through Belgium. "This was a happy period for all of us," recalled Lanham. "It was full of laughter and heady with victory. . . . we were standing virtually on the borders of the Fatherland [within 900 yards of the Siegfried bunkers] and Ernest was at his gayest and wittiest." Privately Ernest was writing love letters to Mary. The days with her in August had been the happiest of his life, he wrote, without disappointment or disillusionment.

. . . I am just happy and purring like an old jungle beast because I love you and you love me. . . . we will fight . . . against loneliness, chickenshit, death . . . sloth . . . and many other worthless things—and in favour of you sitting up straight in bed lovelier than any figure head on the finest, tallest ship. . . . Dearest Mary. . . . Please love me very much and always take care of me Small Friend the way Small Friends take care of Big Friends. . . . Oh Mary darling I love you very much.

The sunshine and blue skies turned to mist and freezing rain as the grinding assault continued. During many gloomy nights punctuated only by the rumble of distant gunfire, Ernest and Lanham talked for hours about their childhoods, their parents, their women, their dreams and fears. It was during this period that the colonel heard Ernest refer to Grace as "that bitch" and speak of his father's cowardice. Hadley, revered though she was in his memory, did not escape criticism. "He told me how his wife (the first one) lost his volume of short stories on the way to join him in Switzerland," recalled Lanham. "He said that this nearly did him in. Even in the retelling of the story I could see his rage mount. It was certainly not the poor woman's fault, but I always got the impression that he thought it was, and that he had never forgiven her for it and never would."

Ernest's deepest rage, however, was reserved for Martha and for her behavior at the London hospital. "His hatred of her was a terrible thing to see," wrote Lanham. In a letter to Patrick at boarding school, dated September 15, Ernest expressed his consuming bitterness.

Haven't heard from the Marty since letter dated in June. . . . I am sick of her Prima-Donna-ism. When [in London] head was all smashed and terrible headaches etc. she would not do anything for a man that we would do for a dog. I made a very great mistake on her—or else she changed very much—I think probably both—But mostly the latter. I hate to lose anyone who can look so lovely and who we taught to shoot and write so well. But have torn up my tickets on her and would be glad to never see her again. . . . Thought I should write you about Marty so you would know what the score is. . . . When I was in such bloody awful shape in London . . . Capa's girl Pinkie was awfully good to me and so was another fine girl named Mary Welsh. I saw her again in Paris and we had fine time. Think you would like. Have nicknamed [her] Papa's Pocket Rubens. If gets any thinner will promote to Pocket Tintoretto. . . . Very fine girl. Looked after me, in worst time ever had.

In his self-pitying state of mind, Ernest neglected to mention the abuse he had heaped upon Martha. This omission would not come as a surprise to her. She knew, when she told him at the hospital that she thought him contemptible and considered herself free and separate from him, that he would never forgive her. She left him and that was unforgivable. "He lied about me as hard as he could ever since —all the nonsense about my ambition and hard-heartedness."

Ernest's shrill disparagements of Martha's coverage of the war were ludicrous. The truth was quite different. When she came off the hospital ship after the Normandy invasion, she had been arrested by the P.R. office of the American Army for not having the proper papers. (Her papers, as second correspondent for *Collier's*, allowed her to visit rear areas only.) As punishment for having gotten herself over to Normandy she was ordered to an American nurses training camp in the English countryside and told she could cross to France with the nurses whenever they left for a base hospital in France. Martha sat this out for a day, then climbed over a wire fence, hitchhiked to the nearest military airfield, told a pilot a sad story about wanting to see her fiancé in Italy, and got an illegal lift to Naples. "I had no papers, no travel orders, no PX rights, nothing. I was a gypsy in that war in order to report it," she said. And she reported it well and bravely, with different units of the British Eighth Army, with the Poles in the Adriatic, with the French in central Italy, "sharing the dangers and hardships that were the lot of all the soldiers and the Italian population, whose country was fought over mile by mile." Harold Acton, the British literary figure, praised her articles as the best written and most acute of all the ones submitted to him when he was reading cables at the Hotel Scribe. Acton believed they compared favorably with the work of Ernest and that she was a good influence on him.

Martha came through Paris on her way back from Italy after filing a dispatch from Florence that was published in *Collier's* on September 30, 1944. "It is a good thing to remember," she wrote, "how brave the Italians were when they knew what they were fighting for." In the vicinity of Florence, which was under German attack, she persuaded a British officer to take her with him in an armored car when he met with the Partisans. Later she billeted herself in the Hotel Excelsior where there was no food and no electricity but a young English captain played Chopin by the light of a kerosene lamp.

Ernest, who had returned from the Siegfried Line and was living at the Ritz with Mary, called Martha at the Hotel Lincoln—he always knew where she was though she did not know where he was. "He *insisted* that I have dinner with him; I did think we could talk about divorce. Instead he had a band of his young soldier pals from 'his' regiment and in front of them insulted and mocked me throughout dinner. They were miserable and slowly left and when I could, I got up from the banquette seat where I'd been hemmed in and fled." Capa found her in tears and tried to comfort her. What gave Ernest the right to punish her, when he was having a relationship with another woman? Capa asked sensibly. "This was the first time I had heard of Mary Welsh, and I was overjoyed. It meant he *had* to give me a divorce."

On November 3, Martha wrote Ernest from Holland that it was time for some final action. How else could he and Mary plan for their future, or she for hers? "We are honest people, Bug," she continued, "and this is a no-good silly arrangement. It is not our style. . . . I think it would be best for you to get this finished with me."

Since Ernest had already publicly renounced her and was infatuated with Mary, one would expect him to appreciate Martha's attempt to make peace. But he could not accept the idea that she would walk away from him so easily. Hadn't Hadley exacted a hundred days' trial before consenting to her divorce? And Pauline fought for three years before giving up. His pride was badly hurt, but his Cuban friends and his sons have suggested that he still loved her, still wanted her.

In Paris, Ernest had started a sporadic correspondence with Pauline, perhaps in anticipation of his return to Cuba and participation in the life of his sons. "I read Papa's letter with great interest," Pauline wrote to Patrick. "If the war in Europe is won I am inclined to think Papa will do it. Do you think he might send us some nice wines, white and red? Also, new bicycles? I sit and think of all the fine things he might send us, but I guess better not ask. He might think I was just a gold digger and not interested in the noble work that takes up all his time if I think he has time to run errands for people in America the land of plenty."

Her life was bound up in the house, the garden, the meandering pace of village life. She went to New York or San Francisco for glitter and excitement but wartime travel restrictions kept her home most of the time. In January 1944 her father, Paul Pfeiffer, had died. Spring, as she wrote Patrick, had brought a rash of "more or less small catastrophes." Her mother, visiting Pauline as a new widow, sprained her back. The pool pump was out of commission. And the electrical wiring in the old house had to be replaced by two electricians "who look like something out of a chain gang—they follow each other about in lock step, leaving a smoking trail of cigarette butts. They work only at meal times, so that we have no current to cook with, and they appropriate all the electric globes for 'test lights,' they say, but they are never seen again."

With the fall came the hurricane warnings. The worst blow hit on the night of October 23, 1944. "Not only 17 trees in the garden went down flat," Pauline reported to Pat, "but your old mother did too and I must say I don't know whether it is worth putting any of us back on our feet. I feel as though I had been beaten by rods." By the time she went north in November most of the debris had been removed and winter planting started. This time her travels were not for pleasure but for a checkup at the Mayo Clinic to find out if some nagging pains were due to the onset of arthritis. "Just a line to relieve your mind," she wrote both sons on November 15. "In case you have worried, which you probably haven't, the doctors say I am fine and will not be all crippled up." She returned to Key West to find the weather absolutely perfect ("having wrecked everything, weather now saying see how fine I am,") and word from France that Ernest might sail at Christmas.

At the Ritz, Mary and Ernest were quarreling and making up. When some of his friends from the 22nd Regiment made a drunken spectacle of themselves by vomiting all over her bathroom, and then were rude to Clare Booth Luce at dinner, Mary was furious. Ernest accused her of insulting the brave men of the 22nd. Mary retorted that they were drunks and slobs, and with that he cuffed her lightly on the jaw.

Another quarrel was set off by his interference with her work. When a morning call came from Wertenbaker, Ernest gave Wert his views of her assignment instead of handing the receiver to her. It was not until he noticed her angry look that he gave her the phone. She reminded him forcefully that she needed no help from him when it came to her work. But at the same time she was beginning to admit to herself that Ernest was becoming more important to her than her job and that a career of wifehood was what she really wanted, especially if it was constructed in behalf of a man as compelling as Ernest was at that time.

One day, as they were having lunch at the Ritz, a courier brought the news that Jack Hemingway (who had graduated from officers candidate school and was now with an OSS team attached to the 30th Infantry Division) had been wounded and captured the day before in the mountainous region near Montpellier. Ernest began to concoct bizarre schemes to rescue his son, and Mary finally suggested that perhaps she could go to division headquarters at Nancy and determine Jack's whereabouts. Ernest agreed that she should be the one to make such a trip. Mary, the innocent *Time* reporter, could make inconspicuous inquiries. Wertenbaker arranged her travel orders and an Army jeep and driver picked her up in front of the hotel on the morning of November 7. Communication with Ernest would be uncertain since he was leaving in a few days for Lanham's command post in Germany. But she promised to write him a full report.

A week later, back in Paris, Mary wrote him all that she had learned. Jack's assignment was training partisans to infiltrate enemy positions. During a daytime reconnaissance with his captain and a French partisan, the partisan was killed from German fire and the two Americans were wounded. From a captured German soldier who had been present, Jack's intelligence chief learned where the Americans would be incarcerated. After his release at the end of the war, Jack filled in a dramatic detail. The Austrian officer in charge of the Alpenjäger unit that captured him knew Ernest and Hadley and their two-year-old child in Schruns in 1925. Recognizing his name, the officer had ended the interrogation and shipped Jack to a hospital at Alsace.

Ernest meanwhile had joined Buck Lanham's regimental command in the Hürtgen forest. For three weeks Lanham's crack troops, the heroes of Normandy, threw themselves against the giant German artillery of the Siegfried Line. "The days wore on," wrote Lanham grimly, "the casualty lists mounted, and the 22nd ground ahead, yard by bloody yard." Bill Walton, who was there also, noted Ernest's behavior as being "especially gay, without internal conflicts, happily free of the complications of women." Walton may have been right. Ernest did seem better equipped to deal with murderous gunfire, wild animals, and stormy seas than some of the personal problems that afflicted him. But the ordeal at Hürtgenwald formed the grist of his nightmares for years to come. Half a fresh armored infantry battalion was killed in the first ten minutes of the attack on Kleinhau. In the assault on Grosshau a few days later, over 40 percent of Lanham's replacements were lost before they could even join their platoons. Eventually, however, the Germans began to falter. "I was on the phone with a blow by blow account which I relayed to EH as it came in," recalled Lanham. "The crisis passed. The Germans surrendered in mass. It was a terribly close thing."

Ernest's censored letters to Mary and to Patrick gave few details about the battles, but it was evident that he was sick of the carnage and longing for home. "But after this one," he wrote Pat, "am going to . . . Cuba, fix up grounds . . . write book. . . . The Mart [Martha] wants to stay on in Europe. . . . we don't fight anymore. Once I was gone she wanted back very much [could have been wishful thinking, since Martha gave scant evidence of this]. But we want some straight work, not be alone and not have to go to war to see one's wife and then have wife want to be in different war theatre in order that stories not compete. Going to get me somebody who wants to stick around with me and let me be the writer of the family." Mary, going about her assignments in the dismal Paris winter, wondered if she could be that somebody. In spite of lingering doubts about giving up her hard-won independence, she asked Wertenbaker for an indefinite leave of absence and wrote Ernest on November 14 that she would try living with him in Cuba.

But when he returned to the Ritz with a severe pneumonia he was often nasty to her in private. One day when she was feeling low herself and in need of comfortable small talk over a bottle of cognac, he told her that she looked like a "spider." Withdrawing in injured silence to her own room she wrote sadly in her diary that maybe they were not meant for each other after all. He knew nothing of affection. Why had other women hung on to him, if he drove them to bitchery as he was doing to her?

On December 16 Ernest learned that the German high command was launching a major counterattack against the American First Army's position near Luxembourg. Barton's 4th Division would take the first impact. Feverish with pneumonia and sweating, Ernest rushed off with a jeep and driver on the morning of the 17th. But by the time he reached divisional headquarters the worst of the attack was blunted. When he went around to Lanham's command post, a luxurious mansion formerly owned by a priest-collaborator, Lanham ordered the regimental doctor to treat him with massive doses of sulfa. Ernest recovered quickly and on December 22 was well enough to visit some of the battle sectors.

The end of 1944 saw one last skirmish between husband and wife. Late in the morning of December 31, Bill Walton checked into the Luxembourg City Hotel, which was the local Press billet. In the lobby he noticed a stunning woman whom he recognized from pictures as Martha Gellhorn. "You'd notice her a mile away," said Walton, "because of her elegant hair, the tawny-gold color. And her bearing, like that of a fine race horse." After a few moments they struck up a conversation and agreed to visit a nearby unit. The city had not been destroyed but was being strafed by German pursuit planes. On their way back in the late afternoon they went sledding in the park with the local children. There were laughs and spills and Martha was good company. Bill invited her to dinner and was looking forward expectantly to a merry evening. But when he went back to his hotel room to change, there was Ernest, sitting on his bed, knowing nothing of the day's events.

"I have a date with your wife tonight," said Walton. Although Ernest had told him, when they were at Hürtgen together, all about his affair with Mary and what a terrible person Martha was, Walton was not sure how Ernest would react to such an announcement.

Ernest saw a chance for mischief-making. "I'll come along, too," he said, grinning.

The evening was a disaster. Ernest berated Martha wildly and she gave it back to him. Walton began to feel like a spectator at a tennis match. At one point he tried to stop Ernest by insisting that he would not tolerate such insults directed at a woman, but Ernest only retorted that you couldn't expect him to hunt an elephant with a bow and arrow. Walton thought Martha behaved well under the circumstances and he was immensely relieved when the dinner was over.

But there was more. Back at the hotel he realized in dismay that Ernest was planning to be his roommate for the night, and that he was not yet through with Martha. Ernest stripped to his long johns and borrowed a mop and a bucket from the maid's closet. With the bucket on his head for a helmet and the mop over his shoulder, he prepared to storm Martha's room. "Go away, you drunk," she ordered from behind her locked door. Walton was secretly pleased to see Ernest finally retire in defeat.

By mid-January, back in Paris, Ernest was in a better mood, and in fact more good-tempered than Mary had ever seen him. In his absence she had told herself rather sternly that she must not expect some perfect relationship in paradise if she did go to Cuba, as she tentatively planned to do. She was thirty-six and had two failed marriages. Pain and conflict were inevitable, certainly, with " . . . such a complicated and contradictory piece of machinery as Ernest."

Walton was also at the Ritz during this period. He saw the frisky playfulness between them and heard Ernest express his gratitude over and over for the love-making he was enjoying with Mary. "He talked about it a lot," said Walton, "and he was proud of her, this cute little girl on his arm as he swept into the Ritz dining room. Mary did not play up to him as the famous man of letters—she acted as though she had not read much of his work." (According to Leicester Hemingway, she had read everything Ernest wrote.) "Instead," continued Walton, "she treated him as the hotshot warrior, macho man, great in bed." This was the beginning of Mary as pupil, Ernest as teacher. The stories of her father became important, too, for Ernest was a man who was interested in everyone's past, and the notion that she had grown up on a riverboat and lived in logging country appealed to his imagination. "I don't believe they thought much about the future," observed Bill, "at least not at first. The present was moving so fast and was so separate from the future."

But after a few weeks of champagne parties both of them did begin to look toward their future. Mary wrote to Noel that she would now take the necessary first steps for a divorce, and she let her parents know that there was an important new man in her life. Early in February 1945 she went to London on an assignment and to dispose of her furniture. Noel was more vindictive than she had expected. He had ordered the *Time* office to sell her things and then withdrew all the money in their joint bank account.

When it became clear that the Battle of the Bulge had been won, Martha flew from Luxembourg to London. Earlier in the year, after the miserable dinner in Paris, Ernest had written her a note of apology, saying, "I feel the way a man would feel who had spat upon the Holy Grail." (Martha was unmoved by such rhetoric.) During the first week of March, when Ernest was on his way back to the United States, he looked in on her at the Dorchester.

"Though he had previously refused even to talk of divorce, he then came to say Yes, he would get the divorce in Cuba as I wanted. We were both residents so it was easy and legal. I had no intention of leaving the war for weeks in Reno and I never dreamed of asking for anything—money, alimony. I was intensely eager for the divorce so [that] I could get my passport changed back to Gellhorn. I wanted above all to be free of him and his name; and step out of the whole picture fast." Using the same phrases he had used when he had written Mary Pfeiffer about Pauline, Ernest said to Martha, "I'll look after your interests as if they were my own."

Martha was in bed with the flu when he appeared and was relieved that he only stayed for a few minutes. They never saw each other again.

Chapter 27

Mary sailed out of Glasgow on the British liner Aquitania, now converted to a troopship. Her last story filed before she left Europe was a sardonic report for the radio program *March of Time*, about conditions in Germany. It angered her that German civilians had stocked their cellars with food and their children looked plump and healthy, when the children of France were bony and malnourished. On the day Franklin Roosevelt died—April 21, 1945—she was in New York recording for *March of Time* her impression of how the average G.I. in Europe would react to the death of his president. Before flying to Havana she visited her parents, who had moved to Chicago. Her father was working in the accounting department of a local factory. Her mother was involved in Christian Science activities and the feuding between them had softened, or so it seemed to Mary. As she said good-bye to her father, she realized sadly how much he had aged.

Ernest, meanwhile, had returned to Cuba determined to get back into good writing shape. He would preserve the privacy of the Finca and cut back on drinking. But his battered body and black mood made it an uneven fight. He soon became bored with civilian life and homesick for his Army friends. For a man who had been drinking a quart of champagne before breakfast, waiting till noon for his first Tom Collins was a Herculean effort of will. The subdural hematoma suffered in the London accident and then carelessly treated (by his stubborn refusal to stay at rest, plus the steady diet of raw gin) had left him with terrible headaches, hearing impairment, some memory loss, and slowness of speech. And he hated to be alone. "It's not the way people were made to live. . . . " he complained in a letter to Hadley. "Stayed in last night instead of going out to dinner," he wrote Mary on April 17, "because thought there might be mail. But there wasn't. And then was sure there would be some this morning. There had to be. . . . But guess what? There wasn't any mail."

Mary landed at the Havana airport on May 2. Ernest, shaved and neatly dressed, met her with his chauffeur. It was a tense, silent drive to the Finca. Perhaps Ernest was contemplating his past marriages and the complications of bringing a new woman to the house that had belonged to him and Martha. Mary swallowed her disappointment when he showed her to the guest house. Apparently he assumed that she would sleep there, rather than in Martha's old bedroom near his. (Before long she did move into the main house. Martha's room, with its reminders of the former occupant, became Mary's.)

The next day she engaged a village girl to give her Spanish lessons and met all the servants. There were thirteen, including four gardeners. Ernest introduced her to his Cuban friends, who seemed to come for lunch very often. On May 8 there was a sudden burst of shouts and singing in the driveway. Ernest went out to investigate and brought back the news that the war in Europe was over. A terrible feeling of isolation came over Mary. She felt completely estranged from her surroundings and had an overwhelming longing for her life in London.

However, her mood lightened when Ernest drove her to see the *Pilar* at anchor. Standing beside him on the flying bridge, with her hair blowing in the light wind, Mary felt hopeful for the first time. The analogy she drew is interesting. "I felt," she wrote, " . . . that I had returned to the remembered paradise of childhood summers."

The feeling of contentment lasted until Ernest put her into the fishing chair to troll for marlin. She concentrated on following his instructions, but when she brought the small fish to the side of the boat it swam under, the line broke, and the rod sank. Embarrassed by her failure, she burst into tears. Ernest, acting as though the loss of an irreplaceable, pre-war wooden rod was trivial, tried to comfort her, but she knew—and never forgot—how displeased he really was.

Mary had been at the Finca about a month when Ernest's three sons came to visit. They quickly recognized that she was bringing order out of the chaos that had prevailed in Martha's absence. Their initial feelings about Mary varied. Gigi, the youngest at fourteen, did not care for her at first. "She had displaced my true love, Marty." Patrick, much as he loved Martha, had come to believe some of his father's accusations. He knew that Ernest was an effective character assassin; his father's furious misery during the winter of 1943 had come across vividly to Pat. So it was a great relief to see his father cared for once again. Patrick admitted, however, that it was tiresome to have to adjust to yet another Hemingway woman. But he and his brothers were polite, open-hearted young men and found Mary easy to like. She packed delicious picnics for excursions into the countryside and rooted for them at club shooting contests. Jack, old enough to pursue women and drink daiquiris, was an easy companion for Mary on the tennis court and at the Floridita. He did not confuse his loyalty to his own mother, as well as affection for Pauline and Martha, with his father's obvious need to be married.

Writing to the Lanhams early in July, Mary described with great enthusiasm Ernest's renewed health and vigor—stomach flat, headaches gone, appetite healthy. His enthusiasm for everything was infectious. Sometimes she had trouble distinguishing which Hemingway was the son and which the father. In her diary she expressed herself differently. She was beginning to realize the significance of becoming completely dependent upon Ernest, a situation that did not exist with any of his previous wives. He had taken on the support of Mary's parents and was sending them money regularly to supplement their small savings. On June 19, he wrote a courteous, old-fashioned letter to his future father-in-law. "My only ambition is to make her a good husband when we can be married and if you need a son around for any purposes ever please remember you have one." Mary appreciated such gestures but continued to worry that he would come to resent the burden.

The trips on the sea were wonderful, but the raucous shooting parties at the Club de Cazadores irritated and bored her, as did the empty conversations of the wives who did not share her interest in world affairs. She was too new in Ernest's life to make any significant changes at the Finca. Twenty cats still left their odors and excrement all over the house. Gallons of chlorine put the unfiltered pool in murderous condition for eyes and skin. The rose garden was a maze of brambles. Fifty pounds of ice daily could not properly refrigerate the food stored in the ancient icebox. Every time Ernest caught her writing in her notebook he referred to it caustically as the Horror Diary. When on August 31, 1945, she finally flew to Chicago to wind up her divorce proceedings, she asked herself, only half-jokingly, whether she was ready to give up her newly won freedom for another marriage.

Her six-week absence from the Finca worked to Mary's advantage. Ernest began to act on every suggestion she had made for the improvement of the house and grounds. There were enlarged gutters to improve the storage of water, new furniture for the thirty-eight-foot living room, a small house for the cats. His letters were full of promises—to work hard, to treat her as a full partner in all their projects, to love her always. He acknowledged that he wrote better letters than he talked or acted, and he showed unusual sensitivity to the apprehension she felt about giving up her independence. He complained about being lonely, but that condition was at least partly solved when Buck Lanham, now a Brigadier-General, and his wife, Mary "Pete," visited for two weeks in September.

With Buck, Ernest was content to reminisce about the war and enjoy the fishing and the shooting. With Pete Lanham he took on more controversial subjects—bullfighting, world politics, his past and present associations with women. After several afternoons spent drinking wine with him, Pete noticed that Ernest had few good words for any woman except Mary, with his most passionate dislike reserved for Martha Gellhorn. "My feeling," said Pete, "was that she was the one woman in his life—besides his mother—who ever stood up to him and defied him." Ernest told Pete a silly tale about being in mortal danger at the London hospital after his accident, when the doctors had to locate Marty at a cocktail party to get her permission to operate. According to Ernest, Martha told them to do whatever they wanted with her husband and refused to leave the party. But he did concede that she was as brave as a lion.

His attitude toward Pauline seemed to Pete to be one of colossal smugness. She had stolen him from her friend, Hadley, and there was nothing he could do to stop her. "When women start on that sort of thing they can't be stopped," he explained, adding that

Pauline's wealth made her impossible to resist. As for leaving her ten years later, he blamed that on Pauline's refusal to follow him into Spain! While he was risking his life, Pauline was frolicking on the Riviera, so naturally he fell in love with the brave, lovely correspondent. When he asked Pauline for a divorce and she protested, he replied blandly, "Well my dear, those that live by the sword must die by the sword."

Early in October when she returned from Chicago, Mary agreed to take over the management of the house, garden, food larder, and the accounts, and to type Ernest's manuscripts and take care of correspondence. All financial decisions would remain in his hands. She was ready to put all her energies into making a success of their marriage. It was a relief to be financially secure. Although they were not yet married, she now assumed that she had some proprietary rights and set up a few of her family pictures on Martha's desk. To her consternation, Ernest seemed very upset and she bristled in return. Instead of confronting him, she wrote him a note—her way of defending her point of view when they quarrelled. "In all this place you are master. . . . I only wanted some small thing that could look like it was mine." In his study a handsome, framed photograph of Martha was still in place.

The hostility toward Martha that Ernest had expressed to Pete seemed to vanish when he spoke of her to Mary. Then he only talked of her love for his sons and her efforts to please them and make them happy. Martha's imprint on him was as permanent as Agnes von Kurowsky's thirty years before. He would not let go of the pain of the rejection. On July 23, he wrote Lanham that marrying her had been the biggest mistake of his life. But he must not blame her for his stupidity. He admired her for her bravery in Spain and the good job she did in Finland. It was the last war that ruined her for him, though he qualified that indictment with a thought to the effect that a horse who could win a race in 1937 might not win one in 1944.

On July 26, Martha had said in an interview in St. Louis that she would be divorced from Ernest Hemingway in the fall. She was impatient for Ernest to start the divorce proceedings, as they had agreed in March. Finally he did so, suing her for desertion, and the decree was granted on December 21, 1945. Martha read about it in an item in *Time*. "Under Cuban law if you divorce someone for desertion," she said, "you have a right to everything that belongs to both parties." Ernest kept everything that was hers—the typewriter on which she had written all her books, her second-hand car, her tennis racket and clothes, the four or five hundred dollars in the bank, even the cashmere long underpants and shotgun.

When Mary objected to living with Martha's furniture, Ernest authorized the Finca carpenter to build some new pieces. He told Mary that he would let Martha know that her furniture was being stored and that he would pay the storage fees until he heard from her. (Mary later wrote that Ernest paid such fees for fifteen years.) Martha said that she never received a word from Ernest about the furniture, that she would have "sold it like a shot," for she had little money at the time. She was, however, very much interested in reclaiming her family silver, china, and glass, inherited by her mother and handed on as a present to Martha. Edna Gellhorn wrote Ernest a tactful letter, pointing out that Mary would surely not want table silver with Martha's family monogram. "Can you imagine such a thing?" Ernest said to Pete Lanham, who had no difficulty in agreeing with Marty.

Eventually Martha paid for the shipment, though it arrived so poorly packed that the crystal was shattered and the china badly chipped. Martha, then living in a modest rented house in Cuernavaca, Mexico with her adopted baby son, Sandy, and two Mexican servants, was supporting this household by writing commercial short stories with happy endings, a type of fiction she called "bilge" stories.

As the time approached for setting the wedding date, Mary was assailed with last-minute doubts. In the afternoon she loved him, in the evening he was a boor. She lashed out at him for not taking her to the gay parties that Jack attended, for depriving her of the chance to be a roving reporter, for subordinating everything to his work. His theory now, he wrote in desperation to Lanham, was that all women worth sleeping with were difficult. No matter that he was thoughtful and polite, not drinking, not gambling—everything he did sent her into tantrums.

Using a shopping trip as her pretext, Mary flew to Miami to visit Bill Lyons of Pan American and his wife, Maruja Braden, to whom she confided her anxiety. Ernest, suspecting that the shopping might be an excuse, began to send flowers and cables—how much he missed her, how easy it would be to set the date. Mary pondered Maruja's advice, which was to marry him if she really loved him. She began to remember how dull her previous husbands had been and reasoned that it was impossible for Ernest to be dull. And her year's apprenticeship had prepared her well. For the complexities of living with Ernest, there could be no further preparation. So she returned to Havana and set the date—March 14, 1946.

The marriage ceremony, a two-stage affair, took place in the office of a Cuban lawyer. Before lunch Mary and Ernest heard a complete reading of the Spanish version of the Napoleonic Code as it pertained to the property rights of each party. After lunch they spoke their vows before a small group that included Patrick and Gigi and Winston Guest. There was a champagne reception. As the hours passed, Ernest became quarrelsome and Mary irritable. On the drive back to the Finca they argued furiously, and Mary went to bed wondering if she should pack up and leave in the morning. But in the morning the air was soft and fragrant, Ernest was full of apologies, and Mary's prenuptial jitters were over. She organized the vegetable garden and brought in milk-producing cows, studied navigation as well as Spanish verbs, and began target-shooting. Only rarely did she think about the old exciting life in London. The Finca generated its own excitement, as when Ramon, the cook, brandished a bread knife at Justo, the butler, and Justo retaliated with Ernest's pistol.

Then in July she missed her period. She was delighted. At thirty-eight she had wondered if she could become pregnant. Together with her own desire for a child was the intriguing possibility that she might be the one who would give Ernest a daughter. "Think Mary probably having baby," reported Ernest to Lanham on July 20. "Can't tell for sure, but signs point that way . . ."

The presence in his life of a new wife and the promise of another child did not take the edge off Ernest's interest in former wives and older children. When Jack became infatuated with the international beauty, Nancy de Marigny, the former Nancy Oakes, and followed her to her family's Nassau estate, Ernest wrote a scorching letter to his lovesick son. This crisis opened up a fresh correspondence with Hadley, who gently reminded the irate father that those problems were part of growing up. She commiserated with Ernest that such distractions were taking his mind off his work. "But it has always been so," she reminded him, "that when you were really going white hot, some problem would be on hand for you to settle, involving numerous epistles etc."

Hearing that Pauline was planning a cross-country motor trip for herself and their sons, Ernest fired off a letter in that direction, too. "How good a driver is mother? How far has she ever driven?" he demanded of Patrick. "How much in towns? How long hauls?" Knowing of at least one narrow escape with Pauline at the wheel, Ernest maneuvered Jack into making the trip with them. Then he "sweated out" twenty-seven days waiting for mail. Whenever there was a phone call or a telegram, he anticipated news from the coroner. He wrote Lanham on July 14 that "some people" showed a lack of responsibility in not insisting that the boys write him once in a while.

This last was a dig at Pauline, of course, who shrugged off the grumbling and thought the arrangement with Jack peachy. "I trust you are as excited as I am about Bumbi joining our troupe," she wrote her "men" on May 30. "It was Papa who arranged it, being worried about our general safety, I think. Anyway it was very thoughtful of him. . . . "

Ernest apologized to Buck Lanham for getting "black at the joint" in recent letters but blamed his foul mood on the "open wound" of loving women. "What suckers we are for them. . . . as long as they have mens and womens, will have plenty problems." Pete Lanham had concluded after her visit to the Finca that Ernest hated all women except the one who was currently a good sex partner. The reverse may be closer to the truth—that Ernest liked and admired many women, but could not make the necessary adjustments in close relationships. In the same letter to Lanham he referred to his mother as being as dangerous dead as most women alive. "I know I'd never go to her funeral without being afraid that she was booby-trapped." Carol Gardner, when reminded of Ernest's periodic harangues against Grace, expressed the belief that his true feelings were more ambivalent.

Nothing seventy-four-year-old Grace Hemingway was saying or doing seemed to warrant such hostility. Her letters were colorful as always—with more invocations to the Almighty than appealed to Ernest, but she never forgot to thank him for his financial help and always asked after his wife and children. In 1943 there had been

Mary and Ernest on the daily shoot, Sun Valley, 1946.
From the John F. Kennedy Library

loving greetings to Martha and in 1944 an anxious letter of inquiry when she heard on the radio that he had been injured in an auto accident in London. During the months when he was touring the battlefields she had sent letters to various cities hoping that one of them would reach him. On March 25, 1945, she had written of reading in the newspapers that he would be marrying again and inquired about Mary Welsh.

In the late summer of 1946 Ernest and Mary drove to Sun Valley. It was hot and dusty on the western roads, there was little air-conditioning, and the motels were often ramshackle, but Mary made it through the 120-degree heat with nothing worse than some slight dizziness to remind her that she was pregnant. On August 18 they checked into the Mission Motor Court near the railroad yards in Casper, Wyoming.

Early the next morning, while Ernest was repacking the car, Mary awoke in terror, feeling as though she had been "gored." The pain inside her abdomen was so excruciating she could only writhe and moan. An ambulance was summoned, and after being dimly aware of receiving an injection she awoke many hours later on the operating table to the sound of Ernest's voice and the sight of his rubber-gloved hands milking plasma through a tube into her left arm. It was an ectopic pregnancy and her left Fallopian tube had ruptured as she slept in the motel. The only way to stop the hemorrhaging was with surgery; plasma and fluids were administered all day by the house staff so that the doctor could safely operate.

Ernest wrote later:

> Dr. told me it was hopeless; impossible operate; she couldn't stand shock; to tell her goodbye (useless manoever since she unconscious). I got asst. to cut for a vein and got plasma going (they were very short handed and the plasma tubeing had bubbles in it and a too tightly plugged air vent and wouldn't flow). I took over the plasma administration, cleared line by milking the tube down and raising and tilting until we got it flowing, and by the latter end of the first pint she was comeing back enough so that insisted they operate.
>
> To skip again: She took 4 bottles of plasma during operation, two blood transfusions after, been under oxygen tent ever since and now today [Sunday, August 25] is feeling fine.... They removed the ruptured tube and other tube and all other organs are intact and OK.
>
> But Buck it was closest one I've ever seen. Dr. had given her up— and taken off his gloves. Certainly shows never pays to quit.

Three days later Ernest wrote Lanham again, apologizing in case his friend thought him a braggart. "Was only trying to give you the play by play and was still fascinated by how much can be done to f—— fate rather than accept it."

No one who witnessed the crisis had anything but tremendous respect for Ernest's quick action. The anesthetist, the doctors, and Mary herself knew that he had saved her life. As disappointed as she was to lose her baby, Mary's appreciation for Ernest seemed to swell into an everlasting and unshakeable trust. Nothing he could do to her, either inadvertently or with premeditation, would destroy that gratitude. She had seen him at his solid best—quick-thinking, modest, effective, and it put into permanent perspective the occasional bullying, the vanity, the sudden gusts of cruelty.

On September 13 Ernest drove a humbly grateful Mary to Ketchum, where a four-bedroom cabin was reserved for them and the boys. (The Sun Valley Lodge had not yet been converted to peacetime status from its use as a naval hospital.) Tillie Arnold's first sight of Ernest's new wife was to watch him lift her out of the car, like a limp doll, and set her down in a rocking chair in the Arnold kitchen, where she dozed happily before the warmth of an old iron cookstove. After a week of rest she was strong enough to go on the daily shoots for duck, pheasant, mountain quail, and partridge. "I make breakfast," reported Ernest in his letter to Lanham of November 2. " . . . and Mary cooks supper. She can cook like hell. Learned it in England cooking for ex-husband who only liked an over-cooked chop (dry) really and is haveing wonderful time with this succulent basic food."

Late in the fall, Al Horowitz, the publicist for Mark Hellinger, brought the film treatment of "The Killers" to Sun Valley for Ernest to see. Horowitz noticed how tenderly Ernest treated Mary at that time, but he also noticed that when business matters were discussed he sent her out of the room. Mary did not act offended but seemed to accept this as Ernest's preference. Perhaps she took his generosity to her parents as a fair trade-off. On their way back to Cuba in November, Ernest invited Tom and Adeline Welsh to New Orleans, which they had never seen, and took them to the races and to the good French restaurants. On Thanksgiving he ordered a turkey and trimmings and iced champagne to be served in the Hemingway suite.

For Christmas Ernest invited Sunny, now married to Kenneth Mainland, and her young son, Ernie, to the Finca for a few days. Except for the flow of wine and the presence of certain Spanish customs, the hospitality reminded Sunny of Grace Hemingway's open-handed ways on Kenilworth Avenue. There were servants in the kitchen, uninvited guests for lunch, and bountiful food. To his sister the similarities were obvious, though it might not seem so to

Ernest. Everyone noticed how much Ernest was drinking at this time. In spite of his resolutions when he came home from the war, his intake was enormous. Both Jack and Patrick remember him slumped down over the dining room table after several hours of wine-drinking with the Basques.

In January Mary decided to build a tower addition to the house. It would include housing for the cats, a study for Ernest, and a roof-top sun deck for her, with work rooms built into the sloping hillside. She was making sketches and consulting with a building contractor when Patrick became ill. He had taken a year off since graduating from the Canterbury School and was living at the Finca while preparing for his college boards. During Gigi's Easter vacation from school, Pat had returned to Key West, where the two boys were in a car accident. Gigi cut his knee and Patrick complained of a headache, but he came back to the Finca as planned to take the college board tests scheduled for April 12 in Havana. On the 14th he was feverish and irrational and during the night turned violent.

While Ernest was trying to figure out what to do about Patrick, Mary received an urgent call that her father had been hospitalized for a badly neglected cancer of the prostate. She flew to Chicago feeling like a traitor but believing her parents needed her more than Ernest. From the hospital room at St. Luke's in Chicago, while watching over her emaciated, fearful father, Mary received daily letters from Ernest, who explained that Pat's condition was most likely the result of an undiagnosed concussion that caused some intracranial bleeding. He had called in local doctors for the diagnosis and then assumed all responsibility for the boy's daily care. The household was organized like a hospital, wrote Ernest. His Basque friends helped with the nursing, but Ernest administered all the rectal feedings when Patrick refused to eat and slept on a mattress outside his door.

On April 16 Pauline flew to Havana and wrote Mary in Chicago that she expected Patrick to recover in about two weeks. (Her hopes were premature. Patrick did not recover fully until July.) When Mary returned to the Finca in the middle of May, Pauline was still there. During Mary's absence, at her suggestion, Pauline had moved into her bedroom. Now Pauline moved to the Little House and Mary took over again.

Ernest, enjoying the attention of two wives, wanted to assume that they could become friends, although he still resented the alimony payments to Pauline of $500. a month. When he peeped into her checkbook one day and saw that her balance was $9068.43, he was furious. He cited it to Perkins as an example of her greed and vengeful nature. Pauline, according to Patrick, did "play the game of money for keeps." She would never give up the alimony payments because she had contributed substantially to the finances of the marriage and wanted back what she was entitled to when he left her.

As for her politeness to Mary, that was simply a case of good manners. She was a guest in Mary's house and her son was a patient there. But actually Mary and Pauline had little in common beyond the fact that Ernest had once been her husband and now was Mary's. Pauline saw clearly how Mary danced to his tune. Remembering how she had done the same, she probably took some satisfaction from being free of his orders. Some months later, when Mary and Ernest stopped over in Key West for a few days and Mary observed Ernest in the role of guest in the house where he had once been master, Pauline neatly pricked Ernest's self-esteem. She referred dryly to the nice house she had but said of course she couldn't run it properly by herself. It needed the authority of a man. "There's nothing in this world to match the male prerogative. His right to come and go . . . especially go. . . . " Beneath Pauline's banter were the old wounds, never healed.

Chapter 28

With Toby Bruce at the wheel of a new blue Buick Roadmaster convertible, Mary and Ernest drove west to Sun Valley in September. This time their accommodations were at the lodge and for Mary this meant no cooking and cleaning—at least for the present—only room service in suite 206 and lazy afternoons in front of their private fireplace. Hunting was minimal, as Ernest followed his doctor's orders not to go into the high country until his blood pressure came down. (It had been 215/125 after Patrick's siege.)

To make room for their Christmas visitors, however, Mary and Ernest moved out of the lodge in December and rented three cabins in Ketchum—one for themselves, a second for Ernest's sons, and a third for the Cubans who had been so devoted when Patrick was ill. Mary took over the job of preparing meals for them. Having already learned how to cook game, she now learned about pies, often baking half a dozen in a single day. Lillian Ross, who had sought Ernest's help with her *New Yorker* profile of Sidney Franklin, came over for Christmas dinner. Noticing that Mary was worn out but too proud to ask any of the men to help clean up, Lillian went into the tiny kitchen to wipe dishes. Mary accepted her help but seemed subdued. She was making the rueful discovery, not new but often forgotten, that Ernest's wives could easily become a piece of "his backdrop." But in her fierce determination to be the perfect wife, she did not protest such behavior. Perhaps she really did believe him to be so extraordinarily gifted that he must not be judged as other men are judged.

By the time Ernest returned to Key West in February of 1948 he had decided that the winter just past would be their last in Idaho for a while—too many tourists, too few old friends. During the spring he talked about a trip to Italy, his first since 1927, and in the summer he told Mary to work out the details. She booked their passage on a small, well-built German craft, the *Jagiello*, turned over to Poland after the war, arranged for the Buick to be shipped over as well, and took charge of the packing.

In the book bag was a Scribners review copy of Martha's latest novel, *The Wine of Astonishment*. After June 1947, when Max Perkins had died suddenly of pneumonia complicated by heart failure, Charlie Scribner became Ernest's conduit for news about Martha. From Scribner he had learned that she was writing a full-length work about the closing days of the war. When Ernest wrote Scribner that he had a new housemaid named Martha and it was a pleasure to give her orders, he inquired whether Charlie had seen her (Gellhorn). "She stopped at the office in April [1947] while I was away," replied the publisher. "Marty had written a novel about the war, and both Max [Perkins] and Wallace Meyer thought that the first two-thirds of it were extremely good. It told of an American colonel who toured around the warfront with his chauffeur and had love affairs, drinking bouts and the usual sort of thing, all of which they said was very effectively done and very masculine." Neither editor, however, was pleased with the final third, which, according to Scribner, was a tale of horrors about the death camps. The girls had been dropped from the story, Scribner continued, and it was pretty dull to read about war if there were not a few women mixed in. On December 26, 1947, he had written Ernest that Martha was polishing the book. "She hopes to have it in my hands by the middle of February [1948] so that it can be published in the early summer and not be overshadowed by publishing in the same season as you."

The Wine of Astonishment is the story of two soldiers: the over-worked, dedicated battalion commander from the small Georgia town, Lieutenant-Colonel John Smithers, and his handsome, la-conic twenty-two-year-old driver—the Jew, Jacob Levy, who is from a middle-class, storekeeping family in St. Louis. Through the device of long interior monologues the reader understands their past, eavesdrops on the anguish and occasional joys of the present, and learns something of their hopes and fears for the future. As a journalist and observer, Gellhorn's eye and ear are as sharp as ever.

> The German artillery rolled over them in furious cracking waves, and his [Levy's] head felt as big as a balloon, growing high and naked above his shoulders. Then the artillery would stop and the silence was unnatural and threatening. The strange mists of the forest floated in rags through the trees or crept upwards from the ground; the smoke of a phosphorus shell stood fixed in a white plume; branches split and fell; mud-covered figures moved in the shadows; and the silence became as cold as the cold colorless sky.

Martha's editors at Scribners might have wished for her to ease up on the brutality of the final scenes, believing that moral outrage is not as commercial as seduction, but Martha's own stunned disbelief and shame and horror over the reality of Dachau could not be contained. "*The Wine of Astonishment* was my way of getting Dachau out of my system," she later explained. When Jacob Levy, having seen for the first time the stinking, hollow-eyed, near-dead remnants of Nazi barbarism, vengefully drives his jeep into a crowd of stout, laughing German villagers, it is Martha herself who is crying out in protest.

Ernest complained that the action took place over terrain he considered his private preserve—Hürtgenwald. Martha does not know where he picked up such an idea. Her book had nothing to do with Hürtgenwald; she used Luxembourg, which she knew well from weeks there during the Battle of the Bulge, and *invented* the combat scenes. Her greatest compliment as a professional came from the editor of the *U.S. Infantry Journal,* who wrote that they had no record of this action and would she please inform them of its date and locale for their records.

The critics did not care one way or another. "Her war is *A Farewell to Arms,*" wrote the *New York Herald Tribune* reviewer, "a kind of intimate drama in which nothing is sacred but an individual's integrity." Myles Green in the *Times* wrote on October 17, 1948, that "ten years of first-hand observation of the fighting fronts in Europe and Asia have gone into this taut . . . tender book." And the *San Francisco Chronicle* described her as one of America's most impressive woman authors."

The *Jagiello* sailed out of Havana on September 7, 1948, and docked in Genoa two weeks later. With an Italian chauffeur at the wheel of the Buick, Ernest showed Mary the full beauties of northern Italy, visiting places he had not seen in twenty-one years—Stresa, Como, Bergamo, and finally Cortina d'Ampezzo, where he had first skied with Hadley in 1923. At Cortina Ernest and Mary met a titled Venetian sportsman, Count Federico Kechler, who invited them to fish with him at his favorite lake just across the border in Austria. He was an admirer of Ernest's work and expressed a desire to introduce the Hemingways to his friends in Venice.

Ernest's original plan was to spend the winter in Portofino, with only a brief stopover in Venice. But he was so pleased with Cortina that he told Mary to find them a house for the ski season. She rented the Villa Aprile, adjacent to the slopes, and then they continued on to Venice. The moon was just coming up over the Grand Canal as their water taxi docked at the five hundred-year-old Hotel Gritti Palace across from the Church of Santa Maria della Salute. Mary was disappointed that Ernest fell asleep immediately after dinner, instead of taking a walk with her. But in the morning, and for many days afterward, she made up for it. A tireless sight-seer, she visited the museums and palaces, poked through the old shops, and happily lost her way in the maze of tiny bridges and meandering canals.

Count Kechler introduced the Hemingways to the Franchettis, whose paternal head, Count Franchetti, was a famous hunter who had given his children Kenyan names or nicknames. The young barone was known as Nanyuki and his good-looking sister was Afdera. Nanyuki invited Ernest and Mary to his duck-shooting preserve along one of the northern lagoons. As the vivid reds of the afternoon sky faded to a hazy twilight, clouds of ducks flew over the blind and Ernest quickly brought down eighteen. Mary, encumbered with a heavy, borrowed gun, shot very badly, hitting only one. Her relationship with Ernest was so bound up in wanting to please him that the afternoon was spoiled for her.

There was no longer any question of leaving Venice between now and December 15, when they would go back to Cortina. Ernest was beginning to write of Venice as "absolutely god-damned wonderful." The Gritti Palace was the fashionable center of things and he enjoyed socializing with the aristocratic Venetians who frequented it, but for a prolonged stay he preferred a quiet place where he could work, and that was convenient to duck-shooting. On the island of Torcello, a half-hour's fast motorboat ride from Venice proper, was the Locando Cipriani, a luxurious small inn and restaurant owned by Guiseppe Cipriani, who also owned Harry's Bar. The restaurant was excellent and the half-dozen suites on the second floor lavishly furnished. There was nothing else on the island but an old cathedral and some marshland full of water fowl. On November 4 Mary and Ernest moved over to Torcello, and Mary unpacked and rearranged everything for Ernest's comfort. Two weeks later she left him to visit her friends, Alan and Lucy Moorehead, in their fifteenth-century house outside Fiesole.

It was in the company of the Mooreheads that Mary met Bernard Berenson, the eighty-three-year-old art historian and connoisseur, and it was to Lucy Moorehead that she stoutly defended her decision to forego her career in favor of the move to Cuba and marriage to Ernest. There were many advantages, she insisted to Lucy, in being " . . . simply a wife, and not a harried and competing career woman."

From Torcello Ernest had written her that he was working hard and missing her harder, but to Lanham he had taken a rather cynical view of his married life. The best approach to women was to compliment them, he wrote, make love to them, and then keep them off-guard. Early in December, however, at the Franchetti hunting lodge near Latisana, he met a young woman whose innocence and romantic background called for something entirely different—a gentleness and respect that Ernest was still capable of generating. She was Adriana Ivancich, the eighteen-year-old daughter of Dora Betti and the late Carlo Ivancich.

Adriana's Ivancich ancestors on the island of Lussino in Dalmatia, under the government of the Doges, had been the owners and captains of merchant vessels that sailed as far as the North Sea. During the Napoleonic era Anton Luigi Ivancich moved his fleet headquarters to Venice and the family became one of the five most important in the city. The heroic deeds of Ivancich seafarers were honored by a succession of royal heads of state, including the Emperor Franz Joseph and the Archduke Maximilian. The family's status and wealth reached its peak during the time of Adriana's grandfather Ivancich, who owned the Grand Hotel when Queen Victoria was a guest, as well as a palazzo in the Calle de Rimedio. One of his projects, which proved to be very costly, was to bring much-needed electricity to a part of Venice that was without it. His sisters, Adriana's great-aunts, were famous for their beauty and their literary salons. One sister, Yole (Marchesa Biaghini Moschini), inspired the Italian writer Antonio Fogazzaro to produce his most important novel, *Piccolo Mondo Antico.* Another sister was so friendly with D'Annunzio that he gave her the nickname Graziana.

By the time of Adriana's birth on January 1, 1930, the Ivancich wealth had declined somewhat, due to bad investments and the ravages of the first World War. But the family continued to be held in great esteem by the Venetian establishment, especially Adriana's father, Carlo, who was granted the title of Grandissimo Ufficiale Dottore by the government for his many good works in behalf of the community. He was a man of dignity and strict moral standards and very exacting—Adriana recalled that he always carried two watches, one across his chest and another in his pocket to check on the accuracy of the first. Her mother, Dora, had the delicate beauty of a cameo and was much loved by her Venetian friends for her kindness and wit.

Adriana was one of four children. Gianfranco and Francesca were ten and eight years older than Adriana, who was close in age to the youngest, Giacomo. The family home continued to be the palazzo acquired by Adriana's grandfather in the Calle de Rimedio, a few blocks east of the Piazza San Marco. It had been designed by Palladio and built in the late sixteenth century, and still displayed the tapestries, paintings, and gilded furniture collected by former heads of the family.

Until the time of the Second World War, life in Calle de Rimedio was placid and orderly. Then events occurred with fierce swiftness. "I was ten years old when the war started," Adriana wrote in later years. "I didn't know what it was but I remembered that I cried. . . . I saw the soldiers leave and never come back. I didn't yet know what death meant. . . . Then Gianfranco left also and I saw my mother cry." Gianfranco, assigned to the Italian tank corps, fought with General Rommel's forces in North Africa at the Battle of El Alamein, and after being wounded in the autumn of 1942 was evacu-

*Mary the "tireless sightseer" in
Venice, 1948.*
From the John F. Kennedy Library

*Adriana Ivancich and friends.
Venice, 1949.*
From the John F. Kennedy Library

ated to Italy and hospitalized on the seaside near Lido. In July 1943 the Allied Forces invaded Sicily, and by September 8 Italy officially went over to the Allies, although all of northern Italy was still controlled by the German Army. As American bombing intensified around Venice and Trieste, Adriana counted sixty separate attacks in the vicinity of the family's country villa near the village of San Michele on the lower Tagliamento River.

During this period, Adriana's father began to work with the partisans and arranged for supplies of grains and foodstuffs from his country estate to be delivered secretly to the various groups supporting the Allies. Her mother, as a volunteer nurse at the central railroad station of Venice, found ways to save a few Venetian Jews from being shipped to their deaths in the concentration camps. Gianfranco persuaded the hospital authorities to discharge him although he was not altogether recovered from his wounds, so that he could join the American OSS. By early 1944 he was chief of all partisan activity in the Veneto. Adriana, a young teen-ager and well aware of the dangerous activities of her father and brother, wanted to do something, too. Gradually she was given simple tasks that usually involved carrying messages from one house to another—simple but nonetheless full of risk. As she walked through the familiar streets and along the canals, she reminded herself that the penalty for aiding the Allies was certain death and tried to imagine what she would do if she were caught.

During most of 1944 and 1945, up until the end of the European war in May, the destruction of northern Italy was widespread and devastating, for the Germans were giving ground very grudgingly. Because of San Michele's location near a bridge that crossed the lower Tagliamento on the direct road to Trieste, the village was attacked repeatedly from the air. The Ivancich estate was finally destroyed in the spring of 1945. Carlo Ivancich and Gianfranco, who were in the house at the time, were able to escape on their bicycles, but Gianfranco was wounded again.

The hardest blow to the family came in June. The increased revolutionary activity during the closing months of the war led to extreme factionalism among the partisans and infiltration by criminal elements. On June 12, 1945, the body of Carlo Ivancich was found by Gianfranco in a rubble-strewn alley in San Michele. His murderer was never apprehended but the family believed that he was killed, not by thugs, but because he had discovered that one of the partisans had been using party money for his own ends.

Dora Ivancich never recovered from the brutal death of Carlo. Finances could be at least partially rebuilt, but nothing could restore the strength and stability provided by her husband. Gianfranco, a young man of quiet charm and good looks, was badly shaken by the death of his father and repeated threats to his own life. He tried various occupations but none lasted. The dislocations of the war had been too much for him. Venice was a traditional community, however, and in spite of their troubled situation the Ivancich family did not lose their entrenched position. With the income from a few remaining properties Dora was able to hold on to the palazzo in Calle de Rimedio, educate the younger children, and reestablish a continuity in their lives. Adriana received her secondary education at the Liceo Classico, was presented to society on her eighteenth birthday, and then was sent to Switzerland for six months to perfect her French. "It was a shock meeting the American girls," she said, "for I realized that one could have more than two parents [because of the number of divorces]. For me it was all new. They had boy-friends and they painted their nails and they had money."

Adriana had only recently returned from Switzerland when Count Carlo Kechler, a friend of Gianfranco, invited her for a weekend of hunting at the private preserve of the young Barone Nanyuki Franchetti. The Franchetti lodge near Latisana was not far from the Ivancich property at San Michele. Adriana walked about the grounds of her bombed-out house and then waited at the cross-roads outside the town, where Count Kechler would pick her up. As cars slowed down and then speeded up she watched anxiously, for it had started to rain and she began to worry that Carlo would forget about her. Finally, after an hour of waiting and walking back and forth, she saw an American Buick slow up and then stop. It was blue, a chauffeur was at the wheel, and a strange man sat beside him.

"I'm sorry I'm late. We stopped along the way," called Count Carlo from the back seat, adding, as Adriana climbed in, that when Ernest talked about the war he forgot about time. "By the way," he asked, "do you know Ernest, Ernest Hemingway, the writer?" He motioned to the broad-shouldered man sitting in front.

So this is Hemingway, thought Adriana, the one all of Venice is talking about. Why, he is an old man. When he turned around, however, and she saw the alert expression in his eyes and he smiled his crooked smile, she decided that maybe he was not so old after all. The men offered her a drink from Ernest's red flask. She demurred. Ernest urged her, saying that the whiskey was good for circulation. She replied that her circulation was excellent, thank you, and began to feel more relaxed as the conversation continued. Ernest drank a toast to her as the girl who waited for them under the rain and then referred to Carlo's having told him that she once lived across the river and that the Americans had bombed her house. "I hope you'll forgive us," he said.

"It is not the fault of anybody," she replied. "War is war."

Ernest cursed war and then quickly apologized for his language as that of an old soldier. Carlo remarked that besides being a soldier Hemingway was a very good writer.

"I know," said Adriana, "but I have not read even one of his books." She stopped, afraid that she was being rude, and said she was sorry.

Ernest told her not to be sorry, that she could not learn anything good from his books. She replied that there was good in everything, as long as one looked for it, and then, to herself, hoped he would not notice the banality of her remark. What was good today, said Ernest, was that they met in spite of the rain and that they would go hunting together in the valley. He raised his flask again, to Adriana's health.

As Adriana Ivancich described for her mother the events of her weekend at Nanyuki's hunting lodge, she pointed to little pen-and-ink sketches she had made of the various guests. Here was Carlo with his big nose, there was Hemingway's stomach. She said how nice this Mr. Hemingway was. On the day of the shooting it had rained again and when she was drying her hair in front of the large kitchen fireplace he had spoken kindly to her, apologizing that she was the only woman on the shoot. He explained that his wife, Mary, had been expected but at the last minute could not come because of a headache.

"And I want to tell you, Mama," added Adriana, "that he has invited me to Harry's Bar."

Dora was hesitant. Was it proper for Adriana to accept an invitation from someone she had just met, a foreigner? (Harry's Bar had become an acceptable place for Venetians of good families to congregate. Even young women were permitted to go there unescorted.) Adriana brushed aside her mother's objections. Of course it was proper. Mr. Hemingway wanted her to meet his wife, and everyone would be there, and they would talk about the hunt again, and besides, in less than a month she would be nineteen.

Since making her formal debut less than a year before, Adriana had caused quite a stir in Venice. Partly it was her appearance—a striking combination of coloring, bone structure, and classic Italian breeding. Her hair was a rich black, long and full and lustrous. Her eyes were an unusual green, lively with curiosity, and her nose was narrow and Roman. She had interesting hollows under her cheekbones and a curving mouth that smiled easily even when her expression was watchful. Her figure was good and her stride vigorous. The terror of the war, which touched her most directly with her father's death and the way in which he was killed, gave her youthfulness a haunting quality. Apart from her looks and personality there was a bright, quick intelligence. She had not had a particularly impressive education—a Catholic girls school and six months in Switzerland. But she read seriously, had written poetry since she was fourteen, and could draw very well.

Adriana did go to lunch at Harry's Bar and she did meet Mary, who paid scant attention to her, noting only that she was girlish and respectful and that Ernest was already calling her "daughter." After Mary left for Cortina to prepare the ski chalet, Ernest saw Adriana a few more times, still in the company of her friends, who would gather around him at Harry's Bar or in the lobby or on the terrace of the Gritti. Again Dora asked how it was that Adriana was so friendly with this married man. Again Adriana tried to reassure her. "But his wife is always coming and going," she explained, "and he invites my friends, and we walk and talk and it makes him happy."

But what did they talk about for so many hours? It was not so easy, said Adriana. Often they did not understand what Ernest was saying. His American slang was different from the English they were accustomed to, and his habit of lowering his voice and whispering out of the side of his mouth as though he were telling state secrets made it difficult, too. But when he laughed, they laughed, and that seemed to please him.

Ernest drove up to Cortina to join Mary in time for Christmas, and for a while everything was just as she hoped and expected it would be—she could cook up an occasional meal in her own kitchen with willing maids to clean up after her, and there was good skiing on the slopes that fell away from her front yard. On January 20, however, while they were skiing in fresh snow, she fell and broke her right ankle. Nothing went well after that. In February Ernest was in bed for two weeks with a heavy chest cold, and in March, when Mary was out of the cast and exercising gingerly, Ernest's eye became infected, and the infection quickly spread across his face. The condition was diagnosed as erysipelas, a potentially contagious, infectious disease of the skin and subcutaneous tissue. Ernest was hospitalized in Padua and given massive doses of penicillin to bring down a fever and reduce the severity of his infection. It was late March before he and Mary were back in Venice.

While Mary revisited her favorite museums, Ernest once again sought out the companionship of Adriana, and not always in the company of her friends. He was fascinated by her eighteenth-century upbringing in a twentieth-century Venice that clung to the mores of the past, and he continued to call her daughter. By this time of his life, Ernest was "Papa" to most of his friends and family, and "daughter" was the form of address he favored for women. Such terms were a logical extension of his paternalism and fed his need to think of himself as the grizzled, battle-weary veteran. In the case of Adriana, however, the paternalism was a convenient mask for some new—and perhaps unwelcome—erotic longings. Adriana, however, does not believe that she confused Ernest with her father. "People have wondered if my affection for Hemingway came out of my need for a father," she wrote in 1980 in her memoir, *La Torre Bianca (The White Tower)*. "It is not so. My father, though of rigid morality, gave me deep understanding and love. It was he who encouraged me to write poetry. They are from different cultures. Papa had courage like my father, but used it in a different way." Adriana believes that she did try to remind Ernest of the distinction. When he wanted to buy presents for her, she protested. "You cannot do that," she reminded him, "for I am not your daughter."

It was during this same period—early spring 1949—that Ernest met Gianfranco Ivancich. "That is Gianfranco, my brother," said Adriana to Ernest, pointing to a slight, dark-haired man walking toward them in the vicinity of San Marco. Gianfranco had been in

New York for six months and only lately had returned to Venice. Adriana had already explained his situation to Ernest—how he had been wounded as a soldier and as a partisan, how it had been difficult for him to get resettled after the war, and that now there was a possibility of a position for him in Cuba. Ernest was immediately drawn to him. "He walks like an Indian," he said, and noticed how Gianfranco's absent-minded air changed swiftly to a pleased smile when he saw his sister. After Adriana performed the introductions and Gianfranco went on his way, Adriana and Ernest resumed their walk. "I like that boy," said Ernest. "I will see him in Cuba." Adriana was startled to realize the coincidence. Of all the possible jobs to be offered to her brother, the one he received would now take him to Cuba, to Havana, where Hemingway, her new friend, lived. "You can count on me from now on," repeated Ernest. "I will see him in Cuba."

Before leaving Venice late in April Ernest invited Adriana and Gianfranco to have lunch with him and Mary at the Gritti. Mary's comment in her diary was that Adriana and Ernest "were busily launching a flirtation." Adriana, who had gone out of her way to convince her mother that Ernest's interest in her was harmless, preferred to think of it as a friendship. "For me he was a much older man," she emphasized later, "even though there was something of the big child about him. At times I even felt the desire to protect him against himself. But 30 years was for me a lifetime. I never thought of being in love with him. I appreciated his kindnesses and his attention. We were friends. I learned much from him."

Ernest's feelings as the jaded, much-married older man aroused by the sensuousness of an eager, responsive girl were much different from Adriana's. Thirty years his junior, and of a conspicuously different background, Adriana could only complicate his life. But the fantasy had taken hold of him—the fantasy that he could have her. This became evident when he returned to work on a novel that he had begun in Torcello and now continued at the Finca. Published later as *Across the River and into the Trees*, it is the story of Richard Cantwell, a middle-aged American colonel stationed in Trieste after the Second World War. Cantwell's war record is similar to that of Buck Lanham, but his personal habits resemble Ernest's. The woman whom he passionately desires but cannot marry because she is Catholic and he is divorced is a nineteen-year-old

Venetian countess named Renata. " . . . she came into the room, shining in her youth and tall striding beauty, and the carelessness the wind had made of her hair. She had pale, almost olive colored skin, a profile that could break your, or any one else's heart, and her dark hair, of an alive texture, hung down over her shoulders." In Ernest's imagination Adriana Ivancich now became the worshipful mistress of the cynical, much-battered Cantwell. Their climactic love scene is played out in the midnight shelter of a listing gondola under an old U.S.O.D. Army blanket.

When Buck Lanham came to the Finca in June, prior to his departure for a new station in Europe, he was surprised by what he perceived as Mary's increasing submission to Ernest's exhibitionism. Ernest would sit around the pool or at meals and brag about his sexual conquests (real or imagined), and Mary, covering her embarrassment, would act as though she were proud of his manliness. It disturbed Buck that she should degrade herself so in the face of Ernest's bad manners. One night when the conversation turned to Venice she made some remarks to the effect that all the women wanted to go to bed with Papa, but she was the lucky one who had him all to herself, and such riches made her feel a little guilty. Lanham knew she believed that she owed her life to Ernest, but it appeared to him and to others that she was enduring far more at his hands than obligation warranted. A Cuban sportsman who fished with Ernest agreed with Buck, at least in regard to her abasement. To him it sometimes seemed that she made herself practically a slave to his wants. He never heard her criticize Ernest publicly, whatever the provocation.

Why Mary—the gutsy, mischievous reporter—slid so readily into the role of submissive wife is a matter for some conjecture. Beyond the power of Ernest's personality and the obvious gratitude she felt in behalf of herself and her parents is the possibility that youthful worship of her father, coupled with the recognition that her mother did not meet his needs, made her particularly susceptible to Ernest's set of demands. In any event his well-being seemed her reward for the continued obeisance. She was at her very best aboard the *Pilar*, where she never had to dress up and could bask in Ernest's approval of her skill as fisherwoman and sailor. Not since Jane Mason had any of his female companions adapted so readily and with such zest to the fishing life.

They began to talk of another winter in Paris and Venice, but first Mary flew to Chicago to see her parents. Ernest's penchant for letter-writing was never more apparent than during these weeks of Mary's absence. Writing to Grace Hemingway, who at seventy-seven required the care of a full-time nurse-companion, he reported on the activities of his three sons, all then in Europe, and referred to the book he was working on as one that would be very good. To Mary, he wrote that she should proceed with "Operation Mink Coat," and then, in a tone of contrition, explained that his flirtations were harmless, " . . . like going in the cage with the big cotsies. . . . I only play for keeps with you. . . . " A Venetian noblewoman who had paid him much flattering attention in the winter past now received a word count on the new book—1,641 words on Monday, 1,176 words the week before. He wished she were at the Finca so that she could read it. Had she seen his boys? They were in Venice with their mother, a lovely woman but very difficult at times.

Pauline, who had gone to Europe in the summer with Gigi and Patrick, did not think of herself as difficult. Had she not been hospitable to Mary when the latter wished to flee the burdens of the Finca? Were not both Patrick and Gigi a credit to their father, who had left most of their rearing to her, even while enjoying their good-humored companionship when and as it suited him? In Paris, Pauline visited Hadley, who had moved with Paul back to Crécy-en-Brie in 1945 when Paul took over the editorship of the Paris edition of the *New York Post*. Patrick was surprised to see how friendly his mother and Hadley were. "Perhaps," remarked Patrick years later, "it was because they were well out of the running and could relax."

Hadley was grateful to Pauline for her many kindnesses to Jack, who in the spring had been married in Paris to a young woman from Idaho, Byra (Puck) Whitlock. The Honorable David Bruce, ambassador to France, who had been his commanding officer in the European Theater of Operations, was Jack's best man, and Alice Toklas, who had attended his christening, now came to his wedding. "She brought a fine piece of silver for the bride," recalled Jack, "and was like a busy little bird, coming through the reception line three times, always bubbling with enthusiasm." Jack, who described himself as something of a lost soul in the postwar world, had reenlisted in the army, and took Puck with him to Berlin on his first assignment. "Pauline was the only one in the family," he said, "who took the trouble that year to come and see us." Continuing on to Venice Pauline and the boys met some of the young people from the Franchetti and Ivancich families. Patrick thought Adriana very attractive, but in his mature Harvard judgment, Afdera Franchetti was the schemer, "a real Italian siren, with four or five boyfriends always hanging about."

Ernest told Adriana how pleased he was that the boys had met her. Mary and he would be in Paris about the 6th or 7th of November. From Paris they hoped to go to Venice and shoot a little with Nanyuki. His book would be finished, but there would be some revising of proofs. He was nostalgic for Venice and for her and hoped that she would write to him. She did not have to worry about writing in English because he read Italian almost as well as he spoke it badly.

Mary returned from Chicago with a five-thousand-dollar mink coat on her arm, and Ernest wrote Lillian Ross the next day that with Mary back there would be discipline in the house once again —meals on time, life to be taken seriously. "I like to have her back," he said, "though I love the real wild life."

In taking on the role of manager, which she performed very well, Mary forfeited some of the playfulness that had attracted Ernest. Did he no longer perceive her quite so clearly as the "Pocket Reubens" whom he had taken to bed with such gusto in 1944? Their sex life was satisfactory, but Ernest craved other stimulation as well, especially in the isolation of the Finca. Mary was inquisitive about nature and liked to collect facts and read best sellers, but Ernest began to perceive her level of cultural sophistication as superficial. Mary's intellectual growth had come from her experience as a curious, energetic, working reporter. When she gave up her career to take care of Ernest and his household, she forfeited most of the opportunities that had enlarged her horizons.

How interesting those wartime opportunities were came to light again in a novel published at this time by her former close friend, Irwin Shaw. In *The Young Lions* Shaw drew a picture suggestive of Mary Welsh. The fictional Louise has bright hair and a "small elegant body," works in wartime London for the Office of War Information and " . . . seemed to know every bigwig in the British Isles. She had a deft, tricky way with men, and was always being invited to week-ends at famous country houses where garrulous military men of high rank seemed to spill a great many dangerous secrets to her. . . . After the war . . . she would run for the Senate or be appointed Ambassadress to somewhere. . . . " Ernest was angry over the similarities to Mary, but Shaw's description is a reminder, perhaps, that she had led a very different sort of life before she settled down in Cuba.

In mid-November the Hemingways flew to New York, taking a suite at the Sherry-Netherland for a few days before sailing to Europe. It was during this period that Lillian Ross gathered most of the material for her *New Yorker* profile of Ernest. When the profile eventually appeared in the magazine it became highly controversial, largely because, in Lillian's view, she had portrayed too closely Ernest's "enormous spirit of fun." In transcribing literally his joking Indian talk, in which he dropped his articles, she was supposedly ridiculing him. Her impression of Mary was literal as well, and it contributed to the view that Mary had become, in her zeal to be the perfect wife, little more than a good drinking companion and the partner who unpacked, ordered lunch, and kept the lists.

On New Year's Eve, 1949, Mary and Ernest dined early and alone at a hotel in Nervi, south of Genoa. Ernest was gloomy, for he missed the attentions of the companions who had toured the south of France with them—Peter Viertel and his wife, and Aaron Hotchner, a young editor from *Cosmopolitan* who had impressed Ernest as being intelligent and conscientious. But as soon as they reached Venice Ernest was cheered by the presence of Adriana.

Mary attributed Ernest's infatuation with Adriana to his romanticized memories of Italy from his youth and a need to act out the fictional love affair he had created for Cantwell and Renata. But such reasoning did not catch the essence of Adriana herself. The elder Cipriani's son, Arrigo, who was a young teen-ager in that winter of 1950, is of the opinion that Adriana's qualities as a mature woman —the aristocratic style and poise, the poignant sense of a past, the vibrant beauty, the quick mind (Ernest called it her "fast brain")— were exactly the same when she was young. It would not be difficult, he reasoned, to visualize a mature man such as Hemingway being smitten by her.

Again Dora questioned Adriana about the frequency of Ernest's attentions. "You see this man Hemingway too much," she said. "It is not normal, a married man, older than you. I don't forbid you to see him, but from time to time, not so many dates." Adriana protested. Ernest enjoyed her company, and that of her friends, too. It made him feel young, and it protected him from dull admirers who bored him.

"You have to consider what people might think," pressed her mother. Now Adriana was angry. What did it matter what people thought? It was an obsession, this concern for what people thought. Perhaps her mother should meet Hemingway and judge for herself. Dora agreed.

"It is high time that I met him," she said. "We will invite him for lunch."

"So Ernest came to lunch at Calle de Rimedio," recalled Adriana, "and he was dressed in blue, neatly, wearing a tie, and he talked very slowly so that my mother could understand him." Joining them was Adriana's Aunt Emma, who remembered that in 1923 while visiting her friend, Renata Borgatti, at Cortina d'Ampezzo, she had met Renata's American acquaintance, Hadley Hemingway. She remembered the afternoon in the hotel dining room when there was an empty place at the table for Hadley's husband, who was writing upstairs and would be late for lunch. "You will hear from that young man one day," Renata had said. A few minutes later Hemingway joined them. Ernest, too, remembered the incident, and there was much pleasure at such a coincidence. Adriana, listening to all the chatter and the nods of recognition, was relieved. Now her mother's doubts would be dispelled. Papa was not a stranger after all, but an old acquaintance of the family.

During the two months that followed, Adriana saw Ernest frequently in Venice and twice in Cortina for skiing. They developed a private shorthand language. "Joke" meant not serious. "Mistake" was the code word for kiss or any other display of affection. They spoke to each other of many things, including their mutual concern for Gianfranco, who was now working in Havana. "He has in his heart only you and your mother," said Ernest, "and does not care about the rest. He is very affectionate to me and I feel close to him. That makes it easier for us, brings you closer to me." When she told him of her brave great-aunt Clotilde who had sat quietly drinking tea as the bombs fell in San Michele, he asked to meet the lady, now in her nineties. So Adriana took him to visit Clo, who offered him vermouth and then reminded him how important it was for the whole world that Venice be preserved.

At Harry's Bar one day Carlo Kechler teased Ernest about Adriana, warning him to beware of her—that girl with the green eyes who was like a crazy horse. No, said Ernest, she was not a crazy horse, but a great black one. From then on, one of Ernest's names for Adriana was Black Horse.

The first time that Adriana went to Cortina was for the weekend of an international ski competition. Mary, watching what was happening, felt helpless to say anything. "Ernest was weaving a mesh which might entangle and pain him," she wrote in her diary. "But I was sure that no cautionary phrases of mine could arrest the process." Adriana's second visit was in response to an invitation from Venetian friends to be their house guest and she stayed in Cortina until summoned back to Venice by her mother. Ernest, who was not skiing, volunteered to drive her to Venice. Mary stayed behind on the slopes, going out every day with an instructor until for the second time in as many seasons she fell, this time injuring her left ankle.

When she returned to Venice, wearing a walking cast, Ernest told her that he wanted to invite Adriana and Dora to Cuba. His excuse was that it would be nice for them to see Gianfranco. Knowing what really motivated him, Mary was cold to the idea but saw no way out. She did, however, remind him that for propriety's sake the invitation should be a joint one. Ernest agreed, and Dora Ivancich and a woman friend were invited to Harry's Bar for lunch. Ernest wandered off with his cronies, leaving Mary to represent him. In her position she could not be expected to feel kindly toward Adriana's mother, and her description in *How It Was* is highly derogatory. According to Mary, Dora seemed vague as to who she, Mary, really was. She was "gray of hair, eyes, manner and wardrobe," and "seemed relieved" when Mary said she and Ernest had not been married "in the Church." Mary was sarcastic about Dora's careful English and thought it "utterly irrational" that the high-born Venetian woman should be interested in visiting such a backwater as Cuba.

Mary and Ernest departed from Venice with a cautiously worded reply from Dora that she appreciated their invitation and would consider it for the future. In Paris Ernest stayed in bed, suffering from bronchitis, while Mary shopped and dashed about. He did not visibly improve until Adriana arrived during the week of March 15. She had come to Paris to study art for a few months and to live with a school friend, whose family were prominent Parisians. Adriana's introduction to Charles Scribner, who was in Paris on a visit, was a triumph. Earlier in the winter Ernest had encouraged Adriana to submit some sketches to Scribners for the book jacket of *Across the River and into the Trees*. Without knowing that she was a friend of Ernest's, Scribner had selected her pen-and-ink drawing of Venice over all other entries and now so informed her. Ernest proudly called her his partner and hosted a grand luncheon at La Rue Royale the day before he and Mary were to sail from Le Havre. Late that afternoon Adriana went for a walk with him and they had a drink at an outdoor table at Deux Magots.

The conversation began innocently, as Ernest asked Adriana whether she noticed the resemblance between her mother and the Mona Lisa. "It is my good luck," he said, "that you are not the daughter of the ancient one."

Then they watched the passers-by, with Ernest making jokes about the various types. At that point, wrote Adriana, he gazed straight ahead, not looking at her, and said that any of the men, if they saw her and were not stupid, would want to marry her. "Since I am not stupid, I would feel the same way.

"But you have Mary," said Adriana.

"Ah, yes, Mary. She is nice of course, and solid and courageous." But he added that a couple could travel a part of a road together and then take two different directions. It had already happened to him. This time, he promised, it would not happen. "I love you in my heart and I cannot do anything about it."

"From his voice," said Adriana recently, "I knew that he was terribly serious and suddenly I felt paralyzed, unable even to stretch my hand out to sip the gin-and-tonic that sat in front of me on the table. It was like waiting for an avalanche, an avalanche that would break from the mountain at any moment."

Ernest said again that he loved her and that, in the language of Dante, he wanted only her good. "I know what you need to be happy. I will live to make you happy."

"All I could think of at that moment," she said later, "was that everything was ending, our beautiful friendship was over, finished, the avalanche was falling."

But then his voice changed. "I would ask you to marry me, if I didn't know that you would say no." So the avalanche did not fall. Outside there was still the sun. People still were walking. And she knew that the dangerous moment had passed. They could look at each other safely.

She stood up. They smiled at each other. Ernest stood up, too. "Now let us take a walk along the Seine," he said.

Chapter 29

In New York, Mary had a thorough medical check-up to find out whether there was any chance of a normal pregnancy after the narrow escape at Casper three years before. The answer was not encouraging. Her general health was excellent, but her remaining Fallopian tube was so "occluded" that the chances of getting pregnant were slight. It was several days before she could break the news to Ernest. She felt like a "failed member of the human race" and blamed herself for a situation that was beyond her control. It was in this dejected mood that she arrived back at the Finca, and it could not have been easy to watch Ernest's euphoria at finding three letters from Adriana awaiting him.

"It is seven hours that your boat ran away from me," she wrote in halting English, "and I have to say this makes me rather sad. . . . I have so many things to say that I prefer to skip them all—you understand, don't you?" At 1:00 A.M. she was writing again, this time in Italian. If she had seemed cool in his presence, now that he left her she was experiencing a strong sense of loss "I don't know why I write you so much. . . . perhaps, because being used to talking to you for hours, I must also write you for hours. . . . Take good care of Mary; she is good and dear and deserves the best in the world." The next morning she wrote for the third time, complaining that all topics were forbidden to her. She could not thank him, for he found gratitude annoying. To remind him to watch out for Gianfranco was useless, for he would do that in any case. "The only topic left is to talk about you, and ask what goes on in your book, just like the girl of Figaro did! Do you understand, Papa, I don't have anything to say—this is just an excuse to send you a few words across the Ocean."

On April 10 Ernest replied. " . . . if you were here, Ay as one says in Spanish, if you were here." The next day he wrote a second letter. One of the things he missed the most was the sound of her voice. There were no other voices that sounded like hers in the world. And, on the 15th: would she please get her papers in order, and "carry them as a gift to me?"

The rush of letters was interrupted briefly when Pauline and Patrick with his fiancée, Henrietta "Henny" Broyles, arrived at the Finca to seek Ernest's blessing for the marriage that would take place in June after Patrick graduated from Harvard and Henny from Radcliffe. "My father was quite nice about it," recalled Patrick, "even though it probably offended his sense of tradition that I had no visible means of earning a living." But Henny was presentable and Patrick had the feeling that everyone was enormously relieved he had not gone to pieces [after his illness of 1947] and were afraid to cross him for fear of triggering something awful. Patrick was neither too young nor too self-absorbed to be unappreciative of Mary's kindnesses—the fine luncheon she served, her effort to put him and Henny and Pauline at ease. It troubled him that Ernest was rude and cutting to her, and he was keenly aware of the element of brutality in their relationship. Patrick suspected that Mary was not as tough as she represented herself and felt that his father was taking advantage of her determination to take whatever he dished out.

After Patrick's departure, Mary looked forward with much pleasure to a visit from one of her own relatives, a favorite cousin. But Ernest's behavior turned increasingly petulant. He would refuse to eat his dinner, even to the point of placing his heaping plate on the floor for the cat. One afternoon he kept the women waiting for hours at a local restaurant and then walked in with one of Havana's leading whores on his arm. Mary broke down and gave vent to her pain and bewilderment.

Again she composed a note. It sounded like an ultimatum. "As soon as it is possible for me to move out, I shall move." But she did not leave. Instead she assigned most of the blame to herself, continued to run the house, and watched for some sign that his passion for Adriana was subsiding.

No such sign appeared. He kept up a feverish correspondence with Adriana and was nastier than before with Mary. When Gianfranco lost his job Ernest promised Adriana he would look after her brother. In one letter he promised that in any situation, if only one of them could be happy, he would always want hers to win; he would withdraw from the race. In another he wrote that it was 3:30 A.M. and he could not sleep for missing her. When she wrote that Italian men were becoming aware of her, he replied that although he could not help loving her he hoped that she would marry the finest man in the world that she could truly love.

One of the reasons for Adriana's increased popularity was the rumor that she was the heroine of Hemingway's new book, a rumor that she herself, perhaps not inadvertently, had started. She recalled:

> It was during the time that my maid began to look for a husband for me. She would describe this one as the faithful type or that one as nice because he had more money, and we would laugh about it. One of them was the Count Guido and I told her it was impossible. He did not know I existed. All he ever said to me was "how was Gianfranco and where was Gianfranco?" But one day I met him on the street and when he asked the usual question I said that Gianfranco was fine, and also Hemingway was fine. "What, you know Hemingway?" Now he was interested. Of course I know Hemingway. I had lunch with him and we talked of many things. "What things?" Oh, he asked me a favor. "What favor?" The favor to use my physical characteristics for his heroine. "You mean you are the heroine?" No, no, that is not what I said. I only look like her. But Guido had already raced off with my news and soon all of Venice was saying that I was the one in the book.

Since May Ernest had been hinting in his correspondence—and not always subtly—that he was in love with another woman. To Charlie Scribner, he had written on May 10 that he would soon start another book to keep his dependents in mink coats, but without being able to give a dime to someone he loved. To Lillian Ross he described himself two weeks later as a character with a broken heart —an old-fashioned term, he admitted to Lillian, but real nonetheless. And when Harvey Breit, a *New York Times* writer, inquired about Renata while reading a prepublication copy of *Across the*

River, Ernest replied on July 17 that it was a portrait—possibly unsuccessful—of someone he loved more than anyone in the world.

Early in August, Mary flew to Gulfport, Mississippi to secure a small house for her parents and then went on to Chicago to help them with the move. While she was setting them up in their new home, Louella Parsons, the Hollywood columnist, reported on the radio that the Hemingway marriage was breaking up over an Italian countess with whom Ernest had fallen madly in love and that they were presently living together at the Finca. An hour after the broadcast Ernest was on the phone, frantically assuring Mary that it was a pack of lies. (The origin of the Parsons item was a story circulated by Afdera Franchetti that she was the model for Renata, that Ernest was infatuated with her, and that she had visited him twice in Cuba.) After his telephone apology Ernest assumed that Mary would forget the whole matter, but when she still appeared angry upon her return to the Finca he wrote Lillian Ross that she was behaving "with all the grace of a garbage woman."

By this time, however, in spite of the gossip, Mary had reverted to her original attitude, which was not to break up her marriage over Adriana. She reasoned that it would be worse for Ernest than for her, if she allowed him to walk out. According to Mary, he would be wracked with guilt and such a love affair would not bring him any emotional peace. But Bill Walton, who knew Mary well, believes that her abject acceptance of Ernest's treatment was too high a price to pay. By refusing to march out when he was so abusive, she lost something upon which there can be no price—her self-respect.

Ernest now called Mary a "camp-follower and scavenger" and said that she had the face of "Torquemada." He would make preparations for solitary fishing trips, lulling her into thinking she would have a few days of peace, only to return the same day, tanked up with daiquiris. Her reactions to such treatment continued to be mixed. At times it only stiffened her resolve not to be driven away. But at other times her mood was one of desperation. On October 13, she wrote Charlie Scribner that she had decided not to stay any longer with Ernest. He was destroying what she believed was her inexhaustible supply of devotion to him. She wondered whether some of his hostility toward her might relate to her not being able to have a child. If Charlie heard of any kind of job she might get in New York, he could let her know about it.

Across the River and into the Trees had been published and most of the reviews were in. Although the book was rapidly becoming a best seller, the professionals were calling it Hemingway's worst novel, a parody of his previous themes, garrulous and tawdry. Mary, noting the dedication, "To Mary with Love," wondered at the irony, at once comic and painful. The Hemingway book she least admired was dedicated to her, and its heroine was none other than her current rival.

Adriana first saw *Across the River* in a book stall, when the freighter on which she and her mother were traveling to Cuba docked in Tenerife in the Azores. In Venice no copies had circulated. (Ernest had forbidden the Italian publication for at least two years.) Gossip had continued to swirl about Adriana and Afdera, with some newspaper writers speculating that Renata was a composite of both young women. Adriana had begun to argue ungraciously with people who accused her of being interested in Hemingway. Sometimes she screamed at them, she had written Ernest, when they told her that no true friendship could exist between a man and a woman. But there were advantages, she discovered. At least she was being treated like an adult instead of Gianfranco's little sister.

When the Italian vessel carrying Adriana and her mother docked in Havana harbor, Mary and Ernest and Gianfranco were out on the *Pilar* to meet it. Gianfranco had not seen his family in over a year, and his normal reserve dissolved in a torrent of Italian when he embraced them on the dock. Ernest's face betrayed his happiness at seeing Adriana, but otherwise he made no gestures of affection, only concentrated on putting Dora at ease. Mary was as friendly as though the visit had been her idea. She arranged a series of parties climaxing in a lavish outdoor gala and pointedly followed her own routine when Ernest showed Adriana the old city, the Club de Cazadores, and his favorite views of the ocean.

A few days after she arrived Ernest gave Adriana a copy of *Across the River* and then a week later asked her what she thought of it. "I hesitated," wrote Adriana, "but then I spoke up. 'The girl is boring. How could your colonel love a girl who is so boring? A girl like that does not exist, if she is lovely and from a good family and goes to Mass every morning. Such a girl would not drink all day like a sponge and be in bed at the hotel.' " Ernest did not agree. Adriana was wrong. Girls like that did exist, he insisted. He had known quite a few. Perhaps in America she replied, but not in Venice. Seeing his face grow sad, she backed off. Probably it was a good book, but she preferred the others.

"For you," he said, "I will write a good book, better than I have ever written before. Wait and see."

Both Mary Hemingway and Adriana Ivancich have written something about the situation at the Finca during the winter of 1950–51—Mary in her autobiography, and Adriana in *La Torre Bianca*. Taken together these accounts provide a reasonable indication (from differing perspectives) of how the various principals were behaving. Mary, holding rigidly to her control, was not going to be goaded into leaving. She had made that clear again and again. Sometimes her efforts to placate Ernest were clumsy, as when she tried to coax him out of a black mood by putting on a record from the musical *Kiss Me Kate* and then urging him to dance with her. Each time she sang the words, "I'm always true to you in my fashion," he grew redder and redder. "Papa moved like a trained bear," wrote Adriana, "and when Mary urged him around the room a second time, he assumed the crouch of a man at bat and hurled a glass of wine past her face into the wall behind her."

Adriana, having entered a situation that compromised her more than the others, believes that Mary owed her a great debt simply because she had not walked away with Ernest. "I could have, you know," she said years later. Instead, she went on dates with young men her own age and gently persuaded Ernest to cooperate with Mary's social plans. From their private conversations and correspondence she knew that he longed for her, and being human she enjoyed such power, but having been raised in a certain way, she conducted herself in accordance with the rules of her world. (To Ernest's Cuban men friends, who were used to enjoying quid pro quo in a love affair, Ernest simply looked foolish, since he was receiving no sexual favors from her.)

Early in December 1950, feeling that Adriana's presence sparked his creativity, Ernest went back to a story he had begun in 1948. The hero is an artist, Thomas Hudson, who owns a house in Bimini, a second in Cuba, and a third in Montana. With his first wife and small son, Tom, Jr., Hudson had lived and worked in Paris. His second wife bore two younger sons, David and Andrew, identical in all ways, save a slight adjustment in age, to Patrick and Gregory. Making little attempt at invention, Ernest relied almost exclusively on his own recollections. Now he moved the scene from Bimini to Cuba and a farmhouse similar to the Finca of Martha's tenure. All the Hudson sons are dead—Tom killed in the war, David and Andrew in an automobile accident along with Hudson's second wife. As the artist lies on the Samoan mat, exhausted from twelve punishing days at sea looking for German submarines, he reads a letter from his hated third wife who is a journalist covering the Pacific Theater of Operations. " 'She's a bitch, Boise,' " says Hudson to his principal cat.

Five years after his divorce from Martha Gellhorn, Ernest was still attacking her. She had already appeared disguised as Cantwell's estranged third wife in *Across the River and into the Trees*, and the colonel's remarks about her to Renata were so rancorous that Charles Scribner had brought up the question of libel. On May 10, 1950, Ernest had replied heatedly that "if Miss Martha were to take umbrage," she would be well advised not to try trading punches with him. At other times, however, his reminiscences of Martha had been tinged with a certain magnanimity, if not affection. "I read Martha's article in The New Republic," he had written Scribner back in 1947, "and thought it was good. . . . She is at her best when she is fighting for something she believes in. . . ." He admitted to Charlie that he liked to know where she was, what she was doing, and how she was getting along.

Martha, on the other hand, wished to know nothing of him and if possible never spoke of him publicly or privately. (She never gave any interviews about their life together until after his death, and then only two: to Carlos Baker and the author.) When she finally realized that he was using Scribners as a sort of "spy post" she changed publishers. "Far from having any curiosity about him, when I saw items in gossip columns I was ashamed for him and ashamed to have been part of his life."

Bill Walton, who had a comfortable rapport with Ernest as well as Marty, saw at first hand how Ernest still could not be objective about her. He had stopped off at the Finca on his way to Cuernavaca and received a letter from Martha. Ernest, who always was up early and saw the mail before anyone else, recognized her handwriting.

For the next two days he berated Walton and accused him of being a spy in his (Ernest's) own house. Bill only laughed and reminded Ernest that he had every right to receive his own mail, and besides, wouldn't Marty be amused to hear how the mere sight of her handwriting on an envelope could unnerve him so.

During Christmas at the Finca, the number of house guests increased. Patrick and Henny arrived, and Gregory, in disfavor for having dropped out of school, brought along a young woman whom he had met while experimenting with dianetics. Gigi, who was uncertain of his father's feelings for him, wished that they could be close again and was sympathetic to the older man's needs. "Adriana is so lovely to dream of," Ernest told his son, "and when I wake I'm stronger than the day before and the words pour out of me." Perhaps the girl was flattered by his attention, reflected Gregory Hemingway in his memoir, " . . . or perhaps bored and just being polite or amused, as only young girls can be amused with an infatuated old man, but certainly not in love with him. But very sweet and considerate and never betraying her inner emotions. Never hurting him."

Patrick did not agree with Gigi. He thought it grotesque of his father to be making a fool of himself over a twenty-year-old girl. He was indifferent to her point of view, having concluded that Ernest could not afford that sort of thing anymore (the process of leaving one woman for another and the emotional damage it wrought). His sympathies were with Mary. He hinted to Dora that Ernest was not as rich as she might think and then needled Ernest about all the things he should give Adriana if he really loved her—such as a car so that she could drive back and forth to Havana.

By permitting Adriana to continue her friendship with Hemingway and then bringing her to the Finca for three months, Dora Ivancich was vulnerable to the criticism of Patrick, Mary, and others. Her family and friends in Venice, however, believed her bad judgment to be the result of the trauma suffered in the war. Adriana, refusing to judge her harshly, has repeatedly stated that she was finally moved to write her own version of her relationship with Hemingway—the details of which she had shielded from public scrutiny—because of Mary's disparaging remarks about Dora in *How It Was.*

According to Adriana's recollection, in January 1951, while Ernest was planning the trip to the mainland he would soon take with Mary and the Ivancich family, Dora received a disturbing leter from Venice saying that the Renata in the book was Adriana. Her daughter merely shrugged at the suggestion; it was nothing new. Hadn't the public been looking all along for the real Renata? Didn't her mother remember that they could not decide between her and Afdera? Dora was insistent, finally handing her daughter a French newspaper with a large picture of Adriana and the caption "Renata, Hemingway's new love."

Dora said tonelessly that she and Adriana must return to Venice—that in Venice, Renata was Adriana.

And that was how it ended. Dora and Adriana moved to a Havana hotel. Gianfranco walked around nervously saying that no one should pay attention to the gossip. Mary said that it was just what she expected and it was too bad that Papa didn't listen to her advice and give the girl red hair and blue eyes and have her come from Trieste. Ernest protested that a story was a story and if people compared it to reality then what the devil happened to the freedom of a writer.

The plans for the trip were changed, since the recent unpleasantness made it impossible for Ernest to go. Mary, however, did agree to tour the deep South with Dora and Adriana and a young Cuban from a good family, Juan Veranes, who had fallen in love with Adriana. Because of Juan, Adriana's leave-taking was not as sad for her as it might have been. There was a poignancy about saying goodbye—she had begun to think of the Finca as her second home—but in her youthful optimism she assumed that one day she would return. Ernest, feeling displaced and lonely in her absence, was comforted by the unusual ease with which he was writing a new story. He had begun it in the early weeks of 1951 and began to think of it as the good one he had promised to write for Adriana. It was the tale of an old Cuban fisherman, Santiago, and his fight to land a giant marlin.

Chapter 30

In Venice Adriana was finding it impossible to lead a normal life, with everyone who understood English translating *Across the River* and snickering over it yet always seeming embarrassed in her presence or her mother's. One Italian editor felt compelled to ask rhetorically whether it would not have been more sensitive of the author, if he really loved the countess, to disguise her features and liberate her from the innuendos. Ernest tried to comfort her, insisting in a letter that she was not the girl in the book. Maybe he should have never met her at Harry's Bar, maybe he should have never met her at Latisana in the rain, though it was good that he did before she got too wet. It would have been the same, he continued, if he had never written a book about Venice. People would have seen them together, seen they were happy. She must try to remember that the best shield against lies was the truth. He sent his regards to her mother and ended the letter on a pensive note. Why, on such a beautiful day, was she not walking into the Finca, shining in her loveliness?

As deeply as he longed for her and wished she were near him, Ernest wrote Adriana no letters in 1951 after the aforementioned one. From June until the end of the year cables and the long distance telephone calls seemed to him like "instruments of the devil." On June 28 Sunny cabled from Memphis that their mother was dead at the age of seventy-nine. A head injury sustained at Oak Park Hospital when an attendant mishandled her wheelchair and caused it to tip over had left Grace's memory severely impaired, and then senile dementia set in. Sunny took her into her own house in Memphis for the last months that she lived. "It was heartbreaking," recalled Sunny. " . . . She would hide from me like a child. . . . " When the family doctor tried to prompt Grace to recognize her daughter, she referred to Sunny as a lovely lady who was taking care of her. On the night that she was hospitalized for the last time, she sat at the piano and played several classical pieces with great gusto. A few weeks later she died in a Memphis Hospital.

Ernest did not attend the funeral, though he apparently told the village priest of her death, for on the day she was buried in Illinois, the church bell in San Francisco de Paula began tolling at dawn. On July 20, 1949, two years before she died, Grace had written Ernest that she still loved him and would rejoice to receive a letter from him. This benign statement from an old woman had only served to stir up Ernest's deep animosities. For several weeks he had expressed his hostility in the most vehement terms to, among others, Charlie Scribner. He had stated that he would play the role of the devoted son if it pleased her. "But I hate her guts and she hates mine. She forced my father to suicide. . . . I will not see her and she knows that she can never come here." He wrote Grace a brief letter on July 30, 1949, to thank her for her birthday wishes—he was fifty on July 21—and on September 17 he acknowledged a shipment of some personal papers from Key West. Among the papers were the baby albums she had kept for her children. Apparently she had sent all of them to Key West long before, but at that time Ernest had not looked at them. "Please let me congratulate you," he had written in 1949, "on diligence and your lovingness for all of us kids when we were young and must have been great nuisances to you."

On the night of her death, Ernest showed the albums to Bill Walton, who was visiting the Finca. He had hidden them in his bottom bureau drawer so that Mary would not find them. He told Walton he feared that if she knew about them she would sell them to *Life*. Nearly a year later—July 4, 1952—he would write Harvey Breit that he had not loved his mother for a long time. He knew that was not a nice thing to say, but at least he was remembering the times when he did love her, before she began to be cruel to his father. In the same letter he made a remark that may have applied not only to Grace but to others: if he was hard on someone it was often from ignorance, and if not from ignorance it was from being "sore."

On July 9, Grace's obituary appeared in *Time.* "Died. Grace Hemingway, seventy-nine, who married a doctor, bore him six children, the second of whom was Ernest Hemingway."

On September 30 another of the gloomy cables was delivered to the Finca. Pauline wired from San Francisco that Gigi was in some kind of trouble with the Los Angeles police and she was flying down to try to get the full story. After she had ascertained the facts she would call back. The next night when it was midnight in Cuba, Pauline put the call through to Ernest from Jinny's house in Los Angeles. Gigi had experimented with some illegal drugs, reported Pauline, but she was in touch with a lawyer who would look after everything. At the time, Gigi hinted to his mother that perhaps it would be simpler if his father were not brought into the picture. " . . . a lot of things would be simpler," replied Pauline, "if you had only one parent." According to Jinny, who recounted the incident to Gigi, the telephone conversation started out calmly enough. Very soon, however, Pauline was shouting into the phone and sobbing uncontrollably. Gregory wrote later:

> My aunt . . . hated my father's guts, and . . . certainly couldn't be considered an unbiased witness. . . . [But] I'd seen papa's ability for destroying people with words, and had even seen him use it on Mother. Once he had written her a letter entitled "How Green was my Valet," with Mother portrayed as Hettie Green, the eccentric Wall Street millionairess, and the "valet" referring to the nature of their former relationship.

After the emotional conversation with Ernest, Pauline went to sleep but awoke at 1:00 A.M. (Los Angeles time) with severe abdominal pain. Only the day before she had told Jay McEvoy that she felt marvelous and was going on all cylinders. At other times, however, she was known to suffer from sudden elevations of blood pressure —sometimes as high as 300—and severe headaches. She was rushed to St. Vincent's Hospital, where she died on the operating table three hours later. The autopsy report indicated that she died of pheochromocytoma, a rare and unusual tumor of the adrenal medulla, which intermittently secretes abnormal amounts of adrenaline, causing the extremely high blood pressure that Pauline had previously experienced. A variety of stimuli could cause the tumor to put out the adrenaline—a sudden stressful incident is often cited —though the cause can be something as innocent as being jostled from behind or having a bad dream. When Pauline's tumor "fired off" during the night, her blood pressure skyrocketed, causing a blood vessel to rupture. Later on, the tumor, of the intermittent rather than constantly secreting variety, precipitously stopped discharging the adrenaline, and her pressure dropped from 300 to 0. She died of shock on the operating table, with the frustrated surgeons looking for the bleeding point in the abdomen where she had originally felt the pain. Ironically, she was scheduled for another visit to the Mayo Clinic where, if the tumor had been diagnosed, it might have been successfully removed.

Five hours later, 9:00 A.M. on the west coast, Jinny cabled the news to Ernest, adding in her wire that she would call him to explain. Ernest waited at the telephone all day; when he heard nothing by nightfall he called Los Angeles. Jinny, badly shaken by the tragedy, remembering how agitated Pauline had been when she talked to Ernest the night before, cut him off coldly, telling him nothing, implying that it really did not matter anymore what he knew or didn't know. Long ago Jinny had been his friend, though it was an equivocal relationship—two intelligent people who enjoyed each other's wit but knew how to hurt each other, too; and in rather complex circumstances, they were rivals for Pauline's devotion. Ernest was convinced that Jinny had turned Pauline against him, not only because of his infidelity but because she was the lesbian who distrusted men. Now he was furious with Jinny but for the moment, at least, swallowed his wrath. Pauline, whom he had once loved, was dead at the age of fifty-six. He wrote Scribner the next day that he had the full sorrow of Pauline's death. "I loved her very much for many years and the hell with her faults."

As soon as Gigi could borrow some money against his inheritance he brought his wife Jane and their infant daughter to the Finca to visit Ernest and Mary. Since graduating from the Canterbury School in 1949 with a four-year straight-A average, Gigi had experienced difficulties. After leaving St. John's College in his freshman year and refusing psychotherapy, he experimented with drugs and married against his father's wishes. (Pauline, according to Patrick, had been enthusiastic about the boys' marriages, as she was hoping to become a grandmother.) Gregory grieved over his mother's death. "But time tends to heal," he wrote. "Besides, from being a poor aircraft mechanic . . . I was suddenly a rich young man, having inherited a small fortune from my mother. I'd been left exactly the same amount as my brother, which surprised me because I had always been sure that she loved him more."

At first Gigi and Ernest got along well. Then, feeling expansive one afternoon, Gigi referred to the trouble he'd gotten into as not really so bad. To his horror and shame Ernest said bluntly that it really was bad, because it had killed his mother, the implication being that her worry over Gigi had triggered her fatal attack. Patrick, whose love and respect for Ernest did not prejudice his ability to be fair, was disturbed that his father could be so vindictive. He assumed that Ernest's pride as a father was assaulted and he also thought that Ernest might be angry over not being remembered in Pauline's will. She had left money to his son, Jack, but not to him —no casual decision, since Pauline was not casual about money. With the same deliberation and forethought she had decided that the original manuscript of *A Farewell to Arms*, which Ernest had given to her Uncle Gus Pfeiffer in appreciation for his generosity, should revert to Patrick and Gregory after Gus's death. She persuaded Gus to put such instructions in his will. But by the time Gus died so had Pauline, and Ernest, with some justification, harrassed the boys to give it back to him. Patrick wanted to hold out, believing that some day that manuscript would be the single most important thing their father could have given them. But Gigi caved in, hoping to earn back Ernest's good opinion.

For a time it looked as though 1952 was following sadly in the wake of 1951. On the morning of February 11, Charles Scribner died of a heart attack. When Max Perkins had died in 1947, Ernest had mourned him as one of his most " . . . loyal friends and wisest counsellors in life as well as writing." He had written, " . . . it was like haveing a part of yourself die." Now, four years later, the man who had filled Perkins's shoes so gracefully was dead, too. Ernest and Mary were spending the month at sea and learned of the tragedy when Mary went ashore to make a routine call to the Finca. Ernest wrote Vera Scribner how stunned and heartsick he was.

Mary asked me if I couldn't tell her something that would help her to reconcile herself or anything to console both of us because it was very bad. I told her the best thing was to think of how you and Charlie loved each other and how kind you were to each other when you were here and how proud he was of his children and his work and of you. . . . Now my dear and good friend is gone and there is no one to confide in nor trust nor make rough jokes with. . . . "

Before the news of Scribner's death had reached them, Ernest and Mary were having a wonderful time. They caught enough fish to fill the freezer, read half a dozen books in the shade of the *Pilar*'s wide canvases, and dropped anchor in the waters of Mary's favorite islands. That they rarely made love on these excursions did not seem to trouble her. The excitement of the sport was stimulus enough, and the metaphor she chose—Ernest as big "cogwheel," herself as little one—confirms once again her willingness to be his ever-adaptable companion.

One recent satisfaction to Ernest was the advance reception—both critical and financial—that was enjoyed by *The Old Man and the Sea*, which Mary had put into final typescript the previous summer. Everyone who read it was ecstatic. Now, in May 1952, *Life* promised to pay $40,000. for the right to publish the entire text in a single issue, and the Book-of-the-Month Club made it their main selection with a guarantee of $21,000. The only matter left to worry Ernest was the unsatisfactory dust-jacket design that arrived in the mail from Scribners. Immediately he cabled Adriana to come up with an alternative. Remembering the afternoon during her visit to the Finca when Ernest had driven her to a site above Cojimar, Adriana was able in a very short time to do an impressionistic view, in white, blue, and brown, of the cluster of shacks and fishing boats set against the endless stretch of blue sea. "I have never been prouder of you. . . . If I could only have been there to celebrate with you when you had finished. . . . It would have [been] tragic to have a book without your cover. But it was only you and your wonderful speed and promptness . . . that made it possible," Ernest wrote in his letter of May 31, 1952. "You are wonderful, daughter, and I thank you very much and love you very much. . . . "

Response to the book was tremendous. Five million copies of *Life* were sold within forty-eight hours. Friends were calling Ernest

The "remembered paradise of childhood summers." Mary on the Pilar, *ca. 1955.*
From the John F. Kennedy Library

from all over the world and readers were writing to him at the rate of eighty to ninety letters a day. People who saw him personally were apt to burst into tears. It was "worse than Pagliacci," said the author happily.

Mary suggested that they go to New York to celebrate. As gamely as she had adapted to country life, she still missed the city, and this seemed a logical time to take a trip. But Ernest would not budge, and although she protested that she did not want to go alone, finally she did, and enjoyed it immensely. Ernest wrote Bernard Berenson on September 13 that Mary was making the small triumphs that he didn't like. "Somebody should have [them] . . . when we win, or seem to. . . . "

When she returned to Cuba late in October, Mary found Ernest busy with plans for a vastly more ambitious trip—a shooting safari in East Africa. The idea was stimulated by a letter from Patrick, who had moved to Tanganyika and was negotiating for a 3,000-acre ranch in the southern highlands. Ernest alerted Philip Percival to the possibility of organizing a second Hemingway safari and then devised ways of financing the trip without going into debt. He gave the option on the film rights of *Old Man* to Leland Hayward and made a deal with *Look* to allow their photographer, Earl Theisen, to accompany them to Africa to do a picture feature. For this he would receive $15,000. for expenses. His own 3,500-word narrative would bring in another $10,000. The negotiations with Hayward proved to be protracted and frustrating, as the producer tried to sign Spencer Tracy up for the role of Santiago and bring him down to the Finca to meet Hemingway.

In the spring a fresh load of visitors arrived—Leland Hayward, his wife, Slim, and Spencer Tracy came in from Miami on April 4, Jack and Puck and their small daughter a few days later. Easter Sunday was Mary's forty-fifth birthday and rather than going fishing she chose to look after little Muffet. They splashed in the pool. Mary prepared supper for the child, read to her out of a book from her own childhood, and tucked her into bed. Mary was reluctant to admit her disappointment in not having a child of her own. She even suggested that it was probably just as well, since so many of her friends' children were turning out badly. But that was the rationalization of a tough, uncomplaining Mary who believed good sportsmanship to be the ultimate test of character. Whether their having a child together would have made Ernest more considerate of her is open to question. Mary believed that it would have, especially if she had given him a daughter.

During this period of the early fifties Ernest wrote frequently to Berenson, now eighty eight, although the two men would never meet. When the art historian, who knew and liked Martha Gellhorn, wanted to hear more about Ernest's relationship with her, Ernest, writing on May 27, 1953, was more even-handed and less vengeful than usual. He was contemptuous of himself for acting the fool in their relationship but admitted that he had been in love with her. He described her excellent qualities of generosity and devotion to what she believed in but repeated the old accusation that she loved war, even "the trappings" of it. He called himself a damn fool for leaving his wife and children and attributed much of his unhappiness with Martha to his own guilty conscience, which led him to heavy drinking.

There was a tone of respect in the letter, both for their love and for her, that was different from before. He wished her luck and envied Berenson that he saw her. Ruminating further, he suggested that perhaps he had not been a good husband to her, though he did teach her as much as she could learn about writing. "She tried hard to like the things I care for such as shooting and fishing and the Sea," he wrote, ". . . and she was lovely to my children who all loved her." He referred again to how beautiful she was and how he was moved every time he saw her. Berenson must never show her this letter nor tease her nor hurt her feelings. "She belongs with me now to les temps perdu. Not lost in one sense."

If Martha belonged to his past, Adriana was still very much in his present. "It is two years now that I have not been there [Venice] and that is twenty years too long," he had written Berenson in an earlier letter. "Today is a gloomy wet day and that makes me more homesick." Although he tried to console Adriana about the gossip that followed them, he was not consoled himself when he saw how it inhibited their freedom to see one another. Dora Ivancich did not want Adriana's name on the jacket of *The Old Man and the Sea* and probably would not like them to go to Venice either, wrote Ernest to Adriana. He had not seen her for two years and that was terrible for him. But her good was what he cared about. Many people would love her in her life, but no one more than him. It rankled that he might be in Europe for two months and still not see her. The fact that he had loaned Gianfranco some money for his Cuban farm did not mean that she was under any obligation to him. She must never view him as her "monied aunt." He loved her and missed her, almost as if he had suffered amputation, but if it was a bother to see him, he would understand. They could not always see one another.

For Adriana the glare of publicity was bringing embarrassments more bruising than mere tongue-wagging. Much to her distress a lascivious American masquerading as Ernest's friend tried to make an assignation with her. Her friend Count Carlo tried to comfort her. It was not her fault, he pointed out, that she had been born in

Venice instead of New York. In New York she would have been on television as the woman who fascinated a writer, and her sponsor would have been Coca-Cola! Reluctantly she was beginning to agree with the Italian editor—it would have been better for her if Ernest had not borrowed her physical features for his Renata. And there was the sober realization that her connection to Hemingway, the famous and brilliant Hemingway, would have destructive consequences for her relationships with ordinary young men and even hinder the possibility of a successful marriage. "No one will love you as much as I do," Ernest had written her repeatedly. So far, his prediction seemed depressingly true. "I loved Juan [Veranes] but when I returned to Italy I gave him up for Enrico [another beau], who left me for a Venezuelan," she wrote later. "I thought I loved Nikki [a local suitor] and he was killed in an auto accident."

In her artistic life, however, Ernest's encouragement and attention stimulated Adriana to take herself seriously and to be productive. Her illustration for *The Old Man and the Sea* was singled out as the best book cover of the year. And in the fall of 1953 Mondadori published her slender volume of poems, *I Looked at the Sky and the Earth*. It was coincidence and not favoritism that Hemingway's Italian publisher had been the one to give her a contract. As when Charles Scribner selected her sketch for *Across the River* without knowing of her friendship with Ernest, so Mondadori only knew her as an eager, unknown poet. After her manuscript had been repeatedly passed over by other editors to whom she submitted it, Adriana carried it to Milan herself and barged into Alberto Mondadori's office unannounced. In order to be polite, Mondadori riffled through the pages quickly. Then he looked more carefully. Finally he told her to leave the manuscript with him so that he could consider it at leisure. Some weeks later he accepted it for publication.

Adriana was chagrined to learn that Gianfranco would tour Europe with Ernest and Mary but that she would not even get to see them. But she obeyed orders "like a good girl," for she was not yet at the point in her life when she could make her own rules. She was still "the good family daughter." Meeting the Hemingways on the dock at Le Havre late in June was Gianfranco and his friend, Adamo, who would drive the rented Lancia. Ernest sat in front and Mary and Gianfranco in the back, packed in among the clothes, cameras, and guidebooks. (Although Mary wrote politely of Gian-franco, she had good reason to resent him as Adriana's brother. Sometimes she flirted with him, as a way of getting back at Ernest. Other times she was irritated with him as the Finca's permanent boarder and recipient of her husband's generosity. But with her nearly infinite capacity for adjusting, she made the best of it.)

On this trip, as she sniffed the sweet fragrance of apple orchards and the freshly mown hay, Mary was reminded of her first journey through Normandy in August 1944, when the flags were waving outside the village cafés and the roads were clogged with convoys. After a few days' rest in Paris, the four travelers climbed back into the Lancia for the drive south. It was a misty July 3 and the damp-ness went to the marrow. They crossed the border at Irún and like Hadley and Pauline before her Mary made the ritual journey through the land of *The Sun Also Rises*, faithfully describing in her diary the square stone farmhouses of Navarre, the forests of beech trees north of San Sebastian, and the Basque shepherds watching over their flocks. In Pamplona a friend of Jack Hemingway's—Peter Buckley—alerted Ernest to the presence of a brilliant new matador, Antonio Ordoñez. Mary was as ecstatic over his performance as Hadley had been with his father's, Ordoñez senior, in 1925. "He did the most brilliant passes," she wrote in an unwitting imitation of Ernest's style, "slow and sure. . . . he was luminous between the great horns, and the bull died bravely."

At the conclusion of the Fiesta, Gianfranco left for Venice and Adamo drove Mary and Ernest on to Madrid. "We stayed at the Hotel Florida where I had lived with Martha during the siege of the town and there were no ghosts," Ernest wrote later to Berenson. As the day of his fifty-fourth birthday approached, Mary went on a hunt for presents, persuading a jeweler to take the gold and jade medallions from an antique bracelet for a pair of cufflinks. After returning to Paris to gather up their stored luggage, they drove to Marseilles to board the British vessel, *Dunnottar Castle*, for the voyage to Mombasa.

From September 1, 1953, when the Hemingway safari left Philip Percival's Kitanga Farm for the Southern Game Reserve in the Kajaido District forty miles south of Nairobi, until January 26, 1954, when she flew out of Entebbe, Uganda, with Patrick, Mary kept a diary that recorded—among other things—the sounds and smells of Africa, the landscape and the weather, the habits of animals and birds, and the life of the Masai. She liked the workman-like clothes, the well-prepared food, the long gin-drinking in front of the fire. She and Ernest always found an excuse to finish a bottle. Either the hunting was good, which rated a celebration, or it was bad and the disappointment was drowned in gin.

In contrast to their chaste life on the *Pilar*, in Africa Mary compared their love-making to "little private carnivals." Ernest praised her in blunt terms to Lanham, to his sons, and to others whom he trusted. At various times he had complained about Pauline and Martha as sex partners, but even when he was flirting with other women or pining for Adriana, he reported that Mary was good in bed. Mary's own needs seemed well-served by Ernest and she was proud of her ability to satisfy him sexually. In her autobiography she recorded the entry Ernest made in her African diary on December 20, 1953. Their thrice-daily love-making at Torcello, he wrote, had been "the loveliest time Papa ever knew of."

Philip Percival had come out of retirement to direct the safari, and Mary, like Pauline twenty years ago, thought him wonderful. Assisting him on an impromptu basis was a young British conservationist from the Kenya Game Department, Denis Zaphiro, who was so taken with Ernest that he attached himself to the group. Earl Theisen was standing by for the pictures of a triumphant Hemingway grinning over his fallen game. On September 10, the day that they were to move on to Kimana Swamp, Ernest shot his first lion. But it was not a good show. Mary, creeping along behind him, heard the shot but no roar and no fall. The wounded beast disappeared into the brush, a dangerous circumstance. Later in the morning Denis finished him off with two shots and Ernest received the congratulations of the safari boys. The next day, Mario Menocal, Sr., who had come from Cuba to hunt with the Hemingway party for six weeks, felled his lion with one bullet. The comparison became disturbing. Ernest, whose normal skill was entirely adequate to African shooting, was performing ineptly. Menocal, a seasoned sportsman but not the world-famous author Theisen had come to photograph, was having a phenomenal run of luck—at least he modestly attributed it to luck.

Mary was too loyal to dwell on Ernest's difficulties. She called Mario their good provider for the game he routinely brought into camp but barely hinted that she might be getting continuous hell from Ernest for his troubles, which was the way it came across to Menocal. Occasionally Ernest was contrite for his callous treatment of her. But most of the time he rationalized that she could take it and what he was doing could not be all bad since she looked healthy and happy.

Mary's own shooting was dismal at first and only slightly better as time passed, no matter how much she practiced. But having chosen to be worshipful little brother, out to please heroic big brother, she was not going to let him down. Each time the village boys brought news of lion tracks, Mary scrambled into the land rover with the men and crawled through scrub and grass in the roasting sun behind the trackers. Sometimes they would come upon the lion and she would fire, only to hit the dirt in front of him. Sometimes he would not appear at all and she would dream about him at night. At last, on the late afternoon of December 5, a thin, irritable male was lured from his den. With Denis shouting instructions she got the lion's left shoulder in her sights, lost him, then found him again and sent the bullet of her Mannlicher 6.5 into his right hind leg. Denis's larger bullet broke his spine. Hearing the noise and shouting, everyone at the base camp drove out to the bush, shouting and singing and beating on tin pans. They had waited a long time to celebrate Memsa'ab's *piga* (hit).

By this time Ernest had decided to go native. He shaved his head, carried a spear, dyed his English wool jackets and Abercrombie shirts the Masai orange-pink, and began to flirt with the local women. When Mary flew with Roy Marsh to Nairobi for holiday shopping, Ernest invited Debba, his favorite, and several of her friends into his tent for a celebration so vigorous that the cot collapsed. When Ernest chose Debba for his fiancée, Mary tartly suggested that Debba have a much-needed bath.

Ernest's Christmas present to Mary was an aerial journey over the Serengeti Plain, Lake Albert, and Murchison Falls in a Cessna 180. On the first afternoon, as they flew over Ngorongoro Center, Ernest pointed out the spot where Pauline had killed her lion in 1933. Roy Marsh, the pilot, dipped low enough for Mary to take pictures. At noon on the third day, January 23, as they circled Murchison Falls, a flight of ibis suddenly crossed the path of the plane. The pilot dived deeply to avoid the birds but then struck an abandoned telegraph wire that stretched across the gorge and crash-landed among low trees and bushes. Miraculously the plane did not catch fire and Roy ordered them out safely. Mary tried to help the men set up a camp on a nearby rise in the terrain, but after a few staggering trips back and forth to the plane in the pounding heat she gave up and lay down on top of her raincoat on the hard sand. By nightfall most of the gear had been removed from the aircraft and a stack of firewood gathered to see them through the night. For supper they drank whiskey and ate bits of corned beef from the meager supply of tinned food. There were a few feeble jokes. Ernest called it an unscheduled chance to camp out, and Roy offered to bring Mary some engine oil to cleanse her face in lieu of cold cream. But mostly they were aching and cold and worrying about attracting elephants.

In the early morning stillness Roy constructed a huge wooden arrow that pointed to the fallen plane, and Ernest searched for more firewood. Mary was still resting when Ernest reappeared with the news that he had spotted a large white boat coming up the river below them. They waved their raincoats frantically but could not get the attention of the passengers who by that time were sauntering ashore. They could not make a dash from their campsite for the boat landing for fear of running into elephants. Then some passengers from the ship climbed the hill toward them. The boat was the *Murchison*, chartered for the day by a British surgeon from Kampala. The East Indian skipper agreed reluctantly, and for an exorbitant fee, to take Mary, Ernest, and Roy aboard as passengers.

It was late afternoon when the *Murchison* reached its home port of Butiaba on the eastern shore of Lake Albert. A pilot was waiting to fly the Hemingway party in his old-fashioned De Havilland Rapide biplane to Entebbe, where an impatient press corps was waiting. The word had gone around the world that Ernest and Mary were dead. A BOAC Argonaut, crossing near the falls, had reported the wreckage and no sign of survivors. Mary, exhausted from the ordeal, wondered why they could not sleep in Butiaba and fly out the next morning. But the pilot seemed eager to get started and they taxied off, lifted, set down, lifted again, "like a grasshopper," and set down again, "bumping" crazily, wrote Mary. Finally they crashed to a stop, the plane creaking and cracking, and flames shooting up outside the windows. Mary fumbled with her seat belt and then escaped through a window cracked open by Roy Marsh, who squeezed behind her. Ernest, too bulky for the small window, butted his way through the jammed door.

Ernest had saved himself from burning to death, but his skull was fractured and he suffered grievous internal injuries that were not diagnosed until he reached Venice weeks later. (Among the injuries were a ruptured liver, spleen, and kidney, temporary loss of vision in one eye and the hearing of one ear, a crushed vertebra, paralysis of the sphincter, and first-degree burns.) Mary, having survived two crashes with nothing more than a few sprains and some broken ribs, could think of nothing beyond the fact that they were alive. They were driven from the airstrip to the town of Masindi, fifty miles away, where several bush pilots who had been searching for them rushed them into the hotel bar for a celebration. Too tired to wash away more than the worst of the blood and dirt, they went to sleep to the sound of hyenas howling outside their windows. In the morning Ernest's pillow was soaked with cerebral fluid. A local doctor cleaned them up a bit and Roy Marsh, who was going to fly to Entebbe, arranged for a railway company car and chauffeur to drive Mary and Ernest. Before departing she persuaded the hotel manager to cash her check and sent a cable to reassure her parents in Gulfport.

When they reached the Lake Victoria Hotel in Entebbe, Mary was ready to crawl gratefully into bed. Ernest, however, kept moving, although he was reeling from the concussion and bleeding internally. Fortified with gin, he talked with airline officials and the press, read cables, and considered how to write up the affair. Patrick arrived from Dar es Salaam with 14,000 shillings and Mary dragged herself down to the bazaar to buy a few essentials—a sweater for Ernest, a basket carryall for herself. Everything they owned that had not burned up in the biplane was stored in Nairobi, which would now be their destination. On January 28, 1954, seven days after taking off on the sight-seeing flight, Ernest flew to Nairobi with Roy Marsh in a new Cessna. Mary could not bring herself to act with such gallantry and refused to fly with Roy. It was one of the rare times in her life when she was sick with fear. She flew instead on a regular East African Airways plane with Patrick.

The first telegram to reach Mary in Nairobi was from Noel Monks, and his concern touched her, especially as Ernest was being more than usually difficult. He greeted well-wishers from his bed before she was even awake in the morning, refused to go out for meals, and drank constantly against the advice of his doctors. Dirty laundry was tossed into corners, empty whiskey bottles lined up on side tables. To escape the general slovenliness and the pounding, repetitive conversation that droned on day and night, Mary attended to the mechanics of replacing burnt documents and bringing snack food to the room. Ernest had some insight into his behavior but could not seem to stop himself. "Due to the cerebral thing," he wrote Berenson, ". . . I say terrible things and hear myself say them. It is no good."

Things were so bad that Mary was glad to get out of Nairobi for a while, if only to make the arrangements for a fishing holiday on the Indian Ocean that had been planned before the crashes. Patrick and Henny drove up to Mombasa to assist her and to navigate the fishing boat, *Lady Faye*, to Shimoni. Percival and Denis and a reassembled safari crew traveled to the new camp with Mary. When Ernest flew down with Roy Marsh she was distressed to see how little he had improved. Although he made the old jokes, he was worn down by pain and spent most of the time sitting in the shade of a veranda.

After the Percivals left, everything deteriorated. Denis decided he was coming down with malaria. The hot winds blew with gale force. Ernest had periodic tantrums that came on without warning. One afternoon he took an unreasoning dislike to the dugout canoe of a neighboring native and shattered it with a piece of driftwood. Mary quickly apologized and promised to reimburse the owner. At breakfast on March 3 Ernest picked a quarrel with Patrick that was so absurd and unfair that Patrick excused himself from the table. At this point Pat concluded that Ernest's concussion and his nonstop drinking were more damaging than anyone realized. When he saw his father in November he had looked well and was clear-headed and sensible, but now he was just very strange. Leaving Shimoni the next day Patrick worried that the condition might not be reversible. A few days after that, Mary and Denis came in from fishing to find Ernest collapsed in his veranda chair, dazed, shaking, and horribly burned all up his legs, stomach, and chest. A bush fire had erupted south of the camp and he foolishly insisted upon joining the firefighters. With his equilibrium still so poor, he had stumbled and fallen into the flames. Mary and Denis applied ointments and bandages and gave him seconal and whiskey. He refused to budge from his chair until camp was dismantled and he boarded the *Lady Faye* for the journey back to Mombasa.

In the weeks that followed the second crash, Ernest had been greatly comforted by letters from Adriana. To conserve money, the women of the family had spent the summer quietly at San Michele. ". . . we try to restore, little by little, this kind of house," she had written. ". . . we dig in the earth in front of the house, we paint chairs, we restore statues, we attach prints to the walls." When the rumor of Ernest's death went around the world, Adriana's feelings, as reflected in her letters of that period and in her memoir, became much more intense. On January 25, the day that her maid came into her bedroom to say that the Hemingways had been killed in Africa, she cried and cried, her heart "heavy like a stone. . . . La vida es una puta," (Life is a bitch) she thought. She upbraided herself for letting gossip ruin everything. "I will publish the letters," she raged, "and show the truth, how much they humiliated him and made him suffer." Then she recalled how she prayed to the Lord that the tragedy had not really happened. It was not fair that she had suffered so much: ". . . hunger and fear, the loss of my father, the loss of San Michele." She remembered a childhood incident in Capri when her pet goat, whom she was leading on a rope, fell. She was terrified that he would choke to death. The more he struggled, the more the rope tightened. But like a miracle, he freed himself from the noose and came back to life. "Are miracles only for children?" she wondered sadly.

Getting up from her bed, where she had been grieving, Adriana walked over to her desk to read, once again, Ernest's letters of the winter. The last one to reach her before the crashes was one in which he described another story of Venice that he wished to write, the real story of their love, a difficult story, yet delicate and discreet. "I cannot do anything but love you," he had written. "I will love you always in my heart and in my heart I cannot do anything about it." A week after escaping with his life, Ernest wrote that he never loved her so much as in the hour of his death. And on February 15 he wrote again, rationalizing that perhaps Mary would understand what had happened to him when he met Adriana, that it was just something that struck him like lightning at the crossroads in Latisana in the rain. He promised her that when he next saw her in Venice he would not act stupidly or cause her any embarrassment.

Adriana in the library at Calle de Remedio, 1963.
Adriana Ivancich

"I went over to my window," Adriana wrote "and gazed out at the rooftops, at the smoke that curled out of the chimneys, and at the birds beating their wings as they flew through the curls of smoke. At that moment the bells of San Marco struck the hour." There were shouts from someplace in the house, and the telephone rang in Adriana's room. On the wire was her great-aunt Clo, who said excitedly that the Hemingways were alive.

Hearing that the ship carrying the Hemingways from Mombasa to Venice had now docked and that Ernest and Mary were at the Gritti, Adriana told her mother that she wished to see them. Dora acquiesced. "It is better that you go with my permission than without it," she said. So Adriana rushed to the hotel. Her recollection is of an emotional reunion in Ernest's room, and that Mary was not present. Ernest had lost twenty pounds, his hair was white, and his big frame looked shrunken. He enveloped her in a tight hug, then looked at her fondly. Adriana struggled to hold back the tears. They talked briefly about the accidents but most of what he said, as recounted by her, related to the damage the book had wrought.

"I'm sorry about the book. . . . You are the last person I would have done any harm to," he said. "You are not the girl in the book . . . and I am not the colonel that died in the car that went on the road from Codroipo to Latisana." He spoke again about the gossip and said that the best ammunition against lies was the truth. Adriana nodded, still fighting back her tears. He repeated that he loved her and wanted to live so that he could see her again, and she listened, knowing that it was all coming to an end.

He moved toward the window that faced the Grand Canal, his back to her. The sun was setting. Against the pink light that suffused the sky and the water his figure loomed larger and darker. "Probably it would have been better," he said, "if I had never met you that day under the rain." He turned to face her. "Two tears shined in his eyes," she wrote. "Other tears fell on his cheeks. 'Look, daughter, look,' he said. 'Now you can tell everybody that you have seen Ernest Hemingway cry.' "

Chapter 31

Mary left Venice ahead of Ernest in mid-April 1954 for a holiday that would take her to Paris, London, and the spring ferias in Seville and Ronda. The separation was to give her a respite from his irascible temperament. She rejoined him a month later in Madrid, feeling much better but disappointed to find him still looking weary and ill. On June 6, they sailed for Havana, their twenty-four pieces of luggage having swelled to eighty-seven! Finally Ernest was listening to his doctors and cutting down on his drinking, but Mary did not notice any appreciable improvement in his treatment of her. When she could not remember where in the suitcases his favorite pocketknife was, he yelled out in the ship's dining room that she was a thief! Taking no notice of the insult that sent a hush across the nearby tables, she calmly finished her coffee.

As their ship approached Havana, Mary realized that thirteen months was too long to be away from home. She had barely started to unpack, however, when the news came from Gulfport that her father was very ill again and her mother too weak to look after him. In the sweltering Delta heat she dismantled their cottage and moved them to a mansion-turned-nursing home. It was clean and well-managed, the menu was varied, and the attendants kindly. Even so, Mary was apprehensive. The patient faces of her elderly parents were a silent accusation. She rationalized that her job was to look after Ernest, and she could not also look after them. But a sense of guilt dogged her.

She returned to the Finca in time to celebrate Ernest's fifty-fifth birthday. He was now strong enough to do some fishing and he returned to his writing. On the morning of October 28, he woke her with the news that he had been awarded the Nobel Prize—"The Swedish thing," as he sheepishly called it. Mary jumped up to hug and kiss him, her mind flashing to the kitchen and the realization that the place would soon be mobbed. The news was already being broadcast over local radio. Three American wire services, along with Swedish correspondents and Havana reporters, were calling for interviews. Cuban and American television people would be on hand to take pictures. Ernest spent hours talking to the press. A dozen people were served lunch. In the afternoon he broadcast a short speech for local consumption.

During the next few months tourists came to the Finca in droves. Ernest tried to convince himself that such intrusions would soon end. He knew that the publicity, coming so soon after the plane crashes, was bad for him and bad for his work. He had already made it clear that he would not go to Stockholm to accept the prize in person and on Saturday, December 11, his official acceptance speech was read at the Nobel Prize proceedings by the U.S. Ambassador, John Cabot.

> No writer who knows the great writers who did not receive the prize can accept it other than with humility. . . . For a true writer each book should be a new beginning where he tries again for something that is beyond attainment. He should always try for something that has never been done or that others have tried and failed. Then sometimes, with great luck, he will succeed.

Mary received New Year's greetings from Denis Zaphiro in Kenya. ". . . I can still see you dancing in the carpet of white flowers," he wrote, "whirling round and round. . . . You were laughing happily like a small child surrounding itself with make-believe, wrapping the moment up forever in joy. . . ." Such moments had been all too rare in Mary's life since the accidents. On February 17, 1955, came one of the saddest moments of all—the phone call from Gulfport that her father was dead at eighty-five. She had scarcely unpacked after returning from the funeral when her mother began to make new demands. She was unhappy in Gulfport and wished Mary to move her back to Minneapolis. Mary tried to discourage this but Ernest said that she might as well give in or there would be no peace, and at the end of July she went to Gulfport to supervise Adeline's move. Mary was grateful to Ernest for his consideration. Suddenly they seemed close again. When that happened she could cope with anything.

During the fall Ernest developed a kidney infection and went to bed for two months with nephritis and hepatitis. After recovering he tried to work but was bitterly disappointed with his lack of progress and resented Mary's determination to protect his privacy. When Jack and Puck Hemingway moved to Havana so that Jack could join the Cuban office of Merrill Lynch, Puck felt that Mary resisted visits from her and Jack. Mary and Ernest were alone a great deal—especially when the weather was bad. It was inevitable for Ernest to become bored. He craved stimulus and wanted to learn from others, as well as teach them. Whoever called up from Havana was immediately invited for lunch—not by Mary but by Ernest— and friends who did show up were encouraged to stay for days, even weeks.

In March 1956 a Hollywood crew arrived to film the land sequence for *The Old Man and the Sea*. In June Earl Theisen of *Look* came to the Finca to do a photographic study and Ernest agreed to write the text and picture captions. With the $5,000. that *Look* would pay him he could take Mary to Spain. He was worried about her health. She had a persistent anemia that had not yet yielded to treatment. After she had blood transfusions, he wrote Berenson, they would come to Europe.

Two weeks later he was moved to write Berenson again, this time to explain his current sentiments about Martha, who was seldom far from his thoughts. A visit from Alan Moorehead, who reported seeing her in London, stirred up old animosities. Ernest repeated his oft-stated complaints: that Martha was too ambitious, and that she had made a fool of him. But he was glad, he wrote Berenson, that she had married a man who was rich and known to be extremely nice.

Ernest did proceed with his plan to take Mary to Spain, and they sailed from New York in late August 1956 on the *Ile de France*. Their chauffeur for this European tour was another friend of Gianfrano's. Their hotel in El Escorial, some miles north of Madrid, was the Felipe Segundo. In the crisp fall air Mary enjoyed a relaxed pace of sight-seeing and late morning breakfast trays. Not so Ernest. He drank punishing amounts of liquor and wine, held court for friends and the strangers and sycophants who now besieged him whenever he appeared, and seemed to have no concern for his health. It was not until Mary required medical attention for an attack of colitis that he agreed to be examined as well. His cholesterol level and blood pressure were high and his liver was functioning badly. Reluctantly he promised to cut down on alcohol and follow a low-fat diet. They returned to Paris on November 17 and sailed back to New York after the New Year.

Nearly four months of torrential spring rains kept the number of house guests at the Finca to a minimum in 1957. In the summer Denis Zaphiro brought regards from Patrick, who was now a professional white hunter. Ernest was reasonably satisfied with his older sons but continually aggravated by Gigi. When Gig sent his father a tele-gram of congratulations for winning the Nobel Prize, Ernest, knowing that Gigi had suffered financial reverses, sent him a check for $5,000. But as Gigi's problems compounded, Ernest lost all patience with him.

In the fall Mary persuaded Ernest to fly with her and Denis to New York. Ernest agreed, although he claimed to find the city sterile. Mary was sorry to see Denis sail back to Africa—he had become her friend—but back at the Finca in November she tried to be satisfied with a reasonable amount of harmony between her and Ernest. Then, on the last day of the year, Western Union tele-phoned another of the messages that brought bad news—Adeline Welsh, who had been living in a nursing home in Prescott, Wiscon-sin, was dead. Quickly Mary made all arrangements long-distance and then flew to Wisconsin for her mother's funeral. Returning to Chicago on the train she was comforted by the snowy landscape outside the window. If she felt a sense of isolation that comes from the death of a surviving parent, she made no mention of it in her diary.

Since his return from Paris Ernest had been experimenting with a work that was emerging as a memoir. "If the reader prefers, this book may be regarded as fiction," he wrote in the preface to *A Moveable Feast*. "But there is always the chance that such a book of fiction may throw some light on what has been written as fact." The heroine of these Paris sketches is Hadley of the "gently modeled face," selfless and devoted. When Ernest uses the words "my wife," they strike the reader with a special poignance, coming as they do from the pen of a man who has gone on to three more wives, who is burned out, quarrelsome, and aging too rapidly. " . . . my wife and my son and his cat, F. Puss, all of them happy and a fire in the fireplace. . . . " Ernest felt lucky in those times but like a fool did not knock on wood, though "There was wood everywhere in that apartment. . . . " Writing of the false spring that came to Paris ahead of the bitter March rains, he wonders how he could have been so foolish, so innocent, so full of confidence. He had seemed not to know that " . . . nothing was simple there, not even poverty, nor sudden money, nor the moonlight, nor right and wrong nor the breathing of someone who lay beside you in the moonlight."

It is a moving tribute, romantic and idealized and no doubt deeply felt. But the underside of this paean to Hadley is a self-serving attack on Pauline. In the final manuscript, signed by Ernest with the dates January 12–February 15, 1961, and published posthumously by Scribners in 1964, Ernest describes Pauline as the

> . . . unmarried young woman [who] becomes the temporary best friend of another young woman who is married, goes to live with the husband and wife and then unknowingly, innocently and unrelentingly sets out to marry the husband. When the husband is a writer and doing difficult work so that he is occupied much of the time . . . the arrangement has advantages until you know how it works out. The husband has two attractive girls around when he has finished work. One is new and strange and if he has bad luck he gets to love them both.

In the Hemingway collection at the Kennedy Library are the unpublished "starts and incompletes" that preceded this final draft. Many of these fragments enlarge upon Ernest's regret for the breakup of his first marriage, his anger at Pauline for precipitating it, and the bitter memories of his own misery. But there are other deleted passages that express a much different point of view about Pauline, one that implicitly supports Ernest's remark to his brother and others that she may have been the best wife of all.

> . . . I never worked better nor was I happier [than he was after Hadley remarried and he felt free of remorse]. . . . I loved the girl [Pauline] truly

and she loved me truly and well. And we had as good a life together for many years as early Paris had been. . . . There is no mention in this book of Pauline on purpose. That would be a good way to end a book on these days except that it was a beginning not an ending. . . . That part, the part with Pauline, I have not eliminated, but have saved for the start of another book. . . . It could be a good book because it tells many things that no one knows or can ever know and it has love, remorse, contrition and unbelievable happiness and the story of truly good work and final sorrow.

Ernest never wrote that book, and his final words about Pauline are the hard judgments of the published version of *A Moveable Feast*, which is an irony since she alone of all the women he loved never transferred her loyalty to another man, whatever the occasional gibes she sent forth or the small acts of revenge to which she succumbed.

Hadley, on the other hand, whose position, because of *A Moveable Feast*, is the most honored, formed a more enduring and more satisfying bond with Paul Mowrer than with Ernest. After Paul retired from journalism he and Hadley bought an old farmhouse in New Hampshire, with a view of Chocorua Mountain that reminded Hadley of the Matterhorn. The area offered the outdoor recreation that they both loved and shared—hiking, fishing, bird-watching. Paul wrote poetry and Hadley played the piano. With congenial friends they formed amateur musical groups. For Hadley there were no regrets. It had happened for the best.

So conflicted was Ernest, however, about his role in his first divorce, that he wrote in acid tones about former friends, blaming the Murphys for introducing him to Pauline and Dos Passos for introducing him to the Murphys. Dos, his former friend, is singled out as the pilot fish, " . . . sometimes a little deaf, sometimes a little blind . . . [with] the irreplaceable early training of the bastard and a latent and long denied love of money. . . . " who introduced the innocent Hemingway to the predatory rich. Such a hatchet job cannot be explained away entirely, however, by Dos's connection with Pauline and the Murphys. In 1948 Katy Smith Dos Passos had been killed in a horrible automobile accident, when Dos Passos, losing his perspective in the setting sun as he drove her from Provincetown to Boston, crashed into a parked truck. Katy, almost decapitated, died on the way to the hospital. Dos was permanently blinded in his right eye.

Ernest never forgave Dos for Katy's death. His logic was that Dos, with his bad eyesight, should never have been driving in the first place. As if that weren't enough, in 1951 Dos had published a novel, *Chosen Country*, based on Katy's recollections of her summers at Horton Bay and her highly personal opinion of the youthful Hemingway. Ernest raged over the contents. "He's killed her off," he groaned, "and now he's stealing my material." But if Ernest was angry that he showed up in Dos Passos's book as a surly youth with dirty fingernails, perhaps he should have blamed Katy, not Dos.

The two women who come in for the most biting criticism, besides Pauline, are Gertrude Stein and Zelda Fitzgerald. With Stein it was a straightforward act of revenge. In her own autobiography, published in 1933, Gertrude asserts that she and Sherwood Anderson had more or less created Hemingway, the writer, and that Ernest, being "yellow," could not face Anderson after he betrayed his friendship by writing *Torrents of Spring*. Ernest in turn draws an unflattering portrait of Gertrude as a hysterical lesbian helplessly dependent on her companion, Alice B. Toklas.

With Zelda, however, it was more than revenge. In Scott's behalf, Ernest had taken for himself the right to judge her, as he had always considered himself fit to judge people. With women like Zelda (and perhaps Grace Hemingway), whom he perceived as dominating their husbands, it was one-sided judgment—no mercy, little consideration for extenuating circumstances.

By this time the Fitzgeralds were both dead, Scott of a heart attack in 1940, Zelda in a hospital fire in 1948. Ernest's private opinion since the Paris days had been that Zelda was pathologically jealous of Scott's work and talent, that she was secretly pleased when he got drunk, because it stopped him from working, and that she derided him sexually (this on Scott's testimony). Now he declared in his manuscript that Scott would not write anything more that was good until after he knew she was insane. It was left for Zelda's biographer, Nancy Milford, to look for other reasons than Zelda's instability alone to explain the tangle of the Fitzgerald marriage. Zelda's jealousy of Scott's work came out of her own desperate search for an identity. And Scott's jealousy of Zelda extended to a form of ownership in which he claimed her life as the raw material of his fiction.

Mary read the sketches for *A Moveable Feast* as Ernest wrote them and then typed the finished drafts. If she was troubled by the intensity of his longing for Hadley, she kept a tight lid on her emotions. Her pragmatic nature helped her settle for what was possible. After his miserable treatment of her during the Adriana period, when she declared passionately that she would never leave him unless (in her words) he came in, sober, in the morning and asked her to, she limited her expectations. In return for a degree of civility, she would be whatever he required. If, in addition, he could do some good work, which he now apparently was doing, that gave her satisfaction.

Ernest's feelings for Mary, however, seemed to be deteriorating. Although he praised her in his letters and they enjoyed some good times now and then, there were more times when he acted like a man who was trapped and squirming for a way to escape. He was old and sick and she was his keeper and he resented it bitterly. Mary was too strong to be driven out and the worst of it for Ernest was that he was afraid to be without her. It was Jack Hemingway who remarked that his father would have made a wonderful old man except that he had never learned how to be one.

Chapter 32

When Mary and Ernest left Cuba for Ketchum, Idaho in September 1958, Fidel Castro and his revolutionary forces were hiding out in Sierra Maestra and the streets of Havana were unusually quiet. Fulgencio Batista, the Cuban dictator, had reinstated censorship to hide the fact that his government was being hard-hit by the rebels. From their servants and from the local villagers, Mary had heard sickening reports of terror and reprisal.

Soon, political events reached a climax. Batista fled the country and Castro formed a new government. On January 2, 1959, twenty-four hours after the leftist victory, Herbert Matthews, on the scene as a *New York Times* writer, cabled Ernest in Idaho that the Finca was safe. Mary was disappointed that Castro did not immediately call for elections, but she agreed with Ernest that the new regime could not possibly be as brutal and corrupt as the old one.

They left for Cuba in mid-March, Ernest having already settled the problem of where to relocate if it ever became too difficult to live under Castro. He had acquired the Robert Topping property in Ketchum for $50,000. It was a two-story concrete chalet standing on a hill overlooking the Wood River. Mary thought it hideous in design and coldly depressing but for the moment was more concerned about the conditions of the Finca. To her great relief, she found that Matthews was right. Nothing had been damaged, the fresh pool water beckoned, and the garden was in full bloom.

But Ernest gave her no time to relax. He accepted the invitation of an old friend, Nathan "Bill" Davis, whom Mary had never met, to visit him and his wife, Annie, at their estate on the Costa del Sol. From the hacienda in Spain, the Hemingways and the Davises would follow the summer ferias, after which Ernest would do a major piece for *Life*. Antonio Ordoñez, Ernest's young favorite, was competing in a series of *mano a mano* corridas with his brother-in-law, the veteran Luis Dominguín. Listening to Ernest's enthusiasm, more that of an eager youth than a man nearing his sixtieth birthday, Mary cooperated, as usual, with his feverish timetable. By April 22 they were in New York and a few days later sailed on the S.S. *Constitution*.

At the port of Algeciras across from Gibraltar, Bill Davis was waiting for them. He stowed their twenty-one pieces of luggage in a Ford sedan, provided them with a picnic lunch, and drove them to La Consula in the countryside west of Malaga. The nineteenth-century mansion rose gracefully behind twin iron gates. Vases of fresh flowers stood in corners and on the polished surfaces of the oak furniture. Fine prints and paintings from Davis's collection were displayed on the white walls. A suitable writing table was located for Ernest's convenience.

During the first ten days at La Consula he roughed out the preface to a new school edition of his short stories. In its initial form the essay was highly discursive, with Ernest commenting informally about the origins of various works. In writing of "The Short Happy Life of Francis Macomber," he asserted that he had known Margot Macomber very well in real life. "I invented her complete with handles from the worst bitch I knew (then) and when I first knew her she'd been lovely. Not my dish, not my pigeon, not my cup of tea, but lovely for what she was and I was her all of the above which is whatever you make of it."

Ernest had not seen Jane Mason since the late thirties. How much he thought about her during the twenty intervening years is not known, but he heard about her from people who did see her. She divorced Grant Mason in 1939 and married John Hamilton in 1940. In 1945 she divorced Hamilton and two years later married George Abel, who was head of the European division of *Time/Life*. To friends that marriage appeared to be a good one. Jack and Puck Hemingway reported seeing her in Paris. "She looked great—

happy, lively, beautiful," they recalled. But it was not until she divorced Abel to marry Arnold Gingrich that Jane found emotional contentment. Years before on Bimini, Arnold had fallen in love with her, and in 1955, nineteen years after they met, they were married.

On the 13th of May, the Hemingway party departed for the ferias at Madrid, Cordoba, and Seville. Normally indefatigable, on this trip Mary was soon hanging on the ropes. Wherever they went they were surrounded by people. Lunch was at four in the afternoon, dinner at midnight. With Davis at the wheel of the Ford, Ernest on the passenger side, a canvas bag of wine between them, and Annie Davis and Mary in the back, they zigzagged across the face of Spain, driving all night, just as the matadors and their cuadrillas did, to make the next afternoon's fight. As he roared into the circuslike atmosphere with an enthusiasm that was becoming manic, Ernest took up the cause of Ordoñez. Mary, feverish and coughing from a respiratory infection, dropped out after Seville and returned to La Consula.

A few days later, much sooner than expected, Ernest and Davis also returned to La Consula, after Ordoñez was severely gored. On June 25 they took off again, as Antonio resumed his schedule—Zaragoza, Alicante, Barcelona. In Ernest's absence Mary began preparing for the lavish party she would give on July 21 for Ernest's and Carmen Ordoñez's joint birthdays and worked up an article for *Sports Illustrated* on Antonio's injury and his recuperation at La Consula. The money from the article would help to finance the party. (Her only other published articles since her marriage had been an occasional photographic essay on life at the Finca with Ernest—one in *Look* in 1950 and a second in *Today's Woman* in 1953.)

The group that would accompany Ernest for most of the summer had formed. Bill Davis did the driving and Aaron Hotchner had been summoned from New York. A nineteen-year-old Irish journalist, Valerie Danby-Smith, who had sought Ernest out for an interview, was seldom far from his side. Her creamy complexion, pink cheeks, and tangled dark hair reminded some people of Goya's Duchess of Alba. As the cavalcade moved to Pamplona, Mary drove with Annie Davis in her car while Valerie sat in the front seat of the Ford between Ernest and Bill. Hotchner rode in the rear seat with the wine, luggage, maps, and picnic supplies. Accommodations in the crowded village were primitive, hardly more than barren dormitory-style rooms, segregating men from women. Ernest averaged three hours of sleep a night, rarely even bothering to return to his room but curling up in the front seat of the Ford. There were seldom fewer than twenty friends—or strangers—at mealtime, with Ernest footing the bill. His massive head with its white beard rose above the crowds who constantly pressed in upon him. The curly white locks were combed forward to hide his baldness. He drank for hours at a stretch. In addition to Valerie, who now assumed the position of private secretary, two schoolteachers from America were made "prisoners" of his mob.

"I was increasingly repelled," Mary wrote, "by the dirty tables, the sour smell of spilled wine . . . and Ernest's endlessly repeated aphorisms." Several times she went off alone to read and rest and nibble on a piece of fruit. Annie Davis found Ernest's adolescent cavorting mildly contemptible, as when he charged into the women's quarters waving a whiskey bottle and displaying his nakedness. Peter Buckley, who was a member of the party and knew Ernest on other occasions to be kind and self-effacing, was disturbed by his rudeness to Mary. Buckley believes that his treatment of her was even worse than she would ever admit. On the afternoon that they went to the Irati River for swimming and a picnic, Mary cracked a toe as she scrambled over some sharp rocks. Ernest, watching her hobble past him, with her toe painfully squeezed into a stiff hiking shoe, nodded to her as though she were a stranger and then turned back to Hotchner to exclaim over the delicious cold food.

If Mary was shaken by such callous treatment, she controlled her anger, writing only that something was changing in him or her or both of them. For the next few days, back at La Consula, she threw all her energies into putting on a first-class birthday celebration. (Ernest's remarks published later in *Life* had a curious twist. "It was quite a party and I might not have noticed I was sixty if Mary had not made it so important and so pleasant. But that party drove it in.") Flamenco dancers entertained to the accompaniment of soft guitars. Japanese lanterns turned the darkness into a fairyland. There were target-shooting booths, photographers, and fireworks. The champagne came from Paris and the Chinese vegetables from London, and Mary cooked the sweet-and-sour sauce for the turkey. The guests gathered from all over Europe and the United States. They included Buck Lanham, David and Evangeline Bruce, Gianfranco and his wife, the Peter Buckleys, Dr. George Saviers from Sun Valley and his wife, and all the celebrants from Pamplona including the American schoolteachers and Valerie Danby-Smith, who sat beside Ernest at the long banquet table.

As the guest who knew Mary the longest, Buck Lanham saw much that was troubling. It was obvious to him, as to everyone present, that she had worked tirelessly to create something special and memorable for Ernest, and equally obvious that he was going out of his way to be cruel to her. He whined that she was spending all his money, when Lanham knew that she had earned most of it from the *Sports Illustrated* article. He accused her of not really breaking her toe and to his men friends referred sniggeringly to their love-making of the night before as just the remedy for her complaints. Lanham felt that he was in the presence not of the towering figure who had indelibly impressed him during the war but of a foolish old man trying to renew his youth with a young girl who could not have developed any real affection for him. Where was Mary's pride, he wondered, that she could allow herself to be so demeaned? Mary was aware of Lanham's concern, for she knew him to be an upright and honorable man. But the only thing she said to him, in a rare moment of candor, was that Ernest's skills as a lover were no longer as noteworthy as he boasted to his friends.

On July 30 at Valencia the first *mano a mano* got underway. (Until that time the two matadors had appeared in separate bull rings on different schedules.) Ernest, Valerie, Davis, and Hotchner traveled from town to town in a new Lancia delivered by Gianfranco. Sometimes Mary and Annie followed, other times they dropped out. After she retired to La Consula for two weeks, Mary received a few tender notes from Ernest, but when she rejoined him late in August she acknowledged that she seemed to have become "inaudible" to him. Even so, the tone of her diary is that of a careful reporter, taking notes on the behavior of a madman with whom she has a nodding acquaintance. When he turned on her savagely after she made some simple request and compared her to his mother who had driven his father to suicide, she recorded the scene without comment.

For the first time since 1950, however, she admitted to herself that she might not be able to stay married. As was her habit, she expressed her misery in understated terms—"pique" was her word.

She would not do anything rash because she still loved Ernest and their home. They separated early in October, Ernest staying in Paris for a while, Mary flying home. From the Finca she mailed another long examination of their problems. Itemizing the instances of neglect and criticism of her, she asked whether he really had any more need of her in his life and offered to move to New York, where she would rent an apartment of her own.

Ernest cabled that he still loved her and to postpone such a drastic decision. At the airport in Havana, accompanied by Carmen and Antonio Ordoñez, he presented her with a diamond pin. Mary wasn't sure that another present meant anything was going to change, but she concentrated on being a proper hostess and flew out ahead of Ernest and the guests to put the Ketchum house in order. The Ordoñez visit was brief, and after their departure Mary began to believe that a quiet routine of work and recreation would have a beneficial effect on Ernest. The weather was perfect—golden sunlight, bracing air—and Ernest returned to working on the piece for *Life*.

But Mary's optimism was dashed by yet another of her unfortunate injuries. On the afternoon of November 27, while shooting ducks with Ernest and George Saviers, she tripped over a root on the slick, frozen ground. Her left elbow took the brunt of the fall, the bones cracking, to quote Dr. Saviers, like the shell of a turkey egg hit by a mallet. Ernest was childishly unsympathetic. During the drive to Sun Valley Hospital he scolded her for moaning from the pain, which was excruciating. He was annoyed that she had to stay overnight after the surgery. And in the weeks that followed he grumbled constantly that he was doing the work of servants (driving to the market, helping her to undress, and so forth). A week before Christmas the elbow had to be broken and reset because it was not healing properly.

After the New Year, heavy snow blanketed the slopes and Ernest fumed that he could not get the exercise he needed. Mary noticed how little he was sleeping, and though he was laboring over the notes of the summer, what resulted displeased him. She continued to assume, however, that this mood would pass, as others had. But then something happened which she conceded was different.

At the Arnolds' one snowy night, as everyone was enjoying a roast beef dinner, Ernest began to notice that there were lights inside a local bank down the hill. As he stared out the window toward the distant building, he concluded that someone was checking his accounts. "They" were trying to get something on him, he insisted. Tillie Arnold suggested that "they" were the cleaning crew, but he ignored her. When Mary pressed him to explain, he said that the FBI was investigating him.

Later, on the way home, he became so concerned about the heavy snowfall that Lloyd finally stopped the car to put chains on the snow tires. As jarring as the evening was, Mary refused to theorize beyond the admission that it was strange. "I would never presume to intrude on his private brain," she said heatedly in an interview many years later. "All I could say is what he said. . . . I would consider it bad form to presume anything about what really went on inside his head. I would never speculate about what Ernest was actually thinking when he said something." Such an unwillingness to speculate surely put her at a disadvantage when she was faced with such erratic behavior. Her mindset was for the concrete, not the intuitive, and she had always given priority to facts. If the facts were contradictory, her tendency was to wait for something clear-cut to emerge.

In February the flowers around the Finca were in bloom, but the house was freezing as cold winds blew in from the north. Mary had daily physical therapy for her aching and stiffened elbow. Ernest spent more and more hours on the *Life* article, expanding an assignment that called for 10,000 words to 100,000. He summoned Valerie Danby-Smith from Dublin to take care of his typing and correspondence. Mary welcomed her cordially, grateful for anyone who could divert Ernest.

Aaron Hotchner, who came in June to help Ernest prune the manuscript, noticed that he had, at least for the moment, let up on his abuse of Mary. In all other respects it was a grinding four days. Ernest protested every one of Hotchner's suggestions for deletion, handing him incomprehensible lists of objections, yet at the same time he seemed anxious to deliver an acceptable draft to *Life*. Finally they produced an abridged version of 60,000 words and Hotchner prepared to carry it to New York. On the way to the airport Ernest confided his anguish about money. For years he had accepted advances from Scribners to meet tax payments but this year the idea seemed to terrify him. Pleading poverty, he persuaded Hotchner to try to change the contractual arrangements with *Life*. Hotchner, who had made many deals for Hemingway, knew that he was now a rich man but rationalized that he was expressing insecurities from the days when there were long droughts between sales. In New York he negotiated with the managing editor of *Life* to pay Ernest $90,000. instead of the $10,000. originally agreed upon and located an apartment for the Hemingways to use when they came to Manhattan.

Ernest had decided that he must return to Spain to make a final swing with Ordoñez, select some photographs, and verify a few unsubstantiated facts. Mary had no wish to go and he did not try to change her mind. With most of her friends no longer in Cuba, she decided to wait for him in New York. Assuming that she would return in a few months she packed up nothing but clothes.

In Miami there occurred another of those paranoid episodes to which Mary applied the misnomer "disproportionately large tizzy." Valerie, who was traveling with them, had not renewed her visitor's visa. Ignoring everyone's assurance that there would be no trouble, Ernest called the Office of Immigration in Key West repeatedly for clearance, and even when these officials made light of it he was not mollified. Finally he gave in and boarded the plane. For Mary and Valerie and all the luggage, three compartments were reserved on the Miami-to-New York train.

The apartment rented by Hotchner was an imposing two-story townhouse. Mary eyed all the possibilities for redecorating, but Ernest seemed scarcely aware of his surroundings. For the first time in his life he wanted no mention made of his birthday. He set up a card table in the living room for conferences and Mary prepared his meals. Valerie, who was staying at the Barbizon Hotel for Women, came over frequently, but he was too depressed to take an interest in her or anything else. The only time Hotchner remembered a smile breaking through his mask of apprehension was when Charles Scribner Jr. and Ernest's editor, Harry Brague, praised "The Dangerous Summer" and the Paris sketchbook as simply wonderful. Like Mary, Hotchner clung to such moments as evidence that his friend would soon recover his old spirit. But most signs pointed otherwise. Ernest prepared dozens of lists for himself, for Hotchner, and for Mary before finally boarding the overnight TWA jet for London and Madrid on August 4. And with a sudden manic delusion, he put a price of $900,000. on some Nick Adams stories that 20th Century-Fox wanted to buy for a film.

Mary now looked forward to a respite from the excruciating tension, even admitting that an interlude without Ernest could be pleasant. But on August 8 there was a radio report that he had taken ill in the bull ring at Malaga. Although she could not confirm this news with any of the wire services, Mary immediately booked two separate flights. After the 8:00 P.M. flight had left, but before 10:00 Associated Press announced that Mr. Hemingway had denied the earlier report. Moments later a cable from Granada verified the dispatch. "REPORTS FALSE ENROUTE MADRID LOVE PAPA." Mary cried with relief and then spent the rest of the night calling to reassure worried friends who had heard the same bad news.

Among the people Mary phoned were Toby and Betty Bruce. Betty, who worked at the library in Key West, made a remark about Hemingway's illness in the presence of another librarian—a tall, jolly, attractive woman. To Betty's surprise the woman, Agnes Stanfield, asked if it was true that Ernie had suffered a heart attack. Betty said that anyone who referred to Ernest as "Ernie" must have known him very well and for a very long time. Agnes said yes, she had known him quite well, in Italy, during the First World War. She had some wonderful photographs of the two of them in Milan and would be pleased to give them to Betty, if she was in touch with Ernest.

During the war Agnes had worked in New York at the Fifth Avenue blood bank. After the war she and her husband, now returned from service, had moved to Key West. So it was a quirk of geography that for nearly fifteen years Agnes had been living less than a mile from the Hemingway house on Whitehead Street and ninety miles from the Finca.

Subsequently Betty Bruce wrote Ernest about the photographs, assuming that he would be interested. Instead he said that she should send them to Scribners. Now Betty was embarrassed. How could she explain his rebuff to Agnes? When she did, stumbling a bit to sound tactful, Agnes burst out laughing. Of course he would be angry. He had never forgiven her, she explained, for turning him down when he was nineteen.

After Ernest's reassuring cablegram on the eighth of August his letters began to sound worse and worse. Mary continued to blame

The house in Ketchum, Idaho, overlooking the Wood River.
From the John F. Kennedy Library

The final days. Ernest and Mary with Tillie Arnold (back to camera), 1961.
John Bryson

his problems on fatigue and overwork. Yet even after Valerie flew to Madrid to act as his secretary, the tone of his letters remained desperate. "I wish you were here to look after me and help me out and keep from cracking up," he wrote on September 23. Still Mary could not grasp the reality of what was happening. Years later she admitted sadly that she had not picked up the warning signals.

Ernest flew out of Madrid on an ancient *Constellation* that took fourteen hours to cross the Atlantic. He explained to Aaron Hotchner, who had come over to visit him for a week, that the slower plane, being less crowded, might give him better security than the new, more popular jet aircraft. From Bill Davis and Annie, Hotchner learned what a nightmarish two months they had endured. Ernest had been irritable beyond belief, and so suspicious that he believed Davis wanted to drive him off a cliff. Along with the others, Hotchner had watched helplessly while Ernest postponed the flight for four days, staying in bed most of the time.

When Ernest came off the plane in New York, Mary found him less agitated than he had reportedly been in Spain, but withdrawn. She tried to pry him loose from seclusion, but he only murmured that unknown agents were after him. The question of consulting a psychiatrist was apparently not raised. Though he used the word "crack-up" in referring to his own situation, he could not admit the need for a "head doctor." The old prejudice—that one fought out such conflicts alone, that it was cowardly to seek help—still dominated his thinking. So he rejected the one possibility that might have offered him some relief. Mary, knowing this, was unwilling to challenge him. Instead she summoned all her organizational and persuasive powers to get him on the train for Idaho. Perhaps in the safety of his own house (many people, including his sons, have since noted the fortresslike character of that residence) he would be able to shed some of his delusions.

That was not to be the case, however. In Ketchum he did rally briefly, enough to dictate a few letters and to send Valerie the money for her tuition at the American Academy of Dramatic Arts. But the fixation about the FBI continued to haunt him. He was convinced that he was poor. Even when Mary phoned a vice-president of Morgan Guaranty Trust for a report on all of his various accounts and persuaded him to listen on the extension, Ernest insisted that the banker was "covering up something."

At this point, in mid-November 1960, Mary was ready to admit that something was terribly wrong. When Hotchner offered to consult a prominent New York psychiatrist, who might be able without seeing the patient to suggest the proper approach, Mary agreed. The psychiatrist, Dr. James Cottell, arranged for Ernest to be hospitalized at the Mayo Clinic in Rochester, Minnesota. His first choice was the Menninger Clinic, but Mary knew that Ernest would not go there voluntarily. Dr. Cottell said that his physical complaints justified his being admitted to the Mayo Clinic. After he was examined the psychiatrists could enter his case.

In the utmost secrecy (Mary, as much as Ernest, feared the adverse publicity) Ernest was flown to Rochester on November 30. Mary followed by commercial airliner and bus. They took the name of Mr. and Mrs. George Saviers. From her room at the Kahler Hotel in Rochester, Mary wrote Patrick that his father was there for a thorough examination and that most of the tests so far looked good. She said nothing to Patrick about Ernest's emotional state but merely suggested that he had been hospitalized because of high blood pressure.

Believing that some of Ernest's depressive symptoms resulted from the prolonged use of reserpine, an antihypertensive drug used to lower blood pressure, the medical doctors at the Mayo Clinic discontinued the drug. (Dr. Gregory Hemingway ["Gigi"] pointed out in 1976 that the depressive effects of reserpine can last for months after the drug is discontinued, but he was not sure that this fact was known in 1960.) But when Ernest continued to suffer from delusions and feelings of persecution, Dr. Howard Rome, a senior consultant in the Section of Psychiatry, prescribed and administered a series of electric shock treatments. For Mary it was a dismal time. She lived alone, taking her meals alone as well. Her consuming worry was that Ernest might beguile Dr. Rome into believing he was cured when he wasn't. Much later, among Ernest's papers Mary found a memorandum never delivered to her that dramatically illustrated his paranoia. The letter was his pathetic effort to free Mary of any complicity in the imagined illegal acts for which he expected to be prosecuted by the FBI.

On January 22, 1961, Ernest was discharged. The doctors did not deny that he still clung to some of his delusions, but his growing desire to return to work was, for them, the predominant element in their positive evaluation. His return to Ketchum, however, and to the pressure of work, was disastrous. Mary made her usual herculean efforts; she prepared appetizing meals and set up an outdoor regimen. Ernest followed the doctors' advice not to drink and went faithfully to his writing table every day. He stayed there for hours and hours, moving the papers back and forth, hardly aware of his surroundings and writing nothing. One of the most heartbreaking episodes was his effort to respond to a request from a woman in Washington who was putting together a volume of handwritten tributes to President John F. Kennedy. Every afternoon after lunch he was at his desk, moving his pen uncertainly across the blank pages in an effort to put a few sentences together. The tension was so unbearable that Mary could not stay in the room with him. It took him a week to write a four-line tribute.

As Ernest became more reclusive and fearful, he developed a fresh worry—the conviction that his Paris manuscript was vulnerable to lawsuits. He decided suddenly to call Hadley, who was spending the winter at a ranch in Arizona. "I was called to the phone," she wrote later, "away from my lunch. I ran to the cabin. Curiously enough I had been thinking of Ernest, although I had not heard from him in a long time. It was E. and I felt happy to hear his voice. He said 'hello Tatie,' and that he was pleased to get in touch with me but though all he said was kind and friendly, the tone was sad and utterly mirthless." Ernest went on to describe the book he was doing about their early years and asked what she could remember of certain people. They talked on for a while and Hadley supplied some addresses. They spoke of Jack and Puck and their children and how nice it was that Jack was successful in his business. After the conversation ended, Hadley continued to be troubled by the hopelessness beneath Ernest's polite questioning.

Every day at noon Dr. Saviers stopped by to check Ernest's blood pressure. As they sat beside each other on the sofa in the living room, the doctor would offer bits of homely philosophy. What he was trying loyally and sensibly to do, even though he described himself as a plain country doctor, was to offer some simple psychotherapy. Sometimes Ernest's cheeks would be wet with tears as he explained pitifully how he could not write anymore. It just wouldn't come.

In the evenings as they prepared to go to bed, Ernest would become more voluble, reproaching Mary for imagined misdeeds—

later, "and the burden on her was impossible." Mary brought some of this upon herself when she insisted upon taking exclusive responsibility for Ernest's care. But whatever her degree of devotion, she did not perceive the depth of the crisis and would not commit him to a mental institution against his will.

Late in June she made her last trip to the Mayo Clinic, was ushered into Dr. Rome's office, and was shaken to see Ernest sitting there wearing street clothes, "grinning like a Cheshire cat." Dr. Rome was discharging his patient. All of Mary's fears had materialized. Ernest had indeed conned the doctor into believing he was recovered. But with her husband gazing at her a few feet away, she could do nothing except capitulate. George Brown, Ernest's friend who ran a Manhattan gym, flew out to drive them back to Idaho.

The first day's trip by rented car was uneventful. But by the second day Ernest was worrying about the wine they were carrying, convinced that state troopers would arrest them. Then he began to insist that if they did not stop at noon (for the night) there would be no motel space. Mary and George never argued but worked around his anxieties until on the late afternoon of June 30, 1961, they reached the Ketchum house.

After Ernest's first suicide attempt on April 21, Mary had taken the precaution of removing all the guns to a storage room in the cellar. She did not hide the keys because she decided that "no one had a right to deny a man access to his possessions." With other keys, they remained on the windowsill. It was a decision that in retrospect would bring her terrible grief and guilt.

The next night the Hemingways took George and Mary Saviers to downtown Ketchum for dinner. When Ernest decided that the two men in city clothes at a nearby table were FBI agents, Mary simply shrugged. She had heard so much of that that it had become almost a meaningless refrain. At bedtime she undressed in her large bedroom. From the back bedroom Ernest joined her in some loud singing of Italian folksongs. His "Good night, my kitten" carried no note of anxiety. Many nights he shared her big bed. This night he slept alone in the smaller room.

At nearly half-past seven the next morning, a cloudless Sunday, Mary was awakened out of a deep sleep by what sounded like the banging of two bureau drawers that had been pulled out too far and let fall to the floor. She rose on one elbow and called out to Ernest.

There was no answer. She ran to his room. He was not there, though his bed had been slept in. She rushed down the staircase. In the front entryway the body of her husband lay, clad in the red "Emperor's" robe she had sewn for him long ago in Italy; a shotgun was between his legs. Blood and disintegrated flesh speckled the hallway ceiling. She ran immediately for George, who was asleep in the guest house, then called the Sun Valley Hospital for any doctor who was on call.

No more than fifteen minutes later, Dr. Scott Earle arrived and determined after a brief examination that Ernest had died of a self-inflicted wound to the head. Shaking violently in every muscle, Mary called friends, who bore her away from the scene. Before taking a tranquilizer she permitted herself a few moments of anger at the violence that had all but destroyed her. But after one night at the Sun Valley Hospital to escape the punishing phone calls, she recovered her composure and it did not seem to her a conscious lie when she told the press that Ernest's death had been "accidental."

In two days the family assembled: Ernest's three sons, his sisters (all save Carol) his brother, Leicester, and a few close friends, including Gianfranco Ivancich. Mary had restored the house to order and not even a stain remained. She had seen to it that all planes were met, that meals were served on time, that the funeral arrangements were organized. Accepting the natural death theory, the officiating priest permitted Ernest to be buried in hallowed ground. With radio and television reporters crowding the entrance to the tiny cemetery and broadcasting a running commentary of the events to an interested world, Mary wrote out entrance permits for the invited participants. Immediately following the graveside service, Alfred Rice, Ernest's lawyer, disclosed the contents of the will. Everything was left to the widow—all cash, securities, real estate in the United States and abroad, and the copyright to all Ernest's published and unpublished works. She would be a rich woman.

For twenty years Mary managed the affairs of the Hemingway estate with shrewdness and tenacity. Soon after his death she negotiated with the Castro government to remove Ernest's literary properties and personal papers safely to the United States and then made a gift of La Finca Vigia to the people of Cuba. She took the full responsibility for reviewing the manuscripts, deciding which of them should be published and which ones withheld. The former included *A Moveable Feast, Islands in the Stream,* and, most recently, *Selected Letters, 1917–1961,* edited by Carlos Baker. Beginning in 1972 she placed all the letters, notes, photographs, and manuscripts in the Kennedy Library and subsequently established the Hemingway award under the aegis of the P.E.N. club for the best first novel in the field of American fiction.

It was not until 1966, when Aaron Hotchner revealed the true circumstances of Ernest's death, that Mary publicly acknowledged the fact of his suicide. In an interview with Italian journalist Oriana Fallaci, published in *Look,* she stated bluntly to the surprised Fallaci that " . . . he shot himself. Just that. . . . For a long time I refused to admit it even to myself. . . . I've never discussed it with a psychiatrist, but I suppose it had something to do with self-defense. . . . admitting the truth would have snapped my nerves." In an uncharacteristic show of emotion, she compared her loss of Ernest to being cast in the darkness of an endless tunnel, and repeated how all alone she was, " . . . alone with publishers, lawyers, alone with the responsibility of Ernest's books, alone with my loneliness."

She was bitter about Hotchner, insisting to Fallaci that he had no right to expose Ernest's disintegration, especially for commercial purposes. Six months earlier she had filed suit to prevent distribution of *Papa Hemingway,* Hotchner's account of his friendship with Ernest, to be published by Random House. Mary contended that Ernest's conversations, which Hotchner used in his book, were protected by common-law copyright, that use of the material was a violation of the trust and confidence placed in Hotchner by her husband, and that, finally, the book violated her own right of privacy in its various allusions to her. In February 1966 Justice Harry B. Frank, of the New York State Supreme Court, delivered an eight-page decision siding with Hotchner. The most important question raised by Mary—the right of privacy—was struck down vigorously. "The right of the public to know" and "the freedom of the press to inform," said Justice Frank, must stand "above considerations of individual privacy in conjunction with factual publications . . . whether authorized or not." He added that Mrs. Hemingway's own right of privacy had been waived because of the fact that she was a "newsworthy person." Her appeal was denied by the Appellate Division but the case dragged on until 1968 when the New York State Court of Appeals finally dismissed her suit.

When asked why she did not remarry, Mary might respond lightly that no one had asked her, then add that sometimes she regretted it, for she did not like to be alone, especially at night. But she kept to a frenetic pace, just as she had done in Ernest's lifetime, and whether out of the loneliness or unresolved conflicts that she could not confront, began to drink more heavily than at any time in the past. She gravitated between the house in Ketchum and an apartment in New York and visited new parts of the world—Australia, Russia, Antarctica, Alaska—as well as Ernest's haunts—Paris, Venice, Spain, Kenya.

Mary did return to journalism, on a free-lance basis, but her subject was always Hemingway—his manuscripts, his travels, his habits. In 1976 she published her autobiography, *How It Was*, and went on a strenuous book tour across the country to promote it. The critics were generally not enthusiastic. It is hard to imagine that Mary, tough as she is, was not hurt, even though on a literary level the criticism was probably justified. As a journalist she had insisted that facts must speak for themselves, but she loaded the pages with unnecessary details and then zealously guarded them against the efforts of an editor. (She took the manuscript away from Scribners, who wanted to make many changes, and gave it to Knopf, who agreed to print it as she had written it.) The book has a certain rough honesty and inadvertent humor, as when she explains that she kept her diary of dates, places, birds, fish, people, and daily weather reports because she thought such data would be useful to Ernest, only to find out that he needed none of it—he had a "tape-recorder" in his head. Stuck with the diaries, she decided to publish them.

Most exasperating to the reader is Mary's extreme reluctance to pause for reflection or examine her feelings. (The burst of passion in the Fallaci interview was not to be repeated.) But this is a matter of character, not style. In not allowing Scribners to tinker with it, she may have provided a better perspective on her basic personality than if, at some editor's urging, she had written a sophisticated psychological analysis.

Mary's recent public appearances have been rare. She did not attend the dedication of the Hemingway Room at the Kennedy Library in 1980 and her attorney, Alfred Rice, acts as her representative in all matters having to do with the Hemingway Foundation. In 1979, however, she acquiesced to a visit from the author. On a quiet, hot September afternoon the two women sat together on the deck of the Hemingway house in Ketchum. Mary was small and frail in blue slacks and floral print blouse. Her elbow was in a sling. She had injured it again—the same elbow that had cracked after a fall in the icy woods in 1960. Her lovely skin was weathered and heavily veined, her eyes red-rimmed and watery. But her voice was still musical, and she seemed faintly amused that anyone would travel so far to see her, especially since she could remember so little about the past. The afternoon waned, and the sun moved closer to the crest of the mountains. Someone in the house brought Mary a cocktail. During one heavy silence she pointed to the fluffy clouds drifting across the brilliant blue of an Indian summer sky. During another, she identified a tiny bird that perched briefly on the wooden ledge. When the visitor persisted with her questions, Mary only shrugged and repeated what she had been saying most of the afternoon. "Read my book," she said. "All you have to do is read the book. It's all there."

Notes

Letters and manuscripts used in the text may be located in the following library holdings, either as originals or accurate copies:

Colby College Library, Waterville, Maine: Ernest Hemingway to Waldo Peirce.

Franklin Roosevelt Library, Hyde Park, New York: Martha Gellhorn to Eleanor Roosevelt.

Houghton Library, Harvard University, Cambridge, Massachusetts: Ernest Hemingway to Harvey Breit.

Humanities Research Center, University of Texas at Austin: Ernest Hemingway to Adriana Ivancich; letters of Grace Hemingway.

I. Tatti, Berenson Archive, Settignano, Italy: Ernest Hemingway to Bernard Berenson.

John F. Kennedy Library, Boston, Massachusetts; Hemingway Collection: letters of Agnes von Kurowsky, Duff Twysden, Elizabeth Hadley Richardson (Hemingway Mowrer), Grace Hemingway, C. E. Hemingway, Jane Mason, Pauline Pfeiffer (Hemingway); A set of five albums of Grace Hemingway, 1888–1917; Ernest Hemingway, "Starts and Incompletes," *A Moveable Feast*.

Lilly Library, Indiana University, Bloomington, Indiana; Hemingway Collection: Ernest Hemingway to his family, 1918.

Mugar Memorial Library, Boston University, Boston, Massachusetts; Gellhorn Collection: Martha Gellhorn to Ernest Hemingway (restricted).

Newberry Library, Chicago, Illinois: Ernest Hemingway to Sherwood Anderson.

Princeton University Library, Princeton, New Jersey. Sylvia Beach Collection: Ernest Hemingway to Sylvia Beach, Mary Hemingway, and Thomas Welsh. F. Scott Fitzgerald Collection: Ernest Hemingway to F. Scott Fitzgerald. Ernest Hemingway Collection: Ernest Hemingway to Janet Flanner, Arnold Gingrich, Isabelle Simmons Godolphin, Guy Hickok, Howell Jenkins, Hadley Mowrer, Evan Shipman, and Henry Strater. Patrick Hemingway Collection: Aunt Harriet to Pauline Hemingway; Ernest Hemingway to Patrick Hemingway, Pauline Hemingway, and Mary Pfeiffer; Mary Pfeiffer to Ernest Hemingway; Pauline Hemingway to Partick and Gregory Hemingway. Charles T. Lanham Papers: Ernest Hemingway to General Charles T. Lanham. Harold Loeb Papers: Ernest Hemingway to Harold Loeb. Charles Scribner Archives: Ernest Hemingway to Maxwell Perkins; Ernest Hemingway to Wallace Meyer; Ernest Hemingway to Charles and Vera Scribner; Charles Scribner to Ernest Hemingway. W.B. Smith Collection: Ernest Hemingway to William B. Smith.

Beinecke Rare Book and Manuscript Library, Yale University, New Haven, Connecticut; Collection of American Literature: Ernest Hemingway to Grace Quinlan and Gertrude Stein.

The details of Ernest Hemingway's life are drawn, for the most part, from Carlos Baker, *Ernest Hemingway: A Life Story*. Authors whose books have contributed materially to the lives of the women are Alice Hunt Sokoloff, *Hadley: The First Mrs. Hemingway*; Marcelline H. Sanford, *At the Hemingways*; Madelaine H. Miller, *Ernie: Hemingway's Sister "Sunny" Remembers*; Leicester Hemingway, *My Brother, Ernest Hemingway*; Michael S. Reynolds, *Hemingway's First War*; Bertram Sarason, *Hemingway and the Sun Set*; Mary Welsh Hemingway, *How It Was*; Adriana Ivancich, *La Torre Bianca*.

Unpublished letters identified in the text by date will not be cited again in the notes.

List of Abbreviations for the Notes

AI	Adriana Ivancich
AvK, AS	Agnes von Kurowsky Stanfield
BB	Bernard Berenson
BK	Bernice Kert
CB	Carlos Baker
CHG	Carol Hemingway Gardner
EH	Ernest Hemingway
ER	Eleanor Roosevelt
GH	Grace Hemingway
Greg H.	Gregory Hemingway
HR, HH, HM	Hadley Richardson Hemingway Mowrer
JH	Jack Hemingway
JM, JG	Jane Mason Gingrich
MG	Martha Gellhorn
MHM	Madelaine Hemingway Miller
MWH	Mary Welsh Hemingway
Pat H.	Patrick Hemingway
PP, PH	Pauline Pfeiffer Hemingway
STLPD	*St. Louis Post Dispatch*
NYHT	*New York Herald Tribune*
NYT	*New York Times*

For further abbreviations, see Bibliography.

Chapter 1

21 EH on GH: Maj. Gen. Charles T. Lanham to CB, Dec. 7, 1966; Mary Lanham to CB, June 1, 1964; Tillie Arnold to BK, Mar. 14, 1979; John Dos Passos, "Young Hemingway: A Panel," *Fitzgerald/Hemingway Annual:* 1972, p. 136.

22 "My mother": CHG to BK, May 8, 1979.

22–23 "You tend to"; "Come quick": Marcelline Sanford, *At The Hemingways*, pp. 54, 53.

23 GH to Ernest Hall: June 5, 1887; Aug. 20, 1899; July 15, Sept. 8, 1900.

27 "From the start": Leicester Hemingway, *My Brother, Ernest Hemingway*, p. 22.

"She would certainly": CHG to BK, May 8, 1979.

27–29 GH on EH as child: GH, *Albums 1* and 2.

31 ". . . no reason why": Sanford, *At The Hemingways*, p. 105.

34 "my grandfather": EH, "Now I Lay Me," *SSEH*, p. 365.

36 simple elixirs: Ben Euwema to CB, Dec. 1964.

GH lying a bit: Pat H. to BK, Aug. 23, 1978.

Chapter 2

37 "If there was an imbalance": CHG to BK, May 8, 1979.

"My mother was": MHM to BK, Jan. 24, 1978.

38 "I proved": Sanford, p. 90.

39 "She just bowlderized": EH to CB, Aug. 27, 1951 (priv. coll.).

41 "like a baby": MHM to BK, Jan. 24, 1978.

41–42 "It will be only"; "As the boxing"; "a dainty": GH, *Albums 5*.

43–44 ". . . plump brown"; ". . . the thing": EH, "Fathers and Sons," *SSEH*, pp. 497, 491.

46 "Nick could get"; "He touched": EH, "Summer People," *NAS*, pp. 218, 227.

47 "The fellows said": EH to parents, Jan. 30, 1918.

47 "funds"; "We all have": Carlos Baker, *Life Story*, pp. 19, 36.

48 outlandish stories: Vincent Sheean to CB, Aug. 22, 1965.

49 In her last letter: GH to EH, May 20, 1918.

Chapter 3

50 "My mother was": Michael S. Reynolds, *The Agnes Tapes: A Farewell to Catherine Barkley*, in typescript, unpub., Oct. 1, 1970.

51 "no ladies": AS to BK, Jan. 27, 1978.

53 "had all the earmarks": Henry S. Villard, "In a World War I Hospital with Hemingway," *Horizon*, Aug. 1978: 88.

55–56 GH letters to EH in Milan: GH to EH, May 27, June 11, July 21, Aug. 5, 1918.

page

56   gold star mother: Pat H. to BK, Aug. 24, 1978.

57   "drank brandy": Reynolds, *Tapes.*
         "I think he was"; "I was on night": AS to BK, Jan. 27, 1978.
         "I knew he had": Villard, "In a WWI Hospital": 89.

58   when he read the book: Villard to CB, Feb. 1, 1962.
         "You be nice": AS to BK, Jan. 27, 1978.

61   "And we weren't allowed": Reynolds, *Tapes.*

61–62   Nurse Jessup; "the dreadful thought"; "solemn as an oyster": AvK to EH,
             Oct. 20, 21, 22, 28, 1918.

63–64   "I was looking"; "My idea": AS to MWH, Mar. 5, 1962.

65   "missus": EH to Wm. B. Smith Jr., Dec. 13, 1918, *S. Lett.*, p. 20.

66   "Yesterday I walked": AvK to EH, Jan. 15, 1919.

67   "very gentle": Reynolds, *Tapes.*
         "Of course you understand": AvK to EH, Feb. 3, 15, 1919.

67–68   burned letters and transfer of Carracciolo: AS to BK, Jan. 27, 1978.

Chapter 4

70   ". . . the first one": EH, "The Snows of Kilimanjaro," *SSEH*, p. 64.
         "Vaguely he wanted": EH, "Soldier's Home," *SSEH*, pp. 147, 148.

71–73   "Ernest is very"; "I want the view"; "He is . . . willing"; "the big shutters":
             Sanford, pp. 194–198.
         Grace Cottage letter: GH to Ed Hemingway, undated.

74   waitress on the dock: Kathryn Dilworth to CB, July 10, 1964.
         "The boards"; "Jim stirred"; EH, "Up in Michigan," *SSEH*, pp. 85, 86.

77   "Ernie went along"; "the air was BLUE": Madelaine H. Miller, *Ernie:
             Hemingway's Sister "Sunny" Remembers*, p. 67.

79   "He had been": CHG to BK, May 8, 1979.
         "I'm rating": EH to Grace Quinlan, Nov. 16, 1920.
         "Japs keep out"; Mary Bethune: GH to EH, Dec. 8, 1920, Jan. 19, 1921.

79–80   "I took Sun": EH to GH, Dec. 22, 1920, *S. Lett.*, pp. 42, 43.

Chapter 5

86–87   "hulky bulky"; "How did I love"; "panting"; "Maybe the nicest"; "nice
             over and"; "I understand"; "The only thing": HR to EH, Nov. 8, 11,
             20, 30, Dec. 15, 1920; Jan. 15, 23, Mar. 8, 1921.

88   "The moment she entered": L. Hemingway, *My Brother, Ernest Heming-
             way,* p. 71.

88–89   "the female bird"; "wholesome": Edmund Wilson to CB, Jan. 10, 1953.

89   "very parfit": HR to EH, Jan. 24, 1921.
         Ernest as prince: HM to BK, May 19, 1976.
         "She wants me": EH to GH, Dec. 22, 1920, *S. Lett.*, p. 42.
         "Anybody else": Sanford, p. 209.

page

89–90   "Don't you expect"; "You are mine"; "Rome sounds"; "pure madness":
         HR to EH, Jan 1, 18, 1921.

90   "bold penniless"; "I'm not at all": Alice Sokoloff, *Hadley*, pp. 21, 22.

90   "It makes"; "Guess he": HR to EH, Jan. 28, Feb. (undated) 1921.

91   "Ernest": Sokoloff, p. 20.

91–92   "unusual"; "Terribly low"; "How I love": HR to EH, Feb. 5, 11, Mar. 8,
         1921.

92   "wait around and make hoards": Sokoloff, 22.

         "For Ernest and my sister": HM to CB, Apr. 1965.

         Ernest and Hadley kissing: W.D. Horne to CB, Dec. 1962.

92–93   Hadley on senior Hemingways: HM to CB, July, 1962, HR to EH, Apr.
         30, 1921.

93   "I never expected": Sokoloff, pp. 26, 27.

         "together"; "Corona"; "Don't see how": HR to EH, Apr. 13, 22; June 23,
         1921.

94   "Guy loves a couple": EH to Wm. B. Smith Jr., Apr. 28, 1921, *S. Lett.*, p.
         48.

         "I was dull": HM to BK, May 19, 1976.

95   ". . . can't we give": HR to EH, June 7, 1921.

         Hadley too old: Donald M. St. John, "Interview with Hemingway's Bill
         Gorton," *Connecticut Review*, 1968. Rep. Bertram Sarason, *Hemingway
         and the Sun Set*, p. 159.

         "PARTNERS"; "if I hadn't": Sokoloff, pp. 32, 33.

96   "apparently forever"; "You practically": HR to EH, July 12, June 11, 1921.

97   "Already": HR to GH, July 12, 1921.

97–98   "Wish I were"; "mortage"; "wonderful times"; "I wish": HR to EH, Feb.
         19, July 8, Aug. 6, 7, 1921.

98   collapse of Commonwealth: EH to Grace Quinlan, Aug. 1921.

99–102   EH's mood: GH to Marcelline Hemingway, Aug. 18, 28, 1921; EH to Grace
         Quinlan, Aug. 19, 1921, *S. Lett.*, p. 54–55.

102–3   "He enjoyed"; "Nick kissed": EH, "Wedding Day," *NAS*, pp. 231, 232.

103   "busting": HH to GH, Sept. 22, 1921.

104   "He could smell": HM to CB, July 1962.

Chapter 6

106   "took turns": HH to GH and Dr. H., Dec. 28, 1921.

         "all in all": Sokoloff, p. 42.

107   "heart and nervous system": Malcolm Cowley, *A Second Flowering: Works
         and Days of the Lost Generation*, p. 57.

         ". . . we've been walking": EH and HH to S. and T. Anderson, Dec., 1921,
         S. Lett., pp. 59–60.

107–8   incident with *addition*: Sokoloff, pp. 43, 44.

109–11   "The steep winding staircase": HM to CB, July, 1962.

113   "at Pound's feet"; cantankerous": HM to CB, July, 1962.

         "beautiful": Sokoloff, p. 50.

114 "immigrant hair"; well-behaved children: EH, *AMF*, p. 14.

   ". . . a great deal": Gertrude Stein, *The Autobiography of Alice B. Toklas*, p. 213.

115 "You can either"; "steerage": EH, *AMF*, pp. 15, 16.

   "Pablo, go home": JH to BK, Mar. 1979.

115–16 "It was easy"; "The act [they] commit"; "In the night": EH, *AMF*, pp. 25, 20, 21.

115 ". . . I always wanted": EH to W.G. Rogers, July 29, 1948, *S. Lett.*, p. 650.

116 EH-Smith quarrel: Bill Smith to EH, Baker, *Life Story*, p. 88.

117–18 scene at Enghien: EH, *AMF*, pp. 49–52.

118 "excellent manners": HM to CB, July 1962.

119 "He seemed to": Maj. Gen. E.E. Dorman-O'Gowan to CB, Feb. 24, 1961.

   "When you and Chink": EH, *AMF*, p. 54.

   "We tramped": HM to BK, May 19, 1976.

120–22 "human blister"; "We were welcomed"; "wonderful": HM to CB, July 1962.

122–23 fishing trip to Germany: EH, "A Paris-to-Strasbourg Flight," *TDS*, Sept. 9, 1922: 8; EH, "Crossing to Germany," *TDS*, Sept. 19, 1922: 4; EH, "German Inn-Keepers Rough," *TDS*, Sept. 5, 1922: 9.

123–24 Hadley's mood: HM to CB, July, 1962; Sokoloff, 56; HH to GH, 1922.

124–25 "whored"; "Armenian slut"; "back at the apartment": EH, "Snows of Kilimanjaro," *SSEH*, pp. 64–66.

125 Ernest cheating: W.B. Smith Jr. to CB, Apr. 1964.

   Hadley beautiful: EH to Bill Horne, July 17, 1923, *S. Lett.*, p. 86.

Chapter 7

126–27 "I love you": EH to HH, Nov. 28, 1922, *S. Lett.*, p. 74.

127 "She had cried": EH, *AMF*, p. 74.

   "That painful subject": HM to CB, 1965.

128–29 Christmas Day: EH, "Christmas in the Swiss Alps," *TSW*, Dec. 22, 1923: 19.

129 EH's letter to Agnes: AS to CB, Mar. 29, 1965.

130 glimpse of Carracciolo: AS to BK, Jan. 27, 1978.

131 "A short time after": EH, "A Very Short Story," *SSEH*, p. 142.

132 " 'It's hell, isn't it' ": EH, "Cross Country Snow," *SSEH*, p. 187.

133 ". . . whenever he missed": Sokoloff, p. 61.

134 ". . . she walked along": EH, "Cat in the Rain," *SSEH*, pp. 168–70.

   Ernest's assertion: Baker, *Life Story*, p. 580.

135–36 " 'I'm going' ": EH, "Out of Season," *SSEH*, p. 176.

136 "was an almost": EH to F. Scott Fitzgerald, Dec. 24, 1925, *S. Lett.*, p. 180.

   "It was a kind": Baker, *Life Story*, p. 109.

   "I also liked": HM to CB, July 1962.

137 "It's just like": EH to Wm. D. Horne, July 17, 1923, *S. Lett.*, p. 88.

"Music was pounding": EH, "World's Series of Bull Fighting," *TSW*, Oct. 27, 1923: 33.

138   "embroidering": Sokoloff, p. 63.

"Hemingway posing": Sylvia Beach to CB, undated.

139   "We are going": EH to Wm. D. Horne, July 17–18, 1923, *S. Lett.*, pp. 88, 87.

Chapter 8

140   "He is greatly": HM to GH, Sept. 27, 1923.

141   "but then pulled together": HH to Isabelle Simmons, Oct. 12, 1923.

"à la Rudolph": HH to GH, Oct. 18, 1923.

"it is too horrible": HH to Isabelle S., Oct. 12, 1923.

". . . against the law": EH to Sylvia Beach, Nov. 6, 1923, *S. Lett.*, p. 98.

"squawling": EH to parents, Nov. 7, 1923, *S. Lett.*, p. 99.

142   "chuck journalism": EH to Gertrude Stein, Nov. 9, 1923, *S. Lett.*, p. 101.

"Most of all": HH to Dr. and Mrs. Hemingway, Dec. 8, 1923.

143   Ed Hemingway reaction: Sanford, p. 218, 219; I.S. Godolphin to CB, Oct. 22, 1964.

145   "would have done": Sokoloff, p. 71.

"I did not read": Baker, *Life Story*, p. 126.

146   "up-ended": EH, *AMF*, p. 83.

". . . never before": Harold Loeb, *The Way It Was*, p. 190.

147   "I have no doubt": St. John. Rep. Sarason, p. 201.

"pink and white": HM to CB, 1967.

147–48 "attractive"; "prissy"; "He felt I was": Kitty Cannell to CB, Oct. 13, 1963.

148   be a king: HM to CB, July 1962.

149   "We went through": EH, *SAR*, 108.

150   "hard factual": Baker, *Hemingway: The Writer as Artist*, p. 117.

151   ". . . He always worked": EH, "On Writing," *NAS*, p. 238.

"first distinction": Baker, ed., *Hemingway and His Critics: An International Anthology*, p. 58.

"We will probably": EH to Edmund Wilson, Oct. 18, 1924, *S. Lett.*, p. 129.

152   Paris art scene and Florida land: GH to EH, Dec. 16, 1927.

153   "She is the best": EH to Howell Jenkins, Nov. 9, 1924, *S. Lett.*, p. 132.

154   "In short words": Loeb, p. 220.

155   "He was too assured": Nancy Milford, *Zelda*, p. 150.

"unreadable": Baker, *Life Story*, p. 238.

"I'll bloody well": A. Scott Berg, *Max Perkins, Editor of Genius*, p. 199.

156   Pauline in apartment: Cannell to CB, Oct. 13, 1963.

"I was talking": W.B. Smith, Jr. to CB, Apr. 3, 1964.

156–57 Biography of Duff prior to move to Paris: Sarason.

158   "When she laughed": HM to CB, July 1962.

159   "I heard a laugh": Loeb, pp. 249, 250.

page

159–60   Duff and Harold in apartment and on train: Loeb.

        "sadness"; "I have nothing"; "the thought of"; "for a doubtful": Loeb, pp. 266, 272, 275, 280.

160   "Pat and Duff"; getting tight: EH to Loeb, June 21, 1925, *S. Lett.*, p. 164.

        "a great joy"; "Pat broke": Loeb, pp. 282, 284.

161   "question of Hem": Donald Ogden Stewart to CB, Mar. 2, 1962.

162–64   Loeb's account of quarrel: Loeb, pp. 291, 294, 295.

165   "quite a dish": St. John. Rep. Sarason, p. 195.

        "hair . . . brushed": EH, *SAR*, pp. 22, 26, 203.

Chapter 9

168   "Ernest my dear": Duff Twysden to EH, Sept. 1925.

        "You must make": Baker, *Life Story*, p. 156.

169   "double-cross": John Dos Passos to CB, Apr. 1962.

        "detestable"; "wet blanket": HM to CB, 1967.

170   "the rich": EH, *AMF*, p. 205.

171–72   Pauline Pfeiffer's biographical data drawn from Otto Bruce, Jack Hemingway, Patrick Hemingway, Jay McEvoy, and Karl Pfeiffer to BK, various dates.

173   new girl: EH, *AMF*, p. 208.

        breaking contract: HM to CB, 1967.

173–76   "Oh my soul"; "I feel he"; "I've missed you": PP to HH and EH, Jan. 16, 17, 21, 1926.

176   "She was always": HM to CB, July 1962.

        "a mad thing": PP to HH, Feb. 4, 1926.

176–77   "grand"; "where we went": Baker, *Life Story*, pp. 164, 591.

177   "Everybody kidded": John Dos Passos, *The Best Times: An Informal Memoir*, p. 159.

178   "about the colour": PP to EH, Mar. 12, 1926.

178–79   the Loire Valley trip and scene with Ernest: HM to CB, July 1962.

179   "I was in love": EH, "The Art of the Short Story," June 1959, rep. *The Paris Review* 79: 97.

        ". . . one day of": EH to Dr. Hemingway, May 23, 1926, *S. Lett.*, p. 207.

180   incident at Monte Carlo: Ada and Archibald MacLeish to CB, Mar. 9, 1965; Mary Hickok to CB, undated.

180–81   "Here it was": HM to CB, 1967.

Chapter 10

182   "We went to Madrid": HM to CB, 1967.

        "Today's still": EH to PP, July 26, 1926.

page

"close to what's elemental": Baker, *Life Story*, p. 172.

183   "We were returning": EH, "A Canary for One," *SSEH*, p. 342.

"Emperor Tiberius": Sokoloff, p. 90.

184–85   "I am feeling very comfortable"; "I think maybe"; "printing": PP to EH, Sept. 24, Oct. 5, 8, 1926.

185   ". . . the deliberate": EH to PP, Dec. 3, 1926, *S. Lett.*, p. 234.

"Nothing faked": Archibald MacLeish to CB, Nov. 4, 1963.

186   Her letters were; "We are one": PP to EH, Oct. 12, 11, 1926.

186–87   Early October; oil drilling in Piggott; *Vogue* letter: PP to EH, Oct. 12, 14, 15, 23, 1926.

187   Ernest, dispirited: EH to PP, Oct. 1926.

"madhouse depression" letter: PP to EH, Oct. 25, 1926.

189   ". . . I pray for you": EH to PP, Nov. 12, 1926, *S. Lett.*, p. 223.

190   "I would include": EH to HH, Nov. 18, 1926, *S. Lett.*, p. 228.

"made it easy": JH to BK, Mar. 1979.

191   "I didn't know": HM to BK, May 19, 1976.

Chapter 11

195   "THREE MONTHS"; "and as I": PP to EH, Nov. 25, 1926.

196   "I'm really tougher": Cannell to CB, Oct. 13, 1963.

197   "They were as"; "that book": L. Hemingway, p. 100.

GH criticism of *SAR:* GH to EH, Dec. 4, 1926.

". . . I'm trying in all"; "absolutely": EH to parents, Mar. 20, 1925, *S. Lett.*, p. 153; Feb. 5, 1927, *S. Lett.*, p. 244.

198   discomfiture in Oak Park: GH to EH, Oct. 4, 1926.

"It won't be very"; "Since I know now": PP to EH, Nov. 29, Dec. 3, 1926.

199   Ernest "a handful": JH to BK, Mar. 1979.

"I liked the": Paul Scott Mowrer, *The House of Europe*, p. 556.

199–200   Ernest and Jinny: Pat H. to BK, Aug. 1978.

200   "Naturally I didn't": EH to I.S. Goldophin, Mar. 5, 1927.

200–201   the Italian tour and apt. at 6, rue Férou: CB notes based on PP to EH, Mar. 15, 17, 19, 20, 23, 1927.

legality of Hadley's marriage: Sokoloff, p. 92.

Paul Mowrer and EH at lunch: Mowrer to CB, 1962.

202   GH views on marriage, her success in art world: GH to EH, Jan. 21, Feb. 20, Mar. 6, 1927.

203   "but my dear Ernest": Mary Pfeiffer to EH, May 1927.

203   stained their faces with . . . juice: Pat H. to BK, Aug. 1978.

204   copying a story: EH to Mary Pfeiffer, June 10, 1927.

"having one day"; "my *time*": HH to I.S. Goldophin, Aug. 13, 1927.

205   "I came to love": JH to BK, Mar. 1979.

206   "I am feeling": PH to EH, Feb. 3, 1928.

Chapter 12

page

209   "Little Pilar": PH to EH, May 20, 1928.

       "The town was shocked": Mary Pfeiffer to PH, Sept. 8, 1929.

210   "You would best": L. Hemingway, 107–8.

210–11 EH and fatherhood: EH to Guy Hickok, July, 1928; EH to Waldo Peirce, July 23, 1928.

212   information about Duff: Clinton King to CB, Mar. 18, 1964.

213   "strong as a goat": EH to Waldo Peirce, Aug. 23, 1928, *S. Lett.*, p. 285.

214   Ed Hemingway's suicide; family details: CHG to BK, May 8, 1979; Sanford.

215   "Dad had always told": Miller, p. 115.

216   "I would esteem": EH to Henry Strater, Dec. 22, 1928.

216–17 influence . . . prizes and honors; Grace renting rooms and examining accounts: GH to EH, Sept. 24, Oct. 5, 25, 1929.

218–19 "That was what"; " 'I'll say just' "; " 'Oh darling' "; " '. . . why don't you' ": EH, *FTA*, pp. 105–6, 299–300, 327.

219   "Remember especially": PP to EH, Oct., Nov., and Dec. 1926.

       "How is Pauline?" Michael Reynolds, *Hemingway's First War*, p. 18.

223   "splendid"; "apotheosis": Baker, *Life Story*, p. 204.

224   "The heat was": American Red Cross correspondence with John C. Buck, 1957.

       "Short men": AS to BK, Jan. 27, 1978.

       "We are avoiders": AvK to Clara Noyes, Nov. 1928.

       "Times have": Clara Noyes to AvK, Dec. 1928.

225–26 Patrick's birth; Hadley at Versailles, Crécy-en-brie and Annecy: HH to EH, June, July 10, Aug. 4, 10, Sept. 6, 1928.

226   "He gave me": HM to BK, May 19, 1976.

       "If Ernest": I. S. Godolphin to CB, Oct. 22, 1964.

Chapter 13

227   thousands would starve: EH to Waldo Peirce, Mar. 1930.

228   "It's the best": EH to Guy Hickok, May 1930.

       "long pondered answer": HH to EH, Jan. 26, 1930.

229   Pauline and Ernest's wills: Pat H. to BK, Aug. 1978.

       "The poor fellow": PH to GH and Sunny, undated.

230   his Hemingway grandmother: Pat H. to BK, Aug. 1978.

       "only thing in life": EH to Fitzgerald, Nov. 24, 1926, *S. Lett.*, p. 232.

230–31 misunderstandings between GH and EH, GH to EH, Feb. 6, Mar. 9, 1930.

231   "a passion"; "If he wrote"; "He had died": EH, "Fathers and Sons," *SSEH*, pp. 489, 490–91.

231–32 GH widowhood: CHG to BK, May 8, 1979.

232   "haunted house": McLendon, p. 60.

page

233   sailing plans: EH to Mary Pfeiffer, May 13, 1931.

233–34   "I hate to"; "each more lovely"; "Spending still"; "I think you"; "nice, small girl": PH to EH, May 31, June 1931.

234   "very much": EH to Waldo Peirce, Nov. 10, 1931, *S. Lett.*, p. 343.

         Ernest's superstitions: Toby Bruce to CB, Mar. 1965.

         "I want your": HH to EH, Apr. 16, 1931.

234–35   Allen and EH in Madrid: Jay Allen to CB, Mar. 6, 1963.

235   the Gris purchase: Caresse Crosby, *The Passionate Years* (New York: Dial Press, 1953), p. 284.

235–36   Jane Mason's biographical data supplied by Anne Cazeneuve to BK, 1979 and 1980, and Jane Gingrich to BK, 1979.

Chapter 14

239   "There is no"; "If this book": EH to Pfeiffers, Jan. 5, 1932, *S. Lett.*, p. 350.

240   "utterly satisfying": Baker, *Life Story*, p. 228.

         "one of the boys": Mario G. Menocal Jr. to BK, Feb. 9, 1979.

242   further data on Jane Mason: JG and Anne C. to BK, 1979, 1980.

         "Ernest loves Jane": Baker, *Life Story*, p. 228.

243   "Next year": PH to EH, June 26, 1932.

244   "Well Pauline": EH to Hickok, Oct. 14, 1932, *S. Lett.*, p. 372.

244–45   "Three things"; "I would sooner": EH, *DITA*, pp. 103, 122.

245   "juvenile romanticism": Baker, *Life Story*, p. 242.

         "the book sheds": Anthony Burgess, *Hemingway and His World*, p. 63.

246   "Ernest was supporting": CHG to BK, May 8, 1979.

         GH response to elopement; deed to Windemere; EH fishing: GH to EH, June 30, 1931, Apr. 5, 1932, Mar. 20, 1933, July 17, 1933.

247   "no papa"; "The place"; "lousiest": PH to EH, May 18, 21, 27, 1933.

248   "Finest life": EH to Janet Flanner, Apr. 8, 1933, *S. Lett.*, p. 387.

248–49   Turgenev and Jane Mason, Pat H. to BK, Aug. 1978.

249   "Not on the boat": JH to BK, Mar. 1979.

         JG, EH, and marriage: JG to BK, May 9, 1979.

         car accident in Cuba: JH to BK, Mar. 1979.

249–50   Jane's injury and Kubie: G. Grant Mason to CB, Feb. 10, 1966.

250   "much nuttier"; "happy, healthy": Baker, *Life Story*, p. 228, Foreword, x.

251   "builder-upper": Dos Passos to CB, Apr. 1962.

         "I don't expect": EH to Mary Pfeiffer, Oct. 16, 1933, *S. Lett.*, p. 397.

252   "a different life": Clinton King to CB, Mar. 18, 1964.

         "we met together": Sarason, p. 47.

252   Duff and Clinton in N.Y.: Maria Rogers to CB, Jan. 1962.

253   "It was a fine place": EH, "A Paris Letter," *Esquire* Feb. 1934: 22, 156.

Chapter 15

254   "Pauline and I": James McLendon, *Papa: Hemingway in Key West*, p. 99.

254–61   PH and EH on safari: "African Diary of Pauline Hemingway," Dec. 22, 1933 to Feb. 18, 1934 (unpublished), courtesy Jay McEvoy; EH, *GHOA*, Foreword, 17, 41–44, 73, 86, 94–95, 290.

262   "Poor little lambs": McLendon, p. 105.

       "I entered": Marlene Dietrich, "The Most Fascinating Man I Know," *This Week*, Feb. 13, 1955: 8–9.

263   "much of what's": Greg H., *Papa: A Personal Memoir*, p. 19.

       "Patrick is"; "It was Papa's": PH to EH, May 31, June 2, 1934.

       "A Philco radio": HM to EH, Apr. 11, 1934.

264   "I will be so glad"; "I would like": PH to EH, June 11, Sept. 20, 1934.

265   "Darlings": JM to PH and EH, Sept. 3, 1934.

       "lit royale": Dos Passos, *The Best Times*, p. 219.

       Miró never returned: JH to BK, Mar. 1979.

Chapter 16

268   Pauline as second mother: JH to BK, Mar. 1979.

       "He is a lovely": PH to EH, June 14, 1935.

       "It seems to me": HM to EH, May 9, 1935.

       "Do you know": JH to BK, Mar. 1979.

269   The Hemingway sons and Ada Stern: Pat H. to BK, Aug. 1978; JH to BK, Mar. 1979; Greg H., *Papa*.

270–71   analysis of EH by Kubie: Lawrence S. Kubie, M.D., "Principles of Psycho-analysis As Applied to the Modern Literature of Neuroticism" unpublished.

271   series of letters between JM and Kubie: July 13, 1935, plus enclosures.

272   Sidney Franklin and Pauline: Jay McEvoy to BK, Feb. 19, 1979.

273   "The hardest thing": EH, "Old Newsman Writes: A Letter from Cuba," *Esquire*, Dec. 1934: 25–26.

       "good" love: Lewis, *Hemingway on Love*, p. 64.

       "Pauline has"; "real old melancholia"; "have been going out": EH to Mary Pfeiffer, Jan. 26, 1936, *S. Lett.* pp. 434, 435, 436.

274   "Mrs. Mason": EH to Dos Passos, Apr. 12, 1936, *S. Lett.*, p. 446.

275   "clearly bent": Jackson Benson, *Hemingway: The Writer's Art of Self-Defense*, p. 147.

       "Perhaps what Mrs. Macomber": Warren Beck, "The Shorter Happy Life of Mrs. Macomber," *Modern Fiction Studies*, Nov. 1955: 35, 37.

276   Jane and Arnold: Arnold Gingrich, "Horsing Them in with Hemingway," *Playboy*, Sept. 1965: 123, 256–58.

       "selfish chap": Pat H. to BK, Sept. 17, 1979.

277   "Jinny has": EH to Mary Pfeiffer, Jan. 26, 1936, *S. Lett.*, p. 435.

page
277–78   ". . . he had written her"; "you said"; "caretaker"; "I'd have gone": EH, "Snows of Kilimanjaro," *SSEH*, p. 54–65.

278   AS's divorce and remarriage: Reynolds, *Tapes*.

280   dullest bitches: EH to M. K. Rawlings, Aug. 16, 1936, *S. Lett.*, p. 449.
      "The week was funny"; "Goddamn editor"; "Maybe what": Arnold Gingrich, "Scott, Ernest and Whoever," *Esquire*, Oct. 1973: 151–54, 374–80.

281   "collected writers"; "dull and upright"; "aren't built that way": EH, *THAHN*, pp. 150, 238–40, 244–45.

282   the thought flashed: MG, Oct. 31, 1980.
      Ernest as slovenly, and beautiful blonde: McLendon, 163–64.

Chapter 17

285   "marvelous men": MG, Oct. 31, 1980.
      "loving, merry"; "my plan for life": MG, Feb. 15, 1982.

286   "nothing ever happens": Gellhorn, *What Mad Pursuit* (New York: Stokes, 1934).

287   "The great beauty": MG, Feb. 15, 1982.

288   "Enlarge this book": *STLPD*, Oct. 3, 1936.
      "Her stories are quite": *The Spectator* (London), May 22, 1936.
      "alarming and vile": MG, Feb. 15, 1982.

288–89   Eleanor Roosevelt in "My Day": *Kansas City Star*, Aug. 5, 1936; *St. Louis Globe Democrat*, Sept. 19, 1936.

289   "Who is this Martha": *NYHT*, Sept. 25, 1936.

290   "She was very grumpy": MG, Feb. 15, 1982.

291   Ernest's interest in Martha: Jonathan Latimer to BK, Apr. 5, 1979; Bruce to BK, Jan. 1978.
      inhibited her intimacy: JG to BK, May 9, 1979.
      "The world was": Pat H. to BK, Aug. 1978.

292   Martha and EH in railway car: MG, Feb. 15, 1982.
      "It rains and freezes": MG to PH, Jan. 14, 1937.
      "I'm trying to have"; "the horrible dinner": PH to EH, Jan 13, 17, 1937.

293   "She reminded me": Latimer to BK, Apr. 5, 1979.

294   "This is from": EH to Mary Pfeiffer, Feb. 9, 1937, *S. Lett.*, pp. 457, 458.
      "I hope we get": MG to EH, Feb. 8, 1937.
      "You do get your": ER to MG, Jan. 16, 1937, Joseph Lash, *Eleanor and Franklin* (New York: W. W. Norton & Co.), p. 431.

295   "She has made": *STLPD*, Mar. 17, 1937.
      "The French fonctionnaire [sic]"; "Since few people": Gellhorn, *FOW*, pp. 10, 11.

296   "seeing and writing": MG to CB, June 2, 1966.
      "You will not be"; "I absolutely": Ted Allan to BK, Feb. 5, 1981.

296   Martha and Ernest at Gran Via: MG, Feb. 15, 1982.

297   EH's attentions felt like a command: MG, Oct. 31, 1980.

page

hot-water tank: Sefton Delmer to CB, Feb. 9, 1966.

"I tagged along": Gellhorn, *FOW*, p. 12.

298   "huge, stony": Gellhorn, "Only the Shells Whine," *Collier's,* July 17, 1937: 13.

299   "I think it was": MG, Oct. 31, 1980.

Chapter 18

301   "There is evidently"; "At the moment": PH to Max Perkins, Mar. 6, Apr. 22, 1937.

302   "I suppose I will": MG to EH, June 1937.

        "Gellhorn seems": Eleanor Roosevelt, "My Day," May 29, 1937.

304   Ernest's speech: Baker, *Life Story,* p. 314.

        "astoundingly": MG to ER, 1937, undated.

        "bigger than his own cause": MG to CB, June 2, 1966.

        "The writers who": Henry Hart, ed., *The Writer in a Changing World,* (New York: Equinox Cooperative Press, 1937), pp. 63, 67–68.

304–5   "It seemed to me": Prudencio de Pereda to CB, July 18, 1967.

305   "Emergency Ambulance Committee": MG to EH, July 2, 1937.

        "stayed there a lot": EH to Mary Pfeiffer, Aug. 2, 1937, *S. Lett.,* p. 460.

        "I am the scribe": MG to ER, July 18, 1937.

306   "cuckoo idealist": MG to EH, July 24, 1937.

        ". . . in that pre-historic": Gellhorn, "On Apocryphism," *Paris Review* 79, p. 290.

307   "a strange thing"; "Even in war": Gellhorn, "Men Without Medals," *Collier's,* Jan. 15, 1938: 10.

        ". . . he made good jokes": Gellhorn, "On Apocryphism": 301.

307–8   "It is a very": Gellhorn, "Zoo in Madrid," *HOA,* pp. 125, 127.

308   " 'I've tried to be' ": EH, *THAHN,* pp. 183, 185, 186.

309   " 'Listen, I want to' "; ". . . thousand breakfasts"; " '. . . I've been to' ": EH, *TFC,* pp. 57, 82, 83.

Chapter 19

310   "The smoke from"; "No matter how": Gellhorn, *FOW,* pp. 25, 20.

311   ". . . you may know"; "I hope": MG to EH, Dec. 1937 (Paris and the *Normandie*).

312   "He seemed amazed": Jay Allen to CB, Mar. 6, 1963.

        Hôtel Elysée: William Bird to CB, June 1962.

313   "Don't be sucked in": PH to EH, Apr. 1938.

        "She spoke as": *STLPD,* Jan. 29, 1938.

314   Martha gives up tour: MG, Feb. 15, 1982.

315   Ernest boasting about Martha: General Charles T. Lanham, *Memoir* (1963, unpublished).

"dress rehearsal": William White, ed., *By-Line: Ernest Hemingway*, p. 288.

316   Ernest as lover: MG, Oct. 31, 1980; Feb. 15, 1982.

". . . my daily bread": MG to ER, Apr. 24, 1938.

"write to Ernest": Jay Allen to CB, Mar. 6, 1963.

317   "too quiet": PH to Mary Pfeiffer, June 11, 1938.

episode in nightclub and after: McLendon, pp. 185–86.

quarreling on road: Pat H. to BK, Aug. 1978.

"To Marty": Maxwell Perkins to EH, Apr. 7, 1938.

318   "cable for . . . passport": McEvoy to BK, Feb. 19, 1979.

"Czechoslovakia is"; "All these people": Gellhorn, "Come Ahead, Adolf," *Collier's*, Aug. 6, 1938: 43, 45.

319   ". . . The English": Gellhorn, "The Lord Will Provide for England," *Collier's*, Sept. 17, 1938: 37.

". . . free as air": Gellhorn, *ASF*, p. 288.

"There were over": Gellhorn, "Guns Against France," *Collier's*, Oct. 10, 1938: 35.

320   ". . . sick of conflicting": EH to Perkins, Oct. 28, 1938, *S. Lett.*, p. 474.

"he listened": Gellhorn, "The Third Winter," rep. *FOW*, p. 35.

321   loss of democracy: Gellhorn, "Obituary of a Democracy," *Collier's*, Dec. 10, 1938: 12, 13, 28–30.

"They're just like us": Gellhorn, *ASF*, p. 88.

"Myself alone": MG to ER, Feb. 3, 1939.

Chapter 20

322   Make the bastard pay: Pat H. to BK, Aug. 1978.

jealous small boy: McEvoy to BK, Feb. 19, 1979.

"Who should go": JH to BK, Mar. 1979.

323   incident of knife: Pat H. to BK, Aug. 1978.

"like royalty": *Los Angeles Times*, July 16, 1978.

324   mood of GH: GH to , Sept. 7, 1935; Dec. 30, 1936.

325   "I owe him"; "I am really not": MG, Oct. 31, 1980.

326   ". . . there would be"; "She would walk": Gellhorn, "Luigi's House," *THOA*, pp. 9, 16.

Martha supporting herself: MG, Oct. 31, 1980.

"followed your man": Gellhorn, "Luigi's House," *THOA*, p. 1.

327   "I thought I was so good": PH to EH, June 23, 1939.

328   "I think": EH to Mary Pfeiffer, July 21, 1939, *S. Lett.*, pp. 491–92.

". . . like your and my": EH to HM, July 26, 1939, *S. Lett.*, p. 493.

329   "knock-out punch": Pat H. to BK, Aug. 1978.

330   Early the next morning: Lloyd Arnold, *High on the Wild with Hemingway*, p. 23.

page

331   "barrel of fun": Tillie Arnold to BK, Mar. 14, 1979.
331–32   "What old Indian"; "Keep your eyes": Arnold, pp. 70, 71.
332   "as interesting as"; "Suddenly the whole": Gellhorn, "Slow Boat to War,"
           FOW, pp. 46, 54.
333   ". . . rather than lose": Gellhorn, "Bombs from a Low Sky," *Collier's*, Jan.
           27, 1940: 41.
           "This is the height": Gellhorn, "Blood on the Snow," *Collier's*, Jan. 20,
           1940: 9, 11.
334   heroine, Maria: Baker, *Life Story*, p. 328.
335   "I imagine": EH to Perkins, Dec. 8, 1939, *S. Lett.*, p. 498.
           "can't eat": EH to Clara Spiegel, Dec. 9, 1939 (priv. coll.).
           Pauline's behavior; "Here is": EH to HM, Dec. 1, 19, 1939.
336   "Virginia's version": EH to Mary Pfeiffer, Dec. 12, 1939, *S. Lett.*, p. 499.
337   "Your father and I": Mary Pfeiffer to EH, Dec. 1939.

Chapter 21

338–39   "I, the undersigned": MG to EH, Jan. 19, 1940.
339   "hausfrau": MG to Clara Spiegel, Jan. 29, 1940 (priv. coll.).
           title of *ASF*: Audre Hanneman, *Ernest Hemingway: A Comprehensive Bibli-
           ography*, p. 109.
340   "material is so poignant": *NYT*, Mar. 10, 1940.
           "novelist . . . legend": *Time*, Mar. 18, 1940.
341   "We talked and talked": MG to HM, Apr. 19, 1940.
           "permanent gloom"; "which I won't": MG to Clara, Apr. 15, 1940 (priv.
           coll.).
342   "You never had it"; "She had high": EH, *FWBT*, pp. 305, 22, 25.
           "so damned happy": EH to Perkins, Apr. 21, 1940.
           "ghastly hard"; "grim, grinding": MG to Clara, May 17, 1940 (priv. coll.).
343   "He loved my mother": MG, Oct. 31, 1980.
           "You can stand me up": Baker, *Life Story*, p. 350.
344   rich bitch: EH to Perkins, Aug. 26, 1940, *S. Lett.*, pp. 515–16.
           "Papa would suffer": Greg H., p. 92.
345   ". . . Good but": EH to Charles Scribner, ca. Oct. 21, 1940, *S. Lett.*, p. 519.
346   "war, pestilence": EH to Clara, Aug. 23, 1940 (priv. coll.).
           "I want that": Tillie Arnold to BK, Mar. 14, 1979.
           "I understand it"; "that woman": EH, *FWBT*, pp. 338–39.
347   "amoeba-like"; "give and take": Edmund Wilson, "Hemingway: Gauge
           of Morale," in John McCaffery, *Ernest Hemingway: The Man and His
           Work*, p. 254.
           Ernest's heroines: Baker, *Writer as Artist*, pp. 109–11.
348   "PICTURE US TWO": Arnold, p. 111.
           "I do not believe": MG to CB, June 13, 1966.
349   "I felt a driving": Gellhorn, *TWMA*, p. 19.
351   Jack as dependent: EH to HM, Dec. 26, 1940, *S. Lett.*, p. 521.

354   "This is a place": Gellhorn, *TWMA*, p. 21.

       "To our lovely": The Hemingway Collection, JFK Lib., Boston.

Chapter 22

355–56   "U.C. took to"; "U.C. used to": Gellhorn, *TWMA*, pp. 23–24.

356–57   "If you considered"; "Suddenly, from"; "The DC-2 behaved"; "volcanic": Gellhorn, "Time Bomb in Hong Kong," *Collier's*, June 7, 1941:13; "Flight into Peril," *Collier's*, May 31, 1941:21, 85.

357–60   "Glowing with"; "an ever-growing"; " 'We're all living' "; "I wondered"; "Thinking it over"; "A platoon": Gellhorn, *TWMA*, pp. 29, 30, 31, 32, 34, 35, 38.

360   "jolted forward": Gellhorn, "These Our Mountains," *Collier's*, June 28, 1941:16–17.

       "said in the darkness": Gellhorn, *TWMA*, p. 43.

       "After you have": Gellhorn, "These Our Mountains": 40.

360–61   "I shouted above"; "I cannot"; "We thought Chou"; "He saw the": Gellhorn, *TWMA*, pp. 49, 53, 60, 56.

361–62   "The Dutch are"; "if you relax": Gellhorn, "Fire Guards the Indies," *Collier's*, Aug. 2, 1941:20–21; "Singapore Scenario," *Collier's*, Aug. 9, 1941:20–21.

362   communal shower: EH to Bernard Berenson, Mar. 6, 1953.

       longing for a daughter: Ramon Lavalle to CB, Mar. 24, 1966.

363   "regards": EH to PH, June 9, 1941, *S. Lett.*, p. 524.

       Jinny's influence: Pat H. to BK, Aug. 1978.

       "I have to have": EH to PH, July 19, 1941, *S. Lett.*, p. 525.

       "It was fun": Ellis Briggs to CB, Feb. 27, 1964.

364   "What I did not": MG, Oct. 31, 1980.

       Martha Hemingway: Tillie Arnold to BK, Mar. 14, 1979.

       ban on sweaters; publishing Martha: EH to Perkins, Aug. 26, Sept. 12, 1941.

365–66   "A tattered Indian child"; ". . . paralyzed by": Gellhorn, *FOW*, p. 107.

366   "This winter": MG to Clara, Nov. 10, 1941 (priv. coll.).

366–67   MG holiday in Florida; "well-written"; "There will never": MG to EH, May 19, 20, 22, 23, 29, 30, 1942.

368   "The President loved": MG, Oct. 31, 1980.

       "He has the": EH to PH, June 9, 1941, *S. Lett.*, p. 524.

       "I'll show you": Greg H., pp. 91–92.

369   "During that terrible"; "with the mild"; "sideshow": Gellhorn, *TWMA*, pp. 64–65.

       "Operation Friendless"; "Don Quixote": Greg H., p. 68.

Chapter 23

370   "am embarrassed": MG to EH, July 26, 1942.

371   "I seem to be"; Proust: MG to EH, Aug. 1, 2, 1942.

page

371–72   "I hadn't felt"; "Since I was": Gellhorn, *TWMA*, pp. 82, 90, 91.

372   "Marty, my Marty": EH to Evan Shipman, Aug. 25, 1942, *S. Lett.*, p. 538.
"Good bye Miss": EH to HM, July 23, 1942, *S. Lett.*, p. 537.

373   "We'll have to divorce": MG to EH, Oct. 23, 1942.
"the way things": EH to Pat H., Oct. 20, 1942.
". . . with a little": EH to HM, July 23, 1942, *S. Lett.*, p. 535.

374   "Spain!": Jay Allen to CB, Mar. 6, 1963.
"there was always": Pat H. to BK, Aug. 1978.
Pauline and marriage: Greg H. to BK., Sept. 1975.

375   car into ditch: MG to CB, Apr. 30, 1963.
"rot and rubbish": MG, Oct. 31, 1980.
"making the ground": MG to CB, June 2, 1966.

375–76   housebroken cobra; "I guess I": MG to EH, Dec. 26, 1942; Jan. 10, 1943.

376   "like in the good": EH to Max Perkins, Apr. 1943.

377–78   "After this trip"; "It was a great success"; "having no natural": MG to
EH, June 3, 6, 13, 1943.

379–80   "in this perfect"; "I wish we"; "You have been"; "brutalization"; "I would
like"; "I will almost": MG to EH, June 28, 1943.

381   Ernest going to war: MG, Oct. 31, 1980.
Ernest baiting Martha: Greg H. to BK, Sept. 18, 1975.

382   "with my body": MG, Feb. 15, 1982.
"expected no praise": MG, Oct. 31, 1980.
"should be of": EH, *Men at War* (New York: Crown, 1942), p. xv

383–84   ". . . I am yours"; her bad management; "In my heart"; "I don't mind":
MG to EH, Oct. 1, 12, 13, 15, 1943.

Chapter 24

385   "shaming and silly": MG, Feb. 15, 1982.

386   "deadly"; "First you wait"; working children: Gellhorn, "The Bomber
Boys," *Collier's*, June 17, 1944:60; "Children are Soldiers, Too," *Collier's*,
Mar. 4, 1944:21, 27.

386–87   "It's like being"; "I wish you could"; "Everyone knows you": MG to EH,
Nov. 14, 20, 21, 1943.

389   straight off the *Pilar:* EH, *IITS.*
"I never had so": EH to HM, Nov. 25, 1943, *S. Lett.*, pp. 555, 556.

390   "What does this mean?": MG to EH, Jan. 15, 1944.

391   "even the Unknown": EH to Dawn Powell, Jan. 31, 1944 (priv. coll.).
"ARE YOU A WAR CORRESPONDENT": MG, Oct. 31, 1980.

391–92   "I was not received"; "Therefore I was"; "hideous and insane"; "He was
going": MG, Feb. 15, 1982.

392   "Oh no . . . I couldn't do that"; "It was a very good": MG, Oct. 31, 1980.

393   "Introduce me"; "I don't know"; "This war may": Mary Hemingway,
How It Was, pp. 94–96.

Chapter 25

page

397–98 ". . . It was freezing"; "safe angle"; "If he really"; "Q-boat"; "ceaseless, crazy"; "wonderfully exposed": MG, Feb. 15, 1982.

398 "stature and status": M. Hemingway, p. 96.

399 "Maybe it was not": MWH to BK, Sept. 1979.

400–401 "abstemious" and "conservative"; ". . . through the steps": M. Hemingway, pp. 43, 49.

402 British Wren: Pat H. to BK, Aug. 1978.

403 "writers": M. Hemingway, p. 81.
"She was full of": William Walton to BK, Apr. 1980.

404 "Mary had been": Connie Bessie to BK, Apr. 17, 1980.

Chapter 26

405 Martha and Ernest and the invasion: Gellhorn, "Over and Back," *Collier's*, July 22, 1944:16; EH, "Voyage to Victory," *Collier's*, July 22, 1944:11–13, 56–57.

406 "I acted as": MG, Feb. 15, 1982.
"I'm leaving for Italy": MG to EH, June 7, 1944.

406–8 "was the first female"; "whipping boy"; "I never learned": M. Hemingway, pp. 102, 117.

408 "Papa can be more": L. Hemingway, p. 192.
"This was a happy period": Lanham, *Memoir*, p. 12.

408–9 "I am just happy": EH to MW, Sept. 13, 1944, *S. Lett.*, pp. 569–70.

409 "He told me"; His hatred": Lanham, p. 17.
"Haven't heard from": EH to Pat H., Sept. 15, 1944, *S. Lett.*, pp. 571–72.

410 "He lied about me"; "I had no papers": MG, Oct. 31, 1980.
"sharing the dangers": MG, Feb. 15, 1982.
believed they compared: Harold Acton, *Memoirs of an Aesthete* (New York: Viking, 1970).

411 "He *insisted* that"; "This was the first time": MG, Feb. 15, 1982.
still wanted her: Mario Menocal to CB, Nov. 18, 1970, Pat H. to BK, Aug. 1978.

411–12 Pauline in Key West: PH to sons, Mar. 1, Oct. 5, 23, Nov. 15, Dec. 6, 1944.

413 Hürtgenwald: Lanham.
"especially gay": Walton to CB, Apr. 2, 1964.

414 "But after this one": EH to Pat H., Nov. 19, 1944, *S. Lett.*, p. 576.
"spider": M. Hemingway, p. 143.

415 "You'd notice her" incident on Dec. 31: Walton to BK, Apr. 1980.

416 ". . . such a complicated": M. Hemingway, p. 142.
"He talked about it"; "she treated him": Walton to BK, Apr. 1980.
she had read everything: L. Hemingway, p. 200.

417 "I feel the way a man": EH to MG, undated (priv. coll.).
"Though he had previously": MG, Feb. 15, 1982.

Chapter 27

page

419   "It's not the way": EH to HM, Apr. 24, 1945, *S. Lett.*, p. 591.

        "Stayed in last night": EH to MW, Apr. 17, 1945, *S. Lett.*, p. 588.

        "I felt": M. Hemingway, p. 158.

420   Hemingway sons and Mary: Greg H., p. 96; Pat H. to BK, Aug.
        1978.

        "My only ambition": EH to Thomas Welsh, June 19, 1945, *S. Lett.*, p. 592.

421   "My feeling": Mary Lanham to CB, June 1, 1964; May 10, 1966.

422   ". . . In all this place": M. Hemingway, p. 178.

        Martha's divorce: *STLPD*, July 26, 1945.

422–23 "Under Cuban law"; "sold it like": MG, Oct. 31, 1980.

423   "Can you imagine": Mary Lanham to CB, June 1, 1964; May 10, 1966.

        "bilge" stories: MG, Feb. 15, 1982.

        His theory: EH to Lanham, Jan. 20, 1946.

424–25 "But it has always": HM to EH, July 30, 1946.

425   "How good a driver": EH to Pat H., Apr. 13, 1946.

        Whenever there was; "black at the joint": EH to Lanham, July 14, 20, 1946.

427   "gored": M. Hemingway, p. 189.

        "Dr. told me it was"; "Was only trying": EH to Lanham, Aug. 25, 28, 1946,
        S. Lett., pp. 609–11.

428   like a limp doll: Tillie Arnold to BK, Mar. 14, 1979.

        "I make breakfast": EH to Lanham, Nov. 2, 1946, *S. Lett.*, p. 613.

        business matters: Al Horowitz to BK, Jan. 9, 1979.

429–30 Pauline and Mary: Pat H. to BK, Aug. 1978.

430   "There's nothing in this world": M. Hemingway, p. 215.

Chapter 28

431   "his backdrop": M. Hemingway, p. 214.

432   "She stopped at"; She hopes": Scribner to EH, July 9, Dec. 26, 1947.

433   "The German artillery": Gellhorn, *WOA*, p. 29.

        "*The Wine of Astonishment*": MG, Oct. 31, 1980.

434–35 "absolutely . . . wonderful": Baker, *Life Story*, p. 468.

435   ". . . simply a wife": M. Hemingway, p. 231.

436   "I was ten": Adriana Ivancich to EH, 1950 (undated).

439   "It was a shock": AI to BK, Oct. 1980.

439–40 Meeting at Latisana and aftermath: Ivancich, *La Torre Bianca*, pp. 7–15.

441   "But his wife": AI to BK, Oct. 1980.

442–43 "People have wondered"; "I like that boy": Ivancich, pp. 136–41, 55–58.

443   "launching a flirtation": M. Hemingway, p. 246.

        "For me": AI to BK, Oct. 1980.

444   ". . . she came into": EH, *ATRIT*, p. 80.

        Ernest's boasts: Lanham to BK, Apr. 23, 1976; Lanham to CB, undated.

445   "Operation Mink Coat"; "going into the cage": M. Hemingway, p. 245.

446   Ernest wrote: EH to AI, Oct. 1949.

"I like to have": EH to Lillian ross, Sept. 18, 1949.

EH perception of Mary: Walton to BK, Apr. 16, 1980.

"small elegant body": Irwin Shaw, *The Young Lions*, p. 382.

447   "enormous spirit": Lillian Ross, *Portrait of Hemingway*, p. 16.

Adriana's qualities: Arrigo Cipriani to BK, Oct. 21, 1980.

Winter of 1950 in Venice and Cortina: AI to BK, Oct. 1980.

449   "Ernest was weaving"; MWH on Dora: M. Hemingway, pp. 254, 256.

450   Adriana and Ernest in Paris: Ivancich, pp. 96–101; AI to BK, Oct. 1980.

Chapter 29

452   "occluded"; a "failed member": M. Hemingway, pp. 260, 261.

"It is seven hours": AI to EH, Mar. 21, 22, 1950.

453   "As soon as": M. Hemingway, p. 262.

454   Correspondence with AI: EH to AI, June 3, 1950, *S. Lett.*, p. 699; June 16, 1950.

"It was during the time": AI to BK, Oct. 1980.

455   "with all the grace": EH to Lillian Ross, Oct. 5, 1950.

abject acceptance: Walton to BK, Apr. 1980.

"a camp-follower"; "Torquemada": M. Hemingway, p. 276.

456–57   AI and *ATRIT*; EH dancing: Ivancich, pp. 136–40, 162–66.

457   "I could have": AI to BK, Oct. 1980.

Ernest's Cuban men friends: Mario Menocal, Jr., to BK, Feb. 9, 1979.

458   " 'She's a bitch' ": EH, *IITS*, p. 203.

"I read Martha's article": EH to Scribner, Oct. 29, 1947, *S. Lett.*, p. 630.

"Far from having": MG, Feb. 15, 1982.

Walton at Finca: Walton to BK, Apr. 1980.

459   "Adriana so lovely": Greg H., pp. 111, 112, 113.

He thought it grotesque: Pat H. to BK, Aug. 1978; Sept. 17, 1979.

460   Disturbing letter from Venice: AI to BK, Oct., 1980; Ivancich, pp. 201–2.

Chapter 30

461   Maybe he should: EH to AI, Mar. 18, 1951; Apr. 12, 1952.

"instruments": Baker, *Life Story*, p. 495.

462   "It was heartbreaking": Miller, p. 130.

"But I hate her": EH to Scribner, Aug. 27, 1949, *S. Lett.*, p. 670.

"Please let me": EH to GH, Sept. 17, 1949, *S. Lett.*, p. 675.

Ernest had hidden: Walton to BK, Apr. 1980.

463–64   Pauline's illness and death: Greg H., pp. 6–12.

464   Jinny and EH: Pat H. to BK, Aug. 1978; Sept. 17, 1979.

". . . I loved her": EH to Scribner, Oct. 2, 1951, *S. Lett.*, p. 737.

page

465   "But time tends": Greg H., p. 7.
        ". . . loyal friends": EH to Scribner, June 28, 1947, *S. Lett.*, p. 622.
        ". . . it was like": EH to Wallace Meyer, Feb. 21, 1952, *S. Lett.*, p. 750.
466   "Mary asked me": EH to Vera Scribner, Feb. 18, 1952, *S. Lett.*, 749.
        "cogwheel": M. Hemingway, p. 294.
        "I have never been prouder": EH to AI, May 31, 1952, *S. Lett.*, pp. 762, 763.
467   "worse than Pagliacci": Baker, *Life Story*, p. 505.
468   "Somebody should have": EH to BB, Sept. 13, 1952, *S. Lett.*, p. 781.
469   "It is two years": EH to BB, Jan. 24, 1953., *S. Lett.*, p. 801.
        "monied aunt": EH to AI, July 19, 1953.
470   "I loved Juan": Ivancich, pp. 308–14.
        "like a good"; "the good family": AI to EH, June 21, 1953.
471   "He did the most": M. Hemingway, p. 329.
        "We stayed": EH to BB, Aug. 11, 1953, *S. Lett.*, p. 823.
472–74 "private carnivals"; "the loveliest time"; "like a grasshopper"; "bumping":
        M. Hemingway, pp. 351, 369, 382.
476   "cerebral thing": EH to BB, Apr. 4, 1954.
477   ". . . we try to restore": AI to EH, June 21, 1953.
477–79 AI hears false report; scene at Gritti: Ivancich, pp. 303–24; AI to EH, Jan.
        25, 1954.

Chapter 31

480   sense of guilt: MWH to Lanham, Mar. 16, 1960.
481   "The Swedish thing": M. Hemingway, p. 410.
        "No writer": Baker, *Life Story*, p. 528.
        ". . . I can still": M. Hemingway, p. 416.
482   sentiments about Martha: EH to BB, Aug. 16, 1956.
483–84 "If the reader"; "gently modeled face"; ". . . my wife and my son"; "There
        was wood"; ". . . nothing was simple"; ". . . unmarried young woman":
        EH, *AMF*, Preface, pp. 7, 31, 38, 57, 207, 208.
484–85 ". . . I never worked better": EH, *A Moveable Feast*—Starts and Incom-
        pletes, *Hemingway Collection*, JFK Lib., Boston.
485   ". . . sometimes a little deaf": EH, *AMF*, p. 205.
486   "He's killed her off": Pat H. to BK, Aug. 1978.
        "yellow": Baker, *Life Story*, p. 240.

Chapter 32

489   ". . . I invented her": EH, "The Art of the Short Story," *Paris Review*
        79:93.
491   "I was . . . repelled": M. Hemingway, p. 471.
        Annie Davis found: Lanham to CB, undated.

page

rudeness to Mary: Peter Buckley to BK, Apr. 13, 1980.

"It was quite": EH, "The Dangerous Summer," *Life,* Sept. 12, 1960: 68.

492   It was obvious to him: Lanham to CB, undated.

"inaudible"; "pique": M. Hemingway, pp. 475, 476.

494   "I would never presume": Interview, *The Student,* Wake Forest University, Winter 1978: 23.

495–96   "large tizzy"; "REPORTS FALSE": M. Hemingway, pp. 485, 488.

496   Agnes and EH: AS to BK, Jan. 1976; Betty Bruce to BK, Jan. 1976.

498   "I wish you were": M. Hemingway, p. 490.

"covering up something": M. Hemingway, p. 493.

500   "I was called": HM to CB, Apr. 1962.

503   "grinning like a Cheshire cat": M. Hemingway, p. 500.

keys on . . . sill: MWH to CB, Aug. 3, 1964.

"no one had a right"; "Goodnight, my kitten": M. Hemingway, p. 502.

504   self-inflicted wound: Dr. Scott Earle to CB, Aug. 7, 1964.

"accidental": M. Hemingway, p. 503.

funeral arrangements: Miller, pp. 139–42.

in hallowed ground: JH to BK, Mar. 1979.

Ernest's will: *New York Times,* Aug. 25, 1961:4.

505   ". . . he shot": Oriana Fallaci interview, *Look,* Sept. 6, 1966: 62–68.

"The right of the public": John Tebbel, "Papa's Troubled Legacy," *Saturday Review,* April 9, 1966: 31.

506   "tape-recorder": M. Hemingway, p. 535.

Bibliography

I. *The Writings of Ernest Hemingway*

Across the River and into the Trees. New York: Scribner Library/Contemporary Classics. 1970. *(ARIT)*

By-Line: Ernest Hemingway. William White, ed. New York: Charles Scribner's Sons. 1967.

"The Dangerous Summer." *Life* Sept. 5, 12, 19. 1960.

Death in the Afternoon. New York: Scribner Library/Lyceum edition. 1960 (first edition 1932). *(DIA)*

A Farewell to Arms. New York: Scribner Library/Contemporary Classics. 1969. *(FTA)*

The Fifth Column & Four Stories of the Spanish Civil War. New York: Charles Scribner's Sons. 1969. *(TFC)*

For Whom the Bell Tolls. New York: Scribner Library/Contemporary Classics. 1968. *(FWBT)*

Green Hills of Africa. New York: The Scribner Library/Contemporary Classics. 1963. *(FWBT)*

Islands in the Stream. New York: Charles Scribner's Sons. 1970. *(IITS)*

A Moveable Feast. New York: Bantam Books, by arrangement with Charles Scribner's Sons. 1963. *(AMF)*

Nick Adams Stories. New York: Charles Scribner's Sons. 1972. *(NAS)*

Selected Letters: 1917–1961. Carlos Baker, ed. New York: Charles Scribner's Sons. 1981. *(S. Lett.)*

The Short Stories of Ernest Hemingway. New York: The Scribner Library/Omnibus Volume. 1966. *(SSEH)*

The Sun Also Rises. New York: Scribner Library/Contemporary Classics. 1954. *(SAR)*

To Have and Have Not. New York: Scribner Library/Contemporary Classics. 1970. *(THAHN)*

Selected Articles—*Collier's, Esquire,* North American Newspaper Alliance (NANA), *Toronto Daily Star (TDS), Toronto Star Weekly (TSW).*

II. *The Writings of Martha Gellhorn*
  "On Apocryphism." *Paris Review* 79 (25th Anniversary Issue). 1981.
  The Face of War. New York: Simon & Schuster. 1959. *(FOW)*
  The Heart of Another. New York: Charles Scribner's Sons. 1941. *(HOA)*
  Liana. New York: Charles Scribner's Sons. 1944.
  A Stricken Field. New York: Duell, Sloan & Pearce. 1940. *(ASF)*
  Travels with Myself and Another. New York: Dodd, Mead. 1978. *(TWMA)*
  The Trouble I've Seen. New York: W. Morrow & Co., 1936. *(TIS)*
  The Wine of Astonishment. New York: Charles Scribner's Sons. 1948. *(WOA)*
  Selected Articles—*Collier's.*

III. *Other Works Consulted*
  Arnold, Lloyd R. *High on the Wild with Hemingway.* Caldwell, Idaho: Caxton Printers. 1968.
  Baker, Carlos. *Ernest Hemingway: A Life Story.* New York: Charles Scribner's Sons. 1969.
  Baker, Carlos. *Hemingway: The Writer as Artist.* 4th ed. Princeton, N.J.: Princeton University Press. 1972.
  Baker, Carlos, ed. *Hemingway and His critics: An International Anthology.* New York: Hill & Wang. 1961.
  Barea, Arturo. *The Forging of a Rebel.* New York: Reynal & Hitchcock. 1946.
  Beach, Sylvia. *Shakespeare & Company.* New York: Harcourt, Brace. 1959.
  Benson, Jackson J. *Hemingway: The Writer's Art of Self-Defense.* Minneapolis: University of Minnesota Press. 1969.
  Berg, A. Scott. *Max Perkins: Editor of Genius.* New York: E.P. Dutton. 1978.
  Book Review Digest. New York: H.W. Wilson Co. 1925, 1932, 1940, 1941, 1944, 1948, 1950.
  Burgess, Anthony. *Ernest Hemingway and His World.* New York: Charles Scribner's Sons. 1978.
  Callaghan, Morley. *That Summer in Paris: Memories of Tangled Friendships with Hemingway, Fitzgerald, and Some Others.* New York: Coward-McCann. 1963.
  Catalog of the Ernest Hemingway Collection. John F. Kennedy Library. Boston: G.K. Hall & Co.. 1982. vols. 1 and 2.
  Cowles, Virginia. *Looking for Trouble.* New York: Harper. 1941.
  Cowley, Malcolm. *A Second Flowering: Works and Days of the Lost Generation.* New York: Viking. 1973.
  Donaldson, Scott. *By Force of Will: The Life and Art of Ernest Hemingway.* New York: Viking. 1977.
  Dos Passos, John. *The Best Times: An Informal Memoir.* New York: New American Library. 1966.
  Dos Passos, John. *Chosen Country.* Boston: Houghton Mifflin. 1951.

Eastman, Max. *Great Companions: Critical Memoirs of Some Famous Friends.* New York: Farrar, Straus & Cudahy. 1959.

Flanner, Janet. *Paris Was Yesterday: 1925–1939.* New York: Viking. 1972.

Glassco, John. *Memoirs of Montparnasse.* Toronto and New York: Oxford University Press. 1970.

Greenberg, Clement. *Joan Miró.* New York: Quadrangle. 1948.

Hanneman, Audre. *Ernest Hemingway: A Comprehensive Bibliography.* Princeton, N.J.: Princeton University Press. 1967.

Hanneman, Audre. *Supplement to Ernest Hemingway: A Comprehensive Bibliography.* Princeton, N.J.: Princeton University Press. 1975.

Hemingway, Gregory H., M.D. *Papa: A Personal Memoir.* Boston: Houghton Mifflin. 1976.

Hemingway, Leicester. *My Brother, Ernest Hemingway.* Cleveland: World. 1962.

Hemingway, Mary. *How It Was.* New York: Knopf. 1976.

Herbst, Josephine. "The Starched Blue Sky of Spain." *Noble Savage* 1 (Spring 1960).

Hotchner, A. E. *Papa Hemingway: A Personal Memoir.* New York: Random House. 1966.

Ivancich, Adriana. *La Torre Bianca.* Milan: Arnaldo Mondadori Editore. 1980.

Lewis, Robert W. Jr. *Hemingway on Love.* Austin and London: University of Texas Press. 1965.

Loeb, Harold. *The Way It Was.* New York: Criterion. 1959.

McAlmon, Robert. *McAlmon and the Lost Generation: A Self-Portrait.* Robert E. Knoll, ed. Lincoln: University of Nebraska Press. 1962.

McCaffrey, John K. M., ed. *Ernest Hemingway: The Man and His Work.* Cleveland and New York: World. 1950.

McLendon, James. *Papa: Hemingway in Key West.* Miami, Fla.: E.A. Seemann. 1972.

Matthews, Herbert L. *The Education of a Correspondent.* New York: Harcourt, Brace. 1946.

Mellow, James R. *Charmed Circle: Gertrude Stein & Co.* New York: Praeger. 1974.

Milford, Nancy. *Zelda: A Biography.* New York: Harper & Row/Avon edition. 1971.

Miller, Madelaine Hemingway. *Ernie: Hemingway's Sister "Sunny" Remembers.* New York: Crown Publishers. 1975.

Montgomery, Constance Cappel. *Hemingway in Michigan.* New York: Fleet. 1966.

Mowrer, Paul Scott. *The House of Europe.* Boston: Houghton Mifflin. 1945.

Regler, Gustav. *The Owl of Minerva: Autobiography.* London: Hart-Davis. 1959.

Reynolds, Michael S. *Hemingway's First War: The Making of* A Farewell to Arms. Princeton, N.J.: Princeton University Press. 1976.

Ross, Lillian, *Portrait of Hemingway.* New York: Simon & Schuster/Avon edition, 1961.

Sanford, Marcelline Hemingway. *At the Hemingways: A Family Portrait.* Boston: Atlantic-Little, Brown. 1962.

Sarason, Bertram D. *Hemingway and the Sun Set.* Washington, D.C.: NCR/Microcard editions. 1972.

Shaw, Irwin. *The Young Lions.* New York: the 1st Modern Library ed. 1948.

Sheean, Vincent. *Not Peace But a Sword.* New York: Doubleday, Doran. 1939.

Sokoloff, Alice Hunt. *Hadley: The First Mrs. Hemingway.* New York: Dodd, Mead. 1973.

Stein, Gertrude. *The Autobiography of Alice B. Toklas.* New York: Random House/Vintage edition. 1960.

Tomkins, Calvin. *Living Well Is the Best Revenge.* New York: Viking. 1971.

Turgenev, Ivan. *Torrents of Spring.* Trans. from the Russian by Constance Garnett. London: William Heinemann Ltd. 1927.

Westbrook, Max. "Grace Under Pressure: The Summer of 1920" (unpublished).

Acknowledgments

Carlos Baker: From *Ernest Hemingway—Selected Letters, 1917–1961*, edited by Carlos Baker. Copyright © 1981 The Ernest Hemingway Foundation, Inc. Copyright © 1981 Carlos Baker. Reprinted with permission of Charles Scribner's Sons and Granada Publishing Limited. From *Ernest Hemingway: A Life Story*. Copyright © 1969 Carlos Baker; copyright © 1969 Mary Hemingway. Reprinted with the permission of Charles Scribner's Sons and William Collins, Sons & Company Limited.

Martha Gellhorn: From her unpublished letters. Copyright © 1983 by Martha Gellhorn and reprinted by her permission. From *Travels With Myself and Another*. Copyright © 1978 Martha Gellhorn. Reprinted by permission of Dodd, Mead & Company, Inc. and by permission of Martha Gellhorn.

Jane Gingrich: From her unpublished letters. Copyright © 1983 by Jane Gingrich and reprinted by her permission.

Ernest Hemingway: The quotation on page oo is reprinted from *To Have and Have Not* by Ernest Hemingway, with the permission of Charles Scribner's Sons. Copyright © 1937 Ernest Hemingway; copyright renewed 1965 Mary Hemingway. From the unpublished letters of Ernest Hemingway, reprinted with the permission of Alfred Rice acting for Mary Hemingway. From *A Moveable Feast*, an unpublished passage, reprinted with the permission of Alfred Rice acting for Mary Hemingway. From *A Moveable Feast*. Copyright © 1964 Ernest Hemingway Ltd. Reprinted with the permission of Charles Scribner's Sons and Jonathan Cape Ltd. From "The Snows of Kilimanjaro." Copyright © 1936 Ernest Hemingway; copyright renewed 1964 Mary Hemingway. Reprinted with the permission of Charles Scribner's Sons and Jonathan Cape Ltd.

Gregory Hemingway: From *Papa: A Personal Memoir*. Copyright © 1976 Gregory H. Hemingway. Reprinted by permission of Houghton Mifflin Company and the author and the author's agents, Scott Meredith Literary Agency, Inc., 845 Third Avenue, New York, New York 10022.

Pauline Hemingway: From her unpublished letters and her unpublished African diary. Copyright © 1983 Patrick Hemingway and reprinted by his permission.

Adriana Ivancich: From her unpublished letters. Copyright © 1983 Adriana Ivancich and reprinted by her permission.

Hadley Mowrer: From her unpublished letters. Copyright © 1983 Jack Hemingway and reprinted by his permission.

Mary Pfeiffer: From her unpublished letters. Copyright © 1983 Patrick Hemingway and reprinted by his permission.

Agnes Stanfield: From her unpublished letters. Copyright © 1983 Agnes Stanfield and reprinted by her permission.

Index